WHERE TO OBTAIN HELP AND TRAINING

Dr. Mosse offers suggested solutions to her readers - methods of instruction which will prevent or remediate various types of learning disorders. Featured prominently among her recommendations is the use of the unified, multi-sensory, intensive phonetic approach described in *The Writing Road to Reading,* by Romalda & Walter Spalding. References to it are made on pages: 75, 82, 93, 102, 114, 122-123, 138-139, 185, 191-195, 196-209, & 231.

Accredited thirty-hour training courses, teachers' manuals and phonogram cards necessary to teach this method are available through:

The Riggs Institute
4185 S.W. 102nd Ave.
Beaverton, Oregon, 97005
(503) 646-9459

IN APPRECIATION

The Riggs Institute, a non-profit, educational organization, gratefully acknowledges the assistance of Dr. George L. Mosse and a grant from the Mosse Foundation which has made possible the paperback edition of these timely volumes.

THE COMPLETE HANDBOOK OF CHILDREN'S READING DISORDERS

You can prevent or correct learning disorders

HILDE L. MOSSE, M.D.

VOLUME 1
VOLUME II

Riggs Institute Press
4185 S.W. 102nd Avenue
Beaverton, Oregon 97005

Distributed by
TEACHERS COLLEGE PRESS
Columbia University, New York
ISBN 0-8077-2983-3

About the Author:

Dr. Hilde L. Mosse was a physician who specialized in child and adolescent psychiatry, prior to which she practiced pediatrics. For over twenty years, Dr. Mosse served as a school psychiatrist for the New York Bureau of Child Guidance and the Board of Education. She was the co-founder (with Dr. Fredric Wertham) of the Lafargue Clinic in Harlem and was Clinical Associate Professor of Psychiatry at New York Medical College. Dr. Mosse was well known in both Europe and North America for her articles on childhood depression, the effects of mass media on children, criminal and violent behavior of children and adolescents, and reading disabilities. In 1964-65 she was a Fulbright Professor in Child Psychiatry at the University of Marburg in the Federal Republic of Germany. She was a fellow of the American Psychiatric Association, the American Orthopsychiatric Association and the New York Academy of Medicine. Dr. Mosse was presented with the Watson Washburn Memorial Award for excellence in education by The Reading Reform Foundation at Houston, Texas, in 1980, in honor of this book, *THE COMPLETE HANDBOOK OF CHILDREN'S READING DISORDERS*, the "capstone of her life's work".

Dr. Mosse died in New York City on January 15, 1982, following a lengthy illness. Her original publisher, Human Sciences Press, reports that she did not live to see either of her original two volumes of this book in print.

Selected Publications by Hilde L. Mosse

- Aggression and Violence in Fantasy and Fact
- The Misuse of the Diagnosis Childhood Schizophrenia
- Linear Dyslexia: A New Form of Reading Disorder
  (with C.R. Daniels)
- Reading Disorders in the United States
- The Influence of Mass Media on the Mental Health of Children
- The Importance of Clinical Diagnosis in the Management of
  Seriously Disturbed Children
- Individual and Collective Violence
- The Psychotherapeutic Management of Children with
  Masked Depression
- Terrorism and Mass Media

In German:　　　　　　　73
- Die pathogene Bedeutung der Ganzheitsmethoden
  (The Pathogenicity of Whole-Word Methods)
- Massenmedien

Copyright © 1982 by Hilde L. Mosse
Published by Riggs Institute Press
4185 S.W. 102nd Avenue, Beaverton, Oregon 97005

Printed in the United States of America
3456789   987654321

Library of Congress Cataloging in Publication Data

Mosse, Hilde L
  The complete handbook of children's reading disorders.

  Paperback reprint. Originally published: New York : Human Sciences Press, c1982.

  Bibliography: p.
  Includes index and forwards.
  1. Dyslexia. 2. Reading disability. 3. Learning disabilities.
  4. Learning disabled children— 5. Education—Reading.
  I. Title. [RJ496.A5M67   1987]   618.92'8553   87-23500
ISBN 0-942311-00-0

Contents

FOREWORD

by

Dr. Lendon H. Smith

Pediatrician, Author, Lecturer

Now here is a book that fulfills the promise of its title, **COMPLETE** Handbook. I am sure that some potential buyers (and readers) might be discouraged, not just by the size and weight of the whole 700+ pages, but by the nit-picking detail of the subject matter. How many pediatricians have seen or would know what to do if they did see a child who was a non-reader and a schizophrenic? But at least with this book at hand they would be able to look up these rare, odd syndromes, conditions and combinations. Then the doctor would appear to be at least slightly knowledgable when referring a child to some local diagnostic citadel.

How about the teachers who are confronted daily with "challenges?" They have given the students their best shot and 80% learn to read, seem to enjoy learning and pay attention. But what about those 20% who just refuse to "fit in?" They simply **do not learn how to read**. Why? These teachers would find their non-learning students here in this handbook and might be more efficient at sending these problems off to the correct facility for help, or better yet, learn to teach the non-reader themselves.

How about parents who know their child is bright enough to learn to read? What's the matter with the school? They could scan the index until they found their child and then would go to the appropriate professional or clinic for a more definitive diagnosis and treatment plan.

How about the pediatrician, the general practitioner or the family practice doctor who is faced with a 7 year old who cannot read but looks okay - or at least average? Their numbers are legend: pale with circles under their eyes, hemoglobin test a low normal, a little maladroit, but all within normal limits. There is no clue in the examination that anything is wrong. What does the professional do? It would be best to read this book, or at least the first line of every paragraph to get the drift of Dr. Mosse's thrust: make an accurate diagnosis first. Doctors are supposed to know everything.

How about psychologists, psychiatrists, social workers and school counsellors who are overwhelmed with medical literature and biased by their own training? They assume that if the medical doctor has ruled out any physical problem, what is left is a clear cut neurosis or at least the reading difficulty has an emotional basis. These professionals can find something wrong with every family's dynamics. But do emotional or psychic imbalances explain reading disorders or are the children disturbed and show emotional symptoms **because** they cannot read? These professionals will feel comforted and supported by Dr. Mosse's book because she uses terms that they are familiar with. She is right; emotional overlay must be diagnosed and dealt with along with any reading therapy. She did the most unique method of investigation of reading problems; she actually went into the classroom and watched the teacher teach and the children learn. Or not learn. Dr Mosse knows what she is writing about.

How about the reading therapist who knows that if the phonetic method had been used as the basic learn-to-read method, there would have been few if any referrals from the schools and his/her job would be in jeopardy? When the reading therapist uses phonetics, about 90% or more can learn. Why is the phonetic method used only as therapy for the older non-reader and not used in the primary learn-to-read situation?

Can you believe this book will help all these people? There is something in here for everyone. For some it may be more than they want to know. I was flattered because I could understand most of what Dr. Mosse wrote. She also included some of my cherished beliefs: (1) there is too much use of stimulant medication without an accurate diagnosis, (2) there is a lack of the use of phonetics as the basic method of learning to read, (3) not enough therapists, parents and teachers are aware that a good diet is a prerequisite for the ability to concentrate, and (4) there is a lack of a definitive diagnosis before treatment is begun.

The reader can find himself, his child, his patient and his pupil in this book, and its not difficult to do. She has given us some easy steps to find the answers. An adequate index of contents allows the parent/teacher/therapist to zero in on his particular interest, concern or problem.

I was delighted to find that Dr. Mosse recognizes that organic problems can appear clinically as if psychologically induced. And then there are normally appearing and acting children who just don't get it; they have great difficulty reading a word! So the teacher would be the first to recognize - but maybe not pinpoint the cause of the non-reading. But where have the parents been? Shouldn't they have figured out that their child's development was not even close to the average? And shouldn't their doctor have done more than say, "It's just a phase; he'll outgrow it." Dr. Mosse has provided clues all over these pages that fairly scream out to parents, teachers and doctors that something needs to be done for the child at risk.

Because she was an M.D. psychiatrist and had made her life goal the understanding, diagnosis and treatment of non-reading children, she emphasizes that a specific diagnosis should be made in each case. She felt that a clinic approach involving the parents, the pediatrician, the social worker, a psychologist, a psychiatrist, and a reading therapist would be the minimum professional staff to study the child but a neurologist, an ophthalmologist (I would look for a developmental optometrist) and perhaps an otologist should be consulted. An ombudsman would be essential for the execution of the recommendations of the staff.

How does the child learn? Is he auditory or visual? Is he kinesthetic or whatever? Is his cortex working? Where does one start? Dr. Mosse provides us with some steps to figure out the direction to take.

Don't let the weight and length of this book discourage you. Read the index and the table of contents first. Then jump into some section that appears to be familiar and get used to Dr. Mosse's style. (You'll love what she has to say about comic books and television.) You'll have to admit that she makes a lot of sense. You will come to appreciate her insights and welcome her easy style that makes sense out of something as complicated as the way the brain works.

Happy hunting.

SECOND FOREWORD

by

Barbara Bateman, Ph.D., J.D.

Professor of Education, University of Oregon

When Dr. Mosse's *Complete Handbook of Children's Reading Disorders* reached my desk this term, I was teaching a course in Learning Disabilities. Each chapter in Dr. Mosse's book had to be shared with my students and we found ourselves neglecting the assigned text in favor of the *Handbook*. Dr. Mosse tells it "true" and she tells it very well.

One of her most striking messages is that the large majority of our reading disabled children have been victimized by the sight word method and related curriculum practices. Never has this vital message been conveyed with more authority and experience.

According to the U.S. Department of Education (Wills, 1986) about 25% of high school students drop out before graduation and of those who do graduate over 30% are illiterate. Thus, we are apparently teaching only somewhat over one half of today's students to read. The statistics on writing and arithmetic are no more encouraging.

Dr. Mosse observed that "it will not be possible to stem the epidemic of reading disorders unless corrective measures are based on the clinical method" (p. 12). Her work is a comprehensive, readable, and practical presentation of the clinical method and the wide ranging body of knowledge on which it is based and to which it contributes.

In today's milieu of specialization and fragmentation, the breadth and integration of Dr. Mosse's experience and knowledge are strikingly welcome. In this work, professionals, students, parents and all practitioners can find useful and accurate information about every aspect of reading, writing and arithmetic disorders.

Dr. Mosse's description of a thorough clinical examination is a model of careful, wide-ranging thoughtful inquiry too seldom seen in practice. Dr. Mosse's approach is the antidote to narrow, limited diagnoses. Too often reading disorders are "diagnosed" only thru psycho-educational tests. Realistically, Dr. Mosse observes that not every single child with a reading disorder can be practically diagnosed by the total clinical method, but observes that the knowledge she and others have acquired through the method is reliable and valid. That knowledge base, derived from both research and clinical practice, is the focus of this book. After the in-depth diagnostic process is described, Dr. Mosse presents descriptive chapters on writing disorders and arithmetic disorders with an organic basis. She divides reading disorders into those with an organic, psychogenic, or a sociogenic basis. In this day of disputes among those who would label all learning disabilities due to one cause—whether inadequate teaching, minimal brain dysfunction, or heredity—her approach of recognizing all has the solid ring of truth and practicality.

Sociogenic reading disorders are far more numerous than psychogenic and organic in our society and others where damaging teaching philosophies and practices, mass media domination and violence are rampant.

Dr. Mosse indicts the sight word method, comic books and destructive television programming. She moves on from the problem to the solution and many readers will find inestimable value in the chapter on treatments. That chapter concludes on a positive note. "The prognosis for the treatment of all reading disorders is excellent. Only a small number of children with the severe organic type cannot be completely cured."

This book ought to be required reading and a constant reference source for every parent, teacher, clinician, therapist and administrator concerned with helping prevent and treat school failure. And perhaps most of all, it should be reading by every college professor who teaches others how to work with children who have disorders in reading, writing, or arithmetic.

My personal list of books I recommend to people who want to help children with learning disabilities has now grown to two: Suzanne Stevens' *Classroom Success for the Learning Disabled* and Hilde Mosse's *Complete Handbook of Children's Reading Disorders.*

Acknowledgments

Grateful acknowledgment is made to the authors and publishers for permission to reprint excerpts from the following material:

Adey, W. R. Neural information processing: Windows without and the citadel within. In L. D. Proctor (Ed.), *Biocybernetics of the central nervous system.* Boston: Little, Brown and Company, 1969.

Chall, J. S. *Learning to read: The great debate.* New York: McGraw-Hill Book Company, 1967.

Critchley, M. *The parietal lobes.* London: Edward Arnold Publishers LTD., 1953.

Freud, A. *Normality and pathology in childhood.* New York: International Universities Press, Inc., 1965.

Hecaen, H. Cerebral localization of mental functions and their disorders. In P. J. Vinken and G. W. Bruyn (Eds.), *Handbook of clinical neurology* (vol. 3). Amsterdam: Elsevier/North-Holland Biomedical Press B.V., 1969.

Jarvis, V. Clinical observations on the visual problem in reading disability. In *The psychoanalytic study of the child* (vol. XIII). New York: International Universities Press, 1958.

Jenkins, J. J., Schuell, H., & Jiménez-Pabón, E. Aphasia in adults. Hagerstown, Maryland: Medical Department Harper and Row, Publishers, Inc. 1964.

Kline, M. *Why Johnny can't add: The failure of the new math.* New York: St. Martin's Press, 1973.

Lowe, H. R. The whole-word and word-guessing fallacy. In C. C. Walcutt (Ed.), *Tomorrow's illiterates.* Washington, D.C.: Council for Basic Education, 1961.

Pearson, G. H. J. A survey of learning difficulties in children. In *The psychoanalytic study of the child* (vol. VII) New York: International Universities Press, 1952.

Rabinovitch, R. D. Reading and learning disabilities. In S. Arieti (Ed.), *American handbook of psychiatry (vol. 1). New York: Basic Books, 1959.*

7

Simpson, E. *Reversals: A personal account of victory over dyslexia.* Boston: Houghton Mifflin Co. 1979.

Spalding, R. B., & Spalding, W. T. *The writing road to reading.* New York: William Morrow & Co., 1962. 1969.

Stern, C. & Stern, M. B. *Children discover arithmetic.* New York: Harper and Row, 1949, 1971.

Vereeken, P. Inhibition of ego functions and the psychoanalytic theory of acalculia. In *The psychoanalytic study of the child* (vol. XX) New York: International Universities Press, 1965.

Vinken, P. J., Bruyn, G. W. (eds.). *Handbook of clinical neurology* (vol. 4). Amsterdam: Elsevier/North-Holland Biomedical Press B. V., 1969. The articles listed below have been reprinted:

Benson, F. D., & Geschwind, N. The alexias.

Grewel, F. The acalculias.

Leischner, A. The agraphias.

Lhermitte, F., & Gautier, J. C. Aphasia.

Sperry, R. W., Gazzaniga, M. S., & Bogen, J. E. Interhemispheric relationships: The neocortical commissures; syndromes of hemisphere disconnection.

Walcutt, C. C. The reading problem in America. In C. C. Walcutt (ed.), *Tomorrow's illiterates.* Washington, D.C.: Council for Basic Education, 1961.

Illustrations

Figure 3.2, The evolution of the alphabet, courtesy of the Picture Collection of the New York Public Library.

Chapter 1

Examination

I have a sickness about reading.
—Chief complaint
of 10-year-old boy

The aim of this book is to describe how careful clinical examination of children can disentangle all the different factors involved in the causation of reading disorders, and can provide a valid basis for practical and useful diagnostic categories, the only realistic guidelines enabling treatment and prevention.

The Journal of the American Medical Association, in an editorial dealing with reading disorders, deplored "a regrettable tendency to substitute terminology for fact and hypothesis for experimentation," and pointed out that "the physician and the educator have had views so diametrically opposed that they have found it difficult even to communicate with one another" (Editorial, J.A.M.A., 1968). I have worked with teachers all my professional life and found no communication difficulty when practical, concrete work with a child was involved.

In this book I want to discard empty speculation and present what is essential for the understanding of reading and its pathology, using as a basis careful examinations of real children with their all too real reading troubles, that is, using the clinical method. Theoretically as well as practically, child psychiatry is well suited to bring the findings of physicians and educators together and to be the focus of a necessarily interdisciplinary approach. Reading disorders affect all theories of human behavior; in practical clinical work they challenge our ability to diagnose, treat, and prevent—that is, to apply the clinical method successfully.

The Clinical Method

The clinical method is the only method that makes it possible to study a person as a whole, with all the subtle ramifications involving different psychologic and somatic levels. It consists of a thorough psychiatric examination and includes: psychologic tests; observation within the family, in the classroom, and in a play or talking group; and longitudinal follow-up studies. Examination of parents and siblings, taking a social history including home visits, and investigation of the work and economic background all are indispensible parts of this method.

The correct application of the clinical method requires not only knowledge of descriptive psychiatry and of psychoanalysis, but also familiarity with a wide range of social, historic, pedagogic, and economic facts and trends. It is the only method that permits us to arrive at carefully developed, valid results (Mosse, 1969).

The study of reading disorders actually presents the most severe test for the clinical method; it is a touchstone of scientific psychiatry. Reading disorders can be demonstrated objectively; it is not necessary to rely only on the patient's subjective report. It can also easily be shown whether the diagnosis and the treatment based on it were correct: the patient either does or does not learn how to read.

Because the reading skill requires intact vision and hearing as well as intact performance of the involved parts of the central nervous system in combination with equally complex psychologic factors, reading pathology becomes a test of our ability to understand and disentangle the individual causes of the reading disorder in each case. To achieve this end accurately, we must take into account developmental, experimental, and clinical psychology, brain pathology (especially aphasic disorders), conditioned reflexology, clinical neurology, education, language—and, of course, psychopath ology. In a considerable number of cases unconscious motivations and processes are also important, thus we must always consider the possible application of psychoanalytic principles.

Even though for practical reasons it is not possible to apply the clinical method to each one of the great masses of children who have reading difficulties, its results are so reliable and valid that they form a solid foundation for generalizations. As a matter of historic fact, progress in psychiatry was never achieved without it. Such important and divergent discoveries, for instance, as that of the organic brain disease General Paresis and its causation by the syphilitic spirochete (which led to successful treatment and to its virtual eradication), and that of the pathogenic and pathoplastic (form-giving) impact of mass phenomena such as mass media, were based entirely on the clinical method (Kraepelin, 1921; Wertham, 1966,1978).

Dr. Paul B. Beeson (1977) stressed the importance of this method in a paper, "The Development of Clinical Knowledge," in which he wrote: "The best clinical investigation deserves to rank as a science along with any of the other disciplines."

It will not be possible to stem the epidemic of reading disorders unless corrective measures are also based on the clinical method. Reports are accumulating that document failures of many of the recently established and funded special reading programs. Teaching techniques will remain unsuccessful and tests and statistics misleading unless they are built on the sound foundation of clinical diagnoses.

The clinical method has established a body of knowledge on which the work of all professionals working with children in the field of reading can and must be based. It is this body of knowledge I am going to present in this book, beginning with how children should be examined.

My work with psychologists, social workers, reading and speech therapists, guidance counselors, and teachers has convinced me that they all can profit from studying how a clinical examination is performed. They can then apply those aspects that they find pertinent to their work.

Importance of Detailed Observations

The key to understanding reading disorders is the careful, thorough, and detailed examination of the child. Observing details is very important for correct and corrective teaching as well as psychiatric evaluation. A diagnosis of disturbed basic functions is our first goal. Mistakes both clinical and educational that are made in practical work with children, as well as errors in theories, can usually be traced to incomplete examinations of children, which invariably lead to faulty diagnoses. Frequently the simplest observations are either omitted or not recorded, thereby invalidating an entire, often elaborate, theoretical structure.

The tendency to base complex and far-reaching theories on minimal observations of children is not unique to the field of reading; it pervades all of child psychiatry (Mosse, 1958a). In reading this tendency has gone so far that researchers' diagnoses, and their conclusions based on these diagnoses, can often be proven erroneous when the evidence (e.g., the concrete reading performance of the children) as presented by the researchers themselves is analyzed (Diak & Daniels, 1961; Gurren & Hughes, 1965). Even Thompson's much praised book, *Reading Disability, Developmental Dyslexia* (1966), includes not one case of a young elementary school child personally examined, diagnosed, and followed up by the author, who is a psychiatrist. It contains only the cases of two boys, aged 14 and 19, who were personally examined by Dr. Thompson.

Even clinical studies dealing with different diagnostic categories may, on close scrutiny of the actual case examinations and histories, be found to describe children who suffer from exactly the same type of reading defect. Frequently such diagnoses as Dyslexia, Developmental Dyslexia, Congenital Dyslexia, Specific Dyslexia, Alexia, Developmental Alexia, Congenital Word-Blindness, and Inborn Reading Disorders of Central Origin are synonyms; they describe cases with the same symptomatology. (See section in Chapter 2, Classification, p. 14.)

What must be done is a step-by-step factor analysis of the child's reading performance, always proceeding from the simple to the complex, from the observable to the hidden.

Role of Parents and Teachers

Ideally, each child with a reading difficulty should be examined individually by a remedial reading specialist, but this is not possible. Because children's reading difficulties are so common and so frequently overlooked, the help of parents and teachers is essential to establish the facts. They are the only adults in constant contact with the child, and unless they find out that the child has a reading difficulty, no one probably ever will. Referrals to reading specialists and psychiatrists necessarily depend on them.

It is a pity that both parents and teachers have been intimidated and discouraged in many ways by those "experts" who portray reading as impossibly complicated. The following statement by administrative educators is an example of this: "Reading facility is a kind of quintessence, a distillate produced by the communication process. The search for the almost magic formula for success in reading must, therefore, go beyond the crucibles of the resultant broth deep into the cauldrons of the language potions and ingredients from which it springs." One can understand why this inspired *The New Yorker* magazine to the sarcastic remark: "Maybe it's just silly to learn to read." (Footnote, *The New Yorker*, March 18, 1967).

Tests for Parents

I suggest the following tests to parents: Let the child read to you from any book that interests him, not necessarily from one he brings home from school; some children, especially in the first grades, memorize the books they are studying in school, but cannot read one word outside the context and sequence in this book. This is called position reading (see Chapter 2, p. 112). Then let him write what he has read—not copy, but write. This means you have to dictate it to him. Contrary to the prevailing educational theory, reading and writing belong together; they reinforce each other. In this way the parent can find out whether the child has difficulties and even where they lie, can discuss this with the teacher, and can get expert help if the school cannot help correct the defects.

Parents and teachers need no expert to tell them that a child's reading is defective and needs immediate attention when he reads a story and cannot distinguish "tree" from "three"; when he sees the word "eat," and reads "food"; when he proudly writes "ghounte" on the blackboard and reads it as "couldn't"; when he points to a place on a map, asks where it is, is told to read what is printed over the area, then names the letters correctly and reads it as "America"; when he reads "really" instead of "ready"; when he brings a neat workbook home with clearly and correctly written instructions and stories and cannot read one word of what he has written. All of the preceding are actual case examples of children referred for various reasons—but not for reading disorders, which had been overlooked.

Role of Teachers

Individual and group conferences with teachers invariably showed that the teachers had two main worries: what to do about disruptive children, and how to help the large number of children in their class who had difficulties learning to read. These complaints were always the same, regardless of the school's neighborhood. As a rule, the teachers, especially the younger ones, were baffled by this situation and confused about what to expect from the children. And they just could not understand why certain children had reading difficulties.

Frequently these teachers could not even determine exactly how many children in their classes had reading difficulties because they were uncertain as to whether a child was just slow in developing and/or had a below-average IQ and therefore was reading as well as could be expected, or whether he had a reading disorder needing correction. The teachers had apparently not received concrete practical help from their supervisors and had not been taught how to analyze a child's reading performance. As Rosswell and Natchez so clearly show in *Reading Disability: Diagnosis and Treatment* (1964), in most cases teachers are perfectly capable of making a reading defect diagnosis, provided they are taught properly in teachers' colleges and in-service courses.

Sometimes rigid school rules make such a diagnosis most difficult. For instance, when the school psychologist Clesbie R. Daniels and I, in the course of our study of the reading disorder Linear Dyslexia, suggested to teachers that they have the child read aloud, watch his eye movements, and record his reading errors, we were frequently told that it was against the school's rules to let children read aloud, especially in the early grades. These teachers begged for suggestions. We had to explain to them that it is impossible to give specific and therefore effective suggestions for corrective reading without a prior diagnosis, and that this cannot be done without observation of oral reading.

I have now studied over 1,000 children and adolescents; 445 of them (367 boys, 78 girls) had reading disorders. There may have been more. I find in going over the records of the early years of my practice that I used to rely primarily on school reports and on results of group reading tests given in the school. If these indicated that the child's reading was satisfactory, I accepted the evaluation. Careful follow-up during psychotherapy and through frequent reexaminations taught me that these tests and reports are most unreliable. Even individual psychodiagnostic testing may fail to detect significant defects in the child's reading. This led me to refine my own techniques and to scrutinize with greater care the child's reading and writing performance during classroom observations and in conferences with teachers, guidance counselors, social workers, and psychologists.

Inaccuracy of Group Reading Tests

Each child referred to me for examination had a graded reading score on his school record card. I learned to pay no attention to these scores because they were usually the result of a group test and differed considerably from the individual tests given by psychologists and remedial reading specialists working with me. These group tests unfortunately appear to have mathematical accuracy because they not only refer to grades but to months within each grade; for instance, 3.2 means that the child reads at grade 3 plus 2 months. This seeming accuracy leads too often to the scores' acceptance as absolute truths by parents, teachers, principals and all other professionals working with children. (See Chapter 6, Sociogenic Reading Disorders.)

No reading curriculum in any school is so rigidly structured that it progresses at a standardized pace from one month to the other. The group test scores refer only to word-list tests and have no practical connection with the child's true reading ability or deficiency. Parents should therefore not be reassured when they are told that their child's reading progressed 3 points in 1 month: from 3.2 to 3.5. Where these test scores are accepted uncritically, they may do the child great harm because they may color the teacher's judgment of the child's ability and obscure reading disorders at the very time when they are most easily corrected, namely at the very beginning.

It was only in 1967 that extensive educational research raised fundamental questions about the reliability of group "reading" tests and revealed that teachers had begun to question them. Jeanne S. Chall, in her book *Learning to Read: The Great Debate,* which is based on the most thorough study ever done of how children are actually being taught, reports that "most teachers and principals have little faith in the standardized tests now given periodically in every school. . . . The standardized reading tests often mask some of the important outcomes of reading instruction because they measure a conglomerate of skills and abilities at the same time" (p. 312).

Ever-increasing numbers of children referred to the various clinics, psychiatric hospitals, and courts I was connected with, and to me in my private practice, had reading disorders, either connected with the chief complaint or independent from it. Reading problems took on such overwhelming importance that I decided to look for them in each child and adolescent I examined, regardless of the reasons for their referral. In many cases my psychiatric examination established for the first time that there was a reading difficulty that had remained completely unnoticed, or had been noticed but neglected, or had been minimized and ignored. This was true for children from all backgrounds, economic classes, and skin colors, whether I saw them in mental hospitals, on pediatric wards, in courts, schools, mental hygiene clinics, or in private practice. Testing of reading ability is therefore a routine part of my examination of all youngsters, whether preschool, school, or college age. Reading trouble can go undetected until the person enters college.

Because the understanding of a child's reading disorder depends entirely on the way he is examined, I will describe the technique in detail. Every quotation of what a child said is accurate, word for word. I take notes during the examination and treatment of every patient.

Principles of Examination

When examining a child, I keep certain basic principles in mind. Psychiatry is the art of listening, of decreasing the patient's anxiety so that he can talk about his thoughts and feelings freely and if possible spontaneously—or express them in other ways. If it is a small child this may take the form of play, drawing, or painting (Gondor, 1954; Rambert, 1949; Wertham, 1966). The examiner must create a calm and peaceful atmosphere and be in a relaxed and receptive mood. Only thus can we convey our readiness and eagerness to understand the patient and establish the kind of friendly yet detached contact we need.

The relationship established must differ from that of teacher to student or judge to defendant. The many children and adolescents referred by schools and courts usually expect to find the same tense, and to them often humiliating, atmosphere from which they have come, where they were in the limelight being judged. They must find something quite refreshingly different. Our aim is to observe and listen, not to grade and judge. This very contrast may serve to engender a feeling of security even in the most anxious and excited youngster. Having had the occasion to examine patients under most difficult and stressful circumstances—in jails, courts, hospitals, and schools—I have found that this feeling can be achieved, provided privacy can be established within a room or cubicle with closed doors.

Caution Regarding Physical Contact

We must keep in mind throughout the examination that some degree of emotional detachment, and especially complete physical detachment, is essential to avoiding causing the youngster to feel repulsed, smothered, and/or attacked. Children, especially when they are in trouble, are usually overwhelmed by the emotional (both verbal and physical) reactions of the adults around them. They need to establish some distance to collect their thoughts and feelings. This applies not only to corporal punishment, but to the habit many adults have of expressing their concerns and affection by embracing or otherwise fondling a child. Many children fear and resent this because they feel defenseless against it and may even experience it as an attack (consciously or unconsciously). There may be an erotic tinge to this adult gesture, which the child senses and fears. Many a teacher has been shocked by being rebuffed or even struck when he or she put an arm around a child in a friendly gesture.

Twelve-year-old Paul came to my office one day in a furious mood. His shirt was torn, by the guidance counselor according to Paul. He had been walking down the hall on his way to my office when the guidance counselor had stopped him to find out why he was not in his classroom. While talking to him, she had put her arm on his shoulder. He had turned with his fist ready to hit her, and that is how his shirt had been torn. He assumed that she was going to pull him back into the classroom. He was still angry at her when he came to see me, shouting, "Does she think money grows on trees? My mother doesn't have the money to buy me new shirts all the time!" It was difficult to calm him down and to make him understand that all she wanted was information, and that he tore his own shirt because he had immediately assumed a hostile intent on the part of the other person.

This reaction was characteristic for Paul in his relationship with everyone outside his immediate family. One of the goals of psychotherapy was to give him insight into the origin of his chronic irritability, defensive attitude, and morbid suspiciousness. This boy was a nonreader who felt deeply ashamed, inferior, and doomed to failure in life because of this handicap. As is true for many children with reading disorders, he tried to hide his defect and was always afraid of being found out. This was not the only reason for his behavior disorder, but it was a constant source of conflict and distress that permeated all his reactions. If the guidance counselor had not touched him, he would have explained to her why he was in the hall, she could have found out whether or not he was breaking any rules, and he might have obeyed her. The social worker and I discussed this incident with her, and there was no recurrence.

The importance of keeping a physical distance from troubled youngsters was brought to my attention dramatically by the tragic murder of a dedicated Youthboard worker by members of the youth gang who called themselves "The Untouchables," after the television serial. Guidance counselors and teachers who knew the boys told me that they felt that these boys, who actually had liked the worker, may not have started to hit him if he had not touched them—also unquestionably in a friendly gesture. These boys had been drunk and therefore especially irritable and prone to sudden violent actions. Most of them, incidentally, were poor readers and academic failures.

Adults show a lack of understanding of children when they assume automatically that because they have cordial feelings toward the child and want physical contact, the child must feel the same way. Forced closeness and cordiality results in the child's withdrawal and may make valid examination results impossible. Therefore I never touch a child physically, except where hyperactivity or destructiveness become dangerous and cannot be controlled in any other way. My aim is, of course, to touch him emotionally.

EXCEPTIONS.   There are exceptions to the rule of no physical contact. Some young children may be very shy, timid, and anxious, and may need reassurance. Holding the adult's hand might make it easier for a child to separate from his or her mother, or classmates and teacher. For such children the walk to the doctor's office may seem terribly long, and they need this type of physical contact to decrease their anxiety. One may be able to sense this; if uncertain, it is best to reach out one's hand so that the child is free to hold on to it if he wants to.

Problems in Relation to Physical Examinations

Because physical distance facilitates a psychiatric examination, psychiatrists, including child psychiatrists, should not do a physical examination before, during, or after their contact with the patient—except under specific circumstances. A hospital setting often makes such an examination mandatory. I have made it a rule to undress and examine a child physically when there is the slightest suspicion of abuse. All children who come to their examination filthy and with torn clothes fall into this category, since I have detected signs of cruelty in many of them.

One such child was a 6-year-old girl referred to the hospital clinic from first grade because she paid no attention in school and learned nothing. The odor of her filthy clothes was overwhelming. The resident and I undressed her and found her arms covered with second-degree burns that were infected. She told us that she got burnt when she and her 10-year-old sister tried to cook for themselves and their 8-month-old brother because their mother was lying in bed, sick and unable to move. This child's mother was a heroin addict. Her neglect of her children amounted to abuse.

Importance of Confidentiality

In order to put the child at ease so that he feels free to say what is really on his mind and does his best when his intellectual achievements such as reading are tested, we must assure confidentiality. I tell each child that what he says is confidential and ask him what the word means. Many children do not know the meaning of this word. In child psychiatry and in teaching we assume too readily that the child understands the words we use or that our words have the same meaning for him as they have for us. I have learned always to determine whether the child understands what I am saying, not only with children whose native language is not English.

Children usually understand the words "private" or "secret," but not "confidential." Even after making sure that he understands what I mean, I add that whatever we say to each other will not go back to his parents or his teachers, unless there is something he would like me to tell them, because it is sometimes easier for a grown-up than for a child to talk to mother, father, or teacher. I also find out whether he knows what a psychiatrist is and assure him, if necessary, that I am not the kind of doctor who gives "needles." Some children associate this unpleasant experience with all doctors, and may be tense throughout the entire examination because they are expecting injections.

Note Taking

While the child talks and sometimes also plays, I observe him and take notes, holding the folder so that he cannot see what I am writing. I explain to him that this is my way of remembering what he says, and that by going over my notes after he has left I can think more deeply about him and try to understand him better. I make clear that the notes are my own and that no one else has access to them. In my experience with examining over 1,000 children and adolescents, only *one* child, a 12-year-old girl with acute paranoid schizophrenia, ever objected to this procedure.

Initiating Spontaneous Responses

If the child does not start by talking spontaneously, I ask a general question. I never start by asking about reading or any other sensitive subject likely to arouse turmoil and anxiety, unless the child himself brings it up. Even then I might suggest that he tell me about it later, and ask him about less painful aspects of his life first. This is a sound technique even where the examination has to be done under extreme pressure, for example, in jail. One should never start with the offense, but cover more neutral ground first. It takes time to establish a good relationship and earn the child's trust. One must give the child a chance to get to know the examiner better before one can expect to get a valid, truthful picture.

Diagnostic Assessments While Listening

While listening, I try to assess the child's general level of intelligence, attention span, mood, capacity for emotional contact, ability to express himself verbally, clarity of speech, anxiety level, excitability, and suggestibility. I also try to evaluate how truthful he is, how much he dramatizes, whether he can distinguish fantasy from reality, fact from fiction.

Speech Evaluation

I listen to the child's speech with special care to find out if it is clear, slurred, indistinct, or unintelligible for other reasons. Speech disorders are frequently associated with reading disorders and far too often are overlooked. Hearing disorders often have the same fate, especially when they are mild. A minor hearing defect may cause a major reading disorder. Pediatricians, neurologists, child psychiatrists, and other professionals caring for children should therefore train themselves to listen carefully to all details of the child's speech. It is possible to tell that a child or an adult is hard of hearing just by listening to him or her talk. Referrals to ear specialists and speech therapists depend on such astute observations (see Speech Disorders, Vol. II, p. 403).

Importance of Scars

As a part of my general observation, I look for scars on the child's face, neck, and arms—on all exposed parts of his skin. This is done inconspicuously and is not like a close physical examination. Asking about the origin of scars is a routine and very important part of the examination, and it almost invariably leads to the revelation of incidents in the child's life not told in any other context. It also shows his relationship with siblings and other children: many boys have what I call "battle scars" all over their faces, and can tell me stories of incessant battles with siblings and/or other children. Scars may also be the only clue to the identification of a "battered child," whose parents or other adults are treating him cruelly, who may even be in danger of being killed.

Asking about scars also reveals the child's general attitude about violence, which is of crucial importance for understanding his behavior. Sometimes it breaks the ice and initiates free and spontaneous talk in a tense and fearful or hostile child.

Getting Vital Information

While the child talks and plays, I interrupt to obtain the necessary information about specific aspects of his past and present life, and also to ask him to explain what he just told me whenever I find it unclear. I then ask him to describe what he meant in greater detail to me so that I can picture it clearly in my own mind. He can draw it if he likes, or dramatize it with dolls or puppets.

Practically all children, even 3-year-olds, can talk about intimate and often quite complicated thoughts and feelings, and I rarely have to rely only on their play and on my interpretation of it. We are apt to forget that children love to talk as soon as they have learned how, and that the older they get, the harder it is for them to find adults with enough time and interest to listen to them. Medical schools, teachers' colleges, and universities are generally inclined to ignore this fact and to train their students primarily to observe and interpret small children's play, drawings, and paintings, when it may be simpler and more reliable to ask the child. The exclusive use of play interpretation may lead to errors.

Description of Child's Home and Daily Life

I always ask the child to tell me about his home in great detail, about all dramatis personae, the physical setting, the economics, the daily life. I have a separate heading for sleep, including bedtime, how early or late it is, how long it takes him to fall asleep. Far too many children habitually go to bed so late that they are always sleepy and fatigued in class; this alone may be a major cause for their reading difficulty. Bedtime is commonly a time of stress for the entire family, especially with young children, and the child's description of it may bring out characteristic interaction among the different family members.

ELICITING SPECIAL FEARS AND HALLUCINATIONS.   While he talks about his experiences with sleep, the examiner can easily lead the child into revealing sleep difficulties and fears of the dark, of seeing "ghosts," "spirits," "painted faces," and into talking about hearing frightening noises, feeling skeletons touching him, hearing God or the devil talk to him. Children may try to conceal these experiences from adults for fear of being laughed at or called "crazy." These hypnagogic hallucinations usually are within normal limits and benign, but they may indicate severe psychopathology; this line of questioning can make such distinctions more obvious. It also facilitates questions about dreams, any dream he happens to remember or a dream he has had repeatedly.

DREAMS.   Even though an analysis of dreams is obviously not possible during one session, it does give a quick insight into the depth of the child's conflicts and anxieties. Children with reading disorders do not dream simply about reading or even about school, and it is not possible to infer a reading disorder from dream analysis, not even where the reading problem is the chief complaint. (See section in Chapter 5, Dreams, p. 253.)

PUNISHMENT AND GUILT FEELINGS.   I ask about all aspects of punishment: who administers it, how (beatings; "she just yells at me," etc.), and what type of behavior makes parents and teachers angry and leads to punishment. While talking about this, the child quite naturally reveals his own guilt feelings.

I cover the child's health history, his experience with illness and pain, with doctors, hospitals, and clinics, and his feelings and thoughts connected with this.

Sexual History

I do not ask about sexual thoughts and feelings unless the child brings them up spontaneously or the history requires this sort of information. This topic is surrounded by so much hypochondriasis, such feelings of shame and guilt, that it is most difficult for the youngster to talk about it truthfully. The very questions we ask are inevitably also suggestions and may therefore be harmful to the child. More than one session is usually required to establish a relationship of sufficient depth that these difficulties in communication can be overcome. (Mosse, 1966(a), 1970).

School History

The child's school experiences form necessarily a key part of the examination. He will talk freely about them only if he is really sure that what he says will not go back to his teachers. Here he reveals his general attitudes toward learning, explains what he finds difficult and what easy, and also how he feels about his teachers and the other children in his class.

Reading History

The child at this point may start to talk about reading on his own because it is an important part of his daily classroom life. This affords the opportunity to find out what his feelings about reading are and what experiences he has had with it, even before I test his achievement. Some children feel so ashamed about their reading failure or are so angry that they do not mention it at all. In these cases a question about comic books usually breaks the ice.

MASS MEDIA. I always ask children about mass media (comic books, television, movies) because they are companions in most households and are important in the lives of all children. Frequently they are the key to the child's world. A child may refuse to talk or answer only in monosyllables, until comic books are mentioned; then his face lights up and he starts to talk with excitement and animation and sometimes so fast that it is difficult to follow him. This may be the first time he uses sentences and shows that he can tell a story coherently. He may confuse reality, television, dreams, and fantasy to such an extent that an important aspect of his emotional disturbance is suddenly revealed.

Comic Books. Often the only way a child can be made to talk about his reading habits is by asking what comic books he likes and noting how he tells the stories in them. Children with reading disorders usually say that they tell the stories only by the pictures. Many children carry comic books around with them; if this child has one, it will be even easier to bring this topic up and ask him to show how he reads it. By observing children's eye movements during routine clinical work, Wertham discovered a new form of reading disorder he called Linear Dyslexia. All children should be examined for this condition. (See section in Chapter 2, Linear Dyslexia, p. 127.)

Comic Book Reading Test. Clesbie R. Daniels and I developed a technique to observe and record children's eye movements and reading errors during comic book reading. Either place a mirror on the page opposite to the one the child is reading to observe his eye movements, or just ask him to point to the picture he is looking at. A number is written next to each picture and each balloon as the child looks at them, so that one has a permanent record of what the child looked at first, second, and so on. The words are numbered as he reads them, and the errors are noted. In order to have a clearer record it may be better to write on a separate sheet of paper the words he reads, and later to compare them with the text in the balloons. The child's eyes zigzag of necessity when he tries to follow the text in the balloons conscientiously, so that the comic book test can lead us only to suspect Linear Dyslexia. It must always be confirmed by formal testing during regular paragraph and page reading. (See section in Chapter 2, Linear Dyslexia, p. 127.)

Television. Some information about the child's reading habits can also be elicited when he talks about television. We must suspect a reading disorder when he says that he never reads a book on his own but spends all his free time watching television. In some respects television makes it harder for children to learn how to read because they are so conditioned to respond to the live or animated action on the screen where everyone talks, that they may tend to ignore anything communicated on the screen with letters, which may help them to learn to read and spell. Children may also find that reading is not exciting, interesting, or relevant enough.

Yet television provides such intensive emotional and intellectual stimulation that children become interested in ideas and topics they never heard of before. The enormous interest in science fiction books, for instance, was initiated and kept alive by television. Television has thus stimulated reading in children as well as adults. Fourteen-year-old Teddy, whose reading problem was not due to difficulties with the techniques of reading, but to lack of practice because of complete lack of interest, surprised me one day by asking me what "raw material" is. He had heard this term on television and became interested in it. This gave me the opportunity to arouse his interest in reading about raw material, a fascinating topic to him.

Book Reading. At some time during the examination I ask each child whether he has ever read a whole book. If so, I ask him to name the title of the book, to tell me something about the content and whether he liked it, or what type of book or story he prefers. Even if the child says he has read a book and seems to have understood it, and even if he was not referred because of a reading disorder, I still let him read a page to be sure he can read. An increasing number of children either say they have never read a book or talk about it in such a way that one suspects they have never actually read one and are bragging to make a good impression. I ask such children whether they can read a whole page and observe whether they really can.

The Formal Testing Phase of the Examination

The free talk and play part of the examination has now been completed, and I start more formal testing. As a transition I often use the Duess Fable test to learn more about sensitive areas of the child that may not yet have been touched. It consists of open-ended stories which the child is asked to complete (Mosse, 1954).

Examination of Lateral Dominance

As a change of pace I now investigate the child's laterality. I ask him to lift up the hand he eats and writes with and to tell me which hand it is. Some children can distinguish their hands but cannot name them correctly. I also ask him to fold his hands to see which thumb is folded on top, as this indicates the dominant hand. To determine eye dominance, I fold a sheet of paper so that it forms a telescope, let him pick it up with one hand and look through it with one eye only. I also ask him to shut both eyes and to try to open just one; this is the dominant eye. This is a routine part of my examination even though, contrary to Orton and others, I have not found a significant correlation between reading disorders and mixed eye/hand dominance, lack of the development of dominance, or forced use of the nondominant hand. Apparently most children with these conditions learn to read and write perfectly well if taught properly. They may require more careful training in the very beginning in the left-right direction, and may take a little longer. (See Hand Dominance and Organic Writing Disorders, Chapter 3, p. 179.)

There does seem to be a correlation, however, between certain reading disorders definitely of organic origin, and difficulty not only with laterality, but with orientation in the general environment. For this reason I always examine children with reading problems for this type of defect and also ask their parents whether the child can find his way home or gets lost, and whether he gets confused about directions in the home, on the street, or in school, especially in the halls going from one classroom to the other (Birch & Belmont, 1965; Rabinovitch, 1959,1968).

The Mosaic Test

My formal testing starts with the Mosaic test because it is nonverbal and unstructured and seems more like play to the child. He usually enjoys doing it and does not feel self-conscious or pressured. I find this test, as interpreted by Wertham, indispensible both for clinical work and research.

TEST MATERIAL. The child psychiatrist Margaret Lowenfeld developed a Mosaic test set that she originally obtained from Czechoslovakia. Wertham added oblong pieces. The set consists of colored pieces, which can be made of plastic, wood or aluminum. Commercial sets are usually made of plastic, but aluminum with color baked on in an enamel finish is the most suitable material because the pieces are light, sturdy, easily handled, and unbreakable. I have seen good sets made in hospitals and clinics in occupational therapy or other workshops because they are not always available commercially.

The pieces are ¼-inch thick and there are six colors: black, blue, red, green, yellow, and off-white or eggshell. Each color is presented in six shapes, as follows:

Squares—1 ⅛ in. on each side, four pieces of each color

Equilateral triangles—1 ½ in. on each side, six pieces of each color

Diamond-shaped pieces—1 ⅛ in. on each side, eight pieces of each color

Triangles—1 ⅝ in. on the base, 1 ⅛ in. on each of the other two sides; eight pieces of each color

Triangles—⅔ in. on one side, 1 ½ in. on the second side, 1 ⅜ in. on the third side; 12 pieces of each color

Oblongs: 1 ½ in. by ¼ in.; 12 pieces of each color

These pieces are used on a tray that measures 16 in. by 10 ½ in., having a raised margin about ½-in. wide to keep the pieces from sliding off as they are used. A brown piece of paper is put on the tray so that the completed mosaic can be traced and colored. Another method of recording this test is photography.

PROCEDURE.   The child or adult is shown the pieces in the box. The examiner takes out a sample of each shape and then of each color and shows them to the child, explaining that all shapes come in every color, and every color in each shape. It is important not to name the shapes or the colors and only to show the samples; otherwise the child's color discrimination and color naming cannot be tested.

After this the child is asked to make anything he wants to on the tray, and that he can use as many or as few pieces as he likes, take as much time as he needs, and indicate when he has finished. The time he takes should be recorded.

When he has finished, he should be asked whether he has given it a title, what he had in mind to do, whether it came out that way, and whether he likes it (Ames and Ilg, 1962; Dörken, 1956; Wertham, 1959; Zucker, 1950).

TESTING COLOR DISCRIMINATION.   Using the mosaic pieces to test the child's color discrimination adds to the value of the Mosaic technique.

When the child has finished his mosaic and has titled and explained it, I point to pieces of different colors on his mosaic and in the box and ask him to name the colors. Some children can distinguish colors perfectly but cannot name them. To test for this, I point to a piece on the tray without naming its color, and ask the child to pick a piece of the same color out of the box.

When I detect color blindness or other, less clear-cut color-discrimination difficulties, I administer the Ishihara test to establish a definite diagnosis and also refer the child to an eye specialist. This technique enabled me to diagnose color blindness where no one had noticed it before, and to discover other less common color-discrimination defects.

CLINT, 7 YEARS OLD: SEVERE UNDIAGNOSED CONGENITAL RETINOPATHY. This boy had been referred by his school because of disruptive behavior and inability to learn to read. With the help of the Mosaic test I discovered color-discrimination defects and referred him to an ophthalmologist, who diagnosed a congenital retinopathy (high myopia with congenital dystrophic retinal changes), which was treatable. With successful treatment of his eye disease his disruptive behavior ceased and he learned to read.

COLOR BLINDNESS. Color blindness, which affects 3% of boys and 0.2% of girls, is a handicap whose existence seems to have been forgotten. This is shown by the replacement of black chalkboards by green ones in all modern schools and colleges in Europe as well as in the United States. Color-blind youngsters cannot read what is chalked on green boards because they see it as gray on gray.

Seven-year-old Perry first brought this problem to my attention. He was in psychotherapy with me privately for hyperactivity on a neurotic basis. He was so distractible, hyperactive, and preoccupied with fantasies that he could not concentrate long enough to learn how to read. (See section on Hyperactivity, Vol. II, pp. 611.) He told me that his closest friend was also in trouble for not doing his work properly. This friend could sit still and concentrate, but could not read what was on the chalkboard because he was color-blind, and the board was green. I checked up on this story and found it to be true.

I have seen a number of children get into undeserved trouble in school because their color-blindness was undetected. This may even endanger their lives because they cannot distinguish the red from the green traffic light.

It is especially important to look for color-discrimination defects in children suffering from reading disorders because such defects are sometimes found when the reading difficulty is of organic origin. The reason for this is that the pertinent brain areas are located in the parietal lobes near the angular gyrus, which lies at the center of the region where correlation of the different functions that enter into the reading process takes place (Critchley, 1953).

The Mosaic test is especially helpful for understanding reading disorders because of its reliability in confirming or ruling out major pathologic processes. It may show organicity where no other test does. It can even distinguish cortical from subcortical localization and is of special help where apraxia is suspected. It can clinch the diagnosis of mental deficiency and help to differentiate it from schizophrenia and neurosis. It sometimes indicates depression and severe, potentially violent conflicts and explosiveness more clearly than any other test.

The reason for the reliability of the Mosaic test within broad diagnostic categories is Wertham's method of investigation. He correlated in very large numbers of patients the mosaic designs made by adults and children with definite diagnostic categories. In this way he found that adult and child patients with organic brain disease make designs characterized by "a disorder in the organization of the designs" and that two kinds of lesions can be distinguished, a "cortical" and a "subcortical" pattern (Figures 1.1, 1.2).

ORGANIC MOSAIC TEST PATTERNS.   In the chapter "The Mosaic Test" in *Projective Psychology* (1950), Wertham described the cortical pattern in the following way.

Patients with senile dementia, severe cerebral arteriosclerosis, dementia paralytica, Korsakov's psychosis, or severe encephalopathy following trauma express their cortical defect in an inability to achieve a good configuration. There is a dismemberment and dissolution of the Gestalt. Patients with dementia use very few pieces, and they like to represent very simple, elementary geometric forms such as a circle or a star. They are likely to use shapes inappropriate for their goal and they tend to use color indiscriminately. The combination of using a very simple pattern and of being unable to achieve a good configuration is typical. Sometimes subjects with diffuse cortical brain disease make a number of very small incomplete designs. In the most advanced conditions of dementia, patients merely place a few scattered pieces on the board. (pp. 248–249)

I have found cortical Mosaic patterns in a number of children with an organic reading disorder. Most, but not all, also had other organic symptoms, especially aphasia. (See section in Chapter 10 on Aphasia, Vol. II, p. 382); and cases Alfred, Vol. I, p. 99, and Morris, Vol. II, p. 568.)

Wertham described the "subcortical" pattern in the following way: "It is characterized by 'stone-bound' designs. At the expense of an inner plan the patient follows the impetus inherent in the shape and color of the pieces put down so that the whole response becomes reduced to a more mechanical or automatic level." He explained this performance by stating:

In the normal brain there is a plastic utilization of inner and outer stimuli. The patient with impaired brain function becomes excessively dependent on outer stimuli at the expense of his inner goal. If one follows the successive utilization of the stimulus of each new piece as the patient makes the "stone-bound design," the "bondage to the stimulus" ("Reizgebundenheit," as Goldstein called it) becomes apparent. "Stone-bound" designs may be seen in such diverse clinical conditions as postencephalitic Parkinsonism, cerebral arteriosclerosis, congenital spastic paraplegia, and Jacksonian epilepsy. (p. 249)

The Mosaic test performance itself can in this way be considered a neurologic sign. I have found this pattern in many children with an organic reading disorder with or without other organic symptoms. (See Inability to Shift Freely from One Activity to Another, Vol. II, p. 480; and cases Emilio, p. 157; and Leon, p. 101, Vol. I.)

FIG. 1.1.   Girl, age 14. Cortical Mosaic design, no title. She tried desperately to "make something," but could not achieve any gestalt. Lack of red and prominence of black pieces indicates depression. She suffered from a degenerative disease of the brain of unknown origin. (Color plate of Figure 1.1 follows p. 224.)

Drawings

While I trace and color his mosaic, I ask the child to draw. This saves time and keeps me busy so that the child does not feel that my attention is completely focused on him. Tests should be observed unobtrusively in any case.

I use the Koch Tree Test and the Figure Drawing Test. I always start with the tree because it seems the easiest form to draw and is less charged emotionally. When the child has finished it, I ask him to draw a person; then, depending on whom he drew first, to draw a person of the other sex, all on separate sheets of paper. These two projective techniques give insights into different aspects of the child's personality and often show defects characteristic for children with reading disorders. (See Common Features of Handwriting Analysis and Drawing Tests, p. 197.)

Testing Reading

I use the drawings as a starting point to test reading, writing, and spelling, because they belong together. A child reads better when he can also write and spell what he reads, and he writes and spells better when he reads a lot and well. The reading skill consists of a succession of conditioned reflexes that are reinforced in this way. (See Conditioned Reflexes, p. 69.)

FIG. 1.2.   Mosaic of a 9-year-old boy with an organic reading disorder and congenital nerve deafness in one ear. The Mosaic was the only test indicating an organic impairment. *Title:* "I can't call it anything because I don't think it looks like anything." Typical *stone-bound* design indicating subcortical impairment. The shape of the design is entirely determined by the first piece put on the tray. The following pieces are put on each other's surface. *The pieces* determine the shape of the design. The patient is *stimulus-bound.* (Color plate of Figure 1.2 follows p. 224.)

TESTING SEQUENCING.   I ask the child to write his name, age, and the date on the back of one of the pictures he drew. This occasion is used to find out whether he knows the days of the week and the months of the year and can recite them in correct sequence. Many children with reading disorders can not do this. If there is a genuine difficulty in learning distinct sequences or series, an organic impairment may be present. Before we can make this assumption, however, we must establish that the child has been taught the days of the week and the months of the year. Some children lead such chaotic lives that one day seems like the other, and it makes no difference to them what day or what month it is; they therefore pay no attention to them and do not learn to recite them.

TESTING CLOCK READING. The same considerations as above l
for children who cannot tell time. I let each child read a watch or a
the child cannot tell time, I let him copy the drawing of a clock face, _
draw one without a model to find out where the difficulty lies. (See Clock
Reading Disorder, Chapter 3, p. 164.)

TESTING LETTER, NUMBER, WORD RECOGNITION. By writing his name,
the child writes the two words he is most familiar with and has known how
to write the longest, since kindergarten. These are the first words almost any
child learns to copy, particularly the first name: the last name is generally
learned only when it is short. I have learned not to take for granted that the
child understands how the different lines and squiggles he writes come to
signify his name. I therefore ask the child to point out the word that says his
first name and the one that says his last name. I do not use the words "first"
or "last," but rather say the names.

Some children show confusion even on this elementary level; many more do
not recognize all letters in their names, either by sound or name. I always test
for this by pointing to one letter at a time (out of sequence of course) and
asking the child to name it and sound it out. I also name the letters and let
him point to them; then I make the sound of the letters and let him point them
out.

This detailed testing is necessary because these functions are distinct facets
of the writing and reading skill. The child may learn one but fail to learn the
other; or he may not have been taught either one. We must make a precise
determination; otherwise we can neither diagnose his defects correctly nor help
him overcome them. Some children, for instance, can name the letter correctly
only when they see it, but cannot find it when they hear it said. If properly
taught, a child does not notice that the reading and writing skill consists of
so many minute parts. The teacher, however, must know about them in order
to be able to train the child in such a way that he does not develop any defects,
and in order to be able to recognize and eliminate defects as soon as they occur.

For this purpose I have made a list of functions that must be tested so that
a reading disorder diagnosis can be made. This list is based entirely on the
clinical method, and was developed while testing and retesting hundreds of
children with or without a reading disorder.

We must find out whether a child can:

1. Recognize letters and numbers when he sees them as letters or numbers
2. Sound out letters
3. Name letters
4. Find letters when someone else says their name or makes their sound
5. Recognize a group of letters as a word and read it out loud
6. Understand the word

7. Read a word silently
8. Spell a word orally
9. Keep his eyes on the line while reading and perform the return sweep to the beginning of the next line correctly, without skipping lines
10. Copy letters and words
11. Write letters and words to dictation
12. Write letters and words spontaneously

While carrying out such detailed examination, we must be aware that the child's mounting feelings of frustration and anger may interfere with his performance. Older children, especially, may feel insulted when asked to write letters. This reaction can be avoided or minimized only if a good relationship has been established before this testing is done.

When I have the slightest doubt about the child's ability to write, recognize, name, or sound out letters, I dictate them at random, not in alphabetical order, because he may have merely memorized them mechanically within this sequence. (See Sequence Writing, Chapter 3, p. 141.)

Next, I dictate words and sentences, and after that I ask the child to write anything he would like. Some children have such severe defects and such resistance against writing that they say they cannot write anything. In this event I remark that I know they can write *one* word at least, and that it happens to be one they usually like a lot. I mean the word "I" and tell them if they don't guess it. This usually breaks their resistance and they enjoy writing "I." I then try to find out whether they can put any words together by dictating such two-letter words as "me, no, be, in, on, it." Often children with a severe organic reading and writing disorder cannot do this even after the sound of the letters has been explained to them. Children whose defect results only from the curriculum practice of not teaching phonics to beginning readers, write these short words correctly as soon as the connection of letter with sound has been pointed out. If the child cannot write these words, I print them to see whether he can read them.

SENTENCE DICTATION. The sentences I dictate are short and simple and are selected so that they evoke pleasant images for the child, for example, "I like my mother and my father. I am a little (nice) boy (or girl). I like to swim. I live in a house. My home is big. We like to go out. I like to ride on a horse." I dictate only one or two of these sentences, as indicated in each particular case.

It is well known that children with reading disorders make typical errors. One 6-year-old girl simply wrote "i m a g" for "I am a girl." A 9-year-old boy wrote "mn" for man, "hocs" for house; another 9-year-old boy wrote "I a tan" for "I am tall." Many write "siwn" for "swim," "gril" for "girl," "ma" for "am," and reverse letters horizontally or vertically. Some children turn the paper in such a way that they write straight upwards instead of left to right.

The above examples show directional confusions. They are called "reversals" when letters are rotated around their horizontal axis—m becoming w, b becoming p, and so on; and "inversions" when letters are rotated vertically, b to d, q to g, and so on. These children also tend to read "saw" instead of "was," "on" instead of "no," and the like. (See Directional Confusion of Letters and Words, Chapter 2, p. 91.)

The words "house," "home," and "horse" are especially helpful for the understanding of the child's reading problem. I always dictate them and write them to let the child read them. Children who confuse these words or stop after writing the "h" and ask "how do you spell it?" invariably have not been taught phonics properly or, as is unfortunately the prevailing curriculum practice, have been taught only the beginning consonant.

Millions of viewers of a Sunday television program run by the Board of Education of New York City ("The Superintendent of Schools Reports") witnessed a demonstration, no doubt unintended, of this faulty curriculum practice on November 23, 1969. The teacher held a so-called flash card with the word "horse" on it up to the class for the children to read. All children promptly yelled "house." The teacher did not explain their error to them, but only taught the beginning sound. When later she held up the picture of a trumpet with the word "trumpet" under it, the children read it as "horn."

This highlights the importance of asking each child, as well as his parents and teachers, exactly how he has been and is being taught to read. It took years of painstaking examination of children to make me realize that reading and writing disorders were not necessarily signs of psychopathology or organic defects, but may instead be consequences of inappropriate teaching methods. Until I actually observed sight/word teaching in classrooms, it had not occurred to me that anyone would attempt to teach a child how to read while withholding from him the information that letters and letter combinations stand for sounds. When I realized that this had become the standard curriculum in most schools for beginning readers in kindergarten and first grade, I had to revise my diagnoses of reading disorders.

TESTING NUMBER READING AND WRITING. Asking each child to write the date on the back of his drawing helps in evaluating his number reading and writing ability. However, he may just be copying what he saw the teacher write on the chalkboard that same day. His number reading and writing should therefore be tested along with his letter concepts, since he may make reversals or inversions on his numbers also. Letting him read and write numbers is part of an assessment of his arithmetical reasoning, which should be tested in detail when there is even the slightest doubt about his performance. (See Chapter 4, Testing the Ten Basic Arithmetical Acts, p. 227.)

Handwriting Sample.   Testing the child's writing also provides a sample of his handwriting that I can analyze. This is a useful projective technique that has been much neglected. (See Chapter 2, Handwriting Analysis, p. 209.)

TESTING PARAGRAPH AND PAGE READING.   I test the child's paragraph and page reading with the Gray Oral Reading Paragraphs. Since I know them by heart, I can easily observe the child closely and record his errors. The style of some of the stories is old-fashioned for modern American children, and they are usually not familiar with some of the words, for example, "scarcely," "reared," "industrious," "brilliancy," "dignifying." This enables us to observe how the child approaches words he has never heard or read before. It is important in any case to ascertain which words are unfamiliar to children in each reading test or book one uses. We must be aware of what words are not being used any more, and also be familiar with dialects and the current uses and meaning of words for children. I have for years made lists of such words. This knowledge is essential not only for correct evaluation of tests in general, but, more importantly, for our understanding of the child during the general psychiatric examination and particularly during psychotherapy.

Miles Peep-Hole Method.   I have mounted the Gray Oral Reading Paragraphs on cards so that I can use the Miles Peep-Hole Method to observe the child's eye movements while he reads. A small opening is made near the middle of the page between two lines. I hold the card against my face so that I can look through the opening while the child faces me and reads (Blair, 1956, p. 26).

I usually first observe the child's eye movements casually while he reads sitting at my desk, with this card or a book in front of him. When I notice that he loses his place on the line, skips lines or can't find the beginning of the next line, points at each word as he reads it, or moves his head along with the text, I suspect eye movement trouble and use the Mirror or Peep-Hole test. (See Chapter 2, Linear Dyslexia, p. 127.)

Eyesight Assessment.   I refer the child with such difficulties to an ophthalmologist in any case. Many children need such referral, not only when they have eye movement difficulties. Observing the child during reading and writing affords the opportunity to form an opinion about his eyesight. Often I have suspected that a child might need eyeglasses, and have been the first person to have noticed it. This happens even with children as old as 11 or 12 years of age, and is as true for clinic practice as private practice. It is my impression that neglect of a medical eye examination is, next to lack of dental care, the greatest failure in children's medical care.

School eye examinations are unreliable. Children hate to wear glasses, so many of them memorize the different letters or other signs on the eye charts by observing others before it is their turn to read them.

Statistics as reported by pediatricians Falvo and Flanigan confirm my impressions. In their paper, "Child Health Assurance Program" (1979) they refer to statistics collected for an ABC-TV program with the title "A Case of Neglect," which was aired on July 17, 1974. It stated that 12 million children in the United States still receive no health care, that two-thirds of poor children never see a dentist, one-fourth have uncorrected visual problems, and one-fifth to one-half have a hearing deficit. Their own data collected from 1975 to 1977 show that there has been no improvement.

EVALUATION OF ERRORS. It is helpful to know the pitfalls and common errors in the reading material one uses. Each error must be recorded and analyzed separately while the child is present so that one can ask him about it. The words "Pray, puss," for instance, in the third paragraph of the Gray Oral Reading Test frequently present the first obstacle. They are both unusual for the child and can be read only phonetically, by a child who has learned how to sound letters and blend them. Some children leave out "puss" or only whisper it, giggle, or blush because this word also has a "dirty" meaning. In the vast literature on reading disorders one rarely finds an exact and detailed analysis of the child's actual reading errors. Yet diagnosis as well as treatment must be based on such an analysis.

TESTING COMPREHENSION. To test the child's comprehension I ask him to define some words he has read and to tell me the story he has just read in his own words, while I cover the paragraph so that he cannot refer to it.

TESTING SILENT READING. I no longer use silent reading tests because I find them worthless for my purpose. I test the child's silent reading ability by having him read a paragraph or chapter in a book I know, or one of the Gray Oral Paragraphs, and ask him to tell me what he has just read. Useful reading error analyses can be made only with oral reading. With the help of tape recorders it has now become possible to give oral reading tests even to large groups of children. To avoid embarrassing any of them, one can let each child read alone in a room or cubicle.

READING POEMS OR STORIES WRITTEN BY THE CHILD. We cannot take it for granted that a child can read a poem or a story he wrote himself, but should always ask him to read it to us. Children bring such stories to us proudly. They are frequently mimeographed and published in the classroom or school newspaper. However, this does not necessarily mean that the child actually wrote it. Rather, he may have dictated it to the teacher who wrote it on the chalkboard for him to copy; the child may not necessarily be able to read it. Teachers may do this not only to save time, but to help children who suffer from reading, spelling, and writing disorders. This may create the illusion that the child can read when he can only dictate and copy. (See Teaching of Writing, Chapter 3, p. 184.)

Test Evaluation and Treatment Plan

I do not try to make a formal evaluation of the child's reading grade. The tests are not scored. My concern is to find out exactly what aspect of the reading skill the child has trouble with, irrespective of age or grade, or even level of intelligence, because this alone determines what kind of corrective teaching and therapy he needs. A high school student who has trouble reading "Pray, puss," who reads "scarely" instead of "scarcely," "even" instead of "ever," "place" instead of "palace," needs training in phonics irrespective of his grade or intelligence level.

My examination of the child lasts about 3 to 3½ hours, and usually includes a brief session with each parent alone, then with both parents together. At this time I discuss my diagnostic impression with them, and we develop a treatment plan. After that, I see the entire family together to observe their interaction and to share pertinent aspects of the diagnosis and especially the treatment plan with the child. It is important that the child not feel left out of decisions involving his life, and that parents and child are together when the treatment plan is being discussed so that misunderstandings, which are so apt to occur, are kept at a minimum. If the child seems very anxious or still in great turmoil, I see him again briefly alone at the very end.

This procedure is flexible and depends on the circumstances under which I see the child. In a mental hygiene clinic the social worker usually has seen the parents, and I have read the complete social history before I see the child. In my private practice I usually see the parents first without the child. As a rule, I have read the psychologic examination report and conferred with the psychologist before I examine the child. This is the best and most efficient procedure, since it saves time and greatly facilitates my task of evaluating all the facts, pulling the diverse observations and reports together, arriving at a diagnosis, and working out a treatment plan.

All children referred for reading disorders need individual psychodiagnostic testing. Sometimes the psychiatric examination must first determine whether such testing is indicated. But child psychiatrists should be capable of determining on their own whether the child needs reading treatment and whether this should be done individually or can be successful in a group, usually a special class; or whether it can be accomplished by the classroom teacher. It is also the child psychiatrist's task to refer the child for other examinations and tests, especially an electroencephalogram (EEG).

Diagnostic Importance of Electroencephalography

The EEG is of great value for the diagnosis of brain diseases, for example, encephalitis, brain tumors, or convulsive disorders. It should, however, be evaluated like any other test, namely as only *one* piece of evidence among others, never as the *only* determining factor. For, even though the neuropsychiatrist Hans Berger invented the EEG as long ago as 1924, the correlation of abnormal or unusual EEG tracings with clinical symptoms and diseases has still not been completely worked out, especially in children. This test is very difficult to administer to a child, the margin of error is great, and the limits of the normal reading for different ages has not yet been clearly defined.

False negative results can occur, even when the EEG has been done under the most favorable conditions and evaluated with the utmost care. Brain disease or defect has been demonstrated in such cases by other means. False positive results also occur, with a frequency estimated by various investigators as high as 10%. No one can demonstrate organic cerebral defects or diseases by any other means in these cases, and neither do follow-up studies show any evidence for organicity.

The famous neurosurgeon Paul C. Bucy put the EEG in its proper perspective. In an editorial in the *Journal of the American Medical Association* (1956) he stated:

> The electroencephalogram is not, independently, a trustworthy diagnostic instrument. No one, by this means alone, can make a satisfactory diagnosis of epilepsy, a brain tumor, or a traumatic injury to the brain. The electroencephalogram by itself is also inadequate evidence on which to base treatment or to render a medicolegal opinion. It is a matter of common experience that the information gained from electroencephalographic tracings may be grossly misleading and that great care must be exercised in correlating such records with all other clinical and laboratory data and in evaluating the electroencephalograms accordingly.

The neurologist David B. Clark also warns in W. E. Nelson's *Textbook of Pediatrics*: "One should not commit himself irrevocably to a diagnosis whose sole support is an electroencephalogram" (1969, p. 1273).

These admonitions to use the EEG with caution have unfortunately gone unheeded. Far too many children are labeled "organic" or "brain damaged" because of an abnormal EEG, without any corroboration clinically or through other tests. The EEG has been much too widely accepted by physicians and laypersons alike as *the* crucial test for organicity.

Parents, teachers, and school principals are now apt to demand an EEG and to look on it as the final judgment. It is far from infallible, however, and may not even be necessary for the determination that the child's reading disorder has an organic cause. A negative EEG alone does not indicate that the child's psychologic symptoms and/or his reading disorder are psychogenic; nor does a positive EEG necessarily mean that they are organic. Clinical examinations and psychologic tests are needed in addition to an EEG to determine cerebral causation with certainty. This is clarified in great detail in Chapter 2, p. 43; Vol. II, p. 453.

Children's Reactions to an EEG

It is of the utmost importance to explain this test to the child before administering it. He should also be given a chance to reveal all the questions and doubts he has on his mind before, during, and after the test. An EEG causes great anxiety and stimulates fantasies that are often profuse and frightening. Children have told me that they were afraid their brain would blow up. An 11-year-old boy refused to keep his appointments at the child psychiatric clinic because he thought his brain was radioactive and would spread radiation. Other children had similar fears, undoubtedly influenced by comic book and television stories. None was psychotic. Simple, truthful explanations could have prevented these harmful psychologic reactions.

Summary

The data collected with the clinical examination here described make it possible to disentangle those factors that enter significantly into the causation of the child's reading disorder. It is a multilevel examination that touches on all aspects and all layers (conscious, preconscious, and unconscious) of the child's personality, as well as the familial and social forces around him. It forms the basis for the practical diagnostic classification that is presented in the following chapters. Special tests for specific symptoms are described in the sections devoted to each symptom.

Chapter 2

Reading Disorders on an Organic Basis

1. The Organic Bases of Reading Disorders

All children whose reading disorder is due to the malfunctioning of those parts of the brain that must be intact for reading and writing are victims of organic reading disorders. With few exceptions, they are unable to *learn* reading. These disorders constitute distinct clinical syndromes, even though their etiology is most difficult to establish and must remain tentative in most cases. They differ from the psychogenic and the sociogenic group of reading disorders. They may occur either as features of general disorders such as mental deficiency, epilepsy and other convulsive disorders, cerebral palsy, schizophrenia, and so on, or by themselves. (See sections where their relationship to the above-mentioned disorders is described, Vol. II, pp. 411, 422, 429, 431.)

Reading disorders on an organic basis are frequently presented as the only type of reading disorder, especially in studies by neurologists and other physicians. Authors with an exclusively psychoanalytic point of view, on the other hand, tend to minimize their existence and to explain these children's symptoms as symbolic expressions of unconscious processes. Pearson's *A Handbook of Child Psychoanalysis,* however, takes a more cautious view. It states that psychoanalysis may not be successful in "specialized learning difficulties" and suggests that "parents should be warned that the analysis is only an experiment and may not result in any increased ability to learn" (1968, p. 48). Still, Pearson makes no differential diagnosis, and does not even mention an organic group. Yet a close scrutiny of clinical statements presented in some psychoanalytic publications shows that the child concerned apparently had an organic reading disorder. This can be deduced from details in the description of the child's symptoms without even having examined him (Mosse, 1967).

The failure to diagnose that a child's reading disorder has an organic basis may do great harm. When such a child's reading difficulty is misdiagnosed as psychogenic and he is consequently treated with psychotherapy or psychoanalysis, a new psychopathologic process is set in motion. He becomes deeply discouraged because his reading does not improve, and frequently gives up any effort to cope with it. Many of these children subsequently become chronically anxious, insecure, and depressed, doubting their intellectual ability generally. Others deny and suppress their reading difficulty altogether, lying and inventing stories they say they have read.

Some children even begin to doubt their sanity, a most serious consequence. They feel that they must be severely and perhaps hopelessly sick mentally because they just cannot learn to read, and they may be afraid to confess this fear to parents, teachers, or therapists. Organic symptoms do indeed have psychologic implications and consequences just as do all other physical symptoms, and many children with an organic reading disorder need psychotherapy. This does not mean, however, that these symptoms have psychologic causes. One must distinguish between the nature of a symptom and its cause. A psychologic symptom may have a psychologic or an organic cause. (See General and Unspecific Psychopathology Frequently Associated with Organic Reading Disorders, Vol. II, p. 453.)

The diagnostic and therefore therapeutic fate of children whose reading disorder has an organic basis depends far too often on the theoretical point of view or conviction of their examiners, be they pediatricians, psychiatrists, neurologists, psychologists, or educators. For decades the dominant theoretical trend was psychologic, but this changed to a general organic orientation. The medical term "Dyslexia" has become fashionable among psychologists and educators. Dyslexia, translated from its Greek and Latin origin, means only reading difficulty; it does not refer to any causation. This term has nevertheless come to be widely used in describing organic reading disorders; it is even more widely misused to excuse the failure of the schools to teach reading properly. For if all reading failures are "organic," teachers cannot be held responsible for them.

The following is part of a mimeographed statement given to worried parents by the principal of an elementary school with a poor reading record:

> When Johnny can't read—and 15% of the 36 million U.S. elementary school children are at least two years behind in reading capability—Johnny's parents usually blame the teachers or their techniques. Teachers often snap back that Johnny just won't try. In perhaps 2,000,000 of these cases, researchers are now discovering, neither school nor student is at fault: Johnny can't read because of a neurophysiological disorder, most often called "dyslexia."

This 2,000,000 figure is frequently cited, but the data on which it is based are never discussed. Diagnostic criteria and terminologies vary so widely that no valid statistics on the number of children suffering from organic reading disorders can possibly exist. The core group with severe organically based pathology is relatively small, but a large group of children with minor defects usually remain undetected. Such minor defects may remain subclinical and never develop into a symptom when these children are raised and taught carefully. They develop into clinical symptoms and even lifelong handicaps only in educationally, emotionally, and socially neglected children. This is one of the reasons reading disorders are more prevalent in schools attended by disadvantaged children.

The term "Learning Disability" (LD) has become widely used, probably because it is noncommittal as to the nature and the causes of the disability. It obscures the important issues rather than clarifying them. Children with this diagnosis do not suffer from a global learning disorder, but rather have problems learning reading, writing, and arithmetic. Their learning ability with regard to other skills and subjects is not diminished; indeed, they learn something new every day in many fields, as do all other children. Their very specific learning defects can and should be isolated, given a precise diagnosis, and treated appropriately.

The diagnosis, treatment, and prevention of organic reading disorders hinges on understanding the organic matrix that makes reading possible.

The Organic Basis of the Normal Reading Process

Reading is not a purely psychologic process and cannot be understood as such. This is equally true for clinical, educational, and experimental psychology. Animal psychology is not pertinent at all, because the brain areas necessary for reading do not exist in animals, not even in the highest primates. Reading is an exclusively human faculty belonging to the highest neurophysiologic performances of the brain. The reading process shows that there is no dichotomy between mind and body. (See The Engram, p. 64, and Vol. II, Psychosensory Restitution Phenomenon Under Physical Changes During Attention, p. 521 ff.)

It must be stressed that reading is not an inborn neurologic function like walking, seeing, hearing, or speaking. It is sometimes erroneously compared with them and even with color vision. The physician Lloyd J. Thompson, for instance, makes the following statement in *Reading Disability, Developmental Dyslexia:*

> All gradations of reading facility are passed through by the average normal child as he develops from age five to ten. Also, there is a similar continuum of development or maturation in color vision, motor coordination, tone acuity, et cetera, without a definite line drawn to distinguish those persons who lag behind in any of these respects while progressing in others" (1966, p. 51).

This is unfortunately also what teachers are being taught. Typical is this statement by a professor of education: "Each youngster has his own personal private time table for growing in reading (as well as walking, talking and teething)" (Artley, 1955).

Reading is a complicated skill that must be learned, preferably early in life, and consistently practiced. The areas in the brain needed for reading are present in all children. They remain dormant, however, unless and until the child learns to read. They are not prepatterned and do not become active spontaneously at a certain stage of the child's development like walking or talking but instead become coordinated, integrated, and active only through reading. That is why good teaching and appropriate teaching methods are of such fundamental importance for reading and for the prevention of all types of reading disorders—organic, psychogenic, or sociogenic. Walking does not have to be taught; teething and color vision cannot be taught.

If properly taught, most children learn to read with such ease that later on they do not remember when and how they learned it; thus they have no painful associated memories. When they think back on it as adults, it seems a simple skill indeed. Its complexity is revealed only when difficulties arise, for example in adults who lose it due to organic lesions of the brain such as infections, injury, vascular accidents, degenerative diseases, or tumor, and in children who have trouble learning it. Reading is impossible unless all parts of a complex brain mechanism are intact, properly coordinated, and able to operate at a required speed. It is not an isolated, circumscribed function of the brain, but a highly complex performance.

Reading involves so many different functions that have to be integrated and timed properly, that a number of areas and a wide region of the brain have to be intact in order for us to be able to read fluently. All the senses are involved, not only vision and hearing, either directly or through associations. A child who reads the word "apple," for instance, cannot understand what it means unless he has seen, touched, smelled, manipulated, and eaten an apple, remembers these sensations when he reads the word, and can visualize an apple. Visualization—that is, visual and acoustic image formation and kines-thetic sensations—also enter into reading; so also do the motor acts of speech and eye movements and the power of abstraction. The brain has to make all these parts of the reading process instantly available when needed.

What is involved in this process was most clearly explained by Wertham in the following way:

> To see, to recognize, to touch, to grasp, and to name an apple is relatively easy. But to read the word APPLE, to recognize the letters and the meaning of the whole word, to understand its significance, and to pronounce and write it, belongs to the highest neurophysiologic performances of the brain. A great deal enters potentially into this performance: associations in the sphere of hearing, touch, smell and taste; power of abstraction, visualization, kinesthetic sensations. The question of the surface of the apple and of spatial relationships is also involved (Mosse & Daniels, 1959, p. 830).

Writing and spelling are an integral part of the total performance. They should therefore be studied and taught together with reading. (See chapters below on spelling and writing.)

THE CEREBRAL READING APPARATUS.   There is no specific reading center in the human brain. The correlation of the different functions that enter into the reading process involves a rather wide region. Peripherally it reaches into different areas of the brain. Its center is in the angular gyrus (Brodman's area 39 and Vogt's area angularis). Wertham found that area 39 is of fundamental importance for reading because it is located at a point equidistant from three important projection fields: the visual field in the occipital lobe, the acoustic field in Heschl's transverse gyrus in the temporal lobe, and the tactile field in the postcentral gyrus in the parietal lobe. This is a strategic location for the integration and the "clocking"—that is, timing—of all functions needed for reading (Conrad, 1949; Mosse & Daniels, 1959). Not only must these cortical fields be intact and integrated properly with each other, but their connections with other parts of the cortex, with subcortical structures, sense organs, and peripheral nerves, must also be in working order. Signals and communications must be able to flow unhindered and with the necessary speed in afferent and efferent directions.

The location of the angular gyrus and area 39 is indicated in textbooks of neuropathology and the neurosciences. However, its importance for reading is usually mentioned only briefly as part of the association areas whose lesions cause different forms of aphasia (House, Pansky, & Siegel, 1979, p. 474; Liebman, 1979, pp. 68, 69; Noback & Demarest, 1977, pp. 6, 202, 207, 208). (See Figure 2.1.)

Biocybernetic studies have shown that the transmission of impulses in the central nervous system is not a linear but a circular process. Norbert Wiener, who originated the scientific method he called Cybernetics, and others have applied communication engineering to the study of the brain. The most dramatic practical results of these studies have been in the field of reading. Devices for the blind have been constructed which convert print into audible tones or into touch with the help of optical scanners and photoelectric cells. Wiener and McCulloch suggested that the brain might also use a "scanning apparatus" with a "well defined, appropriate anatomical structure" for vision and hearing. Although these are only assumptions, the refinement of such prostheses which are brain analogues—that is, constructed to imitate brain functions—is of great importance for clinical practice as well as neurophysiology. ("Medical News: p. 1323, 1973; "Medicine Around the World: Artificial Vision," 1974 M.D. P. 63; "Substitutes for Sight," M.D. p. 49–51, 1970; Wiener, 1965, p. 22).

The Kurzweil reading machine is the most advanced and practical of these analogues. It is a desk-top machine that will be improved to be as small as an attaché case. The Kurzweil reading machine consists of an optical scanner on which printed or typewritten material is placed, a computer, and a small control unit with 30 buttons. A program tape is inserted which is as small as a regular cassette tape.

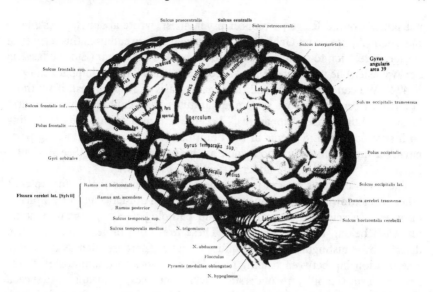

FIG. 2.1.   Left side of the brain showing the gyri and the sulci. The center of the reading region lies in the angular gyrus, in area 39. This is a cyto-architectonic field, which consists of different cell layers and can be detected only with the microscope. It is located at an equal distance from the visual field in the occipital lobe, the tactile field in the postcentral gyrus in the parietal lobe, and the acoustic field in Heschl's transverse gyrus in the temporal lobe. This location is crucial for its functions. Heschl's transverse gyrus is located inside the temporal lobe and is not visible on this picture.

The scanner searches the page, finds the top line, and moves across the text, line by line. It takes an electronic picture of each word, which the computer analyzes into letters. The letters are then blended according to phonetic rules into spoken words, which are heard over a speaker or through a headset. The machine's pronunciation is not clear yet: the words are sometimes difficult to understand. But controls make it possible to have a word repeated and/or spelled and to vary the pauses between words. Pitch and resonance of voice and speed of reading can also be changed. The machine can recognize over 200 styles of print. It imitates a number of operations of the cerebral reading apparatus and is being used as an aid not only for blind children and adults, but also in the treatment of reading disorders. (Kurzweil, 1980; see also Information Theory, Vol. II, p. 504, under Attention Disorders).

Biocybernetic researchers use the term "apparatus" to describe how the brain carries out specific actions. The same term has also been used by neurologists and psychiatrists to describe those parts of the brain involved in such specific actions as reading, speaking, hearing, seeing, writing, and other manual skills. Konrad Rieger, a pioneer psychiatrist, wrote about *Apparatuses in the Brain* (Apparate im Gehirn) as long ago as 1909. Freud used this term even earlier, in relation to speech, in 1891. In his book *On Aphasia* (Zur Auffassung der Aphasien) he wrote about the "speech apparatus" (Sprechapparat) (1973, p. 474). We can still understand the organic basis of reading best, if we think in terms of central nervous system apparatuses. One could also use the term "system," but I prefer "apparatus," because it indicates that we are dealing with specific action. Systems in the brain consist of large interlocking parts having a more diffuse function, such as the reticular system. (See Reticular Formation, Vol. II, p. 502 under Attention Disorders.)

The brain contains several interconnected apparatuses that influence each other. Breakdown of these apparatuses causes the apractic–agnostic–aphasic disorders. In scientific clinical and brain pathologic terms, organic reading disorders belong to these disorders. These are more or less circumscribed defects to be distinguished from diffuse organic disorders such as dementia. The relationship between reading disorders and apraxia (manual skill disorder), agnosia (inability to understand what one sees), and aphasia (speech disorders) will be described in detail. (See p. 150 ff.; Vol. I, p. 95; p. 382, Vol. II section on speech disorders.)

Classification of Organic Reading Disorders

The diagnostic terms used by physicians, psychologists, and educators all over the world differ, but they describe the same type of reading disorder. The most widely used term is Dyslexia ("Dyslexie" in French). "Alexia" or "Alexie," which in its literal translation from Latin means complete inability to read, is also found frequently, and so is "Analphabetica Partialis." These terms stem from adult neurology.

To indicate that the reading disorder is specific for children and prevents them from learning to read, qualifying words are added to the adult terms. These are: "specific," "developmental" ("Dyslexie d'evolution" in French), "congenital," "hereditary," "inborn." The qualifier "developmental" requires special explanation since different definitions of this term have caused confusion. The prevailing meaning is that the reading disorder affects a brain that is developing—that is, the brain of a child. Lauretta Bender and her followers, however, define it as "developmental lag." Bender speaks of "developmental lags in language like dyslexia." What she means by this is a "specific maturational lag." Her concept of "developmental" thus refers to a neuropathologic theory of the causation of organic reading disorders in children. (Bender, 1973, pp. 528, 530) (See Developmental Lag Theory, p. 54.)

The term "hereditary" is sometimes used to describe this entire organic group. Heredity can indeed be demonstrated in a number of these children, but this constitutes a special group. (See Heredity, p. 58.)

Two terms were invented especially for organic reading disorders in children. The most widely used all over the world is "Word Blindness." Denmark has a famous "Ordblinde" Institute, which treats only children suffering from severe forms of organic reading disorders. I have visited it and observed the painstaking work done by its devoted teachers. This term is so popular because it describes the most striking symptom of these children, namely their inability to read and write a word. Many of them can learn with great effort to recognize, say, and name individual letters, but when they see them grouped together, they cannot read the word, even though they can say, understand, and use the same word correctly in their conversations, and understand it when someone else uses it. As 8-year-old William told me: "Like butterfly. I can say it, but I can't read it. If I don't have the picture, I can't tell what it says."

Children who have not been taught to read and write phonetically—that is, by learning the sounds of letters and letter combinations—may have the same symptom. The word-picture or sight-word method of teaching beginners to read may cause a form of Word Blindness (Diak, 1960). The teaching methods employed by the child's teachers must therefore always be carefully investigated before making the serious diagnosis of Word Blindness on an organic basis.

Another especially coined term is "Strephosymbolia," meaning "twisted symbols." It was introduced by Orton and is now used only sporadically by his followers. It reflects Orton's theory that reading disorders are "characterized by confusion between similarily formed but oppositely oriented letters, and a tendency to a changing order of direction in reading." He used "Strephosymbolia" interchangeably with "Developmental Alexia" (1937).

Some psychiatrists and neurologists divide their cases of organic reading disorders into two groups and use different diagnostic terms for each. This complicates the terminology even further and makes communication among all professionals working with these children, which is so essential, difficult and almost impossible. Rabinovitch assigns the term "Primary Reading Retardation" (Developmental Dyslexia) to those cases where the reading disorder is inborn, often hereditary, and of obscure origin. He calls all other cases "Secondary Reading Retardation" and divides them into two groups: (1) children with "frank brain damage manifested by clear-cut neurologic deficits"; and (2) others whose capacity to read is "intact but is utilized insufficiently for the child to achieve a reading level appropriate to his mental age." He equates "secondary" with "exogenous" and puts some organic and all psychologic and sociologic reading disorders into the "Secondary Reading Retardation" group. He has done important work in this field and helped nonmedical professionals to understand and treat these children, but his classification has increased the confusion (Rabinovitch, 1968, p. 5).

Critchley proposed the diagnosis "Symptomatic Dyslexia" for reading disorders in children with neurologic disorders such as diplegia, spasticity, double athetosis, or after encephalitis, brain injury or cerebrovascular disease (Critchley, 1968 (1), p. 20; 1970, p. 22). [See sections in Vol. II on cerebral palsy p. 431; athetotic movements and encephalitis under Hyperactivity, p. 585; and cases Richard (subdural hematoma), p. 129, Eddy (athetotic movements), Vol. II, p. 586, Morris (head trauma), Vol. II, p. 568, and Adrian (encephalitis), Vol. II, p. 616.]

The official classifications used in hospitals and mental hygiene clinics for statistical purposes are not very helpful either. Dyslexia, Alexia and Specific Reading Disorder are the diagnostic terms for reading disorders in children as well as adults as listed in the *International Classification of Diseases,* 9th Revision (1979) of the National Center for Health Statistics of the United States. The *Diagnostic and Statistical Manual* of the American Psychiatric Association, published in 1968 (DSM II), did not even mention reading disorders. It only carried "Specific Learning Disturbance" in its list of "Special Symptoms."

Some child psychiatric clinics and hospital departments use the classification of psychopathologic disorders proposed by the Committee on Child Psychiatry of the Group for the Advancement of Psychiatry in 1966. Here, "Reading Disability" is listed within the group of the "Developmental Deviations" under "Deviations in Cognitive Functions." These include "developmental lags or other deviations in the capacity for symbolic or abstract thinking," indicating that the "developmental lag" theory of the causation of all reading disorders has been accepted. This classification suggests that all reading disorders are organic in nature, as "problems in reading" are also mentioned in the text under "Chronic Brain Syndromes." It does not recognize the important social and educational fact that the overwhelming majority of reading disorders fall into the psychogenic and sociogenic groups.

DSM III of the American Psychiatric Association, published in 1980, accepts this concept. It lists "Specific Reading Disorder" under "Specific Developmental Disorders." Psychiatric residents and Fellows in child psychiatry are sometimes instructed to classify reading disorders under "Organic Brain Syndromes" or "Neuroses," depending on the nature of their patient's reading disorder. In practice, this distinction may not depend much on the actual symptoms of the child, but rather reflect the residents' or their supervisor's theoretical orientation. As children are primarily referred for disturbing behavior and not for a learning disorder, and because the classification of reading disorders presents such problems, these disorders are frequently not mentioned in the final diagnostic classification that is used in mental hospitals and psychiatric clinics for statistical purposes, so that all psychiatric statistics are unreliable in this respect.

All children in this organic group also have writing and spelling disorders, and this should be reflected in the diagnosis. One can simply add to the term the qualifying words "writing" or "spelling," or use the neurologic terms "agraphia" or "dysgraphia," and "dysorthographia" for spelling disorder. Abbreviations are frequently used. "LRS," for instance, is popular in all German-speaking countries. It stands for Lese/Rechtschreib-Schwäche, meaning reading/writing weakness. (See Vol. I on spelling p. 115, and Chapter 3, writing, pp. 142.)

ARITHMETIC DISORDERS ON AN ORGANIC BASIS. Many children with an organic reading disorder also have an arithmetic disorder. Testing of this ability is frequently neglected, so that these disorders are often overlooked.

The term used by neurologists for arithmetic disorders is "Acalculia." (See section on Gerstmann Syndrome, p. 175, and Chapter 4, Arithmetic Disorders.)

Pathologic Basis of Organic Reading Disorders

Great confusion surrounds the term "organic." This is not the educators' fault, but that of those psychiatrists and pediatricians who talk in vague general terms about the "brain-injured child," "perceptual disorders," "developmental lags," "minimal brain damage or dysfunction," when reading, like speech and manual skills, is a mental tool that can be attributed to special parts of the brain. A child who has an organic reading/writing disorder suffers from specific defects in the functioning of his cerebral reading apparatus that interfere with his ability to learn to read and write. Because these defects are not diffuse and vague, but are very specific, they can be isolated and concretely diagnosed and treated.

The term "organic," as used in medicine and especially in neurology and psychiatry, refers only to the brain and to other parts of the central nervous system. Where this term is used, diseases in other parts of the body are called "somatic." "Organic" therefore means pertaining to the brain. It also means nonpsychologic—that is, the disorder is not caused by traumatic experiences in the patient's life that caused psychologic damage.

"Organic" does not necessarily mean that a lesion shows up neuropathologically either macroscopically or microscopically. A disorder may have an organic etiology even when we cannot demonstrate with our present methods any pathologic changes in the brain. Clinical methods of examination that make it possible to infer the presence of an organic disorder or defect will be described in detail.

I want to stress that "organic" does not necessarily mean unalterable. Modern studies have shown that the brain has powers of compensation, realignment, and self-restoration. "Organic" does not mean that the child's fate is sealed and that he is doomed, as far too many parents, teachers, and even clinicians think.

What we know about the brain mechanisms underlying reading and writing stems largely from the examination of its pathology in adults as well as children. The patient's symptoms depend on which portion of these mechanisms is malfunctioning. The localization of the cerebral defect can often be inferred from certain features in the clinical picture. However, such correlations can never be as accurate as the localization of a defect in a car engine, for example. They must remain approximations. The brain does not operate in isolated units, but this does not mean that we cannot pin-point anatomically specific areas in the brain that have very specialized functions. For even though, as Wertham observed, "lesions of considerable intensity and extent can occur in the central nervous system without clinically demonstrable interference with function" (Wertham & Wertham, 1934, p. 362), damage to certain crucial shunts or sidings invariably causes loss of function. Brodmann's area 39 in the angular gyrus in the parietal lobes, which is located at the center of the reading region, is such a shunt. Any kind of damage to it causes Alexia (complete inability to read), and at least a partial Agraphia (an inability to write). This does not mean that the neurophysiologic basis for reading is located in area 39 exclusively. This area is only one part, even though a crucial one, of the entire cerebral reading apparatus. (See The Cerebral Reading Apparatus, p. 44.)

The confusion surrounding the very concept of organic reading disorders stems primarily from one of the most difficult problems in medical science—namely, the correlation of cerebral lesions with clinical symptoms. It is an error to assume that the only acceptable proof for the organic causation of a symptom is a gross anatomic or microscopic histologic lesion of the brain. As Wertham, in his classic study of the correlation of brain lesions with psychopathologic phenomena in *The Brain as an Organ,* points out, "in proportion to the extraordinary complexity and differentiation of the finer functions mediated by the central nervous system, histologic lesions are very gross" (1934, p. 358). He also stresses that "it will be increasingly necessary to supplant histological pictures with parasitological, serological, heredobiological and clinical (not purely neurological) data" (1934, pp. 340, 341).

The full implications of this forward-looking scientific observation have become clear only since the phenomenal advances made in biochemistry and molecular biology that led to the discovery of inborn errors of metabolism and other cellular and humoral pathology, and of the neurotransmitters (Noback & Demarest, 1977, p. 22). This does not mean, however, that histologic examinations have become unnecessary, but that they must be evaluated in proper perspective. Wertham also emphasizes this. He writes, "The neurohistological facts are only a link in a chain of data, a necessary link, however, without which coordinated etiological research is not possible" (1934, p. 341). As a matter of fact, the electron microscope has revived interest in histology and opened entirely new vistas in this field.

The elevation of clinical data that are not purely neurologic to a status equal to all others is of profound importance for organic reading disorders in children. Certain clinical symptoms (and especially combinations of symptoms) in and of themselves indicate that the reading disorder has an organic origin. Some psychologic tests must also be viewed in this way. A cortical or subcortical pattern on the Mosaic test, for instance, is an organic clinical sign of diagnostic weight equal to a neurologic sign.

When a child like 9-year-old Michel, after attending school regularly for 4 years, still has trouble copying letters, can name all printed letters but cannot sound them out; when he cannot even read one word; when he can write spontaneously only the words "LooK" and "DiCK" (in exactly this way), and can read them only hesitantly; when he makes a "stone-bound" Mosaic design; and when intelligence tests indicate that his intelligence is average in all other areas—then we can assume we are dealing with organic defects, that is, with defective functioning of those parts of the brain that make reading possible, even though routine neurologic examinations showed no other demonstrable organic symptoms, as is the case in the majority of such children.

These clinical data are especially crucial in children's reading disorders, because we lack autopsy information. These disorders are not fatal diseases after all, and we must study them and deal with them without waiting for the results of postmortem examinations.

Causes of Organic Reading Disorders

A great deal is known about the special vulnerability of the brain of the fetus and the infant, for example, to anoxia (lack of oxygen). The reactivity of the central nervous system at this stage is very different from that of adults and old people (Wertham, 1934, pp. 286, 287). The brain continues its complicated process of development even after birth. Migration of immature cells and formation of mature cells continues; spongioblasts continue to migrate and to form glia cells; neuroblasts continue to form ganglion cells. The myelinization of fiber tracts has not been completed and continues during the first few years after birth. In the angular gyrus it is thought to take place between the first and the eighth month after birth.

Iron, melanin, and lipofuscin pigmentation of certain nerve cells are absent during infancy. Lipofuscin pigment, for instance, is not present in cells of the lateral geniculate body, a structure assumed to be of importance for reading and writing (see p. 95). The expansion of the entire parietal lobes, where areas vital for reading and writing are located, apparently continues until the child has reached 10 years of age (Critchley, 1953, p. 14). We do not know precisely, however, what these data mean in clinical terms, and cannot correlate them definitely with reading disorders. For even though the brain continues to develop after birth, this does not mean that organic reading disorders are due to "developmental lags."

THE DEVELOPMENTAL LAG THEORY.   The developmental lag theory has introduced a general vagueness, confusion, and uncertainty. The concept of developmental lag assumes an automatic process of maturation, independent from all the intrinsic and environmental factors that impinge on a child. It is frequently interpreted to mean that if the child were just left alone, all his defective faculties would still develop; thus nothing is done for these children at a time when their reading disorder is easiest to correct. Lauretta Bender's definition lends itself to this procrastination: she writes that she means "a specific maturational lag," which she defines as

> a concept of functional areas of the brain and of personality which maturate according to a recognized pattern longitudinally. A maturational lag signifies a slow differentiation in this pattern. It does not indicate a structural defect, deficiency, or loss. There is not necessarily a limitation in the potentialities and at variable levels maturation may tend to accelerate, but often unevenly (Bender, 1973, p. 533).

This implies a potential for eventual differentiation of a healthy pattern, so that the lag will disappear.

Children do indeed mature at different rates, and we must take this into consideration in our diagnoses and our therapeutic plans. However, reading and writing are learned skills. Their acquisition and development differs even from speech, which sometimes develops abnormally late without being impaired. A child who can hear and whose cerebral speech apparatus is healthy and only needs to mature to function normally, does not need formal teaching to learn to talk. Everyone around him is a "teacher." All he has to do is listen to what everyone around him says, and to repeat it. Speech is an inborn faculty on this elementary level; reading is not. A child is born with the capacity to learn reading and writing, just as he has the capacity to learn to drive a car or pilot a plane. These capacities do not develop spontaneously like speech, but rather depend on specific instructions. Some children learn to read so fast and at such an early age, sometimes before they go to school, that it seems to be a "natural" development like talking. These children nevertheless went through a learning process, picking up the necessary information with such speed and ease that neither they themselves nor their parents noticed when and how they learned to read. They figured out the necessary techniques largely on their own and guessed a lot. However, they still need specific instruction to write, spell, and read above the level of simple children's books.

The developmental lag theory has been so generalized by Lauretta Bender and others that it hinders our diagnostic and therapeutic task. Bender sees childhood schizophrenia also as a "maturational lag" and stresses that this "at times makes even the differential diagnosis difficult" (Bender, 1973, pp. 529, 530). This has blurred the distinction between organic and nonorganic disorders to such an extent that children are being committed to mental hospitals with the diagnosis of "childhood schizophrenia" when they are actually suffering from severe but treatable organic disorders such as the apractic–agnostic–aphasic disorders, to which organic reading disorders belong. These disorders thus remain forever untreated because they are not recognized. I have examined many such children and witnessed the harm this has done. There will be examples of such missed diagnoses throughout this book. (See cases Elaine, age 6, Vol. II, p. 391 and 398 under Speech Disorders; Clemens, age 12, Vol. II, p. 550 under Attention Disorders; Chester, age 8, Vol. II, p. 631 under Hyperactivity; and statistics under Hospitalization, Vol. I, p. 254. For differential diagnosis of schizophrenia, see Vol II, p. 478 under Inability to Tolerate Disorder; Vol. II, p. 487 under Perseveration; Vol. II, p. 564 under Concentration Disorders; Vol. II, p. 581 under Distractibility; Vol. II, pp. 630 and 679 under Hyperactivity; Vol. II, p. 676 under Irritability.)

Whether organic reading disorders in children are caused by immaturity or by a "developmental lag" affecting the cerebral reading apparatus remains doubtful. I have found no evidence, however, that an organic reading disorder in a child is a pathologic process that progresses or regresses, or that changes spontaneously. It is rather a static condition, little affected by the child's general maturation. Although it may be progressively more cleverly covered up, it remains throughout life unless corrected early, and may be so severe that it cannot be completely cured. (For cover-up methods, see section on word reading, pp. 72 and 112. For prognosis, see case descriptions and Chapter 7, Treatments.)

THE BLOOD–BRAIN BARRIER. Another factor in the special vulnerability of the brain of the fetus, the newborn, and the infant is the hematoencephalic —that is, blood–brain—barrier. Its task is to protect the brain by keeping out many toxic substances entirely and by letting others through only at a very low pace. It is, as Himwich and Himwich state in *Comprehensive Textbook of Psychiatry,* "of great importance in many problems, including the utilization of food stuffs by the brain, the therapeutic use of drugs, and the pathologic effect of viruses and toxins on brain tissue" (Himwich & Himwich 1967, p. 63). Its localization and the exact biochemical mechanisms through which it functions are not yet known. Clinical studies and animal experiments have, however, established that it is much more permeable during fetal life and at birth than later on, and that it loses its intactness at any age when the brain is injured, when the vascular system is damaged or malfunctioning, during infectious diseases, when there is carbon monoxide poisoning, and so on. This means that the brain of the fetus, the newborn, and the infant is vulnerable to many more somatic disorders and toxic substances than that of older children and of adults. It also means that research on brain damage during these ages and of its consequences later on is incomplete unless the role played by a still poorly functioning blood–brain barrier is taken into consideration. Far too many studies in this field do not even mention it.

INTRAUTERINE AND PERINATAL PATHOLOGY   The fetal brain is suscepti-ble to substances or infections that may present no danger to its mother. Examples are the disastrous effect of German measles on the fetal brain, the effects of heroin, methadone, alcohol, smoking, nutritional deprivation of the mother during pregnancy, and the effect of drugs such as thorazine taken by the mother. There are as yet no follow-up studies showing whether children whose brains were damaged in any of these ways had reading disorders later on. Chess, Korn, and Fernandez (1971) report on a follow-up study of children with congenital rubella conducted by the New York University Medical Center. This study found that learning problems "were showing up in a number of them (children) as they grew older" (p. 65). This might be a reference to reading disorders, but the report did not clarify it. Unfortunately, many statis-tical studies use such vague categories as "learning problems" or "learning disorders," "inadequate schoolwork," "poor school performance," and the like. Reading disorders are specific in their symptomatology, and can only be correlated with fetal brain infections or other damage when they have been diagnosed with precision. (See also "Malnutrition During Pregnancy Causes Learning Disabilities Among the Offspring," *Obstetric and Gynecologic News,* July 1, 1979.)

Kawi and Pasamanick undertook such a study. They reviewed the prenatal and perinatal records of 205 boys with verified reading disorders assumed to be of organic origin. A comparison of these records with a control group of boys who read well showed that their mothers had a "significantly larger" proportion of premature births, of toxemia of pregnancy (preeclampsia, hyper-tensive disease), and of bleeding during pregnancy (bleeding before third trimester, placenta previa, premature separation of placenta). These are com-plications apt to lead to fetal anoxia. The authors stress that these findings seem to strengthen their hypothesis that there exists "a continuum of repro-ductive casualty with a lethal component consisting of abortions, stillbirths and neonatal deaths, and a sublethal component consisting of cerebral palsy, epilepsy, mental deficiency, and behavior disorders in children." They came to the conclusion that "some of the reading disorders of childhood constitute a component of this continuum" (Kawi & Pasamanick, 1958, 1959).

Such correlations are difficult enough to prove in an individual child. Statis-tical proof is less reliable in this respect even when well researched, as in this study. The conclusions of these authors do not apply to all children with pre-or perinatal pathology. For, as Pincus and Glaser state in "The Syndrome of 'Minimal Brain Damage' in Childhood," "some children can sustain organic damage varying from very mild to severe and still remain behaviorally otherwise normal" (1966, p. 29). This applies also to reading disorders. A child's brain may have undergone a toxic, traumatic, infectious, or any other insult during his fetal life, at birth, or later on, and the child still may not develop a reading disorder. The reason for this may be that the disorder did not damage the cerebral reading apparatus or that the damage healed completely before the child was old enough to learn to read.

The children we examine have of course survived intrauterine illnesses, birth injuries, and other pre- or perinatal traumas. The symptoms we see are the result of scar formation or of other cerebral changes, depending on the nature of the original pathology. s The reading disorder of a child with a history of perinatal damage may also have been caused by factors other than direct injuries to the cerebral reading apparatus. A prolonged period of anoxia, for instance, may cause an attention or a memory disorder. Such a child may have trouble with reading because it is difficult for him to concentrate long enough to learn, or because his memory is impaired. (See Vol. II, Anoxia under Attention Disorders, p. 565, and Memory Disorders, Vol. I, p. 70.)

Head Injuries. Head injuries during birth and later on may cause a reading disorder. The consequences of intracranial hemorrhages are often especially severe and long-lasting. The neurosurgeon William Sharpe, who pioneered in the diagnosis, treatment, and prevention of birth injuries, developed as long ago as 1918 a spinal puncture test for the diagnosis of intracranial hemorrhages in infants during the first week after birth. He recommended that such a hemorrhage be treated right away so that cerebral palsies might be prevented (1954). That intracranial neonatal hemorrhages are relatively common, especially in premature infants and in association with the respiratory distress syndrome, was found by Schoenberg, Mellinger, and Schoenberg in a large statistical study involving 10,850 live births from 1965 through 1974 (1977). Where such birth injuries are left untreated, there may be lasting effects, as in the case of Richard, who had severe neurologic symptoms in addition to a reading disorder, and who developed intractible convulsions later on, at the age of 13. (See case of Richard under Linear Dyslexia, p. 129; case of Morris in Vol. II, section on concentration, p. 568; and Vol. II, section on cerebral palsy, p. 428).

Organic reading disorders highlight the importance of good medical care for pregnant women, excellent obstetrical management, and conscientious care of the newborn. (See case of Emilio in section on writing disorders, p. 169; and Eddie, erythroblastosis fetalis, in section on reading disorders specific for hyperactive children with choreiform movements, Vol. II, p. 586.)

It must be stressed that the determination that a child's reading disorder has an organic basis should never be based on a history of intrauterine or perinatal damage alone. The reading disorder of even these children may have a psychogenic or sociogenic basis. This was the case in two boys, age 7 and 9, out of the 19 children (3 girls and 16 boys) in my study who had been through unquestionable prenatal or perinatal pathology.

HEREDITY.   Clinical evidence has been accumulated in various countries showing that the same kind of organic reading disorder may affect several members of the same family, and that it can be traced through several generations (Weinschenk, 1965). A search for reading disorders of the child's relatives through several generations is therefore always indicated. Such tracing is very difficult to do; this group may therefore be larger than it appears (Hermann, 1959; Hallgren, 1950).

The neurologist Macdonald Critchley put special emphasis on this group. In his important book *The Dyslexic Child* (1970), he wrote: "To anyone experienced in clinical diagnosis, it seems impossible to overlook the very real heredofamiliar incidence in cases of specific development dyslexia" (p. 90). He incorporated this genetic aspect in his classification of these reading disorders by defining them in the following way: "This syndrome of developmental dyslexia is of constitutional and not of environmental origin, and it may well be genetically determined" (p. 24). (See also 1968 (2), p. 165).

The hereditary form of organic reading disorders affects boys almost exclusively. That is why a sex-linked gene has been suggested as its mode of transmission. The intelligence of these children is, as a rule, average or superior; only a few mental defectives are included in this group. Their arithmetic and mathematical ability is not affected, but some of them also have an organic speech disorder. Twin studies, for example, those by the Scandinavian researchers Hallgren and Norrie, have shown a 100% concordance in monozygotic (identical) twins (Critchley, 1970, p. 90). This is further proof that an organic reading disorder may have a genetic basis; the size of such a group is unknown. Klasen (1970), in her study of 500 children with all sorts of reading disorders published in *The Reading Disorder Syndrome (Das Syndrom der Legasthenie)*, found hints of a hereditary factor in 39.7% of 392 children. This study was based on records of children examined and treated at the Ellen K. Raskob Institute in Oakland, California. I found definite evidence of heredity in only 10 of the 222 children in my study whose reading disorder had an organic basis. All were boys, ages 6 to 10. Psychogenic and sociogenic reading disorders cannot, by definition, be hereditary. (See case of Doug in section on Spelling, p. 97.)

THE ROLE OF HEMISPHERIC DOMINANCE.   Orton and his followers assumed that a causal relationship existed between left-handedness, lack of development of hand dominance, or cross-dominance (right-handedness and left-eye dominance or vice versa) and organic reading disorders. It was Orton's theory that the two hemispheres enter into a struggle with each other for dominance from infancy onward, and that where this struggle continues, stuttering, mirror-writing, and reading disorders result (1937).

Anatomically, there is no difference between the two cerebral hemispheres. The concept of "dominance" is relevant only in relation to certain specific activities and functions. Both hemispheres, for instance, control all motor movements, each being responsible for one side of the body. Because the motor and sensory fiber tracts of arms, legs, eye muscles, and so forth cross from one side of the body to the opposite cerebral hemisphere, each hemisphere is responsible for the opposite side of the body in this respect. The concept of dominance in relation to motor activity stems from the observation that one hand is stronger and more skillful than the other. The emphasis is on *skill.* Both hemispheres are equipped to mediate *all* hand and arm activities on the opposite side of the body. Only the finer, more difficult, and complicated activities requiring greater skill, such as writing, seem to depend on one hemisphere alone, which we then call "dominant."

Considerable confusion could be avoided if the activity for which the hemisphere is dominant were added whenever dominance is discussed. It is assumed, for instance, almost throughout the voluminous literature dealing with reading that the dominant hand indicates which hemisphere is dominant also for other performances. But the cerebral areas responsible for hand dominance do not necessarily lie in the same hemisphere as those controlling speech and reading. We cannot know with certainty, for instance, that the cerebral dominance for speech and reading is in the right hemisphere of a left-handed child. It may not even be in the left hemisphere of a right-handed child, although this is much more common (Noback & Demarest, 1977, p. 213). Where no hand dominance has been established, we don't know which hemisphere is dominant for other functions either. But dominance as such is not intrinsically related to any pathology anyway; rather, it is a physical manifestation of brain organization and not a symptom of illness or defect. Left-handedness, for instance, may be inconvenient, psychologically or socially unacceptable, and a handicap in some professions, but it is not related to any organic pathology. Left-handed children are perfectly capable of learning to read, write, and speak. (See Hand Dominance and Organic Writing Disorders, p. 179.)

Which hemisphere is dominant for reading is actually of no consequence for the child. Brodmann's area 39 and the entire reading region, as well as all speech areas, exist in both hemispheres. Why they are activated and developed more in one hemisphere than in the other is not known. It can be assumed that these highest and most complicated neurophysiologic performances are easier to establish if one hemisphere specializes in them. There is much recent evidence that both hemispheres work together more than was previously assumed.

The question of cerebral dominance for reading, speech, and motor skills assumes importance only in regard to pathology. We know that cerebral control of reading, speech, and, to a lesser degree, writing and arithmetic, is unilateral because lesions in only one hemisphere cause alexias (reading disorders), aphasias (speech disorders), and certain types of agraphias and acalculias (writing and arithmetic disorders, respectively). However, some patients with such lesions can relearn speaking, reading, writing, and arithmetic abilities, at least partially; and unless we find that these lesions have healed, we must assume that the other hemisphere was capable of taking over. Such retraining is easier in patients who are left-handed or where no dominant side has ever been established. Their hemispheres are evidently more flexible in this respect (Hecaen & de Ajuriaguerra, 1964). This contradicts the assertion by many students of organic reading disorders that such children are especially vulnerable and prone to develop reading disorders. Since we do not yet understand all aspects of these mechanisms, it is inappropriate to employ measures and therapies directed entirely to improving the dominance balance as Doman and Delacato do (Delacato, 1959; "The Doman-Delacato Treatment," 1968; Doman, Spitz, Zuckman, Delacato, & Doman, 1960). (See also Vol. II, pp. 435.)

Eye Dominance. Eye dominance is also of no consequence for reading and good vision. In this sense there is no dominance for vision; each eye is represented in both hemispheres. We must always keep the basic anatomical facts in mind that only fibers in the median part of the optic nerve cross to the opposite hemisphere. The lateral fibers originating in the lateral part of each retina do not cross; their cortical projection fields are on the same side. (See Tachistoscopy, Vol. II, p. 510.) Injury to Brodmann's area 19 in the occipital lobe (the visual sphere) in one hemisphere therefore does not cause total blindness. Orton himself rejected "vague concepts of visual superiority" (1937, p. 55), and stated that "master eye" referred to eye muscles (i.e., motor dominance, not visual dominance). Eye preference tests are usually muscle tests. Unfortunately this is not always clearly stated and understood.

There is also a complicated relationship between visual preference for one eye and this eye's visual acuity. The ophthalmologist H. K. Goldberg stressed this in *Vision, Perception, and Related Facts in Dyslexia.* He wrote: "Eye preference is usually but not necessarily associated with preferential visual acuity. In those persons, whose vision is affected, the better eye need not be the preferred one" (1968, p. 104). None of this has anything to do with hemispheric dominance or with reading disorders.

Dominance for Speech. The cerebral dominance for speech is also important for reading. A close functional and anatomical proximity exists between the cerebral reading and speech apparatuses. Both must function well and interact with precision in order for the child to learn to read and write without difficulty.

Historically, hemispheric dominance was first observed in relation to speech when autopsies showed a lesion in only one hemisphere in patients suffering from aphasia. We now know that both hemispheres are more flexible in this respect. The simple elements of speech such as vocalization, for instance, apparently remain localized in both hemispheres throughout life. Penfield could produce arrest and arousal of vocalization in the case of a conscious human subject by appropriate stimulation of the cortex of either hemisphere (Critchley, 1953, p. 415).

There is also evidence that both hemispheres are flexible regarding their ability to develop speech dominance, especially before the child has learned to talk. Experience with the consequences of hemispherectomies (surgical removal of an entire hemisphere) in children showed this. Such operations have been performed successfully in children with severe unilateral pathology.

Stutte (1965) studied six such children, one boy and five girls, ages 8 to 19. The right hemisphere was removed in two children, the left in four. The boy had a prenatal brain trauma with cyst formation; one girl also had a cyst due to asphyxia. The four other girls had unilateral brain atrophies, following vaccination encephalitis, after head trauma at the age of 6 months, and after prenatal trauma. All improved. Those whose brain pathology started after they had at least learned to repeat words had a transitory aphasia after the operation, but spoke again later on. Stutte reported that he knew of no child in whom complete aphasia resulted from this operation, irrespective of which hemisphere had been removed. He concluded that "severe anatomic and functional damage to one hemisphere in the pre-, peri-, or early postnatal period can be compensated for by the other hemisphere to a large extent" (p. 94). He added that the ability of one hemisphere to substitute for the other seems to be greatest up to the age of 8. Other clinical studies also indicate that the cerebral speech apparatus can develop in either hemisphere under certain conditions and up to a certain age, given variously as 8 or 10 years. Cerebral dominance for speech is assumed to have been established in most children by the age of 10. This probably also applies to dominance for reading.

Dominance for Musical Ability. Musical ability and reading are closely related, and so are their disorders. Reading requires a certain rhythm and tonal changes, and these factors are also involved in the ability to read music. Children with good musical ability and a feeling for rhythm generally learn to read with greater ease than a child who is not musical. I have found that many children with organic reading disorders have no musical ability at all. They cannot carry a tune; some of them are completely tone deaf. This alone makes it harder for the child to learn to read, especially English, because so many sounds differ only minutely. This affects spelling and pronunciation. The combination of organic reading disorders and lack of musical ability, with or without tone deafness, does not mean, however, that children with these disabilities cannot learn to read; lack of musical talent *alone* never causes a reading disorder. (See Vol. II, sections on musical ability and on rhythm disorders; and case of Alfred, Vol. I, p. 99.).

How very complicated and little understood the relationship between the hemispheres is with regard to musical ability is evident in this finding by Grinker and Bucy (1949):

> Lesions of the anterior portion of the superior temporal convolution result in auditory musical agnosia from which recovery takes place by assumption of function by the opposite side even though it be the right or minor lobe" (p. 373).

Someone with such a lesion can hear but cannot understand music. Such a patient cannot sing or play an instrument, a disability disastrous for musicians. There is other evidence, however, that cerebral dominance for musical abilities may not be in the same hemisphere as that for speech. But this question is far from settled. In their book, *Left-handedness: Manual Superiority and Cerebral Dominance,* Hécaen and Ajuriaguerra (1964) concluded after an exhaustive study of the cases published in the international literature: "Motor amusia, like sensory amusia, may depend on lesions of either hemisphere, although the left is more common" (p. 141). As the example I quoted from Grinker and Bucy shows, either hemisphere can take over the musical function when its projection field has been injured on one side (see Vol. II, Musical Ability Disorder, p. 434).

The question of hemispheric dominance of musical ability has become of practical as well as theoretical importance for reading disorders only because Doman and Delacato base their treatment of children's reading disorders on the assumption that what they call the "tonal area" is in the "subdominant hemisphere" (Delacato, 1959). In *The Treatment and Prevention of Reading Problems* (1959), Delacato therefore recommends that children going through this remedial program "first of all should not listen to music and secondly should not sing" (p. 25). His aim is to "establish [the] dominant hemisphere" (p. 24). As far as the localization of musical ability is concerned, this theory has no scientifically valid foundation. Neither is it possible to "establish dominance." Nature does this, and all we can do is to find out which hand is dominant in the child we examine and then train that hand. We can and must train speech and reading where they are defective, but we cannot influence which hemisphere will develop control over the cerebral speech or reading apparatus. As far as musical ability is concerned, it is not antagonistic to speech. One is associated with the other and they are interrelated in a healthy child. Speech requires rhythm and variations in loudness and in tonal quality. ("The Doman-Delacato Treatment," 1968; Doman, Spitz, Zuckman, Delacato, & Doman, 1960).

Modern clinical and experimental studies indicate that the right hemisphere is more efficient than the left in nonverbal and spatial faculties. Apparently it remembers *Gestalten* (forms or shapes) such as faces better than the left. This seems to apply to both right- and left-handers. Sperry, Gazzaniga, and Bogen (1969), among others, made these observations on patients whose hemispheres had been severed surgically by commissurotomy. They also found that parts of the reading process were not confined to one hemisphere alone. They reported that

> The minor [i.e., right] hemisphere can read printed names of objects as well as comprehend simple verbal instructions presented by ear. It is also able to spell simple 3 and 4 letter words with the 4 inch high, solid, cut out letters presented in a scrambled pile to the left hand out of sight. After the left hand has succeeded in spelling words like hat, cat, milk, coat, et cetera, the subject is unable to name the words he has just spelled, but can print the same word with the left hand, the entire performance being screened from sight throughout" (p. 286).

They also found evidence for the "presence of conscious awareness and intellect at a level characteristically human with fairly high order mental processes including abstract thinking and reasoning" (p. 286) in the severed right hemisphere. It also appeared that this hemisphere possesses "distinctly human emotional sensitivity and expression" (p. 287). They came to the following conclusions about the relationship between connected hemispheres: "The specialized non-verbal and spatial faculties of the minor hemisphere would normally reinforce, complement and enhance the verbal and volitional performances of the major hemisphere"(p. 288).

This and other clinical and experimental evidence supports Critchley's (1953) observation that "unilateral predominance is not an exclusivism, and can be modified if necessary, the two hemispheres being flexible in this respect" (p. 415). Therefore, unless we can find a tumor or any other unilateral lesion, we have no basis for the assumption that the cerebral defect in organic reading disorders in children lies either in the dominant or in the nondominant hemisphere or has anything to do with cerebral dominance.

Existing neuropathologic and clinical studies have not established any significance of cerebral dominance for organic reading disorders in children.

Role of Memory

Anyone who has tried to teach reading to a child with a severe organic reading disorder knows that what he seems to have learned in the morning may be completely forgotten that same afternoon or on the following day, in spite of strenuous and sincere efforts by the child to concentrate and to learn. This applies even to small basic steps for reading. For instance, child and reading therapist may feel certain that he has finally managed to be sure of the form and sounds of the letters "n" and "o" and that he can say "no" when he sees them or writes them down next to each other, left to right. All too frequently, however, the child sees the word "no" that same afternoon or several days later and is completely baffled by it. Such a child suffers from a memory defect that is the cause of the greatest and most irritating frustration for him and his teachers.

It is a pity that memory defects either are not mentioned at all or are referred to only superficially in books on children's reading disorders. These defects play a major role in all forms of reading disorders, organic or psychologic. Many reading difficulties of these children can be understood and successfully treated only as defects of specific types of memory. For instance, a child who gets the horizontal and/or vertical direction of letters and numbers mixed up, who reads and writes "W" instead of "M," "p" instead of "g," "6" instead of "9," and so on, cannot *remember* the correct forms. The memory of these children is usually defective only in relation to reading and writing. It is a very specific, circumscribed memory defect. Their intellectual memory is otherwise intact; so is their speech memory, motor memory, memory of emotions, and all other forms of memory including their ability to remember their own life experiences as well as what others have told them about it, television shows and other fiction, and so on. The understanding of these children's specific memory defects requires knowledge of the memory process.

THE ORGANIC BASIS OF THE MEMORY PROCESS.   The brain has the faculty of retaining stimuli and experiences coming from within the body or from without, of storing them, and of making them available for recall. Retention, storage, and recall are basic elements of memory. The smallest unit of this process is called a memory trace or an engram.

The Engram.   Richard Semon (1923) first introduced the term "engram" to the scientific study of memory. Painstaking clinical and anatomical human and animal research on different continents gave him the idea that any stimulus, physical or psychologic, originating outside the organism or coming from within changes the part of the brain it reaches chemically, electrically, or in some other so far unknown way. He stressed that one must assume that such a change takes place, even though we cannot prove it experimentally. He called this change an "engram," which means, translated from the Greek, something that has been engraved or written in. The reactivity of that part of the brain is different from then on. Its capacity to react has been altered permanently.

However, one stimulus rarely, if ever, enters in isolation; also, stimuli as a rule enter by more than one route and pass over more than one receptive area in the brain. Semon therefore suggested that synchronous stimuli produce a "simultaneous engram complex." The excitation caused by a stimulus also takes a certain amount of time. Since new stimuli are usually added before the previous excitation has completely subsided, engrams may have a successive association with each other. Semon defined associations as links formed by different engrams or engram complexes that are established simultaneously. Consecutive associations are only a minor form of this complicated process. He felt certain that the formation of engrams and of their associations continues throughout life. Once established, they are not extinguished until death. The brain's engram storage persists as long as the organism is alive.

Semon proposed the idea that engrams remain in a state of latency and that they are activated by the repetition, in whole or in part, of the original stimulus or of the experience that produced the engram complex. It is interesting in this connection that Smith Ely Jelliffe called his evaluation of Semon's work "The MNEME, The Engram and the Unconscious" (1923). In this paper he stressed that just before his death, Semon began an investigation of the unconscious, and that he had acknowledged receiving the stimulus for this from the work of Freud. Jelliffe also emphasized that Semon showed "the close relation of mind and body as really representing the same group of life processes only viewed from two different standpoints" (p. 338) This is important for reading, because the reading process is partly physical and partly psychologic. The engram as defined by Semon can be assumed to form one of the links between the two. (See Vol. II, section on Psychosensory restitution phenomenon, p. 527 ff.)

Modern neurophysiologic research, including information theory, tends to confirm Semon's original ideas. For instance, W. Ross Adey suggests at an International Symposium on Biocybernetics of the Central Nervous System (1969) that cellular wave phenomena might be associated "with both 'write' and 'read' phases of storage," and that "neuronal excitability would then be determined by previous experience of these particular patterns of waves." He then poses the question: "How do these wave trains lead to long-term changes of a chemical, structural nature, such as would be assumed to underlie a memory trace?" (p. 23). We still cannot answer this question. The nature of an engram is still not known, but we must assume that it exists. As Brobeck wrote in 1973, "the exact nature of the changes in the memory trace remains unknown. There are, however, a number of studies that shed some light on this fascinating problem" (p. 157).

Engrams form the indispensable basis of the reading process. The child must establish especially close and reliable engram complexes to be able to read, and their recall must become automatic. (See Conditioned Reflexes, p. 78.)

There are great individual variations in the speed with which memory is acquired, most of which remain within normal limits. Speed is usually dependent on the child's interest and motivation and on the level of his intelligence. The higher these are, the faster his retention. However, the memory of some children with an organic reading disorder and/or other organic symptoms is slow in spite of their average or superior intelligence. This slowness often affects only their organically impaired activities such as reading and writing. (See section on Slowing Down of All Reactions, Vol. II, p. 460.)

HYPERMNESIAS.   Hypermnesias are exceptionally accurate, fast, and extensive feats of memory. They are quite specific and do not involve all forms of memory. A child with a photographic memory may, for instance, be able to read an entire page instantly, and to remember every word on that page. These are special talents and they are not confined to mentally healthy children: some mentally defective children also have hypermnesia. These children may, for instance, be capable of reciting long poems just by listening to them a few times, without being able to read or to understand them. Some of them also perform complicated calendar calculations or other tricks with numbers requiring a fast and accurate memory. These are the "idiots savants." Children suffering from early infantile autism often also have such specific hypermnesias. (See Early Infantile Autism, under Speech Disorders, Vol. II, p. 391, and under Inability to Tolerate Disorder, Vol. II, p. 478.)

RETENTION DIFFICULTIES.   All sorts of interferences from without and within—somatic, cerebral, or psychologic—may inhibit retention while the capacity of the child's brain to form lasting engrams and to store them is intact. These interferences are part of everyday life and are not necessarily pathologic. The process of attention plays a crucial role here: a distracted or distractible child may not have enough time to form lasting engrams because they are not clearly and permanently "written in." A child must learn to concentrate on what he is supposed to or wants to remember. Otherwise only fleeting engrams are formed.

MEMORY AND THE ATTENTION PROCESS.   Engram formation requires stimuli that can be clearly perceived or experienced in some way. A house seen clearly or a tune that can be heard distinctly is easier to remember than an object shrouded in mist or music heard through noises. It is not known how strong a stimulus must be to leave a lasting engram. We do know, however, that repetition is an important factor and that attention plays a major role. The process of attention changes perception into apperception. It provides an additional clearness that facilitates engram formation. Without it, we perceive many things, but we do not *notice* them. Penfield stressed this close link between attention and memory. In "Engrams in the Human Brain, Mechanisms of Memory" (1968), he wrote: "Only those things to which a man paid attention are preserved in the record or added to the automatic mechanism. The sights and the sounds and the somatic sensations that he ignored are not preserved in any engram form" (p. 840). (See Vol. II, Clearness, under Attention Disorders, p. 514.)

The Role of Concentration. Concentration is the highest form of active attention. A concentration disorder, whether organic or psychogenic, invariably affects the child's memory. Such a child may therefore have memory defects even though his brain's capacity for memory formation may be intact.

The ability to concentrate is of such fundamental importance for memory and therefore for learning because engrams are best formed, retained, and recalled when attention is actively concentrated on whatever the child or adult is supposed to remember. Retention and recall, two basic components of the memory process, are therefore impaired by a concentration disorder. Unless concentrated attention is focused on the material to be remembered, its memory image will be vague and inaccurate, its retention unstable, and recall unreliable. It will therefore take much longer to learn such material. Learning in this context means to form and retain a memory image so clear and stable that it can be securely stored and accurately recalled. This takes longer because more repetition is required when less attention is paid. Only such clear, accurate, and stable images can form a reliable memory basis for learning reading, writing, arithmetic, and other subject matter, and only the process of attention provides the required images. The selectivity of the attention process lifts the material out of all other stimuli so that it can be distinguished from them, become clearly outlined, and accurately perceived. The clearness provided by attention is one of its most important effects. Sensory impressions become clear only when attention is focused on them, otherwise they fuse with each other into a confused and confusing general impression. This also affects recall, which is facilitated and speeded up when the original memory image was precise and clear. (See Vol. II, Selectivity, Concentration, and Clearness under Attention Disorders, pp. 514, 518, 554.)

The following example shows how important concentration is for recall.

A child built an electric lamp in school while learning about electricity. He took it home, put it away, and forgot all about it. When he came across it again and tried to light it he found that it did not work. He was at first sure he had forgotten how he had built it. While inspecting it and concentrating intensely on its mechanism, however, he suddenly remembered exactly how he put it together. This recall was possible because while he built the lamp he had concentrated his attention on his work, so that his memory images were clear. Children and adults can give many such examples from their daily lives.

This type of recall, however, applies only to memories stored in the mental layer Freud called the Preconscious. The recall of memories repressed into the Unconscious is more complicated. It is often facilitated by deliberately averting attention and by letting it wander freely, as the psychoanalytic method of free association requires. (See Vol. II, section on Free-Floating Attention, p. 545.)

Children who seem to pay no attention at all, who are restless, fidgety, run around the classroom, or daydream while sitting quietly at their desk sometimes surprise their teacher by suddenly giving a correct answer. This shows that they learned something in spite of their inattention and indicates that retention can occur under such unlikely circumstances. These children's attention apparently stopped wandering elsewhere long enough to pick up at least some of the material they were supposed to learn. Knowledge picked up in this casual way, however, is usually not very sound and soon forgotten. Its engram is too vague and unstable.

RECALL DIFFICULTIES. Penfield defined memory as "The power or the process of reproducing or recalling what has been learned." He emphasized that engrams "may be summoned consciously or automatically for the purpose of recognition, interpretation, perception" (1968, p. 840). He defined perception in this context as "the automatic interpretation of the present as judged by past experience" (p. 834). It is important to realize that the process of recall is to a large degree automatic and involuntary. Penfield suggests that its organic basis lies, in part, in certain areas of the temporal cortex which he called "interpretive cortex." He writes: "It seems evident that the interpretive area of cortex is part of an automatic mechanism which scans the record of the past. It makes subconscious automatic judgments that have to do with the individual and his environment" (p. 840). He bases these assumptions on his extensive neurosurgical work and on electrical stimulation from point to point over the cerebral cortex of conscious patients (p. 835).

Clinical and experimental studies indicate that engrams are less vulnerable than the mechanisms that transmit the information they contain. Engrams are apparently retained throughout life; their long-range storage is well protected. Memory difficulties are usually due to transitory recall impairments for organic or psychologic reasons.

For instance, vascular spasms or other interruptions of blood supply may prevent recall temporarily.

Anxiety, anger, and preoccupations normally interfere with the recall of specific engrams or engram complexes. Recall difficulties on a neurotic basis are more severe and long-lasting because they are the result of repressions thoughts, feelings and experiences into the unconscious.

VISUAL AND AUDITORY TYPES OF MEMORY. Engram formation is facilitated or made more difficult depending on the route through which a stimulus enters the brain. There are differences in this respect between visual and auditory routes. It is important for teachers and parents to find out by which route the child learns best, the visual or the auditory. Many children of the visual type cannot learn anything they only hear. They must see it in pictures or in print. They can't, for instance, remember even simple sequences such as the days of the week when teachers or parents just say them and have the child repeat them. An auditory child, however, can learn them with ease this way. He may not be able to learn anything visually, however, and this becomes an ever greater handicap to him the older he gets, because he has to learn more and more through reading and through other visual material such as maps, diagrams, and so on. Unfortunately he is also destined to be poor in mathematics. This subject can be understood and remembered only visually. (See Chapter 4, Arithmetic Disorders.)

These memory types are inborn. Training the auditory route in a visual child or the visual route in an auditory child helps, but it does not change his basic type. Most children find out for themselves to which type they belong. This is fortunate because a child may develop a reading or other learning disorder if he himself or his teachers are not aware of his memory type. Not all children have a special memory type. Some can learn equally well by either route.

Unfortunately, courses on education and books on reading, child psychology, child rearing, and related topics do not usually mention these important neurophysiologic and psychologic facts. (See Automatic Memory, p. 69.)

LOCALIZATION. The storage of the enormous number of engrams retained from fetal life onward must necessarily occupy large parts of the brain on all levels and in both hemispheres. Memory is to some extent involved in almost all activities of the brain. The reading and speech apparatuses, for instance, cannot function without the information contained in numerous engrams and engram complexes. One of the reasons why area 39 is such an important shunt is that it apparently transmits, coordinates, and integrates information contained in engrams important for reading and spelling and, to a lesser degree, for writing.

Autopsy findings and observations during and following surgery have shown that the integrity of the temporal lobes in both hemispheres is vitally important for memory. The hippocampi are especially sensitive in this respect. Bilateral lesions in these structures invariably cause a memory disorder. Penfield de-

69

'ory disorder caused by such lesions or by surgical removal.

...terference with the function of the hippocampal system produces ..ade and antegrade amnesia of a peculiar type. There is loss of memory . events for some years previous, with a fair preservation of memory of the distant past. There is also inability to recall (or possibly to record) all the succeeding conscious states of mind from the date of the hippocampal lesions onward (p. 838).

[See also Noback & Demarest, 1977, pp. 173, 174 (diagrams), 178, 179.]

However, these are not the only structures underlying the memory process. As Hecaen (1969) writes in "Cerebral Localization of Mental Functions and Their Disorders,"

It may well be that any lesion affecting the circuit formed by the hippocampus, Ammon's horn, fornix, hypothalamus, mammillary body, mammillothalamic tract, thalamus, and cortex, is liable to derange the mechanisms subserving the recording of memories (p. 16).

Because of its widespread localization throughout both hemispheres, memory storage is very well protected. Retention and recall are more vulnerable. The memory disorder of children with an organic reading disorder is almost exclusively one of retention. Recall is not as frequently involved. A child who can retain the information necessary for reading will have no trouble storing it, unless his brain has severe and widespread lesions in both hemispheres, for instance due to degenerative diseases.

Memory Disorders

Diffuse cerebral disorders such as dementia, encephalitis, meningitis, hemorrhages and other circulatory disturbances, atrophies, degenerative diseases, all cause memory defects. Retention and memory for recent events are the first faculties to be affected. Recall is also often involved. (See case of Adrian, encephalitis, Vol. II, p. 616, under Hyperactivity.)

ANOXIA. Anoxia (lack of oxygen) is one of the many causes of an organic concentration disorder as well as a memory disorder. Anoxia is especially important because it may affect an infant's brain before, during, or after birth. The pediatrician McKay points out that anoxia is "the leading immediate cause of perinatal death or of permanent damage to central nervous system cells which is manifest later as cerebral palsy or mental deficiency" (1979, p.

423). (See Vol. II, sections on cerebral palsy and on mental deficiency, pp. 428, 410). It is important to add that there are apparently less severe forms of anoxia which do not cause such profound and diffuse brain damage. It is assumed that such less severe anoxia sometimes causes organic reading, writing, and arithmetic disorders and other organic symptoms in children whose general intellectual capacity is not impaired and who do not have cerebral palsy.

Anoxia also causes concentration difficulties and therefore impairs retention in adults and children climbing or working in high altitudes; it also affects children and their teachers working in poorly ventilated classrooms.

AMNESIAS.　Any head injury leading to a loss of consciousness leads to amnesia for the time the patient was unconscious. It usually also causes retrograde amnesia for a varying length of time before the injury. Convulsions, spontaneous or induced as in electric convulsive treatment (ECT), have the same effect. A child suffering from epilepsy or another convulsive disorder usually forgets what he learned for a varying length of time before a seizure, and does not remember what happened while it was going on. Epileptic fugues and twilight states are especially distressing in this respect. The child or adult does not remember anything that happened during such an abnormal mental state. A convulsive disorder that does not respond to treatment slows down the child's retention and recall during the intervals between convulsions as well, and this gradually leads to an irreversible memory disorder. (See Vol. II, Convulsive Disorders p. 422. See also case of Morris, Head Injury, under Concentration, p. 568.)

Chronic alcoholism also causes episodes of amnesia, or "blackouts." The youngest alcoholic I have examined was 14 years old. Alcoholism, like other addictions, affects ever younger children. (See p. 285.) (Mitchell, Hong, & Corman, 1979.)

Psychogenic Amnesias.　Episodes of amnesia, fugues, and twilight states may also have a psychogenic basis. They are infrequent in children but must be taken into consideration when the differential diagnosis is determined. Some children have amnesia during a temper tantrum or during other angry outbursts.

Role of Psychologic Factors.　In the memory process organic and psychologic factors are closely linked. The content of what children or adults forget is determined psychologically. They forget words, feelings, experiences, and so forth, according to their individual interests, life experiences, or psychopathology. Psychologic factors do not cause organic memory disorders.

They are not pathogenic for these disorders. However, they are to a certain degree pathoplastic—that is, they may determine the form the memory disorder takes.

KORSAKOV SYNDROME.   Rare in children, the Korsakov syndrome may occur after a head injury, carbon monoxide poisoning, a fever delirium, or other traumatic, toxic, or infectious conditions. It also occurs in severe vitamin B deficiencies, for instance pellagra or beri-beri. Chronic alcoholism is its most frequent cause.

Confabulation.   A characteristic symptom for the Korsakov syndrome is confabulation, which involves a severe defect of retention, of memory for recent events, and of recall. Sufferers cover up their memory gaps with very elaborate stories, and are convinced that these stories really happened.

Confabulation on a Psychogenic Basis.   Confabulation can occur alone, without any organic defects. It may not be entirely accurate to call this confabulation, but the clinical manifestations are very similar. It is especially frequent in children with a reading disorder, whether or not it is organic in origin. Such children fill their reading gaps with elaborate stories, maintaining that they have actually read these stories. They also invent the text they were supposed to have studied. Many such children do not lie deliberately, but instead deceive themselves. Frequently they really believe that the story they are telling is what they actually read.

PHYSICAL DISEASES AND MEMORY DISORDERS.   Physical diseases and disorders not originating in the brain can cause a memory disorder, a concentration disorder, as well as other brain symptoms. They do this indirectly, by causing circulatory, metabolic, endocrine, nutritional, and other changes that reach the brain and damage it. The brain is, of course, involved in all bodily functions, normal and abnormal. It is immediately informed of all bodily changes and plays a role in all pathologic and healing processes. These are functions of a normal, healthy brain that operate entirely automatically, without our conscious awareness and beyond our control. Most somatic (in contrast to organic) disorders and diseases do not interfere with the brain's normal functioning. There are toxic, metabolic, endocrine, nutritional, and other somatic disorders, however, that can damage a basically intact brain and cause organic symptoms, for instance a memory disorder, by breaking through the hematoencephalic (i.e., blood–brain) barrier. No conclusion can be drawn about the harmlessness or harmfulness of *any* substance (therapeutic drug, food additive, etc.) for the brain at any age, unless it is known whether or not and under what circumstances the substance penetrates the blood–brain barrier. (See Blood–Brain Barrier, p. 00.)

Hunger and Malnutrition. Hunger and malnutrition are among the somatic disorders that affect the brain indirectly and seriously impair the ability to concentrate and to remember. Both affect many more children than statistics indicate. These disorders are not necessarily identical. A chronically hungry child is, of course, malnourished, but not every malnourished child is underfed. Chronic diseases, for instance, may cause malnutrition, because of lack of appetite or poor absorption of food. Malnutrition is also often caused in a child by an unhealthy diet resulting from poor dietary habits of the entire family or from the child's own neurotic food preferences, or by defective infant formulas. An entirely novel set of factors beyond the control of any individual or family must also be considered when such a child is examined, namely food additives. Their effect is described in detail in Vol. II, section on Concentration (p. 554) and Hyperactivity (p. 630).

Fatigue. Fatigue is another somatic condition that causes concentration difficulties and impairs memory. It affects retention and recall. (See Vol. II, Fatigue under Concentration Disorders, p. 562 and Fatiguability, p. 272.)

Chemical Brain Damage. It is not sufficiently appreciated that chemical damage to the brain may cause a concentration disorder, a memory disorder, and other organic symptoms. Drug abuse, alcoholism, and bromide intoxication are the most frequent causes of this kind of damage. Bromides, alcohol, LSD, heroin, cocaine, methadone, barbiturates, dexedrine, marijuana, tranquilizers, and so on, affect the brain chemically. Different chemical changes within the brain produce the effect of these drugs on thoughts and emotions. These changes also affect the attention and memory processes and may cause a concentration and a memory disorder, among other organic symptoms. (See Vol. II, Concentration, p. 554.)

Drug Addiction and Abuse. The innumerable studies of drug users do not sufficiently stress the effect of these drugs on memory, if they mention it at all. Even marijuana alone, taken habitually over a long period of time, may cause a memory and a concentration disorder. The psychoanalysts Kolansky and Moore stressed this in their paper, "Clinical Effects of Marijuana on the Young." This study is outstanding because it is based on careful clinical examinations. The authors state that, after having withdrawn from marijuana, "these patients seem to be left with a residual of some memory difficulty and impairment of concentration. One patient has shown this for two years at the time of this writing" (1972) (See Vol. II, Concentration, p. 565 ff.)

Endocrine Disorders.   Hypothyroidism, which is due to the deficient production of thyroid hormones, affects memory. It slows down retention and recall. Cretinism is its severest form. Infants born with this disorder invariably become mental defectives unless they are treated to restore normal thyroid balance during the first months of their lives.

Memory Aids (Mnemonic Devices)

Mnemonic devices are indispensable for learning. They create fast and reliable engrams.

Memory is not formed in a vacuum. A new fact is best remembered as part of a familiar sequence or framework. Understanding is therefore the best memory aid. New material should be built on something the child already knows. However, there are innumerable items, such as house and telephone numbers, names, difficult spellings, medical terms, and so forth, that do not lend themselves to easily remembered explanations.

AUDITORY AIDS.   Rhythms, melodies, chants, and word or sound associations are memory aids. The pun "Spring forward, fall back" helps us remember our twice-yearly time changes.

MOTOR AIDS.   Letting what one sees or hears, for instance a lecture, a tune, a text, pass through one's motor apparatus by writing it down, by singing, by saying, or at least by articulating it, defines it more clearly, underlines it, establishes it as something worth noticing and remembering. That is why motor acts such as writing, typing, or reading out loud are excellent memory aids.

When we want to remember a telephone number, for instance, we say it out loud several times.

Taking notes is a type of motor aid. Children should be encouraged to take notes as soon as they can write adequately. This is not easy to do but it is an excellent way to learn to listen, to write, to think, and to remember, all at the same time. The prevailing teaching practice of simply letting children listen and later on copy from the blackboard is not at all helpful in this respect.

Some children, just like adults, can best remember what they hear when they repeat it silently to themselves. This applies to lectures, conversations, and so on. They can learn to do this very quickly. It is best to suggest this memory aid to them because they might not discover it by themselves. (See Vol. II, section on Distractibility, p. 581.)

There is a certain danger in the mindless use of memory aids. Children who learn something only by rote may not really understand what it is all about. Many children I examined sang the alphabet song happily and accurately without knowing what it meant. They could neither read nor write all the letters. Some did not even know that the song was about letters.

A motor memory aid I have found to be especially helpful for children with learning disorders is described by Spalding and Spalding in *The Writing Road to Reading* (1969). It tends to prevent the confusion between "b" and "d," so frequent in so many children with or without a reading disorder.

Romalda Spalding stresses that these two lower-case letters should never be taught at the same time because that is confusing. She instructs the teacher to hold up a card with a "d" on it and to sound "d." The teacher should then explain that this is a short letter with a tall part, and point a finger at the round part to show that this part comes first, before the tall line. After this visual and auditory demonstration, Spalding uses the following motor memory aid: she has each child say "d" and feel his upturned tongue with the back of his mouth making a circle as he says the sound of this letter.

The children are taught that in contrast to "d," "b" begins with a line, and that in saying "b" the lips make a straight line. Spalding makes the important point that "the kinesthetic feel of these two letters can keep children from reversing them" (p. 55).

Spalding has a number of other helpful memory aids. For instance, the senseless sentence, "Her first nurse works early." This contains all five different spellings of the sound "er." She tells her students to memorize it (p. 86). Such rote memorizing is helpful. These spellings cannot be explained and learned simply by understanding them.

VISUAL AIDS. Diagrams, maps, pictures, and especially films are indispensable memory aids. Films in particular have made the sciences, history, social studies, geography, and all other subjects understandable and memorable as never before. They are the greatest advance in memory aids. Caution must be exercised with regard to teaching reading, however, because to read is not only a visual and auditory, but also a motor act.

To teach reading through pictures, even moving pictures, may promote illiteracy rather than fluent reading. There is no way that seeing a picture of a house above the word "house" can teach a child to read, spell, and write. It can only confuse a beginner by misinforming him that h o u s e has something in common with the picture of a house when it actually represents the sounds of the word "house." Reading the word should evoke the *memory image* of a house. The child must learn that h o u s e has nothing in common with a real house. Films do not improve such an erroneous way of teaching, neither does television.

The harm done by this word/picture teaching method is documented in the analysis of the pathology of the reading and writing process.

TACTILE MEMORY AIDS. These aids are often a great help for children with a reading disorder. They remember letter forms better when they make an outline with their finger in the air or can feel them on sandpaper. A sandbox can also be used. These methods are also helpful for beginning readers. The Open Court Readers (1963) recommend their use.

MEMORY BY ROTE.   Rote-memory learning is appropriate only for a limited number of topics that are difficult to remember any other way, for example, the alphabet, days of the week, months of the year, multiplication tables, certain spellings, and so on.

Rote learning may conceal a reading disorder. I have examined many children who had memorized their readers and other books read aloud in school or by their parents at home. When given a different book, they read fluently without realizing that the text and their words did not match. This is called "position reading." These children are usually nonreaders and nonwriters. (See Position Reading, p. 112; and 8-year-old boy, Vol. II, under Hyperactivity, p. 630.)

Memory Tests

All children suffering from reading disorders should have memory tests. Not even the Stanford-Binet is thorough enough in this respect, even though it evaluates memory in greater detail than the Wechsler Intelligence Scale For Children (WISC). The special memory scale developed by Wechsler for adults is more reliable even for children.

ROLE OF ATTENTION TESTS.   Tests designed to evaluate attention also test memory. How much of a text a child can read, understand, and recall in a set period of time tests his memory as well as the length of time he can sustain intellectual attention.

To test both faculties one can ask the child to remember some dates, names, or addresses about which he will be asked later on. One can also show him different pictures and find out how many of them and what details he remembers after a while. The tachistoscope is sometimes used for this purpose. (See Vol. II, p. 510 under Attention Disorders.)

This type of test must be evaluated with special care. This is because a patient of any age with a severe defect of retention may actually have seen the objects on the test card, but may have forgotten instantly what he actually saw; then he may report seeing nothing or fewer objects than he saw. When shown the same cards hours or days later, he may say that he has already seen them. One must assume that an engram was formed, but that the patient had no immediate access to it.

It frequently also happens to healthy adults and children that they cannot remember something and are certain that they never saw or otherwise experienced it, and then suddenly their memory comes back. This fits in with the theory that once an engram is formed, it is retained forever, that the process of engram formation cannot be reversed, and that forgetting means transitory lack of access to memory traces for organic or psychologic reasons. That is why the memory of patients even with the severest brain pathology fluctuates so strikingly.

It is also important to find out whether a child can retain a "set" of attention. This is a fixed, stable attitude of attention that is focused exclusively on one task. A child who cannot retain a "set" cannot remember the thread of a story or a text long enough to understand it, follow it, and learn it. (For tests, see pp. 506–512 under Attention Disorders.)

The visual, auditory, motor, and tactile memory of children with a reading disorder should be tested separately. They may remember the shapes of letters better with one modality or the other. Some children remember letters and words better when they are outlined on their hands or back—that is, through touch. Some children's memory in this respect is improved when they dance letter forms or indicate them with motor movements. Remedial reading teachers use these methods. (See p. 78 under Conditioned Reflexes.)

Careful and detailed observation by parents, teachers, and clinicians and by the child himself is also essential for the evaluation of memory.

SPECIAL MEMORY DIFFICULTIES OF CHILDREN. Some children have trouble only with remembering numbers. (See Chapter 4, Arithmetic Disorders.)

Many children with an organic reading disorder have trouble memorizing the days of the week and the months of the year, and also learning to read the clock face. These children invariably have difficulties orienting themselves in regard to time. A digital watch or clock helps them. (See section on Clock Reading Disorder, p. 165.)

Many of these children also have difficulty remembering landmarks they need for space orientation. They get lost on the street and in the school building. This may be the first obvious sign of a more generalized memory defect.

Automatic Memory

Reading requires not only that the child's ability for general and specific memory formation be intact; the child must also be capable of forming the special type of memory needed for perfectly smooth and fast reading. His memory must function with great speed and without his being aware of each step needed. Reading must become an automatic act, performed without thinking about the technique involved. Included in this automatism must be an automatic correction of errors. The neurophysiologic mechanism that makes this possible is the formation of conditioned reflexes. The reading skill consists of a succession of reflexes whose development is governed by the laws of Pavlov's conditioned reflexes (Mosse & Daniels, 1959).

It is important to distinguish the terms "automatic" from "unconscious." Automatic brain mechanisms have nothing in common with the mental layer Freud called the Unconscious. If one wants to fit automatic brain mechanisms into the Freudian model of mental mechanisms, they might be considered part of the Preconscious, which Freud defined as having a mental quality of "passing into consciousness with no difficulty" (1946, p. 26). This is in contrast to the Unconscious which, according to Freud, is strictly separated from the conscious by a layer he called "resistance." There is a fluid boundary between Freud's Conscious and Preconscious layers just as there is between automatic and conscious performances of the brain. (See Vol. II, Free-Floating Attention under Attention Disorders, p. 545, and Automatic Mechanisms, p. 470.)

Reading disorders can be caused by an inability to form the necessary conditioned reflexes or by the establishment and practice of wrong reflexes. It is therefore important to understand what conditioned reflexes are and how they are developed.

Conditioned Reflexes

Conditioned reflexes are, according to Pavlov, special forms of associations (1956, p. 256). The terms "association" and "reflex" are often used interchangeably; the same neurophysiologic mechanism is being described. A conditioned reflex depends for its formation entirely on an unconditioned reflex. The reflex action is the same in both, but the stimulus initiating this action has been changed from an unconditioned to a conditioned one.

All human beings are born with the same types of unconditioned reflexes: inborn, hereditary, and automatic neurophysiologic reactions that do not have to be learned. Pavlov found that they are the basis for all involuntary alimentary, sexual, and some other inborn functions on which instinctive behavior is based. These unconditioned reflexes appear with absolute regularity and are independent of previous experience. That is why they are called "unconditioned."

The best-known example of an unconditioned reflex action is salivation in response to the unconditioned stimuli of smelling, tasting, or chewing food. Pavlov based important experiments on these unconditioned alimentary reflexes. He used a bell as the conditioned stimulus and found that after a certain number of repetitions the bell alone elicited salivation. His experiments showed that almost any stimulus chosen at random could be used for conditioning provided certain rules were observed.

Both the unconditioned and the conditioned stimulus had to be activated together and in always the same sequence (first the new, conditioned stimulus, then the unconditioned stimulus), and this had to be repeated many times before the unconditioned reflex action was able to respond to the conditioned stimulus alone, without the help of the original unconditioned stimulus. In this way it became possible to plan and thus control unconditioned biologic functions. Based on his experimental work, Pavlov came to the conclusion that conditioned reflexes provide the neurophysiologic basis for certain higher performances of the brain. He showed that unconditioned reflexes do not necessarily require cortical activity, but that conditioned reflexes always do.

He called the conditioned stimuli "signals" and concluded that they exist on two levels: (1) a primitive level before the child has learned to speak; and (2) a higher level, after the child has learned to say and to understand words. Words, according to Pavlov, function as conditioned stimuli or signals of the highest order. He called them the "second signal system," which he thought formed the basis for the development of the highest and most complicated mental functions. Reading, according to him, is part of this "second signal system" because it is "graphic speech" (1956, p. 312).

THE NEUROPHYSIOLOGIC BASIS OF READING. Applying Pavlov's discoveries to the neurophysiologic basis of reading, this means that we must establish a conditioned reflex or an automatic association in the child, which starts with the letter (or a fixed combination of letters representing *one* sound) as the conditioned stimulus, and ends with the child's saying the letter sound.

Speech is the unconditioned reflex action that must be conditioned to respond to the new visual "signal." The unconditioned reflex, which all children have in common, consists of the repetition of the speech sounds they hear. It is, of course, not exactly like the unconditioned reflex of salivation when smelling food. It is a higher level neurophysiologic reflex that requires activity of the entire cortical, subcortical, and peripheral speech apparatus; this apparatus must, in addition, have reached a certain level of maturity to be able to function. It starts to function only when the child is about 11 months old.

The unconditioned stimulus that sets this apparatus in motion is acoustic (the hearing of speech sounds); the unconditioned reflex action is kinesthetic–motor (speech). For reading, the child must be conditioned to respond with speech to a visual instead of an acoustic stimulus. This means that the conditioned visual stimulus must eventually take the place of the unconditioned acoustic stimulus in order to elicit the spoken response.

CONDITIONED VISUAL STIMULI. Before learning to read, the child has already been conditioned to respond with speech to a large number of other visual stimuli. In Pavlov's terms, he has begun to develop an extensive "second signal system." The naming of objects is such a conditioned reflex. That he can say the word "apple," for instance, when seeing an apple, is due to conditioning that took place when he heard the word "apple" said repeatedly and regularly when he himself or someone he observed held an apple or pointed at it. This simultaneous conditioned visual and unconditioned acoustic stimulus eventually established a special type of close association—an engram complex—in the child's mind between the apple he saw and the word "apple." Only after such an engram complex had been firmly established could he say "apple" immediately upon seeing one.

IMPORTANCE OF ENGRAM COMPLEXES.   The formation of such an engram complex is crucial for the establishment of these high-level conditioned reflexes. The engram complex acts as a switch or relay, directing the visible apple to the spoken word "apple." It makes the conditioning of the reflex possible. Such an engram complex consists of two images, a visual image of the apple and an acoustic image of the word "apple," and of a close connection between them. The formation of visual images is called "visualization." Speech–acoustic images are called "mental" or "inner" speech; other acoustic images are called "inner hearing."

IMAGE FORMATION.   The formation of such mental images is one of the brain's most important and least understood functions. We do not know their exact neurophysiologic and anatomical basis, but we can infer their existence through extensive psychiatric, neuropathologic, psychologic, and experimental observations. The images needed for naming objects and for the basic technical act of reading are simple compared with complex ideas, feelings, and experiences. It is the capacity to form images that underlies memory formation and thinking, as well as the ability to create something new and original.

AUTOMATIC CORRECTION OF ERRORS.   We know that the reading conditioning process does not end with the child's saying the word "apple." Cybernetics has taught us that reflexes transcend the linear reflex action that proceeds from stimulus via the engram complex to response. Reflexes function in a circular way in which cause and effect change roles constantly. The effect of the conditioned reflex is the saying of the word, which then becomes a cause by setting in motion a reverse activation of the entire reflex. This is called a "feedback" response, which checks and automatically corrects the reflex.

When the child hears himself say the word "apple" he automatically retraces the steps of the reflex via the engram complex back to the visual stimulus, namely, the apple. He matches the sound of the word he just heard himself say with the acoustic memory image he had formed of it, and following this he matches this acoustic image with the visual image of the apple, and ultimately with the real apple he is looking at. This assures not only that his pronunciation of the word is correct, but also that the word refers to the correct object. He does not do this deliberately, nor is he aware of it. This feedback takes place with great speed, and the different steps remain below the threshold of consciousness.

Only those children who have difficulty in establishing these reflexes should be made aware of the separate steps and should be instructed to practice them. The practice of "inner" speech and of visualization is a good treatment technique for children with reading disorders and also with certain speech disorders, provided they really have image-formation difficulties. (See Vol. II, p. 543 under Attention Disorders.)

In children with a healthy central nervous system we can observe some signs of the process of conditioning and image formation. When we observe such children from the age of 11 months onward (or from whatever age they start to speak), we hear them talk to themselves when they are alone, especially just before they fall asleep. They repeat all the words they heard during that day. This is how they practice, quite spontaneously. Eventually we hear them only whisper, and finally we can't hear them anymore but can observe that they practice silent speech with lip and tongue movements without making a sound. This is the last stage before they have formed such reliable images that they can think and fantasize without even a remnant of speaking (Luria & Yudovich, 1971, p. 29; Moolenaar-Bijl, 1948, p. 214).

The beginning reader has to go through a similar process. The conditioned reflexes needed for reading, however, are much more difficult to establish. The visual stimuli are letters, which are two-dimensional abstract forms that bear no immediate relationship to objects or feelings and whose only meaning is the sound. It must be explained to children from the very beginning that letters represent speech sounds that are a part of every word. This explanation is quite indispensable because not all children can deduce this on their own.

I have examined too many children of all ages up to high school who had reading disorders because they did not fully understand this basic fact. It either had not been explained to them properly or not stressed consistently enough. Learning, even the acquisition of automatic functions such as conditioned reflexes, *always* requires understanding; the highest and most advanced parts of the cerebral cortex must always be activated, otherwise learning cannot take place.

To show a child a group of letters and to tell him that this means "house" —as is done in those kindergartens and first grades where children are introduced to reading with so-called "sight words"—confuses them, interferes with the formation of conditioned reflexes, and teaches them a lie. The letter sequence h o u s e stands for the word "house" and not for the house they see; pictures do that, but not letters.

To achieve conditioning with the greatest possible speed and accuracy the child must know exactly, step by step, what he has to learn. He must be told, for instance, that the letter "S" stands for the sound "S" and for nothing else, and that he must learn to say "S" when he sees "S." Whether single letters or a fixed combination of letters forming one single sound are taught, the conditioning process is the same. The child must be helped to form an automatic association between the seen letters and the spoken letters. The formation of such an association is the key to reading (Schmitt, 1966).

The formation of such a conditioned reflex requires that the child experience the visual and the spoken letter together repeatedly, without interference by any other stimulus, and always in the same sequence, namely by looking at the letter briefly before saying it. The teacher should make certain that the child is looking at the letter while the teacher sounds it and the child repeats it, or later on when the child reads it on his own. The teacher's pronunciation must act as the child's feedback correction until his own feedback system is working. That is why it is so important to let the child read aloud at first and to correct his pronunciation right away. It takes time for a conditioned reflex to be established, and it can not possibly function until the child has developed reliable visual and acoustic images and formed a close connection between them. Silent reading cannot achieve this.

The best way to teach this skill is by having the child write the letters and make the sounds as he writes them. Writing fixes the forms of letters faster and more firmly in the child's mind than reading because it combines the senses of vision and touch with motor, kinesthetic, and proprioceptive (arising from striped muscles, tendons, joints) sensations. Simultaneous writing and speaking fixes the visual and the acoustic images of the letters more firmly in the child's mind than any other method, strengthens the connection between them better, and forces the child into the correct left-to-right sequence from the very start. No other teaching technique establishes the necessary conditioned reflexes with greater speed, accuracy, and reliability. Another reason reading is best taught through writing is that the reading feedback is exactly what the child must do when writing—namely, proceed from his own sounding of the letter via the engram complex to the visual signal (i.e., the letter), so that he can write it down. With dictation he has to proceed from someone else's sounding of the letter, and when he writes spontaneously, he has to start from his own acoustic memory image of it. All this strengthens the entire reflex. For this reason, the beginning reader should not be permitted to write something he cannot read or to read something he cannot write, and should always say, or at least articulate, the letters and words while he writes them down. The current practice of silent copying from the blackboard violates these principles. [See sections on Teaching Writing (p. 184) and on Distractibility (Vol. II, p. 581).]

WORD READING.   The reading of words becomes reliable only after the child has acquired conditioned reflexes to letters and to fixed combinations of two, three, or four letters forming one single sound. Spalding calls these fixed combinations "phonograms" (Spalding & Spalding, 1969, p. 18). The neurophysiologic basis for reading a word is the formation of a sequence of conditioned reflexes. Only in this way can the visual representation of a word become the spoken word. It is this connection between the seen and the spoken word that presents such difficulty for most children with organic reading disorders, and it is this connection that must be taught properly; otherwise perfectly healthy children do not learn it either.

For word reading, each letter or phonogram must elicit its specific speech sound with lightning speed, so that the child can quickly say one letter after the other in correct sequence, from left to right. The linear arrangement of the letters makes the reading of a word possible. If the letters were scattered all over the page, we could not read them.

LINEAR READING. The child must learn linear reading from the very beginning. He must be taught to sound the letters carefully, one after the other, from left to right, and not to skip a letter or a line. This slows reading at first, but is absolutely essential for the fixation of the required conditioned reflexes and for their combination with eye movements. Special fiber tracts connect the eye muscles, which move the eyes, with the organ of hearing in the inner ear. This makes it possible to look at the source of a sound with great speed. It also facilitates the connection of eye movements with reading (House, Pansky, & Siegel, 1979, p. 194). Reversal of letter sounds within words and reversal of entire words is frequently due to defective linear reading. (See Linear Dyslexia, p. 127.)

Speed and accuracy of reading, and ultimately of understanding, depend on the completeness of this early conditioning. It works in the following way: when the child is supposed to read the short word "me," for example, he pronounces the letter "m." It must be stressed that he has learned the sound of "m" and not its name, because for reading and writing he needs to know the sound; the name can only interfere with conditioning. As soon as he hears himself pronounce "m" and senses that his pronunciation is correct, he moves his eyes to the next letter, "e," selects the pronunciation of it he has been told to use or which had been indicated for him on the letter (e has two sounds, as in "end" and in "me"), says it, and corrects it if necessary. It is unlikely that he will have to go through these separate conditioned reflexes for very long when he reads such a short word. He will very quickly learn to say "me" and become conditioned to the entire word, but the first separate conditioning is an indispensable phase he has to go through. Not only does this assure correct pronunciation of all words, but it also guarantees left-to-right linear reading because the child's attention and eye movements are forced into the required left-to-right direction, and a special association is established between feedback sensation and eye movements from the start. No eye movement takes place until feedback confirmation of the sounding of the letter has been established. (See section on Linear Dyslexia, p. 127.)

This transition from one conditioned reflex to the other can be compared with the mechanism of a typewriter. Its carriage does not move until the letter is pressed down (Schmitt, 1966, p. 80). The connection among vision, speech, and eye movements becomes fixed through this cyclic mechanism. With practice, it can be carried out with great speed and eventually becomes automatic. If this basic training for reading is done properly, no reversals will occur in healthy children, and reversals will be prevented in very many children whose organic defect is only mild. It might take longer for them to establish these automatic responses, and they may have to practice harder; but in the end, the reading process will become automatic for them as well. (See sections on Automatic Mechanisms, Vol. II, and on Teaching of Writing, p. 176, and Vol. II, p. 470.)

BLENDING.   That the child learns to pronounce the word as a unit whose sound differs from the sounds of the individual letters is due to a synthesis called "blending," which the child performs on a higher level. If the word he is reading is familiar to him, he will recognize it while sounding the letters and quickly say the word, pronouncing it exactly as he does when using it while speaking. It must be stressed that he recognizes the word's sound first, before he can recognize its meaning. We read, after all, *before* we know what we are reading. If the word is new for the child, he will try to blend the letter sounds using acoustic memory images of words he already knows.

The ease with which children learn to blend varies. *One* example, dramatically presented, may be sufficient for some children to understand and remember the technique of blending for the rest of their lives; others need months. Some children with organic reading disorders have difficulty with it, especially when they also have hearing or speech defects. If taught well, all children except the very few with the severest forms of organic reading disorders should be able to blend by the end of the first grade. The prerequisite for this is careful conditioning and clear explanation of the reading technique. I have examined many children from the elementary grades through high school who did not know what blending was all about. It had apparently never been explained to them. The expression on their face of sudden excited understanding when I explained to them that letters stand for sounds and how these sounds blend into a word is unforgettable. This was a breakthrough experience for many of them which they should have experienced in the first grade. I undertook this explanation for diagnostic purposes, namely to determine whether their reading disability was organic or due to faulty teaching. To test whether this really was a breakthrough, I gave them first short and then longer words to read, and they could frequently read them after only this single explanation. Of course all these children had to be referred for remedial reading anyway because they still had to learn the sounds of all letters and phonograms. This is what the "visual," "sight/word," "global," "word perception," "word picture," "whole word" method of teaching reading to beginners leads to. There are young men and women in high school to whom reading remains an eternal mystery because no one ever explained to them its basic, indispensable elements, and the necessary conditioned reflexes were never established.

CONTOUR READING. Many of these mistaught youths sweep their gaze around each word in a desperate effort to deduce its sounds and meaning from its contour. We know that patients with brain pathology who knew how to read before their disorder started, use this same technique as an aid to reading. Neurologists call this symptom "Westphal's Maneuver" after the neurologist who described it first (Critchley, 1970, p. 3). It is a shame that a technique used with little success by desperate patients is taught to healthy children as part of the "sight word" method, where it is called a "configuration clue." When we observe a child doing this, therefore, we cannot assume that it necessarily indicates an organic reading disorder; it may be due to faulty conditioning.

Once the reading of words has become automatic, the child can say them immediately upon seeing them. As he formerly did with letters, he moves his eyes to the next word only after he has experienced the feedback confirmation for his saying the entire word aloud. Only when this more complicated conditioning has been established can flawless reading even of unfamiliar words take place, and only then can the linear progression from one word to the next without reversals and without omission of any word be guaranteed. With practice, a new association will be formed between the visual image of the entire word, which has become a conditioned stimulus, and the sound of the word. Only when this stage has been reached can the word be read as a whole, and only this step makes almost instantaneous understanding of the word possible. (See sections on Silent Reading, p. 112, and Linear Dyslexia, p. 127.)

The gnostic part of the word (i.e., its meaning) is activated as soon as the child hears himself saying it. Understanding comes through *hearing* the word; it cannot originate in any other way. This step cannot be skipped. With practice, an instantaneous association is formed between the acoustic and the gnostic part of the word. Only then can the child read aloud fluently and with understanding and only then has the basis for silent reading been established. The understanding of the word strengthens the feedback sensation, makes reading pleasurable, and creates a feeling of satisfaction and self-assurance in the child. Only then can he be quite sure that he is reading correctly. Eventually he learns to use his memory image of the sound of the word alone as his feedback sensation to confirm that he is reading correctly, and only then is he ready to read silently. (See section on Silent Reading, p. 112.)

These complex memory images of words are more sensations or feelings, than precise intellectual pictures, even when the words evoke pictures—for

instance, the word "house." They require the participation of sensations arising in sense organs, inner organs, the autonomic nervous system, and the
musculoskeletal system. The cortex, subcortical structures (especially the
thalamus), and other relevant parts of the central nervous system are activated.
These images remain, at least in part, below the threshold of consciousness;
expressed in psychologic terms, we know the unconscious is almost always
involved.

Some children with organic reading disorders cannot form conditioned
reflexes to visual stimuli, but are capable of developing associations between
tactile, kinesthetic, or proprioceptive sensations and speech sounds. That is
why some children who are not blind can learn to read only by touch, like blind
children who use the Braille method. Some can learn by feeling the outlines
of letters pasted on various materials; others can learn by writing letters in the
air, which gives them kinesthetic sensations, or by manipulating three-dimensional letters, which stimulates tactile and proprioceptive sensations. It takes
longer to read in this way. However, many of these children can change to
visual stimuli after they have established reliable associations between tactile,
kinesthetic, or proprioceptive sensations and acoustic stimuli—that is, letter
sounds.

OBSTACLES TO READING CONDITIONING.   The ease and speed with which
a child can be conditioned to this special visual code (i.e., letters are a code
representing speech sounds, just as musical notes are a code representing pure
tones) depend on three main factors: the responsiveness of his particular
nervous system, the clarity of the teaching technique, and the nature of the
code.

The responsiveness of the child's nervous system depends on the intactness
of his organic reading apparatus as well as on his general health. Fatigue,
vitamin deficiencies and malnutrition of any type, anemia, and other chronic
physical illnesses slow down conditioned reflex formation and may even extinguish reflexes which had already been established. It is well known that young
children may forget how to read after a severe and prolonged illness. (See
sections on Hunger and Malnutrition, p. 561, and Fatigue, Vol. II, p. 562.)

Conditioned reflexes can also be extinguished by disuse unless they have
been very firmly established. This is what happens to children frequently
during long summer vacations or during any other prolonged absence from
school. Unless these reflexes are constantly reinforced, they begin to fade. This
is one reason it is so important to assign teachers to chronic pediatric wards
in hospitals and to homes where chronically ill children are confined. It is also
why reading should be taught so well and made so exciting that it becomes
a pleasant part of a child's life.

Conditioned reflex formation requires clear signals that do not vary. This cannot be done with chewing gum in one's mouth. Both the visual and the acoustic stimulus must be exactly the same, at least in the beginning. This is why the clarity of teaching techniques is of such vital importance. The visual signal must always look the same and the speech sounds sound the same. It is therefore best to teach the same letter forms in the beginning. Starting with lower-case letters is easiest because their transformation into script is not too difficult in English and in other languages that use Roman letters for both print and script. Where script differs fundamentally from print, as for instance in Russian, children have to learn two totally different forms for each letter. This is, of course, much more difficult to teach and to learn.

Some textbooks such as *Teaching Reading with Words in Color* and some self-teaching devices use different colors for different letters or indicate the different letter sounds with different colors, so that each letter contains two signals: its form and its color (Gattegno, 1968). This confuses children to such an extent that either no conditioning takes place at all or the child becomes conditioned to only *one* of the stimuli, the form or the color. Pavlov has demonstrated this phenomenon in many experiments. The vast majority of children will become conditioned to the color only, because color excites children more than form. These children then read all red letters, for example, as "S," if "S" was shown red. I have observed such errors in conditioning and witnessed children struggling to disentangle form from color.

Pictures are another form of interference that renders impossible the formation of these basic reflexes. The child must see the signal clearly for what it is: a form and not a picture. Where he is shown "flash cards" with a picture above a word—that is, with a word and a picture shown at the same time, the necessary conditioning the child needs for reading cannot take place at all. This is the main reason the word/picture method of teaching reading to beginners is so devastating, and why comic books that train the child to picture gazing and to relying on pictures to tell stories are so damaging for reading (Mosse, 1962b). (See Linear Reading, p. 83, and Damaging Aspects of Mass Media, p. 275.)

The sounds of letters and of letter combinations should be pronounced clearly and should always sound the same. Noises interfere with the formation of this part of the conditioned reflex. Conditioning should ideally be done in a quiet room without yelling. This is very difficult to achieve in a crowded classroom. Teachers and parents, however, should be made aware of the fact that conditioning cannot be accomplished while the television set is going, and the radio and/or the record player are blaring. Noisy classrooms and homes not only interfere with small children's learning to read and write. They also make children of all ages tense and restless, so that it is very difficult for them to concentrate. It is a pity that this has to be stressed at all, it seems so obvious.

School and home visits, however, show that adults need to be educated about this basic rule which facilitates learning. (See Vol. II, p. 000 under Attention Disorders.)

The need for a clear and unified pronunciation of the speech part of this conditioned reflex highlights a fact that has so far not been faced squarely by any American school system, namely that most American children and their teachers do not speak formal English anymore, and that their pronunciations vary. This is true not alone for children who habitually speak another language at home, such as Pennsylvania Dutch or Spanish, but even more for those who speak one of the many distinctive American dialects or slangs.

Probably 50% or more of all children now belong to this group. What child nowadays, for instance, says "ask," "going to," "himself," "escape" clearly? It sounds more like "ax," "gonna," "hisself," "excape." These children must be taught the formal sounds of English letters and of phonograms even while they are being taught to read. It should be made clear to them from the very beginning that many sounds they are learning to say differ from the sounds they use in their daily speech, and that it is necessary for them to learn these formal English sounds because all books, newspapers, magazines, laws, signs, instructions, job applications, and so on are written in this way. It is about time we face the fact that formal English is a new language for very many American children. Reading disorders, even to the severe degree of "word-blindness," can be caused by this foreign language aspect of formal English. We must not take it for granted any longer that the sounds of letters and fixed letter combinations are always pronounced in the same way by all teachers and by all children, and we must realize that this affects the teaching of the basic reading skill adversely. This is especially troublesome because of the nature of the English code.

SPECIAL PROBLEMS OF CONDITIONING TO READING ENGLISH.   The visual code differs in different languages. The English code is much more complicated and therefore infinitely more difficult to learn than that of many other languages. Not only does one stimulus (letter) stand for several different sounds, but the same sound may be represented by completely different stimuli. The letter "a," for instance, stands for three sounds, as in "as," "same," or "want," and the "a" sound in "same" can have seven different visual codes, namely a, e, ai, ei, ay, ey, eigh. This same sound is represented in French, Italian, German, Spanish, for instance, by only *one* letter, "e." This is the reason so many different reading teaching methods have been developed in English-speaking countries in an attempt to get around having to teach this complicated code step by step. None of them has a chance of success unless it establishes the conditioned reflexes I have described *at the very beginning*. Conditioned reflexes become more firmly established the earlier they are practiced. They then become fixed permanently and are very difficult to extinguish. This is why some adults cannot learn to pronounce words in another language properly when they read it. They continue to pronounce the letters as they learned to do in their native language. French people, Italians, Germans, and Spaniards, for instance, tend to continue to say "e" as in "me," whenever they see the letter "i." Unfortunately faulty conditioned reflexes also become fixed. It is therefore essential for the teacher to correct the child's pronunciation until it is clear that the child can correct himself. Silent reading should be introduced much later than is common practice in current curriculums, because the danger of establishing wrong reflex reactions is too great (Mosse, 1963(b), 1965).

From the study of a large number of children with every kind of reading disorder, and from theoretical deductions, I have made an analysis of the reading and writing process. I found that we can distinguish 11 separate acts for reading and 3 for writing. These acts are, of course, connected, but they must be tested separately for a reading and writing defect diagnosis. All of them overlap, but they can be disentangled from each other. This is important, because failure to perform any single one or a combination of them may cause a complete breakdown of reading and writing.

The performance of arithmetic also depends to a large degree on the perfect functioning of the cerebral reading and writing apparatuses. Organic arithmetic disorders therefore occur frequently in combination with reading disorders. The analysis of the reading acts will therefore include arithmetic. A separate chapter will circumscribe arithmetic disorders. (See also Constructional Apraxia, p. 159, and Gerstmann Syndrome, p. 175.)

The complexity of the cerebral reading apparatus means that it is vulnerable, but it also means that innumerable avenues are available to replace a lost function or compensate for it in other ways. In order to find these avenues, we must have an exact, step-by-step knowledge of how this apparatus works. Only then can we devise corrective and preventive measures that have a chance of succeeding.

2. The 11 Reading Acts

1. Seeing and recognizing the lines seen as a letter
2. Sounding the letter
3. Finding the letter when someone else sounds it
4. Naming letters
5. Finding letters when they are named
6. Recognizing a group of letters as a unit, that is, a word
7. Blending the sounds of this group of letters, reading the word aloud
8. Understanding the word
9. Silent reading

10. Spelling
11. Linear reading

Proceeding from the simple to the complex, from healthy performances to malfunctioning, I will outline the different reading and writing acts and correlate them with that part of the organic reading and writing apparatus that makes their operation possible. The symptoms caused by their malfunctioning will then be described, as well as techniques for correction as well as prevention. I will also describe symptoms that in certain instances are associated with organic reading/writing disorders: some, such as speech disorders, apraxia, and agnosia, are due to breakdown of other, interconnected cerebral apparatuses; others are due to proximity of the underlying cerebral areas.

While outlining the reading acts separately, one must keep in mind that the cortex analyzes all incoming sensations (from outside as well as from within the body), stores information, and directs all responses, and that the part of the cortex that has this task with regard to reading is situated in the parietal lobes, centered in Brodmann's area 39 in the angular gyrus, and involved in *all* aspects of reading. I therefore need not mention it repeatedly with each functional anatomical analysis and correlation.

The following is an outline of the 11 reading acts.

1. Seeing and Recognizing the Lines Seen as a Letter.

This requires the ability to see, to focus the eyes properly, to distinguish forms, to separate figure from background, to recognize two-dimensional forms, to recognize the letter as abstract (i.e., as not representing an object), to recognize it as a letter, and to know that this form is called a "letter."

Repetition and practice are required for all children to learn the exact shape of a letter, what part is at the top or at the bottom and what part is on its right or on its left side, and that in a word the letter sequence runs from left to right. The left-to-right pattern is not inborn and biologic, but originated in a historic tradition that varies in different countries. Hebrew and Arabic, for example, are written from right to left. Many oriental languages are written from the top to the bottom of the page, then from right to left, as in Korean and Chinese. Ancient Greek and Roman had an intermediate stage in which one row was written right to left, the next left to right. This was called boustrophedon, meaning as the ox turns when a field is plowed, one row right to left, the next left to right. (Schuell, Jenkins, Jiménez-Pabón, 1975, p. 128.)

Some children require a longer time to learn this reading act and need more practice than others. Such difficulties are within the limits of normal development. Most but not all children with organic reading disorders have great difficuly with it; some of them never feel quite sure about the direction of letters and the letter sequences within words. (See Directional Confusion of Letters and Words, p. 99.)

ORGANIC BASIS OF THE ACT. The involved parts of the central nervous system are the eyes—that is, the sense of vision with its cortical projection field in the occipital lobes (area 19) as well as areas surrounding it which make the understanding of what one sees possible. Spatial orientation, located in the parietal lobes, and kinesthetic sensations are also involved (Noback & Demarest, 1977, p. 142, Figure 16.1).

2. Sounding the Letter

3. Finding the Letter When Someone Else Sounds It

This requires the conversion of letters (i.e., two-dimensional forms) into sounds made by speech—in other words, into motor acts. It is important to realize that speech sounds differ not only from pure tones made by singing or playing musical instruments, and from all sorts of noises made by air conditioners, footsteps, cars, but they are different in many other ways. The child must be able to distinguish all these sounds; otherwise he has difficulty with speaking and reading.

ROLE OF HEARING. A child who cannot hear clearly and cannot analyze various sounds cannot learn to speak clearly because he cannot repeat accurately what he hears. He is also headed for a reading disorder. Inability to distinguish sounds may be due to partial deafness because of defect or disease in the inner ear affecting the organ of hearing. The pathology may also lie in the fiber tracts connecting this organ with the cortex, in subcortical structures lying in their path, or in cortical projection fields for hearing and speech (Liebman, 1979, p. 51, Plate 14-1, & p. 68, plate 19-1).

The hearing of every child with an organic reading disorder should therefore be tested thoroughly. Testing should include audiometry because it is so important to determine not only how loud a tone must be to be heard by the child, but also the tone's position on the scale. A pure-tone as well as a speech audiogram should be administered. Such an analysis of the hearing of speech is absolutely essential, because so many of these children cannot analyze speech sounds accurately, while they can distinguish pure tones without difficulty (Newby, 1971, p. 353).

Augusta Jellinek was among the first to stress in publications, lectures, and case conferences at the Lafargue Clinic and elsewhere, that deficiency in hearing higher tones often causes speech and reading disorders because it makes speech sounds, especially consonants, less distinct (Jellinek, 1948, p. 107).

The extreme importance of diagnosing this type of hearing defect, especially in children, was revealed in a study by Philip E. Rosenberg and his group at

Temple University Medical Center. He examined a large number of children between the ages of 1 and 5 years, whose speech did not develop properly. Many of them had been misdiagnosed as aphasic, autistic, or retarded. All of them developed a reading disorder. What they actually suffered from was a "relatively simple but easily missed type of hearing problem," namely, "high frequency, sensorineural hearing loss." Their hearing in the low frequency was entirely normal. They heard vowel sounds clearly, but did not hear most consonants. Rosenberg stresses that many techniques for diagnosis and treatment of this type of deafness are available. He concludes that if these children "were diagnosed and treated properly, a small segment of the apparently dyslexic population would disappear" (Rosenberg, 1968, pp. 53–59.)

RELATIONSHIP BETWEEN CEREBRAL HEARING, SPEECH, AND READING APPARATUSES. The intimate connection between reading, hearing, and speech is reflected in the brain by the close anatomical proximity and intimate connection between the areas and apparatuses responsible for all three activities. The acoustic field in Heschl's transverse gyrus in the temporal lobes is part of all three. Motor areas in the frontal lobes are involved in speech and reading, specifically the posterior portions of the middle and inferior frontal convolutions and the lower end of the precentral gyrus. They are located in that part of the frontal lobes that adjoins the postcentral gyrus and other parts of the parietal lobes (Liebman, 1979, pp. 68, 69, Plate 19-1; see Fig. 2.1 of this book).

Lesions in the motor part of the speech center, which is located in frontal as well as parietal lobe areas, lead to motor or expressive aphasia in which the patient cannot say words clearly or at all, even though he hears and understands them. This disorder is frequently associated with a reading disorder, as are all other types of aphasia. Children with any type of aphasia invariably have a reading disorder if the insult to these specific parts of the brain took place before they learned to speak and read. The cortical association of the reading and the speech apparatus is so close that an "Aphasic Zone" that overlaps area 39 has been outlined. A lesion in any part of this zone causes various forms of aphasia combined with reading and writing disorders. (Vick, 1976, p. 375). (See section on Speech Disorders, Vol. II, p. 382.)

PURE TONES AND THEIR RELATIONSHIP TO SPEECH AND READING DISORDER. Another localization is also important in this respect, namely that the recognition and understanding of pure tones has a different projection field from that of spoken sounds. A lesion in the posterior part of the first and second temporal gyrus, for instance, results in a defect in the understanding of words, yet sounds are recognized (Grinker & Bucy, 1949, p. 373). That is why some aphasic children can sing. I am stressing this localized neuropathology, which is primarily based on examinations of adults, because it shows that certain symptoms we find in children may have organic causes, even though these children have no tumor or other verifiable and demonstrable anatomical lesions in their brains. The very combination of a reading disorder with a speech and sometimes also a hearing difficulty means that there is an organic basis for the reading disorder. It is a frequently found combination of symptoms, that is, a syndrome. (See Musical Ability Disorder, Vol. II, pp. 434, 384ff.)

4. Naming Letters
5. Finding Letters When They Are Named

Knowing the names of letters does not help the child with reading English, because the names of all consonants differ from their sounds, and the names of all vowels indicate only one of their sounds. Learning the names of letters first, before learning their sounds, confuses children. It is therefore better to teach their sounds first, as the Spalding, Open Court, Cureton, and some other methods do. The child can learn the names later. He needs them to recite the alphabet and for spelling, but he is better off spelling with letter sounds until some basic conditioning has been accomplished. The most prevalent curriculum practice unfortunately continues to be the teaching of letter names first, and frequently not to teach any letter sounds until a "sight vocabulary" has been memorized by the child.

The popular children's educational television program, "Sesame Street," has made the same mistake. I watched a section dealing only with the capital letter F. It went something like this in ditty form: The letter F can be fast; the letter F can be flat; the letter F can be flowers. Nothing was said about the sound of this letter. It was called "ef" throughout. What children should have been taught was the sound of F and its connection with other sounds in a word. It would be possible in a television show to suggest that a child ask his parents for a lined piece of paper and then show him how to write the F and suggest that he say "fff" while he writes it down.

LEARNING THE ALPHABET AND OTHER SERIES. Some children with organic reading disorders manage to learn the sounds of letters and their names, but have trouble memorizing the alphabet. As a rule, they cannot memorize the days of the week or the months of the year in correct sequence either, or, in arithmetic, the multiplication tables. This inability to memorize distinct sequences is an organic symptom. It is not only a specific memory defect but indicates a general difficulty with serial ordering. On intelligence tests these children cannot repeat the required number of digits forward and especially backward. The spelling difficulty that most children with organic reading disorders have may also be due to this inability to perform serial ordering; a word consists of a distinct series of letters. This serial ordering inability seems to be confined to series of items connected only in an abstract way. These same children can usually remember sequential rules of ballgames and of other games requiring concrete, practical action. They may have trouble with more complicated games such as chess. Some children with this difficulty can memorize the alphabet by singing it, sometimes without realizing what it means— that is, they either do not connect it with letters at all or not with the appropriate letters. This can also happen to children with a normal central nervous system. I have observed it in very young children who learned the alphabet song before being taught to read or write letters. Teaching the alphabet in sequence was not part of the elementary school curriculum for many years, and many children I examined could not recite it. All rote learning was considered harmful. Pressure was exerted on schools to teach it again, and most children can now recite it. This does not mean that they can read and write all letters, however; we must test them to determine this.

SEQUENCE WRITING AND READING.   Some children remember letters only when they see them or write them in alphabet sequence. This is an organic symptom called "sequence writing or reading." It was one of 7-year-old Luis's symptoms. He could not even write *one* letter outside the alphabet, but had to go over the entire series of letters preceding the one I dictated. He could not do this mentally at all. When I asked him to write the letter "k," for instance, he wrote down all preceding letters slowly and carefully, and only then, with a sigh of relief, could he write "k."

The five reading acts described so far are the foundations for the more complex reading acts that concern the reading of words. These are as follows.

6. *Recognizing a Group of Letters as a Unit, That Is, a Word*
7. *Blending the Sounds of This Group of Letters, Reading the Word Aloud*
8. *Understanding the Word*

There is a visual, an acoustic, a kinesthetic–motor, a gnostic (understanding), and a spatial–sequential aspect to this group of acts.

VISUAL AGNOSIA.   Some children have trouble recognizing that the letters they see belong together, that they form a distinct group, even though they recognize each letter and even though they are not blind. These children are suffering from special forms of visual agnosia.

Agnosia, translated from its Greek origin, means lack of understanding. It was Freud who proposed this term in 1891 in his book *On Aphasia* for "disturbances in the recognition of objects" (Freud, 1973, p. 465). This is an organic symptom where the peripheral vision is intact, but the understanding of what is seen is defective. Neurologists call this symptom "literal alexia" when it is restricted to a lack of recognition of letters, and "verbal alexia" when entire words are involved. This is the visual part of organic reading disorders in children which helped to establish the term "word-blindness" (Brain, 1961, p. 114; Weinschenk, 1965, p. 121).

Most children with organic reading disorders can accomplish these specific visual acts quite well. Their difficulty lies in connecting the visual with the kinesthetic–motor acts needed for word reading.

Visual agnosia is assumed to be caused by a malfunctioning of cortical regions surrounding the visual centers in the occipital lobes, or of subcortical structures that mediate peripheral vision with the understanding of what is seen.

Critchley diagnoses such cases as suffering from an "agnostic type of dyslexia." He found that "an element of metamorphopsia [which means a change in the form of what is seen] of central origin may occur in some of these patients and this can either be responsible for the dyslexia, or at least it can aggravate it." He states that a magnifying lens can sometimes help these patients (Critchley, 1970, p. 3).

BLINDNESS FOR VISUAL MEANING. Some children who cannot learn to read because they do not understand what they see suffer from what the neuropathologist and psychiatrist Lise Gellner termed "blindness for visual meaning." This is a form of visual agnosia that apparently occurs only in children. Gellner and I were acquainted and often discussed the patients under our care both at the Lafargue Clinic and privately.

Localization. Gellner studied children diagnosed as mentally defective or autistic in England and the United States. She also did neuropathologic examinations of the nervous systems of children with these symptoms who had died. She concluded from her clinical observations and from these pathologic examinations that the damage apparently lay in subcortical regions. She implicated especially the lateral geniculate bodies which integrate vision with the inner organs via the autonomic nervous system, and with the cortex (House, Pansky, & Siegel, 1979, pp. 176, 178, 449, Figures 8.4, 8.5, 8.7, 8.8, 8.9, & 8.11; Liebman, 1979, pp. 54, 55, Plates 15-1, 15-2).

These children can see but they behave in many ways like blind children, because they cannot understand or learn by looking. Children learn to recognize and understand an object by the way it looks, sounds, feels, tastes, by its shape, and by its use. That is why young children need to look, listen, touch, bite, and manipulate. Meaning-blind children cannot comprehend what something means when they only see it. They must therefore touch, bite, manipulate, and drop objects (so that they can hear what sounds they make) in order to learn what they are all about, and they must continue this infantile behavior much longer than normal children. They may be punished unjustly for these "babyish habits" unless their impairment is at least suspected early. These children cannot concentrate on visual tasks and have a weak visual memory. They often avoid reading for these organic reasons, and this avoidance is easily mistaken for lack of interest or motivation for psychologic reasons. They fatigue easily when they are forced to learn by vision.

As mild or even minimal "blindness for visual meaning" is much more frequent than severe forms, familiarity with its symptoms is very important. Eye examinations are negative even though the fibers of the optic nerve which connect the center of the retina (the fovea) with the cortex apparently do not transmit impulses properly, so that color vision is affected (House, Pansky, & Siegel, 1979, pp. 180, 181). These children cannot match colors. They see things better on the side and in the background for the same neuroanatomical reasons. They may tilt their heads accordingly, especially when trying to read. Teachers who observed just such behavior have asked me what it meant. They were inclined to think that the child had just mischievously acquired a bad habit. I explained that this habit could be due to an organic impairment and that the child should have a pediatric examination as well as thorough eye, neurologic, and (depending on the findings of these specialists) possibly also psychiatric examinations.

These children can understand and imitate movements and get a special pleasure from watching moving objects. They can sit for hours and watch passing cars. They love to watch trains and planes and fast movements on television shows. Of course all young children love to observe this type of fast movement, but children with this special form of visual agnosia are intensely preoccupied with it and fixated on it in an abnormal way. They do not like to look at picturebooks and often cannot recognize two-dimensional objects which they can recognize perfectly well in their three-dimensional form. They are good at manual skills which they can learn without looking. Once this condition has been explained to the teacher, such a child can safely be taught complicated manual skills. He must be instructed in ways similar to those used for teaching a blind child.

The pleasure these children get when watching fast movement and when moving themselves, and the excitement this generates, makes controlling them at home and in school sometimes very difficult. Such children are often referred not primarily for a learning disability, but for hyperactivity. To diagnose such a child as suffering from a motor impulse disorder on an organic basis is to miss the point. This symptom is also easily misdiagnosed as psychogenic, but it is not caused by psychologic trauma. Successful remedial techniques can only be developed and planned through a precise diagnosis of the special visual agnosia underlying the child's reading disorder and his disturbed behavior. (See Vol. II, Hyperactivity, p. 630.)

Remedial Techniques. Meaning-blind children can learn to read only by listening—that is, phonetically. They can copy only mechanically, and must learn to write and to spell by listening. They have "wandering eyes," which means that their eyes wander all over the page and cannot be trained to move steadily along the line of print without the help of lines, finger pointing, or a cover card. These children have a severe organic form of Linear Dyslexia. Even when they use techniques to steady their gaze, their visual performance fluctuates. Even a mild upset of their autonomic nervous system impairs their visual performance. (See Linear Dyslexia, p. 127.)

Where this meaning-blindness syndrome is severe, it presents such a serious handicap that these children function on the level of mental deficiency. Many present such management problems that they are eventually sent to mental hospitals or institutions for mental defectives. The symptoms are fortunately mild in the majority of children, and a reading disorder may be its most distressing manifestation (Gellner, 1953, 1959; Mautner, 1959, p. 4; Wing & Wing, 1971, p. 258).

INABILITY TO READ THE WORD AT THE END OF A LINE. Wertham observed that some patients cannot read the word at the end of a line after intoxication, strokes, food poisoning, or trauma. There are two forms of this reading disorder. In one, the patient cannot read the word at all; in the other, he or she reads very slowly and figures out the word with great effort. This is a definite symptom that appears only in organic disorders (Fredric Wertham, personal communication).

INABILITY TO SEE WORDS CLEARLY. Some children complain that they cannot read because the words seem blurred, that they seem to merge into each other, and that they cannot see the letters clearly. This may be due to near-sightedness or other defects of vision. It may also be due to eye muscle pathology, namely fusion, convergence, or accommodation defects. In these cases the action of eye muscles in both eyes are not properly coordinated and/or they do not respond with the necessary speed; or the ciliary muscles react too slowly so that accommodation is not timed properly. Routine eye examinations do not always show these defects, especially when they are mild; thus they are often not diagnosed (Eames, 1968, p. 138; Taylor, 1957).

Doug, 9 Years Old: Undiagnosed Fusion and Accommodation Defect. Doug was referred to me for neurotic symptoms. He had complained since the day he entered school that there was something wrong with his eyes, but no one believed him. He had been examined by a number of ophthalmologists who assured his parents that there was nothing wrong with their son's eyes. For this reason parents and teachers alike were certain his complaints were neurotic.

When I examined him I found that he was suffering from an organic reading disorder with Linear Dyslexia. I suspected a fusion and possibly an accommodation defect as contributory causes. Since opthalmologists had found no defects with their methods, I referred him to an optometrist, who found a severe fusion as well as an accommodation defect requiring special visual training.

Optometrists are nonmedical professionals specializing in these defects. Fusion and accommodation difficulties do not necessarily interfere with the child's ability to learn to read. This depends on their severity and on their coupling with other defects, organic or psychopathologic. Sometimes only the speed of reading and of copying, especially from the blackboard, are hampered; or visual tasks not connected with reading may be affected. (See Figure 11.2 in Vol. II.)

A brilliant college student of physics who had worn eyeglasses since elementary school, for instance, noticed he had these defects only after having been drafted into the Navy. He found that he could not learn to distinguish different types of warships when they were flashed in quick succession on a screen. He just could not recognize their distinguishing features at that speed. Children with such defects sometimes cannot recognize words flashed before them on "flash cards." They get low marks undeservedly unless the correct diagnosis is made.

Role of Comic Book Habituation.   When we examine children who complain that words are blurred and seem to merge, or when we observe that they cannot tell where one word ends and the other begins, we must also consider other causes. I have examined many children with these complaints. Some blended all sounds of letters on each line and completely missed the cohesion of words, making it impossible for them to understand what they read. The vast majority of these children had no organic reading disorder. What made word reading and writing so difficult for them was their comic book habituation, which had started years before they entered school. Comic books had not only conditioned them to picture gazing and to looking for pictures to explain the text, but also to seeing print as *one* cohesive unit. The reason for this is that the text in comic book balloons is printed in capital letters only, and that the words are so crowded into the unevenly shaped balloons that there is only very little space between them and sometimes none at all. The distinct Gestalt of words is also destroyed in other ways. Some balloons are filled only with letters to indicate sounds and noises but not words, for instance "AYEEEEE!", "BAROOOM!", "ARRRGH!", "VROOM!", or "EEYAAA!"; and letters are strewn all over some pages. This faulty preschool conditioning, which usually continues during the school years, makes it very difficult for children to learn word reading and writing, so that the aforementioned symptoms result. (See Comic Books, Chapter 6, p. 275.)

DIFFERENT LEVELS OF UNDERSTANDING. Based on his own experience, Freud described the different levels of understanding in his book, *On Aphasia:*

> Everybody knows from self observation that there are several kinds of reading some of which proceed without understanding. When I read proofs with the intention of paying special attention to the letters and other symbols, the meaning of what I am reading escapes me to such a degree that I require a second perusal for the purpose of correcting the style. If, on the other hand, I read a novel, which holds my interest, I overlook all misprints and it may happen that I retain nothing of the names of the persons figuring in the book except for some meaningless feature, or perhaps the recollection that they were long or short, and that they contained an unusual letter such as x or z. Again, when I have to recite, whereby I have to pay special attention to the sound impressions of my words and to the intervals between them, I am in danger of caring too little about the meaning, and as soon as fatigue sets in I am reading in such a way that the listener can still understand, but I myself no longer know what I have been reading. These are phenomena of divided attention which are of particular importance here, because the understanding of what is read takes place over circuitous routes (1973, p. 463).

The role of fatigue in undermining understanding is very important. It affects children with organic reading disorders more than others because of their increased fatiguability. (See Vol. II, Fatigue, p. 562 under Attention Disorders, and Fatiguability, p. 672.)

DIRECTIONAL CONFUSION OF LETTERS AND WORDS. Directional difficulties are also called mirror-writing and -reading. However, these children do not read or write mirror images of texts. Healthy children can do that with some ease just for fun, as tests carried out in various countries have shown. Children with the symptoms referred to here are much too confused about the direction of single letters and of letter sequences in words to be able to read texts normally, from left to right. Mirror-reading and -writing is completely beyond them.

Children with an organic reading disorder have two types of directional confusion. They write and read vertical mirror images of letters, that is, they get the right and left direction of letters mixed up. They read "d" for "b," "p" for "q," or vice versa; or they get "p," "q," and "g" mixed up, and so on. These mistakes are called *reversals.*

The other directional confusion involves horizontal mirror images of letters. Here, children get the upper and lower parts of a letter mixed up. They confuse "M," "m" and "W," "w"; "T," "t" and "F," "f"; "C" and "G"; "h" and "y"; "u" and "n"; "p" and "b"; "d" and "q"; and sometimes also "a" or "g" with "e." They also confuse the numbers "9" and "6," "5" and "2." These are called *inversions.*

Reversals are discussed in all studies dealing with reading disorders. Inversions are usually not even mentioned, yet they are a frequent symptom and indicate a more severe form of organic reading disorder that is more difficult to treat. Many children have reversals in the normal course of learning to read, but they do not have inversions. This type of rotation around the horizontal axis is *always* the symptom of an organic reading disorder. However, it is not present in all children with this type of reading disorder (Barger, 1960, p. 4 ff.).

Children with severe forms of organic reading disorders make reversals as well as inversions. They also change the letter sequence within words in reading and writing, and often start to read or write at the bottom of a page or at the right side of a line.

Reversals. When testing a child who has difficulty with reversals, one should keep in mind that he tries hard not to reveal his reading and writing difficulties. That is why so many of these children write capital "B" when asked to write this letter. This is an evasion because it is much easier to remember the form and direction of capital "B" than of lower case "b." When such a child is then asked to write lower case "b," he either refuses or writes very slowly and hesitantly, with a tortured and questioning look on his face. And what he usually writes is "d." I have observed this sequence many times. Children love to write capital "B," just as they like to write the number "8." I use this opportunity to explain to the child that the round part of "b" points in exactly the same direction as the two round parts of "B." Such simple memory aids should be used much more consistently and repetitively by parents and teachers.

Reversals change the sounds of letters. That is the reason these children read "dill" instead of "bill," "bull" for "dull," "get" for "pet," "got" for "pot," and vice versa. Their reading and writing mistake can only be understood and corrected through familiarity with reversals and inversions.

Numbers are not necessarily misread when they are seen or written in their reversed form. For instance, a "4" remains a "four" even when seen or written like this: .

Inversions. Children with inversion problems make characteristic mistakes in word reading. They read "if" for "it," "we" for "me," "put" for "but," "ou" for "on," "gnu" for "gun," "wade" for "made," and so on.

Children with either or both directional confusions tend to transpose letters within words. They read "was" for "saw," "on" for "no," "tell" for "let," "devil" for "lived," "ma" for "am," "dog" for "god," "won" for "now," "tub" for "but," and so on.

All of these children suffer from a severe spelling disorder. They make such typical mistakes as spelling "gril" instead of "girl," "siwm" instead of "swim," "hsoue" for "house," "chiar" for "chair," "potnet" for "potent," "from" for "form," "rnu" for "run," "Thrusday" for "Thursday," and many more. These mistakes get worse the longer the words and the higher their grade. Those with an especially severe organic reading disorder sometimes sound letters at random, not systematically from right to left or left to right. This results in a complete jumble, unless the child manages to guess the word. These children's linear reading is defective. They suffer from Linear Dyslexia. (See section on Spelling, p. 115, and Linear Reading, p. 118.)

Beginning of Directional Confusion. One can sometimes make the diagnosis of a tendency to directional confusion by observing how children write when they start, in kindergarten or first grade. Some start all letters and parts of letters with an upward stroke. They avoid downward strokes and lift their pencil or crayon up high to start their next stroke again from the bottom instead of continuing smoothly with a downward stroke.

These children get the form of capital "N" mixed up in a typical way. They make an upward stroke, then lift up their pencil and start another upward stroke from the bottom of their first stroke. Then they lift up their pencil again and start with a new stroke at the bottom, connecting its upper end with the last stroke. Their "N" then looks like this: И. That is also why their "M" turns into a "W." These are not inversions. Only through such close observation can the correct diagnosis of a child's directional confusion be made.

Many of these children start writing at the very bottom of the page and write straight upward. Even when their paper has lines, they turn it by 90 degrees so that the lines start right in front of them. They write on each line vertically upward. When they have finished writing on the entire page, they rotate it back so that when they hand it to the teacher it seems to have been written from left to right. This directional difficulty is therefore often not noticed. I have observed it innumerable times during inconspicuous classroom observation and when examining children individually. This may become an ingrained habit that lasts throughout life, unless it is noticed in its very beginning and corrected right away. It should not be permitted to become a fixed habit because it slows writing and damages reading, especially linear reading, which must proceed on a horizontal line from left to right.

The early detection and immediate correction of vertical writing is important also for the prevention of reversals and inversions. A child's tendency to write vertically indicates that he is heading for directional difficulties in reading. Such a child should be taught reading and writing with special care. If this were done, many organic reading disorders could be prevented.

Advantages of Cursive Writing and of Teaching Reading Through Writing.
Children with any form of directional confusion learn directions of letters and words better when taught cursive writing. For instance, "b" and "d" cannot be confused when this style is used, and it also forces the child into a fluid left-to-right direction. Thus teaching writing first, and teaching reading through writing before the child is given printed texts, prevents reading disorders. The Spalding method, with its stress on direction using the clock face as a guide, is one of the best (Spalding & Spalding, 1969) (See Comparative Study of Conventional Teaching Methods with the Phonetic Spalding Approach, p. 340.)

Disadvantages of Sight/Word Teaching. Directional confusions are very frequently not noticed in the very beginning and remain unnoticed far too long because of whole/or sight/word teaching. Children can read words correctly while still seeing the letters as inverted or reversed. Whole/word reading cannot properly be called "reading" in any case. The child just *says* the word matching the picture. That is why a child may say "arm" correctly under the picture of an arm or connect the picture of an arm with the word correctly, while he still sees the word thus:ɐɹɯ.

Children also memorize each word exactly as they see it, so that their inversions and reversals become fixed while the teacher remains ignorant of their directional mistakes. Some mistakes of such a child may also remain obscure when the sounds of letters and fixed letter combinations are taught first, unless writing is taught before reading. Such a child may, for instance, sound the letter "S" correctly while seeing it as reversed: Ƨ.

However, typical mistakes in reading and writing will bring the child's reversals and inversions to the attention of a teacher who begins with writing long before a sight/word teacher can notice them. The child will, for instance, say "u" instead of "n," or get "b" and "d" mixed up. Those children whose directional confusions are so severe that they begin to read at the right side of the page will come to the attention of parents and teachers regardless of the teaching method used.

Inversion of Drawings. Some children also draw upside down. They start their picture at the bottom of the page and proceed to draw the roof of a house or the head of a person first, and legs, windows, and so on, later. It is important to make sure that this is a genuine inversion and not done as a joke or in anger. Pearson was first to describe such children, a girl age 6 and a boy age 5 (1928).

Inversion of Pictures. Some children with directional confusion of letters also hold books upside down and read in this way. Some very few of these children also turn pictures in books upside down. This starts on the first day they are given a picturebook, namely, before they enter kindergarten. They will not turn that book right-side-up, but insist on the inverted position. Apparently they cannot recognize the picture any other way. Reversion (a confusion of right and left) does not seem to enter into this. These children can recognize people, animals, buildings, or whatever else they see; they can even tell picture stories.

These pictures are usually recognized in their entirety, so that it is difficult to determine whether reversals are present. The child sees the total Gestalt of a house, for instance. The recognition of what the picture represents is not influenced by what part is on the right and what is on the left. The child can recognize a house whether the door or the chimney is on the right or the left side.

These same children have no trouble recognizing pictures hanging on the wall just as they are, right-side-up, or the moving pictures on television, or live animals, or people. Their inversions are entirely confined to two-dimensional forms that are relatively small and do not move. (See case of Alfred, age 7, p. 000.)

Localization. The developmental lag theory is widely used as an explanation for reversals and inversions, but it does not apply. The normal development of a child does not include any stage where he sees anything upside down or with its right and left side reversed. It is important to realize that these children reverse or invert very specific forms only—those that are small and stationary. All other visual impressions in these children's lives are seen right-side-up and not changed vertically. A specific defect must exist in their central nervous system causing these specific directional changes.

We know since the studies of Johannes Kepler in 1604 that the image of the outside world we perceive on the retinas of our eyes is inverted and reversed. The rays from the right side of an object fall on the left side of the retinas of both eyes. The rays from the left side reach the right retinal sides. The world around us is perceived upside-down, left side on the right, right side on the left. We know that this visual perception is instantly and automatically converted to a right-side-up position, with right and left sides and upper and lower parts corresponding exactly to the object we are looking at. This conversion is an inborn faculty, even though extensive studies have tried to prove that it is learned in infancy. All children, without exception, are born with it (Best & Taylor, 1943, p. 1667; Brückner & Meisner, 1920, p. 59).

This conversion does not take place in the eyes. Eye diseases do not cause reversals or inversions. Such directional changes have been observed only after brain disease or injury. For example, an 8-year-old boy has been described who developed this condition after a bout with the measles; a 20-year-old man suffered from it after a head trauma (Pearson, 1928).

It must therefore be assumed that this conversion takes place in the cerebral cortex. Images perceived by the retinas of both eyes are transmitted to the visual fields in the occipital lobes, and from there to areas in the parietal lobes. There are also connections with the frontal and temporal lobes. It is assumed that the parietal lobes are crucial for a flawless conversion of these retinal images, so that we see the world as it is.

The spatial disorientation of children who reverse and/or invert letters or look at picturebooks upside-down is strictly limited to these items. It can therefore be assumed that the cerebral malfunctioning on which it is based is limited to those parts of the parietal lobes that are responsible for the automatic upright and correct right and left perception of these small, stationary, two-dimensional forms. As far as letters are concerned, one can assume that the impairment lies somewhere in the angular gyrus, in or near Brodmann's area 39. This is the parietal part of the cerebral reading and writing apparatus (Figure 2.1).

These directional difficulties have been connected with lack of development of hemisphere dominance. Barger and others observed that the majority of these children are left-handed, have mixed lateral dominance (right hand, left eye, etc.), or dominance has not been established. This seems to apply to the severest forms only (Barclay, 1967; Barger, 1953, 1959, 1960, 1977). (See The Role of Hemispheric Dominance, p. 58.)

Barger Mirroreading Board. Dr. William C. Barger, a neurologist and psychiatrist, developed a treatment device designed especially for children suffering from these directional confusions. It is called the Barger Mirroreading Board and it consists of a mirror placed in such a way that a book or any other text can be placed in front of it outside the view of the child. The child only sees the mirror image of the text. Its left-to-right progression is not altered. Barger describes it in the following way:

> Printed material can be so placed before the mirror that the horizontal axis of some letters, and the *vertical* axis of all print are reversed and inverted. The child views the image of the print in the mirror while the actual print is concealed from his eyes by a barrier over which he peers into the mirror. The normal top of the actual print is placed at the bottom edge of the looking glass (Barger, 1953, p. 160).

I worked closely with Barger at the Bureau of Child Guidance of the New York City school system while he was developing his technique. He was at that time also the only school psychiatrist assigned to work with aphasic children. He was instrumental in organizing the first public school in New York City entirely devoted to the education of these children. They always had severe reading and writing disorders, so that the Mirroreading Board was put to its severest test. Many of them responded to it better than to any other technique. It improved not only their reading but also their speech.

I gave the Mosaic test to many of these children. All made clear-cut organic patterns of the cortical or subcortical type, and often of both types. Severe anxiety was indicated on the majority of these mosaic patterns. (See Speech Disorders, Vol. II, p. 382.) But the Barger Mirroreading Board primarily helps less severely handicapped children, namely those who have organic reading disorders without aphasia. An exact indication for this technique has not yet been worked out. Barger states that only children with mixed lateral dominance benefit from it. It is my impression that it works best with children who have inversions. Sometimes even relatively brief periods of reading with this Mirroreading Board can be a turning point that opens the child's mind so that he can understand the reading process and can learn it through regular right-side-up material from then on.

A test that indicates whether or not the child has a good chance of being helped by the mirror is to let him copy the text he sees in the mirror. This is done by giving him a sheet of lined or unlined paper. A child who will benefit from treatment with the mirror will invariably copy the text in correct up-down and left-to-right direction, even though he sees only its mirror image. He does this spontaneously, without having been told to copy in this way. His inversions and reversals have suddenly disappeared. Adults and children who have no reversals or inversions cannot copy such a mirrored text without the greatest difficulties. I have observed this phenomenon many times and have no satisfactory explanation for it. The mirror apparently helps the child in a thus-far unknown way to achieve the normal direction of letters.

To treat a child with the Mirroreading Board requires special training. It is only a transitional treatment device; children are treated with the mirror for only weeks or months, and gradually normal texts are substituted.

Jose, 9 Years Old: The Barger Mirroreading Board.   The experience of Jose, whom I examined when he was 9 years old, shows the value of the Barger Mirroreading Board. He was of at least average intelligence but a complete nonreader. He had a speech defect due to a mild receptive aphasia. He could repeat sounds correctly but could not distinguish all of them. For instance, he could not distinguish between the sounds of "n" and "m." The teachers thought that he did not hear well, but the ear specialist found no hearing loss. When I examined him he was irritable and depressed. He had anxious dreams, pulled at his hair, and picked at the skin of his arms. He had been in seven different schools, because his family of seven could find no place to live. For years, they had lived together in one or at most two furnished rooms, which were vermin- and rat-infested and had no heat. When I examined him, he had just moved into a housing project with his parents, his younger brother, and three younger sisters. He had his own room for the first time in his life. I made the diagnosis of an organic reading disorder with a mild receptive aphasia and a neurotic reaction to this learning disorder and to severe social and economic pressures. His family was closely knit, totally devoted to one another. Jose's father felt guilty for failing to live up to his children's needs and expectations. Jose was especially close to him. I recommended psychotherapy, remedial reading, and speech therapy. Jose received speech therapy from the school's corrective speech teacher, remedial reading from the school's corrective reading teacher, and psychotherapy from the school psychologist who was a trained psychotherapist. The school social worker did casework therapy with Jose's family. I reexamined him when he was 11 and again when he was 13 years old and going to junior high school. Only one of his reading teachers had been trained in the use of the Barger Mirroreading Board, but her teaching had been the turning point for him. She had unfortunately died, and we could not find any other teacher for him who knew how to use this device. Jose described his experience with the Barger Mirroreading Board in this way: "When Miss V. put the letters in front of me, I could read them backwards, it seemed easier to me. Then she taught me with the mirror, then the other lady kept on teaching me how to read without the mirror, then I kept on getting better without it." His high school teachers reported later on that he liked to tell them and the other students proudly how he had been taught to read with a mirror. He continued to visit the clinic to report on his progress. During such a visit (he was then 17 years old), I asked him who or what had helped him most during those five years when different people worked with him. I ask this question routinely as part of my follow-up examinations. Jose answered without any hesitation: "The mirror, the teacher who taught me to read with the mirror." It is not unusual for patients of all ages to remember one dramatic event, one concrete turning point rather than the subtle and gradual effect of psychotherapy. This does not mean that psychotherapy was not effective or even crucial to their recovery. The Barger Mirroreading Board did not cure Jose of his organic mirror-reading and -writing disorder, but it initiated his improvement and made a complete recovery possible. I saw him last when he was 21 years old and came to the clinic to show off his new Navy uniform. He wanted to let us know that he had been accepted by the Navy.

Barger's device is in use in many countries of Europe, in Israel, Japan, and Argentina, as well as in numerous clinics and colleges in the United States.

Alfred, 7 Years Old: He Looked at Picturebooks Upside-Down. Children with inversions and reversals of letters who also look at picturebooks upside down are exceptional cases. A child is only rarely referred with the chief complaint that he does "mirror-reading." Seven-year-old Alfred was such a child. His parents were inclined to think that his peculiar way of reading and writing was due to "sibling rivalry," that it was caused by jealousy of his 9-year-old sister who, as they told me, was "efficient in everything." His father was a professor of biology and his mother a computer analyst. Reading seemed so simple to them and was such a basic part of their lives that they were quite bewildered by their son's struggle with it.

Alfred's difficulties were concentrated in the following areas:

1. Writing. He had been taught to write with his right hand from kindergarten on even though dominance had not been established at that time. The teacher had to put a dot on his left hand to help him remember which one it was. His parents observed that he rotated some letters vertically, others horizontally. He habitually rotated "S," "F," and "Z" vertically and "a" horizontally; and he also confused the numbers 3 and 5, whose vertical mirror images resemble each other when they are not written clearly. The parents also reported that Alfred made the same mistakes when he copied letters from the blackboard. When I examined his writing he wrote very slowly and made a great effort to write accurately. He wrote "mathor" instead of "mother," "diy" instead of "boy," and "howes" instead of "house," later putting a "u" between the "o" and the "w." The letters "b" and "d," "m" and "w" were confusing for him and he usually did not know which one belonged to the word he was writing.

2. Reading. His mother told me that he concentrated too hard on each word so that he forgot what the text meant. She had noticed that he read "was" instead of "saw," "on" for "no," "spik" for "skip," and that he preferred holding books upside-down. He started doing this when he got his first picturebook at about 2 years of age. He could recognize the pictures but was not sure of this until he turned the book upside-down. He never had any difficulty recognizing anything right-side-up, for instance pictures on walls, family photos, toys, people or television shows. When I asked him to read for me during my examination, he said spontaneously: "It is easier to read upside-down for me." I asked him to try to read right-side-up, and he tried hard, reading slowly and with great effort. He pointed at each word because he was afraid of losing his place. He said that he lost his place very often, skipped lines and got completely confused. He read "sawns" instead of "swims," "little" instead of "lost," "tall" instead of "tell." In these words he seemed to recognize only the letters "t" and "l" with certainty. He read "e" as "a," a typical mistake made by children with both inversions and reversals. The horizontal

rotation of "e" looks similar to upright "a" only if it is also rotated vertically.

Alfred fatigued so rapidly that he could barely finish two lines of the first Gray oral reading paragraph. This early fatigue is characteristic for children with reading disorders on an organic basis. It is not caused primarily by the psychologic stress these children have to endure—even though this does play a role—but by the tremendous strain on their organic reading apparatus. (See Vol. II, Fatiguability, p. 672.)

3. Speech.   Alfred started to talk somewhat late (at 18 months of age) and could say only a few words, which his parents found very difficult to understand. He did not use sentences until he was 3 years old, and he did not pronounce them clearly either. He still spoke somewhat slowly and pronounced his words carefully. His parents described his pronunciation as "deliberate." His words became unclear when he spoke fast, which indicated that he had a mild form of cluttering. He could not pronounce "R" until the age of 6, and had trouble with the pronunciation of "G." He said "wlass" instead of "glass." According to the parents' description, this did not seem to be simply baby talk, but a difficulty with distinguishing and repeating certain sounds.

This speech defect had disappeared without treatment by the time I examined him. He spoke fluently, freely, and clearly during the examination. He repeated words well, but stumbled on nonsense syllables. This was not due to a hearing defect because his hearing had been tested by an ear specialist and found to be normal. Alfred had a speech history typical for many children who suffer from an organic reading and writing disorder with or without mirror symptoms. As I describe in the section on aphasia, the inability to repeat nonsense syllables together with Alfred's type of speech history indicates a mild receptive aphasia.

4. Spatial Orientation.   Alfred had trouble finding his way outside his home. He habitually looked in the wrong direction for cars, to the right when they were supposed to come from the left and vice versa. He was therefore always in danger when he crossed the street alone. His school was only a few blocks away from his home, but he got hopelessly lost one day on his way home when no other child was with him. He took only *one* wrong turn and wandered about desperately for hours until he was picked up by the police. His parents had looked for him without success. This directional difficulty is found in very many children with reading disorders on an organic basis or with other cerebral pathology where the parietal lobes are affected.

5. Right–Left Orientation.   Alfred had difficulty distinguishing and naming the right and left parts of his own body and on other people. His mother reported that he frequently put his shoes on the wrong feet. When I asked him which hand he wrote with, he lifted up his right hand, but when I asked him to tell me which hand this was, the right or the left, he could not name it, and said: "It is hard to tell which hand it is, because I don't know right from left."

He could hammer and perform some other manual skills with either hand, but could write much better with his right. When folding his hands, his right thumb was on top of the left, which indicated right-hand dominance, but when I gave him a rolled-up piece of paper to look through, he picked it up with his left hand and looked through it with his left eye. As I have mentioned in Chapter 1, both tests (folding of hands and looking through a telescope) are given to determine hand dominance. That each test result differed reflected the fact that no hand dominance had been established. Eye dominance, however, seemed to be located in the left eye. Alfred preferred to use his right hand for writing; he felt it was more skillful in this respect. This was the hand that had been trained to write from the beginning and was therefore better able to perform this one skill. Orton and his followers suggest that where no hand dominance has been established, the child should learn to write with the hand that corresponds to his dominant eye. It is, however, hazardous to change the writing hand of a child like Alfred, whose right hand has already been trained and who himself has confidence in the writing ability of this hand. A change may increase the child's mirror confusion; he may also begin to stutter. I therefore recommended that he continue to write with his right hand. (See section on Handedness, p. 179.)

6. Manual Skills Other Than Writing.   Alfred's parents said that he was clumsy with his hands, that he did not have "his sister's dexterity." He could not throw or catch a ball with either hand and had only recently learned to tie his shoelaces. He did puzzles well and liked to play with his construction toys. His sense of balance seemed to be good, and he enjoyed riding his two-wheel bike. This information is important because children with organic writing disorders sometimes have apraxia and occasionally balance difficulties. These children often find it most difficult to learn to tell time. They cannot draw a clock face or read it. Albert had this difficulty. He could neither draw a clock face nor tell time: this may not have been an organic symptom, however, but due instead to immaturity. Many children cannot tell time until they are 8 years old. I concluded that Alfred's hand-skill difficulties were much too mild for a diagnosis of apraxia.

7. Musical Ability.   Many children with organic reading and writing disorders cannot carry a tune; some are tone deaf, others cannot repeat even a simple melody. They cannot learn to play an instrument or even enjoy listening to music, and some cannot learn to read music. They have a note-reading disorder together with their letter-reading disorder. This may not be of any practical importance for the child's life, but it indicates the extent of the cerebral areas involved. Alfred had no musical ability at all. (See Vol. II, section on Musical Ability Disorder, p. 434.)

Alfred's Mosaic test showed that it was difficult for him to construct the form he had in mind, indicating a cortical defect. His Mosaic design showed in addition to this that his intelligence was average or superior, that he had an active fantasy life and a tendency to depression (his color preferences were blue and black). His drawings had features typical for children with reading and writing disorders. They showed feelings of insecurity and marked anxiety (extensive shadings). He was so uncertain about his body image that he refused to draw a body. He drew a stick figure and said, "I made it the easy way." I encouraged him to draw a body, and he drew an oval form with no neck or shoulders. The arms were sticks coming off the body at differing heights and angles. The hands were large circles with five round fingers attached to them. This hand drawing was unusual and indicated his preoccupation with his hands, which he felt were important but poorly connected with his body. These prominent hands also indicated a desire to use them actively and aggressively (in a constructive or destructive sense). The legs on his drawing of a boy (which was the first figure he drew) were not sticks but pants. Both were shaded, indicating anxiety. The female figure he drew had stick arms and legs. (See section on drawings, p. 214.)

Alfred's parents felt that he was "a very happy boy." His teachers had no complaint about his behavior. They were not even concerned about his reading and writing and had not referred him. They should all have recognized the severity of his reading and writing difficulties and seen to it that he got special help.

My impression was that Alfred was much more troubled about his learning difficulties and about conflicts with his parents and especially his sister than his parents realized. He presented a happy facade only; behind it he was tense, anxious, insecure, and unhappy. I explained this to his parents. My diagnosis was that he was suffering from an organic mirror-reading and -writing disorder with Linear Dyslexia, combined with a mild receptive aphasia and a difficulty with spatial orientation. A psychologic reaction to his handicaps and to his strenuous efforts to hide his disabilities and his true feelings was evidently just beginning.

I recommended remedial reading therapy and a reexamination after about 6 months of this remediation to evaluate its effectiveness and to determine whether psychotherapy would be indicated in addition. I conferred with his teachers and later on with his remedial reading therapist.

The prognosis for a complete cure of Alfred's reading and writing disorder was excellent. The reasons for this were that his disorder had been diagnosed early, and that remedial therapy was started right away. My clinical experience has convinced me that where these factors exist, children whose intelligence is lower than Alfred's, whose family relationships are less favorable, and who live under social and economic stress can also be cured of such severe organic reading and writing disorders. The public school Alfred attended had taught him to read and write from kindergarten on and had explained the connection of letters with sounds from the beginning. Had he been subjected to sight/word teaching first and had writing been started only in the middle of the first grade, as is such frequent practice, his disorder would have become much worse and more difficult to treat. Alfred was privileged compared with many other children because his parents had time for him, could always answer his questions about reading and writing accurately, and their social and financial status guaranteed that he would receive skillful therapy. It seems to me that all children are entitled to this help, regardless of their parents' social and financial position; I know that far too few are receiving it.

Leon, 11 Years Old: He Looked at Picture Books and Texts Upside-Down.
Leon was as intelligent as Alfred and suffered from the same type of organic mirror-reading and -writing disorder with a mild receptive aphasia. His family situation, however, was most traumatic and tragic. All his life he had lived under the severest social and economic pressures. His mother had deserted the family, so that he and his three sisters had lived without her since he was 8 years old. All four children had lived with their father or with foster grandparents from then on. These grandparents were frequently ill and his father did not always make enough money to support the family, so that there was sometimes not enough food or clothing; welfare department assistance was needed. Leon spoke Spanish at home and had to learn English as a second language when he entered school. Fortunately his teachers showed such interest in him that they referred him to an excellent school social worker when he was 8 years old who asked the school psychologist for assistance in evaluating his learning and emotional difficulties. The psychologist diagnosed his reading disorder, started to treat him right away, and arranged special class placement for him. His social worker helped him and his entire family with intensive casework treatment throughout the years. At the time of his referral, his older sister was in psychotherapy with me for a severe neurotic reaction.

I examined Leon when he was already 11 years old to evaluate his progress and to help with further planning. By then his reading was up to his grade level, but he had residual symptoms of his organic reading disorder, namely spelling difficulties, Linear Dyslexia, and the great ease with which he still could do horizontal mirror-reading. While reading the Gray oral reading paragraphs to me, he suddenly asked, "May I read upside-down?" I told him to go ahead. He then read much more fluently than he had read before, and his linear reading was flawless. He had pointed at each word while reading right-side-up; now he read entirely without pointing. He had not mentioned to anyone before that he preferred to read upside-down. This type of horizontal mirror-reading very often remains undiagnosed because the children do it only when they are alone or with other children, whom they trust more than adults. They are afraid to reveal this habit for fear of being laughed at or considered "crazy." Leon told me that he collected comic books and that he still preferred looking at them upside-down, whether he looked at the pictures or read the text. He said that he had looked at picturebooks upside-down "since I was a baby." He made an organic pattern on the Mosaic test. It was a "stone-bound" design indicating a subcortical difficulty. Leon's speech was clear both in Spanish and English, and his spatial orientation was good. Another residual handicap was that he still could neither draw nor read the clock face. I am sure that under more favorable family and social conditions Leon's organic reading and writing disorder would have been completely cured even before he reached the age of 11.

POSITION READING.   Children with any kind of reading disorder may memorize words by their position on the page. They cannot read them in any other context or when they see them alone. Some of these children even memorize entire stories or texts after the teacher or other children have read the book or text out loud in class or after someone else reads it to them orally. When given something else to read they just rattle down the text they memorized. They do not seem to notice that what they read does not match the words in the text. (See Memory Disorders, p. 70; and Tantrums with a Case Example under Hyperactivity, Vol. II, p. 598.)

OTHER COVER-UP TECHNIQUES.   Position reading is one of the cover-up techniques children with any kind of reading disorder are likely to use. They also use their imagination and may do this so well that their reading disorder is overlooked.

Some children do exactly what adult and child patients suffering from aphasia do when they are supposed to say a word they cannot say. For instance, when they are supposed to say "gun" they might say "chewing gum," or any other word that sounds remotely like it. These children say any word they can imagine that seems to have anything remotely in common with the word they are supposed to read. That is why some current teaching methods that do not insist on absolute accuracy of word reading are so damaging. They encourage cover-up techniques in all children, not just in those whose cerebral reading apparatus is defective.

There is a hierarchy of acts within the reading process, from relatively simple to ever more complicated ones. The higher and more complicated the act, the later it is learned by the healthy child, and the more difficult it is for the child with an organic reading disorder. Silent reading is a higher performance than reading aloud; it is much more difficult to do.

9. Silent Reading

Children call silent reading "reading in my mind." Like many other formulations invented by children, this one expresses a complicated process in a simple way, exactly as the child experiences it, and comes right to the central point. Silent reading is indeed based on images that exist only in the mind. It is mnemic reading, which means that it is based on the formation of memory images of how words sound when they are spoken. As I discussed in the section on the formation of conditioned reflexes, engram complexes between the group of letters forming the word and the sound of the word must have been firmly established before silent reading becomes possible. Without this foundation, children substitute guessing for reading, and this disturbing habit may last throughout their lives. A consequence of this lack of a firm foundation is that many children never feel entirely sure of their reading or feel sure when they should not. They may read words wrongly or read the wrong words for years and may completely distort and misunderstand the meaning of these words, unless their reading is constantly checked by oral reading and also by writing spontaneously and to dictation. Because this is not stressed sufficiently in current curriculum practice, severe reading disorders are obscured and their diagnosis is delayed. Children can acquire an astonishing facility with guessing and with filling in the right word or marking the right answers on silent reading tests. They can also pick up the content by ear when they are supposed to give a report on a text they were supposed to have read silently by themselves. Silent reading should therefore be introduced much later than is the current curriculum practice. A child should not be permitted to read silently before he and the teacher are sure that he can pronounce every word he is supposed to read silently, and can read it orally.

Twelve-year-old Darryl understood the importance of this when he told me, "If you read in your mind, you might say the wrong word." This was his explanation of why he still liked to read his homework out loud to his mother. These were his own words, and he chose them carefully. He deliberately said, "the wrong word" and not "the word wrong." He was not worried about mispronouncing a word, but wanted to be sure that he was reading the right word, so that he would understand the text correctly. He had fortunately learned that the meaning of a word depends on its sound and not its configuration. He had overcome his organic reading disorder, which I had diagnosed when he was 7 years old.

The difference between the silent and the oral reader is that the oral reader actually hears his own pronunciation of the word, whereas the silent reader hears only the memory image and sensation of it (Schmitt, 1966, p. 85.). Silent reading is based on "inner" or "mental" hearing and speech. The silent reader whispers or starts to read aloud only when he tries to figure out an unfamiliar word. The silent articulation of words, which in the beginning accompanies silent reading, can be dropped only after intensive practice, so that in the end the child reads faster than he speaks. This is, of course, the ultimate goal but it cannot be reached until the technical basis of the reading process has become completely automatic, so that the child no longer has to focus his attention on it. Only then is he free to concentrate fully on the content of the text, and only then can the highest cortical structures be activated so that understanding and the forming of associations can take place on the highest level, and so that even creative thinking becomes possible while reading. Perfect silent reading is done without lip and tongue movements. It is really silent and much faster than oral reading.

Silent reading requires a certain level of intelligence. Mentally defective children usually cannot learn it. Some children with below-average intelligence also find it very difficult to do, and they may never learn to read complicated texts silently. Very many children of all levels of intelligence never get beyond the silent articulation stage and should not necessarily be forced beyond it.

SCANNING. Teachers place too much stress on overcoming articulation and on the speed of reading to the point where they teach "skimming" or "scanning" in the early grades. It is much more important for the child's entire intellectual and character development to be taught to read accurately and thoroughly rather than rapidly and superficially. Accuracy is what he needs for acquiring any knowledge and for developing intellectual as well as emotional reliability. It is better to give fewer reading assignments so that the child has time to enjoy and absorb what he is reading. This early pressure for speed, skimming, and scanning, confuses many children and makes reading so unpleasant for them that some turn away from it forever. Practically all curriculum manuals, however, recommend the early teaching of "scanning" and "skimming." These words are often used interchangeably. *Webster's Dictionary* injects the word "careless" into its definition of skimming ("To make a rapid or careless examination, as of a book"), and carelessness is what these children learn. I agree completely with Spalding who states that "speed reading, which is currently being widely taught, is suitable only for children who have really learned to read; that is, to read accurately. It is no substitute for the basic teaching of the language subjects. Time spent speeding up inaccuracies is wasteful" (Spalding & Spalding, 1969, p. 251). I would add that a student must first have learned to recognize what is important before being taught to scan, which means to leave out what is unimportant.

Some children learn on their own to read an entire paragraph or even an entire page almost instantaneously while looking at it. This can, of course, only be done silently and without articulation. Those who learned to read accurately in the beginning do not scan, but read and remember every word on such a page. Not all children can learn to do this; it apparently requires a special visual talent that is sometimes called "photographic memory." However, this is not entirely a visual performance, but also requires speech acoustic images.

Some children with organic reading disorders have great difficulty with silent reading, and many cannot get over the articulation stage or must always read out loud or at least whisper. There is a group of children with organic reading disorders, however, for whom silent reading is easier to do than oral reading. Their accuracy, however, is questionable and must always be carefully tested. Adults and children with aphasia who knew how to read before the aphasia began usually have difficulty with oral reading, but may be able to read silently and to understand what they read (Benson and Geschwind, 1969, p. 133).

10. Spelling

The next higher reading act, spelling, is a high-level performance and very difficult to learn.

English spelling is like a map of the history of English words; it continues to carry letter groups that are leftovers from their Greek, Roman, Celtic, German, and, of course, English origins. They represent sounds long since forgotten. The spelling has remained static while the sound of the words has changed. Each variation of the spelling of the same sound therefore indicates the historic derivation of the word that requires this particular spelling. Where the "f" sound, for instance, is spelled "ph," or the "s" sound "ps," the word has a Greek origin. In modern Greek and in some other derivative languages the "p" and the "s" are still both pronounced separately in words such as psychiatry. The silent "gh" in eight or might, for example, indicates the German origin of the word, which once contained a hard, guttural "g" sound. This historic derivation of spelling should be explained to children since it makes both teaching and learning of spelling more interesting and helps children to remember it better. A child always remembers (i.e., learns) better what he understands; it also trains his thinking. (See also discussion of the English code, under Conditioned Reflexes, p. 88.)

Spelling requires the firm fixation of both the acoustic and the visual memory image of letters and words, as well as linear reading. Where linear reading is defective, the child cannot spell correctly because the letter sequence in his visual image of the word fluctuates and varies, so that he gets the sequence mixed up when he spells. Such confusion of the letter sequence may also have other causes. Children with an organic reading disorder sometimes cannot learn this sequence because they have difficulty with serial ordering in general, and children with a healthy central nervous system may have the same symptom because they did not pay attention in school for neurotic or other psychologic reasons or because they were not taught properly. (See Attention, Vol. II, p. 564; and Vol. I, p. 78 under Conditioned Reflexes and Teaching of Writing, p. 173.)

For spelling, the child must be able to transform his memory image of the group of letters forming the word into speech or writing. This transformation is made possible by the engram part of the conditioned reflex, which links the sound of the word with its visual representation. The child can be expected to spell correctly only after conditioned reflexes to letters and words, including feedback sensations, have been firmly established, and have been just as firmly linked with eye movements. (See Conditioned Reflexes, p. 80.)

One must distinguish three types of spelling: oral spelling, writing to dictation, and spontaneous writing. Writing is described in great detail in the section on writing. Both oral spelling and writing to dictation start from hearing the word said. Spontaneous writing starts from the speech acoustic image of the word. The end result is either speech (in oral spelling) or the kinesthetic motor act of writing. When spelling orally, the child hears the word said or says it himself. He then automatically retraces the steps of the conditioned reflex he has established; he proceeds from the speech sounds he heard to the engram complex that links the acoustic image of the word with its visual image.

This represents the original "signal" to which he has been conditioned. All he needs do after this is pronounce the letters one after the other as he sees them "in his mind," provided he remembers the signals exactly as he learned them. Spelling depends on the linking of letters with speech sounds; it cannot be learned by linking words with pictures or entirely visually, at least in the beginning. That is why children taught with the whole-word or word/picture method either cannot spell at all or are very poor spellers. Children must be taught the speech acoustic synthesis of words.

The best way to teach oral spelling to beginners is to have the child say the word himself, after the teacher has said it, and to have the child say the word as a unit again *after* he has spelled it. This method is slow, but it gives the child a reliable foundation and helps him understand and remember the acoustic cohesion of words. Only after the child has reached the highest reading level, where he can read without or with only minimal articulation can he begin to learn spelling more visually. The prerequisite for this is that the child does a lot of reading. After having read a word many times he will sense misspellings when he writes them; it will not "look right" to him and he will then look it up or ask someone how it is spelled.

Children with a spelling disorder (Dysorthographia) make typical mistakes. They leave out letters, transpose them, or condense them. They spell "gril" instead of "girl," "siwm" instead of "swim," "m" instead of "am," "Thrusday" instead of "Thursday," "schuled" instead of "scheduled," "hre" instead of "hear." None of these mistakes is made exclusively by children with organic reading disorders so that this diagnosis cannot be based entirely on a Dysorthographia, at least not in children. But when a child with a background of good teaching who can concentrate well and whose intelligence is not defective consistently makes spelling errors, the diagnosis of an organic type of Dysorthographia is indicated.

Some of these children can read, but most of them have a reading disorder. All, of course, find it difficult to write from dictation or spontaneously because they cannot spell. Some such children can learn to spell orally, but when they see in print or in writing what they have just spelled orally, they cannot read it. That is why oral as well as written spelling must be taught and why both types of spelling must be tested separately. We should not assume that a child can spell in writing what he can spell orally, or vice versa. Many children can spell only by writing the word down. Others spell well orally, but make mistakes when writing the word. (See case of Alex under Slowing Down of All Reactions, Vol. II, p. 463).

Severe spelling disorders are typical for children with an organic reading disorder. They are difficult to treat and are usually the last symptom to disappear along with Linear Dyslexia. Some such children never learn to spell, so that a spelling disorder remains as a residual symptom throughout their life.

A severe organic spelling disorder is sometimes treated most successfully by ignoring it. These children need a prolonged period of remedial reading therapy before they can and should be expected to spell. Their parents and their teachers should be advised not to force them to spell any longer, but to help them. Forcing such a child only increases his feelings of failure and depression, discourages him even more, and makes him dislike reading and writing. He should be permitted to give all his reports orally, in his own words, and should be told how the words are spelled when he has to write them down. The parents should either let the child write his homework with his own spelling or should dictate those words to him that he cannot spell. This often removes a major area of tension at home and improves his relationship with his parents, so that he is no longer torn by conflicts and anger and can learn better in general. The teachers should be asked not to grade his papers for spelling, and to permit him to look up the spelling of words in his classroom work. To have such a child spell out loud before the entire class only embarrasses him and worsens all his psychologic, and with them, his organic symptoms. I have examined and treated high school and even college students who were perfectly capable of studying for their degrees provided they got this kind of help. I have even seen students manage to get through medical school in spite of this handicap. I remember one medical student whose disability came to my attention when I discussed children's reading disorders in the senior course on child psychiatry. The students started to giggle and to point at this one student who admitted that he suffered from a hereditary organic reading disorder. He still could not spell properly and had trouble reading long words. His family had diagnosed his disorder even before he entered school. They knew the symptoms only too well because his father, several of his uncles, and his grandfather had the same condition, and all had helped him overcome his handicap and to live with what he could not conquer. Later on his fellow students had pitched in to help him. He described how he had trained himself to memorize his lessons entirely by ear, and how he used the tape recorder to help himself. His grades were excellent.

Because spelling errors are so persistent in children with organic reading disorders and so resistant to cure, one can sometimes suspect that an adult who reads well but makes many spelling mistakes may have had such a reading disorder as a child. Doug's father belonged to this group. Doug came to me for psychotherapy for neurotic symptoms and an organic reading disorder, which I diagnosed when he was 9 years old. It had remained unrecognized through three grades in an exclusive private school. Doug's father, an engineer, sent me many handwritten notes in which he described his son's nightmares and his other troubles during the time interval between our sessions. The numerous spelling errors in these notes led me to suspect that he, too, had had a reading disorder as a child. He told me that he did not remember any difficulty with reading, but that he was very unhappy throughout elementary school. It is possible that this handicap was so humiliating and painful for him that he repressed any memory of it.

The experiences of the medical student and Doug's father both show how important it is to search for reading disorders in the child's family, in his own as well as in preceding generations. (See Heredity, p. 58.)

Organic spelling disorders are so persistent and resistant to cure because spelling requires the intactness of the highest and most complicated parts of the organic reading apparatus, which makes linear reading and image formation possible. Three areas of malfunctioning are primarily responsible for Dysorthographia:

1. Engram complex formation between the visual and the acoustic aspect of the word may be defective or impossible to establish.

2. Image formation itself may be impaired, affecting the visual or the acoustic image of letters and words, or both.

3. Linear reading may be defective.

All three impairments, alone or in combination, lead to a spelling disorder on an organic basis.

SOCIOGENIC SPELLING DISORDERS.   It is important to realize that the overwhelming majority of children who cannot spell have a perfectly healthy cerebral reading apparatus. Their failure is due to inadequate teaching, frequently combined with comic book habituation. Such spelling disorders are sociogenic; that is, they are caused by adverse social factors that affect large masses of children. They are not due to individual psychopathology. Children at all educational levels from elementary school through graduate studies are affected, and this is symptomatic of the breakdown of an entire school system.

THE CRUCIAL ROLE OF TEACHING METHODS. Fundamentally, there are two approaches to teaching reading: The visual or sight/word (also called whole-word, word-perception, word/picture, global) method and the phonetic (also called phonic, analytical, or synthetic) method. In the United States the sight/word method is still being used in almost all schools for the beginning reader—that is, in the first grades of elementary school. It emanated from Teacher's College at Columbia University in New York City around 1926, when the famous educator Arthur I. Gates and his colleagues set forth the edict that phonics should not be taught in the early grades anymore. Since about 1940 most schools have used sight/word teaching as the only accepted and approved teaching method (Mosse, 1962b, 1963c, 1966d). (See History of These Curriculum Practices, p. 273 in Chapter 6, Sociogenic Reading Disorders.)

READING READINESS. At about the same time as the sight/word method, reading readiness tests were introduced. They must also be discussed because it is impossible to understand how children are being taught to read unless one is familiar with both whole-word teaching and reading readiness concepts. The idea underlying both is that learning should be made as easy and painless as possible and that this can only be achieved if the child is mature enough to absorb each new step in education.

The child's readiness to read, however, is not determined by actually teaching reading in a simple, easily understandable way commensurate with his state of maturity. This would really amount to fitting the method to the child and would be an efficient way of finding out which child can learn fast, which one more slowly, and which child not at all. The opposite approach is used, however. A teacher is not allowed to teach a child to read until he has passed a so-called reading readiness test. These tests have nothing whatever to do with the child's interest in reading. They do not examine his ability to distinguish sounds, but rather test almost exclusively his motor and visual aptitudes. The curriculum demands that a child who has not yet passed these "readiness" tests must paint, draw, or play, while the other children in the same kindergarten or class are learning how to read. As a serious consequence of this system, very many children learn to read relatively late, and some are never able to catch up with their grade. By that time, most of them have developed strong feelings of inferiority because their classmates are so much further advanced. I have seen children of normal intelligence who were allowed to start only at the age of 7 years or even later (Mosse, 1962b)!

When a child has finally been declared mature enough for reading, the teacher gives him a primer and shows him cards. On both he sees a word beneath a picture. He has to memorize the word. When he is shown the word again, he is supposed to remember the picture and in this way to be able to say the word. He is also told to observe the configuration of the word. He is not taught the different letters and their sounds, and the teacher does not explain to him what makes up the word, how a printed squiggle comes to represent the word "house." The child is supposed to develop a sound association to a visual stimulus that he does not understand, via another visual stimulus (the picture), whereas language, whether spoken or printed, is based on acoustic associations and conditioned reflexes. (See section on Conditioned Reflexes, p. 78.) It is therefore not surprising that very intelligent children frequently refuse to memorize such nonsense since it is something they do not understand. Children who are not of exceptional intelligence learn with this method only with great effort, provided that they have a good visual memory. It is in any case impossible to learn to spell, read, and write formal English adequately without the knowledge of phonetic principles and rules. This holds true for children with a healthy nervous system. It also helps to prevent spelling disorders in children with a defective cerebral reading apparatus. It is almost impossible to learn to read, write, and spell English with the whole-word method for the very many children who speak either a different language or one of the numerous American dialects at home.

The theory of the educators is that the child ought to learn in a painless way, as much as possible without the experience of failure. One can only agree with this goal. The whole-word method, however, leads to the exact opposite situation. The children lose their initial enthusiasm for reading, writing, and spelling and acquire the habit of guessing at words. Some of them can never overcome this habit. Actually the only children who learn rapidly with the whole-word method are those who have already learned to read and write the alphabet at home, before they enter school. Many children are interested in letters and their sounds as early as the age of 3 years. They learn this like a game, in a playful way, provided their parents have enough knowledge, time, and patience to answer all their questions.

The conventional curriculum prescribes that phonetics may only be taught after the child has acquired a "sight vocabulary" of about 70 to 100 words, usually during the first grade, sometimes as late as the beginning of the second grade. At first, only the beginning consonant is taught; other consonants follow. Vowels are not taught at all. The child is supposed to fill them in when he has succeeded in guessing what the word may be. In this way most children never learn to read or spell correctly, independently, and with a feeling of security. That is why so many high school students cannot distinguish the word "beautiful" from "because," for instance. They have learned only the beginning sound and never really understood how a word comes about.

The fact that children with reading disorders are usually not referred to us for examination and treatment until they reach the third grade is largely due to this curriculum practice.

Sight/word teaching unfortunately persists even in so-called code emphasis methods, a term used by educators to replace and in this way to avoid the word "phonetics." For instance, a textbook of reading instruction that stresses "decoding" recommends "sight-reading words in isolation" and "passage reading by sight" in a sample lesson for "the beginning reading stage" (Carnine & Silbert, 1979, p. 176). All "code emphasis" methods should therefore be carefully evaluated to be sure that they really eliminate all harmful aspects of whole-word teaching.

The harmfulness of the whole-word method was exposed for the first time only in 1955 by Rudolf Flesch in his book *Why Johnny Can't Read.* The pressure exerted on educators since the appearance of that book, and devastating statistics of children with high school diplomas who cannot read, write, or spell have slowly led to the sporadic reintroduction of phonetic methods. But teachers themselves do not learn phonetics anymore and therefore cannot teach it.

I have myself experienced how much fighting rages about the whole-word method. In May 1960, I attended the Congress of the International Reading Association. Teachers, reading specialists, school principals, and administrators were present in our discussion group. But no discussion got started. I finally said that as a psychiatrist I felt I could discuss something they seemed so anxious to avoid. I spoke about the whole-word method as a cause for reading, writing, and spelling disorders. The reaction was astonishing. It was as though a floodgate had opened, and teachers and others spoke freely, openly, and passionately. They described how they (especially the older teachers) had been aware of the great harmfulness of the whole-word method for a long time, but that they had been completely helpless and powerless since they were being forced to use this method. Those teachers who in desperation had the courage to teach phonetics had to do so secretly. Some even had to tell the children to do something else quickly whenever someone entered the classroom. (Mosse, 1962b).

It is a calamity for the children of the United States that a *new* antiphonics movement has been started. As Patrick Groff writes in *The Elementary School Journal* of March 1977,

> This group is spearheaded by Frank Smith, whose books on reading provide the theory and the rationale for this new anti-phonics movement, and by Kenneth Goodman, who censures phonics in most of his writings about the techniques of reading instruction (p. 326).

Unfortunately, this new antiphonics movement wants to ban phonics instruction entirely from any level of the teaching of reading. The old movement opposed only teaching it early and intensively.

In his book, *Understanding Reading* (1971), Frank Smith states clearly that he has never taught children how to read, write, or spell. One might assume that this alone would disqualify him from writing about the teaching of reading to children and, by implication, about children's reading disorders. He is a psycholinguist who has dealt only with adults.

Patrick Groff reports that "teachers who used a method that the new anti-phonics movement would recommend found that the pupils they so instructed developed significantly less ability in reading than pupils of teachers who gave early, intensive phonics to their beginning readers." He concludes that because of the increasing confidence placed in phonics by publishers and editors of widely used basal readers, the future of phonics will be bright. He feels that the new antiphonics movement is just a passing phase (p. 330); one can only hope that his prognosis is correct. (See Vol. II, sections on Perceptual Changes During Attention, p. 514, and on Selectivity of Attention, p. 518.)

THE ROLE OF PHONETIC METHODS.   The Spaldings express the dilemma of English spelling very clearly in *The Writing Road to Reading* when they write that "the written spelling of words is in English the major obstacle to easy writing and accurate reading. The spelling may seem very inconsistent, but, in fact, it follows certain patterns and rules (with few exceptions) and basically uses its phonograms to express the spoken sound in words." They also explain that "English has seventy common phonograms (twenty-six letters and forty-four fixed combinations of two, three, and four letters) to say on paper the forty-five basic sounds used in speaking it" (1969, p. 14).

The Spaldings' solution to the spelling dilemma is their own phonetic method. Under the Spalding method students start in kindergarten or the first grade by "learning fifty-four of these phonograms by saying their sounds and writing them. Then they write, from dictation, as they say the phonogram sounds heard in each of the most used 150 words, write and read original sentences to show their meanings, and, within about two months, start reading books." This is usually around the first of November. It is the authors' opinion that "the failings of most of the phonic methods may be summarized in that they neglect spelling and do not teach the saying and writing of the forty-five basic sounds of the phonograms of the language *before* trying to read" (Spalding & Spalding, 1969, p. 14).

I have observed the success of this phonetic method under the most trying circumstances, namely, in deprived schools with disadvantaged children in New York City's Harlem. Most children in these schools spoke Spanish or a colloquial English at home. Spelling cannot be taught successfully without the consistently careful, clear, and accurate pronunciation of formal English. The sounds should not vary. (See Conditioned Reflexes, p. 187, and Comparative Study of Conventional Teaching Methods with the Phonetic Spalding Approach, p. 195.)

What makes spelling so especially difficult for American children is that the consonants are being slighted and that the sound "uh" is frequently substituted for the true vowel sounds. The Spaldings offer the following plausible explanation: "Our American spoken language has been rapidly deteriorating, and this has probably come about chiefly through the fact that this generation has been given no clear understanding of the phonetic basis of English. The relation between spelling and the pronouncing of every word has not been taught or even explained." They correctly further state that "the habit of using clear, easily-understood speech is a real aid to clear thinking" and that "the standards of accurate pronunciation which a teacher requires of her pupils are really a very important part of their education" (Spalding & Spalding, 1962, p. 233.) (See the English code under Conditioned Reflexes, p. 88.)

AMERICAN DIALECTS IN THE CLASSROOM. The teaching of the phonetic basis of formal English brings up the problem of the role of American dialects in the classroom. An excellent article in the *New York Times* of June 9, 1972 dealt with this important topic. Its title was "English, Not Dialect" and it was written by T. J. Sellers, a former teacher, an editor of *The Amsterdam News* (New York City), and a special assistant to a community superintendent in the New York City school system. Sellers wrote that

> bright young white teachers from good schools and financially secure homes often play down the importance of teaching reading and the other basic "tool" skills to the poor black kids in the ghetto. They see the effort as an endorsement of the establishment. So much of school time ought to be spent playing the bongo drums or rapping, or just listening to masterpieces from the underground press.

He continues that "black teachers and black poets and black editors have joined the crusade to make little black boys and girls happy in their hang-ups with the classroom." I have observed this attitude in white and black teachers many times, and agree with Sellers that this has done and continues to do great harm to black children. I agree with him when he writes that "black dialect should be accepted for what it is, a method of communication between human beings." However, he warns that

> when the dialect of inner city school children is projected as the "language of their culture" and a determined effort is made to justify the "teaching" of the basic structure of distorted English in the formative years, this linguistic approach becomes another innovative nightmare that could retard the progress of generations of poor black school children.

Sellers stresses correctly that

> there isn't anything poetic about being poor, and there just isn't anything exciting or thrilling about the so-called "culture of poverty" to those people who are poor

and trapped in the bleakness of their poverty. And they cannot change their status by pretending that it is exotic and breathtaking to be poor and ignorant and powerless. Perpetuating black dialect is not the answer. Learning to speak and read the mother tongue might be. And I regard the English language as the mother tongue since all of the little boys and girls that I used to teach around Lenox Avenue and 135th Street were English-speaking.

He concludes with the following important statement:

The situation is simply this: The black kids who are in school now will have to compete for jobs with people who have been educated in the accepted culture that prevails in this country. And it is a cruel hoax for teachers or poets or editors or "leaders" to make children feel that a romantic excursion in distorted grammar will help them with this overwhelming task.

It is crucial for any American child, black or white, speaking Spanish or Pennsylvania Dutch at home, to learn adequately to spell, read, and write formal English. Otherwise, he cannot be expected to lead any kind of secure and constructive existence. Many illiterate and inarticulate youngsters are driven into getting their money through crime, far too often with violent methods. There is unquestionably a close connection between inability to spell, write, and read and delinquent behavior. (See section on Juvenile Delinquency, p. 284.)

My experience confirms what Gene I. Maeroff reported in the *New York Times* of August 4, 1973, where he wrote that "supervisors in the City school system say they are observing an increasing number of spelling errors in lessons that young teachers write on the chalk board." The classroom situation is actually worse. I have seen many spelling errors made by teachers in their written reports. One teacher, for example, wrote "audociatic" instead of "autocratic"; others wrote "masculan" for "masculine," "corporation" for "cooperation," "courious" for "curious," and so on. I have also seen wrong or no corrections by teachers of children's spelling errors in their notebooks on their tests. For instance, 8-year-old Darryl got "Excellent" on a spelling test where he wrote "whole" instead of "hole." His teacher did not correct this or any other spelling mistake. Nine-year-old Lora, who had a severe reading and spelling disorder, wrote "He *have*" instead of "He *has*" on a test marked "Satisfactory" by the teacher without correcting any spelling or grammar mistakes.

How can the reading, writing, and spelling disorder of any child be prevented, improved, or cured with such incompetent and uncaring teaching? Darryl overcame his handicap with hard work, individual remedial reading teaching, psychotherapy, and social work with his family. (See details under

Silent Reading and in section on Writing, pp. 112 and 155.) Lora never overcame her disorder completely.

The spelling dilemma in the United States has involved colleges and even graduate schools. As Edwin Newman reported on NBC-TV on February 1, 1975, journalism school students cannot write the English language accurately any more and do not know how to generalize their facts. That is why they have to take tests in spelling and grammar, which many of them fail. Some students he interviewed took these tests six or seven times and failed each time.

Spelling disorders are affecting even elitist colleges and exclusive graduate schools. R. Arthur Gindin, Associate Professor of Neurosurgery at the Medical College of Georgia, studied the spelling performance of his medical students. He asked each student in a freshman course to write a detailed report of their examination of four patients. What he found was an appalling lack of ability to spell and to use the English language clearly and succinctly. The following errors are examples of these students' spelling problems:

affect (for effect)	ecessive
alchohol	explane (as "explane a proverb")
amblitory	fleem (phlegm)
ankel	hospitil
apethetic	illicit (for elicit)
assciated	irratation
aweful	male-nourished
ballance	nasea, nausia (nausea)
bilatteraly	occaisional
cain (for walking)	paralized
dammage	plach (plaque)
dialating	sight (place)
partically (for partially)	squezzing
sever (very bad)	tendacy
suppling	tobbaco
temporial	tremmor
tracks (tracts)	worst (as in "get worst")
disfunction	distruction

Gindin states: "I offer only one conclusion, based on my knowledge of the students: there is no correlation between the writers of the above words and membership in any minority group" (1974).

The Role of Comic Book Habituation

There is no doubt that children who are habitual comic book readers make more spelling mistakes than youngsters who read comic books only occasionally or not at all. Their letters show this. A ninth-grade boy wrote, for instance, that he was a "*colecter* of comic books." His letters showed that he was a very intelligent boy who was even on the staff of the school newspaper.

It is impossible to determine what role comic book habituation may have played in causing the spelling errors of Gindin's group of medical students. I made a point of asking each class of the fourth-year medical students I have taught how many were still reading comic books and how many continued to collect them. Our rapport was such that they did not hesitate to tell the truth. Their answers were surprising, even to me. Half of the entire class usually still read comic books regularly and many continued to collect them, especially "Spiderman."

From a large correspondence with comic book addicts I have collected the following typical spelling errors:

appierance (appearance)	belive (believe)
concent (consent)	desent (descent)
dimentions (dimensions)	erradicate (eradicate)
figgured (figured)	for instince (for instance)
non-discript (nondescript)	payed (paid)
provocitive (provocative)	repitition (repetition)
reveloution (revolution)	recieve (receive)
sentance (sentence)	there (their)

Comic book habituation may not only cause spelling errors, but also a specific reading disorder that Wertham called Linear Dyslexia. (See Linear Dyslexia, p. 127, and Comic Books, p. 275.)

SPEECH TREATMENT AS AN AID TO THE TREATMENT OF SPELLING DISORDERS. I have sent many children with spelling, reading, and writing disorders to the school's speech teachers or to private speech therapists. These specialists have the children practice the pronunciation of separate sounds and of a combination of sounds. This is really a roundabout way of teaching them phonetics, and many of these children benefited greatly. Especially children with mild receptive aphasia learned to distinguish different speech sounds so that they at last had a basis for learning to spell, read, and write.

The highest part of the technical reading process is linear reading. It is learned last by healthy children and is most difficult and sometimes impossible to learn for children with an organic reading disorder.

11. Linear Reading

Focusing both eyes first on the beginning of one line, following it through to the end and returning a little lower to the beginning of the next line is difficult and involves a complex neurophysiologic mechanism. According to Wertham, smooth linear reading including the return sweep to the beginning of the next line requires the intactness of the highest and most complex parts of the cerebral reading apparatus, which must be able to perform the finest and most exact coordination. In adult patients with organic brain defects, where reading is affected, this is the very last function to return under treatment.

Linear reading including the return sweep must become automatic so that the child can read paragraphs, pages, and books without interruption; paragraph and page reading must become *one* automatic habit, and this cannot be achieved without linear reading. It is therefore essential to teach reading and writing on a straight line from the very beginning, and not to let the child write on unlined paper or read words placed in columns underneath each other, which are such common curriculum practices.

Only a few teachers' manuals even mention linear reading, and teachers are, as a rule, not aware of its importance because it has not been explained to them during their training. Yet, a defect in this highest reading act alone impairs reading severely and causes a serious reading disorder that Wertham called Linear Dyslexia. He described this new pathologic condition in the survey of reading disorders he gave in his book *Seduction of the Innocent* (1972b), as well as in other publications. (1954, 1955, 1962).

LINEAR DYSLEXIA. A great deal of experimental work has been done regarding the relationship of eye movements with reading. Eye movements with the return sweep can be photographed and recorded on graphs. This makes it possible to study them in detail (Taylor, 1957). We know how the eyes move normally when reading: in a progression from left to right with alternating pauses and quick movements called saccadic movements. The pauses are called fixations, and it is assumed that reading takes place during these fixations, which last only a fraction of a second. Of course this refers only to silent reading. We can tell when reading takes place during oral reading.

The amount the reader can see during the fixations is called recognition span. The better the reader, the fewer the fixations and the larger the recognition span. Sometimes the eyes move backwards to get a second look at something, either to understand it better or to think about it. Such backward movement is called regression. When one comes to the end of the line, there is a smooth continuous movement back to the beginning of the next line called return sweep.

Harris, in his standard book on remedial reading, describes children who have trouble with this aspect of linear reading. He states that "some children have difficulty in making a return sweep at the end of a line, and so drop down to the end of the next line and follow it back to the beginning before starting to read it" (Harris, 1956). This highlights the importance of teaching linear reading, including the return sweep, from the very beginning so that no child acquires the habit of searching for the beginning of the next line in the manner described by Harris. This method of finding the beginning of the next line can easily become a habit unless teachers observe their student's eye movements carefully and correct them right away.

Some children suffering from Linear Dyslexia use the above method of returning to the beginning of the line in order to overcome their difficulties in reading, but it is only one of the methods used by these children. Many of them cannot even do this; they move their eyes back to the left in a searching, uneven, and unsteady movement and then frequently miss the beginning of the next line.

Linear reading and the return sweep are especially difficult to learn for children who cannot distinguish right from left, or who are uncertain about this. When they come to the end of a line they don't know that they must look back to the left. These children are usually uncertain where to look and thus frequently let their eyes wander all over the page. They are prone to develop Linear Dyslexia. This type of child is usually left-handed or has not developed a dominant hand. He is often uncertain about the right and left sides on his own body and on other people. (See Gerstmann Syndrome, p. 175, and Hand Dominance, p. 179.)

Children use certain typical phrases to describe this reading trouble, for example: "Sometimes I skip a line but I don't know it," or "I jump a line," or, as 12-year-old Lisa said, "I read slow; I get mixed up; I stutter in my reading and I don't hit the line sometimes." Many such children indeed don't notice when they skip one or more lines and continue to read the wrong line. They have no confidence in their reading ability anyway and often think that it is their faulty understanding that makes the text unintelligible. Many such children point with their finger at each word while they read it or move their head from one word to the next. Small children are apt to do this when they first learn to read, but whenever we observe this in older children we must suspect Linear Dyslexia.

If properly taught, the child does not and should not notice that he is learning linear reading. A good, fluent reader is not aware of his eye movements. He does not have to pay any attention to them because they have become automatic so that he can use his entire power of concentration to understand the content of what he reads, think about it, associate with it, be emotionally involved in it, and enjoy it. Children who suffer from Linear Dyslexia are too handicapped to pay much attention to meaning. They would like to read a page or a book, but for them this requires so much conscious effort and so much time that they cannot do it. They perceive each line laboriously and cannot fit it into the whole page. They get fatigued. (See Vol. 2, Fatiguability, p. 672.)

To make sure that a child's linear reading is not defective, one must always test how he reads an entire page and find out whether he has ever read an entire book. This should be part of any psychiatric and psychologic examination, and one should also ask what books and how many the child has recently read. Linear Dyslexia is easily overlooked because children who suffer from it may do quite well on reading tests that involve only words or single paragraphs. This condition is also often misunderstood and therefore overlooked and not treated, so that it remains a handicap throughout the child's life. It is sometimes erroneously assumed that these children cannot concentrate and are not interested. Yet their disturbance is not an emotional one but a disorder of actual eye movements. Nor is it due to a memory defect. Some of these children read hastily and carelessly because they cannot regulate the speed of their reading and are worried about losing their place on the line or on the page; they are tense and cannot read with either pleasure or profit. Sometimes they are able to read a sentence, but they skip words frequently, and then move their eyes back to pick up the missed work; or they may reverse the sequence of words. Their disturbance may be so marked that their eyes zigzag across the page.

In testing the child's eye movements for Linear Dyslexia, I have found two tests particularly helpful; both are easy to perform. One is the *Miles Peep Hole Method* (Blair, 1956, p. 26). (See Chapter 1, p. 34.)

The other method is the *Mirror Test.* A small mirror is placed on the left-hand page of a book while the child reads the right-hand page, or vice versa. The examiner sits or stands behind the child and looks into the mirror, where he can readily see the eye movements. For more exact studies of eye movements, the ophthalmograph can be used. It records eye movements accurately, including the return sweep. However, it is an expensive instrument and for practical purposes is not necessary.

Of course the possibility of visual defects has to be considered during each examination. The intactness of the visual apparatus is especially important for good linear reading, for experiments have shown long ago that "in the long jumps from the end of one line to the beginning of the next, convergence is often inaccurate and requires correction during the first fixation on the new line" (Woodworth, 1938, p. 723). If there is even a suspicion of such defects, examination by an ophthalmologist is indicated.

Linear Dyslexia may exist by itself, without any other organic or psychopathologic condition. It may occur in children with normal or defective intelligence, in those with gross, or with minimal brain or neurologic defects, and also in those who have no organic involvement at all. I have observed it in children with all possible diagnoses, for instance schizophrenia and all types of psychoneuroses and reactive disorders. (Mosse, 1966b; Mosse & Daniels, 1959).

Richard, 10 Years Old: Linear Dyslexia on an Organic Basis. The following is a typical case of Linear Dyslexia in a child with gross lesions of the brain.

Richard was referred at the age of 10 because he was unable to do the work of his grade in school. He had good verbal ability but could not put anything down on paper. He had a very short attention span and, in school, was always out of his seat. He was born with a subdural hematoma that was removed soon after birth. Nystagmus, mild ptosis of his right eyelid, right abducens weakness, mild right facial paralysis, and mild spasticity of his right arm and hand remained. This could be classified as mild Cerebral Palsy. (See Vol. II, Cerebral Palsy, p. 428.)

Richard's vision was adequately corrected with eyeglasses. His intelligence was below average but not defective. He had episodes of restlessness and irritability but no convulsions until he was 13 years of age. With remedial reading and psychotherapy (individual and group) his behavior improved. He was very anxious to learn and was eventually able to read words and sentences.

When Richard was 11 years old, his remedial reading teacher observed that on his own he had developed the habit of using a folded piece of paper with lines on it to cover the rest of the page underneath the lines he was reading. This helped him to avoid skipping words and lines. He asked his teacher repeatedly, "How can you possibly read straight without lines?" After having read the right-hand page of a book, he habitually shifted to the left which he had already read. Because of the increasing severity of his convulsive disorder, which could not be controlled completely with medication, it was not possible to cure him of his Linear Dyslexia.

Treatment with a Cover Card.   The corrective technique used by Richard was not the best. I have observed that very many teachers unfortunately also use it. A folded piece of paper or, much better, an unlined card should be held *above* the line the child is reading, not beneath it. This is the so-called *Cover Card Method* of treating Linear Dyslexia. The reason for this position of the card is that it can steady the eyes, which have a tendency to wander above and not below the line being read, and it can connect the end of one line with the beginning of the next, thus indicating the return sweep and making it easier on the child's eyes. By blotting out all the text that has already been read, the cover card helps the child to concentrate on just that one line he is reading. By holding the card at a slant with the left corner slightly lower than the right, and by pushing it down while he reads, the child steadies his gaze and at the same time pushes his eyes from left to right and down via a correct return sweep from one line to the next. This is by far the simplest, cheapest, and most effective treatment for Linear Dyslexia. An unlined index card the length of a line in a book serves this purpose very well, and I always keep a supply of them in my desk so that I can show the child and his parents how to use it. The child is instructed to keep a card with him at all times and not to read without it until he has been cured of his Linear Dyslexia. (See Vol. II, Distractibility, p. 581.)

Other Treatment Techniques. A cardboard "window" is helpful for children with Linear Dyslexia and other reading disorders. It also helps the child with an attention disorder to focus on the text. (See Vol. II, Attention Disorders, p. 580.) A window is cut in a piece of cardboard just large enough to accommodate about two or three words of one line of text. The card is placed where the child is to read and pushed along the line as he is reading. Many of these children are too awkward with their hands to manage this on their own; the remedial teacher or parent has to help them in the beginning.

Marianne Frostig, a specialist in children's perceptual disorders, describes another method. She writes:

> Some children are able to direct their eye movements quite smoothly along a line, but have difficulty in accomplishing the fast backward movements to the beginning of the line below. These children can be helped if lines are drawn across the page below the rows of print, and slanted lines are drawn from the end of each horizontal line to the beginning of the next. The children are taught to follow the lines quickly with their eyes (Frostig, 1965, pp. 122–123).

A similar technique consists of writing a text with triple spacing on a typewriter and connecting the end of each line with the beginning of the next. As the child improves, double spacing is used.

Elaborate instruments have been constructed, such as the *Metron-O-Scope* and the *Controlled Reader.* The *Perceptoscope* seems to be particularly suitable for learning how to read an entire page. All these devices are very expensive and not readily available. Most patients can be treated successfully without them (Mosse & Daniels, 1959, p. 840).

In many cases the patient efforts of the remedial reading teacher achieve the best results if they are combined with psychotherapy and constructive social service work. A prerequisite is that the therapist understands the symptom. This form of Dyslexia can be cured, provided it is properly diagnosed.

That almost all children with an unquestioned and severe organic reading disorder suffer from Linear Dyslexia is strikingly evident even without individual examinations when one has the opportunity to observe a classroom or even a school full of them. MacDonald Critchley, in a personal communication to me, said that he noticed it during a visit to the Ordblinde Instituttet in Copenhagen, Denmark. I made the same observation at this unusual special school for children with only the severest forms of organic reading disorders, and it came as no surprise to me. I had already seen Linear Dyslexia exactly as Wertham first described it, not only in the United States, but also in Germany. This form of reading disorder probably is not even confined to countries whose language is written on a horizontal line from left to right with lines following each other vertically downwards as in English. It likely can also be found where reading proceeds from right to left as in Arabic, Hebrew, and other languages, and where ideographs (i.e., symbols expressing ideas) are read vertically downwards so that the eyes have to move on a straight line downwards and then make the return sweep upward to the beginning of the next line which is to the left (e.g., Chinese, Japanese, Korean, etc.). We can make this assumption (even though Linear Dyslexia has not, so far as I know, yet been studied in these countries) because the organic defects I am describing are found in children all over the world, so that their symptoms also must follow the same principles.

I have examined a number of children who were taught to read, write, and spell at the same time two languages that use different alphabets and are written in opposite linear directions, for instance, English and Hebrew. A child with even the mildest form of an organic reading disorder cannot cope with these differences. Children with a tendency toward Linear Dyslexia are completely lost. Such a child should be taught to read and write only one of these languages at a time. He can be expected to learn the second language only after he has overcome his reading disorder and mastered the first language.

LOCALIZATION.   Linear reading requires the intactness of the entire cerebral reading apparatus, which must achieve perfect integration with the tracts and areas responsible for eye movements. The cortical projection areas for eye movements are located in the middle frontal convolution of the frontal lobes in both hemispheres. They must be activated in both hemispheres at the same time to function properly. These projection areas lie directly in front of that part of the middle frontal convolutions where the writing center is assumed to be located. This proximity is important because writing requires the finest and most exact coordination of eye with hand movements (Liebman, 1979, pp. 23–24, plate 8-1). (See section on Writing Disorders on an Organic Basis, p. 142, and Figure 2.1.)

LINEAR DYSLEXIA ON A NON-ORGANIC BASIS.   The overwhelming majority of children with Linear Dyslexia have no organic central nervous system defects. As with most other reading disorder symptoms, defective linear reading is not specific for an organic causation of the reading disorder. Extensive studies show that this condition occurs most frequently as a result of faulty reading habits acquired at an early age. Non-organic factors that cause these faulty reading habits leading to Linear Dyslexia are whole-word teaching techniques, which I have already described, and early and excessive comic book reading.

I have already dealt with some of the negative aspects of comic books with reference to reading. I will now describe the specific damage they do to linear reading, causing Linear Dyslexia. This can only be understood within the framework of the total impact comic books have on reading.

Wertham and his group, to which I belonged from the beginning, has studied comic books now for over 30 years, and always paid special attention to their effect on children's reading ability. In spite of the advent of television with its overwhelming influence on children, comic books still play an important role in the lives of many children, from the earliest years on. Practically all children have looked at hundreds of comic books long before they are taught to read, as a visit to most homes and to practically all kindergartens will show. (See section on Teaching of Writing, p. 187, and Figure 2.2.)

When Wertham's *Seduction of the Innocent*, the classic book about the influence of mass media on children, first appeared in 1954, 100 million comic books were being published each month. This was the greatest publishing success in history. The results of Wertham's studies inspired parent organizations all over the country to fight against comic books portraying crime and violence. Their fight was successful for awhile; the most harmful comic books disappeared from the market and the number of comic book publishers declined. Collecting comic books has, however, become a big business, and the worst ones are being reprinted and are again on the market (Mosse, 1977b). (See Comic Books, p. 275.)

Very many children whose parents do not own books derive their idea of what a book is like from comic books. This is of great disadvantage for such children, who are already disadvantaged in so many other ways. The very concept of the book, namely the characteristic arrangement of a printed page, is lacking in a comic book. To understand the negative impact comic books have on reading, one must analyze their structure as well as their content.

Comic book pages contain many pictures arranged in different sizes and shapes, which do not necessarily follow in a sequence from left to right. So confusing is this arrangement that arrows sometimes are used to lead the child's eyes from one picture to the other. These arrows point in all directions, most frequently right to left or diagonally downward. The entire layout encourages wandering of the eyes in any but a straight left-to-right direction. This lack of direction becomes even more pronounced in the text, which is placed inside balloons. Some pictures have one or more balloons, others none. The child who has some reading ability and tries to read the text acquires the habit of reading irregular bits of print here and there in balloons instead of complete lines from left to right. Neither pictures nor text can possibly be followed with linear eye movements. The emphasis is on pictures and not at all on reading anyhow. The text is completely subordinated to the pictures, and only a few words inside balloons are printed in one straight line. As 9-year-old William once explained to us at the Lafargue Clinic: "You'd think this was the end of the sentence, but it isn't. The sentence goes on in the next line inside the round line that makes the balloon." He was so pleased with this discovery of his that he walked around the clinic, holding up his favorite comic book for all to see, pointing out how the sentence went.

FIG. 2.2. This comic book was brought to a conventional kindergarten class by a 5-year-old girl. This page shows that the children's eyes have to wander in different directions when reading a comic book, so they do not learn linear reading. Added is the glorification of violence: shooting, other forms of violent attacks, and fire bombing, which is especially exciting for children. (Color plate of Figure 2.2 follows p. 224.)

I have stressed above that the printing of the text in capital letters only, with little or no space between the words, can interfere with learning to read words. Many comic books use dialect spelling, which makes it harder for children to learn to spell correctly. This is particularly frequent in animal comic books read by very young children. For instance: "BUT CARS RUN-UM OUT OF

GAS," or "EM" instead of "them," "BUY 'UM" for "buying," "BEESNESS" for "business," "DAWG" for "dog," "BAWL" for "ball," "GAL" for "girl," or "OKAY WE GOT'CHA," "AW! TH' POOR GUY'S DELIRIOUS." Here, incorrect pronunciation is added to misspelling. This structural analysis, to which one can add examples ad infinitum, shows that comic books seriously distort all the complicated acts a child has to learn in order to read properly.

In addition, children acquire certain habits that make reading much more difficult for them. One such habit is picture gazing and daydreaming while gazing. This makes it much harder for the child to learn the conditioned reflexes indispensable for reading—that is, to respond orally to abstract visual "signals." It also inhibits the learning of visualization (i.e., the formation of visual images), which is so crucial for reading as well as thinking. One 9-year-old boy who had acquired some skill in reading but still suffered from Linear Dyslexia, expressed it in this way: "I only like to read books that have pictures in them. The reason is that if I read I have to make the picture in my mind, and sometimes the picture I make is not like the real picture." By "real picture" he meant those in comic books, in movies, and on television.

This habituation to picture gazing has conditioned many children so that they rely entirely on the pictures they see. They are not able to, or do not dare to, make their own pictures—that is, to have their own fantasy life. They are conditioned to be captives of the mass media. They also lose interest in having someone read to them, because looking at pictures has robbed them of the art of listening. This picture-gazing habit may persist for many years. Very many children never read the text in comic books, or only some bits here and there. An 11-year-old girl boasted about the speed with which she "read" comic books (she actually only picture gazed) in the following way: "I can finish 15 comic books in an hour, that's nothing; I know a girl who can read 25." She demonstrated this to me. It was speed picture gazing. The text neither attracted nor interested her. Thus comic books not only inhibit reading but motivate and condition children against reading. (See Figure 2.2.)

In our study of children's eye movements during comic book reading, Daniels and I found that the child usually first scans the entire left-hand page downward, then comes up from the lower left part of the right-hand page. His eyes stop at the picture with the most exciting action, where the murder is being committed or weapons are used, or where he finds a sexually stimulating pose. If he reads at all, he is apt to read the balloon in that picture first. It may be the only balloon he reads on a whole page. Children, as a rule, skip some pictures and balloons. Where a child tries to follow the text conscientiously, his eyes zigzag of necessity (Mosse & Daniels, 1959).

Ten-year-old Kevin, in the fifth grade, is a typical comic book "reader." He was referred because he had attempted suicide in school. I found a severe reading disability with Linear Dyslexia, not previously diagnosed.

His parents and teachers complained that he read comic books continuously and exclusively even before he entered school. Observing his eye movements, I noticed that he first scanned the entire first page of a comic book, then stopped at the first picture. He read part of the first balloon, skipping words and reversing "ON" into "no." He did not read all the words in any balloon. What he read could not possibly make sense. I asked him to read out loud and recorded what he said. He seemed interested and obviously tried to do well. He read the following: "GOOD NOW MAY BE YOU SO I CAN THE END OF THIS STORY NO TV NOW? MICKEY JUST ABOUT TO NOT SO THAT MAKES YOU SO HA HA MAKE ME LAUGH." This skipping and scattered reading was not due to an inability to read the words he left out. He could read those words. His trouble was one of eye movements.

Many children with Linear Dyslexia read just as Kevin did. They cannot even stick to the small left-to-right direction inside the balloons. Some read one line left to right, the other right to left. Other children make up the story entirely from the pictures and guess the words in the balloons. Nine-year-old Ronnie read a balloon that actually stated: "CRAZY WOLF . . . MY BROTHER . . . IT IS GOOD TO SEE YOU AFTER SO LONG A TIME!" as "It is good to use your rifle, so get a Indian." This not only shows faulty reading technique, but that comic books have also conditioned this child to expect violence and murder.

MISUSE OF COMIC BOOKS FOR REMEDIAL READING.   As comic book "reading" can produce deeply ingrained faulty reading habits in children with a healthy central nervous system, how much more destructive must it be for children with organic defects! For this reason comic books have no place in any classroom, and they should most certainly not be used for remedial reading. Yet teachers and even reading specialists use and recommend them. A "Superman Workbook" has even been produced, and I have seen teachers handing out comic books to "motivate" children to read. If they would only observe exactly how their students "read" these comic books, they would realize that the result is exactly the opposite of what they intended. For this, they must let the children read the text orally, but comic books are used mainly for silent reading, and no one pays any attention to the children's eye movements anyway. To ask children about the content of the comic book story is meaningless from the point of view of reading. They don't need the text for this, not even in those comic books that are unfortunately widely used to teach history.

Not so long ago I visited a "Reading Skills Center" that was being organized in a public school district to help about 1,000 fourth and fifth graders who were retarded in reading. The reading curriculum specialist in charge of distributing the supplies showed me what she and her colleagues had ordered. Among the materials were hundreds of comic books. These were not the usual comic books children buy and trade; they dealt with the history of black people. The intent was laudable, namely to give the students pride in their own history and at the same time to awaken their interest in reading. These comic books, however, could not possibly achieve either goal. Their very format (which was exactly like other comic books)—with crudely drawn pictures, cheap paper, and smudgy print—could only debase the image of a Crispus Attucks or a Frederick Douglass, and the vocabulary was worthy of any crime comic book, for instance, "YOU KILLED HIM, YOU SHOT CRISPUS," or "PFFLAM" scattered all over a page. That scarce dollars were spent on comic books seemed to me an indication that the outcome of this massive remedial reading effort could only be disappointing, with minimal improvement of the children's reading level. This is exactly what happened.

TEACHING METHODS HINDERING LINEAR READING. Foremost among these harmful teaching methods is the whole-word or word/sight technique. Daniels and I have observed the eye movements of children as they were learning to read by this method: In the beginning they are apt to look at a few words; then they look up at the picture searching for a clue, then down at the words again. They look back and forth along the line or the page for a familiar word (Mosse & Daniels, 1959, p. 838). This indicates that the method contains some of the same potentially harmful features we have already pointed out in comic books. The children are taught to look for what are called "picture clues" and "content clues." They thus remain dependent on pictures much longer than they should and do not get used to linear reading from the very beginning. They learn to memorize word by word, as though we still had a different symbol for each word and the alphabet had not been invented (Flesch, 1955; Terman & Walcutt, 1958). They get accustomed to searching for the context first and not trying to figure out the word they are actually seeing. The result is that they learn to guess and not to think. They memorize word forms mechanically without understanding how a word comes about and what it consists of.

The conventional teaching of phonetics in the later grades does not further linear reading either. Not only the first consonant but also the last is stressed when word reading is taught phonetically. This forces the children to look at the last part of the word first in order to figure out the last consonant. The linear left-to-right direction of a word is thus destroyed.

The popular television program, "The Electric Company," has adopted this way of teaching phonetics. An example is a section where the letters "f" and "t" are taught together. An actor sounds out the word "left." The "ft" is colored differently from "le," so that it stands out as if the two letters belonged together. The actor says, "Left with a *ft* sound in it." Actually there is no *ft* phonogram. F and t are different sounds that have nothing in common. A large group of words ending in "ft" is then emphasized orally and in writing on the program. For instance: craft, raft, drift, lift, swift, and shift. This type of teaching forces the child to look at the last part of the word first, from right to left, rather than from left to right. It also makes blending harder for him because he can learn this only by connecting the sounds of the letters from left to right. (See sections on Blending, p. 84; on Inability to Shift, Vol. II, p. 481; and case of Chester, Vol. II, p. 631.)

TEACHING METHODS ENHANCING LINEAR READING.   Foremost among methods that enhance linear reading is phonetics teaching. Children who have been taught from the first grade (with foundations laid in kindergarten when most children enjoy playing around with different sounds) to sound out words approach reading differently. They do not need picture clues. They sound out each word as they see it and in this way remain on the line. From the very first they know no other method but linear reading. They acquire a feeling of self-reliance and security sooner because they can make out words they have never seen before and thus read on their own. They can *then* be taught easily to read whole words at a time, to increase their recognition span, and to read faster.

TEACHING AIDS FOR LINEAR READING.   The most important teaching aid is to have the child write and read on a line from kindergarten on. Children should not be permitted to write letters with crayons in any direction they choose. This is customary in kindergartens all over the country. Children must be made to understand from the very beginning that writing letters is quite different from fingerpainting or coloring. They should be helped to understand that writing letters and words is a skill that requires special techniques. Learning this can still be a lot of fun, as I have observed in kindergartens where this type of teaching reading and writing was stressed. (See Figures 3.9, 3.10, and 3.11, pp. 199.)

The Spaldings suggest a number of helpful linear teaching aids. They advise, for instance, that the teacher rule lines on the chalkboard about 3 inches apart for children through the second grade, and that the top line should be no higher than the tallest child. They also stress that the teacher should stand before, that is to the left of, what is to be read on the chalkboard, and should place the pointing finger *before* the center of the first letter. The teacher should also stand on the left side later on when pointing to words on paper or in a book so that he or she can slide a finger from left to right over what is being read so that the pointing finger is always at the place where the reading is taking place and remains on the line. The authors stress that this is "very helpful for the children who tend to regress, or confuse, the proper directions of letters" (Spalding & Spalding, 1969, p. 52).

I have observed in my many visits to classrooms that these rules are either unknown or not followed. Many teachers tend to stand at the right side of the chalkboard. This leads the children to look at the right part of what has been written first, instead of at the left.

Another aid is the use of hand motions to indicate the sequence of the syllables in a word. The Spaldings use the word, "consonants" as an example. The teacher, facing the class, makes a downbeat with his or her right hand after the children have said the first syllable (i.e., "con"). After the class has said "-so-" the teacher's left hand makes a downbeat. After "-nants" the right crosses over the left hand for the final beat. The children are encouraged to do likewise on their own. This demonstrates the left-to-right direction visually and kinesthetically.

These authors also suggest that students who are not sure which hand represents the first syllable be encouraged to stand before the word written in syllables on the chalkboard and lay one hand on the first syllable and the other on the second syllable. They point out that some students need this physical sensation of the linear left-to-right direction, and that one should not confuse the child by calling his hands left and right. He should instead be helped to find out which hand comes first simply by having him hold it up (Spalding & Spalding, 1969, pp. 77–78). Indeed many children cannot label their hands correctly, and their directional confusion increases when they are told specifically to hold up their right or their left hand. If properly taught, they can learn the left-to-right direction of syllables, words, and entire texts even before they understand the designations "right" and "left." (See Directional Confusion of Letters and Words, p. 99; and Hand Dominance, p. 179.)

For the prevention of Linear Dyslexia as well as other reading disorders, it therefore seems advisable to give the beginning reader a thorough foundation in phonics. Of course, one should also protect him from exposure to comic books, which can do so much damage to the development of good reading habits.

Chapter 3

Writing Disorders

Writing Disorders on an Organic Basis

Writing can be considered the 12th reading act because writing and reading belong together from the point of view of neurophysiology, pathology, and teaching. Children who can write can also read, but there are children who can read but not write. Their writing disorder may be either organically based or due to a neurotic inhibition. The routine examination of a child's writing is important in itself, but it is also indispensable for the diagnosis of a reading disorder. Some children have learned to cover up their reading disorder so well that it becomes apparent only when their writing is tested. They may have managed to memorize words so that they may seem to read with only minor difficulty; only when their writing is tested can reversals, inversions, and transpositions of letters (i.e., directional and spelling difficulties) be noticed. The reading disorder would have been overlooked if writing had not been tested. A child should therefore always be examined for both a reading and a writing disorder, and the disorders should be diagnosed and studied together. (See Chapter 1, Examination, pp. 31, 32; and sections on Directional Confusion of Letters and Words, p. 91 and on Position Reading, p. 112.)

Another reason for testing writing carefully as a routine part of every examination for a reading disorder is that certain organic disorders that are sometimes associated with organic reading disorders—namely apraxia (motor skill difficulties) and acalculia (arithmetic disorder)—are found only when writing is tested. Specific drawing disorders (of persons, maps, clock faces) are also frequently associated with organic writing and reading disorders. Testing of the child's drawing abilities should therefore be included in every reading and writing disorder examination.

Classification

Organic writing disorders are called "agraphia," which is derived from Greek and means inability to write. Neurologists distinguish a "literal" agraphia where the patient cannot write letters, from a "verbal" agraphia where the writing of words is affected (Weinschenk, 1965, p. 121). Some neurologists and psychiatrists call writing disorders in children "developmental agraphia". Agraphia is part of Gerstmann syndrome when it is combined with finger agnosia (inability to locate one's own fingers), disorientation for right and left on one's own body and on others, and acalculia. (See Gerstmann Syndrome, p. 175.)

Diagnosis

Organic writing disorders are difficult or impossible to diagnose in children while they are learning to write because their writing, with its initially poor form and its directional confusion, may look exactly like the writing of a child with an organic defect. The diagnosis must therefore take into consideration the child's age and the level of his emotional and physical development, especially of his motor apparatus and of those parts of his peripheral and central nervous system needed for writing. The child's intellectual capacity is of special importance in this respect, since writing difficulty may be the first indication that his intelligence is defective. Children with mental deficiency usually require much more time than other children to learn to write. Some of them learn to master this skill quite well, but can use it only within the limits of their defective intelligence; others have a specific organic writing disorder just like children with normal intelligence. Just as in organic reading disorders, the diagnosis of mental deficiency must always be considered and ruled out. (See Vol. II, section on Mental Deficiency, p. 410.)

An organic writing disorder should therefore be suspected only where the writing difficulty is severe and has persisted for an unusually long time in spite of careful teaching. One must also be certain that the writing disorder is not just the reflection of a reading disorder, namely that it is not simply due to poor spelling. (See section on Spelling, p. 115.)

A child with a severe organic writing disorder, however, can sometimes be spotted very early. An example of the ease with which this can occasionally be done is the writing of a 6-year-old girl, which I picked out by looking through the pile of papers on the desk of a first-grade teacher (see Figure 3.1). I did not know this girl. When I asked the teacher about the child whose writing seemed to indicate a severe organic defect, she said that she had already referred her to the school psychologist for testing. When she mentioned the girl's name I remembered that I had examined her brother, who had such a severe organic reading and writing disorder that I had recommended his transfer to a class for brain-injured children. This shows how important it is to observe all siblings of children with organic reading and writing disorders with special care, because several siblings may have been exposed to the same pathogenic factors, even though these factors may be unknown, or their disorder may have a hereditary basis. (See section on Heredity, p. 58, and case of Doug, p. 97.)

This girl's teacher had indeed observed her carefully and made a timely referral. It is important to make the differential diagnosis among delayed development in a child of normal intelligence, mental deficiency, and an organic reading and writing disorder early, so that remedial measures can be planned while the child is still a beginner. Every child who cannot learn to write letters during the first grade should have a psychologic examination and, depending on its outcome, a neurologic and a psychiatric examination as well. These differential diagnoses cannot possibly be made on the basis of group tests or with other abbreviated methods.

FIG. 3.1.   Writing of 6-year-old girl in 1st grade. I picked it out from a pile of work on a teacher's desk as indicating a severe organic impairment. Girl's brother also had an organic writing and reading disorder.

The Organic Basis of Writing

The Cerebral Writing Apparatus

The neurophysiologic basis of writing is a combination of motor, acoustic, kinesthetic, praxic, visual, and gnostic elements. The cerebral writing apparatus overlaps partially with the reading apparatus. Just as there is no reading center, so there is no writing center either; but there is a motor area in the middle frontal convolution in the frontal lobes that is crucial for the motor activity of writing. It is located between the motor area for eye movements which lies in front of it, and the anterior central gyrus behind it which contains the motor areas for arm and hand. Next to these lies the motor area for mouth movements (Liebman, 1979, pp. 19–20, Plate 7–1). This motor writing area integrates all movements needed for writing. Area 39, which is of such importance for reading, also plays an important role in writing. Lesions in this area always cause writing as well as reading disorders, whereas lesions in the motor writing area affect writing only. Not only that part of the parietal lobes where area 39 is located is important for writing, but also those other parts where the projection fields for spatial orientation and for manual skills are located. (See Figure 2.1, p. 47.)

Organic Basis of Manual Skills

A precondition for writing is, of course, that the arm is not paralyzed and that the motor tracts connecting the motor areas in the cortex with the arm are intact and functioning. The crucial role the hand plays in writing as well as in other vital skills is reflected in the brain by its extensive cortical representation, which is not strictly limited to the anterior central gyrus. Critchley reports that "electrical stimulation over a very wide area will produce motor or sensory effects referred to the hand—even though this area is not rigidly predetermined on a point-to-point principle," and that "very extensive ablations or lesions are necessary to abolish entirely all power of movement from the hand" (Critchley, 1953, p. 210). Just as the cortical areas needed for reading exist only in man, so are the hands with their hairless palms, their long and mobile thumb, the wide abductive range of their fingers, and the ample pronation and supination of the forearms with their wide cortical representation peculiar to man. Fine manual skills are a uniquely human faculty. We cannot understand man's highest neurophysiologic performances such as reading and writing by studying animals. This is at present a popular approach, which must lead to a dead end so far as these performances are concerned. As a matter of fact, the development of the hand through the use of tools and by other types of manual labor played an important role in the transition from ape to man, as Engels has shown (Engels, 1954, p. 228).

In order to write, the child must be able to see two-dimensional forms clearly, to distinguish figure from background, to hold a pen or pencil properly, to guide his hands with his eyes, to move one hand and his eyes from left to right on a line and be able to time all these movements properly; he also must steady his notebook or paper with the nonwriting hand and move them upward as needed; he must have an appreciation of the spatial relationships among his head, his arms, the surface he is writing on, and the surface he is copying from. Kinesthetic and tactile as well as proprioceptive (namely, arising in muscles, tendons, joints) sensations are involved in writing.

When copying from a blackboard which is at some distance from the child's desk, his far vision must be intact, and convergence, accommodation, and fusion have to work properly and at the necessary speed so that he can see clearly what he is writing when he looks down at his paper. All this requires the intactness of all afferent visual tracts arising in his eyes and proceeding via subcortical structures to the visual areas in the occipital lobes. From here, impulses must travel without interference and at the required speed via association tracts to pertinent areas in the parietal lobes and to the motor areas in the frontal lobes, which can then direct the motor movements of the arm, hand, and eyes. The opposite route, from fingers via subcortical and cortical areas to the eyes, must also be in complete working order so that impulses and messages can constantly flow in both directions to check on and correct the entire activity of writing.

Fine proprioceptive and kinesthetic sensations play a special role in writing. The labyrinth (the organ of balance) in the inner ear and the cerebellum, which coordinates fine movements with different positions of the body, must therefore function perfectly. Children with cerebral palsy, whose cerebellar functions are almost always defective, therefore usually have great difficulty learning to write. Typing may be easier for them. (See section on Cerebral Palsy, Vol. II, p. 428.)

The wide overlapping of the cerebral reading, writing, and speech apparatuses explains why agraphias rarely occur alone, but are usually combined with an alexia, an aphasia, or both. Leischner who has made the most extensive study of agraphias in children to date, found that in all his 60 cases it was part of an aphasic syndrome (Leischner, 1969, p. 155). In some of the children he studied, parietal damage had occurred before they were old enough to learn to write (p. 167). I, too, have never seen an isolated organic writing disorder in a child.

ROLE OF HEMISPHERES.   The cortical areas needed for writing are, just as those for reading, present in both hemispheres. A child can be taught to write with either hand, not only with his dominant hand. Writing is less dependent on the organization of all the pertinent areas in one hemisphere only, and is therefore not always affected by a lesion in the dominant hemisphere that damages reading and speech. Writing requires one hand only, but it is easier to learn and to perform when both hands are functioning. (see The Role of Hemispheric Dominance, p. 58; and Hand Dominance, p. 179.)

Historic Development of Writing

Writing is based on the impulse to draw, which is inborn, spontaneous, present universally in all children, and does not have to be learned. Whereas drawing requires study, practice, and a special talent if it is to rise above its rudimentary inborn stage, writing can be learned without any special talent. As a matter of historic fact, alphabet writing was invented primarily because it is simpler, easier to learn, and can be done faster than any other style of writing. Any child with a healthy peripheral and central nervous system can learn to write letters and numbers.

The invention of the alphabet has played an enormous role in facilitating and speeding up communication between individuals, peoples, countries, and cultures. It was as fundamental for the advance of civilization as was the invention of Arabic numbers. Modern mathematics could not have been performed with the Roman numerals used previously.

Writing and drawing are closely related neurophysiologically, psychologically, and also historically. Drawing was the beginning of writing and reading. Human beings had to overcome an enormous hurdle before they could draw. It was a new biologic and social development for them. Primitive human beings could see and recognize a deer, another person, a fire, how a man killed another man, and the like. All these were three-dimensional objects that animals can also see. What primitive humans could not do was to see and to recognize two-dimensional designs on a flat surface. It must have taken thousands of years before they realized that a two-dimensional form on a flat surface could look like a three-dimensional object. It is possible that observing images in clouds or recognizing shadows planted this idea in their heads. Recognizing the shape and meaning of shadows may have been the first step in reading. The next step must have been that they themselves started to draw all sorts of objects on flat surfaces.

This development occurred only in humans. Animals cannot recognize two-dimensional designs on flat surfaces. For instance, dogs and cats may respond to the audio part of television, but they cannot recognize the picture images.

It is important to note that some children with an organic writing and reading disorder also have trouble transposing three-dimensional objects to a flat surface and recognizing two-dimensional forms. This is a symptom of constructional apraxia, a defect in the function of the parietal lobes. (See Constructional Apraxia, p. 159.)

Cave drawings were the first drawings made by humans. They represented concrete objects, people, and animals. They were the first written messages. Primitive humans did not draw a deer as a deer; it was either a message or had to do with death and burial or with their gods. Eventually these became more stylized and developed into pictographs, where each miniature representation of a person, an animal, an object, or an action stood for a word. The next historic step was the combination of pictographs to form ideographs (i.e., graphic representations of ideas and words). Here, symbols were used to represent words and not sounds, as in alphabetic writing. In Chinese writing, for instance, the symbols for sun and moon are joined to read "bright," or those for a woman and child to obtain "happy." A house and a woman combined read "safe" in both Chinese and Korean to this day.

The first people to change from drawing to writing may have been the ancient Sumerians, who lived in the Tigris-Euphrates valley more than 5,000 years ago. Originators of their script apparently were priests and administrators who needed a system for keeping track of property and activities. Part of their drive to simplify probably came from the urge for greater speed, partly from the writing materials used (triangular stylus on clay tablets), but their cuneiform writing remained basically pictographs or complex ideographs. Babylonians, Hittites, Egyptians, Chinese, Mayas, and Aztecs developed a system of writing much like the Sumerians, but none developed an alphabet.

It is not known exactly when and how the transition from ideographic writing to an alphabet occurred. One theory is that it happened when less-cultured outsiders came into contact with the Egyptians; an illiterate people might have mistaken the names of objects represented by various symbols as simply the sounds of each word. The word "alphabet" itself supports this theory of transition: It is the Greek version of the Semitic "aleph" and "beth," the first two letters of the early Semitic alphabet; "aleph" means ox, and the letter "A" developed from the picture of an ox head; "beth" means house, and "B" started out as a pictograph of a house, and so on, through the entire alphabet (Figure 3.2).

According to Greek legend, Cadmus of Thebes brought the alphabet from Phoenicia about 1500 BC, but most scholars believe it happened later. The biggest improvement made by the Greeks was to give vowel sounds to some of the Semitic letters, all of which were consonants, and to add a few of their own. The Etruscans later took over the Greek letters, modified them, and passed them on to the Romans, who made further changes before giving the Roman alphabet to Western Europe. We still use the same letters to write English ("Words and Science," *MD*, 1959, pp. 77–78). Their forms have remained, but their sounds differ in different languages and have even changed within each language over the centuries. That is the reason English spelling is so very difficult to learn. It has remained unchanged over the centuries while the pronunciation and often also the meaning of words have changed. (See section on Spelling, p. 115.)

Writing requires the formation of conditioned reflexes, which have to connect letters with the kinesthetic–motor act of writing, just as the conditioned reflexes needed for reading connect letters with the kinesthetic–motor act of speech. The visual signal is the same in both. It is actually seen only while copying and must be visualized while writing to dictation or during spontaneous writing. The neurophysiologic route is also the same, via the same engram complex that links the visual form of the letter with its sound. Writing strengthens the visual part of the engram complex, reading the acoustic part; both complement each other. (See Conditioned Reflexes, p. 78.)

The Three Writing Acts

Writing involves three different acts: (1) copying, (2) writing to dictation, and (3) spontaneous writing. These acts must be tested separately for a writing disorder diagnosis, and teachers have to make certain that the child can perform all three. Parents as well as teachers are too apt to assume that a child can write when his notebook shows carefully written words and sentences. Unless they ask the child to read out loud what he has written, they may not notice that he can only copy, but not write to dictation or spontaneously.

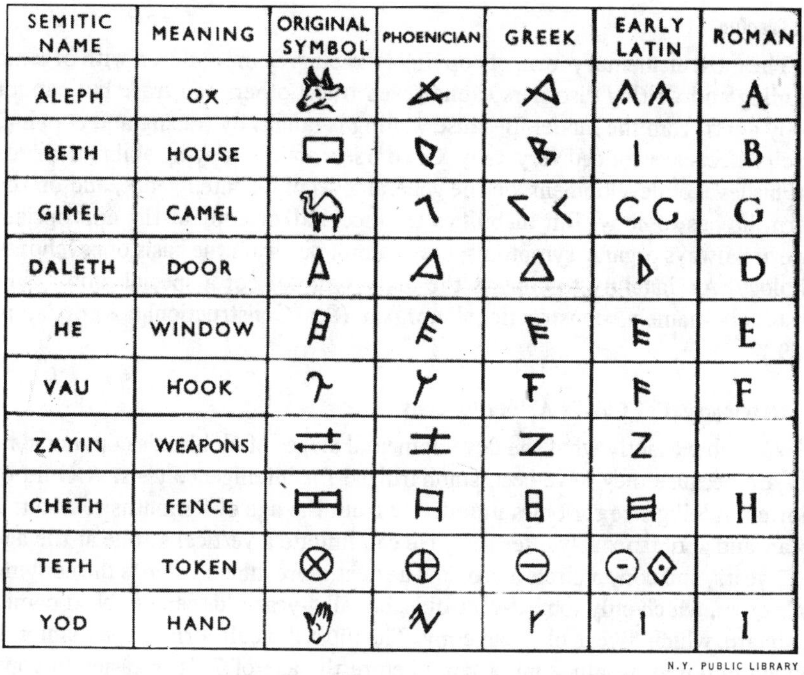

SEMITIC NAME	MEANING	ORIGINAL SYMBOL	PHOENICIAN	GREEK	EARLY LATIN	ROMAN
ALEPH	OX	🐂	↗	A	ΛΛ	A
BETH	HOUSE	⊐	ϙ	฿	l	B
GIMEL	CAMEL	🐪	˥	⟨⟨	C G	G
DALETH	DOOR	Δ	Δ	Δ	▷	D
HE	WINDOW	β	ᴲ	Ⅎ	E	E
VAU	HOOK	Ⴤ	Υ	F	F	F
ZAYIN	WEAPONS	⇄	∓	Z	Z	
CHETH	FENCE	ᗗ	⊟	日	目	H
TETH	TOKEN	⊗	⊕	⊖	⊙ ◇	
YOD	HAND	✋	ᴎ	Υ	ı	I

FIG. 3.2. Historic development of writing from pictographs to ideographs to an alphabet.

Teachers are in the habit of writing homework and other lessons on the blackboard for the children to copy, and this is what such children do conscientiously.

1. Copying

There are two types of copying: the "servile" type where the child copies exactly what he sees, and a more involved type where he copies in his own style of writing, for instance from print into cursive writing. This is more difficult to do because it requires the ability to transcribe from one letter form into another. It is less mechanical and requires some understanding of what is being copied, but can also be done by a child who cannot read.

Isolated copying disabilities have been described in adults who knew how to write before the onset of the cerebral illness or injury that caused this symptom (Leischner, 1969, p. 149). Such a symptom can, of course, not remain isolated in children who are learning to write, but invariably affects all their writing. A child who cannot copy cannot learn to write.

Tracing

The most elementary form of copying is tracing. Some children with organic reading and writing disorders cannot even trace; others can trace but cannot copy apart from the model. Because writing is taught by tracing and copying, such defects are noticed very early. Of course a child's copying ability depends on his level of development, on the general level of his intelligence, and on the form he has to copy. But inabilities to trace and/or copy at the appropriate age are always organic symptoms; they cannot occur on the basis of psychopathology. An inability to copy is the main symptom of a special motor skill disorder—namely, constructional apraxia (See Constructional Apraxia, p. 159.)

Development of Child's Ability to Copy

We know exactly what the developmental stages of children's copying ability are because they have been standardized for intelligence tests. A child of normal intelligence scribbles imitatively from the age of 9 months to about 1 year, and spontaneously after that. He can imitate a vertical stroke at the age of 2 years, and copy a circle at age 3. The next more difficult step is the copying of a cross, which only some 3-year-olds, but all 4-year-olds can do. Next comes a square, which 5-year-olds can copy. The most difficult form is the diamond, which children usually cannot copy before the age of 7. It is easier to copy manuscript letters than squares or diamonds because they are composed only of lines, circles, and crosses. Writing can and should therefore be started in kindergarten (Terman & Merrill, 1937, p. 201).

2. Writing to Dictation

Writing to dictation is a higher level performance than copying. It requires spelling, which means conditioned reflex formation with firm visual and acoustic images. Some children with organic reading and writing disorders can spell orally but have trouble memorizing letter forms so that they cannot write the words or even single letters down on dictation. Others cannot form the necessary acoustic image or cannot connect the acoustic with the visual image. Their defects are identical with those found in organic spelling disorders, with the added difficulty found in some such children, who cannot form the kinesthetic–motor image of letters needed for writing. This inability to form and retain motor movement patterns is part of a motor-skill disorder called ideational apraxia (See section on Ideational Apraxia, p. 159.)

These children often recognize the letters correctly when they see them, but just cannot remember their form when they have to write them. It is characteristic for these children that their performance fluctuates from one day to the next and even within the same day. They may have written a letter or even a word correctly in the morning, but cannot do it in the afternoon. Theirs is a specific memory disorder. (See Role of Memory, p. 69.)

CYRUS, 9 YEARS OLD: HE COULDN'T REMEMBER HOW TO WRITE LETTERS.
Nine-year-old Cyrus is a good example for this difficulty. He had a neglected organic reading, writing, and arithmetic disorder diagnosed by me when he was 8 years old. He had apparently been totally confused by ITA (the Initial Teaching Alphabet, which uses different letter forms for different sounds), which was taught in his first two grades, and had given up trying. After about 6 months of psychotherapy with me and special attention in his classroom by a most patient and understanding teacher, he finally managed to remember how to write all letters, but not how to read them. He was so proud of this achievement that he ran to the blackboard as soon as he entered my office and wrote one line of letters after another, filling the entire board. Then he stepped back, looked proudly at his production and asked me, "What did I write?" He was disappointed when I sounded the letters one after the other as he had written them, and only nonsense resulted. He was delighted when I picked some letters out of sequence and pronounced the word they made. This blackboard writing became a game in his sessions with me and helped him at least to understand what it was he had to learn. It was impossible to provide the remedial reading therapy this boy needed so desperately. His school did not offer it, his mother could not afford it privately, and the waiting lists of clinics were too long. His plight was unfortunately not exceptional.

Writing to dictation can be used as a test to find out whether the child can read and write, and is also an indispensable teaching method for both. The beginner should not be permitted to read what he cannot write, nor to write what he cannot read, and dictation assures that he learns both. It is the surest way to fix the engram complex between the visual form of letters and letter combinations and their speech sounds firmly in the child's mind. It is also an important remedial method for children with all forms of reading disorders, whether or not they have an organic causation.

Dictation forces the child to pay the closest attention to the minutiae of the pronunciation of formal English. Words, and shades of sounds within words, sound different when words alone or when sentences, paragraphs, or entire stories are dictated. The rhythm, sound level, speed, emphasis of the teacher's voice, all affect the sounds of words, even if only slightly. This makes writing to dictation more difficult, but helps the child achieve more confidence in his writing as well as reading. Writing of an entire paragraph must become one automatic habit. For this reason and also because it helps develop linear eye movements with the return sweep, dictation should not be limited to so-called spelling words, as it so often is, but should include paragraphs and stories.

We can always be certain that a child who can write to dictation can also read, but we cannot be sure that a child who can read can also write to dictation. Dictation tests reading and writing at the same time and is therefore superior to all the group reading tests presently in use. It seems to me to be much more reliable and fair.

It is unfortunately not sufficiently appreciated how important dictation is as a remedial technique. Remedial reading teachers usually do not dictate to the child and do not let him write on his own either. Reading improvement programs in college also neglect both practices, as the results show. I know of college students whose reading according to tests was raised to so-called college level, but who could not take notes (which is writing to dictation), write letters, or do any other writing assignment properly because they could not write spontaneously.

3.   Spontaneous Writing

Spontaneous writing is obviously the goal of teaching a child to write. It is the highest neurophysiologic and psychologic performance and more difficult to accomplish than reading. Children should be told in the very beginning that whatever they can say they can write, and that this is what writing was invented for. This will prolong and enhance the enthusiasm for writing that all children have when they enter school, and will enable them to approach the unavoidable drudgery needed to acquire the basic skill with greater interest, and to learn it as fast as they possibly can.

The advent of the tape recorder has taken the thrill out of writing for many children, just as television has taken it out of reading for many of them. It is so much easier to record one's stories and ideas on the tape recorder and to give messages over the phone, so why write? The best way to make writing exciting or at least interesting for kindergarten pupils and first graders is by teaching it so well and so fast that the child soon experiences the pride and satisfaction that come naturally with the mastery of any skill, especially one that makes it possible to create something of one's very own, which can even be done secretly. The little messages children write to each other are evidence for this. Classroom desks and workbooks are treasures of children's notes, many of them illustrated. Their emphasis is on love and friendship (occasionally frankly sexual even in elementary school), but some involve business deals, little intrigues, jokes, anger, or hatred. These are the small joys spontaneous writing makes possible for children (Figure 3.3). On a much higher level, writing more than any other skill forces the child to organize his thoughts, fantasies, and ideas. In this way he learns to think, eventually to think independently and to develop any creative talent he may have. This is true regardless whether the child has an intellectual bent or a more concrete, practical orientation.

Writing Automatisms

When examining a child for defects in spontaneous writing, we must keep in mind that there are writing automatisms that are written without thinking. These are familiar words and sentences that have been learned early in life.

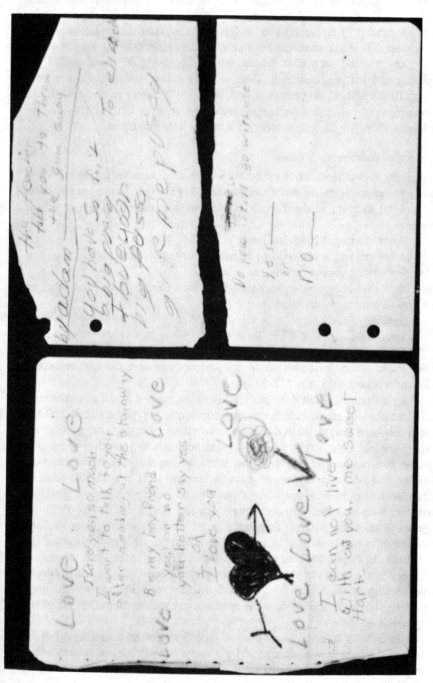

FIG. 3.3. Rewards for being able to write. Secret notes found in desks of a 5th grade class (ages 10 to 11).

They are called "geläufige Reihen" in German, (i.e., familiar distinct sequences or series). These automatisms have been observed primarily in adults where they are retained even after severe damage to the brain areas needed for reading and writing (Leischner, 1969, p. 168). Name, address, and numbers up to 10 are such writing automatisms. We must therefore not be misled into thinking that a child can write spontaneously when he writes his name and address. (See Vol. II, Impairment of Automatic Mechanisms, p. 470.)

Tests of Spontaneous Writing

Testing spontaneous writing requires that we find out whether the child can write sentences, texts, an entire story under the following four circumstances:

1. After listening to the material while someone reads it to him or tells it to him
2. After reading it himself silently
3. After reading it out loud or telling a story spontaneously
4. By writing spontaneously and silently

The child should be able to accomplish all four. We must also test whether he can recognize his mistakes in

1. Spelling
2. Grammar
3. Choice of words
4. Punctuation, including where one sentence ends and the next one starts (Feuchtwanger, 1929, pp. 512–513).

The results of such an examination are much more difficult to evaluate in children than in adults because we can frequently not be sure how well the child has been taught. I have seen papers written by bright college students who were not always sure where one sentence ends and another one starts, whose punctuation did not make any sense, whose sentence structures were erratic, and whose knowledge of grammar seemed to be nonexistent. College professors have been complaining about this for years. We cannot therefore assume, without other corroborating evidence, that a child with defective spontaneous writing suffers from an organic reading/writing disorder. The content of what is written is not as important for this evaluation as the structure. Both are obviously connected to a certain extent and always influenced by the child's level of intelligence, stage of development, and the depth and breadth of his knowledge. A child with average intelligence and good teaching should be able to do some spontaneous writing from the end of the first grade on.

Children with organic reading/writing disorders often make the most pathetic and energetic attempts to write a story, a book report, or any other composition requested by the teacher. (See case of Doug and Figure 11.1 in Vol. II, Perseveration, p. 487.) Their garbled spelling makes only parts of the text intelligible. Yet (as I have mentioned in the section on spelling) it is important to let them write and not to stifle their persistent attempts. It is sometimes possible to decipher what they have written, and teachers and parents should try to do this. The best way to help such a child is to have him write without interruption, ask him to read what he just wrote, and to tell him how to spell the words he misspelled. He can then either correct just these words, or rewrite the entire composition. This takes longer and requires double effort, but it may be best for the child, so that his thoughts are not constantly interrupted by struggling with spelling while he writes.

Spontaneous writing helps all children with their spelling better than rote memorizing of "spelling words," and so does a lot of reading. Repeated seeing and writing of words in an emotionally and intellectually pleasant and interesting content strengthens memory far better than drill. This holds true only where the indispensable minimal technical basis for reading and writing has been mastered by the child.

Importance of Compositions

Composition writing should be a routine part of the entire school curriculum from the first grade on. (See Basic Principles of Teaching Writing, p. 358.) I have observed that spontaneous writing on any subject, freely chosen or suggested by the teacher, is not stressed sufficiently on any level in the schools—whether elementary, junior or even senior high school—in spite of the professed emphasis on "creativity." I mean compositions organized by the child himself, and not the answering of questions printed at the end of a text in a social studies or any other textbook. Thomas Wheeler, who teaches writing and literature to college students, stresses that the "abandoned composition" is a major cause for the inability to write of his and the majority of other college students (Wheeler, 1979, p. 3). I suspect that the mechanization of testing which has almost abolished essay questions, that is questions which must be answered with a spontaneous piece of writing, has something to do with the decline of teaching compositions.

Psychologic Analysis of Spontaneous Writing

The content of what the child writes, whether he invents his own story or writes a book report, tells a lot about him: his thoughts, feelings, conflicts, worries, and preoccupations. An analysis of it should therefore be part of every diagnostic examination. It is, of course, indispensable for psychotherapy. I ask every child and adolescent to let me look at his workbook and at everything else he has written for school or on his own.

DARRYL, 12 YEARS OLD: A SELF-REVEALING ESSAY ON De MAUPASSANT'S *THE NECKLACE*. Twelve-year-old Darryl's book review of *The Necklace* for instance, revealed more about his inner anguish and torturous doubts than about the book he was reviewing. The teacher acknowledged this by commen-

ting: "Good essay on the love of money, but you don't tie it into the story."
Darryl wrote:

> In this story the love for money is worthless. Like in the story necklace was
> worthless. If you are rich or poor love is better than any other thing. This story
> has a great moral. This story was heartbraking. Money sometimes will help you
> but it sometime kill you, like being greedy. Everyone should share and divide and
> don't hide. Money-love is evil. If all people love money this world would be a
> crazy world. Money is good for a lot of things but being greedy and selfish doesn't
> pay for a lot of things. Help yourself don't be greedy.

This is spelled exactly as he wrote it. I had known Darryl since he was 8 years
old. He had an organic reading disorder and a psychoneurosis with recurrent
attacks of anxiety and depression. Remedial reading, psychotherapy, and casework treatment of his mother by the social worker had been so successful that
he had just passed the entrance examination for a prestigious technical high
school. Darryl's deep ethical struggle around greed, selfishness, sharing, and
how large money should loom in anyone's life was revealed in this brief piece
of writing. Darryl was a serious boy who took very seriously all the events in
his life. He was introverted and could not communicate easily. A good, creative teacher would have taken such a revelation as this book review as a
starting point for a free-wheeling class discussion. Darryl and his classmates
were poor and all had basically the same conflicts as he revealed in his book
review. As his psychotherapist, I could help him think his problems through
and find solutions that would make it possible for him to survive in a society
that to a large extent fitted his very definition of "crazy"—namely, one in
which most people love money, are greedy, and don't share. His anguish was
especially acute at the time he wrote the review because his father, a heroin
addict, had very recently pulled out a gun and forced his mother, a nurse, to
give him all her money as well as all the family's pawnable possessions. Darryl
and his sister had witnessed the entire scene.

Of course his teachers did not know any of this, but teachers can help such
children even without knowing all the tragic details of their lives. It may not
even be desirable for teachers to know all their students' life stories, since many
children feel ashamed of and humiliated by their experiences. Darryl and his
sister, for instance, felt very much ashamed of their father's addiction. They
still loved him and did not want anyone outside the family to know about his
affliction (with the exception of the social worker and myself). Still, teachers
can help such children very much by letting them air their thoughts and
feelings in a free discussion of ideas and problems brought up by a story shared
by the class, provided the atmosphere is one of mutual respect, understanding,
and trust. The teacher's most important task during such a general discussion

is to listen, support, and encourage the children's own best ideas and solutions, and to open their horizons to higher and wider viewpoints. Such a discussion about a general problem can help each child with his special problem, if only indirectly. Great writers can express the agony of poverty and the emotions of greed, ambition, hatred, and love better than anyone else; reading what they have to say can help the child rise above his plight and hopefully also to see alternatives to the violent dead-end solutions constantly suggested to him in the mass media (comic books, television, movies). A wise teacher selects books for student review very carefully, so that children can enjoy reading a well-written story, learn about lives and times other than their own, and, incidentally, learn also about themselves.

A child's spontaneous writing lends itself also to other types of psychologic or psychopathologic analyses. A most useful psychotherapeutic technique is, for example, to ask the patient (child, adolescent, or adult) to write a detailed chronologic history of his own life. Such self-written life histories are most revealing. They show not only how the child feels about himself and how he sees himself, but also how he sees all the members of his family and all other people who influenced his life. Such a life history should include a chronologic graph of the main events in his life so that one can see at a glance the chief landmarks of his life and their interrelationships in time. This chronologic relationship by itself sometimes reveals important psychologic connections that may have been forgotten. It was Adolf Meyer who introduced the use of such a life-chart as an aid for the examination and treatment of psychiatric patients (Wertham, 1953b).

Mirror-Writing

Mirror-writing in its literal sense means writing from right to left and rotating all letters and numbers on their vertical axis from right to left. Complete mirror-writing is very rare and may not even be a sign of organic pathology or of any pathology whatsoever. Many children and adults who can write well in the normal left-to-right direction can mirror-write at will. Even though a connection between left-handedness and mirror-writing is widely assumed to exist, right-handers can mirror-write just as well as left-handers. Hecaen and de Ajuriaguerra, in *Left-Handedness, Manual Superiority and Cerebral Dominance* (1964) report the results of a study of 423 subjects aged 6 years to adulthood, whom they asked to write with their left hand starting at the right side of the page and rotating all letters to the left. They found a positive correlation of mirror-writing with age, but not with handedness. The capacity to mirror-write increased with age, probably because of a better understanding of the task. They concluded that "in general, the percentage of mirror-writing in the left-handed is nearly the same as in the right-handed, but one sometimes sees a left-handed subject who can mirror-write just as easily as the ordinary right-hander writes in the normal style" (pp. 88–89). (See Directional Confusion of Letters and Words, p. 99.)

Agraphia and Apraxias

Writing requires a special manual skill. Fingers, hand, and arm must be capable of performing coherent and very fine patterns of movement and of repeating these movement patterns in exactly the same way automatically, without one's having to think about each fine detail of the pattern. Inabilities to carry out such special manual and some other motor skills are called "apraxias." An agraphia may be but *one* symptom of an apraxia, in children as well as adults. This aspect of organic writing disorders in children is usually not mentioned. Yet some forms of organic writing disorders and a number of other organic learning disorders (inability to draw and read maps, inability to draw and read the clock face, one type of arithmetic disorder) are due to apraxia. Unless this is diagnosed, the child's learning and consequent behavior disorder will be misunderstood and mistreated.

Apraxic Agraphia

One form of agraphia is called "apraxic agraphia" (Leischner, 1969, p. 141; Lhermitte & Gautier, 1969, p. 95). The motor power of hand and arm muscles is intact in this condition, and the constructional abilities are undisturbed, but coordination of all the muscles involved in writing is defective. This coordination is controlled by the cerebral cortex, so that this agraphia is due to cortical defects.

Amnesic-Apraxic Agraphia

Another form of apraxic agraphia is due to a severe memory defect. Kurt Goldstein described this form in adults and called it "amnesic-apraxic agraphia." Such patients cannot remember letters or distinguish between letters with a similar form. They can distinguish correctly from incorrectly written letters when they see them, but cannot recognize their own mistakes when they write the same letters themselves. They can compare letters, but cannot write them correctly. Their copying ability is often also defective (Leischner, 1969, pp. 143–144). Adults with this disorder have severe brain disease or injury. I have examined children who, while learning to write, had the same symptoms without gross brain involvement. This form of agraphia exists in children, but is usually not diagnosed because children are, as a rule, not tested for such defects with sufficient care.

Apraxia

A child's agraphia is frequently part of an apraxia that affects other motor skills as well. Three types of apraxia can be distinguished: ideomotor, ideational, and constructional (House, Pansky, & Siegel, 1979, p. 485).

IDEOMOTOR APRAXIA. In ideomotor apraxia, only *intended* movements are defective. Writing is an intended movement for a child who is learning it. It has not yet become a habitual motor pattern. Thus when a child has trouble learning to write, one should test his ability to carry out all kinds of intended movements.

IDEATIONAL APRAXIA. In ideational apraxia the formation of *kinesthetic-motor images* is defective. Children suffering from this type of apraxia can trace and copy letters, but cannot write spontaneously, because they can neither form nor retain the images of the kinesthetic-motor movement patterns needed to form letters. These kinesthetic-motor images of letters are just as important for writing as their auditory and visual images. All three images and their firm association are essential for writing to dictation as well as spontaneously. The kinesthetic-motor and visual images strengthen each other, but they apparently can exist independently. A child who is blind or suffers from visual agnosia can learn to write, at least to a certain extent, through forming kinesthetic-motor images.

A child suffering from agraphia due to ideational apraxia can sometimes learn to write *after* he has learned to read because he is then capable of copying motorically the visual image of the letters, which he formed through reading. This is how some children can at least partially overcome their agraphia. Writing will always be cumbersome for them and they cannot learn script, so it is better to teach them to type.

CONSTRUCTIONAL APRAXIA. Symptoms of ideomotor or ideational apraxia occur only very rarely in children with organic reading and writing disorders. Constructional apraxia, however, is much more frequent. Children suffering from this type of apraxia cannot execute the constructional motor actions needed for writing and other manual tasks.

Their visuomotor coordination is intact, but the constructional drawing element essential for forming a letter does not function (Leischner, 1969, pp. 141, 150). This is a parietal lobe symptom, which Critchley, in his standard book on the parietal lobes, defines as "a difficulty in putting together one-dimensional units so as to form two-dimensional figures or patterns" (Critchley, 1953, p. 172). This difficulty is not just due to clumsiness, lack of talent, or slow development. These children fail in formative activities, in arranging, building, drawing, and writing where they miss the spatial part of the task. They cannot put jigsaw puzzles together, build with bricks, draw, or write from copy; as a matter of fact, the inability to copy is a crucial symptom. These children often have greater difficulty with copying than with writing spontaneously (Critchley, 1953, p. 368).

DIAGNOSIS.   Sometimes the child's inability to build with blocks, tinkertoys, and other building materials may give the first indication that his constructional ability is defective. This is yet another reason why the patient and careful observation of a child's play in the classroom and as part of every educational, psychologic, and psychiatric examination is so important. One should guard against the immediate psychoanalytical interpretations of the child's play that are so popular and often so misleading, and rule out developmental deviations or organic symptoms first. Where this is done, kindergarten teachers can sometimes spot constructional difficulties before the child has started to write. Detailed testing for constructional apraxia should then be carried out.

The child's inability to build must of course always be correlated with his age. His constructional difficulties may simply be due to his immaturity and not to a specific neurologic defect. The child's age and the severity of his inability are decisive factors in even considering the diagnosis of constructional apraxia.

TESTS FOR CONSTRUCTIONAL APRAXIA.

Copying Three-Dimensional Models.   The child's ability to build with blocks or with other three-dimensional models should be tested in the following way:

1. Build a model and let the child copy it while he can see the model.

2. Show him the model and remove it before he copies it. This is more difficult to do because the child must be able to form an image of the model and to retain it long enough to build his copy.

3. If he fails in his attempts to copy, count the number of blocks he needs and put them in front of him.

4. If he still fails, build the model block by block with alternating moves, waiting for the child to put his block on his own building in the way he saw you do it. Here, too, you put the required number of blocks in front of the child before you both start.

Children with constructional apraxia try very hard to make an exact copy and often build it right next to the model. This is called the "crowding-in" phenomenon (Critchley, 1953, p. 180). Some even build their copy partially on top of the model or remove a part of the model and use these pieces for their own building in the mistaken hope that this might help them. According to Critchley, this is an example of the "not uncommon confusion between meum and tuum (what belongs to me and what to you) which some parietal patients display" (Critchley, 1953, p. 180). It is important to understand that such a child does not grab the blocks on the examiner's (or on another child's) building out of selfishness or anger, but that this act is an attempt to overcome a neurologic handicap. Such behavior is frequent in classes for brain-injured children and in classes for mental defectives. It may, of course, also be psychologically determined, but all such children should be examined for symptoms of constructional apraxia and the teachers informed of such a diagnosis. Both the examination and the teacher information are unfortunately the exception and not the rule. Some of these children copy a partial or a complete mirror-image of the model. Perseverations are frequent (i.e., the child repeats parts or even the entire model several times). (See Vol. II, Perseveration, p. 487.)

Copying Two-Dimensional Models. The examination of the child's ability to copy two-dimensional models should use the same principles. First the child should be permitted to look at the model while copying it; later the model should be removed before he starts. Two-dimensional models are all types of drawings (geometric forms, figures, letters, and words). The child should make his copy first on the same piece of paper so that some characteristic apraxic approaches are not missed. Apraxic children often try to make their copy by tracing on the model so that their copy is actually superimposed on it. These children can only trace, but cannot copy. (See Copying, p. 150.)

Other children try to hug the model. They use it as a crutch. Perseverations and mirror-image copies are frequent, just as with three-dimensional models. Apraxic children cannot copy a straight line; their lines are oblique or wavy, too short or too long. They cannot make use of the entire space available to them, whether they draw on the same paper or on a separate sheet; instead they crowd their copies into one corner and make them of a different size from the model. They cannot copy geometric forms such as circles, triangles, or rectangles, and cannot bisect such models into two halves with one straight line either.

Spontaneous drawing also presents great difficulty for these children. The diagnosis of constructional apraxia cannot be based on drawing analysis, but it should be kept in mind when a child cannot indicate a perspective at an age when he ought to be able to. He may, for instance, draw a path leading to a house with two lines running parallel to the door instead of towards it.

Role of Bender Visual Motor Gestalt Test and Wechsler Intelligence Scale for Children (WISC). The constructional difficulties I have just described regularly show up on two tests: the Bender Visual Motor Gestalt Test and the block-design part of the WISC. Both, of course, test many functions other than the child's constructional ability, but every child who makes the constructional errors I have described should be studied further neurologically and with other tests for constructional apraxia. Unfortunately, neither Bender nor Wechsler mention constructional apraxia as a differential diagnostic possibility for the interpretation of their tests, and psychologists report the defects they have observed on these tests only in the most general terms, as signs of organicity or of disturbances in perception, without specifying what functions are affected.

Mosaic Test. One psychologic test is more helpful than all others in establishing the diagnosis of constructional apraxia. This is the Mosaic test as interpreted by Wertham, because it requires the arrangement of specially designed blocks into three-dimensional patterns. (See Chapter 1, Examination, p. 25 ff.) Since this is exactly what patients with constructional apraxia find so difficult to do, it takes them an unusually long time to complete any Mosaic design, and they cannot arrange an adequate form no matter how long and how carefully they try. They sometimes put the pieces in one straight line where angles are called for, or pile pieces on top of each other without being able to make the construction they have in mind. The Mosaic pieces also lend themselves to testing the child's ability to copy three-dimensional models.

APRAXIA WITHOUT AGRAPHIA. Children with organic reading disorders occasionally have minor symptoms of constructional apraxia that do not affect their writing or any other important activity. Such a child may, for instance, still find it difficult to dress himself far beyond the age where other children have such difficulty. An "apraxia for dressing" has been described in adults (Hecaen & de Ajuriaguerra, 1964, p. 296). Some of these children fumble badly with tools and utensils and cannot manage knife, spoon, and fork properly. Somewhat more frequent is a child's inability to tie his shoelaces, which he should be able to do by the age of 7 years. He may also have trouble making his bed, and be incapable of putting together and tying up a package.

DIFFICULTY WITH IMITATION OF MOVEMENTS. One other symptom apraxic children may have is an inability to imitate movements and to do pantomime. They often can imitate movements, but only while they see them, not on verbal command. When asked to make a certain gesture, for instance, while the examiner is making a different one, the child will simply imitate what the examiner is doing. This symptom is called "echopraxia." Some children cannot copy with one hand the attitudes and gestures of their other hand. The diagnosis of constructional apraxia, however, should not be based on any one of such minor symptoms alone. It should not even be considered unless a number of minor symptoms are combined with major defects and verified by a neurologic examination and by tests.

Spatial Disorientation

A careful examination for constructional apraxia is not only important for the practical care of the individual child, but is also essential for solving the larger problems of the relationship between difficulties in spatial orientation and organic reading and writing disorders. In the literature on reading disorders, spatial disorientation is discussed in terms that are much too general. The spatial difficulties of affected children are actually very specific and can be clearly defined. They often involve manual skills only, and fall within Critchley's and Schilder's definition of constructional apraxia. Critchley feels that these patients have "some type of defective orientation in space, but a defect which may not emerge until a motor task is attempted within a visual sphere" (Critchley, 1953, p. 190). Schilder explains these special spatial symptoms in the following way: "One must admit that apraxia can be due to a fault in the transpositions of the conceptions of space to manual activity, without the conception of space being in itself disordered" (Critchley, 1953, p. 196).

Map-Reading Disorder

Some children cannot visualize three-dimensional objects and transpose them into two-dimensional designs. (See section on Historic Development of Writing, p. 146.) This is considered a symptom of constructional apraxia. These children find it impossible or at least extremely difficult to read and to draw maps and blueprints. This learning disorder becomes apparent in the early grades, as soon as the child has to make a plan of the neighborhood in which he lives and is taught other aspects of map making. Such activities are usually included in the curriculum by the second or third grade. A test of the child's map-reading and -drawing ability should therefore be part of the examination of every child with a reading and writing disorder.

I ask the child to draw a plan of his apartment or house and to indicate the location of all doors, windows, beds, and other important pieces of furniture, for instance, television sets. Such a map is useful not only for the diagnosis of constructional apraxia, but also for an understanding of the child's living situation. It shows important details of the child's daily life. Sleeping arrangements, privacy or lack of it, fears of the dark, anxieties connected with going to the bathroom alone at night (which may be the cause of bedwetting), are sometimes revealed for the first time while the child is drawing such a plan. I have every child who is in psychotherapy with me draw such a plan.

Children with a map-reading and -drawing disorder on an organic basis get low marks quite undeservedly unless their learning disorder is recognized as organic and therefore as beyond their control. Teachers should be informed that this learning disorder can be caused by an organic impairment so that they refer such a child for a psychologic, a neurologic, and, if also indicated, a psychiatric examination *early.*

Clock-Reading Disorder

Almost all children with an organic reading and writing disorder find it most difficult to learn to read and to set the clock, that is, to learn to tell time. This may be one more symptom of constructional apraxia. A clock has a complex spatial construction involving not just the ordinary three space dimensions of length, width, and depth (the hands lie above the clock face), but also what the theory of relativity considers a fourth dimension—namely, time. The ability to read and to set the clock requires spatial manipulation and visualization, which must be coupled with the concept of time, partially a spatial concept. Time changes constantly; this means that it is in constant movement, that it changes its place on the clock constantly. To understand the difference between past, present, and future requires a sense of spatial dimensions.

There is a distance between yesterday, today, and tomorrow. A child not aware of this distance experiences daily life as chaotic, confusing, unpredictable, and anxiety-provoking.

A clock-reading disorder is not always associated with a disordered concept of time; learning to read a digital watch or clock helps only those children whose time concept is intact.

DISORDERED CONCEPT OF TIME. Time accompanies all mental activity, whether conscious, preconscious, or unconscious. Lack of a concept of time is always a serious symptom, whether it is based on an organic handicap or, as is infinitely more frequent, on a neurotic process. A child with a reading and writing disorder on an organic basis who has no time concept in addition to a clock-reading disorder is much more handicapped also psychologically than a child with the same disorders whose time sense is not impaired. Some of these children's disturbing and disruptive behavioral symptoms (dawdling, restlessness, and apparent drivenness, which is actually a constant feeling of having to meet an unpredictable deadline at any time) are due to their lack of time sense. These children suffer from a special form of disorientation, in that they cannot judge the passage of time. It is very difficult for them to estimate the approximate hour of the day except by a laborious process of trying to remember when they had their last meal or of some other such clue. Frequently they cannot describe the sequences of simple habitual daily activities.

LOCALIZATION OF TIME CONCEPT. The spatial aspects of this concept involve the parietal lobes. However, memory and intelligence are also indispensable for understanding the flow of time. Parts of the temporal and frontal lobes, therefore, also form its organic basis (Critchley, 1953, pp. 351,352).

The learning as well as the behavioral symptoms of all disturbed children should be carefully analyzed to determine what role the child's disordered time concept plays in their causation. (See Time Sense Neurosis, Vol. II under Hyperactivity, p. 646.)

TESTS FOR CLOCK-READING DISORDER. The child's ability to read and to set the clock should be tested with a toy clock. Of course, one must first find out whether he has been taught to tell time, and whether he is old enough to learn it. Most children do not learn to tell time before 8 years of age. Children with constructional apraxia have great trouble remembering what the difference in the length of the hands of the clock means, and to distinguish minutes from hours. The sequence of the numbers on the clock face also presents formidable obstacles for them. It is not unusual for these children to confuse 15 minutes before the hour with 15 minutes past the hour. All children have this trouble when they learn to tell time, but these children continue to make such mistakes for years beyond the age of 8.

One should also test the child's clock-reading ability by letting him draw a clock face. I have made this a routine part of my psychiatric examination whenever I suspect an organic reading and writing disorder. (See Chapter 1, Examination, p. 31.) This test consists of two parts: first, letting the child copy a clock face and then letting him draw one on his own. These children sometimes can draw a circle, but they cannot insert the numbers in correct sequence. They may crowd them in correct or incorrect sequence into one-half of the dial, or string them vertically underneath each other, often extending beyond the outline of the clock face. This difficulty in correct sequencing and in distinguishing clockwise from counter-clockwise directions are problems most children with a reading and writing disorder on an organic basic have anyway; it is not necessarily caused only by constructional apraxia.

TREATMENT. As one remedial technique to help the child get the feeling of clockwise movement and of clockwise number sequence, I suggest to the child and to his parents that he practice dialing on a toy or a real telephone (while leaving the receiver on the hook, of course, so that telephone service is not interrupted). The intentional movement required of the child is clockwise; the dial snaps back on its own in counter-clockwise direction. This intentional circular finger movement gives the child a visual and at the same time a kinesthetic-motor experience of a clockwise direction. He should practice this with each hand separately. This is only one of many corrective practices for such children. It is easily accessible, simple, and fun for the child to do.

Differential Diagnosis of Clock-Reading Disorders

VISUAL AGNOSIA. Not all clock-reading disorders of children with reading and writing disorders on an organic basis are due to constructional apraxia, however. They may also be due to visual agnosia, an inability to perceive the clock as a whole, to understand what it means, and to make use of its function. How such agnosia affects a patient was described by Wertham. He recounted his own experience with a clock agnosia that was caused by a toxic reaction to scopolamine administered during an operation performed under local anesthesia. His experience was the following:

> When I looked at the clock, I saw numbers in a circle. I recall particularly the 6 and the 7. I said to myself that the position of the numbers on the clock—at the top, the bottom or the side—had a meaning for telling time. But I could not figure out how. I remembered that each number meant something. But I was not sure how one picked a special number. I do not know whether or not I saw the clock's hands. At any rate, I did not comprehend that they pointed to numbers.

This is very much the way children with this type of clock reading disorder feel when they look at a clock (1945, p. 371; 1946, p. 160; 1952, p. 107).

Treatment.   Remedial methods must be structured according to these diagnostic differences. A child who cannot learn to tell time because he has visual agnosia needs a different approach to overcome this impairment than a child whose clock-reading disorder is due to constructional apraxia.

ORGANIC ARITHMETIC DISORDER (ACALCULIA) DUE TO CONSTRUCTIONAL APRAXIA.   Many children with an organic reading and writing disorder have not only a letter-writing, but also a number-writing disorder. Where this number-writing disorder is primarily due to an inability to *arrange* numbers, it is a symptom of constructional apraxia. There are other organic arithmetic disorders such as the acalculia that is part of the Gerstmann syndrome. (See this syndrome, p. 175; number writing, p. 207; and Chapter 4, Arithmetic Disorders, p. 221.)

It is important to realize that a child may fail in arithmetic because he cannot put numbers under or next to each other in correct sequence, and that this may be caused by an organic cerebral impairment. This is not simply due to a confusion of right and left, as is so frequently assumed, but to an inability to make spatial arrangements.

These children cannot write two-digit numbers above 10 correctly, and their mistakes become worse the longer the number sequence is. When told to write 156, for instance, they put down any combination of these three numbers (165, 651, 561, 516, 165), and only accidentally the right one. They cannot write numbers properly in a row underneath each other for additions or substractions either; they thus hopelessly confuse multiplications and especially divisions, because they cannot write the problems down properly unless they copy them, and they cannot understand the arrangement of the different numbers necessary for the problem's solution. The importance for the child's entire future of diagnosing this impairment correctly early is obvious.

Number writing should be tested routinely together with letter-writing ability (See Chapter 1, Examination, pp. 31, 33; and section on number writing, p. 208). These children cannot use the abacus or a bead frame for the same reason—that is, they cannot learn to arrange the beads. They are especially handicapped where "sets" and other mathematical concepts are taught in the lower grades.

Movement-Blindness

A special form of apraxia that only occurs in children is the condition Lise Gellner called "movement-blindness" (Gellner, 1953, 1957, 1959). (See Blindness for Visual Meaning, and Visual Agnosia, p. 165.)

Gellner's hypothesis is that these children's cerebral impairment lies in the midbrain ganglia called superior colliculi. These ganglia mediate the visuosomatic system. According to Gellner, they perform in the following way when they are intact:

> They receive visual fiber tracts emanating from the periphery of the retina, and proprioceptive or kinesthetic fiber tracts from the eye muscles and from all the somatic tissues of the body, that is, from muscles, tendons and joints of trunk and limbs. All the impulses carried in fibers from these two sources are integrated in the superior colliculi. The newly integrated impulse then travels through descending fibers back to the eye muscles and the various somatic body structures, mainly the muscles of the neck, arms and hands, where it produces visual reflexes and is also responsible for all activities based on visuomotor co-ordination (1959, p. 14).

She stresses that the fiber tracts ascending from the superior colliculi to other ganglia and to the cortex are still largely unknown, but that their existence cannot be doubted. (See Liebman, 1979, Plate IX, p. 90; Noback & Demarest, 1977, Figure 16.1, p. 142.)

Gellner assumes that movement-blindness is caused by damage to the superior colliculi that interferes with the production of visuomotor reflexes and with all activities based on visuomotor coordination. She stresses that this interference hampers the development of the child's intelligence decisively because it deprives him of the ability to imitate seen movement, copy visual patterns, distinguish forms, perceive depth, and so on. Some of these symptoms are also found in constructional apraxia, but the total clinical picture is different.

"Movement-blind" children cannot use their hands under the control of their eyes for any activity including writing. Their vision of movement is defective as well as all the movements they must learn to control by their vision. As infants, they do not follow moving lights with their eyes, and blindness is often suspected. However, eye examinations show no defects until the child is old enough for an examination of the visual fields. Only then can the diagnosis of a visual field anomaly be made. Their visual fields are narrowed and hose-shaped. Their retinas sometimes appear less bright than normal, and their visual reflexes are frequently weak. These children sometimes have a nystagmus and convergence defects. Their space perception is always defective.

The infantile eye symptoms of these children are striking and puzzling and prone to misinterpretation. Not only do they not follow light with their eyes, but they move their eyes only in response to sound; they also do not play with their fingers in front of their face like other babies aged 3 to 6 months. There are references to these very symptoms in the literature on childhood schizophrenia and Early Infantile Autism (Fish, 1960; Mosse, 1958 (b); Wing & Wing, 1971, p. 258). These symptoms have even been implicated as predictive indicators of the child's future development of schizophrenia, when they actually indicate malfunctioning of localizable cerebral systems or apparatuses, and not a psychotic process of obscure origin. This kind of misinterpretation of organic symptoms has retarded progress in clinical and educational understanding of these children and consequently in working out successful treatment plans. (See Vol. II, Speech Disorders, p. 381.)

Movement-blind children have great difficulty learning to read. They can only learn it with the greatest effort, letter by letter, and have the severest form of Linear Dyslexia. They cannot steady their eyes to read without deliberately moving their head along the line of print or pointing at each word. They also have great difficulties with the return sweep and lose their place on the page without special assistance, such as cover or window cards. (See section on Treatment of Linear Dyslexia, p. 127.)

Children with movement-blindness cannot learn to write at all because they cannot guide their hands with their eyes. They can and should be taught to type because the typewriter writes the letters for them, and the hand and finger movements required for pushing the letter down and pushing the lever to start the next line are fairly simple.

"Movement-blindness" is such a severe handicap that it invariably has the most serious consequences for the child's intellectual and emotional development, especially when it is not correctly diagnosed. These children, as a rule, are diagnosed as mental defectives or as schizophrenics and institutionalized. Their intellectual impairment and the psychopathologic reaction to it can, however, be contained when the correct diagnosis is made early and a plan for corrective education worked out and also carried out. Where this is done the child can develop those faculties that are intact, and has a chance to function as an independent adult. Gellner had a son who was "movement-blind." He learned to speak, read, and type in two languages and to take care of himself outside an institution. (Gellner, personal communication; Mautner, 1959, pp. 4, 7).

Children with apraxia due to gross brain lesions are usually seen by neurologists and not referred to psychiatrists. A child is only rarely referred with the chief complaint that he has difficulty writing or carrying out other manual tasks. The reading problem is usually of such overwhelming importance that it is the primary reason for referral.

EMILIO, 7 YEARS OLD: AGRAPHIA DUE TO APRAXIA. I have seen only one child whose apraxic symptoms were so severe that they were the main reason for the teacher's original referral in prekindergarten. This child's name was Emilio, and by the time I examined him he was 7 years old. He had already had four psychiatric, four psychologic, two neurologic, and numerous pediatric examinations. None had diagnosed his symptoms as apraxia, agraphia, acalculia, and dyslexia.

Symptoms. Emilio's symptoms could be grouped under the following categories:

1. Manual Skills Including Writing. When Emilio entered the Headstart program at the age of 3 years and 6 months, his teacher's complaints were: "He gets tantrums when he is asked to do anything with paper and pencil. He has no capacity to control his pencil and make it do what he wants. He is not doing well in hand work." The psychologist who examined him when he was 7 years old reported that he had one of the most severe visuomotor defects she had ever seen. At that same age he had an educational evaluation by a reading therapist who found that he could not copy any letter. At that time he was admitted to a class for brain-injured children. His teacher reported that he could not do puzzles, match objects, sort beads according to color, or do any other serial ordering except when he said out loud himself what he had to do next. This is what apraxic and also Gellner's "movement-blind" children do. They realize that they cannot control the movements of their hands visually, and so try to accomplish it by talking to them, that is, orally. They usually succeed with this speech-acoustic, oral control of their hand, arm, and finger movements.

When I examined Emilio he wrote with his left hand. On dictation, he could only write the letter "H" correctly, but could neither name it nor sound it out. He then went to the blackboard and wrote "Emilo" on it spontaneously. However, he could not read what he had written and did not know that this was his first name. After that he wrote "4" but did not seem to know what it meant. Then he proceeded to write "8" and called it "7." This indicated that he at least knew he was writing numbers. After that he wrote the numbers "7," "6," "3," all vertically rotated ($\Gamma, \partial, \mathcal{E}$). He could not read any of them. He had apparently managed to memorize the visual and the kinesthetic-motor images of these numbers and letters, even though some only in vertical rotation, but could not connect them with sounds, and only vaguely with meaning.

Children see their first name in print so many times that they usually recognize it even without understanding the letter–sound connection. Emilio had been seeing his first name for 4 years but still could not always recognize it. He also had a severe drawing disorder. For figure drawings, he just drew a large circle for both the man and the woman. This is what children aged 3 and younger do. Moreover, he could not even draw a complete circle, but left it open. All his lines were wavy and uncertain. He indicated eyes and a nose with small circles and a mouth with a line. Two lines across the lower part of each circle indicated legs, and scribbles across the woman's "legs" were a "dress." Man and woman looked exactly alike. When I asked him how one could tell them apart, he put scribbles across the lower part of the woman's face and said that this was her hair. I then asked him to point to my hair, because I wanted to be sure he knew where hair is located on other people. He pointed correctly, but in his drawing he had confused the upper with the lower part of the face.

I tested his copying ability and found that he could not copy two-dimensional designs. He was 7 years old and still could not draw a circle, a square, or a diamond spontaneously. His drawing disorder was a symptom of constructional apraxia. This diagnosis is easily missed because these drawings resemble those made by much younger children, so that they can be misinterpreted as signs of immaturity in this special task (i.e., as benign developmental delay) rather than as a more serious neurologic disability. Where such drawings are scored with the Goodenough intelligence scale, the result is invariably a very low I.Q., which is misleading, because these children's general intelligence may be much higher, up to average or even superior.

Emilio's hand preference had not been established, but he seemed to prefer his left hand.

His *Mosaic test* showed how valuable this test can be both for descriptive and psychodynamic diagnoses. He took only pieces of one shape and one color. They were red diamonds, which he called "triangles." This indicated that he was "stone-bound" as well as color-bound, which points to a subcortical disorder. That he preferred the red color showed his emotional excitability and explosiveness. He was happily excited and quite restless during the test. He moved the pieces about on the tray constantly, pushed them together and then apart and said, "I am making fishes; this is the water (tray), and fishes are doing this (moves them). I need more fishes to go." When he ran out of red diamonds, he took diamonds of other colors, put each on top of one diamond already on the tray, moved them about in this position, grinned, and said, "They like to kiss." He did not make kissing sounds, but body movements, and it is possible that he was indicating intercourse and not only kissing movements. He covered the entire tray with these kissing fish. He regarded the Mosaic test as a game and would have gone on with it endlessly, so that I had to stop the test.

The "all-over pattern" he made is a sign of emotional immaturity. This is what children aged 3 or younger do on the Mosaic tray. I tested Emilio's color discrimination with the Mosaic pieces and found that he could match and name colors correctly. (See also Mosaic test, under Pathologic Basis of Organic Reading Disorders, p. 51.)

Emilio's Mosaic test indicated a severe organic defect, probably located in subcortical areas, combined with an emotional immaturity and an unusual sexual preoccupation. It ruled out mental deficiency. The use of the Mosaic pieces to portray fish swimming in water is not unusual for very young children, but their kissing and making sexual movements indicates an abnormal sexual trend. Emilio did have neurotic sexual behavioral symptoms. He liked to dress in his mother's or his two step-sisters' clothes and to walk around in his mother's high-heeled shoes. These preferences at the age of 7 may be forerunners of transvestism or of homosexuality or both in adult life, but they may also be only benign and transitory dramatic plays.

2. Spatial Orientation. Even though "poor spatial orientation" was mentioned numerous times in Emilio's voluminous clinic chart, no specific concrete observations were recorded. I found that his spatial disorientation was confined entirely to activities involving manual skills within the visual sphere. He could distinguish the right and the left side on his own body and on others, and did not get confused about directions and locations within buildings and outside.

3. Reading. At the age of 7 Emilio could recognize only a few letters even as being letters. He could not name or sound out any of them. He had only learned to match some letters, but he made different mistakes each time he tried to recite the alphabet, which he had tried to memorize entirely by ear.

4. Speech. He spoke words at about the age of 9 months, and sentences early, at around 1 year. He learned Spanish first, and then English. His Headstart teachers reported that it was hard to understand him in either language. He had a brief period of stammering at the age of 5. When I examined him, he spoke English and Spanish fluently and clearly. The speech therapist, who gave him a thorough examination at the age of 7, also found no impairment.

5. Arithmetic. Emilio could not count until the age of 7, and even then he could count only to 10 and did not know what counting meant. He learned to recite numbers in a certain sequence only by ear, parrotlike, for he could not count objects, not even his own fingers. For instance, when I showed him two pennies he could not count them and was completely baffled when I added one penny and asked him to count all the pennies and to explain what I had

been doing. He just touched one penny after the other and fingered them like a blind child would do, and said nothing. He could not count five pennies either, even though I showed him that this was the same number as his fingers. The neurologist (who had not found any abnormal reflexes or other neurologic signs) and I examined Emilio carefully for finger agnosia, which is sometimes found together with acalculia (See section on Gerstmann syndrome, p. 175.) This examination is most difficult to do in such young children. Emilio's responses were varied and quite unreliable, so that the result of our examination was inconclusive. There was no doubt, however, that he had acalculia (i.e., an organic arithmetic disorder).

6. Intelligence. On his first psychologic examination at the age of 5, Emilio's I.Q. on the WISC was 67 with a Verbal Score of 72 and a Performance Score also of 67. He was given a Goodenough intelligence test, which gave him a mental age of 2 years and 6 months. The psychologist reported that even though he functioned on the level of mental retardation, he had such uneven cognitive development that she suspected "organic deficits." She made an urgent plea for "remediative education *now.*" However, as is the rule rather than the exception, the remedial education she had in mind was not given.

The psychiatrist diagnosed Emilio as suffering from "Minimal Brain Damage with Secondary Mild Mental Retardation" and recommended placement in a class for mentally retarded children. Unfortunately these classes do not provide the specialized corrective education these children need. The teachers cannot be blamed, for they are not being trained to provide this special education. What happens to these children is that their organic defects remain, and the discrepancy between these frustrating handicaps and their adequate general intelligence increases. This sets in motion a severe psychopathologic process with the result that their behavior becomes so disruptive that they cannot function in a classroom any longer and have to be suspended from school. Many of them eventually land in a state school for mental defectives or in a state hospital.

Emilio was saved from this course by a guidance counselor who observed him in his classroom when he was 6 years old and noticed signs of average intellectual functioning. This led her to question his placement in a class for mentally retarded children, and she re-referred him to the mental hygiene clinic for a reexamination. The psychologists who examined him at the ages of 6 and 7 gave him a variety of intelligence and projective tests, and it became clear that he functioned on the mental defective level only on nonverbal tasks. On the Leiter test, for instance, which requires mainly performance, his I.Q. was only 62. On the Peabody Picture Vocabulary Test, however, which is entirely verbal, he got an I.Q. score of 85. His Verbal Scale on the Wechsler Intelligence Scale for Children at the age of 7 was within normal limits. On one subtest (Similarities) he even functioned on the level of an 11-year-old child. On the Performance Scale, however, his score was only 76. His ability to abstract was above average. His performance on the Rorschach Test also was not compatible with a diagnosis of mental deficiency. His Rorschach revealed an inner life and an imagination too complex and varied for such a diagnosis. (See Vol. II, Mental Deficiency, p. 410.)

7. Physical Health and Development.   Emilio was his mother's first and only child, born when she was 16 years old. She was anemic during her pregnancy. Labor was induced at 8 months of gestation and forceps was used. Emilio weighed only 5 pounds at birth and had to be kept in an incubator. He was a sleepy baby and sucked poorly. He was cross-eyed at birth.

Such a pregnancy, birth, and postnatal history may indicate brain injury due to anoxia because of the mother's anemia and the early induction of labor. The latter was probably done because of fetal distress. Unfortunately, it was impossible to locate the obstetrical record.

Emilio had an undescended left testicle which was corrected by an operation at the age of 7. At the age of 2 he had to be circumcised because he could not urinate properly due to a phimosis. He had to wear orthopedic shoes until the age of 7 because of an extroversion of his feet, which was noticed when he started to walk at the age of 13 months.

8. Emotionality.   Emilio was hyperactive, distractible, and had a severe attention disorder. He had been receiving drug therapy for these symptoms, and this chemical restraint had calmed him down. His teacher in the class for brain-injured children reported that he perseverated and that it was difficult to have him change from one activity to another. (See Vol. II, Perseveration, p. 487, and Inability to Shift, p. 481.)

He was very affectionate with adults, especially with his mother, to whom he was very closely attached. He was outgoing and friendly and loved to tell stories and to dramatize them. He liked to make believe that he was either his teacher (female) or Samantha, the funny witch in a TV series. He performed his dramatic acts quite spontaneously and humorously in the classroom. He slept well but had nightmares and talked in his sleep.

9. Family Relationships.   Emilio lived with his mother. His father was much older than his mother and had two daughters, aged 9 and 10, by his first wife who had deserted him. He was put in jail when Emilio was 2, and returned when he was 6 years old. Emilio's stepsisters lived with their (and Emilio's) paternal grandmother. They visited one another almost every day. Emilio's mother worked during the first year of his life, but had to give up work because he was so difficult to raise. She took good care of him: he was always clean, well fed, and well dressed. She was an intelligent woman and devoted to him, but sometimes just could not cope with his hyperactivity. She kept all his many clinic appointments conscientiously.

The welfare department supported both of them until the father returned.

He was a lens polisher and quite capable of taking care of his family financially. Emilio's mother was a very unhappy woman who tried her best to cope with the extremely difficult circumstances of her life, which were essentially beyond her control.

An electroencephalogram done when Emilio was 6 years old was normal. This is a typical and not an unusual finding in children with organic reading, writing, and arithmetic disorders. Only where the child also has a convulsive disorder is a typically abnormal pattern found on the EEG, almost without exception. The EEG should be evaluated just as are gross clinical neurologic signs. Their absence does not necessarily mean that the child's learning disorder does not have an organic basis, and their presence must be correlated with the specific symptoms of each individual child. A child with a psychologically caused reading disorder can also have abnormal reflexes or other abnormal neurologic signs; so can a child who has no reading disorder at all. The same holds true for an abnormal EEG pattern. (See EEG, p. 37, 38; and Vol. II, Epilepsy, p. 422.)

Diagnosis. I made the diagnosis of a severe writing, reading, and arithmetic disorder on an organic basis with constructional apraxia, coupled with neurotic traits.

Neurotic Symptoms. Emilio's neurotic symptoms (nightmares, sleep talking, cross-dressing, attraction to women's high-heeled shoes) were due to psychopathologic processes in his unconscious and had to be evaluated on their own merits. A causal relationship does not necessarily exist between a child's neurotic and organic symptoms. The organic and the neurotic disorder, however, always influence each other deeply, and educational as well as psychotherapeutic planning must take this into consideration. Psychotherapy can only succeed if the therapist is aware of both disorders and of the interaction between them.

I made the following *recommendations:*

1. Emilio should remain in the class for brain-injured children, which he had entered 7 months before I examined him. This class placement had become possible only after a psychiatrist had changed his diagnosis to "Brain-Injured Child."

2. Tranquilizing medication should be continued to lessen his hyperactivity and restlessness so that he could concentrate and therefore learn better. No drug treatment alone, however, can change any child's behavior or learning disorder. Tranquilizers, stimulants, and other so-called psychoactive drugs can be effective only when they are prescribed within the framework of carefully planned remedial education, combined with regular physical checkups, social

casework, and individual or group psychotherapy whenever indicated. (See Vol. II, Drug Treatment, under Hyperactivity, p. 657.)

The key to the improvement of these children is remedial education and training, which must include their parents, especially their mother. Emilio's teachers had been in close touch with his mother, giving her advice about the best educational management at home, and explaining to her how to follow up their teaching, for example, with special exercises.

3. The social worker should continue with casework treatment of the mother. Every mother who has such a handicapped child and who lives in such a stressful family situation needs casework treatment by a social worker. She may also need psychotherapy, depending on the severity of her psychologic reactions.

4. Emilio should receive individual psychotherapy so that his neurotic traits would not develop into a full-blown neurosis and affect his adult sex life.

Gerstmann Syndrome and Its Relation to Organic Writing and Reading Disorders in Children

The Viennese neurologist and psychiatrist Josef Gerstmann published a paper in 1930 with the title "On the Symptomatology of Cerebral Lesions in the Transitional Area of the Lower Parietal and Middle Occipital Convolutions," in which he described a new syndrome which has since carried his name. This syndrome consists of *agraphia; finger agnosia* (a disturbance in the ability to recognize, name, select, and distinguish the various fingers of both hands, one's own fingers, and those of another person); *right–left disorientation* (in one's own as well an in another's body); and *acalculia* (Gerstmann, 1977; Wilkins & Brody, 1971).

Gerstmann syndrome is of interest with regard to organic reading disorders in children. Repeated efforts have been made to find a common causation. Lesions found at autopsies of adult patients who had the syndrome were in the majority of cases located in or near the angular gyrus in the parietal lobes, close to the cytoarchitectonic area 39. (See section on the Organic Basis of the Normal Reading Process, p. 00.) The left hemisphere was affected in right-handed, and the right in a few left-handed patients. It is remarkable that in spite of the close anatomical proximity of the lesions to area 39, reading was usually not impaired, or was affected much less seriously than writing. The cerebral reading apparatus can evidently function independently from writing. Gerstmann characterized his patient's reading symptoms as "neighborhood or marginal symptoms because of their variable appearance and comparative mildness" (Gerstmann, 1971, p. 476). The absence of a reading disorder in these patients was stressed by Schilder, who observed that they "have no difficulties in the perception of direction in reading" (Schilder, 1964, p. 43).

One must therefore question whether a combination of the four defects that make up Gerstmann syndrome with a severe organic reading disorder should still be labeled "Gerstmann syndrome."

Gerstmann syndrome is rare in adults, and even more exceptional in children. There are no autopsy reports on children, so far as I know, but the syndrome has been found in childhood. The neurologists Benson and Geschwind, for instance, diagnosed it in two children, a 12-year-old boy and a 13-year-old girl. The girl read well, but the boy had a "significant spelling disability" (Benson and Geschwind, 1970).

The most prominent representative of the common causation theory of dyslexia in children and Gerstmann syndrome is the Danish neurologist Knud Hermann, who studied the most severe cases of organic reading and writing disorders in children while he was on the staff of the Ordblindhet Institutet in Copenhagen. (See section on Linear Dyslexia, p. 129.) In his book, *Reading Disability,* he suggests that "comparative analysis shows the symptoms of Gerstmann's syndrome and constitutional dyslexia to have so many features in common, that it is very likely that the fundamental disturbance in these two conditions is identical, viz. a defect involving the categorical sphere of function which may be termed directional function" (Hermann, 1959, p. 146). Critchley challenges this suggestion in his book *Developmental Dyslexia,* where he states that "a Gerstmann syndrome is certainly not an integral part of dyslexia" (Critchley, 1964, p. 60; 1970, p. 84). I agree with him, having never seen a child with a severe organic reading disorder who also had Gerstmann syndrome.

Many children with organic reading disorders have the right–left disorientation; fewer have the agraphia, even fewer the acalculia of Gerstmann syndrome or a combination of these three defects. But the finger agnosia is extremely rare. It may be more frequent than is apparent because it is very difficult and sometimes impossible to establish in young children. Their responses vary and are unreliable; the age when a perfect performance can be expected also varies. Another reason is that children are not usually examined for this defect. I agree with Critchley's statement that "negative cases in the literature only too often indicate inadequate examination or even ignorance of what to look for" (1953, p. 219).

Regardless how rarely a complete Gerstmann syndrome occurs in children, it is important for our practical clinical and educational work to know whether a child who is suffering from an organic reading disorder also has agraphia, right–left disorientation, acalculia, and finger agnosia. Diagnostic examinations must include all of these conditions.

Tests for Finger Agnosia

Finger agnosia should be tested for in the following way:
1. Tell the child to point to or to hold up the various fingers of each hand.

2. Ask the child to name the various fingers when they are touched in turn.

3. Let the child point to the various fingers on your hand.

4. Ask the child to perform more complicated tasks (e.g., to put the third finger of his right hand on the tip of the second finger of his left hand, etc.).

5. Let the child draw an outline of his or your hand and tell him to point to the finger corresponding to the one you just touched while he could not see it, for instance by holding his hand behind his back.

6. Touch or move one or more of your own fingers within sight of the child, and ask the child to imitate what you are doing with the corresponding finger on his hand.

7. A mild finger agnosia is sometimes revealed by the so-called Japanese illusion. The child interlaces his fingers and reverses his hands, and then tries to name the fingers the examiner touches (Critchley, 1953, p. 206).

Negative responses on these tests are difficult to evaluate because even adults do not give consistently wrong or right answers. As a rule, they identify thumb and little finger correctly (their own and those of the examiner), but confuse the second, third, and fourth fingers (Critchley, 1953, p. 206). Before examining a child, one must find out whether he knows the names and numbers of his fingers; otherwise one might diagnose finger agnosia when the child simply has not yet learned to name his fingers.

Tests for Right–Left Disorientation

The right–left disorientation of Gerstmann syndrome is not confined to manual tasks within the visual sphere as in apraxia. It involves the sides of the child's own body: he cannot distinguish right and left on himself or on other people. Some of these children are also uncertain of what parts of their body are above or below and what is in front of or behind them or other people.

Mirror-Image Test

The examination for this type of disorientation should include the child's mirror image. Let him look into the mirror and identify his right and left limbs and the sides of his body as reflected in the mirror. These children get completely confused by their mirror image.

Body-Image Disorders

The finger agnosia and the right–left disorientation are disturbances of the body image. In his standard book, *The Image and Appearance of the Human Body,* Schilder describes them as "agnosias concerning the body image (autotopagnosia)" and states: "We deal with true agnosias, not with those concerning a special sensory impression, but with those concerning an object of particular importance, the body-image" (Schilder, 1964, p. 43). Children with such severe body-image agnosias feel insecure because they cannot experience their own body or their surroundings in a stable way. Such children have episodes of profound anxiety and confusion that are easily misdiagnosed as schizophrenic breaks with reality. These episodes, however, are transitory and the child is in good contact with reality as soon as he has calmed down.

MANAGEMENT. These anxiety states and other psychopathologic symptoms caused by body-image agnosias can be avoided by diagnosing the symptoms correctly and by managing the child psychologically and educationally with his body-image disorder in mind. The child should be made aware of his inability to locate certain body parts and to orient himself in relation to other people. He can learn to orient himself with the help of familiar landmarks in his home, on the street, and in school; with scars on his hands or other parts of his body; and with dots put on his hands and distinguishing labels put on the sides of his garments. Some children develop such visual aids spontaneously—on their own—even while no one else notices or understands their handicap.

Body-image agnosias (excluding finger agnosia) frequently accompany children's organic reading and writing disorders. (See section on Hand Dominance and Organic Writing Disorders, p. 179.)

Acalculia

The acalculia of Gerstmann syndrome is a more fundamental arithmetic disorder than the one found in constructional apraxia. It is a severe form of what teachers and psychologists call a lack of "number concepts." A severe number concept lack should always lead one to suspect an organic basis. Children with severe forms of acalculia cannot memorize numbers verbally or when writing them down, especially when more than one digit is involved. They cannot arrange a series of numbers in order of their magnitude when someone else recites them, when they say them on their own, or when they write them down. They even find it difficult to determine which one of two numbers is larger. They cannot recite a series of odd or even numbers, cannot learn the multiplication tables, and cannot count backwards (Feuchtwanger, 1929). (See case of Emilio, p. 169; and Chapter 4, p. 221 Arithmetic Disorders.)

EXAMINATION. An examination for acalculia should include counting of objects and of groups of objects. One should let the child count groups of identical and of different objects. Blocks, small cars, and other toys can be used for this test; random objects in the room or on a desk pushed together so that they form groups will do just as well. Object counting is very important because verbal reciting of numbers may not mean that the child can really count. He may just have memorized the numbers by rote, parrotlike, as Emilio did (see p. 169.) In typical adult cases of Gerstmann syndrome, the acalculia affects calculations done on paper more than "mental" arithmetic. The reason for this is probably that the agraphia that is also part of Gerstmann syndrome interferes with written arithmetic.

Mild forms of acalculia are more frequent than teachers and other professionals working with children realize. Children are, as a rule, not examined for them with sufficient care. The severe form that is part of Gerstmann syndrome is extremely rare, however. (See Chapter 4, Arithmetic Disorders, p. 221.) The agraphia of Gerstmann syndrome does not differ from the organic writing disorders in children I have described in this section.

Gerstmann syndrome as such has no connection with organic reading disorders in children. But its four component symptoms, alone or in differing combinations, are found in association with children's organic reading disorders. This is of interest clinically, for corrective education and in regard to the question of cerebral localization.

Hand Dominance and Organic Writing Disorders

Determination of the Best Hand for Writing

Many children with organic reading and writing disorders confuse both hands because they have no dominant hand or because their hand dominance is poorly developed. It is therefore important to find out which hand they should use for writing. The best principle to follow is to let the child choose his writing hand. He alone can tell which hand does the best work for him and gives him a feeling of confidence and security when he wants to perform any manual task. Once the child has determined this, he should be helped and encouraged to use this one hand only, whether it is the right or the left, and he should be discouraged from switching hands.

The decision which hand to use for writing should be made as early as possible. The issue should never be forced, but should be firmly reinforced as soon as a decision has been reached.

Hecaen and de Ajuriaguerra in their important book, *Left-Handedness: Manual Superiority and Cerebral Dominance,* advance the interesting theory that spatial disorganization may not be inborn, but acquired. They state that the "directional function" can be disorganized in the course of the child's development by many factors, the absence of clear manual preference among them, which makes it impossible for the child to learn to orient himself with respect to his own body (Hecaen & de Ajuriaguerra, 1964, p. 84). If this is true —and clinical and educational evidence seems to support this theory—early and consistent training of one hand through writing should help the child develop spatial orientation. (See section on Role of Hemispheric Dominance, p. 58.)

Children whose hand dominance has been established by the time they enter school, present no problem. They should write with their dominant hand, whether it is right or left. A definite hand dominance has been established in most children by the time they enter kindergarten.

There is no agreement in the various studies about exactly at what age hand preference starts. Gesell found that the right hand was chosen by the age of 2 in 92% of the children he studied. Most studies determine hand dominance at such an early age by the frequency of use, but this may not be the best indicator. The precision and skill with which the child performs more complicated manual tasks later on in life are much more reliable signs. Such early determination of hand dominance is questionable also because oscillations between right- and left-handedness are prevalent until the age of 5 or even later. As a general rule, the more pronounced the dominance, the earlier it is established, regardless whether it involves the right or the left hand. Most studies agree that right-handedness manifests itself earlier than left-handedness and is more stable from the beginning (Hecaen and de Ajuriaguerra, 1964, pp. 12–13.)

It has been clearly established that right-handers are in the overwhelming majority all over the world, regardless of the style and the direction of writing used in their country. Left-handers are a minority everywhere. A great deal has been written about the reasons for this, but they are still unknown. However, it is known that hand dominance is inborn and inherited, but there are different theories about its mode of inheritance.

It is important to understand that there are qualitative as well as quantitative differences in hand dominance. Some children are equally skillful with both hands; others are equally clumsy. The degree as well as the quality of hand dominance must be taken into consideration when an attempt is made to find out which hand the child should use for writing.

Ambidexterity

Children who have no dominant hand and can perform equally well with either hand have many advantages. They should be encouraged to train both hands so that they can develop their bilateral manual talent to their best advantage. This inborn talent is especially important for musicians because it makes it easier for them to play instruments than it would be if they had one hand that was strongly dominant. It is also of advantage to sculptors and painters, and for numerous other skills requiring bilateral manual dexterity, for instance carpentry and other trades. For writing, however, these children should be advised to use their right hand only, because it will simplify their life. The necessary left-to-right writing movements are easier to perform with the right hand. Right-handers can always see what they are writing. Ring books, writing boards on chairs in schools and colleges, and many other writing utensils are based on right-handedness; and so are most tools.

Advantages of Right-Handedness

Children are better off generally with a well-trained right hand. Preference should therefore be given to right-handed writing whenever there is a choice. This also applies for children who perform equally poorly with either hand. Left-handed writing is always more difficult to learn and requires special attention from the teachers. It must be taught carefully from the very beginning so that the child learns to see what he is writing while writing. Children with a weak hand dominance or none at all need a great deal of help and special attention to overcome their initial awkwardness in writing anyway, and this awkwardness is increased when they learn with their left hand.

Left-Handedness

The percentage of left-handers seems to be larger among children with organic reading and writing disorders than among the general population. Left-handedness, ambidexterity, and other dominance variations, however, are not symptoms of any pathology whatsoever. They are physical differences that are entirely within normal limits. If accepted as such and managed sensibly by parents and teachers, they should have no adverse psychologic consequences for the child. They are, however, far too often misunderstood and consequently mismanaged, resulting in entirely unnecessary suffering for the child.

Left-handers face special psychologic and social problems, whether or not their hand dominance is associated with an organic reading disorder. Added to the somewhat greater initial difficulty in learning to write is the fact that their hand dominance is not universally looked upon as normal. Right-handed children often ridicule "lefties" and tend to look down on them. Sometimes, however, they envy them, because left-handedness is of advantage in some sports. Our language also reflects a negative attitude toward left-handedness. A left-handed compliment is insincere or ambiguous and indirectly unflattering. The meaning of the word "left" is derogatory in many languages, as indicated by terms such as "gauche," which means awkward or tactless; "maladroite," which literally translated from the French means bad with one's right hand and is used to indicate clumsiness; and "sinister," (the Latin word for left), which means unlucky, evil, ominous, or disastrous. There is also a superstition that left-handedness is in some magical way connected with homosexuality.

According to Stekel, right and left in dreams refer to ethical conflicts. He expressed this in the following way as quoted by Freud in *The Interpretation of Dreams:*

> The right-hand path always signifies the way to righteousness, the left-hand path the path to crime. Thus the left may signify homosexuality, incest, and perver-

sion, while the right signifies marriage, relations with a prostitute, etc. The meaning is always determined by the individual moral standpoint of the dreamer (1938, p. 374).

Psychopathologic Consequences of the Forced Use of the Right Hand

That left-handed children are permitted to write with their left hand is the result of a long historic struggle that still has not been completely won. Some countries and school systems continue to force all children to write with their right hand. This makes writing more difficult for left-handers and may cause a painful emotional conflict, especially when the child is forced in a sadistic way with threats, ridicule, and corporal punishment. Such forced conversion to right-handedness sometimes causes stuttering, as Orton has shown (Orton, 1937, p. 125). It may also set a neurotic process in motion.

I have been able to trace the origin of some neurotic symptoms in adult patients to conflicts caused by their strenuous efforts as children to suppress their natural inclination to use their left hand for writing and other activities. This had become a major issue between them and their parents, and had aroused feelings of inferiority and hatred (against parents, teachers, and the self) with consequent guilt feelings.

The symbolic meaning of the hand plays an important role in psychopathology generally, and is of special importance for these patients. The hand stands for mastery, for physical and mental strength, power, and adequacy, including sexual adequacy. A boy who is awkward with his hands may worry that he will grow up to be a failure as a man, sexually and in other spheres. Of course, the hand also stands for criminal acts (e.g., stealing or acts of violence). (See section on drawing tests, p. 214.)

An adult male patient of mine could not sign his name on any document while anyone (other than his wife) looked on. His conscious fear was that his hand might shake so that he would smirch his signature or spill the ink and soil the signature and document in some way. He wrote with his right hand.

His analysis revealed that he had repressed into the unconscious what he was really afraid of. He feared that people might suspect him of wanting to write a false name or of purposely making his name unintelligible to cover up criminal activities. He thought of himself as a murderer. Actually he was a meticulously honest and nonviolent man. He suffered from an obsessive-compulsive neurosis with checking and counting compulsions. His central conflict (which was repressed) was his ambivalent relationship to his father. He had simultaneously admired and hated him when he was a child. Death wishes and other violent fantasies directed against his father formed the unconscious image of himself as a murderer who deserved the death penalty. One childhood experience that aroused violent hostility in him was the brutal and unsympathetic way in which his father forced him to suppress his left-handedness. He had no reading disorder as a child, but stuttered for a while. Of course this was not the only conflict with his father that lead to his neurosis, but it played an important role not only by itself but because it prevented a constructive solution of his oedipus complex, which was at its height when the battle around handedness began.

Changes to Left-Handed Writing

The question is often raised whether a child with an organic reading and writing disorder who has been forced to write with his right hand should be changed to left-handed writing. Orton was of the opinion that some children suffering from reading disorders and stuttering could be cured in this way. He even went so far that he put a cast on the arm he did not want the child to use. When he applied this technique in a reform school for delinquent boys, it created such emotional disturbances in and among the boys that it had to be terminated. A cast can become a weapon and such a boy is likely to be the focus of violent fights. In addition, there is no evidence that this drastic measure alleviates either reading disorders or stuttering.

A change of the writing hand can be achieved simply by asking the child to use his other hand and by supervising his writing until he gets used to it. But I have never seen a child whose reading and writing disorder improved by a change of his writing hand alone, and I recommend it only in exceptional cases. Such a change actually carries the great risk of starting a new disorganization of the body image, which so many of these children have barely managed to stabilize.

A change of the writing hand should be considered only under the following conditions:

1. The child is still in attendance in the early grades of elementary school.

2. The child's nonwriting hand is demonstrably more competent than the other hand.

3. The child himself wants such a change (Hecaen & de Ajuriaguerra, 1964, p. 93).

Role of Eye Dominance

The suggestion has been made that a child with an organic reading and writing disorder should be taught to write not necessarily with his dominant hand but with the hand that corresponds to his dominant eye, especially where no dominance has been established. I have found this suggestion to be neither helpful nor practical. Some studies have shown that eye dominance can often be determined by the time the child is 2½ years old, and that it remains constant. Manual dominance, however, fluctuates frequently until the child is much older, and it is not necessarily established on the side of the dominant eye.

One must also distinguish between greater visual acuity of one eye and eye-muscle dominance since they may not be present in the same eye. Most eye-dominance tests test only muscle dominance (See section on Role of Hemispheric Dominance, p. 58.) Eye dominance as described by most clinicians does not mean the eye that is better visually, but the eye with the stronger eye muscles.

Eye and hand dominance are normal physical variations and have no intrinsic relationship with organic reading and writing disorders. I have examined many children who could read and write well, who were either left- or right-handed and whose eye dominance was not on the same side as their dominant hand. I have also examined many children suffering from organic reading and writing disorders who wrote with the hand that was on the same side as their dominant eye. One should observe the child carefully to find out how he performs manual tasks and which hand has the better skill rather than taking eye dominance as a guide.

I want to stress again (as I did in the chapter on examination) the importance of observation and of nonverbal testing for the determination of hand dominance. Verbal determination is quite unreliable. A child may know perfectly well, for instance, which is his "best" hand, but be incapable of naming it. He may also hold up the wrong hand when asked to lift up his right or his left hand. Naming is a performance that differs from carrying out manual tasks. A child may have developed hand dominance before he has learned the designation of each hand. The same holds true for the sides of his body. I have found that directional confusion and lack of hand dominance are sometimes diagnosed in young children who know the sides of their body and have a dominant hand but who cannot name them correctly. They get the words "right" and "left" mixed up, but not the right- or left-sidedness of their body. This naming difficulty may be due to lack of use of these terms in their home —that is, to lack of teaching—or simply to immaturity. In rare cases it may indicate a word-finding difficulty, which is a symptom of aphasia. (See Vol. II, section on Speech Disorders, p. 381.)

Teaching of Writing

Because writing is based on a complicated neurophysiologic apparatus, teaching methods must be structured in such a way that the child learns to use this apparatus with the greatest possible speed and ease and that malfunctioning is prevented. As the cerebral writing and reading apparatuses overlap, good teaching of writing also prevents malfunctioning of the reading apparatus. I go even further and agree with those educators who maintain that the best way to teach reading is through writing. I will outline those aspects of the teaching of writing that need special care and consideration.

Writing should be taught systematically and not casually, as seems to be the prevailing practice. This does not mean that I am generally in favor of rigidly structured teaching and against a more informal approach. It is a basic fact, however, that children can be expected to learn different subjects individually according to their own interest, capability, and pace only *after* the basic skills of reading and writing have been firmly established. They flounder otherwise and their progress in any subject will be uncertain because it rests on shaky foundations.

To write, the child needs good light. He must see clearly what he is writing as well as the blackboard or other copying guide. Unfortunately , it is indeed necessary to mention this, as is shown by the observation of children writing and reading in poorly lit classrooms and homes. Daylight is always preferable to artificial light. This is only one of many reasons why school buildings without windows are hazards educationally, physically, and psychologically. Poor light causes fatigue and puts an unnecessary strain on the child's (and the teacher's) eyes. (See Vol. II, Fatigue under Attention Disorders, p. 562; also Fatiguability, p. 672.)

The child's posture is important in avoiding muscle cramps. Both lighting and posture may seem to be only trivial details, but they influence the speed and ease of learning, and their importance should be explained to the child. The most informal, "relaxed" posture may not be the best in this respect.

There is an optimal distance between the child's head, his arms, and the desk which prevents fatigue and makes relaxed writing possible. Even a casual stroll through any elementary school shows that writing posture is not considered important. Children can be observed slouched in any fashion, often like hunchbacks, at desks, tables, or on the floor, holding their paper at different angles. A posture ought to become a fixed habit, almost like a conditioned reflex. Too many children come to school tired anyway, because they watched television too long and went to bed too late; thus teaching techniques that prevent fatigue assume special importance. (See Vol. II, Physical Changes during Attention, p. 521; and Curative Physical Exercises, p. 534.).

Most handwriting manuals advise teachers how the child should sit and how he should hold his paper. The Spaldings probably make the most sensible suggestions. Here is what they say children should be told:

> Sit with hips against the back of the chair, feet flat on the floor and back straight, with head tall. The straight spinal column supports the head. Keep two inches between body and the desk. Lean forward just enough to see the paper clearly, but keep the head high. Let the chair carry the weight of the body. Do not let the head fall forward because its heavy weight then would be carried by the neck and back muscles. Place both forearms on the desk with elbows just off the front edge and comfortably close to the body.... Keep the side edge of the paper parallel to the arm of the hand that holds the pencil (like the two rails of a railroad track) (Spalding & Spalding, 1969, p. 47).

For the teaching of left-handers who must hold their paper parallel to their left arm, they give this good practical advice: a strip of tape should be pasted near the top of his desk to show the slant for the top edge of his writing paper so that he does not turn it in the same direction as his right-handed neighbors. If such special care were given to all left-handers, they could learn to write just as fast as right-handers.

Both left- and right-handers should also be taught to keep their writing hand *below* the line on which they are writing. They have to twist their wrist if they keep it on or above that line. I have observed such cramped writing with a twisted wrist in far too many children. Writing above the line had become a habit for them. This leads to cramps and pain and ultimately to dislike for and an avoidance of writing.

The child's hand and lower arm should stay in one straight line, and he should never use his writing hand to hold the paper. This is one of the tasks of the nonwriting hand.

Most handwriting manuals make an issue out of the position of the paper. They advise that it be placed straight in front of the child in the beginning when manuscript writing is taught, and at a slant in later grades when the child learns the cursive style. This change confuses many children. To have their paper straight in front of them also forces them to twist their wrist during manuscript as well as connected writing. The slanted position should therefore be taught exclusively. This position is especially important for left-handers, but it also makes for faster writing for right-handers.

It is essential for the teacher to enforce the correct position of the paper because unless the position of their paper is checked carefully, children will write at any slant and may not learn the essential left-to-right direction properly. I have observed entirely too many children writing at ever-changing slants, frequently with a 90-degree rotation of their paper so that they wrote vertically straight upwards. This may be a pathologic organic symptom found in children who reverse letters. (See Directional Confusion of Letters and Words, p. 99.) Most children I have observed writing in this abnormal direction, however, had no organic symptoms at all. Their vertical writing was merely a symptom of careless teaching.

Careless teaching of writing may handicap the child for the rest of his life. It is essential that children are taught so well that writing becomes an automatic habit, and that they learn the linear left-to-right direction from the start.

Linear writing not only helps the child to write legibly and fast, it also supports his linear reading and his spelling and helps prevent reversals and inversions and Linear Dyslexia.

The linear movement of arm, hand, and fingers strengthens linear eye movements. Children should therefore write on lined paper from the very beginning, and continue to use it for all styles and forms of writing (copying, dictation, and spontaneous writing) through elementary school or even longer if they have difficulty with writing and reading on the line, and with performing the return sweep. As a mater of fact, the best way to secure linear reading is by having the child write on lined paper from the very start (i.e., from kindergarten). (See Spelling, p. 115; and Linear Dyslexia, p. 127.)

Writing primers provide lined paper and usually make writing easier for the child by indicating the different proportions of letters with two, three, or four extra lines. However, I found only *one* workbook for teachers that mentioned the importance of linear eye movements. This is the *Open Court Basic Reader for Grade 1:1*. It suggests as part of the daily writing practice to "have the children complete the lines by repeating the sounds, syllables or words that are written at the beginning of each line. Have the children complete each line so that the left-to-right eye movement is firmly established." It adds this warning: "Writing in columns is not recommended because it does not develop the left-to-right eye movement as well" (1963, p. 111). This is sound advice that should be heeded by all elementary and junior high school teachers, but it seems to be unknown to them and to their supervisors. Children are taught in schools all over the United States to write and read words in columns underneath each other. So-called spelling words are always presented in vertical columns on all school levels (elementary, junior and senior high schools), and not even the use of lined paper is routine on *any* level.

Teachers have complained to me that they have trouble getting any paper, lined or unlined. I found out how true and how very troublesome this is when I took over a fourth-grade class to help out during a shortage of teachers. I know of at least one first-grade teacher who bought lined paper for her students with her own money because she could not get any in the public school where she taught.

Lack of Principles for Teaching Writing

So many children of all ages and grade levels that I examined wrote so poorly and were so mixed up about the forms and styles of letters (which they usually intermingled when they wrote anything), that I decided to find out exactly what were the rules for the teaching of writing. This turned out to be a formidable task. I tried unsuccessfully for years to obtain a handwriting primer or any other handwriting workbook for children, which provided a place for them to practice writing letters by tracing and copying them. I could find none at any level of the New York City school system. The manuals I found were for "experimental use," which meant that they were restricted to a few elementary schools and that their use was limited in time.

A principal in whose school I worked for years finally sent me official material on handwriting curriculum practice. I had told her about my unsuccessful efforts to locate such material. As an explanation for my trouble, she wrote me: "Many principals do not like to spend money on handwriting books, as they believe with me that this habit should be inculcated under constant teacher's supervision." This well-meaning theory does not work in practice. The teacher has no time to correct the child every time he writes a letter, and without a printed guide, children have only their own letters to copy from. Copying from the blackboard is not a satisfactory substitute. In addition to this, whole-word teaching has damaged writing too. Children copy words from kindergarten on, before they have been taught to write letters, and each single letter is not practiced with sufficient care. No wonder illegible handwriting results and children confuse and rotate letters much longer than necessary.

The material given to me by this principal, as well as other official statements I have collected over the years, confirmed my impression that writing is taught casually and with little regard for linear writing. A senior handwriting coordinator who was in charge of the handwriting curriculum for an entire district with tens of thousands of children made the following recommendation to teachers in a mimeographed manual: "Children progress from unruled paper —use crayons—then fold paper (4 inches)." Many parochial and other private schools also use this technique in their kindergartens and first grades.

The following excerpt from mimeographed instructions handed to every teacher by an elementary school principal is typical for the teaching of writing all over the country:

When Readiness Is Evident, The Child Progresses As Follows:
A. Writes with crayon on large, unruled paper.
B. Learns to hold the paper vertically and to sit correctly.
C. Begins to write a simple word for which a need has been established.
D. Practices several times a letter in this word which needs improvement, and then rewrites the word.
E. When the above is accomplished with ease, writes on unruled paper folded in spaces of about 4 inches (or a similar space on the blackboard).

Only "at the point of success in the above" is the teacher supposed to let the child write on "lined paper with inch ruling," and to let him skip two spaces between lines of writing. How much easier would it be if each child were given his own workbook with lined pages! In addition, this is typical whole-word teaching. A child has a desperate "need" not for words, but for an explanation of the role of letters, their shapes and sounds!

The use of crayons must also be questioned. Most kindergarten children, and certainly all first graders, are capable of holding a pencil. Why not teach writing with a pencil from the start? Crayons are too crude and wide, and they have the additional disadvantage of introducing different colors, which only confuses most children. I would let children draw and color anything they like with crayons, but use only pencils or chalk for writing. Writing is something special, and one can easily explain to children that it requires special tools.

A large part of the instructions to teachers I have been quoting from is devoted to the size of the child's letters. No advice at all is given about how best to teach letter forms so that the child remembers which parts are on the right and which on the left side. Progress seems rather to be measured by size. Here are the instructions: In the second grade writing should be decreased to "one space of paper ½-inch spacing and ultimately ⅜-inch spacing." The goal is to be reached at the end of the second or the beginning of the third grade, when the child no longer skips spaces between his lines because he has reduced the size of his letters to "slightly less than full space for capitals and tall lower-case letters."

With this type of teaching it is not surprising that so many children do not like to write; they are never really sure of the form and length of their letters, having been further confused in the second or third grade by an equally casual approach to the teaching of cursive writing. The feeling of insecurity when writing also affects reading and spelling. Desk drawers in classrooms and boys' pockets are filled with unruled pieces of paper, often folded in various ways, with letters written helter-skelter all over them. Of course children with even the mildest form of organic defects are always more severely damaged by these practices than healthy children.

Tracing as a Teaching Technique

Instead of stressing the size of letters, careful consideration should be given to a number of really important aspects of the teaching of writing. A decision must be made, for instance, about whether children should trace letters first before copying them. This is a good first step for many children who learn much better by tracing, provided the teacher supervises him closely. One must have observed children tracing to appreciate how many different ways they find to do this; backwards and forwards, round about right to left or left to right, often changing direction abruptly. They are also apt to lift up their pencil at any point, so that they do not experience the complete kinesthetic–motor movement form of the letter, and therefore derive no benefit from tracing. The child needs help to find the best way to trace each letter, and to stick to this one way whenever he traces this letter; otherwise he will not remember its form sufficiently to avoid rotations and other errors. The child should be taught to write each letter without lifting the pencil except, of course, for crossing "f, t, x," dotting "i" and "j," and writing the second part of "k."

Some workbooks for teachers recommend writing in the air in addition to tracing and copying. This is often of benefit for children with organic defects. However, they eventually have to learn to write two-dimensional forms on a flat surface anyway.

Careful consideration should also be given to the selection of the letter style that is easiest to learn. Letter style affects the ease and speed with which children learn to write in the beginning. The initial teaching of cursive writing has some advantages over the manuscript style, because it forces fluid left-to-right movement from the beginning, as well as teaching words as a cohesive unit. It also prevents a confusion of "b" and "d" and "p and q," whose opposite directions in lower-case manuscript style are so difficult to remember for many children. However, the cursive style is more difficult to learn for 5- and 6-year-old children who, in addition, have to remember different letter forms for reading. Teaching manuscript letters first is therefore preferable. Most schools start by teaching printed capital letters informally in kindergarten and in the first grade, but not exclusively; some lower-case manuscript letters are taught at about the same time (Mosse, 1962(b); Mosse & Daniels, 1959).

Writing is always started in an informal way with the child's own first name (his last also, if it is simple), which he copies from his name card before learning any letter and long before the connection of letters with sounds is explained to him. In reading instruction, he gets mimeographed sheets of paper where he has to connect words with pictures—silently, without saying the word. No explanation of the reasons for different letter forms is given here either. (See Figure 3.4.)

Writing is considered unimportant in kindergarten and in the first grade anyway. An "Overview of the Elementary School Curriculum" of the Bureau of Elementary Curriculum Development of the New York State Education Department expressed this point of view. It devoted only these two sentences to writing in the first grade: "The children learn to write their names in large manuscript. By the close of the year, some will be able to write several short sentences" (1954, p. 36). This overview is unclear about the timing of the teaching of small manuscript letters. These it mentions casually only in the two sentences it devotes to the teaching of writing in the second grade, when it states that "they [the children] use capital I and capital letters for names of persons and the first word in a sentence. Their manuscript writing is continued and the quality of their letter formation is greatly improved" (1954, p. 56). It should not take any child, even a child with organic impairments, 2 full years to learn to write 26 letters perfectly (or 40 if the capital letters whose form differs from small manuscript letters are added—namely, A, B, D, E, F, G, H, L, M, N, Q, R, T, Y)! With a good teaching technique, *all* children should know *all* 40 letter forms and write at least short sentences by the end of the first grade, and they should not intermingle capital and lower-case letters as they now do. I have observed this confusion of letter styles continuing through higher grades. This can and should be avoided because it interferes with the fluency of the child's writing.

The best way to teach writing from kindergarten on is to *use one style of letters only.* Where manuscript style is chosen, only lower-case letters should

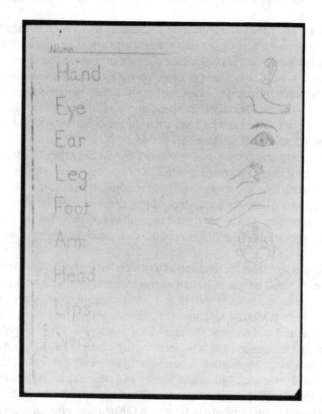

FIG. 3.4. A whole–word exercise: connecting a picture with a word whose composition the child does not know because it has not been explained to him.

be taught. It is easier for all children to learn only one form for each letter in the very beginning. A number of manuals recognize the importance of this.

Romalda Spalding found an especially ingenious solution for this teaching dilemma. She uses only small manuscript letters for beginners, and teaches the direction of letters with the help of the clock face. She starts by explaining these simple basic rules:

All letters sit on a base line. Letters or part of letters are of two sizes. They are either tall or short. Tall letters or tall parts reach to the line above but do not touch it. Short letters or short parts are half as high as tall letters. Manuscript letters are made of the clock face, or parts of it, and straight lines" (1969, p. 54).

Spalding does not teach capital letters until the children have learned all small letters, and the manuscript style she teaches lends itself to easy transformation into cursive writing, so that no fundamentally new letter forms have to be learned later on. This clock-face concept may seem too advanced for 5- or 6-year-olds, but I have seen it work very well indeed. It also helps many children to learn to read the clock earlier than they would otherwise, which certainly is not a disadvantage for them, and is of special benefit for children with organic impairments who have such difficulty learning to tell time. (See section on Clock-Reading Disorder, p. 165.)

By their daily observation of the teacher and of the other children, and by practicing clockwise movements while writing, children with impairments have the best chance to overcome their directional defects *early*. Most of them will still learn at a slower pace, depending on the severity of their disorder. With the exception of the severest cases, however, they will not develop a writing or a clock-reading disorder, and their reading disorder will be less severe.

More important than the decision as to which letter style to use for beginners is whether to teach names of letters or their sounds first, and how to help the child remember the sounds letters and letter combinations represent. Most writing primers teach the alphabet (i.e., the names of the letters first); some teach both sound and name at the same time. Because in English spelling each letter presents various sounds, it is easier for beginners to learn the sounds first, before memorizing their names. As a matter of fact, only five letters, the vowels a, e, i, o, and u, ever sound like their names, and their names are not their most common sounds. (See section on Letter Reading, pp. 89 and 90 ff.)

The only techniques that are in tune with the neurophysiologic, psychologic, and historical basis for writing are those that teach the child in the beginning to say the letters and letter combinations before and while he is writing them, until the necessary conditioned reflexes have been established. (See section on Conditioned Reflexes, p. 78.)

Some teaching methods have children first practice writing letters in the air while saying them, before writing them down. *Open Court* recommends the following daily procedure to the teacher:

> Write the spellings of the new sound on the board in large letters exactly as written in the workbook. As you trace over each one, or as you make the movements in the air, have the students follow your movements in the air. Watch the movements to insure that each student is moving in the right direction. The gross movements give a better feeling for the direction of the motion than the smaller movements, and give the student more self-confidence in knowing which way to move their hands when writing on paper (1963).

These are astute observations. No wonder a fourth-grade teacher remarked, after observing a group of children taught with this technique on an experimental basis in her school that it "seemed like a miracle program in regards to what it did for the children" (Open Court Program Evaluation, 1971)—so great was the contrast to all the other children taught with conventional whole-word techniques.

Lack of Success with ITA

Open Court and other such techniques make it possible to teach even kindergarten children that letters have different sounds, and to pronounce these sounds while writing. It is not necessary to teach a special alphabet whose letter forms differ according to sounds, such as ITA (the Initial Teaching Alphabet). A special alphabet makes writing more difficult for children because eventually they have to learn the regular manuscript and the cursive alphabet anyhow, which means that they have to learn three alphabets instead of two.

My experience with children taught with ITA has been entirely negative. It was used widely for beginning readers in New York City and in other school systems. I have seen a number of third- and fourth graders who were totally confused by it. It seems to be especially confusing for children with even the mildest organic defects. They get so bewildered that they give up trying.

The educational psychologist Gordon L. Barclay, however, reported good results when he taught ITA to a group of seriously mentally ill children in a state hospital. Most of these children had been diagnosed as suffering from childhood schizophrenia. Their reading and their behavior improved so remarkably that most of them could be sent home.

The explanation for this success may be that these children suffered from organic reading, writing, and speech disorders or from behavior disorders, rather than from schizophrenia, and that the special attention given to them combined with remedial reading lessons (which this program gave them for the first time in their lives) had a psychotherapeutic as well as a remedial effect on them. ITA most likely opened their eyes for the first time in their lives to the fact that letters stand for sounds. Before this, all of them had been taught for years unsuccessfully with whole-word methods (Barclay, 1966).

Importance of a Teachable Phonetic System

One difficulty that must be overcome before all children can be taught in an efficient way, by learning letter forms and sounds simultaneously, is that all teachers must learn the phonetic organization of English spelling. This is not now taught universally in education courses in colleges, so far as I know.

Romalda Spalding has developed what is probably the most plausible and useful phonetic system. She teaches writing and reading with the help of "phonograms," which she defines as "a single letter or a fixed combination of two, three or four letters, which is the symbol for one sound in a given word" (1969, p. 18). Her method is based on 70 "common phonograms." This sounds complicated, but English spelling is complicated, and these phonograms actually simplify the understanding and with it the remembering of English spelling.

Once the teacher has mastered the phonograms, she will find that even kindergarten children will respond to them with enthusiasm. Children like to experiment with different sounds, they like to write, and they enjoy forming sounds while they are writing. Their excitement when they discover that they can compose words by putting sounds together in writing is sometimes touching. There are, of course, numerous other phonetic systems.

The attention to minute details that is required to teach writing the way I have described it is not a disadvantage. Spalding is correct in her statement that

> small errors prevent children from learning to write easily, legibly and neatly. They require careful and continued teaching of all the techniques. Children from the beginning need to be taught to follow directives. Success in these writing skills gives children great pride and interest in learning each day's lesson. Each skill builds self-confidence (Spalding & Spalding, 1969, p. 46).

These principles are very elementary and should not have to be stressed, but unfortunately they are not generally adhered to.

The instructions to teachers using "Words in Color," a reading and writing method that has recently become fashionable, are an example for this. Teachers are told that "so long as the signs made on the chalkboard or on paper by the learner are recognizable by him and the teacher as an attempt at forming them, they should be acceptable" (Gattegno, 1962, p. 14). For an illustration of the pathetic letter forms these children produce see Gattegno (1962 p. 15; 1968, pp. 163–166).

Such casual approaches to writing are apt to create writing and reading disorders in children with a normal central nervous system, and magnify the defects in children with even the mildest forms of organic impairments. It is not primarily a question of legibility, but of learning letter forms and sounds with precision and simultaneously, so that a fixed association can develop between them early; otherwise the formation of the indispensable technical basis for reading and writing is unduly delayed. The entire "Words in Color" method turned out to be a disaster in all schools with which I am familiar. It was discontinued after school districts had spent thousands of dollars on it.

Most current curriculum practices damage children by unnecessarily lengthening the time required to learn to read and write. This inhibits the child's general intellectual, and with it his emotional development.

Comparative Study of Conventional Teaching Methods with the Phonetic Spalding Approach

A visit to any kindergarten and first grade where children are being taught with the Spalding method, when compared with the children's performance in conventional kindergartens and first grades, shows the superiority of this method convincingly. The contrast is striking.

I had the opportunity to make such a comparative study of kindergartens and first grades that were especially suited for this purpose. All were situated in the same neighborhood and had the same type of student population. The classes were located in different housing projects. The parents of all children were poor, about half of them were on public assistance, and more than half of the children spoke Spanish at home, so that English was a second language for them. In other words, they were children whom teachers find very difficult to teach.

I visited these classes several times throughout the year. In May, that is 1 month before promotion, when many kindergarten children were already 6 years old, I asked the teachers to let all children write whatever they could, and to let me have what they had written. In this way I obtained tangible evidence of their writing skill.

Conventional Kindergartens

The reading and writing abilities of children in conventional kindergartens, even with the most devoted, kind, and experienced teachers, are minimal. I have visited many such kindergartens in private and public schools, in wealthy and in deprived neighborhoods. The children usually graduate from them with no more writing skill than the ability to write their own first name, and an uncertain and widely varying ability to read some words and write some letters. Unless they pick it up from their parents or infer it from the entirely visual exercises their teachers give them, they cannot sound out any letter or word.

The conventional kindergarten I selected for comparison with a Spalding kindergarten was exactly like all the others. Its two teachers told me that their children could write only their first names, and that some could not even do that; they could only copy it from their name cards.

When I asked them to let all the 19 children present that day write, they made them sit down at two large tables and handed them large pieces of drawing paper, which they tore off some paper rolls. There were no writing books or papers, lined or unlined. The drawing paper had, of course, no lines. Each child took a crayon. No pencils were used. It was a most informal, casual activity. The children ran back and forth, looking for their name cards to copy from, and rarely sat still. Their attitude was one of playfulness and not of study, and their inability to concentrate was obvious. They clearly had not been taught how to concentrate.

Some children wrote their name spontaneously, most copied, and some made mistakes even in copying. They held their paper at differing angles. Those who wrote their first and their last name had no idea where one word ended and another began. All of them intermingled capital with small letters, the sizes and positions of their letters varied, and not all children could read what they had written or explain to me how what they wrote came to say their name. Even 6-year-olds reversed letters, repeated syllables, and were not sure of the left-to-right direction of writing. One 5-year-old girl wrote her first name straight up vertically.

The teachers did not correct any one of the children's mistakes. They told me that writing was not taught in any formal way. Only two children, both 6 years old, a right-handed boy and a left-handed girl, wrote their first names legibly and on a fairly straight line. All other names, whether copied or written on their own, with the right or with the left hand, were difficult to read (Figures 3.5, 3.6, 3.7).

INFLUENCE OF COMIC BOOKS.   As the children finished their writing, a fight broke out between a girl and a boy for the possession of a comic book another 5-year-old girl had brought to school. The boy had taken it from her and started to color it with his crayon. He let me look at it after the teacher had stopped the fight and given me permission to stay with the children for a while. They gathered around me (I suspect the comic book was the attraction) and we talked. It was an especially violent *Supergirl* comic book with the word "murderess" emblazoned three times on its title page. Of course these children could not read this or any other word in the stories, but they did not have to. They could follow the violent stories very well by looking at the pictures. They could watch the gun fights, explosions, fires, hitting, stomping, kicking, killing (Supergirl kills a gorilla and another superwoman), and spin their fantasies around these picture stories even while remaining illiterate. Comic book pictures are designed to tell the story in detail; the text is not essential but is always subordinated to the pictures (see Figure 2.2).

Comic books played a major role in the lives of all these children. They talked about them with great excitement. All of them owned, bought, traded, and collected them. One boy complained that his mother did not like them because his younger (this boy was only 5 years old!) brother tore them up and threw them on the floor, and she had to clean up after him. These poor children spent the few pennies, nickels, or dimes their parents could afford to give them on candy and on comic books. They were steady customers of the comic book industry, good for about $1.50 a month each, or about $285 a year for the entire class. And this was a time when comic books sold for only 15 cents; their price has increased to 50 cents or more apiece!

FIG. 3.5.

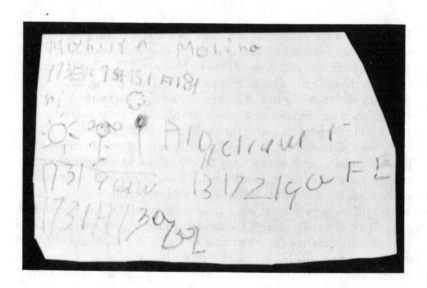

FIG. 3.6.

FIGS. 3.5, 3.6, AND 3.7.   Examples of spontaneous writing of children in May of their kindergarten year, ages 5.8 and 6. They have no clear concept of letter forms or directions. These examples are typical for children in conventional kindergartens all over the United States.

197

FIG. 3.7.

This is not an innocuous pastime: there is a direct relationship between comic books and reading disorders in children. (See sections on Linear Dyslexia, p. 127; and Damaging Aspects of Mass Media, p. 275.) These kindergarten children showed early signs of habituation to picture gazing, and to comic books. They also showed a lack of interest in reading. It is more pleasant and less strenuous to gaze at a picture, to daydream about it, to play at exactly what one has seen in the pictures, rather than to learn to read. The eyes can wander leisurely from picture to picture; they do not have to follow one straight line.

These children's minds were already filled with violent comic book and, of course, also television stories, which had influenced not only their attitude toward reading but also their behavior. Their wildness, restlessness, overexcitement and difficulty in concentrating showed traces of TV and comic book viewing. Here, one could observe the damaging influences of comic books on reading in statu nascendi (in the process of birth), and confirm all of Wertham's tenets, especially his finding that comic books do some of their most pernicious harm long before the child has been taught to read. These observations can be repeated in kindergartens all over the country.

The fact that comic books do such great harm to reading before the child enters the first grade intensifies the need for efficient teaching of writing and reading. It tests the adequacy of teaching methods even more severely, since only a child who can read and write, and enjoys both skills, has a chance not to become a comic book addict or to overcome his addiction where it has already taken hold of him. The earlier he learns to read and write, therefore, the better are his chances.

I discussed their teaching of writing with the conventional kindergarten teachers. They showed me the materials they used. One of their mimeographed worksheets had the words "Hand," "Eye," "Ear," "Leg," "Foot," and others written on one side, and pictures of those different body parts on the other. The child had to connect the picture and the corresponding word with a line. This amounts to a guessing game because the child has not learned letter sounds, and is supposed to recognize the word from its "configuration." On another sheet appeared words such as: "that," "we," "balloon," "grandfather," "table," "in," "giraffe," "moon," "automobile" in lower-case letters with the following caption: "Put a line UNDER the different Word." The capitalization of "W" in "Word" and of the entire word "UNDER" can only be confusing for those few children who could read the words. I was pleased to see at least one writing worksheet consisting of small manuscript letters written underneath each other on the left side of the page, each in a square box. The child was to copy each letter inside empty boxes, from left to right. The same types of worksheets are used in kindergartens and in first and second grades all over the country (Figures 3.4 and 3.8).

The teachers in this conventional kindergarten had many years of experience. They loved the children and believed in what they were doing. They were certainly not to blame for their students' lack of achievement. Both these teachers and their students were the victims of erroneous educational theories and practices. The children in the three other kindergartens in the same school had younger and less experienced teachers and were even worse off. Their classes were less structured and often quite chaotic. The children ran wild, and most of them did not even learn to write their first name.

Spalding Kindergarten

The kindergarten children taught with the Spalding method, on the other hand, sat quietly, relaxed and in a pleasant mood in front of their lined paper. All were alert and attentive, and had obviously learned to concentrate on a given task. They knew me, and this behavior was not just put on to impress me. There were 22 children aged 5 and 6 years. All wrote with a pencil. I had visited this kindergarten before when some of them were still writing with chalk on their own individual chalkboards. I am describing what I observed in May. All children wrote their first name clearly and the words "me," "and," "at," "she," "no," "let," "red," "boy," "is," "ten" correctly as the teacher dictated them. They pronounced the words before and while they were writing them down.

Four children, two 6-year-old girls and two boys aged 5 and 6, had some directional difficulties, but all corrected their errors with some help from the

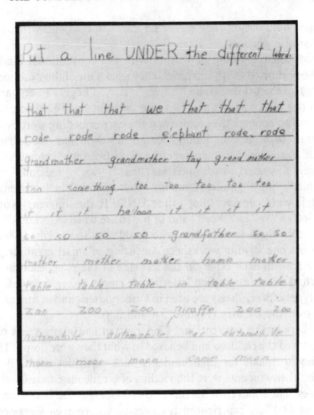

FIG. 3.8. Another example from the conventional kindergarten. These children can neither read nor write. Here is the reason why: Letter writing or reading is not taught. Only the sight-word method is used. Without being able to read the instructions, which in addition intermingle capital and lower-case letters, they have to practice underlining words that look different, that they can neither read nor write spontaneously.

other children. Only one 6-year-old girl made serious mistakes and did not correct them. She transposed letters, writing "ta" instead of "at" and "ehs" instead of "she." The forms and directions of her letters were accurate. This girl had not attended this kindergarten throughout the school year, but had only recently been admitted from a tragically deprived home. Her parents had died, and she and her brother were cared for by an old lady who was not related to them and who spoke only Spanish. Nevertheless, this girl did better than another child in a conventional kindergarten would have done.

I had observed the same kindergarten class earlier in the school year, while the teacher taught them to write the words "high," "might," "night." These words contain the phonogram "igh," which Spalding calls the "three-letter i." This is a plausible way to teach the pronunciation of this letter combination because it helps the children to remember it. All the kindergarten children wrote and read these words before they entered the first grade. What a contrast to students taught conventionally! I have seen far too many elementary and even junior and senior high school students struggle unsuccessfully to read and write just such words.

That potentially serious directional difficulties can be prevented by this teaching method is shown by the following observation: A 5-year-old left-handed girl in the Spalding kindergarten did exactly what a 5-year-old right-handed girl had done in the conventional kindergarten. Both turned their paper so they were writing their name vertically. This also shows, contrary to prevailing theories, that handedness and sex have nothing to do with this directional difficulty, which may be the first sign of a horizontal mirror-writing problem (i.e., a tendency to inversions). Only the Spalding-taught girl corrected the direction of her writing quietly, on her own, as soon as words were dictated. She watched the other children, noticed the line she was supposed to write on, and turned her paper the way all the other children did. She certainly will not have this directional problem anymore when she enters first grade, while the other girl undoubtedly will continue to write vertically.

The Spalding method requires that all children learn 54 phonograms by saying them, writing them, and forming sentences with them, before they are handed books to read. Many kindergarten children in the classes I visited were in the book-reading stage by March.

I showed the writing samples of the Spalding-taught kindergarten pupils to remedial reading teachers, psychologists, and elementary school teachers, and asked them what grade they thought these children were attending. Without exception they put them at the end of the first or the beginning of the second grade; none had ever seen this kind of work done by kindergarten children (Figures 3.9, 3.10, 3.11).

The Spalding first grades I observed were located in the same housing project as the kindergartens. They had been organized by the same remarkable teachers, Helaine O'Shaughnessy and Sylvia Friedman, who were fed up with their students' lack of progress with the conventional whole-word method. They had learned the Spalding method entirely on their own, and had modified it in line with their own practical teaching experience. They received no support whatsoever from the school administrators, who barely tolerated their new approach. Their relative independence was made easier by the fact that their classes were not located in the main school building, but in an annex several blocks away.

All the Spalding-taught first graders, even those children who had not

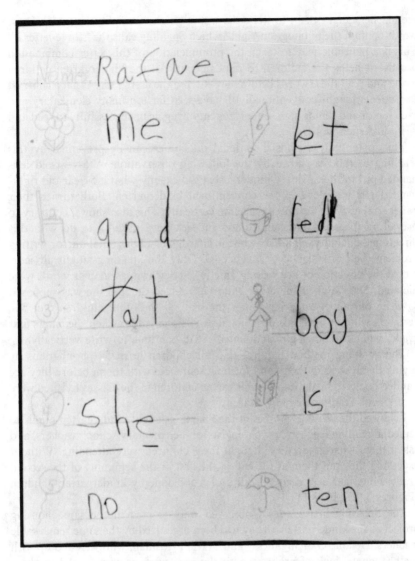

FIG. 3.9.

FIGS. 3.9–3.11. This is how children of exactly the same age (5.8 to 6 years) and from exactly the same neighborhood write to dictation and spontaneously when taught with the Spalding phonetic method. They are far advanced in reading, writing, and speaking English and remain so throughout school unless regressing because of being confused by later sight-word teaching.

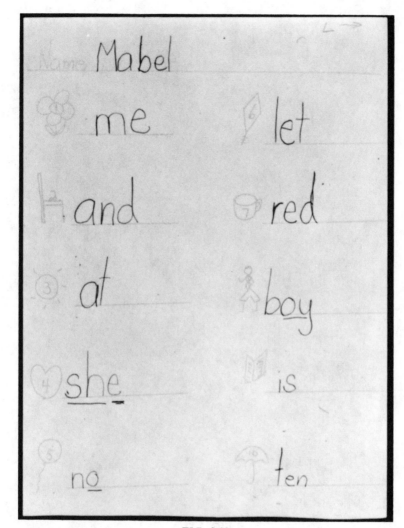

FIG. 3.10

attended a Spalding kindergarten, were in the book-reading stage by March or earlier. By the end of the grade, all read at least at the mid-second-grade level when compared with conventionally taught children, and more than half of them had reached the fourth-grade level in reading. Their writing was far superior to any first and second graders I have ever observed or examined individually.

The 21 first graders whose writing I recorded in May wrote the words "catch," "black," "warm," "unless," "clothing," "teach," "beside," "sight,"

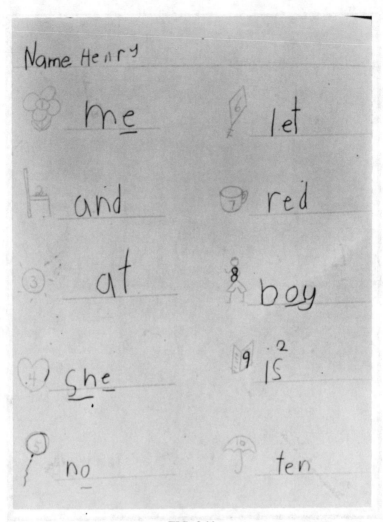

FIG. 3.11

"stood," "fix," "thought," "extra," "brought," "enough," "cough," "through" to dictation without a mistake. All of them knew that "happened" needs an "ed" at its end, which is more than many junior high and sometimes even senior high and college students know.

When I visited the same class earlier during the term, I had noticed that three boys and one girl had special writing difficulties. They formed their letters slowly and with clumsy movements. Their lines were wavy and uncertain, but the form and direction of their letters were always correct. By May they had overcome their difficulties. These four children had also all taken longer to learn the phonograms, but they had caught up with their classmates. These four would undoubtedly have had a much harder time learning to write and read with the official haphazard approach involving sight/word and initial consonants, and would have been headed for a reading disorder. I did not see even one bored child in any of these classes. One must have visited many classes where the official methods are in use, to really appreciate the difference.

I found no comic books either in the kindergarten or the first grade where the Spalding method was used, and not one child was obsessed with comic books. All Spalding-taught first graders and many kindergarten children could read books and were interested in reading without the help of pictures. All of them knew that reading has nothing to do with pictures. They looked forward eagerly all month to the day when the inexpensive paperback storybooks the teachers ordered for them arrived. They kept asking, "When are the books coming?" They took them home to read on their own, and told me that they traded them "just like comic books."

Additional Benefits of Spalding and Other Phonetic Methods

Teaching Reading through Writing

There are a number of important additional benefits of teaching reading through writing with Spalding or other similar techniques. These are discussed next.

1. The child's pronunciation of formal English improves. The teachers of the Spalding classes had wisely insisted that the children's parents participate, and I had the opportunity to speak with some of them. All were enthusiastic about their children's progress and told me that the first improvement they noticed was that their children spoke better. Their diction had improved, and they pronounced even the new English words they were learning clearly and almost without a trace of an accent. This result was of special importance for these parents who were Spanish-speaking and wanted their children to lose their Spanish accent, which had been such a handicap in their own lives.

2. This technique makes it possible to teach children from the beginning that slight differences in sound, as well as the different spelling of sounds, change the meaning of words. In this way, variations in sounds with their corresponding spelling are firmly connected in the child's mind with the meaning of words, so that he learns to understand the words he is writing and reading better and earlier than with other methods.

All Spalding first-graders, for instance, could write and read the word "sight." When the teacher asked them to define it, however, some of them confused it with the word "side": they pointed to their own side. Whole-word methods have no way of impressing such spelling and meaning distinctions on the child's mind, which puts children with organic defects, even mild ones, at a special disadvantage. Fine sound distinctions are most difficult for so many of them, especially when they also suffer from even the mildest form of receptive aphasia, as so many of them do.

3. Many children remember new words and ideas better when they write them down. There is a constitutional difference among children regarding the easiest perceptual learning route: they belong either to the visual or to the auditory constitutional type. This does not mean that a child who can learn better visually cannot also learn by listening, but that the visual route is very much easier and faster for him. However, there are children of either type who cannot learn at all by the other route. One boy in the Spalding class, for instance, could not learn to name colors. He finally succeeded in remembering color names, after he had learned to write them down. He obviously belonged to the visual type. Such a child just cannot remember what he only hears, but must have visual aids. The early teaching of writing is quite essential for such a child, and so is reading. A visual-type child who cannot read or write, is far more handicapped than a child who can learn by listening. He is apt to fall far behind his classmates no matter how good his intelligence. (See section on Role of Memory, p. 70 ff.)

When the Spalding-taught children entered the second grade in the main school building, their superiority to their classmates became evident. Only a few of them forgot part of their writing and reading skills because of the conventional techniques used by the new teachers.

The success of these isolated classes was so convincing even to an initially hostile administration, that the school principal introduced a combination of the Spalding method with the *Open Court Readers* for all children in her school. This lead to the spread of these methods to almost the entire school district.

BOY, 9 YEARS OLD: AN ORGANIC WRITING DISORDER AGGRAVATED BY POOR TEACHING. A fourth-grade teacher asked me informally to help her with a 9-year-old boy who had trouble writing. He could write only when permitted to write very large, with a marker (and not with a pencil), and on lined paper. He came from an intellectual home where he was surrounded with books he could not read.

I observed him while he was desperately trying to fill in a word to complete one of those mimeographed incomplete sentences teachers hand to children. The complete sentence was supposed to be "I want to go home." He had to fill in the word "want," but wrote "what" instead. When I asked him to read the entire sentence to me, he read, "I what to go home." I tested his spontaneous speech and found that whenever he meant "want," he said "what"—i.e., he pronounced "want" as "what." I pointed this out to the teacher, who had not noticed it before, and suggested that his hearing be tested and that he be examined by a speech therapist. Defective hearing or a mild receptive aphasia may have been the cause of his reading, speech, and spelling disorder. His writing difficulty may have been due to a mild apraxia. In any case, his defective pronunciation of formal English would have been noticed and corrected in kindergarten or the first grade had he been taught with a method such as Spalding, or had at least dictation been used regularly from the first grade on.

INADEQUACY OF THE SENTENCE-COMPLETION METHOD. The sentence-completion teaching used by the boy's fourth-grade teacher is a very popular device used in every elementary school in this country. Unfortunately, it is most inadequate. It consists of a mimeographed worksheet with a number of incomplete sentences, and a choice of four words printed under each sentence. The child has to select the word that belongs in the sentence, and write it in the space provided for this purpose. The fourth-grade boy I mentioned had to fill in his own word, but most such worksheets offer multiple choices.

So far as writing is concerned, all this teaches is copying. It is easier for the teacher to hand out these worksheets than to correct compositions or dictation, and this undoubtedly is the reason for the popularity of this device. Added to this "advantage" is that it enables children to work quietly on their own. However, unless each child reads all his sentences orally to the teacher, he may only appear to have read and completed them correctly, when he actually made serious mistakes in reading and understanding.

I have seen numerous examples of this, for instance during a visit to recently established "open" first-and second-grade classrooms, where many children worked with such sentence-completion worksheets. I asked a number of them to read the sentences to me and found that many made serious mistakes. One 8-year-old girl, for instance, read "*Every baby* has to *sleep.*" ("sleep" was the word she had filled in correctly), when the sentence actually read, "*Everybody* has to sleep." This indicated that she confused "d" with "b" and "a" with "o." The very fact that this second-grade girl had to study such a simple sentence showed how far behind she was compared with the Spalding-taught kindergarten and first-grade children, whose school was just a few blocks away from hers.

Prevention of Number-Writing Disorders

Number writing is usually considered to be a part of arithmetic and so simple that it needs no special attention. Yet some number forms and sequences present difficulties for children, especially when they have even the mildest organic defects. Numbers should therefore be taught to beginners with the same care as letters. Saying the number before and during writing it makes it easier for most children to remember their numbers. Writing on a line also helps. Just as with letter forms, some children may learn the direction and forms of numbers better when they trace them and write them in the air first.

Reversals are frequent with the numbers 2, 3, 4, 5, 6, 7, and 9. Inversions may occur with 2, 4, 5, 6, 7, and 9. These children confuse 9 with 6 and 2 with 5. Careful teaching can avoid this in all but the comparatively few children who suffer from the severest forms of organic writing and reading disorders. (See section on Directional Confusion of Letters and Words, p. 99.)

NUMBER-SEQUENCE WRITING DIFFICULTIES.   Learning to write and read number sequences is just as difficult as letter sequences. Some children have trouble with different aspects of it. In order to prevent such difficulties from developing, and to help those children who have number-sequence reading and writing disorders, an analysis of their mistakes should be made.

Tests.   The following five acts should be tested to make sure that the child can write and understand number sequences:

1. Writing all single numbers
2. Reading all single numbers
3. Understanding the arithmetic principles underlying single, double, triple numbers, and so on
4. Writing double, triple, etc. numbers
5. Reading double, triple, etc. numbers

Unless all five acts are tested, fundamental errors in arithmetic may be overlooked. These errors may remain with the child through the higher grades and prevent him from learning arithmetic beyond the number 10, and all mathematics.

READING AND WRITING DIFFICULTIES WITH DOUBLE NUMBERS.   It is especially important for the teacher to realize that there is a difference between reading and writing double numbers. This difficulty involves the left-to-right or right-to-left direction of reading double numbers. This is confusing for healthy children; it is especially difficult for children with organic impairments.

The step beyond the number 10 presents a qualitative leap for every child so far as arithmetic concepts are concerned. Even the child who understands these concepts must learn that the numbers "eleven" and "twelve" have their own special names, and that "thirteen, fourteen, fifteen, sixteen, seventeen, eighteen, nineteen" are read from right to left, whereas all numbers from then on are read from left to right, just as letters (e.g., twenty-one, etc.). Unless this is specifically explained to children, many will make mistakes in numbers reading. This affects their arithmetic. I have examined a number of children whose low scores in arithmetic were due not so much to a lack of understanding of number concepts, as to mistakes in reading number sequences.

Children with organic reading disorders very frequently make mistakes in reading number sequences. It is hard for most of them to learn the left-to-right direction of reading letters. The switch to a right-to-left direction is just too confusing for them. After having memorized these numbers, they may get into the habit of reading all number sequences from right to left.

CYRUS, 9 YEARS OLD: A NUMBER-READING DISORDER. Ten-year-old Cyrus is a good example for this number-sequence reading disorder. (See also case of Cyrus, p. 000 under Writing to Dictation.) He had a severe organic reading, writing, and arithmetic disorder, and had just learned to write and read all letters and numbers and some short words. He wanted to show me that he could at last write "big" numbers. He wrote "56" and called it "sixty-five," "35" and read it as "fifty-three." I could not explain the nature of his mistake to him, because he did not yet understand the difference between the numerical and the position value of a number. He did not comprehend that the number on the left presents a multiple of 10. (See discussion of acalculia under Gerstmann syndrome, p. 175; and Chapter 4, Arithmetic Disorders, p. 221.)

Basic Principles for the Teaching of Writing to Beginners So That Writing and Reading Disorders Can Be Prevented

1. Teach systematically and not casually.
2. Let the child write only on lined paper from the start (i.e., from kindergarten on).
3. Teach the sounds of letters before you teach their names. (See section on letter and word reading, pp. 90ff; and Conditioned Reflexes, p.78.)
4. Teach only *one* style and *one* size letter.
5. Supervise how the child forms his letters. *Let no mistake stand.*
6. Let the child sound out the letters and letter combinations before and while he writes them. Do not let the child write what he cannot read, nor read what he cannot write.
7. No silent copying or silent filling in of multiple-choice words or of sentence completions.
8. Dictate.
9. Let the child write his own sentences and stories as soon as possible.

Handwriting Analysis

Handwriting analysis is called graphology. It is an important projective technique. Once writing has hurdled the beginner stage, its gross and fine aspects become highly individualized and can be analyzed on different levels for a personality profile and as an aid to the diagnosis. However, it can be an aid only. No diagnosis of any condition—whether "within normal limits," psychopathologic, or organic—should be based on graphology alone. It should be part of every clinical examination and should be evaluated within this clinical framework as one more projective test capable of giving limited but often reliable insight, mainly into the child's character structure and certain basic trends. It is a direct and spontaneous creation of the child and more easily accessible than other projective techniques, the Rorschach test, for instance. It should be used more widely than it is at present.

Graphology requires special study just as do other projective techniques such as the Rorschach test. There are different methods of interpretation and various theoretical approaches. It is unfortunately considered a specialty at the margin rather than the center of clinical psychology, and psychiatric textbooks do not even mention it. A so-called test battery, which psychologists administer as a matter of routine to children, adolescents, and adults, usually does not include graphology, and some graphologists practice outside the clinical framework. I find graphology such a helpful aid to the understanding of children and adolescents as well as adults, that I recommend its study to all clinicians. Psychiatrist, psychologists, speech therapists, remedial reading specialists, teachers of special education, guidance counselors—all can benefit from studying the elementary principles of handwriting analysis. I can only here touch on some aspects that are especially important for children with reading and writing disorders.

As outlined in Chapter 1 on examination, I obtain a handwriting sample from every patient I examine and analyze it. I also study the handwriting of all the letters my patients ask me to read while they are in psychotherapy with me. These letters are usually written by their parents or by other persons of importance in their lives.

It is possible to diagnose certain distinctive character traits even without knowing the writer; some elementary handwriting traits are that definite. This blind analysis is more reliable when one knows the writer's approximate age and his sex, because handwriting is unclear in these respects. The handwriting of children can sometimes be recognized if the child is still immature and does not yet write fluently.

Handwriting styles are influenced deliberately by the writer's esthetic judgment. Even children change their style for esthetic and sometimes other reasons, which are mostly playful experimentations. Handwriting remains highly personal in spite of this, and each individual's writing can be identified with great precision when examined with a magnifying glass. Even such short pieces as signatures are difficult to disguise or to forge. That is why graphologists are important witnesses in court, and experts in identifying signatures on old paintings and on historic documents.

For a handwriting analysis, a spontaneous piece of writing is needed, which should be a paragraph or preferably a page long. Cursive writing on unlined paper is more revealing than manuscript style or printing. The more emotionally tinged the text, the more revealing the analysis. Copying or writing to dictation do not provide good graphologic samples. Where only words are available, they should be emotionally meaningful, like the words "father," "mother," or "myself."

When examining a handwriting sample, one should first get a general impression of the entire piece of writing and scrutinize the details later on. Size; general organization; direction; spacing; fluidity; regularity; stability; accuracy of letter forms; legibility; linearity (i.e., staying on an imaginary horizontal line, going up or down, weaving in and out); variations of pressure; relationships of upper, middle, and lower zones to each other—all these distinctive features can be noted while surveying the entire sample. This survey should be done without reading the text. The content is not helpful for this analysis of a person's unintentional graphic expression, which stems from preconscious as well as unconscious mental layers.

Two basically different aspects of handwriting analysis must be distinguished:

1. Signs of organic or somatic diseases or impairments, which are definite clinical symptoms.

2. Indications of psychopathology or character traits, which are less definite and more speculative.

Signs of Physical Diseases or Impairments, Somatic or Pertaining to the Central Nervous System

A child or an adult may not be capable of writing during an acute severe physical illness with high fever, whether or not the brain is directly involved, as in encephalitis. General physical weakness from whatever cause leads to small, tremulous writing with fine, wavy, often interrupted strokes. No physical illness can, of course, be diagnosed by handwriting analysis, but important hints can be obtained.

A change in a formerly normal handwriting can be an important symptom in neurologic and cerebral diseases. In juvenile paresis, for instance, which is a syphilitic infection of the brain affecting children usually after they have learned to write (it is a late manifestation of congenital syphilis where the fetus has been infected by his mother), handwriting change is an early symptom. Irregularities of letter forms appear; letters start weaving above and below the line; eventually the letters are written together, sometimes doubled or tripled, strokes are left out, and the writing becomes increasingly illegible. As the disease progresses, the handwriting deteriorates (Schmidt-Kraepelin, 1920, pp. 30–31).

Not only juvenile paresis, but other progressive brain diseases also involving large cerebral areas including the reading and writing apparatuses, are accompanied by deteriorating handwriting (Vick 1976, p. 333).

Typical handwriting defects of children suffering from different forms of apraxia were outlined in the section dealing with these organic symptoms. Perseveration is another one of these symptoms, which affects handwriting in a typical way. This can be seen in the illustration of the handwriting of 10-year-old Doug, p. 97, in Vol. II, p. 487, in the section on Perseveration (Figure 11.1).

Indications of Psychopathology and Character Traits

VARIOUS PRESSURES.   The pressure used by the writer is meaningful. Even and heavy pressure indicates vitality; light, fine, sometimes uneven and interrupted strokes show lack of vitality and indicate fatigue, lack of confidence, vagueness, indecisiveness. These fine, light strokes may also point to a physical illness.

EXCITABILITY.   Excitability and states of great excitement can be seen in handwriting. Such writing is large and irregular with heavy pressure, big loops, and a fast movement towards the right bumping into the margin of the paper, sometimes ending abruptly and continuing on the next line without regard to the correct division of words at the end of a line. An expansive, exuberant, even manic handwriting looks very similar. One can tell if a child has written a note in great excitement.

DEPRESSION.   One can also get hints of depression from handwriting samples. Depressed children and adults write small letters with fine, uncertain lines that sometimes show small breaks. Depressed patients of all ages make a desperate effort to pull up their downward sagging lines, especially towards the end of a line or sentence.

SMALL WRITING.   Small writing usually indicates anxiety, insecurity, feelings of inferiority, and depression. Small writing with heavy pressure where each letter is carefully and precisely drawn, or even redrawn by retracing it, indicates fear of making mistakes, compulsive preoccupation with details, possibly an attempt to appear above suspicion.

SECRETIVENESS.   Secretiveness or withdrawal from social contact is sometimes indicated by a very small, crowded handwriting where all letters are carefully covered up, (e.g., by low and very long t-bars), and where round letters are circled several times so that they are closed securely. Even normally open letters such as "u" are closed in such handwriting. This may also indicate a tendency to be deceitful. Such interpretations must, of course, be made with caution and be verified by the results of other tests and by the clinical examination.

CHARACTERISTICS FOR WRITING AND READING DISORDERS. Children have the tendency to write small in the beginning, when they feel unsure of their writing. They should be taught, however, to write large, because this makes it easier for them to write clearly and accurately. Small writing with uncertain and often interrupted strokes is typical for children with reading and writing disorders. Their strokes are either very fine or much too heavy; and their letters and words are crowded together as if they were trying to lean on each other. Such heavy, crowded, and illegible writing is often due to the muscular tenseness of children with these disorders. They hold their pencil so tight and their fingers are so stiff that they get cramps in them, so that their hand and even their arm begins to hurt.

SLANTS. The normal direction of handwriting is towards the right. The slant of each single stroke and loop does not necessarily follow this direction. These slants vary in normal handwriting. Perfectly even slants indicate that the writer does not really want to relate to others and makes a deliberate effort to appear well balanced and even-tempered. Anxiety, insecurity, and/or hostility may be hidden behind such writing. A writing whose direction is predominantly towards the right, which is large and well proportioned with strong and fairly even pressure, indicates that the writer feels secure, is at ease socially, and strives towards the future with positive anticipation. A tendency toward impulsiveness is indicated when such handwriting slides downwards into the lower writing zone. Children and adolescents frequently do this. It indicates that they give vent to their emotions freely and uncritically.

When the slant of the writing is directed towards the left, we can assume that the writer has a defensive attitude. His feelings and thoughts are usually turned toward the past, and he is afraid or unwilling to face the future. This slant may also indicate stubbornness and negativism, especially in children and adolescents.

"AGGRESSIVE" STROKES. Sometimes each stroke looks like an exclamation point or gets wider at its lower end. These strokes are written by angry people, and as such, are called "aggressive" strokes. Some children press so hard while they write that they tear the paper. This may mean anger and frustration or an overzealous, overtense attempt to steady the pencil and make exact letter forms. As in all other projective tests, each individual detail has several meanings; it can be interpreted correctly only if all other features are also taken into consideration. Tearing the paper means anger only if the child says he is angry or if there are other indications in the handwriting of anger, impulsiveness, irritability; it means overanxiousness where other features indicate anxiety and compulsive striving for exactitude.

Common Features of Handwriting Analysis and Drawing Tests

Even the evaluation of an entire test depends to some extent on findings in other tests. Some projective tests are more closely related to each other than others in this respect. Handwriting analysis for instance, is very closely related to the analysis of drawings. Both of these projective techniques should therefore be studied and interpreted in conjunction with each other. As I pointed out in the beginning of the section on writing, drawing and writing are closely related neurophysiologically, psychologically, and historically. When they are evaluated as projective tests, the basic principles of their interpretation are also closely related. I use primarily the Koch Tree test and the Machover Figure-Drawing test (Koch, 1953; Machover, 1948).

Pressure, continuity, direction of strokes and lines have the same meaning in both writing and drawing. A tree or a figure drawn with a slant to the left and/or placed on the left side of the paper indicates fixation on the past, preoccupation with the past, fear of the future.

A well-proportioned, large drawing placed in the center of the page or somewhat to the right indicates confidence; a firm grip on reality, a feeling of strength, of being able to face the present and the future. Where the drawing is very large, bumping into the edge of the paper, excitement, expansiveness, dramatization, or a tendency to hysteria are indicated.

Dependency needs, a search for protection and support are indicated in writing and in drawings when figures, trees, or words have to lean on each other or on some other guides, such as the edge of the paper or a wall.

In addition to these basic features, some specific structural details of handwriting and drawings should be compared with each other. When this is done, it becomes apparent that these tests complement each other, that they can underline and stress, or modify the diagnosis of some character traits and psychopathologic trends.

Zones

Most graphologists divide handwriting into three zones—an upper, middle, and lower zone—and pay special attention to the details of the letters in each zone. Even though they analyze the total handwriting, their theory is that each zone specializes in the projection of a different basic aspect of the writer's personality. The bulk of all letters is in the middle zone; loops, lines, bars, and dots occupy the upper zone; and some lines and loops comprise the lower zone.

The correlation of these zones with the projection of different personality levels was made by graphologists in their practical work. They found that the upper zone gives clues to the writer's intellectual, the middle zone to his emotional, and the lower zone to his instinctual life. Of course these zonal interpretations should not be rigidly adhered to, but they are useful for handwriting as well as drawing analysis.

THE UPPER ZONE. The psychologic basis for the different meanings of these zones is that we experience the upper, middle, and lower parts of any graphic expression as corresponding to the upper, middle, and lower parts of our body, and that we feel that certain mental and emotional activities take place in these parts of our body. For instance, we locate intellectual activity and fantasy life in the upper part of our body, namely, in the head. That is why the head in figure drawings and the crown of the tree in Koch's Tree test refer to intelligence and imagination—among other trends projected into them. That is why the upper writing zone reveals something about the intellectual and spiritual life of the writer. The larger this zone is proportionately, the more emphasis is placed by the writer on intellectual and spiritual matters and the more active his fantasy life. This can have positive or negative implications. The loops, lines, dots, and bars in this zone can indicate a clear, piercing, critical, probing intellect that remains within realistic limits. They can also show vague, confused, uncertain thinking with a tendency to daydream. One can sometimes see that the writer makes a strenuous effort to pull his fantasies down to reality, into the middle zone.

Head of Figures and Tree Crowns. A proportionately large head or tree crown has positive or negative implications, which are similar to a large upper handwriting zone. A child with a reading and writing disorder who draws a very large head may be preoccupied with daydreaming, with fleeing into a fantasy world. It may also show confused and uncertain thinking and a feeling of intellectual emptiness. Children who stress the head by making it very large and empty sometimes are worried about what goes on inside their head and doubt their sanity.

Sometimes the outline of the head and/or the tree crown has openings or is so thinly drawn that it is hardly visible. This may indicate that the child experiences breaks with reality. This is a serious symptom found in some neuroses and also in schizophrenia. As I have stressed repeatedly, such interpretations should be made with great caution, and never without corroborating evidence from the same and other tests. The ultimate diagnostic decision should always be left to the clinical examination. A large head may indicate no more than the child's immaturity, because the head is the first part of the body very young children (aged 4 or 5) draw. They draw a huge circle with arms and legs protruding from it, before they are capable of drawing a body.

The upper writing zone is small in children in the beginning, and awkwardly drawn. It gets larger and more complex with practice and increasing confidence, knowledge, and sophistication. Children of preschool age draw a small tree crown. When older children draw such a small crown, it indicates limited intelligence and/or lack of confidence in their intellectual ability. A proportionately small head has the same meaning. It is characteristic for figure drawings of children with mental deficiency, and is found very frequently in children suffering from reading and writing disorders, especially when the disorders have an organic basis. These children feel that they can accomplish nothing with their head. They often say of themselves that they are "dumb" or stupid.

MIDDLE ZONE.   The middle writing zone is thought to express the writer's emotionality and the quality of his emotional and social contact. Open-mindedness and friendly acceptance are indicated by freely spaced words, well proportioned, fluently written, and legible with a general slant towards the right. Large, expansive, fluid writing indicates self-confidence, a feeling at ease socially. Where the middle zone is proportionately very large, showiness, pretension, and a tendency to dramatize are indicated. Such a zone must really be exceptionally large to be considered abnormal, because the emphasis is normally on this zone.

Trunk of Tree, Body in Figure Drawings.   The middle zone for writing corresponds to the trunk of the tree and to the body in figure drawings, with the exception of the body area below the belt (i.e., the abdomen and the genitals), which corresponds to the lower writing zone.

A large tree trunk and the body or the figure drawn larger and broader than the head indicate self-confidence. When this type of body also has strong shoulders and arms that reach out freely with well-drawn hands showing all five fingers, it shows that the child is in good contact, reaches out, and explores freely.

Characteristics for Children with Writing and Reading Disorders.   Children with reading and writing disorders draw such strong, harmonious figures only rarely, and the middle zone of their writing does not show fluency and confidence either. Their words are cramped, constricted, and difficult to read. Their entire body is often tense and cramped while they write and they sit as if they had a stomachache, doubled up, so that their head comes close to the paper. One might think that they are nearsighted and need glasses, but their posture is due to this tenseness. These children draw tiny trees and figures, and sometimes just stick figures. They feel they cannot possibly draw the outline of a body or a tree. Their drawings usually lean on something: edges, margins, lines, or each other.

When they draw bodies on their human figures, they draw them thin and weak and often hide them under clothes that are obviously very much too big for them.

Their drawing of arms and hands reflects their feelings of tenseness, constriction, and awkwardness, as well as their fear of reaching out. Arms and hands are especially sensitive body parts for them, because their own arms and hands are ineffectual. They cannot write properly with them and are frequently also poor in other manual skills.

Arms and hands symbolize mastery of the environment, the ability to reach out to others in a friendly way and to defend oneself when necessary. Children with reading and writing disorders do not feel they can master anything. They feel vulnerable, weak, and defenseless, and often do not dare to strike back. That is why the arms and hands on their figure drawings are weak and thin and hang loosely from the body, or are held tightly and closely to it. They either draw no hands at all or too few fingers. Their arms are only rarely connected with strong shoulders, but come off the body at different points and angles. These poorly drawn figures are usually explained as a reflection of these children's poor body image. This explanation is valid, but too general. Each body part also has its own specific meaning.

LOWER ZONES. The lower writing zone is the simplest. Only a few letters reach into it. It indicates instinctual drives, sexual attitudes, and rootedness. It is small in children's handwriting and there is no emphasis on it, until the child's sexual interest develops.

Adolescent girls often avoid this zone completely in their handwriting. They do not want to cross the line from the middle zone into it and touch (even symbolically) the area where their problems lie. These girls usually draw the thighs on their female figure drawing tightly together, as if to protect the sexual area. The figure-drawing treatment of the abdomen, the genital area, and to a certain extent the feet corresponds to the lower writing zone.

Characteristics of Children with Writing and Reading Disorders. Children with writing and reading disorders usually draw thin legs that often consist only of thin lines, sometimes covered by pants that are much too wide, and frequently without shoes or feet to stand on. This omission reflects their feelings of insecurity, of having no solid ground to stand on, of having been uprooted.

Roots of Trees. The treatment of the roots of the tree has similar implications. The tree can be solidly rooted in the soil with only a few strong roots seen above it, or the roots can be small and thin and visible above ground which means that they are vulnerable, and that the tree is not solidly rooted. Children with reading and writing disorders frequently draw trees that are completely open at the bottom of the trunk, having no roots at all; the ground is often not even indicated by a horizontal line. Such children feel unstable, insecure, and completely without roots. (see Vol. II, Figure 11.3 and case of 6-year-old Eugene under Perseveration, p. 493.)

TRANSITIONS FROM ZONE TO ZONE.   How the transitions from one zone to the other are drawn is important and should be studied. For instance, the lower writing zone should not intrude into the middle zone. The lower loops of letters should be crossed before this zone is reached or at its margin, but not beyond it. Where these loops extend into the middle zone, they point to a tendency to be overwhelmed by instinctual drives. Repression and with it control of instincts are necessary to maintain mental health, and this should be reflected in symbolic graphic expressions. This corresponds to the line of resistance in Freud's model of mental layers. Resistance separates and holds back the instincts and the unconscious from the preconscious and conscious, and prevents them from overwhelming and engulfing all mental life.

Analogous to this, a separation of the trunk from its roots should be indicated in some way, either by drawing a horizontal line showing where the ground starts, or by hiding the roots underneath the ground or in some other way. In figure drawings the genitals should be hidden under clothes, and some line in the region of the waist (usually a belt) should separate the sexual and anal areas from the upper parts of the body.

When letters and parts of letters that belong in the middle zone reach into the upper zone, an imbalance between the emotional and the intellectual spheres is indicated; emotions enter into thinking, and the intellectual control of emotions is weak.

These trends are expressed in drawings by the intermingling of the trunk and the branches of the tree with the crown, without any indication that they are separate structures, and in figure drawings by omission of the neck, which normally separates the head from the body. Children who draw a head that rests directly on the body have trouble with the intellectual control of their emotions.

It must be emphasized that not a single one of the drawing features I have described is specific for reading and writing disorders. The diagnosis of these disorders cannot be made by drawing analysis alone. Children and adolescents who can read and write may produce the same types of drawings, which should be interpreted in the same way. Children can feel uprooted, insecure, incapable of reaching out, constricted, and escape into fantasy for many different reasons, not only because they have a reading and writing disorder.

A special talent for drawing does not rule out a writing disorder either. The child with the greatest talent for drawing I have ever seen had a severe reading and writing disorder. He was so distressed by it that he wanted to kill himself.

Suicidal preoccupation and not his reading disorder was the reason for his referral to me.

Drawings as Screening Devices

The drawings made by children with severe reading and writing disorders on an organic basis are usually so characteristic even within these limitations that they are useful screening devices.

Koch Tree Test

A principal once asked me to take over a class of 34 fourth-graders, ages 9 or 10. These children did not know me and were quite understandably excited and disorganized. In order to get acquainted with them and to get them to sit down and to work on something quietly, I asked them to write their names on a piece of paper, to draw a tree, and to write the word "tree."

I analyzed these drawings and handwritings later on and found that the tree drawings of two boys clearly indicated organic difficulties. Their handwriting was also poor. So far as spelling was concerned, most children spelled "tree" like this: "three." This showed that they got "tree" and "three" mixed up, probably also in reading. This misspelling was so prevalent that it could not possibly be explained as due to some organic disorder (which only two children seemed to have). The confusion of "t" with "th" is typical for normally endowed children who have not been properly taught the connection of letters and letter combinations with sounds.

The Goodenough Test

Figure drawings can also be used as a screening device. Florence Goodenough, in her classic and exemplary study of children's drawings, developed a method of scoring them to measure the child's general intellectual maturity. The Goodenough Intelligence Scale is not used much anymore, but her book, *Measurement of Intelligence by Drawings* (1926), remains a unique study of children's drawings, not only from a historic point of view. It describes the empirical structural analysis of many thousands of children's drawings (boys' and girls') and is well worth studying, even though we now know much more about organic, psychologic, and psychopathologic aspects of drawings.

I find the Goodenough scale useful, especially where the diagnosis is doubtful and an organic defect is suspected. The Goodenough I.Q. of such children is usually quite low and often in contrast to a higher I.Q. on other intelligence scales.

When figure drawings are used as group tests, the drawings of children with organic defects sometimes stand out in great contrast to all the others. It must be stressed, however, that group tests should never be used to make a diagnosis, but only to screen—that is, to find children who are in need of thorough individual testing. All children who show distinct defects in their drawings should be referred for individual psychologic testing and also for a psychiatric examination, if the psychologist determines that this is indicated.

Chapter 4

Arithmetic Disorders on an Organic Basis

Arithmetic, like reading, is not an inborn faculty. The cerebral basis for it is present universally, but it remains dormant unless and until the child acquires this skill.

There is a close relationship between arithmetic and reading and writing disorders. Understanding arithmetic depends to some degree on the child's ability to write numbers correctly, to read them, to write the names of numbers with letters, and to read them also. Reading becomes more important the higher the level of arithmetic, because the child must be able to read instructions. This is even more true for mathematics. I have observed that many children make mistakes in both these subjects because they cannot read and understand the instructions.

I have stressed the importance of the careful and systematic teaching of writing; this is even more true for numbers, because arithmetic depends entirely on correct number forms and placements.

There is also a close relationship between arithmetic disorders and speech disorders. In speech disorders on an organic basis (aphasia) in adults or children, arithmetic is almost always affected.

No pure cases of an isolated arithmetic disorder have been reported in adults with brain disease or defects; they are not so rare in children. A child may have difficulties with arithmetic, and later on with mathematics, without having trouble with any other subject. This may have organic or psychologic causes.

On a higher level, arithmetic and mathematics are unquestionably related to a special talent. Just as there are children who have no musical ability, who are tone deaf, so there are children who lack special talents for number relationships and/or mathematics. They can be taught to perform by rote, but their understanding of the underlying concepts and their creative ability in these subjects is very limited or nonexistent. This has nothing to do with the intelligence level of these children. It is often superior in all other respects.

Classification

Arithmetic disorders on an organic basis are called acalculia. They are classified under Diseases of the Nervous System in medical statistics. This classification in not usually used by child psychiatrists in hospitals, clinics or agencies. They use the *Diagnostic and Statistical Manual of Mental Disorders* (D.S.M.) devised by the American Psychiatric Association. The first and second editions of this manual did not mention arithmetic disorders. They had to be classified under "Specific Learning Disturbance". Fortunately, the 3rd edition contains the category "Developmental Arithmetical Disorder".

Incidence

Children with reading disorders and/or other psychopathology are unfortunately frequently not tested for arithmetic disorders. Their arithmetic performance is always tested in school, but psychologists and child psychiatrists frequently fail to follow this up with clinical examinations to find the cause of the child's failure. Even when an arithmetic disorder has been diagnosed, it may not be classified separately, so that it is not mentioned in the final diagnosis used for statistical purposes. These disorders are therefore very much under-reported and their frequency is not known.

The extent of neglect of the study of arithmetic disorders in children is evident in the fact that, so far as I could establish, there is only one book in the entire international literature on childhood psychopathology that deals exclusively with these disorders. This is *Rechenstörungen: Ihre Diagnostik und Therapie (Arithmetic Disorders: Their Diagnosis and Therapy)*, by the German psychiatrist Curt Weinschenk (1970). I met him when I was a Fulbright lecturer in Marburg, Germany. He showed me the arithmetical defects of a number of adolescent inpatients who were part of his study.

Frequency of Association with Reading Disorders

Studies dealing with the relationship between reading disorders and arithmetic disorders are universally vague with regard to statistics. For example, Critchley and Klasen indicate only in a general way that many children with a reading disorder also have trouble with arithmetic. They do agree that an unknown but large number of these children has no trouble with arithmetic, and that they may even be above average in mathematics, even though this is rare. Critchley expresses it in this way: "Arithmetical retardation may be associated with developmental dyslexia, but not necessarily so." He stresses that "a less well-known defect, but a highly characteristic one, is an inability on the part of the dyslexic to 'spell in numbers'." He states that these children have difficulty writing long numbers with many digits to dictation. They put in too few or too many zeros, and are especially confused about the correct placing of commas. For instance, when told to write 146, they may write 100,46 (Critchley, 1970, p. 45). (See section on Reading and Writing Difficulties with Double Numbers, p. 208, 200, 199.)

So far as my own study is concerned, I found that 31 children (28 boys and 3 girls, aged 6 to 12 years) had an arithmetic disorder on an organic basis. All these children had an organic reading disorder. This amounts to about 14% of the 222 children in my study who had an organic reading disorder. It is impossible to determine whether or not this percentage applies to all children with an organic reading disorder, because of the lack of other such studies.

Localization

The Cerebral Arithmetic Apparatus

Arithmetic disorders have been observed in adults with occipital, frontal, parietal, or temporal lesions. These localizations were confirmed through autopsies. This indicates that the cerebral areas underlying arithmetic ability must be more widespread than the cerebral reading apparatus.

Spatial performances and visualization play a greater role in arithmetic and mathematics than in reading. Visualization is especially important for mental arithmetic, for the understanding of the place value of numbers, and for most mathematical concepts. They cannot be understood entirely through auditory, tactile, or motor routes.

An arithmetic center has therefore been assumed to be located in the occipital lobe of the dominant hemisphere. However, we now know that the cerebral basis for such complicated performances as arithmetic, mathematics, reading, or speech involves more than one single center. The organic basis of arithmetic can be more accurately understood in terms of a cerebral arithmetic apparatus. (See section on Cerebral Reading Apparatus, p. 56.)

The neurologist Henschen, who made one of the first extensive studies of acalculia in adults, was also the first to suggest such a separate apparatus in the human brain, which he called a "calculation system." He came to the conclusion that this apparatus can operate independently of the cerebral apparatuses underlying speech and music. He also stressed that it seems to be independent of general intelligence (Grewel, 1969, p. 184).

Relation to Cerebral Reading Apparatus

The reading and arithmetic apparatuses overlap, but they are also capable of functioning independently. And they are not necessarily impaired together.

A child may be able to understand the calculation and even the place value of a number, for instance, "2." He may also be capable of reading and writing it correctly, while not being able to read or write the word "two." A number has a calculation value that has nothing to do with a word. Its notation does not consist of letters either. The child must, however, be able to say the word "two." Clinical studies show that the cerebral speech and arithmetic apparatuses apparently are more closely connected than the apparatuses underlying arithmetic and reading. Children and adults with organic speech disorders usually have an arithmetic disorder, while organic reading disorders are not necessarily associated with an arithmetic disorder.

Another important difference between reading and arithmetic and their organic bases is that arithmetic has physical underpinnings that reading does not have. A child has two arms, two legs, two eyes, five fingers on each hand, 10 toes, one nose, and so on. He has a distinct physical—namely sensory, motor, and visual—experience of these numbers. Even the complicated concept of zero can be experienced on its most primitive level as a feeling of emptiness or loneliness, for instance when a room is empty because there is no one in it. The concept of plus or minus can also be experienced as a person entering or leaving a room.

The arithmetic apparatus can therefore be assumed to be closely connected with sensory, motor, and visual projection fields in the brain.

When all three apparatuses (reading, arithmetic, and speech) are malfunctioning, the child invariably functions on the mental defective level. (See Vol. II, section on Speech Disorders, p. 381.)

The Role of Hemispheres

The cerebral arithmetic apparatus is apparently also organized in the left hemisphere of right-handed people, just as are the reading and speech apparatuses. However, arithmetic and mathematics are probably less dependent upon one hemisphere than reading and speech. Both hemispheres are flexible in this respect. According to latest studies, the right hemisphere in both left- and right-handers may be of special importance for arithmetic, because it is thought to be more efficient in regard to nonverbal and spatial faculties. It is therefore probably involved in all those aspects of arithmetic and mathematics where spatial concepts are needed. Trigonometry, for instance, requires spatial concepts. (See section on Role of Hemispheric Dominance, p. 58.)

Different Forms of Acalculia

Four forms of acalculia have been differentiated in adults according to the localization of the lesions found at autopsy. However, neurologists who have studied these patients stress that their symptoms cannot and should not be classified so schematically (Grewel, 1969, pp. 188–189). No such studies exist concerning children, because their acalculias are only extremely rarely based on fatal diseases. However, the arithmetical symptoms of these well-studied adult patients are helpful also in evaluating children's acalculias.

Parietal Acalculia

Malfunctioning of parts of the parietal lobes may lead to an arithmetic disorder, with or without a reading and writing disorder. These patients have trouble with the spatial and structural aspects of arithmetic; they suffer from constructional apraxia or the specific arithmetic disorder connected with Gerstmann syndrome. (See sections on Contructional Apraxia, p. 159; and Gerstmann syndrome, p. 175.)

Occipital Acalculia

Malfunctioning of that part of the arithmetic apparatus located in the occipital lobes interferes with visualization, which is of crucial importance for arithmetic, especially mental arithmetic, and for mathematics. These patients cannot do mental arithmetic, although they may be able to solve problems by writing them down. Their ability to understand mathematical problems is also severely impaired.

FIG. 1.1.   Girl, age 14. Cortical Mosaic design, no title. She tried desperately to "make something," but could not achieve any gestalt. Lack of red and prominence of black pieces indicates depression. She suffered from a degenerative disease of the brain of unknown origin.

FIG. 1.2.   Mosaic of a 9-year-old boy with an organic reading disorder and congenital nerve deafness in one ear. The Mosaic was the only test indicating an organic impairment. *Title:* "I can't call it anything because I don't think it looks like anything." Typical *stone-bound* design indicating subcortical impairment. The shape of the design is entirely determined by the first piece put on the tray. The following pieces are put on each other's surface. *The pieces* determine the shape of the design. The patient is *stimulus-bound.*

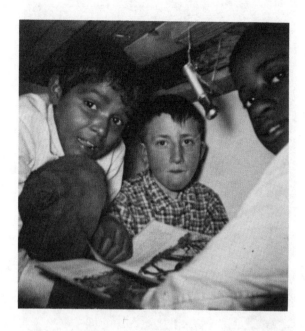

FIG. 7.1. Three 11-year-old boys in play group therapy, reading and listening spontaneously in a "house" they built themselves; they picked the book out of the clinic
library. The boy who is reading is recovering from an organic reading disorder. The
boy in the middle had aphasia; the reading disorder of the boy on the right was
psychogenic. (Photo by Hilde Mosse.)

FIG. 2.2. This comic book was brought to a conventional kindergarten class by a 5-year-old girl. This page shows that the children's eyes have to wander in different directions when reading a comic book, so they do not learn linear reading. Added is the glorification of violence: shooting, other forms of violent attacks, and fire bombing, which is especially exciting for children.

Frontal Acalculia

Frontal lobe lesions sometimes cause a severe arithmetic disorder in adults. These patients may still be able to perform elementary addition and subtraction with concrete objects and numbers. However, they cannot do multiplication or division, because they cannot understand the more complicated underlying thought processes.

Temporal Acalculia

Malfunctioning in the temporal lobes may cause a special form of arithmetic disorder. These patients frequently know the word for the number, but not the number symbol. They have retention difficulties with calculations where number symbols are involved. Their arithmetical memory is affected. (See section on special memory difficulties of children, p. 69.)

A child may have any combination of these symptoms when his cerebral arithmetic apparatus is malfunctioning.

Unspecific Organic Symptoms Affecting Arithmetic

How these symptoms affect the child's ability to learn and to perform arithmetic is circumscribed in detail in the sections dealing with these symptoms. Some basic aspects will be outlined here.

Slowing Down of All Reactions

These children have great difficulty in keeping up with their classmates, because they are so slow. They may also be slow in comprehending the underlying arithmetical structures (Vol. II, p. 460).

Impairment of Automatic Mechanisms

Such children have trouble with the conditioning process needed for arithmetic. It is very difficult for them to solve problems automatically, without repeating the underlying thought process each time, step by step. They also have trouble memorizing by rote (Vol. II, p. 470).

Inability to Tolerate Disorder

These children tend to solve all problems in exactly the same way. Any change in approach creates great anxiety (Vol. II p. 478).

Inability to Shift

Arithmetic is fraught with difficulties for these children. They cannot easily shift; the number 5, for instance, remains 5; it is very difficult for them to think of it in terms of 3 plus 2 (Vol II, p. 481).

Perseveration

Such a child may repeat the same answer many times or continue reciting something by rote long after the teacher has given him another problem. Perseveration may interfere with every step needed for learning and performing arithmetic. (See Vol. II, Impact of Perseveration on Arithmetic, p. 487.)

Attention Disorders

An attention disorder, whether organic or psychogenic, invariably interferes seriously with learning and performing arithmetic and mathematics, because these subjects require more intense concentration than any other. (See sections on teaching arithmetic, p. 222; on Diagnosis of Psychogenic Arithmetic Disorders, p. 501; and Attention Disorders, Vol. II, p. 233.)

Fatiguability

The intense concentration and the elimination of all other stimuli needed for arithmetic and mathematics strains these children's abnormal fatiguability to the limit. It makes the study of these subjects especially cumbersome for them. Arithmetical performance is such a good indication of any person's fatiguability that arithmetic tests are used to test this symptom. (See Vol. II, p. 672; see also Fatigue under Attention Disorders, Vol. II, p. 562; and Tests, Vol. II, p. 510.)

Mental Deficiency

Mentally defective children can cope only with elementary arithmetic. How far they can go is determined not only by the limits of their general intelligence; it also depends on the level of functioning of their cerebral arithmetic apparatus, which may be more or less impaired, independent from their other faculties. However, it does not rise to normal levels. The level of their achievement also depends on how well they have been taught. (See pp. 221, 222 in the section on teaching of arithmetic.)

Exceptional Arithmetical Faculties (Hypercalculia)

Some mentally defective and some aphasic children have superior, however isolated, arithmetical faculties. This superior performance is usually confined to fast mental calendar calculations. They can figure out with exceptional speed on what day of the week any calendar day falls. These children are called "idiots savants." This of course, is an entirely useless faculty; but it has clinical and research importance, because its cerebral basis is still unknown. One can only assume that those parts of the cerebral arithmetic apparatus needed for this particular performance have remained intact for unknown reasons.

There is another form of hypercalculia. It is very rare, and apparently affects the same type of child. When such a child begins to speak, which is usually much later than other children, he talks only in numbers. He does not say any other word. (See section on Hypermnesias under Role of Memory, p. 58.)

Examination

The psychologic tests routinely used invariably have a special section entitled Arithmetical Reasoning. The child has to solve arithmetical problems of increasing difficulty within a set limit of time. The result is expressed in a numerical score indicating whether his performance is above or below average. It does not reveal the child's underlying difficulties. The individual psychologist is left to investigate the underlying defects in arithmetical reasoning. This requires knowledge of the various arithmetic disorders. Unfortunately, this topic is either not taught at all or is touched on only superficially in the training of psychologists. It is also poorly covered during teachers' training, and may be completely omitted from the curriculum of general and child psychiatrists.

To facilitate the examination, diagnosis, and treatment of children with an arithmetic disorder, I have made an analysis of the basic arithmetical operations every child must know to be able to perform elementary arithmetic adequately. These operations can be divided into 10 different acts. They overlap in practice, but the child's performance of each act must be tested for the diagnosis as well as treatment of his arithmetic disorder. Each test should be performed visually, by writing the problem and the answer down or by indicating them with concrete objects: and also entirely orally, to determine the child's ability to perform mental arithmetic.

Testing the 10 Basic Arithmetical Acts

1. *Saying, reading, and writing the words for numbers.* This should be done by asking the child to say how many objects are on the desk or how many fingers he has, or by letting him count without objects, if he is old enough to do this. When it has been established that he says all numbers correctly, reading and writing of number words should be tested.

2. *Writing and reading the figures for numbers.* Testing should include writing to dictation and spontaneously.

3. *Counting.* This should be tested by letting the child count to 10 and beyond, and by making sure that he knows what counting means. When children first begin to count at 2 or 3 years of age, they may do so entirely by rote, without understanding what this word sequence means. Each child should therefore also be asked to count identical objects, different objects, and groups of objects, as described under Gerstmann syndrome (p. 175).

4. *Understanding the relative value of the number compared with other numbers.* The child should be asked which number is smaller, which is

larger, and which comes before or after in a series. This test should first be given using numbers up to 10, and when the child can do this, with larger numbers.

5. *Reading, writing, and understanding the operational signs.* The child's facility with the signs for addition, subtraction, multiplication, and division is tested. This act should be tested together with act number 6 below.

6. *Recognizing the arrangement of numbers to do addition, subtraction, multiplication, and division.* This should be tested by presenting problems to the child in print or in writing, and by dictating them to him. The child may be able to understand them correctly when he sees them in print, and get totally confused when he is asked to write them on his own.

7. *Understanding the significance of 0—its calculation as well as its placement value.* The child should be asked to add and to subtract 0 from a number, and to add a number to 0. He should then be asked what zero means, when 1 or any other number is placed to the left of it, what it means when it is placed between two numbers, and so forth. It is important to realize that the child's answers to the placement question are largely dependent on the way he has been taught. He may, for instance, answer that the 0 in 10 means that there is nothing in the unit-1 column, where units 1 to 9 are located, and that 10 1's were exchanged for one 10. He may further explain that notations of multiples of 10 are made in this second left column. These are excellent definitions, which show that the child really understands the underlying principles. Children taught with the Stern method of teaching structural arithmetic give such answers.

8. *Understanding the placement value of all numbers.* The child should be asked to read, to write to dictation, and to explain multiple numbers of increasing complexity. (See section on Reading and Writing Difficulties with Double Numbers, p. 199.)

9. *Doing arithmetic mentally only, without the use of concrete objects or written material.* A child may be good in mental arithmetic and be incapable of writing the same problems down to dictation or spontaneously, or to do them when he sees them in print. He may have a specific reading and writing disorder involving only the reading, writing, and arranging of numbers. These symptoms, alone or in combination, point to constructional apraxia or the acalculia of Gerstmann syndrome. (See pp. 159 and 175.) Such a child's reading and writing should also be tested. His inability to read and/or write arithmetical problems may be part of a general reading and writing disorder.

10. *Developing the necessary conditioned reflexes, so that these basic arithmetical acts become automatic.* The child needs to do this so he can do arithmetic without figuring out the complicated underlying thought processes each time. A good test for this is timing the child's performance. A child may

also be able to explain his performance in such a way that one can conclude that part or all of it has been done automatically.

The child's reasoning process is much more important than the end result of a given problem. That is why it is essential to ask the child to describe step by step how he figured out exactly what to do.

Some children cannot possibly give any explanation having memorized how to perform each problem without understanding the reason for what they are doing. It is important to determine whether a child is doing this because he may advance to a higher level of arithmetic while still using the same approach, memorizing each act mechanically. He cannot be expected to comprehend higher levels of arithmetic and mathematics, because he has no foundation upon which to build. For this reason the use of calculators in the lower grades is harmful, unless the children are first taught how the results come about. One must keep in mind, however, that there are many arithmetical facts that can only be learned by rote, such as weights and measures and that a dime has the value of 10 cents, a dollar of 10 dimes, and so on.

Differential Diagnosis

It is usually possible to diagnose or rule out mental deficiency, based on the child's level of functioning on other parts of intelligence tests. However, the differential diagnosis among immaturity, victim of poor teaching, an arithmetic disorder on an organic basis, and an arithmetic disorder on a psychologic basis, is difficult to determine.

Developmental Considerations

The child's performance of the 10 arithmetical acts and on other tests has to be matched with what he can be expected to do at his particular age. No correlation between age and understanding arithmetical problems has yet been achieved that meets practical clinical and educational criteria. Performance of the 10 elementary operations varies widely among children of the same age, kindergarten through third grade, whose intelligence is not defective. Special talent plays a role, but is not alone responsible.

Different professionals have different experiences with children of the same age. The experimental psychologist Piaget, for instance, maintains that counting is not much of a developmental landmark, that we should not assume just because a child can count that he is now ready to understand addition and subtraction. He states further that the child is ready for these elementary arithmetical acts only later on, at about the age of 7 or 8, as soon as he understands the "conservation of quantity." Piaget coined this term to indicate the recognition by the child that the quantity of a liquid remains the same irrespective of the form of the vessel; that a piece of clay does not grow when one rolls it; that a number, for example, 7, remains the same whether you see it as 3 plus 4 or 10 minus 3. The book *Teacher's Petit Piaget*, explains this theory in the following way: "This means he must grasp the idea that number represents units, that the units can be put in one-to-one relationships and that the units can be put into sequence" (Charles, 1974, p. 47).

Piaget does not think much of the influence of teaching on the child's development of knowledge. Adhering rigidly to Piaget's theories of development, which means waiting for the child's "readiness," may leave a child without the elementary knowledge he needs. This may handicap him for the rest of his life (Piaget, 1952).

Influence of Teaching

The Stern Method

Teachers who understand the structure of arithmetical reasoning and who also understand the way a child's mind works, have succeeded in imparting knowledge of elementary arithmetic to children long before the age of 7. The method of teaching structural arithmetic to children of all ages from nursery school on, as developed by Catherine and Margaret B. Stern, is probably the best example of this. In their landmark book, *Children Discover Arithmetic* (Stern & Stern, 1971), they show that 2-, 3-, and 4-year-old children can select, for instance, four or six cubes correctly to fit into a specially constructed pattern board. They prove that their technique, using "counting" and "pattern" boards and "unit boxes," makes it possible to teach that numbers consist of units long before the age of 7, and without using "readiness" tests first. Waiting for the child to pass such tests has had the same harmful effect in regard to arithmetic as it has for reading. It has delayed the onset of systematic teaching of these skills unnecessarily, often for so long that the child could not catch up with his classmates for years to come.

The Stern technique makes it possible to teach the concepts of even and odd, of addition and subtraction, and even the zero fact early, before the first grade or at its beginning.

One of their examples is a girl aged 4 years and 7 months who was asked to tell the "story of 6." She started without any help and said, "5 and 1 are just the same as 6, 4 and 2 are just the same as 6, 3 and 3 are just the same as 6," and so on (p. 59). Another girl, aged 4 years and 11 months, was greatly amused when the teacher said "6 and no other block is 6." The child took the 7-unit case spontaneously and said, "And this will be the story of the 7; 4 and 3 make 7 . . . 1 and 6 make 7 . . . 7 and nothing are 7." (p. 60). The Sterns rightly conclude that their record proves "that a child under 6 can easily understand the meaning of addition and subtraction and does not even have difficulty understanding zero combinations" (p. 100).

The Sterns have done for arithmetic teaching what the Spaldings did for reading. They, too, were ignored and attacked far too long by similar entrenched interests, to the detriment of children.

These results of excellent teaching methods are important for the differential diagnosis of arithmetic disorders. I have examined many 11-or 12-year-old children whose intelligence was average or better, for whom division and multiplication remained a mystery, who never heard of a zero fact, and who were not sure of the placement value of numbers. It cannot be assumed that all these children suffered from an arithmetic disorder on an organic or a psychologic basis. Realizing the profound influence teaching may have, these children may be no more than victims of poor teaching. A strict follower of Piaget's theories may diagnose these children as just suffering from delayed development. In the section on the Developmental Lag theory, I point to the damaging effect of this theory on the diagnosis and treatment of children suffering from reading disorders; this also applies to arithmetic disorders. (See p. 54.)

Effect of New Math

It is important in this connection to understand the impact of the New Math method. This method has confused many children so thoroughly that they cannot perform all 10 basic arithmetical acts. They are supposedly being trained to understand computers, but they cannot make simple money transactions. The simple, useful, practical aspects of arithmetic are being neglected. This method was instituted in 1952 and spread to almost all school systems and to many countries. It is far too slowly being modified or abandoned.

One reason for the widespread failure of this method is that it was developed by mathematicians and high–school teachers who had had no experience teaching elementary-school-age children. They were not familiar with their intellectual and emotional characteristics, and thus could not know how such young children learn.

Mathematicians themselves have pointed to this flaw. For example, Professor Begle, Director of the School Mathematics Study Group, made the following remark at a symposium as long ago as 1960: "In our work on curriculum we did not consider the pedagogy." Professor Beberman, another influential mathematician, was more outspoken in his critique. In 1962 he said, "I think in some cases we have tried to answer questions that children never raise and to resolve doubts they never had, but in effect we have answered our own questions and resolved our own doubts as adults and teachers, but these were not the doubts and questions of the children." Two years later, at a meeting of the National Council of Teachers of Mathematics, he warned that "We're in danger of raising a generation of kids who can't do computational arithmetic." He feared that "a major national scandal" may be in the making (Kline, 1973, p. 110).

These warnings were unfortunately not taken seriously and what he feared has happened. New Math has done almost as much damange to arithmetic as whole-word teaching has to reading.

Even the terminology introduced by this method reflects the unclear and therefore confusing underlying mathematical principles. The mathematician Morris Kline calls it "pretentious" (p. 69), "totally unnecessary" (p. 67), and warns that "The introduction of so many new terms and particularly terms which are not suggestive of the concepts they represent, puts an intolerable burden on the memory" (p. 68). He makes these statements in his 1973 book, *Why Johnny Can't Add: The Failure of the New Math.*

The criticism by the Sterns is even more important because it is based on actual teaching experience with very young children. One of their examples is that in spite of a concrete approach to multiplication, "the multiplication facts have to be drilled in the teaching of the new math until they have been learned by rote" (Stern & Stern, 1971, p. 257). They also object to the terminology, writing: "Does it help pupils to grasp the nature of addition to hear that the numbers 4 and 3 are "associated" with 7, which is called the sum? In what way do the sets help them develop clear concepts?" (pp. 88–89). They answer these rhetorical questions in the negative, and conclude with the following observations:

> The experiments with Structural Arithmetic materials lead directly to the concept of addition; moreover, the child studies the addition facts by measuring, thus avoiding many errors. The New Math, on the other hand, still bases addition on counting—a procedure that all too often leads to mistakes (p. 89).

They are especially critical of the New Math approach as a remedial method (p. 301). My own observations agree with this assessment. This method has caused arithmetic disorders; it cannot cure them.

The originators of this curriculum wanted to make mathematics easier for children and therefore more pleasurable. The results are largely the opposite of what they intended.

The Role of Teachers

The teacher's attitude and skill have an important and sometimes decisive influence on the learning process. This is especially crucial for arithmetic, which must be explained carefully step by step so that the students can understand and remember it.

Some teachers do not like arithmetic. They transmit their lack of interest and enthusiasm to their students and may spoil this subject for them. They also often do not know how to explain arithmetical reasoning so that a child can understand it. Frequently they do not take enough time to find out how each child thinks, how he got the end result, so that they can correct hidden errors before they become ingrained habits and hinder the child's progress.

The teachers themselves are often not to blame for their poor results since their own training is frequently defective with regard to arithmetic. They have also been under such relentless pressure to improve reading, that arithmetic has been neglected. Sometimes they are forced to teach outside of license. This is especially harmful for arithmetic and mathematics. How can a social studies teacher, for instance, be expected to teach these subjects, which are so far removed from his expertise?

Lack of teacher training in the use of helpful material such as the Sterns' Boards and Blocks, or Montessori's didactic material, has also hindered successful teaching. I have seen such materials, brand new and very expensive, lie unused in storage closets. Teachers did not know of their existence or had seen them but did not know how to use them. They had not been shown what to do. Sometimes teachers as well as students are victims of administrative incompetence or lack of interest.

It is fortunate that children have an extraordinary imagination and can often help themselves. That is what Ricardo did.

RICARDO, 13 YEARS OLD: HE INVENTED AN INGENIOUS METHOD OF FIGURING OUT ARITHMETICAL PROBLEMS.   I knew Ricardo very well. He had been in psychotherapy with me, and his foster mother had been under the care of a social worker, since the age of 9 when he was in the fourth grade. As happens to so many children with a reading disorder, he had been originally referred to the school psychologist for placement in a class for mentally retarded children. He was actually far from retarded. His reading disorder had an organic basis, and was aggravated by a severe anxiety neurosis. He could not sleep and was at times in such a panic that he confused reality with fantasy. He also had periods of overexcitement when his behavior became disruptive and difficult to control.

During times of great stress and tension he had haptic and auditory hallucinations. This began when he entered the fourth grade. When he went to sleep he felt that someone touched him on the back. He had the same experience several times when someone talked to him. He also heard footsteps of someone walking behind him. When he turned around, no one was there. The voice he heard was always that of a man. It was always a good voice, telling him what to do and what not to do, for instance not to hurt his brother. It alleviated his fears and even helped him with arithmetic. He described it in the following way: "When I'm saying 12 times 12, sometimes he says the right number." He did not know where this voice might be coming from. He told his priest about it, who suggested he say a prayer. It stopped when he touched the crucifix he was wearing; however, he did not really think it came from the devil. He just could not explain it.

Ricardo was an outgoing boy, always in good contact. He was not withdrawn and his behavior was not bizarre. The Mosaic test and other projective tests gave no evidence of a schizophrenic process. They showed marked anxiety and compulsion. I felt therefore that his hallucinations were not malignant. They were benign manifestations of anxiety, which would disappear with psychotherapy.

Fear of abandonment was at the base of his neurosis. He had been seriously neglected and abused before the age of 7. His father had abandoned his mother, who was incapable of taking care of him and his younger brother. She was an alcoholic who left the children to fend for themselves, so that they were often hungry and had to get food from garbage cans. She also punished them cruelly. Once she sat Ricardo on top of an electric stove so that his buttocks were burned. She was eventually sent to a mental hospital, and the boys were placed with a devoted foster mother. However, Ricardo remained very attached to his mother. He gave her all the money he made carrying packages for shoppers and helping merchants clean their store.

Course.   Ricardo's reading improved only with special help from his regular teachers. By the sixth grade, he had caught up with his classmates. The voices stopped, and his other neurotic symptoms subsided with psychotherapy.

Arithmetical Reasoning.   Ricardo had always been interested in arithmetic and his grades had been good. He did so well in general that he skipped the seventh grade and entered the eighth grade of a junior high school at the age of 12. He was 13 years old when he told me spontaneously how he got 99 in a math test when no other student got more than 77. He said:

> I think about people; I take the people on the TV screen when I see a movie. If I am in class, I divide the boys and girls into one whole, the teacher into two wholes or into two and a half, because he is an adult. When math is hard, I take one third or one half out of each student. The halves I took away, I add them all, and I divide by the number I am dividing with. Then I see the result I get. It always comes out right.

It had occurred to him a year or so before that he could use people around him or on the screen to concretize fractions.

His method was imaginative and helpful, but it showed that he could not yet see numbers only as numbers, and that he could not simply imagine that they represented people; he actually had to see them. His arithmetical reasoning was not as advanced as his teachers and the principal thought it was. An eighth-grade child ought to be able to understand numbers as units by themselves. He should no longer need such concretization. A boy as imaginative as Ricci (Ricardo's nickname) should have reached this higher level of arithmetical reasoning. That he had not indicates defects in teaching rather than in his capability.

Ricci kept his method secret for a long time. He only told two girls in his class whom he liked and trusted. He finally got up enough courage to tell his teacher, who said: "Ricci, I can't do that." Ricci told him: "Watch it." Then the teacher said, "Ricci, you are right," and asked him if he could keep the paper to show to the principal. The boy was then called to the principal's office and praised. That was the end of the school's interest. It is a pity that the teacher did not let him explain his method to the entire class. It would have helped both the students and this severely deprived, anxious, and insecure boy. All could then have been helped to rise above such concretizations, never mind how helpful they were. However, all the teacher said was, "Ricci, you must have a good angel. When it comes to math, you do it right. You fool around a lot. But math, you do it right." This boy was fascinated by computers after a teacher had taken the class to a computer center. He intended to learn all about them.

Ricci's arithmetical performance shows that an organic reading disorder, even when combined with a severe neurosis and serious psychologic and physical traumatization in early childhood, does not necessarily interfere with learning and enjoying arithmetic. It also indicates that teachers and other adults caring for a child should make more of an effort to find out how he thinks, learns, and feels, and give him or her a chance to share their ideas with others, so that children and adults can learn from each other.

Ricci's story also demonstrates the value of individual psychotherapy, as well as of social work treatment of the family. These treatments have been under severe attack because they are supposedly not "cost effective" when practiced in clinics and agencies set up to help people who cannot afford private care. This point of view is antisocial and antieducational. It shows prejudice in favor of the wealthy and against the poor.

Diagnosis of Organic Arithmetic Disorders

Organic disorders are determined by the severity and persistence of the child's arithmetic disorder in spite of adequate intelligence and excellent teaching. For instance, an 8-year-old child who cannot perform any one of the basic arithmetical acts, or only the first three, has a malfunctioning cerebral arithmetic apparatus. Specific defects in arithmetical reasoning pointing to organicity are listed in the following paragraphs.

1. Inability to memorize numbers after hearing them, or when reading or

writing them, especially when multiple numbers are involved. (See Gerstmann syndrome, p. 175.)

2.   Inability to do serial ordering or sequencing. This organic symptom has an especially serious effect on arithmetic. These children cannot arrange series of numbers according to their magnitude either mentally or by writing them down. They find it difficult to determine which number is smaller and which larger in a series of numbers. They cannot recite a series of odd or even numbers, and cannot learn the multiplication tables. They also find it difficult to count backwards. They have this symptom in common with many other children with an organic disorder. Numbers 4, 7, and 8 of the basic arithmetical acts are especially difficult for them.

3.   Inability to arrange numbers. Some of these children do not recognize number arrangements as a unit. They confuse vertical with horizontal operations and add instead of multiplying. They may be incapable of arranging numbers in columns and understanding their placement value. It is sometimes possible to diagnose such difficulties in retrospect, years later. For instance, when I asked a 24-year-old young woman where she lived, she answered slowly, "164—The 6 is in the middle, the 4 is on the side." She had forced herself to memorize the placement of these numbers, which were so important for her, because she still had trouble with the placement value of numbers. This woman had a poorly treated or untreated organic arithmetic disorder.

These arithmetical defects are usually part of constructional apraxia. (See section on Constructional Apraxia, p. 159.)

Most children with these symptoms also have a map-reading and a clock-reading disorder. (See sections on Map- and on Clock-Reading Disorders, pp. 155, 165.) They cannot perform the basic arithmetical acts number 6, 7, 8, and 9.

4.   Inability to do mental arithmetic. These children's ability to visualize is impaired. They cannot perform the basic arithmetical act number 9.

5.   The presence of other organic symptoms, for instance a speech disorder, or of the unspecific symptoms already mentioned, also points to an organic basis of the arithmetic disorder.

6.   The prolonged use of fingers for simple daily calculations into adolescence and adulthood points to an untreated organic arithmetic disorder. This is a crutch used by all children in the beginning, except by those few who have a finger agnosia.

7.   Understanding the number arrangements for addition and subtraction, but not being able to add or subtract without using simple, concrete counting methods. For example, an 11-year-old boy could write 26–4 correctly; however, he could not figure this out mentally. He put 26 small vertical lines on the same paper and crossed 4 lines off. Then he wrote the correct result (22) in its correct place. When asked what change he would get if he handed the

salesman one dollar for something costing 69 cents, he started to make 100 lines, but gave up after 29. This transaction was too complicated for him. These children cannot do multiplication or division, because these problems cannot be solved just by counting (Figure 4.1).

It is characteristic for these children that they try hard. They want very much to learn but can't, in contrast to children with a psychogenic arithmetic disorder, who can succeed but don't want to, for conscious or unconscious reasons.

It must be stressed that careful upbringing and skillful teaching can prevent minor malfunctioning of the cerebral arithmetic apparatus from causing clinical symptoms. The same holds true for reading and writing.

Diagnosis of Psychogenic Arithmetic Disorders

Diagnosis of psychogenic arithmetic disorders is determined by the criteria described in the following paragraphs.

1. A contrast between the child's ability to understand and perform all or most of the first nine basic arithmetical acts and his poor school performance. These children usually cannot carry out the 10th act because they have not practiced arithmetic enough to have developed conditioned reflexes.

The underlying reasons may be conscious and deliberate, or due to more hidden psychopathologic mechanisms. Such a child may deliberately ignore a hated teacher or a hated and feared subject. He may just sit in class and daydream, or make believe he is working, when he actually is drawing something or doodling.

A child may also want to annoy or punish his parents by bringing home poor marks. However, most such children are less clearly aware of the reasons for their failure in arithmetic.

2. An attention disorder is the psychopathologic basis for the vast majority of psychogenic arithmetic disorders, just as it is for reading disorders.

Reactive as well as neurotic disorders frequently cause an attention disorder. For instance, the inability to concentrate is one of the major symptoms of reactive and neurotic depressions. Daydreaming and preoccupation with fantasies are symptoms of anxiety and other neuroses.

Arithmetic is more severely affected by an attention disorder than reading, because it requires even more concentrated intellectual attention. It is also further removed from emotions and from the child's immediate interests, such as playing and imagining. It seems to be a remote, cold, and abstract subject. This very fact enables many neurotic children to concentrate on it and even to excel in it, especially when they find it easy. This subject does not touch painful emotions in them.

Mathematics, even more than arithmetic, has long been thought to be so far removed from life and absorbing so much energy, that it can divert attention

FIG. 4.1.   Eleven-year-old boy of average intelligence with an organic arithmetic disorder. He cannot do mental arithmetic at all, and written arithmetic only with the help of lines that he counts. When too many lines are needed, as in the second example, he gives up.

from emotional, especially sexual preoccupations. In one of his early papers, Freud wrote that mathematics had the best reputation by far as a distraction from sexuality. He pointed out in this connection that already Jean Jacques Rousseau had received this advice from a lady who was dissatisfied with him. She told him to restrain his lasciviousness by studying mathematics (Freud, 1947, p. 61).

Arithmetic is actually not that far removed from emotions. Numbers have always had a magical significance; they still play a large role in superstitions. For instance, 13 has a bad reputation and is considered a bad omen; 9 may bring good luck; this probably stems from the 9 months of gestation. Numerologists try to divine a person's fate from numbers, and so on.

3.   An arithmetic disorder may by itself be a neurotic symptom, or it may be part of a neurosis. It must be stressed, however, that it is rarely the only manifestation of a neurosis.

Among the many different psychopathologic mechanisms that may be operative, are those described below.

1.   *Numbers may have unpleasant conscious or unconscious associations.* They may symbolize repressed traumatic experiences. Numbers play an important part in a child's life—for instance, his age, his birthday and those of other family members, holidays, his address, the time when he is supposed to go to bed, when he has to get up, numbers of his school and classroom, and so on.

That numbers play a role in the unconscious is shown by their frequent appearance in dreams. Freud discussed the role of numbers in his *Interpretation of Dreams*. He stressed that arithmetic as such does not seem to appear in dreams, but that numbers by themselves are very important. Often they appear in the form of bills or otherwise within the dream story. They are part of the repressed experiences and thoughts expressed in dreams and give hints of forbidden material. They can therefore cause anxiety in children for reasons that are hidden in their unconscious (Freud, 1938, p. 404; Freud, 1948, pp. 417–421)

2. *The child may have a neurotic attitude towards money.* Money plays a special role in any child's life. It brings him for the first time in his life in contact with something he knows is of vital importance and consists only of numbers. His attitude towards arithmetic therefore tends to be largely influenced by his feelings about money. Most children are quite aware of this and it increases their interest in this subject. A neurotic inhibition against learning arithmetic may be due to a child's conflicts about money, which may have been at least partially repressed into the unconscious.

It is interesting that money is hardly ever mentioned in the vast literature dealing with child psychoanalysis. It is not even mentioned in Anna Freud's classic book, *Normality and Pathology in Childhood* (1965). One might be tempted to suggest that perhaps this is an unanalyzed blind spot.

Child psychoanalytical studies only rarely mention arithmetic disorders or the symbolic significance of numbers, in addition to their omission of money. The few papers dealing with this topic are too general in their interpretations; they often fail to connect the interpretations of unconscious material with the specific symptoms exhibited by the child. This is unfortunately a frequent failing of psychoanalysis generally.

One of the few psychoanalytical articles dealing with this topic is "Inhibition of Ego Functions and the Psychoanalytic Theory of Acalculia," by Pierre Vereeken (1965). Vereeken describes two children in detail, a 6½-year-old boy and a 7½-year-old girl. His analysis leads to the following conclusion:

> The disturbances are not limited to arithmetic alone, but can be seen in all areas of behavior: there is a specific type of blocking, characterized by a lack of motor freedom and a paralysis of mental mobility. These inhibitions serve as a primitive defense against very strong orally colored castration anxieties. Anal factors also play a role. The inhibition of ego functions and arithmetic is especially severe because these functions have not been cathected with stable, neutralized energies. The immobility is also used in the attempt to bring about structuralization and stabilization of their inner world (p. 565).

The children's attitude toward numbers or money is not mentioned. In addition to these interpretations, which follow a rigid theoretical model and fit all sorts of symptoms, one must also question the diagnoses on which they were based.

According to Vereeken, the boy had the following symptoms, among others: "massive perseveration," retardation in "constructive-praxic" activities, "sensorimotor inhibitions"; he did poorly on spatial tasks, could not count backwards, and had difficulty shifting and counting mentally. He could count only when he was allowed to start with 1. All these are typical organic symptoms. The girl's symptoms were similar.

It is unfortunate that in the majority of psychoanalytical studies, all arithmetic disorders are assumed to have a psychopathologic basis. An exception is Gerald H. J. Pearson, who has made the most thorough study to date of children with learning disorders from the psychoanalytical point of view. He sees these disorders as "problems of ego psychology" and uses the classification of "diminished capacity to learn due to organic disorders." However, he does not specifically deal with arithmetic disorders (1952).

In contrast to his followers, Freud has analyzed the conscious and unconscious significance and meaning of money in numerous papers. He traced the symptoms of some of his patients to certain landmarks in the child's development. He wrote that there is an unconscious link between feces and giving or receiving presents and money. He based these interpretations on the child's development, stating that during toilet training the child feels that he is giving a present to his mother and to other loved ones when he lets go of his feces only where he is supposed to, and that withholding stool means that he wants to hold onto what he feels belongs to him.

Freud pointed out that money in myths and superstitions is indeed thought of as dirt. For instance, when the devil gives someone a present of gold, it turns into dirt when he has left. Money is the dirt of hell according to oriental myths, and so on. He developed these interpretations in detail in "Character and Anal Eroticism" (1942a) and "On the Transformation of Instincts with Special Reference to Anal Erotism" (1942b). He stressed that a young child is aware of the fact that he can get money only as a gift, that he cannot earn it until he is older. Freud concluded that "Interest in feces is carried over first to interest in gifts, then to interest in money" (p. 170) (1942b).

Whether or not one agrees entirely with Freud's analyses, clinical experience shows that conflicts regarding money or gifts or both can be repressed into the unconscious and emerge as neurotic symptoms, for instance as an inhibition of learning arithmetic, and of arithmetical reasoning generally.

Treatment Techniques

Educational Treatment

A child with an arithmetic disorder on an organic or a psychogenic basis usually does not recover without individual remedial teaching. These children tend not to respond even in small groups. They have to be given the opportunity to start from the very beginning and to relearn each step slowly, at their own pace. They should also learn in an atmosphere where they feel free to ask any question anytime, without feeling stupid and humiliated. Concrete approaches should be used, which the individual child can understand, regardless of his age. It does not help to use over again the same teaching method that was involved in his failure.

It must be stressed that an arithmetic disorder, whether organic or psychogenic, cannot be corrected with psychotherapy alone. These children have missed so many steps needed to develop arithmetical reasoning that they must be taught the technical part of arithmetic, beginning at the exact level where their failure began. They cannot be expected to catch up with their classmates otherwise.

Much of the advice given by Anne Rogovin for the teaching of mentally defective children, applies also to children with an arithmetic disorder whose intelligence is not defective. In her concrete and practical *Learning by Doing* (1971), she writes that these children "learn best when material is presented to them in concrete situations using concrete objects, always trying to approximate a real situation as closely as possible. Therefore, if they need to know about 'buying and selling' they "play store" (p. 3). However, this may be difficult to carry out with normally endowed older children who might find it beneath them to play such childish games.

Concrete arithmetical materials such as the Stern board and blocks and the games they recommend, help all children suffering from an arithmetic disorder. These materials should also be used as tests to find the level of the child's arithmetical reasoning and to determine which operations he really understands and has not just memorized mechanically.

I have observed the use of these materials by educational therapists and can vouch for their efficiency.

ANGELO, 10 YEARS OLD, NO ARITHMETIC SKILL AT ALL: TREATMENT WITH THE STERN METHOD.   This boy had an organic reading, writing, and speech disorder in addition to his severe arithmetic disorder. He had received reading and speech treatment since the age of 7. His arithmetic disorder had unfortunately remained undiagnosed. He had been left back in the second grade, with no improvement. He was 10 years old and in the fourth grade when I examined him. His speech had improved, but his reading and writing were still not up to grade. He had spelling and directional difficulties and Linear Dyslexia. He also had a clock-reading disorder and could not tell a story fluently. He used short sentences and paused between them, as if searching for words.

His arithmetic disorder was very severe. He used his fingers to count. He could not count further than 10 and achieved this goal only when he started with 1. He could not count when starting anywhere else. This is a typical organic symptom. He also could not subtract. It was impossible for him to do sequencing or serial ordering.

Angelo was an outpatient at a special hospital child psychiatric clinic, organized to help children who presented diagnostic puzzles and seemed to have organic defects. I was in charge of this clinic, which combined the departments of child psychiatry and of pediatric rehabilitation. (See p. 283 in Chapter 6.)

At a staff meeting I recommended that Angelo's reading and speech treatment be continued, and that he receive arithmetic treatment as soon as possible. I also arranged for a demonstration of this form of treatment by an outstanding educational therapist specializing in treating arithmetic disorders. Most staff members had never observed such specialized teaching.

Both Angelo and his therapist seemed to enjoy this demonstration in front of a rather large staff. The boy lost his initial anxiety and became enthusiastic as soon as he made contact wtih the Stern material. At first he had trouble distinguishing the 7 from the 8 blocks. He found even the addition of 5 + 5 very difficult. However, he learned additions up to 10 before our eyes, and slipped easily into subtraction. Some difficulties remained. For instance, he could add 7 + 3 easily with the help of the blocks, but 3 + 7 remained a puzzle. However, he learned some placement facts, for example, that 18 consists of one 10 and eight units, and enjoyed a "long race" of 10 + 10 up to 100.

The therapist explained each step and all the games to us. All participants (pediatricians, psychiatrists, psychologists, educational therapists, a neurologist, speech therapists, residents, interns, and medical students) left that conference with the firm conviction that Angelo was receiving the best possible treatment for his arithmetic disorder, that both his teacher and the material she used were superb.

Psychotherapy

Psychotherapy is the form of treatment indicated for children who have neurotic or reactive symptoms, for instance a reactive depression, in addition to their organic arithmetic disorder. Psychopathology frequently coexists with organic disorders. It does not necessarily subside when the organic disorder has been treated successfully. The psychotherapist has to study all the child's symptoms because they interact and influence each other. Such a child cannot recover from all his disorders unless his psychotherapist and his educational therapist collaborate closely and communicate frequently. Unfortunately this is far too often neglected. A child with an arithmetic disorder on a psychologic basis always needs psychotherapy in addition to remedial arithmetic. (For details see Chapter 6 on Treatment, pp. 279, 288, 290–291.)

Chapter 5

Psychogenic Reading Disorders

The reading disorder of many children is caused by psychologic factors. Their cerebral reading apparatus is intact. Of the 445 children in my study, 177 (36 girls aged 6–16; 141 boys aged 6–15) suffered from a psychogenic reading disorder.

Diagnosis

The diagnosis rests on the absence of organic signs on physical, psychiatric, and psychologic examinations. Nor should there be any indications of organicity on reading and writing tests. These negative signs are important, but they are not the only basis for this diagnosis. A child may have organic symptoms (e.g., a convulsive disorder), but his reading disorder may have a psychologic basis. (See section on Convulsive Disorders, Vol. II, p. 422.)

Children with a psychogenic reading disorder may be able to understand and to perform all or most of the 11 reading and the 3 writing acts and still be poor readers when it comes to reading in the classroom or at home while doing homework. Spelling and linear reading are usually most severely affected, because these children have not practiced reading and writing enough to perform these acts fluently.

It is often difficult to determine whether a child has a reading disorder due to organic pathology; neurotic preoccupation may make it difficult or impossible to pay attention, or poor teaching using sight/word methods may have caused the problems. The errors on reading tests may be exactly the same as those involving organic disorders. Indications of psychogenic causation are discussed below.

1. The contrast between a better performance while the child is alone with an adult he trusts, and his reading in the classroom. This reveals that something in the classroom situation inhibits him. This may be neurotic anxieties and inhibitions or less complicated conflicts with classmates and/or teachers.

2. Rapidity of correction of errors. A child with a psychogenic reading disorder often corrects himself as soon as he has overcome his anxiety and has been encouraged to concentrate. This can be observed during a psychologic or psychiatric examination if good contact has been established.

3. Rapidity of learning basic techniques. When such a child does not know the sounds of letters and cannot blend, he can do it after only brief explanations. I have observed this innumerable times during my diagnostic examination. This indicates that his reading disorder is due to a lack of teaching of phonics. It may have no neurotic basis, unless other findings point to a neurosis that may have played a role in causing the reading disorder, or developed independently. The same applies to reversals in reading and writing.

Many children with a psychogenic reading disorder know the basic techniques, but they read slowly and laboriously because they hate to read for various neurotic or less complicated reasons, and they have not read enough to become fluent. They may have done well in the lower grades but may get very poor marks later on, usually when they reach the fourth grade, where more reading is required.

Two forms of psychogenic reading disorders should therefore be distinguished: an inability to learn the basic techniques, and deficient reading because of lack of practice.

Examination

When examining a child whose reading disorder may be psychogenic, one must keep in mind that his reading defects may not be due to his individual psychopathology alone. Frequent school changes, long absences due to physical illness, poor teaching, inadequate teaching methods, the influence of mass media, and other social factors may also have played a causative role. The interaction between individual psychopathologic and social forces should therefore be determined in all of these children.

A table of the differential diagnosis of organic, psychogenic, and sociogenic reading disorders is part of Chapter 6 on Sociogenic Reading Disorders. (See Vol. I, pp. 251, 252, 253 and Vol. II, pp. 463, [Alex].) (1 and 2)

Causes

Deliberate Nonlearning

The reasons underlying a child's psychogenic reading disorder are often not deep seated and not part of an unconscious process. A child may deliberately refuse to learn to read because he hates the teacher or wants to punish his parents.

Overwhelming Fear of Failure

Some children are convinced that they are stupid. They have been so discouraged and feel so helpless and incompetent that they make up their minds not to try. They think that reading is too hard for them and that they will surely fail. They sometimes think that if they do not try, they can at least assure themselves and everyone else that if they had tried they could have learned to read.

Attention Disorders

An attention disorder underlies the vast majority of psychogenic reading disorders. Reading needs concentration, which is the highest form of active, voluntary attention. A child who has trouble with concentration and with intellectual attention invariably has reading difficulties. Motivation is an important and often crucial part of the attention process. A child may not learn to read because he just is not interested. The symptoms, causes, and treatments of all kinds of attention disorders are circumscribed under Attention Disorders. (See especially Intellectual Attention, Vol. II, p. 540; and Concentration, Vol. II, p. 554.)

Psychopathology Underlying Attention Disorders Interfering with Reading

Daydreaming

A child with superior intelligence whose mind works faster than that of his classmates may find that learning to read, and later, reading, is too slow and therefore boring. Pearson gives a vivid description of such a child. In *A Survey of Learning Difficulties in Children,* which still forms the basis for their classification from the psychoanalytical point of view, he describes the origin of daydreaming and consequently of a reading disorder in a 7-year-old girl with an I.Q. of 160.

He writes:

> In fifteen minutes she would be able to understand and master a particular problem which took the rest of the class, whose I.Q.'s were average or slightly above, about one hour to learn. For three quarters of an hour the patient had nothing to do and in order not to be restless and disturbing spent her time in daydreaming. The daydreams soon became more interesting than was the unsolved problem of the first fifteen minutes and instead of occupying only her unemployed time they began occupying the whole hour. Consequently she learned nothing and at the end of several months her achievements were far less than that of the other members of her class. She also had omitted to learn certain basic fundamentals so that now when confronted by more complex problems, which the rest of the class had the basic skills to solve, she failed utterly. This secondary failure drove her into more intensive daydreaming (1952, pp. 325–326).

This sequence is typical for very many children. It also applies to children with an organic reading disorder who try for a while, then give up and daydream, falling further and further behind their classmates. This explains the frequency of this symptom in both types of reading disorders, as the table in Chapter 6 shows (p. 259–262).

These children get into a vicious circle. Their daydreaming leads to increasingly more serious failure in reading, and this failure drives them into more intensive daydreaming.

THERAPEUTIC MANAGEMENT IN THE CLASSROOM   Teachers who recognize these reactions can prevent the formation of such vicious circles with educational methods, in close cooperation with the child's parents. This is far too often neglected. I have examined many children who were referred for examination and psychotherapy after 1 or more years of failure, whose reading disorder could have been stopped by teachers if they had only recognized the underlying cause. The same applies to children who can't learn because they are too hungry or too sleepy because they suffer from insomnia or do not get enough sleep for other reasons (See Vol. II, Hunger, p. 561; and Fatigue, Vol. II, p. 562.)

Depression

An attention disorder is one of the major symptoms of neurotic or reactive depressions. These depressions may be hidden behind a number of common behavioral symptoms. They are "masked" depressions, which are more frequent in children than the overt form (Mosse, 1974).

That depressions are frequent in children with reading disorders is reflected in my study where 43 children (40 boys and 3 girls) suffered from a depression. The reading disorder was psychogenic in 26 (25 boys, 1 girl), organic in 16 (14 boys, 2 girls), and sociogenic in 1 boy (see Table 6.1).

These depressions were so severe that 12 children (10 boys, 2 girls) with a psychogenic; 10 children (all boys) with an organic, and 1 boy with a sociogenic reading disorder made suicidal threats or attempts (see Table 6.1).

An attention disorder caused by a depression affects the child's reading disorder, whether its basis is organic or psychologic. The underlying depression is usually also the *cause* of the psychogenic reading disorder, whereas it tends to be the *consequence* of the organic type. The depressive attention disorder hinders the child's recovery from his reading disorder; this aggravates and prolongs the depression, which in turn aggravates the reading disorder. This is the vicious circle that prevents the recovery of these children irrespective of the cause of their reading disorder. This highlights the great importance of the early treatment of all reading disorders. An untreated reading disorder invariably causes a depression.

Anger

This is an all-pervading feeling that undermines the attention process. Concentration and intellectual attention are most difficult in a state of anger. A child in a chronic state of anger has great difficulty learning the basic techniques of reading and cannot concentrate on reading even after he knows how it is done. (See Vol. II, p. 678, under Morbid Irritability.)

Sexual Preoccupation

A sexual preoccupation invariably distracts the child and makes concentration on anything else impossible. Sexual feelings are so overwhelming that the child cannot be expected to get his mind on reading. This is only one of a number of compelling reasons why children should be protected from sexual overstimulation.

I was a member of the staff of a clinic for sex offenders, where I found to my dismay that sex offenses against children are usually treated lightly by the courts. I am referring to boys and girls under 12 years of age. Sexual attacks on such young children are major offenses. They may undermine the child's healthy physical, emotional, and intellectual development. This applies to fact as well as fiction in the form of pornographic films, comic books, and magazines. Parents who sell their children into prostitution or for pornographic films, and adults who misuse children in this way, commit a major crime, not just a misdemeanor. (See Vol. II, Sexual Arousal, p. 249, under Attention Disorders.)

Neuroses

Anxiety and other neuroses usually also cause reading disorders indirectly, by undermining the attention process. A child who is preoccupied with his inner life, with neurotic conflicts and anxieties, finds it extremely difficult to concentrate.

However, neuroses do not necessarily cause a reading disorder. Many neurotic children read well and like to read. Reading is a consolation for them. It provides privacy; it allows the child to escape from bothersome people and to retreat into another world. The child can sit quietly while reading, and the world around him disappears.

The reading habits of a 6-year-old girl patient of mine are typical of this behavior. Her central conflict was an overwhelming jealousy of her younger brother. She started to read in kindergarten and read better than all her classmates by the end of the first grade; she was very proud of her ability to read and write. She wrote notes to her mother and left them all over the house; these notes usually complained about the mother's "bad" behavior towards her with hints of the child's jealousy of her brother. She also wrote notes to me, for instance: "I have my school for myself."

This child's interest in reading was an attempt to cope with her deep seated jealousy. By reading so well she demonstrated her superiority over her brother. Her relationship with her classmates was also influenced by her jealousy. She had the need to take the teacher's attention away from them. She had violent outbursts against the other children, and frequently retired to a corner of the classroom to read with a contemptuous look on her face.

However, jealousy of a sibling may also cause a reading disorder. These children are frequently resentful because they have to sit in school while their younger siblings play. Depending on the depth of this neurotic conflict, such a child can sometimes be helped to learn by making reading interesting and easy. The atmosphere in the classroom and the attitude of the teacher are crucial in this respect. (See Importance of Classroom Atmosphere, Vol. II, p. 548.)

That the same trauma or neurotic conflict may cause different and often opposite symptoms, such as a reading disorder in one child and not in another, is typical for psychopathologic processes. They do not operate according to rigid rules. Subtle differences play a major role. Constitutional (physical as well as emotional), psychologic, familial, and social variables—some entirely accidental—influence repression and symptom formation. That is why predictions in child psychiatry are so precarious.

Opposite symptom formation in brothers reacting to a chaotic home and a cruel father is described in the section on Psychogenic Hyperactivity. Ned became hyperactive, his brothers reacted with depression and anxiety. All three had a reading disorder due to lack of attention (Vol. II, pp. 501 ff,).

SCHOOL PHOBIA. School phobia is a severe anxiety neurosis with attacks of phobias (i.e., of deadly fears), with sweating, pallor, tremors, screaming, and a total inability to move on seeing or entering the school building or the classroom. The child does not know why he has such a deadly fear, because it is caused by unconscious processes. Eight children (four boys, four girls) with a psychogenic reading disorder and six children (four boys, two girls) with an organic reading disorder suffered from a school phobia in my study.

A reading disorder alone rarely causes such a severe neurosis. Repressed conflicts within the child's family, especially with his mother, usually form the basis for these phobias.

This neurosis must be distinguished from truancy, which is a deliberate act often caused by a reading disorder. It is circumscribed in Chapter 5 on Sociogenic Reading Disorders.

A Reading Disorder as a Neurotic Symptom

There is no monosymptomatic reading-disorder neurosis, where this disorder is the only symptom. A reading disorder is only one of several neurotic symptoms. It is part of a neurosis and not its only manifestation. Some of the different underlying psychopathologic mechanisms are discussed below.

1. *The reading process itself may have unpleasant conscious or unconscious associations.* It may touch on forbidden and repressed thoughts and feelings. It may have become associated with forbidden sexual curiosity or be experienced as too forceful or even as a violent activity. This may inhibit learning to read indirectly, by increasing the child's anxiety (LaVietes, 1972, p. 389).

2. *Words or single letters sometimes have unpleasant conscious or unconscious associations.* They may be experienced as symbols for forbidden thoughts or wishes. Rabinovitch describes a 9-year-old boy with a spelling

disorder on this basis. During psychotherapy the boy revealed that two older boys in the neighborhood taught him to spell a number of vulgar sexual terms when he was 5 years old. He did not know what these words meant, and proudly repeated his new knowledge to his mother, who became very angry and punished him severely. Rabinovitch concludes that "spelling came to symbolize uncleanliness and danger, and his circumscribed learning block resulted" (1959, p. 862).

According to psychoanalytical theory, reading is a part of the process of sublimation (Silverman et al., 1959, p. 304). It is an ego function. A reading disorder is therefore thought to result from an inhibition of certain ego functions. Some child psychoanalysts have classified reading disorders under "learning impotence." Pearson recommended the use of this term because he felt that such an inhibition "resembles very closely sexual impotence" (1952, p. 344). Actually, reading is, of course, quite different from sexual activity and so is its psychopathology.

The interpretations of reading disorders made by other medical and lay psychoanalysts are often equally speculative. They do not conform to the strict requirements of clinical science Freud observed so carefully. These psychoanalysts use his terminology without presenting any proof that these are really the child's own associations, that they are based on what the child said in his own words or communicated through his dreams or play. Far-reaching generalizations are based on the same shaky foundations.

They have, for instance, implicated "visual shock" due to shocking symbolic meanings of the act of reading words as a cause of reading disorders. Looking is interpreted as a symbol for killing or being blinded.

Such interpretations are made by Vivian Jarvis in a report entitled "Clinical Observations on the Visual Problem in Reading Disability" (1958). She writes:

> There is an emergence, among other things, of symbolic meanings transferred onto the reading process from pathological attempts at a resolution of the oedipal conflict. It is as though eye–phallus, book–genital, teacher–mother recreate afresh the struggle that previously went on at home for the child (p. 453).

She generalizes the role of the Oedipus complex in the following way:

> Bearing in mind also that poor readers are usually boys, we are reminded of Oedipus who blinded himself. It may be that "reading cases" are boys who have blinded themselves symbolically and thus create the problem of vision. As the school has become substituted for the home, so have its activities become sexualized and aggressivized (p. 454).

She also suggests that the reading disorder is connected with the primal scene:

We might further connect the reading situation with the primal scene in the following way. The child learns to read by merging sound (hearing) and sight (seeing). Perhaps early development for the future retarded reader is such that the ear is regarded as a passive organ which can be assailed by sounds during the primal scene for which the listener cannot have the same feeling of responsibility as he would for looking with its active components. He can close his eyes by eye activity, i.e., dropping the lids or averting the glance. He cannot close his ear by ear activity. The ear might be thought of as feminine-passive; the eye as masculine-active. In the reading situation it is as though the reader actually has to rely on sound to further his efforts (p. 456).

Other medical and nonmedical child psychoanalysts have made similar interpretations. Bessie M. Sperry (M.A.), Nancy Staver (M.S.S.), and Harold E. Mann (M.D.), for instance, explain the visual shock of Janet, an 11-year-old girl in this way: "Reading letters is associated with looking at the mother's abdomen with the baby inside, and now we recall the former associations of looking with cutting, with knowing where the baby comes from . . . " (1952, p. 361).

It must be stressed that these interpretations are made only in relation to the structure of words, not to their meaning. These children do not refuse to read such words as "puss" or other words they understand which might have double meanings.

These so-called visual shocks may not be a deep-seated symptom at all. For instance, Sperry and co-workers describe Janet's visual shock in the following way: "She had a great deal of difficulty putting the s's on the ends of words and seeing the first letters of the words. She looked at words in the middle. She could not say correctly small words like "the" (p. 360). These are reading habits frequently found in children struggling with the sight/word method. They are not caused by a neurotic process. (See Inability to See Words Clearly, p. 97.)

There may be even simpler explanations. Children do not like to look at something uninteresting that they do not understand. It is typical of children with reading disorders not to look at what they are reading. Often they look at a word for a second, then look up with an obliging smile and guess wildly, being quite disappointed when they are wrong.

Similar interpretations have been made of writing disorders. In the same report, Sperry and co-workers describe the difficulty of a boy named Patrick with writing the letter "P." They write:

Most often the "P" would appear like a fat zero, strikingly like the zeros on his arithmetic papers, which were conspicuously larger than the other numbers. Sometimes, he left the P out completely. Changing the P into a fat zero expresses his conflict. He is afraid of having a genital like his father's, represented by the

P. He attempts the solution of his conflict either by omitting the P or writing a large zero which represents nothingness, or at best femaleness. He may either be a woman or die (1952, pp. 363–364).

Educators have also tried to explain children's reading and writing disorders with forbidden sexual meanings of letters; for instance, that the "m" may remind a child of a sex organ.

Such interpretations may do great harm, especially when they are made directly to children as Melanie Klein recommends, and not elicited indirectly, waiting for the child's own explanations and insights. This emphasis on sexual interpretations must lead to sexual overstimulation of the child, and often amounts to a seduction. As I stressed in a review of Melanie Klein's *Narrative of a Child Analysis* "The child's world is sexualized, and what he sees and does consists of symbols standing for sexual fantasies, some of them so abnormal that they are only observed in psychotic patients" (Mosse, 1962c).

Neither Freud himself nor Anna Freud had such crudely sexual views of symbol and symptom formation. Anna Freud does not mention reading disorders at all in *Normality and Pathology in Childhood* (1965). She only mentions learning disorders briefly and in a general way in the chapters on "The Infantile Neuroses" (pp. 150, 153, 154) and "Disharmony between Developmental Lines" (p. 126).

She stresses that such a disharmony becomes pathogenic only if the imbalance in the personality is excessive. She states that this applies to children who are failures in school in spite of their good intelligence. She writes:

> In the usual diagnostic examination it is not easy to pinpoint the specific steps in id–ego interaction which they have failed to achieve, unless we look into them for the prerequisites of the right attitude to work such as control and modification of pregenital drive components; functioning according to the reality principle; and pleasure in ultimate results of activity. Sometimes all of these, sometimes one or the other are lacking. Descriptively, the children under discussion are usually classified as "lacking in concentration," as having a "short attention span," as "inhibited" (1965, p. 127).

In Attention Disorders, I discuss the role played by the reality principle, by the attitude to work, by concentration, and by distractibility (Vol. II, pp. 554, 572, 547).

Unconscious processes in parents have also been held responsible for their children's reading disorders. In a paper on "Fathers of Sons With Primary Neurotic Learning Inhibitions", Margaret G. Grunebaum, et al. emphasize that

> While many of these fathers consciously express the wish that their sons could overcome their learning handicap and appear to ally themselves with the goals of therapy, they betray their unconscious need to see their sons as defective and unchallenging by the manner in which they offer to help their sons (1962, p. 465).

Mothers are more frequently blamed for their child's failure, which is supposed to meet their "unconscious needs."

Parents may indeed sabotage their children's progress deliberately or without being aware of what they are doing. However, this affects the child's general emotional and intellectual development, not his reading alone. The child's reaction is often the opposite. Learning to read and reading later on may be one of his defenses against his parents' destructive attitudes. Treatment of the parents alone cannot in any case cure a child's reading disorder.

Dreams

Unlike numbers, letters do not have their own intrinsic historical mythology, their own magic and symbolic significance. They have a personal meaning that is sometimes repressed into the unconscious and revealed in dreams. For instance, the first letter of the father's name or of the names of siblings may appear in dreams standing for these family members.

Words have a much more complicated and personal meaning. They appear in children's dreams in their spoken form. Only very rarely does written or printed material enter a child's dream. Signs, letters, and telegrams tend to appear in adults' dreams. The dreamer usually cannot read and understand what they say. They only hint at repressed, hidden material.

Freud stressed that word fragments, which frequently play a role in dreams, stem from auditory perceptions, and that the seeing of words is a secondary process that has been acquired through reading. In *The Ego and the Id* (1923) he wrote that "the word is in fact a memory trace acquired first through hearing" (1955, p. 248). That is why only the spoken word appears in the dreams of children and is much more frequent than print or writing in the dreams of adults. It was acquired earlier in life and plays a greater role in the unconscious. This applies also to children who can read.

Treatment

Neuroses that involve reading are treated with psychotherapy like any other neurosis. However, if the child's reading disorder is of long standing, psychotherapy alone does not cure it. The child needs reading treatment in addition.

The treatment of attention disorders is described in detail in the section dealing with these disorders (Vol. II, p. 501). Teachers have a very important role to play in helping children overcome such a disorder (Vol. II, p. 544,). The manner in which children are punished is also crucial (Vol. II, p. 550 in the Damaging Roles of Humiliation and Fear). Visualization should be used (Vol. II, p. 543). See also Teaching of Attention (Vol. II, p. 552), Motivation and Education (Vol. II, p. 552), and Concentration Exercises (Vol. II, p. 554).

Home Instruction

The behavior of eight children in my study (all boys aged 7 to 14) was so disruptive that they had to be placed on home instruction. Their severe behavior disorder was not necessarily caused by their reading disorder alone, but was invariably aggravated by it. One of these boys, 6-year-old Jeffrey, suffered from neurotic hyperactivity (Vol. II, p. 656).

Suspensions

Seventeen children (14 boys aged 7 to 15; 3 girls aged 7, 12, and 14) were suspended from school attendance for various lengths of time because of disruptive and violent behavior.

Hospitalization

The behavior of 21 children (16 boys, 5 girls, aged 7 to 15) was so disturbed and disturbing that they were sent to mental hospitals. Four of them (2 boys and 2 girls, aged 8, 9, 10, and 15) were found to be suffering from schizophrenia.

Fourteen children (all boys, aged 7 to 15) were wrongly diagnosed as schizophrenic. This diagnosis was changed to "behavior disorder" or "personality disorder" in the state hospitals or later on when they were followed up on an outpatient basis. I described the plight of three of these boys (aged 7, 9, and 13) in "The Misuse of the Diagnosis Childhood Schizophrenia" (1958).

Three girls, 2 age 12 and 1 age 14, spent a period of observation on the adolescent ward of a city hospital. I was in charge of this ward. All three girls suffered from severe behavior disorders. They improved with psychotherapy, constructive ward management, and remedial teaching in this hospital school. They were discharged to this school and outpatient psychotherapy and social work were continued.

Chapter 6

Sociogenic Reading Disorders

Social factors play a role in the causation of almost all psychogenic reading disorders. Individual and social forces are so closely interrelated that they are difficult to separate. Learning to read is not an intimate personal acitvity like daydreaming. It is a social act for a young child. The inevitable involvement of social factors is what makes reading disorders so different from phobias and other neurotic symptoms. When social factors predominate, the child's reading disorder should be classified as sociogenic.

Classification

Sociogenic reading disorders belong to the reactive disorders, a classification unfortunately not used in the official Diagnostic and Statistical Manuals (D.S.M.) published by the American Psychiatric Association. The classification that comes closest to reactive disorders in these manuals is "Adjustment Reaction" or "Adjustment Disorders." However, reading is not mentioned at all in this connection. Reading disorders are classified only under "Developmental Reading Disorder, 315.00." The emotional and behavioral symptoms of some, but by no means all these children, fit into "Adjustment disorder with depressed mood, 309.00," "with anxious mood, 309.24," or "with disturbance of conduct, 309.30." These classifications are part of D.S.M. III (1980) p. 19. (See p. 42 in Chapter 2, Reading Disorders on an Organic Basis.)

It must be stressed that these children do not have personality disorders and are not sociopaths. Children, adolescents, and adults with disturbing behavior are apt to be put into these diagnostic categories, especially when they commit criminal acts. Children suffering from a sociogenic reading disorder are basically healthy. They are reacting to damaging social factors. The defects are in society, *not* in these children and adolescents.

Diagnosis

The differential diagnosis among organic, psychogenic, and sociogenic reading disorders can be difficult to determine. Mistakes on reading tests are the same, and psychopathologic as well as social factors play a role in all reading disorders. Mistakes typical for all these children are (1) uncertainty about the direction of letters and about their sounds, (2) trouble with blending, i.e., combining the sounds of letters and letter combinations representing one sound into a word, (3) uncertainty about the sequence of letters within words —reading "was" for "saw," "no" for "on"; writing "gril" for "girl," etc.; (4) guessing words following the initial consonant; (5) inventing words or entire sentences with no relation to the text, in other words, covering up the reading disorder, (6) Spelling poorly orally and when writing, and therefore having great difficulty in writing; both dictation and composition are seriously affected.

Children with a sociogenic reading disorder do not necessarily have all six of these reading disorder symptoms, but they invariably have most of them. These symptoms are most severe in children damaged by sight/word methods. These children therefore are most difficult to differentiate from those with organic reading disorders.

General diagnostic criteria are the same as for the psychogenic type: a better performance during individual examinations than in the classroom, rapidity of correction of errors, and ease of learning the 11 reading and 3 writing acts with appropriate methods.

The child's reading disorder is sociogenic when the clinical examination shows that the cause or causes of his reading difficulties lie exclusively in adverse social factors and that individual psychopathology or organic defects are not involved at all or play a minor role.

Examination

Methods to determine the role of social factors are described in Chapter 1, Examination. They include special tests for comic book reading, techniques for finding out the role television plays in the child's life, and the teaching methods used by his teachers. The determination of the social pressures exerted on the child and of the role of violence and prejudice in his life, and an evaluation of his schoolwork are routine parts of every clinical examination (see p. 24).

That damaging social factors alone caused the child's reading disorder can sometimes be established with certainty only after a period of treatment where these social factors are eliminated. For instance, a child whose reading has been inhibited by the sight/word method may learn to read through phonetic methods in a very short time.

The reading specialist Helen R. Lowe gives an excellent example of the cure of such a sociogenic reading disorder. She writes:

Well before 1948 I had become convinced that so-called specific reading disability, as indicated conspicuously by reversals and bizarre misreadings, was largely made, and not born. Moreover, for many students referred by school psychologists, psychiatrists, and teachers as severe cases of mixed cerebral dominance, a simpler explanation was easily found, which lead to a simple remedy. A failure to develop that was due to hereditary causes would not yield to the simple procedures which I find effective with students from kindergarten to college level. They are told, "Oh, you read backwards? Well, don't. It doesn't work. I'll show you how to read forward." This is not psychotherapy nor yet remedial reading. It is, perhaps, nothing more remarkable than horse sense (1961, pp. 105–106).

When a child's reading has been damaged by mass media, such as comic books and television, a period away from these influences may suffice to cure the reading disorder, especially when a lack of interest in reading was its basis. However, most of these children also need reading treatment because comic book habituation may have caused Linear Dyslexia (pp. 127) and severe spelling and writing deficiencies.

Two forms of sociogenic reading disorders can be distinguished, just as in the psychogenic type: deficient basic techniques and faulty, slow, and laborious reading due to lack of practice.

The arrangement of symptoms in Tables 6.1 and 6.2 facilitates the differential diagnosis. It is not a symptom list to be used to feed the child's symptoms into a computer and let the machine figure out the diagnosis. Clinical judgment alone can weigh the relative importance of all clinical findings, of which symptoms are only one part. Computers do not have this kind of judgment. (See Vol. II, Symptom lists, p. 630, 259 ff; under Hyperactivity.)

My statistics are lopsided. The relative frequency of the three types of reading disorders in the general school population is exactly the opposite. Sociogenic reading disorders are by far the most numerous, affecting great masses of children. The psychogenic type is much less frequent, and organic reading disorders are the smallest group by far.

This statistical reversal is entirely attributable to the selection of children and adolescents referred to me. Only the most disturbed and disturbing children ever come to the attention of a child psychiatrist. Children with a sociogenic reading disorder usually do not have the kind of symptoms that lead to psychiatric referral.

The overwhelming majority of children with any type of reading disorder remain in the care of classroom teachers. The reading disorder of a much smaller group is treated in special classes or on an individual basis by teachers specializing in remedial reading treatment. The next smaller group receives private tutoring. Pediatricians, social workers, and psychologists care for even fewer of these children. By far the smallest group is referred to psychiatrists working in schools, agencies, clinics, or in private practice.

Comparison of the Three International Types of Reading Disorders

The symptoms of the organic group of disorders are identical internationally, with minor variations due to differing reading techniques: alphabetical, ideographic, or pictorial. The psychogenic and the sociogenic groups vary according to historic, cultural, ideological, and other social factors. The sociogenic group is by far the largest group in the United States and in other countries where the same harmful factors are operative (Mosse, 1955, 1963b, 1965, 1966c, 1977a).

TABLE 6.1. Differential Diagnosis of Reading Disorders

	Organic 222 Children Ages 5–17 (184 Boys, 38 Girls)	Psychogenic 177 Children Ages 6–15 (141 Boys, 36 Girls)	Sociogenic 46 Children Ages 7–17 (43 Boys, 3 Girls)
Performing the 11 reading and 3 writing acts	Cannot perform several or all of them	Capacity to learn all basic acts	Capacity to learn all basic acts
Attention disorder	Present	Present	Frequent
Interest in reading	Present	Absent or strongly ambivalent	Present
Effort	Present	Absent or sporadic	Present in the beginning
Motivation	Longs to grow up and learn	Frequently prefers to remain a baby and play	Present in the beginning before failure becomes apparent and chronic
Slowing down of many mental reactions	Present	Absent	Absent
Impairment of automatic mechanisms	Present	Absent	Absent
Inability to tolerate disorder	Present	Absent	Absent
Inability to shift freely	Present	Absent	Absent
Perseveration	Present	Absent	Absent
Hyperactivity	Infrequent: 23 (19 boys, 4 girls)	Rare: 6 (all boys)	Absent
Hypoactivity	Infrequent	Infrequent	Absent
Arithmetic disorder	Frequent	Infrequent	Absent
Speech disorder	Frequent	Absent	Absent
Mental deficiency	Frequent	Absent	Absent
Convulsive disorder	Infrequent	Rare	Absent
Fatiguability	Present	Infrequent	Absent
Morbid irritability	Frequent	Infrequent	Absent
Mood disorder	Frequent	Infrequent	Absent
Free-floating anxiety	Frequent	Frequent	Rare
Cerebral palsy	Frequent	Absent	Absent
School phobia	Infrequent: 6 (4 boys, 2 girls)	Infrequent: 8 (4 boys, 4 girls)	Absent
Asthma	Infrequent: 6 (4 boys, 2 girls)	Infrequent: 5 (4 boys, 1 girl)	Absent

TABLE 6.1. Differential Diagnosis of Reading Disorders, Continued

	Organic 222 Children Ages 5–17 (184 Boys, 38 Girls)	Psychogenic 177 Children Ages 6–15 (141 Boys, 36 Girls)	Sociogenic 46 Children Ages 7–17 (43 Boys, 3 Girls)
Gastrointestinal symptoms	Rare (absent)	Rare: 3 (1 boy, 2 girls)	Rare: 1 boy
Headache	Infrequent: 5 boys	Infrequent: 6 (4 boys, 2 girls)	Rare: 1 boy
Enuresis	Frequent: 13 (12 boys, 1 girl)	Frequent: 18 boys	Absent
Conversion symptoms (hysterical neurosis)	Rare: 1 boy	Rare: 3 (2 boys, 1 girl)	Absent
Depression	Frequent (caused by reading disorder): 16 (14 boys, 2 girls)	Frequent (causing reading disorder): 26 (25 boys, 1 girl)	Rare: 1 boy
Suicide threats and/or attempts	Frequent: 10 boys	Frequent: 12 (10 boys, 2 girls)	Rare: 1 boy
Compulsions	Rare	Rare	Absent
Obsessions	Frequent as part of the inability to tolerate disorder	Rare	Absent
Tics	Rare: 3 boys	Rare	Absent
Benign hallucinations due to anxiety	Frequent: 23 (20 boys, 3 girls)	Frequent: 20 (16 boys, 4 girls)	Absent
Telling fantastic tales	Infrequent: 8 (7 boys, 1 girl)	Infrequent: 7 (6 boys, 1 girl)	Rare: 1 boy
Nightmares and other anxious dreams	Frequent: 17 (15 boys, 2 girls)	Very frequent: 37 (25 boys, 12 girls)	Rare: 3 boys
Daydreaming	Frequent after a period of unsuccessful attempts to read	Frequent from beginning of school	Frequent after reading failure becomes apparent and chronic
Attitude toward parents	Tries to please them	Frequently tries to control, annoy, and punish them by poor performance in reading or feels that he is stupid and helpless and cannot possibly live up to their expectations	Tries to please them

TABLE 6.1. Differential Diagnosis of Reading Disorders, Continued

	Organic 222 Children Ages 5–17 (184 Boys, 38 Girls)	Psychogenic 177 Children Ages 6–15 (141 Boys, 36 Girls)	Sociogenic 46 Children Ages 7–17 (43 Boys, 3 Girls)
Attitudes toward teacher	Tries to please, to conform	Tries to be center of attention, sometimes expresses anger at teacher by not learning to read	Tries to conform until reading becomes a major factor in school failure
Attitudes toward classmates	Makes pathetic efforts to work like the other children	Tries to get their attention, to dominate them, or when anxiety predominates, withdraws	Friendly until failure destroys self-confidence and positive self-image

TABLE 6.2. Severity of Reading Disorder and/or Disruptive Behavior in the Classroom Leading to Removal from School

	Organic	Psychogenic	Sociogenic
Home instruction	Frequent: 15 (11 boys, aged 7–13; 4 girls, aged 6–12)	Infrequent: 8 (all boys, aged 7–14)	Rare: 1 (a boy, aged 12)
Suspension from school	Infrequent: 10 (all boys, aged 7–11)	Frequent: 17 (14 boys, aged 7–15; 3 girls, aged 7, 12, 14)	Rare: 2 (both boys, aged 14, 15)
Psychiatric hospitalization	Frequent: 22 (20 boys, aged 7–15; 2 girls, aged 6, 16)	Frequent: 21 (16 boys, aged 7–15; 5 girls, aged 10–15)	Rare: 2 (1 boy, age 13; 1 girl, age 12)

Neo-Illiteracy, A New Epidemic Form of Sociogenic Reading Disorders

Statistical evidence is overwhelming that millions of American children, including those graduating from high school, cannot read. When a disorder affects so many people, one calls it an epidemic. An epidemic is always caused by external forces, not by defects in the individual. This applies to psychologic disorders as much as to physical diseases. When so many children are affected by the same disorder, the explanation cannot possibly be individual psychopathology. Adverse social forces must be investigated as the common cause.

The epidemic of reading disorders in the United States is a new kind of illiteracy because it is not due to lack of schooling. Traditionally, the literacy of a country is measured by the number of children and adults who have attended school. That an increasing number of school children cannot read at all, or so poorly that for all practical purposes they have to be regarded as illiterate, is a new phenomenon (Wheeler, 1979).

The goal of every civilized society is that all its adult members can read the language they speak. A country's literacy rate indicates how much a society cares for all its people equally. It shows whether or not education is provided for all people so that a true basis exists for equal opportunity. The United States has a high literacy rate. Compulsory education for all children was introduced some four generations ago. Yet at a time when many poverty-stricken, underdeveloped countries make great sacrifices and eliminate illiteracy among their youths successfully, the literacy rate among youngsters in the United States is declining.

An undetermined number of these unfortunate illiterate youngsters cannot read or write at all; others can read an occasional word and can copy, but they cannot write spontaneously or to dictation. They cannot fill out job applications or other forms properly, and can barely read street and other signs. It goes so far that they cannot be skilled laborers even if they have the ability, because they cannot read forms, labels, instructions, or contracts fully, or even write more than their name. They cannot spell, or read advertisements where jobs are offered, or write down the addresses where they are to present themselves for work. They may even have trouble finding employment as unskilled laborers, performing the most menial tasks.

The Department of Labor reported as long ago as 1963 that many applicants cannot even pass the simplest task given for jobs as cleaning women and men because they cannot distinguish "rat poison" from "cleaning fluid."

The damage done by this type of illiteracy was stressed in a report by the U.S. Navy. Vice-Admiral James D. Watkins reported that one illiterate sailor alone did $250,000 worth of damage to an engine because he could not read instructions and that a study of 23,000 recruits showed that 37% of them could not read at the tenth-grade level. Seventy percent of these young men could not read well enough to complete boot camp. As a stopgap measure, the Navy started to teach reading and to rewrite instruction and technical manuals so that they can be understood by poor readers ("Admiral Says U.S. Navy Is Hindered by Illiteracy," *New York Times,* July 5, 1977).

By 1969 the number of illiterate youngsters had become so large and the social pressure exerted by this epidemic so urgent that their plight was at last acknowledged in the highest places. *The New York Times* wrote about this in an editorial, "A Nation of Illiterates?":

> The youth who leaves school without being able to read enters society crippled. Worse, his deficiency is likely to impel him to become a drop-out, a frustrated, embittered and easy victim of delinquency, drift and crime. At present, an estimated one-third of the nation's school children are embarked on such a dismal course, and in the nation's big cities, the hopeless army is probably closer to half of the total enrollment (1969).

This editorial supported the "nation-wide war" against reading disorders initiated by Dr. James E. Allen, Jr., who was then United States Commissioner of Education. In a speech before the National Association of States' Boards of Education, Dr. Allen said that one out of every four children had a serious reading deficiency and that three-quarters of the juvenile offenders in New York were at least 2 years behind the norm in their ability to read. He set as a national goal that by the end of the 1970s no person would leave a school system anywhere in the country without the ability to read properly (Rosenbaum, 1969a, b, 1970).

Unfortunately, his timetable was overoptimistic. The neo-illiteracy rate among schoolchildren has increased, not decreased, since then.

Deceptive Statistics

It is an integral part of the reading problem and the confusion surrounding it that what is reported as statistics are actually only estimates. Because of ever-changing curriculum practices and tests no clear-cut unassailable statistics exist. The Office of Education announced in 1969 that they would begin collecting such statistics, an impossible task.

There is no nationally coordinated curriculum in reading, just as there is none in any other subject. Reading levels differ from one school to the next. Reading tests are often not standardized nationally, and can therefore not always be safely compared. Individual schools or school districts spend hundreds of thousands of dollars every few years to buy new reading tests from publishing companies who make periodic revisions of these tests "to ensure that the content of the test may continue to be closely attuned to what is actually being taught in the schools" (*Stanford Achievement Test*, 1964). This is true for all subject areas.

It is inherent in this system that when pupil achievements decline the tests are also lowered; thus such a decline may not necessarily show up in statistics, and neither may a general rise. There is no equivalent to the National Board of Medical Examiners, which sets minimal acceptable standards for all medical students (i.e., for all subjects taught in medical schools). This Board played a crucial role in raising the quality of medical school teaching, which had been severely criticized in the famous Flexner report (1910).

Periodic revision of reading tests should not be necessary anyway, because reading does not change like scientific or vocational subjects. It ought to be possible to agree upon a minimal level of achievement in reading and writing that all children can reach, let's say at the end of elementary school. However, not all elementary schools end with the same grade; it may be the fifth, sixth, seventh, or eighth. It might therefore be better to agree on an age when this reading goal must be reached. I suggest the age of 12 because this gives the schools 6 years in which to teach all children to read and write the language they speak. This ought to be sufficient time even for English. This can be achieved without leaving any child back, provided reading difficulties are diagnosed as soon as they occur and immediately corrected. Six years is sufficient time to achieve this as well.

School administrators keep telling worried parents that an average reading score in any grade means that 50% of the children are expected to read below and 50% above it. This is misleading because it refers only to the way these tests are standardized, not to the child's concrete reading ability. For reading cannot be measured like height, weight, or intelligence with its bell-shaped statistical curve. It is a learned skill and all children can and must be expected to be able to read certain agreed-upon minimal texts, at least in elementary school.

Even though there are no nationwide statistics, the evidence coming from school systems all over the country is overwhelming that the reading ability of children from elementary school to high school has decreased steadily. For example, New York City high school teachers complained as long ago as 1952 that 34% of students entering in the 9th grade and 40% of those entering in the 10th grade were retarded in reading. In 1938 retardation had been 26%; by 1947 it had risen to 34%. The Board of Education failed to see a danger signal in these results, which had been obtained through surveys done by their own high school division, but simply stated that the city's level of achievement was about the same as that for high school students throughout the country. It should not have been reassuring to anyone that the New York City school system only followed the downward trend in the entire nation ("Students Decline in Reading Ability," 1952).

Official reports on students' reading ability and their reflection in the press and in other mass media have not changed since then. They have been depressingly monotonous: "Functional Illiteracy Found High in U.S. in Study at Harvard" (Rosenthal, 1970); "San Francisco, Oakland 'Fail' in Reading

Tests" (Moskowitz, 1971); "Decline Continues in Reading Ability of Pupils in City" (Buder, 1972); ". . . Fleischmann Panel Says System Leaves Thousands of Graduates Unequipped to Hold Jobs or Continue Schooling" (Maeroff, 1972); "A Solution to Falling Reading Scores Continues to Elude Big-City Schools" (Maeroff, 1973); "College Textbooks Being Simplified to Meet the Needs of the Poor Reader" (Peterson, 1974); "On Being 17, Bright —and Unable to Read" (Raymond, 1976); "Study Cites Student Writing Deficiencies" (Fiske, 1977); "City Pupils Remain Behind in Reading—Official Asserts the Tests Suggest Difficulty in Early Grades" (Fiske, 1979); (see also Wheeler, 1979; Hymowitz, 1981).

While it has finally been publicly acknowledged that great masses of children are illiterate—that reading disorders have taken on epidemic proportions —confusion continues to reign in all areas connected with reading. Yet this epidemic cannot be stopped and headlines such as "Federal Education Aid to Poor is Found to Have Little Effect" (Stevens, 1969) will continue to appear; in fact, the very foundation of universal public education will continue to be shaken unless clarity is achieved.

Results of Personal Experience

I was able to study the development of this new form of illiteracy very closely, first as a pediatrician, then as a child psychiatrist. I started my training in child psychiatry while I was still a pediatrician in a mental hygiene clinic run by Dr. Fredric Wertham, who felt that reading and speech therapy should be an integral part of any mental hygiene clinic caring for children. Later, he appointed me to be the director of a Pediatric Mental Hygiene Clinic, one of the first of this type.

Remedial reading specialists and speech therapists were also members of the Lafargue Clinic, a free mental hygiene clinic for adults and children, which I helped Wertham found in 1946. At the Quaker Emergency Service Readjustment Center, of which Wertham was the director, I examined youthful sex offenders whom the courts referred to this free clinic. Many of them also had reading disorders (Mosse, 1958a).

During my work with hospitalized mental patients at the Psychiatric Division of Kings County Hospital, I was in charge of the Female Adolescent Ward and served some time on the Adult and Children's Wards. This gave me the opportunity to examine, diagnose, and treat a large number of children and adolescents with very severe psychopathology. Most of them were referred by the courts and had severe reading disorders.

Kings County Hospital is located in Brooklyn, New York. It had an excellent inpatient day school run by a group of exceptionally devoted and competent teachers. I observed their work, and they participated in all our case conferences. We enlarged this school so that children who had been discharged from the ward could attend it. This proved to be a most successful plan; both the behavior and the reading disorders of the students improved.

I learned a great deal from these teachers. Their success with this school was reflected in their subsequent careers. The principal, Dr. Elliot Shapiro, became one of the most successful and socially active principals in Harlem and was later on appointed an Assistant Superintendent by community demand. Dr. Carl Fenichel became the Director of the League School, a pioneer day school for emotionally severely disturbed children, and Mr. Abraham Sales became the principal of four such inpatient day schools.

I was further involved with reading problems through Dr. William Calvin Barger, who was developing his mirror technique for treating children with certain organic reading disorders and aphasias when I worked with him as a school psychiatrist at the Bureau of Child Guidance of the Board of Education of the City of New York. I observed his work, examined a number of the children he treated, and studied their progress. (See Barger Mirroreading Board, p. 104.)

As soon as I started to work as a school psychiatrist, I made an effort to find out how many children had reading disorders in the individual schools to which I was assigned. I visited the schools, conferring with the principals and other administrators, with guidance counselors, curriculum assistants, school nurses, reading and speech teachers, and individual classroom teachers. I had group conferences with teachers and gave in-service courses to them. I asked the school psychologists and social workers who worked with me about their experiences and impressions. They tried to assist me in getting an estimate of the number of children who had definite reading disorders. Such an estimate was impossible to establish even in schools we knew well and worked in for years.

Sometimes it was even difficult to obtain the results of city-wide group tests because they were not always made public. But even these tests meant very little in practical terms. They did not then and still do not reveal the individual child's total reading performance because they test only silent reading with multiple-choice answers; thus no reading-error analysis can be made with any degree of certainty. The reason for a child's low score can therefore not be determined.

Even the scores themselves are vulnerable to serious doubts. I know of too many children who just guessed and then circled the answers at random or even decided to circle every third word. This leads to completely worthless scores, of course. Many children infer the content of the text from some key words without reading or being able to read all the words. When tested orally, they may not be able to read even this key word. (See Chapter 1, Examination, pp. 31–32.)

As early as 1950 experienced teachers and psychologists who had been teachers told me that all the children they had personally taught years ago used to be able to read by the age of 8, except for those who were definitely mentally defective, and that this had changed. They related it to the *deformalized* program which had been started in the New York City public schools and in most other school systems throughout the nation in about 1935. This new curriculum brought with it the sight/word method of teaching reading. Letters and writing were not taught anymore until the children had acquired a so-called sight-vocabulary of 50 to 100 or more words. The reading-readiness concept was introduced at about the same time. This delayed the onset of teaching of reading for very many children until the age of 7 or 8 because they had to pass a *reading-readiness* test first. This change seemed to have freed teaching and advanced it in many ways, but reading had been adversely affected. ("Curriculum and Materials . . .," 1954, p. 2). (See section on Spelling, p. 199.)

Evidence of the decline of school children's reading ability came to me also from other sources. Librarians and teachers responsible for ordering books told me that third- and fourth-year books were being requested for sixth-graders. Schoolbook salesmen reported that publishing companies had done their own research about reading levels on different grades and had found that they were declining. These findings were especially important for them because they had to readjust their sales.

A department chairman of an exclusive Eastern prep school told me that remedial reading specialists were being employed for the first time in the school's history because too many 14-year-old freshmen could not read properly. This was in 1954, the year Wertham, in *Seduction Of The Innocent,* exposed the profoundly damaging effects crime comic books have on the intellectual and psychologic development of children, especially on their reading [Wertham, 1954, 1972 (b)]. One year later, in 1955, *Why Johnny Can't Read and What You Can Do About It* by Rudolf Flesch was published. It was, according to him, "a little compendium of arguments against our current system of teaching reading" (p. IX). This book opened a passionate, nationwide debate on the validity of the visual or sight/word versus the phonetic method of teaching reading to beginners. Educators reacted with a storm of indignation. Too much economic and psychologic capital had been invested by them, together with textbook publishers, in the sight/word method. They continued to maintain that "children today read as well and perhaps better than children of former years" (Preston, 1962, p. 159). Where statistics were unfavorable to their position, they minimized them or simply denied their importance.

The sad facts have since proven how wrong they were and how right was Flesch. In the November 1, 1979, issue of *Family Circle,* he wrote sadly: "I predicted educational catastrophe 25 years ago, and it has happened. So I've earned the right to say that these frightening prospects are the direct results of look-and-say teaching in our schools" (1979).

Causes of Neo-Illiteracy

Clinical and statistical evidence collected within the past 30 years shows that three clearly definable social factors damage the reading ability of millions of children, whether or not they have organic defects, neurotic symptoms, or are mentally quite healthy. These are: the sight/word method, some aspects of mass media (especially comic books), and an atmosphere of violence at school, on the street, and/or at home.

Damaging Teaching Philosophies and Practices

Teaching means explaining so that the student can understand and remember. It requires "order, clarity and pace" in a lucid definition by Siepmann (1969). It must be a step-by-step process, from basic elementary levels to ever higher and more complicated ones. Unless each lower step has been mastered, a higher one cannot be reached. No teacher can achieve this successfully without a clear understanding of every step involved in this process. Precise definitions are essential for this.

Official Definitions of Reading

There is no agreement even on the definition of reading. Educators have enlarged its meaning to such an extent that it includes subject matter that used to be quite accurately called grammar, philology, English literature, philosophy, psychology, creative writing. The following statement made by a committee of Assistant Superintendents in 1963 sounds persuasive:

> Reading is the deepening of perception and understanding through the intercommunication of minds using the medium of the written word. Reading is much more than mere word, phrase, or even sentence recognition. Reading involves not only the skills of word recognition (such as the use of configuration; contextual clues; and word analysis, which includes phonics as one of the basic means of word attack) but also comprehension, library, work-study, and appreciation skills. Reading includes the development of attitudes, abilities, and techniques whose inter-relationships are many, varied and intricate. Reading has dimensions that go far and above and beyond the literal meaning of the printed word. Reading concerns context in which words expand into ideas and thoughts derived from past experiences. It involves imagination, the thinking, and the feelings of both participants in the communication process—the writer and the reader. Reading is a highly complex process, an expression of the total personality of the individual, and a vital facet of the language arts rather than a separate and discrete curriculum area. Mere word calling is to reading as snapping a photograph is to the painting of a beautiful picture—the one, a mechanical skill; the other, a life-giving art. Thus, all that one brings to the printed page plays a part in determining what he takes away from it ("Sequential Levels of Reading Growth in the Elementary Schools," 1963).

What they say is true, but by their uncritical mingling of lower and higher levels of learning and understanding, the superintendents evade and thereby obscure the entire subject of reading teaching. It is the mechanical skill of reading that the children who appear in the statistics as illiterates have not mastered. They cannot rise above it, and all higher levels remain beyond their reach. This statement is typical for administrative educators all over the country.

In the context of the rising neo-illiteracy, this statement is pretentious and misleading. It is written in a style called "educationese" by *Time* magazine. It denounces phonics as "mere word calling" and downgrades the mechanical skill of reading, which it treats almost with contempt. It expresses a teaching philosophy I have heard repeated over and over again in parent–teacher association and staff meetings when reading difficulties were discussed: namely, that what the child "brings to the printed page" determines his reading ability. This amounts to blaming the child and his parents for his reading failures instead of the school for failing to teach him properly. It is a convenient excuse for poor teaching. It reminds me of those "experts" who maintain that the cult of violence in the mass media (comic books, television, movies) is harmless because it damages only children who are emotionally disturbed anyhow. The same type of reasoning is involved here. The children are blamed, while the adults who are supposed to protect and educate them are exonerated.

These definitions of reading are so very important because definitions are programs, as Walcutt points out in a comprehensive analysis of definitions of reading used by professional educators (1967). The administrative educators who formulate these definitions determine the curriculum of millions of children.

The teaching philosophy that "teaching a child to read is to teach him to get meaning from the printed page" (Hopkins, 1962), combined with teaching of "context clues" and stress on "all that one brings to the printed page" has lead to the practice, now widespread among schoolchildren and college students, of substituting their own words for those used by the author. Many students even alter the content of the text they are supposed to read to suit their own needs. High school and college teachers complain about this habit.

Walcutt gives a typical example for the disastrous results of this educational philosophy. He writes:

Reading is now officially defined as "bringing meaning to the printed page." The reading specialists (who are committed to this definition) assert with absolute confidence and conviction that a child who sees "My father was in a battle" and says "My father was in a war" is *reading* better than the child who comes out with "My father was in a bottle." If reading is "bringing meaning to the printed page," the child who sees "battle" and says "war" *is* doing better than the child who sees "battle" and says "bottle." Obviously the element of sound is now disregarded" (1961, pp. 34–35).

Such substitution of words is exactly what Dr. Kenneth S. Goodman, a professor of education, recommends. He defines reading as "a process of taking in data, making informed predictions about what will follow, checking these predictions as the reader goes along, and, if necessary, making revisions." He states that when a child substitutes the word "pony" for horse, the teacher should not correct him. He reasons that such a child "clearly understands the meaning. This is what reading is all about" (Goodman, 1975 a,b; see also Chall, 1977, pp. 11, 18).

Goodman's theories have unfortunately received wide publicity, to the detriment of children. The conclusion Walcutt draws is quite correct:

> Thus, "bringing meaning to the printed page" has flowered into the notion that meaning exists away from the printed page—a simple and obvious thought which is nevertheless false! Conceptual meaning exists in words, is made from words, and is communicated with words . . . (1961, p. 42).

The reading specialist Helen R. Lowe also stresses this important point. She writes, "The reader discovers; he may not invent" (1961, p. 109).

Another damaging curriculum practice I have heard stressed many times is outlined in Bulletin #7 (1952) from the United States Office of Education. It is the official description of "How Children Learn To Read." It stresses that a child must be taught reading so that his speaking vocabulary will keep ahead of his reading vocabulary (Walcutt, 1961b, p. 111). This has led to the curriculum practice of giving children primers and other reading books where words are carefully counted so that first-grade children learn to read no more than about 300 words. Actually, an average 6-year-old child knows about 10,000 words. Some researchers have found as many as 24,000 different words (Walcutt, 1974, p. 55). The children's ability to read and write all words they use daily and to learn new ones is severely inhibited by this practice.

OFFICIAL CURRICULUM POLICIES.   I encountered confusion and feelings of helplessness in regard to reading among many teachers. They were only rarely given specific practical advice; usually they were told in general terms to "motivate" the child, to look for psychologic deviations, and to try any "word attack" that can hold the child's attention. The reasons for this approach became clear to me during a seminar on "problems relating to curriculum and child guidance" I had to take to qualify for a license as school psychiatrist. This seminar was given by the Division of Curriculum Development and was attended mainly by supervisors. A few specialized teachers were also present.

What they reported about their own practical experiences with the curriculum philosophy and policy outlined to us in this course first created doubts in my mind about its practical and scientific accuracy. I took elaborate notes because of my great interest in the problems discussed in this seminar. The quotations below are taken from my notes.

We were told that teaching must always be done only "in relation to experience," because "experience is fundamental, experience is content also." When teaching the movement of pioneers to the American West, for instance, the teacher should start by asking the children: "Did you ever move?" One basic principle was that teaching should always be done "in relation to the child's individual pattern of growth." This developmental approach had by then (1952) gone so far that some kindergarten teachers had not been permitted to count the children in their class because to count beyond the number 10 supposedly went beyond the children's developmental level. These were, of course, exaggerations of the fundamental principle.

"Developmental" Teaching. "Development" seemed to be a vague concept, consisting mainly of inborn biologic, intellectual, and especially psychologic faculties that had to be given a chance to develop and that were easily suppressed by systematic teaching of skills and other factual material. The fundamental principle in regard to reading was "developing the whole child and not stressing reading is progressive education. We teach developmental reading according to the individual child." This explained why teachers only rarely picked up a child with a reading disorder and referred him or her for further study before the third grade, and why it was impossible to get even estimates of the number of children needing help with their reading.

The feeling prevailed that children learn best without formal instruction. They pick up information best at their own speed and when they are interested (i.e., "motivated"). We were told that children were reading 2% to 5% better than they did 25 years ago as a result of this new approach. A number of principals and teachers disagreed with this. One high school teacher especially questioned these optimistic figures; she reported that a boy had recently come to her on the day he got his high school diploma and had begged her to teach him how to read.

When pressed for practical details about the philosophy and the overall technique of reading, the director of the curriculum division said angrily, "The reading situation is the biggest blind alley. You could solve all the reading problems in the world and still not do anything for kids!" I have heard this contemptuous belittling attitude towards the teaching of fundamental skills such as reading expressed many times since by administrative educators, professors in teachers' colleges, psychiatrists, psychologists, and other professionals working with children. All were being misled by the seemingly liberalizing, progressive, and forward looking educational psychology underlying this curriculum policy. In practice, it had exactly the opposite effect. It was retrogressive, helped create this new form of illiteracy, and generally worked the greatest hardship on social and economically deprived children.

As was discussed in this seminar, these children tested low on reading-readiness and group I.Q. tests. Both tests were and still are used to determine the level of the child's development and his so-called potential. The lower these tests are, the less stress is put on reading. The teacher is actually not permitted to teach reading until the child passes a readiness test. The teaching of reading under this system is minimal in the first grade at any rate. We were advised repeatedly to "get the first grade teachers *not* to stress reading. Give those children a sense of achievement in the first grade, don't *rush* them." Children who test low may not even be taught reading until the middle or end of the second grade. This leads to their falling further and further behind their classmates in reading as well as other subjects. The end result is frequently that they can never catch up with their grade. (See p. 115 under Spelling.)

Another tenet taught in this seminar was that "spelling is an opposite skill from what you do in reading. . . . It is a poor way to learn to spell while learning how to read." Only after observing the practical application of this theory and studying many children with reading disorders did I realize that this meant a complete separation of reading from writing. Writing and spelling were supposed to be taught later than reading, only after a "sight vocabulary" of 100 or more words had been memorized by the child. We learned that where children could not write, the teacher was to take dictation, and that because of this policy "there has not been any writing in the schools in the past 4 years" (since 1948). When visiting schools, I had already noticed the absence of dictation and composition. I had become accustomed to seeing children dictate a story while the teacher wrote it on the chalkboard, and I knew that many children copied such stories without being able to read one word of it (Wheeler, 1979).

Two words were completely taboo: discipline and method. They were ignored and treated as if they were dirty words when participants in the seminar mentioned them. This was at a time when violent behavior among students was beginning to be an important unsolved problem. Children brought knives and whips to school and defaced the school walls and corridors. Several seminar participants asked for a discussion of this vital problem: their questions remained unanswered. Unfortunately, this escalation in blindness to the ever-increasing violence in the schools has continued; this in itself has contributed significantly to the serious incidents of attacks by students against each other and against teachers. (See Juvenile Delinquency, p. 284.)

I had already observed that any mention of teaching methods was frowned upon. A teacher specializing in reading treatment told me about her experience while taking a course in remedial reading at Teachers' College. She asked her professor about the best method to correct a specific reading defect. Rather than giving her any concrete advice, the professor just said angrily, "I would no more teach a child a method of typewriting than one of reading!" No wonder that confusion reigns and that concrete facts about reading disorders are impossible to obtain!

HISTORY OF THESE CURRICULUM PRACTICES. The curriculum policies presented in the seminar I attended had been introduced in most school systems throughout the United States about 1940. Drill of any kind, such as memorizing the alphabet or arithmetic tables, was eliminated. Many school systems, such as that of New York City, adopted the policy of promoting all children, at least in elementary school. This 100% promotion obscured the reading level of very many children and eventually contributed to the high school graduation of illiterate youngsters. It was officially abolished in New York City in 1958 when massive academic failure, especially in reading, created pressure for such a change. However, "social" promotion based on the child's age was actually continued, so that children continue to be pushed up through the grades and many graduate from high school without being able to read.

Suppression of Critical Studies. It remained difficult for anyone working within a school system to make statements critical of curriculum practices with regard to reading or to acknowledge the growing illiteracy. The mere mention of the fact that the teaching of phonics had helped one of my patients, for instance, was cut out of an article on "Creativity and Mental Health" a curriculum journal had asked me to write in 1959 (Mosse, 1959a).

Another example is the experience of a guidance counselor and an assistant principal with special expertise in reading disorders. They were charged with investigating the reading difficulties of all the children who attended special remedial reading classes during the summer. They found that all of them had one reading defect in common: they did not know phonics. Their report was never published. They were called to their supervisors and asked how they dared go against the theory of the associate superintendent.

My paper on "Reading Disorders in the United States" was, as far as I know, the first article entirely devoted to a critical analysis of the sight/word method of teaching reading and reading-readiness tests to be published in an educational journal (*The Reading Teacher* November 1962b, published by the International Reading Association). I suspect that its publication was facilitated by the fact that it had already been published in German in a German medical journal and had been sent to all West German school principals and to many teachers. Its publication also gave *The Reading Teacher* the opportunity to attack my paper (i.e., the point of view it represented). (Preston, Smith, 1962). One of my critics has had to change her mind since then. (Preston, 1962, p. 162). In *Learning To Read, The Great Debate* (1967), Jeanne Chall comes to the conclusion that

> most school children in the United States are taught to read by what I have termed a meaning-emphasis method. Yet the research from 1912 to 1965 indicates that a code-emphasis method—i.e., one that views beginning reading as essentially different from mature reading and emphasizes learning of the printed code for the spoken language—produces better results, at least up to the point where sufficient evidence seems to be available, the end of the third grade" (p. 307).

I was warned as late as 1965 to be careful in my statements and publications because my views differed from the theoretical position of the Elementary School Division. It has been possible to discuss reading methods freely and openly in conferences and publications sponsored by the Board of Education only since 1966. New York City is not unique in this, as I know from attending conferences and visiting schools in other cities and states. It is also important to realize that as a psychiatrist who is looked upon as an outsider anyhow, it was possible for me to speak more freely than for teachers and other school personnel. The pressure on them was, of course, infinitely stronger. (See p. 115 under Spelling.)

Almost two generations have been raised with these damaging curriculum practices. The results are all around us. Mail does not reach us reliably because addresses are not read properly; doorbells are rung for the wrong tenants because someone cannot read names; computer errors are often due to the inability of programmers to formulate and to spell a program accurately; even car accidents may occur because drivers can't read signs. This neo-illiteracy so distressed Walter Cronkite that he made the sad comment: "Perhaps we could say that the trouble for at least some newspapers is that they are being prepared for people who can't read by people who can't write" ("Cronkite Faults Papers and TV, Citing Coverage," 1979).

Summary of Damaging Curriculum Practices

1. Sight/word method
2. Lack of teaching the sounds of letters and letter combinations from the beginning
3. Teaching beginning and end consonants only, vowels not at all
4. Separation of reading from writing; teaching writing too late and without dictation
5. Too late and too sparse use of composition
6. Use of readiness and group I.Q. tests as a basis for the start of the teaching of reading

7. Too early use of silent reading

8. Uninteresting reading texts with too few words endlessly repeated in much too simple stories, written crudely and without any literary value

9. Lack of teaching of at least some basic rules of grammar

10. 100% promotion

Damaging Aspects of the Mass Media

Comic Books

Wertham was first in pointing out that the reading ability of children was declining, that the comic book format played a profound role in this, and that the "undercover extension of the comic book format" was spreading because the publishers were "re-tooling for illiteracy." He gave this title to a chapter in *Seduction of the Innocent,* where he stated that:

> all negative effects of crime comics on children in the intellectual, emotional and volitional spheres are intensified by the harm done in the perceptual sphere. Comic books are death on reading (1972b, p. 121).

He was indeed proven correct in his predictions. Even a casual survey of the newsstands shows an ever-growing number of magazines in the comic book format—that is, the story is mainly told in luridly drawn pictures, with handled balloons scattered over the pages containing the brief text, which consists largely of expletives and is printed in capital letters only.

In the curriculum seminar we were told that teachers had been concerned about the harmful influence of comic books on reading since 1939. To counteract the lure of comic books a curriculum bulletin suggested in 1951: "Through story hours, dramatization and puppetry, the teacher should try to stimulate the children's interest in reading books other than comics." This bulletin also stressed that "comic books are read almost exclusively." However, these suggestions do not make reading attractive to children. They actually have nothing to do with reading. Where I describe the success of the Spalding kindergarten, I show that teaching reading systematically, interestingly, and successfully to children in kindergarten and the first grade forms the only basis for creating excitement about reading. These children look forward every week to the real books distributed by the teacher. Their excitement is just as great as the fascination with comic books of illiterate children (See p. 205 ff).

Comic books affect reading in two ways: they undermine the basic techniques and they destroy interest. They may do damage in the visual sphere so that the child may find it difficult to tell where one word begins and another one ends (See p. 251). Spelling and linear reading are invariably affected (See p. 115, 127). Comic books also condition children to scanning—that is, to too fast, superficial, and inaccurate reading. Comic books are very powerful conditioners indeed. They interfere with learning the importance of accurate reading and of acquiring precise knowledge. (See Vol. II, p. 507 under Measuring Reading Speed, under Attention Disorders.)

It was Wertham who pointed out that comic books are the greatest publishing success in history. By 1954 100 million comic books were published each month. I was a member of Wertham's Lafargue Clinic group where the original studies on the influence of comic books on children were made. We used the clinical method; no one using the same method ever challenged our findings. (See p. 127 ff under Linear Dyslexia.)

Our studies started in 1946. On March 19, 1948 a symposium on The Psychopathology of Comic Books was held at the New York Academy of Medicine. This was the first time a scientific study of comic books was presented. It was organized by Wertham (1948). I gave a paper on "Aggression and Violence in Fantasy and Fact," where I analyzed the effects of comic books on children. The children I examined told me when I asked them about comic books that they select one picture, look at it for a long time, and "imagine that it is real." Alex, a 12-year-old patient of mine at the Lafargue Clinic, expressed it in the following way:

> I look at them hard and keep looking at them. Every time I look at a picture I imagine I am in it. Every time someone gets hurt or shot I can feel that in the place where the person gets hurt or shot at . . . And I feel also like I have the gun in my hand and pull it and it jacks when I shoot. I feel both at the same time. I always like to play it, too, make believe I am the crook, sometimes I play the cop—but I do more of the shooting. I try to play it exactly the way it is in the comic book. My sister plays an actress getting captured. We make her walk on the street, then we catch her, take her to the basement, tie her up. Then we sit at the table and make plans how to get rid of her. In the meantime she is trying to escape" (Mosse, 1948, p. 480).

Alex's response is characteristic of the way children look at comic books, identify with different characters, and dramatize the story. The scenes children prefer are all similar; they actually have no choice. Thus, daydreams and plays are stimulated, all of which have violence as their content. This violence is not a true reflection of what they are confronted with in their daily life. Comic book violence is individualized and highly specialized. People are being hurt in all sorts of ways, with all sorts of weapons, and in all sorts of settings.

I stressed then and I must emphasize now that children's fantasies as stimulated by comic book pictures make them imagine violence as the only way out. For even as the "good" conquers the "evil," it does so by violence only. Alex turns the page and knows there will be a new story with the same people, solving the same problems by slightly varied methods of direct and bloody violence. The same holds true for far too many television stories.

It must be stressed in this connection that the road from daydreams to action is much shorter in children than in adults. Children do carry out their fantasies. One reason for this is that their fantasies are more vivid and lifelike than in adults and that they have yet to learn to distinguish fantasy from reality. Children at the age when they read comic books are particularly inclined to test and experiment. To be inspired to play strangling girls or killing boys can only lead to dangerously destructive reality testing.

How fantasies aroused by comic book stories carry over and affect the school day is shown by the dangerous behavior of 8-year-old Bobby. He was referred to me by the school principal as an emergency for attempting suicide. He told me what really happened: "Me and Pugee were playing Superman. He was Superman and I was the bad man. I had to jump off a cliff." The cliff happened to be the fifth-floor windowsill. Bobby had jumped out of the classroom window suddenly and was hanging on with his fingers. His startled and dismayed teacher had the presence of mind to tell him calmly to climb right back in, which he did. He told me that he didn't think he was in any danger because he had jumped out of that window many times before when no one was watching, landed on the third floor landing and re-entered the school through the third floor window.

To understand the full impact of comic books, one should ask children how many they read or look at each day. Some scan as many as 15 or 20 in a single hour. It is obvious that they cannot read the text at such speed. Others look at one picture after the other slowly without reading the text, using the pictures as a starting point to make up their own stories. (See p. 127 under Linear Dyslexia.)

Children take comic book characters seriously, especially when they also see them on television. Adults usually do not know that many children are convinced that Superman and other such heroes are real. This belief is so prevalent that I have made it a routine part of my examination to ask them about it. Typical is the following remark by an 11-year-old boy:

> Comic books are really true. There was a real Frankenstein. That's what it says in the book, and the book is all true. There was a man; he got bit by a wolf and when the moon comes, he turns into a wolf. He sits on his chair, he looks at his hands; there is a lot of hair, his teeth keep coming out; he takes off his shoes, his feet are growing big.

He insisted that this was true and showed me the page in the comic book where it said, "This book is all true." This boy could not pay attention in school. He had a reading disorder on a sociogenic basis.

The belief that Superman is real may have dangerous consequences. Children have been hurt when they tried to fly like Superman. Often they do not tell their parents what really happened. Adolescents have told me that they had broken an ankle or an arm when they were younger, and that they had told their parents that it was only an accident. They had been ashamed to admit that the injury had occurred while they were trying to fly off a radiator, a fire escape, or even out of a window.

It was Wertham's idea to treat harmful mass media influences as a public health problem, menacing the mental health of children. He presented his findings in 1954 before the famous Kefauver Committee on the Judiciary of the United States Senate—before the Subcommittee to Investigate Juvenile Delinquency (Horn, 1976, pp. 741–760), as well as other legislative committees.

The findings of our group influenced legislation in many states, who passed anticrime comic book ordinances. They were also debated at length in the House of Commons of Canada and England, who passed legislation for the protection of children. These legislative efforts had the goal of protecting the mental health of children. They were not intended to restrict the freedom of the press in any way.

The results of our studies were put to a severe test in 1957 when I testified under oath for the County of Los Angeles, which had passed an ordinance forbidding the sale and display to minors of comic books depicting crime and violence (Ordinance No. 6633, February 15, 1955). The constitutionality of this ordinance was challenged by comic book industry interests. I spent almost 2 days on the witness stand, most of it under cross-examination. I was permitted to bring stacks of material, such as detailed case histories, comic books, books, reprints, photostats; the court also gave me the opportunity to present case histories and explain the harmful dynamics, both conscious and unconscious. I was also given the chance to discuss important theoretical questions, Freudian and otherwise. The case was decided in accordance with my testimony—that is, in favor of the mental health of children. The District Court of Appeal upheld the legality and constitutionality of this anticrime comic book ordinance. This was in February 1959. The decision was later reversed (Kimmis, 1959; Mosse, 1958a, 1959b, 1963a).

Parent organizations all over the country were inspired by our studies to fight against comic books portraying violence and crime. This fight was successful for a while. The worst types disappeared from the market and the number of comic book publishers declined. However, the collecting and trading of comic books has become a big business. The worst of them are being reprinted and are again on the market (Mosse, 1977b).

Schoolchildren of all ages have entered the comic book business, which requires a certain amount of arithmetic but not the ability to read. Comic book conventions have become enormously popular and are attended by thousands of children who expect to spend and make a lot of money. The business angle has assumed overwhelming proportions, with the result that comic books continue to loom large in the lives of what is probably the majority of children.

COMIC BOOK CONVENTIONS. The impact of comic books on children comes to life during comic book conventions, which last as long as 5 days, usually Friday through Tuesday, often during the summer vacation. The ages of convention goers range from elementary to high school and college. Teachers bring entire classes for visits. Many children rent rooms in the hotels where the conventions take place, even when they actually live in the same city. They stay during the entire time and discuss, sell, and buy comic books literally day and night. This often creates conflicts with their parents, who are understandably reluctant to have them stay away unsupervised for so long.

I have visited such a convention. The total intellectual and emotional involvement of thousands of children was evident even before entering the convention halls. Children of all ages crowded the steps leading to the entrance with bundles of comic books on their laps or under their arms, talking excitedly about their wares. Their lives are involved in this business to an extent not realized by most adults. Magazines in comic book format dealing with monsters and with "sick" and obscene picture stories are part of the comic book scene. Taped television commercials and shows are also sold and traded. Lectures, exhibits of cartoons, panels about comic books, amateur art contests, and costume parades "for anyone 12 years or younger" are a part of the attractions.

Children feel not only that they are participating in an exciting and profitable business, but also that their voice is being heard. Actually, they are being manipulated and exploited by a large industry through clever ploys.

To appreciate the commercial value of collecting and trading comic books, the price of single copies of early editions ranges from $200 to $500 for "The Human Torch" #1 (1940), to upwards of $5,000 for the first appearance of "Superman" or the "Submariner." Single copies of comic books that used to cost 10 cents now range from 40 to 75 cents.

Our studies show conclusively not only that children's reading has been adversely affected, but that their fantasy life is being saturated with stories glorifying crime and violence. Children imitate these stories in their play even before they are old enough to enter school. Unintended injuries are the result of such play, which continues when they get older and becomes much more dangerous. Teachers have for years noticed this particularly disturbing result of comic book fascination.

Television

Television is clearly a totally different medium. It is one of the greatest inventions of mankind. President Kennedy stressed this when he said that three new inventions dominate our era: rockets, nuclear energy, and television. Children learn from television, which has made communication between all people on earth possible as never before. They see what goes on in other parts of the world, how other people live, what they think, and how they organize their society. It has enabled children who grew up with television to participate in the cultural and intellectual life of all mankind to an extent not possible before. They learn new words and their reading is often stimulated by shows that interest them and make them want to read more about the topic (Mosse, 1970a).

The constructive aspects of television are unfortunately overshadowed by destructive programs, especially as far as children are concerned. These damaging aspects are the attractive portrayal of crime and violence, the combination of violence with sex, the simplistic story lines, and the very limited vocabulary used repetitively, particularly in shows directed at children. Many violent comic book heros have been taken over by television, for instance Superman, Wonder Woman, Batman, The Incredible Hulk, Aquaman, Spiderman.

Television shows make a deeper impression on children than comic books. Television and films have an immediate impact on the emotions; they reach feelings directly, not via the intellect as reading does. This effect is often subtle and far-reaching; it enters the unconscious sphere (Mosse 1963a, 1970a).

The enormity of this impact becomes clear when one knows how much time children spend in front of the television screen. In an article on "The Child Probers" dealing with the use of children as "guinea pigs for market researchers," David Chagall reports that 2- to 5-year-old children spend 30 hours a week before the TV set, the 6 to 11 group about 27 hours, almost as many hours as they spend at school (1977). Actually many children spend more hours watching TV than at school. They turn on the TV early in the morning before school, when they come home for lunch, and after school as far into the night as they can. They become so preoccupied with television that they daydream in class, have a severe attention disorder, and are not interested in learning to read. These are neglected children, not always physically but certainly emotionally. Their parents are glad that they are quiet and that they have to pay no attention to them (Hanauer, 1965). (See Vol. II: Sleep Deprivation Caused by Television Viewing, p. 601; Television Fatigue, p. 563; Tired Child Syndrome, p. 563.)

Television damages reading by causing an attention disorder. Many children are still so preoccupied with the shows they watched the night before that they daydream about them while sitting in the classroom. There are other aspects of this medium that make it difficult for children to develop their active intellectual attention. Children get used to absorbing entertainment passively; this has a negative effect on independent imagination and thinking. These effects, combined with excessive viewing of violent and criminal acts, affect classroom behavior as well as learning.

The Rev. Jesse Jackson stresses this point. He says, "After a child views enough of these decadent TV shows and motion pictures, he or she is hardly interested in what schools have to offer. Educators, then, are at a grave disadvantage" (1977).

Children cannot be expected to understand what their excessive viewing of violent and criminal acts does to them, how it changes their fantasies, attitudes, and behavior; their very conscience becomes affected; an ethical confusion ensues. They are tempted to solve conflicts in real life also in a fast and furious manner—with fists and weapons—rather than with careful thought, consideration for the feelings of others, and by restraining their emotions.

Richard A. Hawley discusses television-induced tactless, crude, and inconsiderate behavior of his students in "Television and Adolescents: A Teacher's View." He noticed that these adolescents were imitating attitudes and behavior they observed and admired on TV shows. When analyzing the jokes they liked on television, it occurred to him that "many punchlines and visual gags depended on suddenly introducing the idea of injury or violent death." He stresses the cumulative effect of such television shows, which make fun of everything and do not show any decent, humane behavior. He writes:

> Nothing much really happens to a racial or sexual conflict when it is laughed at (a device that is supposed to soften outright slurring and stereotyping), discarded, tolerated, or forgiven. The idea that 'if we can joke about it this way, we have taken a humanitarian stride' is mistaken. There is plenty of evidence, particularly among the student population, that, for one thing, race relations are more strained today than they were a decade ago (Hawley, 1978).

This is also what Wertham stresses: "Complaisance breeds tolerance and tolerance breeds acceptance" (1978).

Shows on television and in the movies have indeed fostered race hatred and all sorts of discrimination in subtle and not-so-subtle ways. An example is Superman and most other super heroes. They belong to the strong, admirable, white super-race. The villains are often people considered inferior in real life; for instance, women, black and Spanish-speaking people, people of Italian descent as in "The Untouchables," and so forth.

The Rev. Jesse Jackson gives a good example of a TV show bound to provoke race hatred:

> One day I found two of my children watching a series in which one of the characters is a Black man. I watched with them. In one scene, he threw a white girl out of a car. In another scene, he and the girl were in bed, making love. Then,

while putting on his fancy cuff links and wearing his ace-deuce cocked hat (pimp paraphernalia), he attempted to convince the girl that she should take drugs. Although she tried to resist, this Black guy, with this street sophistication and demonic mind, prevailed (1977).

Numerous attempts have been made by parent and other groups to diminish violence on television. None has been successful. According to researchers at the University of Pennsylvania's Annenberg School of Communication, there were 15.6 violent incidents an hour in 1977 in children's programs, but that figure rose to 25 an hour in 1978. The definition of violence used in the research project was "that of unambiguous physical violence—hurting or killing a person or the credible threat of hurting or killing" (Study finds children's TV more violent, 1979).

The stimulation of reading by television is not so widespread as it used to be. This distressing development was stressed by Beverly Crandall in an article, "Decline in Reading of the Classics in Public Schools Causes Concern," in the *New York Times* of May 29, 1977. She quotes a teacher saying, "TV is killing us in the classrooms. It has brought about a non-reading generation who would rather watch than read." Not even children who became deeply involved in *Roots* were able to read the book. Crandall reports that Alex Haley's book was assigned at predominantly black Fremont High School in Los Angeles and that a girl who was a junior told her, "We talked about *Roots* for a while in one class, and nobody had read it. It was too long. A lot of us depended on the TV and guesswork to get through." An English teacher at a school in Illinois told her, "The students are used to being entertained. They are used to the idea that if they are just the slightest bit bored, they can flip the switch and turn the channel" (p. 36). This is how television undermines intellectual attention. Almost no one ever works in television programs. Work is not portrayed to be as useful, as admirable, or as exciting as crime.

The harmful aspects of television affect children with any type of reading disorder. They also make it very difficult to help them overcome their disorder. In my study, mass media were a major contributing factor in 58 children (49 boys, 9 girls) with an organic reading disorder and in 77 children (57 boys, 20 girls) with a psychogenic reading disorder. They were a major causative factor in 21 children (19 boys, 2 girls), almost half the total number of 46, with a sociogenic reading disorder.

Violent Atmosphere at School, on the Street, and at Home

Violence in the mass media is part of the violent atmosphere in which children live.

Violence at Home

A child subjected to brutality at home who may be afraid of being crippled or killed cannot be expected to pay attention at school. These are "battered children"; 17 of the children in my study belong in this group (13 boys, 4 girls) (Mosse, 1969, 1974; Wertham, 1972a, 1973). (See Vol. II, Battered Children, p. 561.)

A violent atmosphere at home may also involve the relationship between siblings and between parents. There have been reports that all these violent acts have increased, especially violent attacks of children and adolescents against their parents. Chronic anger, fear, and tension are part of such an atmosphere. It is extremely difficult for children having to survive under these conditions to concentrate on reading or any other subject.

Violence in School and on the Street

What a 12-year-old boy said is unfortunately all too true. He was a gang leader and a truant and had a severe sociogenic reading disorder. He told me, "School is a dangerous place, always has been, and always will be."

What a distraught white mother of seven children living in an affluent suburb told me has become typical: "This is the first time in my life that I am fearful for my children in school." Her 9-year-old daughter had been so brutally beaten by another child that she had to be hospitalized with a concussion. One of her sons, aged 14, was hit so hard that he had to be hospitalized because a ruptured spleen was suspected.

I know from my own work in schools that the fear of physical violence permeates many junior and senior high schools. The Subcommittee to Investigate Juvenile Delinquency of the Senate of the United States found in 1975 that almost 70,000 teachers had been assaulted annually and that hundreds of thousands of students were beaten, robbed, or threatened with violence. As the *New York Times* of March 19, 1976 reported, a federally funded study found "a virtual reign of schoolhouse terror". All violent crimes have increased in the schools, including bomb threats, extortions, and rapes of students as well as teachers (Mosse, 1977 (b), 1978).

Violence has increased to such epidemic proportions because is has never been faced openly and honestly without making any excuses by the officials charged with responsibility for children. What Alfred M. Bloch, a psychiatrist, found is unfortunately true throughout the United States. In a paper on "Combat Neurosis in Inner-City Schools," based on a study of 253 classroom teachers in Los Angeles, he writes:

> The continuum of violence directed toward these teachers included repeated threats of murder and/or rape. Actual physical assault and injury occurred as

did theft, arson, and vandalism of their property.... Campus violence, not specifically directed at these teachers, included bombing of school buildings, theft and destruction of campus equipment, fights between students and gang members, murder, rape and the presence of weapons on campus. Student locker searches revealed drugs, dynamite, knives, ammunition and firearms (Bloch, 1978).

These teachers told him that when they sent violent students to the administrative office, "they usually returned promptly without having been reprimanded. If they assaulted a member of the faculty, they were suspended from school for a few days and then returned, often as heroes to their classmates." When the teachers reported such attacks to the principal he was "indifferent or, worse, fault-finding. Many, like rape victims, were made to feel responsible for being assaulted." They were

usually discouraged from reporting incidents of violence. Although legally required to do so, they received the implicit (and sometimes explicit) message that it was "not in their best interest" to pursue the matter, i.e., that the administrators might consider them unsuccessful. They thus functioned under a two-edged Damoclean sword: the threat to their job security and the ordeal of facing continued classroom and campus violence" (Bloch, 1978).

This atmosphere of violence in the schools has been permitted to fester for over 20 years. Wertham was first to report in speeches and in writing that policemen had to circulate in the halls of some schools (1954, 1972(b)). Circulars from New York City School Superintendents dealt with the assignment of policemen to public schools as long ago as 1958, and with bomb-scare procedures and vandalism since 1959.

Juvenile Delinquency

All types of reading disorders play a major causative role in the violent behavior of school children. The close relationship between violent and nonviolent juvenile delinquency and reading disorders has been well documented. Juvenile-court judges were first to complain that most youngsters brought before them either could not read at all or were so deficient in reading that they were illiterate for all practical purposes. Judges and probation officers were first to question the schools' teaching practices, because they found that a large number of these juvenile delinquents proudly showed them their high school diploma.

The causative chain starts with the fact that the child is not taught reading properly and that his reading disorder is not corrected early enough. Such a child may feel that he is stupid and that he will never be able to achieve anything worthwhile in life, and in this way slide into delinquent behavior. The reading disorder comes first and is the major cause of such a child's violent or otherwise delinquent behavior.

A reading disorder impairs a child's ability to concentrate on any intellectual task, to learn to plan carefully, to postpone gratifications, and to think for himself. It becomes more of a handicap the older he gets. Because he has great difficulty acquiring information independently and developing mature judgment, he remains at the mercy of the mass media.

Many of these children feel that reading does not help them anyhow, that it plays no role in their ability to survive in a violent and hostile atmosphere or to understand their own reactions and those of others. They may come to the conclusion that they can only achieve self-respect and the respect of others by asserting themselves in a violent way, and that this is the only method at their disposal to dominate others and not to be dominated and possibly crushed by them.

Children's attitudes toward reading form an integral part of their attitudes toward work. A child who finds out that he can make money without reading (by stealing, through drugs and other criminal activities) invariably develops a contemptuous attitude to work as well as reading. Muggers have stated publicly that they can make as much as $200 a day (Siegel, 1979). The drug trade yields much more cash for less effort.

The importance of reading dawns on many nonreaders only after they have been locked up in reform schools or jails. Reading treatment is one of the most successful methods of rehabilitation of juvenile offenders. Many studies and autobiographies—for example, that of Malcolm X—have shown this.

Reading disorders and juvenile delinquency feed on each other. A child with a reading disorder who slides into delinquency finds it even more difficult to spend time, energy, and concentration on the correction of his reading disorder. Even children who have mastered the basic techniques tend not to develop their skill after they have entered the exciting and absorbing world of crime.

My statistics reflect this close relationship. 72 (66 boys, 6 girls) of the 445 children in my study were involved in serious violent behavior, including extortion, cutting other children with knives, hitting teachers or the principal, and committing holdups with a toy gun. Twelve additional children (11 boys, 1 girl) attempted murder. They are described in detail in the section on Hyperactivity (Vol. II, p. 604 ff.). The violent act of firesetting was very frequent: 53 children (51 boys, 2 girls) set fires. Firesetting is especially frequent among hyperactive children (Vol. II, p. 609). Gang involvement was also frequent: 48 children (42 boys, 6 girls) were gang members. Thirty-six children (31 boys, 5 girls) were caught stealing.

Drug Abuse

Drug use among children is a tragedy of unequalled proportions. As a TV study showed in 1978, elementary school children as young as 10 or 11 get high on marijuana and are, as they themselves observe, "burnt out" by 16 years of age. This can occur with marijuana alone.

One-third of the children in some junior high and high school classes just sit there and nod, incapable of paying any attention. Often they fall to the floor, unable to get up without help. Some school toilets and halls smell so strongly of pot that one can get a so-called "contact high." This is true for public as well as private schools (See Drug Abuse, in section on Attention Disorders, Vol. II, p. 565 ff.)

All kinds of drugs are available in schools, in addition to marijuana. Children trade or buy cocaine, barbiturates, stimulants, all types of hallucinogenic drugs such as LSD and PCB and heroin. Alcohol consumption has also increased. This drug trade is quite lucrative. I know of a boy in a private high school who made $2,000 in 1 month alone. The drug traffic was known to be so heavy in one public high school that the children called it "the drug store."

A child on any kind of drug loses interest in reading and all other subjects. He may be under the illusion that drugs develop his mind, that they extend his experiences. This is unfortunately what he has been told over and over again. However, the children who are turned on are "like radios tuned to nothing, they play the noise of their own tubes." This is how Donald Barr describes these children's drug experiences in his book, *Who Pushed Humpty Dumpty? Dilemmas in American Education Today* (1971, p. 32).

Drug abuse not only causes a loss of interest in reading; it also fosters violent behavior. In a 1974 article on "Drug Involvement in Criminal Assaults by Adolescents," Tinklenberg et al. report on their study of 50 male adolescents who committed violent assaults, including rape and murder, while under the influence of alcohol, barbiturates, amphetamines, marijuana, and/or glue sniffing. Six of the assaults occurred while marijuana was used either alone or with other drugs. One murder was committed under the influence of marijuana, alcohol, and secobarbital. Amphetamine alone was linked to one murder. Alcohol alone or in combination with other drugs was involved in violent acts more often than any of the other drugs. As Wertham states in *A Sign for Cain,* "Alcohol is the lubricant of violence. How closely alcohol and violence are related can be seen from the fact that among alcoholics, violence, including accidents and suicides, is the most frequent—and preventable—cause of death" (1973, p. 50). The youngest alcoholic I examined was 14 years of age. He also had a reading disorder. (See p. 61 ff. under Memory Disorders.) Onset of alcoholism as early as age 8 has been reported (Mitchell et al., 1979).

It must be stressed that all the various drugs sold to children and adolescents to provide a high affect the brain. Their effect on the brain is what causes the feeling of being high. All these drugs, including alcohol, may cause addiction: that is, their victims feel that they cannot live without them anymore. These youngsters actually have their love affairs with drugs instead of people. Drugs absorb their entire emotional and physical energy. They have been led to believe that drugs make it easier for them to communicate with other people. The opposite is true in the long run. Drugs increase self-absorption and isolation.

An important difference among these drugs is that some of them also cause physical dependence, that is, their withdrawal brings on physical symptoms. No child or adolescent whose central nervous system is still developing and who is still emotionally unstable should have any of these drugs, whether or not they cause physical dependence. All of them interfere with a healthy mental, emotional and physical development.

Treatment

A child with a sociogenic reading disorder needs reading treatment first and foremost. This is often successful in a relatively brief period of time, provided the diagnosis is correct.

When my examination shows that the child's reading disorder has a sociogenic basis due to sight/word teaching, I frequently advise the parents to teach the child phonics, if they themselves know the sounds of letters and letter combinations. The results are frequently startling to both parent and child, provided they have a good relationship. What a mother of a 29-year-old mathematics teacher told me is typical for such a successful cure of a sociogenic reading disorder. She was a lawyer and consulted me about a problem that had nothing to do with her children. She reminded me that she had talked to me 21 years before about the reading disorder of her son. She told me, "He would not be able to read so well now if I had not followed your advice and taught him phonics myself. The teachers had said "Hands off," while I watched him fall further and further behind. They thought nothing of phonics." Her son had attended a suburban public school. The attitude of the teachers described by this mother was typical and has unfortunately not changed sufficiently.

The treatment of many of these children is not quite that simple. When the reading disorder has persisted for several years and the child has developed an emotional block against reading, he needs specialists in reading treatment to overcome his disorder. Some children's psychopathologic reaction to their reading disorder is so severe that psychotherapy, individually or in a group, is indicated.

Children who have developed violent and otherwise criminal behavior need psychotherapy as well as reading treatment. Group therapy or group guidance is often successful, especially when combined with social casework treatment of the entire family.

Alcoholism and other forms of addiction in children and adolescents are extremely difficult to cure. Deterioration invariably occurs unless complete abstinence is achieved. The therapist must find a way to instill in the addict the will to stop.

When the reading disorder is based on comic book or television habituation, these influences must be removed, until the child has learned to read fluently and with pleasure.

Prevention

Prevention rests on the elimination of the causes of the sociogenic type of reading disorder. Sociogenic reading disorders have been largely eliminated in schools that have introduced phonic methods for beginning readers and that teach writing either first or simultaneously with reading. However, the damaging influences of the mass media continue to affect these students. Teachers and parents have the responsibility and to a certain extent the power to eliminate these influences from the lives of the children under their care. This power is unfortunately quite limited. Only concerted and organized social action can really protect all children from being bombarded with alluring portrayals of violence and crime.

Chapter 7

Treatments

Good mass-teaching methods can prevent most sociogenic, many psychogenic, and a large number of organic reading disorders. However, once a reading disorder has developed and persisted for some time, mass methods can no longer correct it. The reading treatment methods are the same for all three classifications, depending entirely on the child's symptoms.

The choice of treatment methods and their success depends on a correct and detailed diagnosis. As has been emphasized repeatedly throughout this book, the treatment these children need can be determined only after meticulous individual diagnostic examinations. This requires a collaborative effort among a number of medical and nonmedical specialists. I want to emphasize that the diagnosis and treatment of reading disorders is an integral part of the medical and educational care to which every child is entitled, or ought to be, regardless of his parent's ability to pay.

In private practice the child psychiatrist, the pediatrician, or the pediatric neurologist are responsible for diagnosis and treatment. To accomplish this they must obtain and study the records of all past pediatric, neurologic, child psychiatric, ophthalmologic, hearing, psychologic, speech, and educational examinations. This requires written reports and telephone consultations, which take a great deal of time. These children's problems are sometimes so complicated, especially when organic symptoms are involved, that a face-to-face conference of all specialists is the most productive procedure. This is difficult to organize in private practice. It requires a great deal of time-consuming administrative work. All these efforts are part of the routine work of mental hygiene clinics.

Role of Clinics

The examinations and treatments children with reading disorders need are so expensive that many parents cannot afford them. Mental hygiene clinics therefore play a central role in diagnosis and treatment. No statistics are available, but the majority of children suffering from reading disorders are probably cared for by such clinics, which are part of hospitals, community mental health centers, social agencies, or schools. When well run, these clinics are actually best equipped to provide the medical, psychologic, and educational care these children need. This is but *one* instance of the superiority of group or clinic practice over individual practice in child as well as general psychiatry.

Organization of Child Psychiatric Clinics
Specializing in the Diagnosis and Treatment of
Reading Disorders

In principle, all children referred to a mental hygiene clinic should be just as thoroughly examined as those sent to specialized clinics. Their diagnostic and therapeutic care requires the same careful consideration. Reading and writing disorders on *any* basis—organic, psychogenic, or sociogenic—can and should be diagnosed by the competent routine work of the regular staff of any mental hygiene clinic. This is what we did at the Lafargue Clinic, where no specialized clinic was organized.

However, so many children are usually referred to child psychiatric clinics and their needs are so urgent that the staff has no time to do the extensive clinical and administrative work needed to help children with the numerous and complicated symptoms often associated with reading disorders, especially the organic type. Special clinics focusing on these children, therefore, have great advantages.

Principles of Referral

Only those children should be referred whose symptoms are so severe and present such diagnostic puzzles that the general child psychiatric clinic cannot diagnose them. These children are too frequently misdiagnosed and consequently mistreated and miseducated. The mismanagement of these children is usually due to the lack of communication between all those who taught, observed, or formally examined and treated the child throughout his life. They do not discuss their findings sufficiently with each other, and there is usually no person specifically designated to study and integrate all findings. The sad story of Elaine who had aphasia, as well as the fate of other children I have described, are good examples for this. (See Vol. II: p. 398 ff; cases of Ned, p. 648; and Mona, p. 625.) A special clinic provides the ideal framework for complete evaluation and integration. It is also excellent for undergraduate, graduate, and postgraduate teaching of the large number of medical and nonmedical professionals involved with the care of children.

Location

A general hospital is ideally suited for such a clinic because all types of specialists are readily available. Clinics located in schools or in other centers in the community can also be organized for this purpose, but a hospital makes it easier to get all specialists together for regular case conferences, which are such an essential ingredient of these clinics.

Staffing

Such a clinic should be run jointly by child psychiatry and pediatrics. Pediatric neurology and rehabilitation should also be involved. A child psychiatrist should be in charge and have the ultimate responsibility for the final diagnosis and for all recommendations. However, diagnosis and treatment planning should be determined jointly at a case conference in which not only all staff members but also the child's teacher, his guidance counselor, and other specialists who had contact with him should participate.

In addition to the child psychiatrist, each child should be examined by a pediatrician, a neurologist, a speech therapist, a psychologist, and a reading therapist (this is usually a teacher with a degree in special education with special competence in reading treatment). An ear-nose-and-throat specialist interested in audiology (testing of hearing, which some speech therapists are also trained to do), an ophthalmologist, and an occupational therapist trained in the diagnosis and treatment of perceptual disorders should also be regular members of the clinic staff or at least be easily available for consultation. Social workers are, of course, indispensable for such a clinic.

I have organized a number of child psychiatric clinics, among them such a specialized clinic. It was located in a general hospital and administered by the Department of Child Psychiatry in cooperation with the pediatric department of rehabilitation. It was part of a medical school.

The pediatric specialty of rehabilitation medicine has special advantages for such a clinic and I can recommend its participation highly. It cares for chronically ill children who are physically and often also neurologically disabled. Most suffer from cerebral palsy (see Vol. II, p. 428 ff.) Many have reading, hearing, and speech disorders, so that these departments employ social workers, psychologists, speech therapists, and occupational therapists specializing in caring for these multiply handicapped children. Their skills are a great asset to such a specialized clinic.

The clinic's pediatric neurologist, the psychologist, the educational therapist, the social worker, and I were members of the Department of Child Psychiatry. All of us, except the social worker, were assigned to the clinic on a part-time basis. The social worker was the only full-time member of the clinic's staff. She coordinated the clinical and administrative work. All psychiatric clinics need one such key person who holds the many facets of the clinic's work together.

Intake was the task of the social worker in consultation with me. She took the social histories, made appointments with all the specialists who examined the child, and saw to it that these appointments were kept and that all examinations were completed before the weekly case conference. She did the telephone and written correspondence with other hospitals and agencies and assembled the various hospital records. She explained the diagnosis and the treatment plan to the parents after the conference together with the child psychiatric fellow. I joined them in particularly difficult cases. She also saw to it that the therapeutic measures planned at the conference were carried out. She did casework treatment of the parents individually or in mothers' groups if this was part of the treatment plan.

Children were referred by the child psychiatric clinic, by the various pediatric clinics and wards, and by outside agencies and schools. The clinic acquired such an excellent reputation that referrals came from the entire city and we soon had a waiting list.

Teaching Functions

Students of many different disciplines learned at this clinic. I examined every child and supervised the child psychiatric fellows who were assigned to the clinic as part of their training rotation. Medical students, pediatric interns and residents, psychologic interns, social work and speech students, all attended the case conferences and observed examinations.

Academic conferences were held at regular intervals on topics such as "Aphasia, Its Definition and Manifestation in Children," "Mirror-Reading and Writing," "Neurologic Examination of Children with Organic Disorders," "Treatment Techniques for Children with Organic Impairments," "Interpretations to Teachers of the Clinic's Diagnoses and Recommendations," "Treatment of Arithmetic Disorders," and many others.

Case Conferences

Each clinic member who had examined the child presented his or her findings. Teachers, guidance counselors, probation officers, and social workers from outside agencies reported their observations.

I presented the child and his parents to the group myself. They knew practically everyone present in the conference room, so that their anxiety was kept at a minimum. I made sure that they left with a feeling of positive accomplishment and hope. As a rule, they had had so many disappointing experiences with clinics, agencies, and schools previously that they were pleased that at last the staff of one clinic cared enough to get all specialists together to talk about their problems and to work out a practical plan to help the child. Far too many staff conferences are held without the participation of a patient and his family. This helps neither the clinic staff nor their patients. The reason for this omission is the fear of harming the patient; however, when done skillfully and with tact, it can be a constructive experience for the patient.

Usually I presented the child alone first, then his parents (we tried to have fathers attend the conference); after that, I presented the child together with his parents, including siblings when they had come. This provided a unique opportunity for the observation of family relationships in this stressful setting and facilitated the diagnosis.

For instance, the cause of the peculiar behavior of 11-year-old John's mother became clear during the conference. Her speech had been slurred when she took John to some of his examinations. The staff members who had examined him then had suspected that she was an alcoholic or a drug addict. Her speech had been clear and intelligible when she spoke to other members of the staff.

During the staff conference she was in good contact and spoke clearly. When I asked her about her changing speech, she said that she had two jobs and had been reluctant to reveal this. She worked nights as a taxi driver and had another job during the day. Her slurred speech was due to fatigue.

Some children behave differently with different members of the staff. Their behavior during the conference, where all staff members can observe them together, is therefore quite significant. The staff conference puts the child in a group situation, which encourages him to behave the way he does in other group settings, for instance in school.

CLARIFICATION OF 7-YEAR-OLD KEN'S MISBEHAVIOR IN SCHOOL. During the staff conference Ken clowned and dramatized exactly as he did in school, just as the teacher had described in her presentation. None of the staff members, including myself, had observed this type of behavior. He had been calm, cheerful, and pleasant with all of us to such a degree that we suspected that his disturbed behavior in school was caused by the teacher's mismanagement. The conference demonstrated clearly that his behavior was due to his own inner tensions, neurotic anxieties, and feelings of incompetence. It was not the teacher's fault.

Some children appear more withdrawn and in poorer contact with reality during the presentation; others are in better contact and less fearful than during their individual examinations.

DANIEL, 9 YEARS OLD: BENIGN HALLUCINATIONS. Daniel talked about seeing "spirits" of dead people at night and seemed preoccupied with religion in an abnormal way for his age during the psychiatric examination. He was less anxious and in good contact during the conference presentation and spoke freely about his fears, which bothered him only at night. It became clear that he only thought he saw "spirits" and that he did not really believe that they were real. This confirmed the result of tests and of previous clinical impressions that he had only benign hallucinations at night caused by neurotic fears and that his "visions" were not a sign of a beginning schizophrenic process.

These case presentations not only help to establish a diagnosis and treatment plan; they are also indispensable for teaching purposes. Many children enjoy them if they are skillfully done, and the parents can be made to feel that they have helped their child and also themselves.

A general discussion followed the case presentation, during which the diagnosis was established and a treatment plan formulated. The conference and its recommendations were recorded by the child psychiatric fellow. I summarized the test results and clinical findings and formulated the diagnosis and recommendations. The time allotted to the conference was about 1½ hours.

The proof of the value of such a specialized clinic lies in the diagnoses it determines. The wide range of diagnoses established by this clinic in one 6-month period alone shows this clearly. Twenty children (3 girls and 17 boys) aged 5–12 years were examined during such a period. Twelve of them had organic reading and writing disorders; seven of these also had an organic arithmetic disorder and an organic speech disorder. One of these 12 had a convulsive disorder. In only one of them could the cause of the organic reading and writing disorder be established with certainty. This was 9-year-old Morris, whose disorder started at the age of 9 following a severe head trauma (see Vol. II, p. 158 ff. under Concentration Disorders). One boy had a school phobia with a neurotic reading disorder. Four 9-year-old boys suffered from severe neuroses that also caused their reading disorder. One 6-year-old girl was a battered child. Neither the Department of Welfare nor the school nor the other clinics the child had attended had recognized her plight and the mortal danger she and her siblings faced. We were first in making the correct diagnosis. The child's inability to learn to read was reactive to her abuse and neglect. She could not be expected to concentrate on learning while under this terrible stress (see p. 17; Vol. II, pp. 561 and 562).

One 8-year-old boy suffered from childhood schizophrenia and had an organic reading disorder (see case of Chester, Vol. II, p. 631 under Hyperactivity).

Not one of these children had been diagnosed and treated properly before their referral to this clinic. The thorough examinations, the clinical coordination and the integration made possible at such a specialized clinic is what these children needed. This is the type and quality of clinical work that must be available if all children so afflicted are to get the medical and educational care they deserve.

Treatment Plans

Once the diagnosis has been made, one has the choice of two kinds of treatment: corrective education and psychotherapy. Many children need both, combined with social casework treatment of their parents. Strictly physical medical treatment is often also indicated and consideration must sometimes be given to psychopharmacotherapy. (See Drug Therapy, Vol. II, p. 657, under Hyperactivity.)

JOSEPH, 9 YEARS OLD: The treatments recommended for 9-year-old Joseph show the type of therapeutic planning most children with severe organic reading disorders need.

The treatment recommendations were based on the following diagnoses:

1. Reading, writing, and arithmetic disorder on an organic basis, combined with free-floating anxiety and a severe concentration disorder

2. Tics of eyelids and lips

3. Psychopathologic reaction to his organic disorders, consisting of flight into fantasy and preoccupation with this fantasy world

4. Asthma

5. Visual defect (left eye deviated to the left when he focused his eyes)

6. Many dental cavities

Recommendations for Further Examinations

1. Pediatric re-examination including allergy tests

2. Eye examination

Treatment Plan

1. Dental care

2. Remedial reading, writing, and arithmetic on an individual basis, to be done by the clinic's educational therapist

3. Placement in an appropriate class in school

If the public school he attended could not provide the special teaching techniques he needed, he should be referred for placement in a class for brain-injured children. The clinic's educational therapist would visit the school, discuss our treatment plan, and make suggestions.

4. Psychotherapy

Joseph talked freely about his thoughts and feelings and was reaching out for help. It could be expected that he would respond well to psychotherapy, which would probably lessen his free-floating anxiety within a few months, and in this way improve his ability to concentrate. The alleviation of his tics, of his fantasy preoccupation, and of his overattachment to his mother would take much longer. Psychotherapy would probably also improve his asthma by decreasing the frequency and the severity of his asthma attacks.

5. Casework treatment of his mother, who did not understand him and whose babying and generally poor management aggravated his disorders.

This would be done by the clinic's social worker, who would also carry the responsibility for seeing to it that all recommendations were carried out.

As this example shows, fulfillment of a treatment plan requires a great deal of administrative, clinical, and educational work. To facilitate communications between all specialists and agencies and to guarantee that the treatment recommendations are really carried out, *one* staff member should be put in charge. The social worker was put in charge of Joseph's treatment plan, but this may not always be the most practical choice. The child's educational therapist or his psychotherapist can also perform this task. Who this should be is best determined at the time the treatment plan is formulated. (See Vol. II, p. 431 under Cerebral Palsy.)

Anyone with practical experience in this field knows that enormous amounts of time are wasted by school personnel, courts, various specialists, and agencies who need information and consultation, trying to reach somebody with current knowledge of the child, unless such a key person is appointed. Ideally, there should be only *one* telephone number on their desk and in their file in regard to this particular child.

Implementation Difficulties

The implementation of such a treatment plan faces many practical obstacles, especially in clinic patients. For instance, scheduling is sometimes very difficult. As so many parents do, both of Joseph's parents worked; they had to provide for four children under the age of 14. In order to keep a clinic appointment, one of them had to take time off from work. Since this meant a loss of pay, they would actually be paying indirectly for clinic care that was supposed to be either free or covered by insurance. Joseph needed so many clinic appointments that this could even jeopardize the job of one of them. He was too young to come to the clinic by himself. Because this is such a prevalent problem, schools should provide at least the educational part of these children's treatment, namely special classes and individual reading treatment.

In Joseph's case, we tried to arrange for paraprofessional staff members to pick him up at school, bring him to the hospital for his pediatric, eye, and dental appointments, and return him to school or home, depending on the time of his appointments. This can, of course, be done only with the parents' written consent. Schools can sometimes provide this vital transportation service for children whose parents work, are sick, or are just too unreliable to keep the child's medical appointments. I know of guidance counselors, school psychologists, and psychiatric social workers who have personally taken children to clinic appointments because the parents were incapacitated for medical or psychiatric reasons. No one, however, has sufficient time to do this on a weekly basis for regular treatment. A way must be found to overcome this obstacle, which deprives thousands of children all over the country of the medical and psychiatric care they so desperately need.

Treatment Plan Failures

There are more complicated reasons why treatment plans are so frequently not carried out. It is unfortunately the rule rather than the exception that even the most carefully formulated treatment plans remain illusory. This is why working in this field is so frustrating. One might know what the child needs and what will happen to his life without treatments; yet one also knows that he will probably not get them. No other branch of medicine would tolerate such conditions. Too few children with reading disorders are diagnosed in the first place and few of these are treated. Reading the voluminous clinic chart of a child or an adolescent usually reveals a number of previous psychologic and psychiatric examinations and treatment recommendations, but too often no treatment at all. This is true for clinic, court, and agency patients and not only for those suffering from reading disorders. Clinics are being set up all over the country for children with organic conditions called "minimal brain damage," "developmental disabilities," or "neurologic handicaps," but this does not mean that these children are also treated. These treatments are expensive and there is a shortage of specialists, but this does not entirely explain or excuse the widespread lack of treatment.

Clinics and schools could be treating more children right now, even within their present budgets. We treated more children in 1 week at the Lafargue Clinic (which was open only two evenings a week and staffed entirely by volunteers who worked without pay) than some full-time clinics with a well-paid staff treat during 5 complete working days. It is a matter of skill, organization, collaboration, point of view, and emphasis, rather than of money.

There are many excellent and hard-working specialists who would like nothing better than to provide the very best treatment for all children who need it, regardless of location (clinic, school, neighborhood center), and even at a personal financial sacrifice, if they could work in an atmosphere where they could function at their best. Such an atmosphere requires the close and friendly collaboration of all clinic staff members, whose interest must be focused on their work with children and parents. A group or collective feeling among all staff members must be formed, regardless of specialty or work assignment, of skin color or so-called ethnic background. I have participated in the organization and administration of a number of clinics and know that such an atmosphere can be created. Such clinics have few broken appointments because child and adult patients sense that the staff is genuinely interested in them, respects them, and does not look down on them. I also know that what prevents so many clinics from treating all the children they could treat is not so much lack of funds as administrative confusion and callousness.

REASONS FOR FAILURE OF TREATMENT PLANS.
1. Incorrect diagnosis leads to an inappropriate plan.
2. Too few therapists are available.
3. Treatments cannot be scheduled.
4. Treatment is interrupted too often.
5. Treatment is terminated too soon.
6. Therapists lack skill.
7. Disorders are so severe that they cannot be completely corrected.

Educational Treatments

The educational part of the treatment plan can use three main forms of corrective teaching: classroom management, special-class placement, and individual reading treatment. I will describe what each form has to offer and under what circumstances it should be recommended.

Classroom Management

Most children with a reading disorder of any type can remain in their regular class while receiving individual reading and other forms of treatment. Children prefer to stay with their friends, with a teacher they like, and in their regular grade. Their parents usually also prefer this, not wanting their child to be treated differently from other children and singled out for special-class placement. Many parents are afraid that a class change might harm their child psychologically and socially. He might lose friends, feel lonely, hurt, inferior, and humiliated. However, a class change is sometimes necessary. The child himself or the parents may ask for it. Such a change should be made only after careful consideration and investigation of all social, psychologic, and educational aspects of the child's schooling.

There are primarily two circumstances that necessitate the change of such a child from one regular classroom to another. One of them is that children with reading disorders, especially the organic type, are often pushed too hard by their parents and teachers and put in a class whose pace is much too fast for them. This happens especially to children who are known to have a high I.Q. Such a child cannot respond to individual reading and other treatments while he is under such severe pressure in school. His class placement must be adjusted to his pace and to his actual academic level. Sometimes a slower class on the same grade level can be found. In exceptional cases, placement in a lower grade may be best for the child. Parents and child are apt to oppose such a plan unless it is explained to them as an integral part of the child's treatment, which is expected to cure his reading disorder. It should be made very clear to all concerned that this is not punishment for the child's poor achievement, but designed to make him feel freer and happier.

Other conditions that make a class change desirable arise out of special tensions that often develop between a child with a reading disorder and his teacher. A teacher who has tried unsuccessfully for months to teach a child to read may eventually see this child as a constant reminder of his or her failure as a person and incompetence as a teacher. The explanation that the child's reading disorder has an organic or a psychogenic basis not caused by the teacher comes as a relief and helps both teacher and child. Where such tensions persist or where the child and his teacher dislike each other for all sorts of reasons, the child is better off in another class with a different teacher, and the teacher is better off without this child. Class changes must also be considered where the child's behavior is disturbed and disruptive.

Placement of a child with a reading disorder in a "resource room" is not helpful. No child with any kind of reading disorder can teach himself to read, regardless of how many "resources" surround him.

IMPORTANCE OF SCHOOL VISITS. Class changes need the approval of the school administration. This is one of the compelling reasons why the child's psychotherapist, his reading therapist, his social worker, or any other member of the clinic staff should visit his school, discuss the treatment plan, observe him in the classroom, and confer with his teachers. Telephone contacts are no adequate substitute for such visits. I have found school visits invariably enlightening about the school, the teachers, and the child. Occasionally a teacher or an entire school is so hostile to what they consider "outside interference" that school visits cannot and should not be made. Under such deplorable conditions it is better for the child that his teacher and his school do not know that he is in treatment for any condition, whether it is a reading or an emotional disorder. Children can be treated successfully without school visits and even without the school's cooperation. Skillful therapy can overcome such obstacles.

INVOLVEMENT OF TEACHERS IN THE TREATMENT PLAN. Teachers need advice about the classroom management and special teaching techniques best suited to help such a child. What special considerations, if any, such a child needs depend on his specific reading, writing, and arithmetic defects, on his behavior, and on the personality of his teacher. As I have stressed in the section on spelling, it is sometimes best to suggest to the teacher ignoring the child's reading disorder and helping him remember subject matter entirely by ear and with visual aids that require no reading (see p. 117). Children with this disorder usually have trained themselves to learn in this way anyhow.

The teacher should not ask such a child to read orally until the child himself asks to be allowed to read out loud. Furthermore, she should not grade the child's written work with regard to spelling, if she lets him write at all; nor should she ask him to spell orally. He should be allowed to give all his reports orally, however.

As soon as the treatment improves his reading and writing, the child himself will want to start to participate in the reading, writing, and spelling work of the other children in his class. He should be encouraged to do this. His participation in classroom and homework assignments should then be increased gradually in length and difficulty, always in close collaboration with his therapist. This is essential for the correct timing of each advancing step. These children are hypersensitive to anything connected with reading and writing, and one false step can undo months of painstaking work of their reading therapist and of their psychotherapist.

It is very difficult for a teacher to have a child in his or her class who requires special teaching and management. The other children understandably resent this special treatment and what they consider special privileges given to this child. It undermines their confidence in the teacher's fairness and sense of justice and may destroy his or her relationship with all the other children. It also disrupts the friendly feeling the children in the same classroom should have for each other, so that the relaxed, conflict-free atmosphere that makes learning possible can be maintained. No one can learn in an atmosphere of jealousy, hatred, and fighting. Most teachers are experienced in handling this problem, though they are not always successful in overcoming it. There are usually far too many children with special learning and/or emotional problems in their classroom anyhow. To solve this group-teaching dilemma, teachers must find a way to explain the reasons for this special treatment to the entire class. This can be done in a tactful way, without humiliating the child in question.

Children have a need not only to be protected and cared for, but also to do the caring and protecting themselves. This is true for boys as well as girls. The teacher can appeal to this impulse in children, ask them for help, and get their cooperation. Such explanations cannot work, however, if they are one-sided sermons. A wise teacher will not just *tell* her pupils what she is doing for this one child, and why, but will also *listen* to them. She will give them a chance to make remarks, ask questions, and offer suggestions. Sometimes the children themselves can figure out better, more practical, and child-adequate solutions to such special classroom problems than adults. Of course the teacher must remain firm about any decisions made (for instance, not to have this child read or spell out loud or do written homework). The teacher will also make clear to the children that these are only temporary measures, that the child is expected to improve with the help of his reading therapist, and that he or she hopes this improvement will happen soon. This kind of optimism helps the child with a reading disorder immeasurably. These children are usually downcast, unhappy, and often so discouraged that they do not really believe that they will ever learn to read and write.

Where such group talks are skillfully done, the children will look up to and admire their teacher more than they did before, and an atmosphere will have been created in the classroom in which a handicapped child can thrive while the healthy children around him will progress at their own, much faster pace.

CLASSROOM MANAGEMENT OF UNSPECIFIC SYMPTOMS ASSOCIATED WITH ORGANIC READING DISORDERS.   It is of fundamental importance for the successful treatment of all reading disorders and the symptoms associated with them that parents, teachers, and the child himself understand their manifestations. A child who understands his handicaps can help figure out how to cope with them.

1. Slowing Down of All Reactions.   Children handicapped in this way cannot react with speed in any situation. They should not be urged to work faster because this causes anxiety, which increases their slowness. Anxiety and excitement worsen this symptom to the point where the child can't do anything. Teaching such children requires great patience, and is difficult to carry out in a classroom situation. Another difficulty of such children is that they can react to only *one* stimulus, *one* request, *one* task at a time (See Vol. II, p. 460).

2. Impairment of Automatic Mechanisms.   These children may require special-class placement or teaching on an individual basis, depending upon the severity of this symptom. It invariably interferes with their learning ability on all levels, because they have difficulty learning by repetition. This causes a severe memory disorder. Such a child must each time deliberately go through every step needed for reading, arithmetic, reciting the days of the week, their own address and telephone number, and so on.

They cannot focus their attention automatically on most activities, but must be taught to focus it deliberately. Many of them can accomplish this only by telling themselves out loud what to do next, step by step. Their classmates need to understand this so that they don't get angry or make fun of them (See Vol. II, p. 462).

3. Inability to Tolerate Disorder.   These children present such severe management problems that they usually need special-class placement or individual teaching. Any new situation, such as a minor change in their classroom routine, a new teacher, or a new child entering the classroom may provoke a severe panic reaction. They need a structured situation. Their daily routine must be predictable. They can function only when they know in advance exactly what they are expected to do. Planning is very difficult for them; free choice unnerves them. The teacher, therefore, needs to explain to such a child step by step what he is to do.

These children find reading very difficult and anxiety-provoking because the arrangement of letters on a page looks like a disordered jumble to them. It does not have a cohesive Gestalt until they have mastered reading (See Vol. II, p. 478).

4. Inability to Shift Freely from One Activity to Another.   These children find it difficult to free themselves from what they are doing or thinking, to stop and to continue with something else. This applies to all activities, whether they find them exciting or boring. It includes emotions: such a child has great difficulty getting over his feelings, such as anger or happy excitement. He needs more time than other children to calm down.

Teaching has to take into consideration that such a child cannot shift quickly, even when he wants to. The more he wants to, the less he can shift. These children are tense and rigid, and are well aware of the fact that they cannot act like other children even though they want to. They are often depressed and cry easily.

They dread anything new because they feel they cannot cope with it. They need a pause before they can start any other activity. They should be permitted to sit quietly for a few minutes before starting another task, and to close their eyes if they want to. Periods of shifting are stress situations when disruptive outbursts of anger and fear can occur. Prevention of such behavior is possible by encouraging such quiet pauses.

Reading and arithmetic present special difficulties for these children because they require a great deal of shifting—for example, from one letter to another, from one word to the next, from addition to subtraction, and so forth. Blending presents special problems. However, this does not necessarily mean that they should be taught with whole-word methods.

They are easily misunderstood and treated unjustly because they appear to be stubborn, rigid, negativistic, and generally disobedient. Actually, they cannot help themselves. They long to be as free and easygoing as other children, but cannot even play free and imaginative games with them. Their frustrations may lead to seriously disruptive behavior unless this symptom is managed carefully.

They have no self-confidence, just like most children with numerous organic symptoms. When they refuse to start a task, one can assume that they are certain that they cannot master it. They need constant reassurance and encouragement above all else (See Vol. II, p. 481 ff.).

5. Perseveration. Teachers are usually familiar with the symptom called perseveration, as their referral notes show. These children cannot stop their perseveration. They usually are aware of this symptom and try to control it.

Perseveration may involve these children's thinking, feeling, and behavior. Reading, writing, and arithmetic are especially severely affected. For instance, children continue to multiply when they are supposed to add and subtract. These children tend to reread words or sentences numerous times, silently or orally. This symptom is especially severe when the text is new to them. Periods present special obstacles: they may reread or rewrite the last word of each sentence repeatedly before putting down a period and continuing. Once they have started to cross out a word, they may cross out all following words, as 10-year-old Doug did (see Figure 11.1 Vol. II, p. 490).

They tend to disrupt classroom work by giving the same answer over and over again and by continuing to answer the same question when the teacher has already asked another one. They seem not to be listening to the teacher, but they do. They usually are aware of their inability to stop, and get very angry at themselves.

Curing perseveration takes time. These children, too, need a peaceful pause where they can sit at their desk without doing anything. It often helps to talk quietly and kindly to such a child alone for brief periods if this can be done in a classroom situation (See Vol. II, p. 487 ff.).

6. Attention Disorders. Teachers should be familiar with the structure of the attention process. Successful teaching of healthy as well as handicapped children depends on it (See Vol. II, pp. 501).

Attention disorders are not uniform; they affect different aspects of this process. Helping these children requires an assessment of what part of the attention process is defective, especially with regard to reading and writing. Teachers should record in detail what tasks the child can concentrate on as well as those he has problems with. This is important information for all his teachers and therapists. They should share and discuss it with each other.

Some basic principles apply to all children. It is important to realize that all children have to be taught to understand what it is they have to notice. Knowing what is important to attend to does not arise spontaneously, but must be taught. This applies to the details of letters and words just as much as to ideas (See Vol. II, pp. 540).

Psychologic studies have shown that a greater number of items can be attended to, remembered, and therefore learned, when they are assembled in groups or arranged in another systematic way. Children can therefore pay attention best when material is presented to them in an organized way and when the teacher explains the principle of its organization. The teaching of disconnected bits of information interferes with the attention process of all children. Their attention as well as their memory is strengthened when they are taught to look for interconnections and principles of organization (See Vol. II, p. 514).

This is important for the teaching of reading and arithmetic. Numbers or letters should never be shown scattered over a page or a chalkboard. The reading process should be explained from the very beginning as an orderly sequence of letters representing speech sounds, grouped together as words. Numbers should be taught in their relationship to each other and not as isolated items. (See Attention Disorders, Vol. II, pp. 507, 516; and Arithmetic Disorders, pp. 240, 241.)

This applies to all subjects. A new topic should be built on something the children already know, if possible as an answer to questions that have already occurred to them. This arouses their interest and increases their motivation (See Vol. II, p. 552).

Attention intensifies all sensations. Children should become aware of these changes caused by attention. Let them experience the increase in clarity and intensity of anything they are looking at, listening to, or touching as soon as they focus their attention on it.

Children with an attention disorder need to practice these experiences deliberately. This can be taught like a game because attention suddenly makes objects look different, more interesting and exciting. These children eventually can practice this by themselves with pleasure. This practice also helps alleviate distractibility.

Figure-Ground Difficulties. Children with an attention disorder on an organic basis usually have trouble distinguishing objects from each other and from their surroundings. They have difficulty distinguishing "figure" from "ground" (See Vol. II, p. 517). Practicing seeing and listening attentively helps them cope with this difficulty, which interferes especially with reading. They have difficulties discriminating letters from their background; thus they should be given reading material that is clearly printed with dark letters on white background. There should be no color or other lines or illustrations that can distract them, since they must learn to ignore everything else they see on a page.

Some of these children do better when they read with a cover card, holding it above the text they are reading so that it blocks out the upper part of the page. A window card may be even more helpful. The window should be so small that the child can see only one word at a time (See pp. 130, 131, Vol. II, 580).

Sometimes it is better to type a text one paragraph at a time on separate sheets of paper, instead of giving the child the book. He should have only one such sheet in front of him when he reads (See p. 580).

Warding off distractions does not come naturally. It requires a deliberate effort, which is strenuous for the child and makes him fatigue sooner than other children who do not have an attention disorder and can distinguish figure from ground. (See Vol. II, pp. 552, 516, 533, 534, 535).

Concentration, which consists of active and derived attention, and intellectual attention are those parts of the attention process that are most important for the learning of subject matter. Children must be helped to develop these faculties to their fullest because higher levels of knowledge and thinking depend on it. These faculties can and should be trained deliberately. One cannot take a chance by waiting for them to develop spontaneously. There are games and special exercises that help children from kindergarten on to develop these faculties. This is important, especially for children with an attention disorder.

Visualization is one of these special exercises. It is pleasurable for children to visualize all sorts of objects, places, stories, with their eyes open or closed. They can practice, for instance, visualizing their room at home exactly as it is. They should also be made aware of the changes that occur when they concentrate all their attention on what they are visualizing, how it becomes more real, colorful, and interesting. This also helps the child to understand why it is sometimes difficult for him to distinguish fantasy from reality. All children have a gift for such lifelike visualizations, which they lose in adulthood. This method helps them to remember letters, numbers, the spelling of words, and so forth. (For more information about Visualization, See Vol. II, p. 543; Concentration, p. 554 ff.; Intellectual Attention, p. 540.)

Strengthening the attention of healthy children and helping distractible children requires the elimination of visual and auditory distractions as much as possible. A distractible child cannot function at all in a noisy classroom. Children should be taught to whisper and not to shout, yell, or run around when they are working together in different groups. Television sets should never be on unless all children are supposed to watch the show.

These principles are not always adhered to. I have visited many noisy classrooms, where the situation was made worse by leaving the door open so that the noise spread throughout the entire floor. This problem is especially severe in open classrooms (See Vol. II, p. 543).

Visual distractions should be limited as much as possible. There should be only *one* item at a time on the chalkboard. Classroom walls cluttered with papers are also too distracting.

A child with an attention disorder should clear his desk completely before starting a new task.

Emotions are an integral part of the attention process. The emotional climate set by the teacher is therefore crucial for constructive management of these children. There should be a peaceful classroom atmosphere, which alone makes it possible for all children to feel secure so that they can concentrate on their work. Negative feelings, such as anxiety, envy, resentment, hatred, inferiority, insecurity, and especially anger, destroy the attention process. Competition tends to arouse such negative feelings and should therefore be avoided (See pp. 546–548).

Any child concentrates best when his interest has been aroused, when he has been motivated to learn. Strong feelings underlie interest and motivation. To arouse intellectual as well as emotional interest is one of the basic tasks of education. It has far-reaching consequences for the intellectual and behavioral development of all children. An interesting task cannot be carried out without self-discipline. Maria Montessori (1964, p. 350) was first in pointing out that self-discipline is best taught indirectly, through interest in work (See Vol. II, p. 548).

That is why the behavior of a child with an attention disorder tends to improve when this disorder improves (See Vol. II, pp. 544–545).

Rhyming is sometimes the only aspect of reading and writing that arouses the interest of such children. Rhymes can then be used for teaching (See Vol. II, p. 558).

Children who are distractible can concentrate better when they use their muscles in some way. They may be least distractible when writing or speaking or doing both. Teaching reading through writing and simultaneously saying the words they are writing is best for them. Oral reading also counteracts distractibility (See Vol. II, p. 578).

How to strengthen the attention process through daily physical exercises is described in the section on Curative Physical Exercises, Vol. II, p. 534. Changes in the muscular system are part of the physical changes occurring normally during attention. They are increased in children with an attention disorder (See Vol. II, pp. 532, 533).

Children with a severe attention disorder cannot divide their attention even after they have learned to concentrate on a task. They can give only their *full* attention, or none at all. Before they can listen to the teacher or to anyone else, they must stop whatever they are doing and look up. When talking to such a child, the teacher should look directly at him and speak slowly, clearly, and briefly. His classmates should be encouraged to communicate with him in the same way (See Vol. II, pp. 577–578).

7. Hyperactivity. Teachers are understandably confused about the diagnosis and underlying mechanisms of this symptom. It has become a fashionable term for children with all sorts of troubles who can't sit still, disrupt classroom work, are sometimes destructive, and are generally difficult to manage and to teach (See Vol. II, pp. 587, 588). The section on Hyperactivity clarifies the differential diagnosis and all other aspects of this symptom (See Vol. II, pp. 585).

The teacher's observations are indispensable for the diagnosis of hyperactivity, just as they are for judging the adequacy of the treatment plan. Any child suspected of suffering from hyperactivity should be referred to private physicians or clinics. The classroom teacher should never be left with the sole responsibility for such a child, not even after the diagnosis has determined that the child can respond to teaching in a regular classroom.

Teachers are forced to cope with far too many hyperactive children in their classrooms without any outside help. This is bound to interfere with the teaching of all the other children, just as it undermines the teacher's efficiency and effectiveness as well as her emotional stability.

A child who is hyperactive and difficult to manage for any reason should be kept in a regular classroom only if he is also being treated on a regular basis with other methods such as reading treatment, psychotherapy, social work treatment of his parents, or drug therapy.

The regular or the special classroom teacher should be able to confer on a continuing basis with at least one other therapist of the child, in person or by phone. The present practice of burdening these teachers with filling out elaborate questionnaires may be helpful for a superficial kind of research so popular today. But it does not help the teacher or the child.

This is also the disadvantage of the use of drug treatment on a massive scale, where neither parents, child, nor teacher have sufficient contact with the prescribing physician. The practice of very many physicians prescribing drugs for hyperactive children is not to re-examine the child on a regular basis, but to check up on him through phone calls. The child is very often re-examined no more than once every 6 months (or even less). (See Vol. II, pp. 661, 662.)

Children on drug treatment should be observed carefully in regard to their appetite, weight gain or loss, growth, just as much as for changes in their hyperactivity and their progress in reading. Teachers' observations in this respect are just as important as those of the children's parents. They should confer with each other on a regular basis.

Teachers should make sure that these children never have access to their drugs. When a child comes to school carrying his own pill bottle, it should be removed from him. No child should be permitted to take pills on his own, and teachers should consent to give out drugs only under very exceptional circumstances. This is not their task. One person should be assigned in each school to administer drugs if they have to be given during school hours. This is best done by the school nurse, a guidance counselor, or an administrator. Because of these children's pathologic interest in keys, and their great facility in stealing them, it is almost impossible to lock drugs up securely in the classroom (National Education Association and American Medical Association, 1974). (See Vol. II, pp. 664, 665).

Classroom management should be based on the fact that a child suffering from hyperactivity cannot control his motor drive even if he wants to. This drive is disinhibited, chaotic, and uncontrollable. Whatever enters the child's vision becomes the target of the drive. It is the motor drive looking for a target, not the stimulus attracting the child (See Vol. II, p. 591). This applies to the organic form of reading disorder only; children with the psychogenic form can control their hyperactivity to a certain degree (See Vol. II, p. 666).

Teachers should also be familiar with the different types of hyperactivity and should help determine whether the child is suffering from the anxious or nonanxious type.

MANAGEMENT OF THE ANXIOUS TYPE OF HYPERACTIVITY. These children respond to the avoidance of all anxiety-producing situations and activities. Holding such a child gently and talking to him quietly to calm him down is usually helpful. It may make him stop running and enable him to sit down and concentrate for a while (See Vol. II, pp. 593, 594).

Lessening anxiety sometimes also helps children who suffer from hyperactivity without anxiety. The hyperactivity itself sometimes makes such a child anxious (See Vol. II, p. 593).

MANAGEMENT OF HYPERACTIVITY WITHOUT ANXIETY.   Any attempt to restrain such a child even gently worsens the hyperactivity. These children wiggle out of any physical restraint. They bite and kick and scream to get free (See Vol. II, p. 594).

An attempt should be made to help such a child to become aware of his excessive motor drive, and to ask him what he himself has found to be helpful in stopping it. Some of these children can stop their hyperactivity when they lean against something such as a wall, a desk, or a chair. Sitting down sometimes also helps, but never completely. Such a child has to squirm and move his legs constantly while he is working. He should be permitted to do this. Punishing him only worsens his hyperactivity. Rocking on a chair is often also a substitute for moving about. These children tend to do this when they are tired and do not have the strength to run around any more (See Vol. II, p. 598).

This pathologic lack of anxiety increases the danger of injury. These children therefore need constant supervision. They cannot be left alone, even on the way to the bathroom, and sometimes must even be supervised in the bathroom. What saves them is their excellent motor coordination, which is typical for these children (See Vol. II, pp. 593, 611).

The teacher should record the child's periods of hyperactivity to determine whether it is episodic or constant and under what circumstances it is likely to occur. This information is basic for constructive management. It should be shared with the child's parents.

The teacher needs information about the child's sleep habits and should impress upon the parents that without continuous, uninterrupted sleep of at least 8 hours every night, the child's hyperactivity cannot improve (See Vol. II, pp. 600–601).

These children cannot do structured work for any length of time. They should be permitted to get up, stretch, take deep breaths, or exercise briefly in some way. Meditation is sometimes helpful. Regular daily physical exercise is essential. Such a child should have a daily gym period (See Vol. II, pp. 594, 666). It is often not possible to manage such a child in a classroom during the entire school day. Half-day schooling should be permitted until the child improves.

Hyperactive children love to watch things that move and like to move objects around. They can sometimes play quietly in a corner of the room, moving cars around, at least for a limited period of time. Games where they can move, be pulled in a wagon, or pull other children sometimes keep their hyperactivity within tolerable limits.

However, they are also interested in anything that flies and may suddenly try to "fly" off radiators, pipes, or closets.

The pleasure they take in pushing chairs around, opening and closing doors rhythmically, turning light switches off and on, and flushing toilets constantly present especially difficult management problems. Such a child can indulge in this type of rhythmic activity for hours. Rhythmic exercises can sometimes distract him from these activities (See Vol. II, p. 596).

Because of these children's interest in matches and in setting fires, special precautions have to be taken (See Vol. II, p. 609).

The management of violent acts committed by these children is complicated by the fact that their destructiveness is sometimes an unintended by-product of their hyperactivity. They bump into classmates while running around wildly. They don't really want to hurt them and are not hostile at all. Their classmates can sometimes be helped to understand this and to react good-naturedly without hitting back. (See Vol. II, pp). 604–605).

These children tend to talk incessantly, expressing their motor drive through their speech muscles. Their answers are often much too fast and may be irrelevant, because of their drivenness. This does not indicate a thought disorder or necessarily a lack of attention (see Vol. II, p. 597).

Their fascination with windows demands that classroom windows be kept closed regardless of the weather. Window guards should be installed. Even then, it is best to watch windowsills. These children move with extreme speed and jump or climb with the greatest of ease.

Not all hyperactive children have a reading disorder, but those with such a disorder have special problems. They may have choreiform eye movements, which make it difficult for them to fix their eyes and keep them on the line, and to perform the return-sweep correctly. Errors in word reading may be due to these involuntary eye movements. The child does not notice them and cannot control them. Teachers should therefore watch the child's eye movements during reading and use the cover card and other methods to help him develop linear reading (See p. 127, Vol. II, pp. 602, 603).

8. Hypoactivity. The most important task of the teacher is to refer a child who is apathetic, lethargic, and without initiative or spontaneity to a physician to rule out physical illness. The symptom may occur with or without a reading disorder. Its association with any type of reading disorder is frequent, especially when the disorder has been permitted to continue for years. These children have given up trying after years of failure and feel they cannot master anything. They need encouragement and an arousal of their interest above all else. They also need individual reading treatment. Usually they no longer can respond in a group situation. Physical exercises sometimes increase their energy (See Vol. II, p. 669 ff.).

9. Fatiguability.   Awareness of the symptom and its ramifications is essential for coping with it. When such a child yawns and is obviously sleepy, his behavior should not be mistaken for boredom or negativism. These children actually need sleep. Reading and arithmetic require such intense concentration for them because these subjects are so cumbersome that they cause fatigue much sooner than in other children. All organic symptoms increase fatiguability.

This symptom alone requires placement in a special class because rest periods usually cannot be arranged in regular classes. Mini-rest periods throughout the day help these children. Many also need an afternoon nap after lunch, at home, or in school. All special classes should provide such rest periods including classes for handicapped children (See Vol. II, p. 672 ff.).

10. Morbid Irritability with a Tendency to Sudden Rages, which May Take the Form of Temper Tantrums.   This symptom is difficult to recognize, understand, and cope with. Irritability is very frequent. It is difficult to deal with under any circumstances because irritable children or adults often do not realize that they are irritable. Morbid irritability is much more severe and serious. It occurs in episodes, suddenly, without warning, and it is often not possible to figure out what precipitated it. Hidden physical and psychologic mechanisms initiate it.

This symptom is involuntary; the child can neither initiate it nor control it. He feels that it comes on without his doing, that it is forced on him. He suddenly feels very touchy. Any trivial stimulus stirs up an unpleasant excitement in him; it destroys his equilibrium and evokes an immediate physical reaction beyond his control. He startles, trembles, turns around, jumps up, cries out, and may start to swear and to lash out wildly. These children sometimes fear that this reaction means that they are going insane.

As with all the other symptoms, the teacher's task is to explain its mechanisms to the child and to his classmates. It is important for everyone to realize that these children are not irritable because they are angry or hostile. Anger is a secondary development caused by self-hatred because of the irritability and by the anger it evokes in others. The worse thing anyone can do is to talk to such a child in an angry tone of voice (See Vol. II, p. 681).

Everyone dealing with the child should also realize that irritability is invariably contagious. One irritable child makes everyone around him irritable. These children want to be left completely alone, away from all stimuli. They should be permitted to work in isolation and to be ignored. This can often not be carried out in a classroom. It is sometimes best to send such a child home, hopefully to understanding parents.

Irritating stimuli should be eliminated as much as possible from any classroom anyhow. Children should not interrupt each other or the teacher. Noises that make it difficult to understand one another should be avoided. So should all interferences with the orderly progression of thoughts and actions. All this cannot always be carried out satisfactorily, but attempts should be made so that at least the normal type of irritability can be minimized.

Violent explosions of these children occur after a prolonged period of irritability that caused smoldering anger and subdued rage, which then errupts after a trivial stimulus. These episodes cannot be stopped after they have started. They take their time and leave the child exhausted, angry, and discouraged. They should be prevented at all costs.

A potentially very dangerous development is suspiciousness aroused by such irritability. Teachers should be alert to this new symptom. Such a child misinterprets harmless noises or other stimuli as deliberate attacks. This requires instant and constant explanations by the teacher that this did not happen with the deliberate intent to harm the child. No such incident should be ignored (see Vol. II, p. 676).

Teasing increases irritability; so does unjust punishment when the irritability is mistaken for deliberate disruptiveness (See Vol. II, p. 679).

11. Mood Disorder. Children who suffer from this disorder on an organic basis have sudden unmotivated mood changes that can neither be predicted nor prevented. They occur in episodes. Teachers are very familiar with the normal variety of "bad" moods. The morbid type is much more severe and cannot be stopped once it has started. These children are cross, cranky, displeased with themselves and everyone else. They grumble, swear, yell out, and are restless. They want to hide and want very much to be left alone. They feel uncomfortable and angry. They cannot explain their "evil" mood; nothing can cheer them up (see Vol. II, p. 684).

Such a child is ready to lash out, to hurt others and himself. He cannot possibly concentrate on any work and fails all tests while in this mood.

These children usually cannot be managed in the classroom during these episodes, because they are not accessible. What makes their management so extremely difficult is that one cannot leave them alone anywhere. They must be watched at all times because they may hurt themselves or others. It is therefore best to send them home, provided a parent is at home who can supervise them (see Vol. II, p. 686).

The mood disappears as suddenly as it came. It recurs invariably, but not at regular intervals.

It is also important for teachers to know that a convulsive disorder may be the cause of such mood swings. These children need thorough physical, neurologic, psychiatric, and psychologic examinations as well as treatments outside the classroom (see Vol. II, p. 685).

12. Free–Floating Anxiety with a Tendency to Panics. All thoughts and actions of these children are tinged with anxiety, which is increased by any situation that normally provokes anxiety in children. Their anxiety may cause physical symptoms such as pallor, sweating, trembling, dizziness, palpitations, and the feeling of imminent fainting. They also have to go to the bathroom very frequently. Their anxiety is so severe that they usually cannot be managed in a regular classroom. In no case should the classroom teacher have the sole responsibility for such a child. He should be thoroughly diagnosed and treated with psychotherapy and drugs, if indicated. These children are also often too anxious to overcome their reading disorder through group teaching. They may need individual reading treatment, at least for a while (see Vol. II, p. 693).

Panics.   Panics are the most serious complication. Inevitably a sign of mismanagement, they can and should be avoided. They are the result of an accumulation of many small frustrations, usually caused by the reading disorder. They may also be provoked by fatigue and by any situation that normally causes anxiety.

A panic consists of a sudden emotional and motor discharge. The child screams, cries, is unconsolable. He may bite or hit himself, bang on his desk, and run home. His conscious awareness is blurred during such panics. He usually does not remember what caused it and what happened during that state. Hitting increases the panic. Holding the child gently, and quietly talking to him sometimes helps. These panics are especially severe in children with a speech disorder, who normally have difficulty communicating.

These children are quite unresponsive and emotionally frozen for some time afterwards. They need to lie down and rest or sleep (see Vol. II, p. 692).

It is important to realize that these panics are not a result of hostility, stubbornness, or negativism. The child should not be punished for them.

Prevention of Panics.   The teacher should be aware of any sign of impending stress, and can ask the other children to assist in this. There are innumerable ways to intervene to relieve tension such as suggesting a changeover to easier work, a familiar task, a period of play, or stopping reading for awhile. The child should be given a chance to recover his equilibrium. It is very important for the teacher or for a trusted child to stay with such a child until one is sure that he is all right.

The child can learn to avoid panics by himself. He can find out when his tension begins, and then stop whatever he is doing. He can tell the teacher that he must rest now and should be permitted to change his activity, to leave the room, or to lie down if he wants to (see Vol. II, p. 692).

It is also important to tell such a child over and over again that his anxiety is not based on any real and present danger.

To misdiagnose a panic as the sign of an ordinary behavior disorder is harmful. When these children are put into classes for emotionally disturbed children, their anxiety is worsened and their panics increase.

Noncompetitive physical exercises have a calming effect. Competition increases anxiety (see Vol. II, p. 693).

The violent outbursts of children with a mood disorder, the rages of children with morbid irritability, and the panic of children with free-floating anxiety make classroom management most difficult or impossible. All three outbursts may look alike, but it is important to differentiate the underlying mechanisms. It must be stressed that this is not the task of teachers, even when they are trained in special education. Pediatric, neurologic, psychiatric, and psychologic examinations of all these children are imperative. So are treatments carried out by one or several of these clinicians.

Punishment of children with a reading disorder associated with one or several of these organic symptoms presents a dilemma, since it has a disorganizing effect on all of them. It increases their anxiety, self-hatred, and feelings of insecurity and incompetence. Any attempt to increase such a child's motivation through humiliation and fear invariably leads to an increase in his symptoms. However, punishment cannot always be avoided. Its destructive effects can be minimized only when it is just and brief, and always followed by forgiveness (see Vol. II, p. 681).

Success is the best medicine for these children. It helps all children, but has much deeper implications for children with organic symptoms. Teachers should try to find ways to enable such children to experience the happiness of success at least once during every schoolday.

SPECIAL READING AIDS. A teacher whose class contains one or more children with a reading disorder needs such aids. These children cannot participate in the work of other groups, and the teacher cannot spend too much time teaching them on an individual basis. Excellent teaching aids are available that help children to learn the different reading acts by themselves. There are special games that are interesting and can be played either by several children or by one child alone. Such materials are often available and listed in catalogs provided by the school system. They can be ordered without using special funds.

Unfortunately, such materials are not always available. I have observed many teachers of regular classes helplessly struggling to teach a baffled and unhappy child. It was impossible for these teachers to obtain the materials they so desperately needed. It is quite possible that these materials were available through another organization within the school system, but the teachers were not informed about them and their usefulness had not been shown to them. This applies to reading just as much as to arithmetic (see p. 225). Lack of availability of basic and indispensable teaching aids pervades most school systems. Teachers frequently are not even given enough pencils or paper for the children. I have visited many classes where teachers bought paper and other such items with their own money. I have made it a practice to buy "Junior Scrabble" and other remedial reading games for teachers struggling to help the children in my care.

Cover Card and Window Card.   These aids are simply 3 by 5 or larger unlined cards. A folded piece of paper will also do. For a window card cut an opening that can accommodate about one word at a time. The cover card is held above the line of print; the window card is pushed along the line the child is reading. Both aid with linear reading and help the child to concentrate on the text. (see p. 130; and pp. 94–97 under Visual Agnosia.)

Rhythmic Ability Disorder.   A child who has a rhythmic ability disorder can be helped if one taps the reading rhythm for him until he can tap it himself (see Vol. II, p. 451).

The Barger Mirroreading Board.   This device was designed for children with directional difficulties. It can be used by only one child at a time under the supervision of the reading therapist. The child cannot use it to study by himself (see p. 95).

Tachistoscopes, Perceptoscopes, Metron-O-Scope, Controlled Reader, and Other Reading Machines.   These devices are very expensive and not readily available. Only a tachistoscope can be made by teachers on their own (Roswell & Natchez, 1964, p. 84). More sophisticated teaching aids have been developed, which use TV screens to present programmed instruction. They can be individualized so that the child can study by himself. Individual reading treatment is still far superior to any device. The reading disorder of the majority of children can be treated successfully without machines (see p. 131).

Speech Treatment.   Sending such a child to speech classes is often helpful. He learns to listen and distinguish different speech sounds, and to pronounce them correctly. (see Vol. II, p. 381 under Speech Disorders.)

Special Class Placement

Special classes are indicated for those children with reading disorders whose behavior is too disruptive for regular classroom attendance or whose organic disorders are so severe and multiple that they cannot function when taught together with healthy children. Special class placement can be on a part-time basis, where the child attends the special class several times each week or once a day, and spends most of his time in a regular class of his grade. This does not help children whose handicap is very severe. They need all-day classes until they have improved. Special classes for these children are rare, so that one is forced to search for classes designated for children with other handicaps which might also help these children.

Many school systems are setting up classes for "brain-injured" or "minimal-brain-damaged" children. Severe and complicated cases such as 7-year-old Emilio (p. 169) often fit into such classes and benefit from attending them. I hope that eventually classes will be set up in all schools that specialize in teaching children with organic reading, writing and arithmetic disorders.

Those who also have a severe organic speech disorder (an aphasia) can be sent to classes or schools for aphasic children. These classes, however, usually accept only children who have almost no speech. Children with milder forms of aphasia, who are much more numerous, would improve faster in classes organized primarily for children with organic reading, writing, and arithmetic disorders who also have speech defects—that is, where aphasia would be treated as an integral part of the learning disorder. Teachers with very special training—some specializing in reading, others in speech therapy—should head these classes, together with teachers for deaf children, who usually run aphasic classes. Even a child with the severe type of aphasia Elaine suffered from would have the best chance to overcome these impairments in such a class. (See Vol. II, p. 398 ff. under Speech Disorders.)

Children with reading disorders whose behavior is too disruptive for a regular classroom are apt to be put in special classes for children with emotional disturbances (called "junior guidance classes," "classes for the emotionally handicapped," "classes for children with severe emotional disturbances," etc.), or in special day schools, which are set up mainly for delinquents. In New York City, these schools are called "schools for socially maladjusted children."

Such class or school placement is often precipitated by the child's suspension from school or by the threat of suspension. These children are referred privately or to a clinic primarily for their disturbed behavior and not because of a reading disorder, which is usually discovered only during their psychologic and/or psychiatric examination. These children, as a rule, cannot function in a regular class unless individual treatment (reading therapy, psychotherapy, psychopharmacotherapy, if indicated) is started promptly and changes their behavior within a short period of time. Many of them can remain in school only if placed in such a special class or school.

These special classes and schools, however, are set up to deal primarily with emotional and behavioral disorders and not with reading disorders. Unfortunately, they do not provide the special type of corrective reading teaching these children need. The teachers of these classes are not specialists in reading therapy although they should be, because the vast majority of their students suffer from severe reading disorders—organic, psychogenic, or sociogenic. As a matter of fact, it was usually their reading disorder that got them placed in these classes and schools in the first place. It either caused their disturbed behavior or aggravated it to the point where they could not function in a regular class any longer. That there is a close connection between juvenile delinquency and reading disorders has been abundantly documented. (See Chapter 6, p. 285 ff, Juvenile Delinquency.) Many of these children eventually land in courts. This makes it even more imperative that they get adequate treatment for their reading disorder *early* in elementary school, so that this tragic turn of their life can be prevented.

CLASSES FOR MENTALLY DEFECTIVE CHILDREN. These special classes play an important role in the lives of very many children suffering from a severe reading disorder, especially the organic type. In the section on Mental Deficiency (Vol. II, p. 410) I point out that the I.Q. level below which a child is considered mentally defective or mentally retarded varies for legal purposes such as special class or school placement, commitment to state schools, competency, responsibility for criminal acts. It is based less on clinical judgment than on historic legal conventions. In New York it is 75. The name of these classes also varies: abbreviations are usually used, such as CRMD (Children with Retarded Mental Development). These abbreviations are supposed to disguise the true nature of the class and to prevent stigmatization of the children attending it. However, this disguise never works. The other children in the school invariably find out that only "dumb" or "crazy" children are placed in these classes. They make fun of them and call them names. Only a healthy school atmosphere where no humiliation of any group of children is tolerated can protect these children from ridicule. In far too many schools children are threatened with being placed in these classes if they don't behave (see Vol. II, p. 419).

As I point out in the section on Mental Deficiency, this diagnosis covers different syndromes with a variety of symptoms and causes. Some, but by no means all, mentally deficient children have a reading disorder. A very large group of children who are not mentally deficient but have organic reading disorders is wrongly placed in these classes. It was their reading disorder that prevented their general intelligence from developing to its fullest, so that their I.Q. score was low enough for their admission to such a class. The I.Q. of a child who also has an arithmetic disorder and a speech defect is depressed even further. Yet, his intellectual capacity may be within normal limits (see Vol. II, p. 419).

These wrong diagnoses and placements are usually due to group testing. Individual psychologic testing by experienced psychologists reveals the true intellectual capacity of such a child. Such individual testing is required in the New York City Public School System before a child can be placed in such a class; this is as it should be. Individual psychologic testing alone can determine whether a group I.Q. score of 70, for example, means that the child is mentally defective or that he has a reading or an emotional disorder or both, and therefore performed poorly on the test (see p. 412).

Tens of thousands of children all over the country are falsely labeled as mentally retarded and placed in these classes because their low group I.Q. score is accepted as a biologic fact. This leads to a devastating educational discrimination against them. They are not expected to learn much and do not get the corrective teaching they so desperately need.

Poor children with a dialect or foreign-language background are hit hardest by this. These are the black, Puerto Rican, or Mexican children who are already discriminated against in so many other ways. No wonder that an ever larger group of parents object to this placement, and that lawsuits have been brought against the schools. The San Diego, California public schools, for instance, were sued for $400,000 in damages by 20 students, 12 of them black, for the years they had spent in ERM (Educable Mentally Retarded) classes. The court granted all misplaced students a token $1 each and the school district agreed to eliminate racial and cultural bias from its placement tests (*Washington Post,* September 6, 1972. See also Capeci, 1978; Lane, 1978). (See section on Mental Deficiency, Vol. II, pp. 414, 416; and p. 11.)

The unreliability of these tests is not limited to racial and cultural bias. Many children with organic reading disorders, whether they are socially disadvantaged or privileged, score low on group I.Q. tests. Whether or not they are placed in a class for mentally retarded children, such a low I.Q. score affects their teacher's judgment of their learning ability. It also limits their parents' expectation of what they can achieve in school and later on in life. This has a deep influence on the child's image of himself.

Damaging Effect of Low Expectations. Numerous studies show that children learn poorly when their teachers expect them to be poor students. The reason for this is that a teacher's conviction that a child's intelligence is so low that he will always remain on the lowest level of academic achievement, leads to poor teaching. The child in turn senses his teacher's judgment of him, if it is subtle, or hears it if it is openly discussed. This shatters his self-image, undermines his self-confidence, and leads to poor learning—which in turn seems to confirm the accuracy of his low I.Q. rating. Such a child is on a downward course from then on, and he will land in a class for mentally retarded children unless someone takes an interest in him and uncovers the educational, organic, or psychopathologic reasons for his school failure.

This is why far too many children are referred to school psychologists for placement in these classes. Caseloads of school psychologists are inflated out of all proportions by these referrals. As few as one out of five of these children may actually belong in these classes. The numbers are staggering in large school systems such as New York City's. I have seen statistics that showed that only about 1,000 out of more than 5,000 children referred for placement in these classes during one school year alone actually belonged in them. Of course, the 4,000 ineligible children needed special help urgently. After all, they were referred because they could not learn and because their teacher could not figure out why and felt helpless. Children suffering from organic reading disorders associated with other organic symptoms can be found in this group. Their plight is usually completely ignored. They are screened out, but far too often do not get into any diagnostic and treatment plan.

False placement in such a class would not be such a disadvantage for a child with a reading disorder, if the teachers of these classes were trained in corrective reading teaching. Such class placement would then help the child. However, most teachers of these classes have no special training in reading treatment. I have observed many of these classes and talked to the teachers. They are devoted to their students; otherwise they would not teach these difficult children. Like too many regular classroom teachers, they are often not given the concrete, practical advice they need. Reading treatment should be a required subject in their training, and speech teachers should be regular staff members of these classes.

Once a child is placed in a class for mentally retarded children, it may be difficult to remove him. He may end up spending all his school life in such classes, which will handicap him for life. Even when a teacher of these classes notices signs of normal intellectual capacity and wants the child retested and removed from the special class, she or he does not always succeed. Unnecessarily cumbersome administrative procedures often make it very difficult to return such a child to a regular class. The temptation to leave things as they are is sometimes very great, especially when the school receives extra pay for each child in such a class, and where this sum is removed when the census declines.

Psychologic re-examination of all children in these classes at regular intervals should be mandatory. Placement of a child in any special class should be a flexible and not a rigid procedure. It also should require the consent and cooperation of the child's parents.

CLASSES FOR PHYSICALLY HANDICAPPED CHILDREN. Public school systems offer a number of special classes for children with various physical handicaps. Many of these children also have reading disorders. Most deaf children and those with cerebral palsy have great difficulty learning to read (See section on Cerebral Palsy, Vol. II, pp. 429, 431.) Teachers in charge of these classes should therefore be trained in reading treatment. Many schools also offer classes for children with multiple physical and gross neurologic handicaps; teachers for these classes also need special training.

"Sight-conservation" classes for children with severe visual defects are helpful for some children with organic reading disorders. I have managed to get some of these children admitted to such classes, even when their sight was somewhat above the norm for placement in this class. Children attending these classes are taught to read and write with very large letters. This helps all children with organic reading disorders, because it makes it easier for them to remember letter forms and slows down their writing movements; this in turn strengthens their kinesthetic–motor memory. As I point out in the section on Word Reading, some children with an organic reading disorder learn best when they are taught as if they were blind (pp.49, 95 and following).

A number of schools offer "health-conservation" classes, which are set up to help children who are undernourished, chronically ill, or convalescing from a serious illness or an operation. Their private physician or the school physician recommends admission to this class. I have found placement in such a class helpful for those children with an organic reading disorder who are undernourished or too thin for other reasons. This type of child is usually tense, fidgity, and always tired. These classes are small. They have special rest and snack periods and give these children, who are usually neglected and sometimes close to being "battered" children, good physical and emotional care. This makes learning easier for them. They also need individual reading treatment and sometimes psychotherapy (see pp. 300–316, Vol. II, pp. 418–420).

ROLE OF FOREIGN-LANGUAGE CLASSES. Children with a reading disorder have great difficulty learning to speak, read, and write foreign languages, especially when their alphabet differs and the direction of the writing is from right to left. The exception is Latin. Eileen Simpson describes the reasons for this in her literate and moving autobiography, *Reversals: A Personal Account of Victory over Dyslexia* (1979):

It was not in English class that I made progress toward literacy but in Latin. Because Latin consonants, vowels, and their combinations represent predictable sounds, and the spelling is not capricious and tricky, I had a friendly feeling toward Latin. I didn't tune out when the teacher taught us about prefixes and suffixes, about infinitives, gerundives, and subordinate clauses. I even began to enjoy playing with words and sprinkled my conversation, often inappropriately, with Latin phrases. If I said that a boy was "e pluribus unum," what I meant was that he was one in a million . . . that conversational crutch "No kidding!" became a more urbane "Mirabile dictu!" I rolled these newly learned sounds around on my tongue as if they were exotic jujubes. It was through this playing with words, I think, that I learned to blend sounds in reading. This blending, carried over from Latin to English, helped me finally to make "fetch" out of "fe etch." I don't say that I was good in Latin, for I wasn't; only that it was good for me. Through Latin, though I didn't realize it at the time, I took a giant step toward becoming a reader (p. 122).

Donald Barr, whose book, *Who Pushed Humpty Dumpty? Dilemmas in American Education Today* (1971), deals with sociogenic reading disorders, calls Latin "the only remedial English course that really works." He stresses that "in Latin, in order to understand anything at all about a sentence, you have to read every letter of every word of it" (pp. 280–281).

Home Instruction

It is sometimes impossible to find a suitable class or special school for children with severe forms of organic reading disorders who also have a behavior disorder. The same applies occasionally to a child with a psychogenic reading disorder. In these rare cases, home instruction may provide the only means of continuing the child's schooling.

It was an important progressive step when public schools began to provide teachers for children with a prolonged physical illness who had to stay in hospitals or at home. Large school systems organized bureaus in charge of special classes in hospitals, and of teachers who were sent to children's private homes. A child's private physician or a school physician had to request such a home teacher. This special school service was eventually extended to include emotionally handicapped children. This was an important step forward in the mental health care of children.

Home instruction should be only a temporary measure while the child is in treatment. The goal should be to have the child catch up with his classmates and to return eventually to a regular class on his age level. One is reluctant to recommend this special education because the child is taught alone and forced to spend all day in a home that may not be the best place for him. However, a child on home instruction does not have to be completely isolated from other children. He can play with his friends after school and on weekends and home teachers often arrange to teach a number of their students together in small groups in homes, libraries, or community facilities.

I was the consultant for a number of such groups. The children had severe organic and emotional difficulties and were very difficult to teach. This form of intensive and flexible small-group teaching provided the only chance for some of them to overcome their reading and arithmetic disorder and to learn to get along with other children and teachers. It kept some of them out of state hospitals.

Some of these children also had speech therapy, and a few were on drugs to restrain their hyperactivity. Not all who needed it could get psychotherapy because no therapist could be found for them. I treated as many as my time permitted.

The families of all these children needed social casework treatment, but some of them did not accept it. Some mothers and fathers just cannot be reached, but this does not mean that schools and clinics should not give these children the best care they have to offer. Children have to be helped to survive in spite of their parents' indifference and neglect.

Teachers of homebound children are another group who should be trained in corrective reading teaching, but are not. The majority of their emotionally handicapped and many of their physically handicapped students suffer from reading disorders, organic or psychogenic.

My experience shows that home instruction works well in carefully selected cases.

Placement Away from Home

A child with a reading disorder (organic, psychogenic, or sociogenic) can and should be treated while living at home. He may need placement in a boarding school, a residential treatment center, or a mental hospital, but not because of his reading disorder. If he is a "battered child," he may have to be removed from his home for his physical safety. Under less dramatic and traumatic conditions, it may be decided jointly by the child's parents, his psychotherapist, and his reading therapist that he would learn and develop better for a number of reasons, if he went to a boarding school. Sometimes the neurotic family interaction is so destructive for the child that he cannot concentrate on his studies while living at home.

Occasionally an adolescent takes the initiative himself and asks to be sent to a boarding school because he feels that he cannot concentrate on his studies while living at home. I have examined a number of such adolescents and found that they were often right. They needed this separation from their family for their mental and emotional growth.

However, when an elementary-school-age child asks to be removed from his home, he signals that he is in severe emotional and often also physical danger, provided that he really means it and does not say it just out of momentary anger, as a threat and a challenge to his parents. These are the children who run away from home. They are depressed, often have suicidal thoughts, sometimes make suicidal threats, and may even attempt suicide, openly or in secret. I have made a special study of childhood depressions and found that a reading disorder that makes the child feel hopelessly stupid and inferior may cause a masked or an overt depression. Childhood depressions are easily missed and often not taken seriously enough. They are, however, benign and transitory provided they are diagnosed and immediate attention is paid to the child's plight. They respond well to psychotherapy and are not necessarily indications for the child's placement (Mosse, 1974) (see Vol. II, pp. 564–565).

It is a drastic and potentially dangerous step to place an elementary-school-age child away from his home. Only careful diagnostic examinations of the child and his family can determine whether it is safe to leave him in his home while a treatment plan for him and his family is carried out. Unless there is unusually severe individual and/or family pathology, all children with reading disorders (organic, psychogenic, or sociogenic) should attend day school and live at home.

Reading Treatment on an Individual Basis

Classroom management or special class placement alone is usually not sufficient for successful treatment of children with any type of reading disorder. These children have such difficulty concentrating and often such an emotional block against reading because of years of failure, that only the undivided attention of one reading therapist can break through this block and help them understand what reading is all about.

Knowledge of the organic cerebral matrix of reading and writing and of the reading process provides the basis for the corrective teaching techniques these children need. Technical details depend on which of the 11 reading and 3 writing acts the child cannot perform.

It must be stressed that just showing flashcards with pictures and whole words over and over again (i.e., repeating the method by which the child could not learn to read in the first place) prolongs the reading disorder indefinitely. I have observed such endless repetitions innumerable times.

What these children need is best expressed by Eileen Simpson, who suffered the agony of an organic reading disorder. She writes:

> What dyslexics need is not to have more of the same kind of training—be it the "whole-word" method which came into fashion in the mid-twenties, or a combination of old and new, "Whole-word" and phonetics—that children have in the classroom. Dyslexics need different training. For them each stage in the process of learning must be broken down into many small steps: each step taught slowly and thoroughly, the learning reinforced by engaging as many sense organs as possible—ear, eye, touch and with it the musculature of the fingers and arms—in what is called tri-model reinforcement. Instead of having had me read aloud the same passage in a story until I made no errors, a remedial teacher would have recognized that I needed to begin at the beginning with the alphabet (p. 90).

It is therefore best not to start with reading when treating a child with a severe reading disorder of any type, but to begin with writing.

Basic Principles for Beginning Reading Treatment

1. The child should not read at all until he can write and sound with certainty all letters, phonograms, and words and sentences containing them.

The teacher should be told not to let him read until the therapist suggests it. (See Teaching of Writing, p. 184.)

2. The child should write on lined paper only—*never* without the support of lines—and preferably with a pencil.

3. Make sure the child knows the direction of all manuscript letters, lower case as well as capital. If he does not, use the clock face as a guide as Spalding suggests (Spalding, 1969, p. 54). (See Teaching of Writing, p. 184.)

4. Let the child sound letters, phonograms, and words before, during, and after writing them. Copying and silent writing are not permitted.

5. Let no mistake stand.

6. Let the child keep a lined notebook with letters, phonograms, words, sentences, and paragraphs he has written himself so that he can study them and refer to them in class. (See Teaching of Writing, pp. 184.)

So much reading treatment fails because the therapists do not teach writing at all and fail to teach phonics systematically. They often use method mixtures to which the child had been subjected before and either caused his reading disorder or contributed to it.

Reading treatment is a specialized form of teaching that requires special training. It is a difficult task that cannot be done by amateurs. College students who volunteer as tutors and many other concerned adults who offer their service to help combat the enormous reading problem are amateurs in regard to reading disorders. They can help children with their homework in subject matter and make the individual child feel happier and more confident, but the teaching of reading, and even more, the treatment of reading disorders, requires special professional training. This should be clear to anyone reading this book.

Reading therapists are either teachers with a degree in special education or psychologists with special training in the diagnosis and treatment of reading disorders. This entire field has been neglected by teachers colleges and by psychology and education departments of colleges, so that there is a great shortage of well-trained reading therapists. This shortage has increased since the advent of "learning disabilities" as a specialty. Courses in these disabilities are much too general and do not teach the specialized knowledge of reading disorders indispensable for their treatment (see p. 43). Academic training alone is not sufficient preparation for reading treatment anyhow. Experience with classroom teaching is essential to understand thoroughly these children's impairments, and so is knowledge of basic clinical concepts.

In order to build a solid foundation for their work, reading therapists should be familiar with clinical work in action. Even though they do not by themselves use clinical methods in the strictest sense, they should know their scope and significance, keeping in mind that knowledge of the broad principles of a clinical specialty does not mean competence to practice it.

Remedial reading teachers were members of the staff of the Lafargue Clinic from the start. Such teachers are by now considered indispensable members of the staff of any well-run child psychiatric clinic. They help these clinics, and the clinics help them to acquire the necessary understanding of clinical work. I have therefore advocated for many years (unfortunately quite unsuccessfully) that all corrective reading teachers (or whatever their changing titles are) of the New York City Public School system should be assigned to the Bureau of Child Guidance or other child psychiatric clinics on a rotating part-time basis for a limited period of time to participate in the work of the clinical team. This would give them more confidence in their work, and more competence in carrying it out. It would help them develop an ever greater variety of techniques to correct the reading and writing defects of each individual child. The clinic staff can learn from them, and they can learn from the clinic staff. All schools should make such arrangements with their own or with community child psychiatric clinics.

Work in a child psychiatric clinic should be part of the training of all "educational therapists," the professional title used most frequently by teachers specializing in corrective education which includes reading treatment. This could be achieved through an internship after the master's degree as a prerequisite for licensing. It should also be a required part of the in-service training of teachers working toward a special license in corrective reading.

The work of the reading therapist invariably has deep psychologic implications and consequences. As Roswell and Natchez point out in their book, *Reading Disability: Diagnosis and Treatment* (1964); "We realize that those who work with children with reading disability apply many of the basic principles of psychotherapy, perhaps without being aware of them" (p. 65). Awareness of the clinical implications of a child's reading disorder is indispensable for the understanding and constructive application of these basic psychotherapeutic principles. An educational therapist, however, should teach, and not psychoanalyze the child or practice other forms of formal psychotherapy with him. Trying to combine both teaching and psychotherapy can only harm the child, sometimes seriously. Such misguided attempts are unfortunately being made. This does not mean that the reading therapist need not understand the child; good teaching must be based on understanding in depth both the reading process *and* the child. To do the work well, a reading therapist need not undergo a personal psychoanalysis, unless he suffers from a severe neurosis for which this form of therapy might be indicated. A thorough knowledge of the symptoms and the underlying mechanisms of all types of reading, writing, and arithmetic disorders will provide the most reliable basis for the understanding of those basic principles of psychotherapy that the reading therapist should know.

Carefully conducted individual reading treatment alone, without special class placement and without psychotherapy, can cure most children suffering from any type of reading disorder. This can sometimes be accomplished in one single school year, depending on the severity of the disorder, the length of time it was ignored, and the strength of the child's emotional block against reading and writing. Which child can benefit from this form of corrective education alone, depends entirely on the diagnosis. (See case of Alfred, p. 107.)

Roswell and Natchez express the feeling of all reading therapists when they state that "this type of remedial treatment can be one of the most provocative, stirring experiences in the child's life" (p. 77). I want to add that it can also be a significant turning point in his intellectual and with it his emotional development (the two cannot be schematically separated). An 8-year-old boy expressed this turning point experience best when he told his reading therapist, "You turned my brain on!"

Treatment Course

The lack of communication between the different educational and medical specialists that so often hinders a correct diagnosis may also prevent successful treatment. Reading treatment may take several years, so that the lines of communication must be kept open until the child is cured.

This is apparently the exception rather than the rule, as pointed out in a study done by the City University of New York. Dr. Lee Ann Truesdel found that children pulled out of their classrooms for tutoring learned things totally unrelated to what they were taught in their regular classes. One boy was taught reading by the phonetic approach in the classroom. In his special class he was taught to memorize words without paying any attention to the associations of sounds and letters. A ninth-grade student who read on the sixth-grade level had to miss classes in mathematics, gym, and English so that she could attend a special reading program. In her regular English class she was learning composition and grammar; in the special class she learned only to read specific words through some elaborate techniques including recording cassettes and videoscreens (Kleiman, 1979). Such lack of communication can only confuse these children and worsen their reading disorder. It may handicap them for the rest of their lives.

As I have described previously, not all children with an organic reading disorder can be cured. Residual symptoms, primarily a spelling disorder, may remain throughout life. (See case of Doug, pp. 118, 490.) Some of these dren may need help with reading and writing throughout their school and college career and sometimes also at work, especially when they are under pressure to read and write faster and more than usual, for instance before a test. These youngsters often prefer to continue to see their original reading therapist every few months and to return to him or her in times of crisis.

Importance of Continuity

The importance of regular and continued treatment cannot be overemphasized. It should not be entirely interrupted even during the summer vacations. The memory of all these children is impaired with regard to the technical basis for reading and writing. If the treatment is interrupted for too long a time, the reading therapist may have to start from the beginning because the child has forgotten all he had learned.

This memory weakness must be taken into consideration when making the decision whether to end the treatment. Treatment should not be terminated until the child, his therapists, and the school are certain that he can read and write fluently and with ease and pleasure. The basic techniques of reading and writing must have become so automatic that the child no longer has to pay any attention to them. He must understand the reading process so well that he can develop it further on his own and read the increasingly more difficult texts required in the higher grades and eventually at work or in college. To dismiss a child from reading therapy after he has passed a reading test on his grade level is not good enough. This unfortunately is the usual procedure. He may fail the same test 2 months later without continued treatment, having forgotten most of what he had been taught. One can only be certain that the memory defect has been overcome when there is proof that the conditioned-reflex basis for reading has been firmly established—that is, that the underlying technique has become automatic. This requires the observation of the child's reading and writing (to dictation and spontaneously) over a prolonged period of time, in addition to special tests (see pp. 74 ff., 82).

Danger of Premature Termination

Treatment is unfortunately much too frequently terminated prematurely for other reasons as well. It may, for instance, be simply dropped informally after the summer vacation without consultation with the school. All the adults may have too many other problems on their mind at the beginning of school in the fall, and they may not have taken the child's reading problem very seriously anyhow. Staff changes sometimes also lead to premature termination of treatment. The reading or the speech therapist may leave the school or the clinic and not be replaced, or the child psychiatric resident who was the child's psychotherapist may finish his residency, and the new residents may have no treatment time for "old" cases. A family moving away from the school's and the clinic's district may also end the child's treatment. There may be no clinic in the child's new neighborhood; the clinic may have a long waiting list or no educational therapist; or the clinic may refuse to accept him, usually for administrative rather than clinical reasons. This lack of continued treatment is a dilemma all mental hygiene clinic patients face, regardless of their age and of their diagnosis.

Private treatment tends to be more continuous, provided the parents can afford to pay the different specialists, who may want to see the child as often as several times a week.

Importance of Availability of Treatment

I want to emphasize again that individual reading treatment should be available to all children who need it, regardless of their parents' ability to pay, and especially to elementary-school children. No child should have to live through the agony of having to go through elementary school with a reading disorder that has been neither diagnosed nor corrected. The 5 or 6 years a child spends in elementary school should give the school personnel enough time to find out that he has a reading disorder and to see to it that it is corrected. If this were done, no child would enter junior high or high school with an undiagnosed and untreated reading disorder (organic, sociogenic, or psychogenic), as tens of thousands of children now do.

Reading therapists should either be employed by the schools directly or by child psychiatric clinics outside schools. The schools should provide quiet rooms for individual reading treatment for the use of outside reading therapists as well as their own. Only in this way can this vital service be provided for all children, including those whose parents cannot pay for it privately. No treatment should, of course, be done without the parents' knowledge and consent.

What I am suggesting may seem utopian because of the shortage of reading therapists and of money to employ them. All available reading therapists are at present overwhelmed with children needing their services. Their caseloads can be reduced only with fundamental changes in mass reading teaching methods along the lines I am suggesting. If these methods are not changed and improved nationwide, the task of correcting reading and writing disorders will remain unmanageable even with a large increase in reading therapists. Only under these static conditions, so tragic for the children, do my suggestions face insurmountable obstacles.

Systematic Noncompetitive Physical Exercises

Children with any type of reading disorder can benefit from this exercise treatment. All of them have an attention disorder and these exercises help them learn to concentrate. Special curative physical exercises are indispensable for children with a neurotic or an organic reading disorder. Distractibility, hyperactivity, and body-image problems cannot be cured without them. A detailed description of these exercises is provided in Vol. II under Attention

Disorders, pp. 534. I want to stress again that classroom teachers, as well as teachers of special education and of physical education, should be familiar with them, recommend them, and apply them. Neurologists, pediatricians, child psychiatrists and psychologists should also include them in their treatment planning (See Vol. II: p. 666 under Hyperactivity; p. 543 under Distractibility; p. 681 under Irritability.)

Pharmacotherapy

Drug therapy is used extensively for children with "learning disabilities" or MBD (Minimal Brain Dysfunction). The indications are, unfortunately, never clearly defined, as I point out in the section on Drug Treatment of Hyperactivity (Vol. II, pp. 658–659). However, drug treatment can help the child only indirectly with his reading disorder. Drugs can calm down an anxious, excitable, or hyperactive child and help him to improve his concentration and his intellectual attention. They can also improve the sleep of a child who has insomnia, so that he is more alert and attentive in school. Such a child still will not learn to read if he does not want to for neurotic and other reasons, if he is bored, does not understand the reading process, or has a malfunctioning cerebral reading apparatus. This form of treatment should therefore never be used alone. Children who are so disturbed that they need drug treatment also need reading treatment, preferably on an individual basis.

It must also be stressed that the improvement of a child's behavior through drugs does not mean that his reading disorder, his hyperactivity, or his other symptoms have an organic basis. The very administration of drugs presents a strong suggestion. Children are suggestible: A child may fall asleep because he is convinced that the drug will make him sleepy; he may become much less anxious and feel more secure because he thinks at last something is being done to help him, and that the drug will have this effect. So far as stimulants are concerned (dexedrine, Ritalin, Cylert, etc.), overstimulation of the child's sympathetic nervous system can have an organic or a psychologic basis (see Vol. II, p. 661).

Details of drug treatment and its undesirable effects, as well as prevention of harm by stimulant drugs are circumscribed in great detail in the section on hyperactivity. General principles of drug administration may be found on Vol. II, pp. 657–659; their misuse and overuse, and successful educational treatment without drugs are described on Vol. II, pp. 661–662. For information about tranquilizers, antianxiety drugs, and sedatives, see Vol. II pp. 663–664.

I want to stress again that the purpose of drug treatment should be explained in detail to the parents and the child separately, and that the child should never have access to drugs. Under no condition should he be sent to school with a pillbox. Drugs should be administered to the child only by adults, preferably his parents.

Children and their parents must understand that the ingestion of drugs should not be taken lightly. It should not be given playfully, like candy. The increase of drug abuse among elementary-school children shows that children have been misled into thinking that drugs can do no harm and bring only pleasure.

For drug treatment of free-floating anxiety, see Vol. II, p. 663, of Irritability, see Vol. II, p. 682; of Mood Disorder, Vol. II, p. 686.

Parental Guidance

All forms of reading treatment have the best chance to succeed when the child's parents are involved in the treatment plan. They should understand the difficulties and the goals of treatment and be advised how to help their child. It is usually best if they leave the child alone and do not help him with homework, unless he asks for assistance. Eileen Simpson stresses this point, based on her own experience as well as experience with counseling such parents. She writes that by the time parents consulted her, "nightly lessons had deteriorated into shouting and crying scenes." She recommends to all these parents "that they leave the actual training to the remedial reading teacher" (1979, p. 209). (See also case of Doug, p. 118.)

An exception to this rule is spelling. When such a child asks parents or siblings to spell a word for him, they should do it, rather than referring him to the dictionary or forcing him to figure it out on his own (see p. 117).

What all these parents should do is to read to their child regularly, every day. That is how Eileen Simpson and many of her co-sufferers learned to appreciate literature long before they could read. However, says Simpson, to be effective, the parents themselves have to read well and to enjoy reading aloud (1979, p. 209).

When a child's parents are unable or unwilling to participate in the treatment plan, the child should be treated anyhow. A reading disorder can be cured even without the parent's cooperation. However, their consent is required.

Psychotherapy

Psychotherapy and Education

Psychotherapy, literally translated from its Greek origin, means treatment with psychologic methods. Educators also use psychologic methods, but they are fundamentally different. Understanding these differences is vital so that these methods do not become antagonistic and destructive for the child. The goals of education and psychotherapy coincide, but the means are different and they should not collide.

Psychotherapeutic methods should never be antieducational. That is why it is so important for the psychotherapist to keep educational as well as therapeutic goals in mind, and why educators and psychotherapists should not work parallel to each other, but instead should collaborate with each other and integrate their approach. Unless this is done, the child may be exposed to unnecessary conflicts and confusions that delay recovery from his psychopathology, while also damaging his progress in reading.

Some minor but important and effective psychologic methods are used by educators as well as psychotherapists whether or not they are aware of it, as they should be. Awareness is a precondition for the successful use of all psychologic methods, even though teachers and psychotherapists put different emphasis on them and use them in different contexts. These minor methods are: suggestion, reassurance, persuasion, and verbalization.

SUGGESTION.   Anna Freud describes suggestion as one of the "inevitable consequences of the analyst's temporary position of power and emotional importance in the patient's life." She considers it one of the "so-called 'educational' side effects of analytic treatment" (1965, pp. 227–228). It is a powerful method not only for psychoanalysts, but for all psychotherapists and for teachers and educational therapists as well. They should realize that every question they ask carries a suggestion with it, as do all their statements, requests, explanations, and interpretations.

REASSURANCE.   Anna Freud stresses that reassurance is "inseparable from the presence of and close intimacy with a trusted adult" (1965, p. 228). It helps the child overcome anxiety and feelings of inferiority and incompetence, it strengthens his self-confidence, and makes him more independent. It is an indispensable method for both teacher and psychotherapist for a child with a reading disorder on any basis.

PERSUASION.   A good teacher uses persuasion skillfully with many reluctant students, especially with those who have trouble with reading. Psychotherapy cannot be successful without it, especially with children and adolescents.

VERBALIZATION.   Teachers use verbalization when they encourage the child to talk or write about his feelings and to discuss his thoughts, ideas, doubts, and conflicts. This is one of the many reasons it is so important to teach a large and varied vocabulary as well as the accurate use of words. Giving names to obscure emotions and figuring out vague ideas has a liberating, therapeutic effect. This method forms an important part of all forms of psychotherapy. Anna Freud mentions it especially as an important therapeutic tool (1965, p. 227).

THE CHILD'S RELATIONSHIP WITH HIS TEACHER.   From the child's point of view, his relationship with his teacher is easy to understand even though it may arouse complicated feelings. The child knows where he stands: He is supposed to listen, obey, do the work the teacher asks him to do, look up to him or her, and accept her or his guidance during the schoolday.

Teachers work in a setting, an atmosphere, and a frame of reference that stresses learning—that is, purposeful intellectual activities and deliberate control of behavior. Although feelings are of course involved, they get less attention and are subject to restraints. Intellectual rather than emotional expression is encouraged.

The teacher's task is to impart intellectual knowledge. For the child, this does involve feelings and complicated relationships to her and to the other children in the class. It furthers the child's healthy and harmonious intellectual as well as emotional growth, but in a structured setting with a time limit. The teacher's involvement with the child usually does not extend beyond one school year; it affects one age level only.

Teachers must of necessity concentrate on the healthy, teachable aspects of the child's personality. They cannot be expected to and should not try to unearth hidden, possibly pathologic thoughts and emotions. Their relationship with the individual child needs to be somewhat distant and detached, especially as they see him primarily in a group, as part of their class.

THE CHILD'S RELATIONSHIP WITH GUIDANCE COUNSELORS AND EDUCATIONAL THERAPISTS.   The child's relationship with those educators whom he sees on an individual basis is much closer, but remains within the educational framework with its stress on learning, namely on conscious, self-controlled efforts by the child. Never mind how free the relationship, it still takes place within a clear-cut, easily understandable structure. This is as it should be. The child needs this structure to learn reading and other subjects, as well as constructive behavior in the classroom. It helps him ward off distracting impulses, thoughts, and feelings—and the anxiety they arouse.

THE CHILD'S RELATIONSHIP WITH HIS PSYCHOTHERAPIST.   This relationship is quite different. It is unique, intimate, not shared with other children, complicated, full of conflicts, and often quite mysterious for the child. It is based primarily on feelings, and involves hidden thoughts and emotions that are active, at least partially, in the child's unconscious. The structure of the child–psychotherapist relationship is loose and is determined entirely by the child's needs, questions, direct and indirect communications. It is not subject to any instructional plan. The therapist's task is to help the child understand his own feelings, thoughts, and motivations so that he can find his own ways of getting out of his dilemmas and of overcoming his symptoms and psychopathology.

Guidance counselors and educational therapists should not permit a child to develop this type of extremely intimate and complicated relationship with them, because it invariably leads to a destructive experience for the child. It confuses him, he becomes preoccupied with it, and it cannot be resolved in a constructive way in an educational setting.

I have seen guidance counselors and educational therapists slide quite innocently into such a relationship with a child, without being aware of what was happening to them or to the child. I have unfortunately also seen children who were deliberately encouraged by these educators to form such an attachment. Educators can guard themselves against falling into this sort of relationship with their students by having a clear understanding of their own task, and by studying the fundamental Freudian concepts of the different mental layers, the structure of the personality, and its pathology. Knowledge of some fundamental clinical facts will give them a better perspective of their own role.

There are at present far too many amateurs without any clinical knowledge and experience practicing "psychotherapy" based only on their own analysis. This has been harmful especially for children and adolescents.

DIFFERENCE BETWEEN FREUDIAN TRANSFERENCE AND ADMIRATION OF AND CONFIDENCE IN AN EDUCATOR.   A distinction must be made between transference in the Freudian sense and the achievement of trust and confidence necessary for guidance and educational treatment. It is a difference not only in quantity, but also in quality.

Many experiences a child has in school touch the unconscious in some subtle way. In this sense, teaching, educational guidance, and treatment also influence it indirectly. However, only psychotherapy is equipped to involve the unconscious deliberately by using special methods to uncover repressed thoughts, feelings, and experiences—provided this is necessary to cure the child's psychopathology. A Freudian type of transference develops, where the child relives current and previous painful love relationships in his relationship with his psychotherapist. The child is never entirely aware of this transfer of very strong feelings to the therapist. It is a neurotic relationship, a transference neurosis. This reliving, together with the therapist's explanations, is supposed to lead to a resolution of the child's conflicts and to enable him to overcome his symptoms and psychopathology.

It must be stressed that it is very often not necessary to uncover the unconscious for a good therapeutic result. It may be harmful, especially for children and adolescents, and should be undertaken only under the strictest indications and only by psychotherapists who have mastered the skill of resolving this transference without injuring their patients.

Psychotherapy requires two seemingly opposite considerations. The psychotherapist must become close enough to the child to enter his world and to influence him. It is important that the therapist tie the child to himself or herself, while at the same time guiding him away gently so that this tie does not become a burden for the child, smother him, and prevent him from acquiring self-confidence, self-reliance, and ultimately, independence. The therapist must not give in to the temptation common to adults, to show their love and at the same time satisfy their own needs for love and power, by making the child utterly dependent on them.

Becoming close to a child and at the same time setting him free is an art. Teachers, guidance counselors, and educational therapists need to master it too, although on a different level. They stand "in loco parentis" (in the place of the parents) for a limited period of time. They cannot replace parents, however, and they should not try to. The power of their influence on the child lies precisely in the fact that they are different and have a different, much less intimate relationship with him.

Indications for Psychotherapy

GENERAL CONSIDERATIONS.   Whether a child with a reading disorder can benefit from psychotherapy at all depends not only on the nature and severity of his psychopathology, but also on his emotional maturity, the level of his intelligence, and his ability to talk—that is, to communicate complicated thoughts and feelings verbally. Psychotherapy cannot be done with an aphasic child who cannot talk at all or say only a few words, or who cannot understand what is said to him.

A child's intellectual capacity should also be within normal limits, otherwise he cannot respond to psychotherapy. The child's I.Q. rating alone, however, cannot determine this. Some mentally defective children have a richer and more flexible intellectual and fantasy life than others, and psychotherapy may help them. As a general rule, however, psychotherapy of truly mentally defective children has little hope of success. For even though child psychotherapy deals to a large extent with emotions and uses nonverbal and indirect methods of communication such as drawing, painting, and play, the child must still be capable of putting feelings and thoughts into words, sentences, and gestures, and of understanding what the therapist says. (See cases of Joseph, p. 296; Alfred, p. 107; Kirk, Vol. II, p. 606 and Ned, Vol. II, p. 648.)

INDICATIONS FOR PSYCHOTHERAPY OF CHILDREN WITH AN ORGANIC READING DISORDER.

1. A child's psychologic reaction to his organic reading disorder and other organic symptoms may be so severe and complex that it cannot be resolved with corrective education alone. For instance, he may develop a depression, disruptive behavior, or neurotic symptoms.

2. The organic reading disorder may set a neurotic process in motion. Psychotherapy is the treatment of choice for neurosis.

Nine-year-old Jose, for instance, whose plight I describe under Directional Confusion of Letters and Words, had the neurotic symptoms of hair pulling (trichotillomania), skin picking, and anxious dreams. He was treated with the Barger Mirroreading Board and psychotherapy. (See p. 105.)

3. A child may also have neurotic symptoms that are not necessarily caused by his organic symptoms. They must be evaluated and treated on their own merits. Seven-year-old Emilio, 10-year-old Richard, and 12-year-old Darryl are examples of this type of neurotic symptom (See pp. 169; 129; 113).

Timing of Psychotherapy

In most cases, psychotherapy should be started at the same time as corrective education. However, some children need psychotherapy as the initial treatment to enable them to respond to corrective teaching. The task of psychotherapy in these cases is to remove conscious and unconscious obstacles that block the child's reading, and to arouse his interest and curiosity. This initial psychotherapy is quite crucial and indispensable for many children with either an organic or a psychogenic reading disorder.

Psychotherapy may also be indicated later on, after educational treatment has started. The child's teacher or his educational therapist or both may have come to an impasse with the child and his progress may have stopped. These children usually need psychotherapy because it alone can break through their neurotic anxieties and inhibitions, which obstruct their learning ability. Where there is any doubt, the child should be re-examined by the psychiatrist or the psychologist or both, so that all factors can be carefully weighed to determine whether psychotherapy is the method of choice to help the child resume his progress in reading.

The psychotherapy of the following symptoms is especially important for children with reading disorders.

Psychotherapy of Anxiety

What psychotherapy does especially well and can often accomplish within a short period of time is to alleviate all forms of anxiety. "Free-floating" anxiety, which is diffuse and affects all levels of the child's personality, or specific phobias are therefore good indications for psychotherapy. It does not matter whether the anxiety is caused by organic symptoms or is psychologic in origin. (See case of Joseph, p. 296.)

However, there are exceptions. Some children with severe organic symptoms suffer from a malignant form of anxiety that does not respond to psychotherapy. I have seen this form only in children who had multiple organic symptoms in addition to an organic reading disorder. This anxiety, which Lauretta Bender calls "basic primary" anxiety, can be contained only with drug therapy combined with special management at home and in the classroom. The same applies to severe forms of schizophrenic anxiety.

It is important to realize that the disappearance of a symptom such as anxiety in response to psychotherapy does not necessarily mean that its cause was psychogenic; neither does its response to drug therapy mean that it was organic.

Psychotherapy of Violent Behavior

Group or individual psychotherapy can eliminate such behavior if it is done skillfully and is based on the realization that violence is contagious, that violent play during the psychotherapeutic session stimulates violence in the child's daily life. Playing with guns or playing darts is not a curative method; it is not a form of catharsis that relieves the hostile feelings underlying violent behavior. The psychotherapist should search carefully and in great detail for the origins of the child's anger and hostility, both those he is aware of and those repressed into the unconscious. The child should be made to realize that he may not be able to control his feelings, but that he can control their violent expression. He can learn to distinguish these two processes.

ROLE OF GUILT FEELINGS. Exploration of the patient's guilt feelings is an indispensable part of psychotherapy. It is especially important for children and adolescents who behave violently. Wertham stresses this in *Dark Legend,* the study of an adolescent boy who killed his mother. He writes:

> A feeling of guilt may be unconscious in two senses. In the first place, the feeling itself may not be experienced as guilt at all, but as vague anxiety which cannot be assuaged. In the second place, the cause of this feeling may have been repressed from consciousness (1966, p. 135).

Psychotherapy must pinpoint the sources of guilt feelings and their disguises, then help the child understand them and deal with them in a nonviolent way. This is essential for the prevention of suicide and other self-destructive acts as well as destructive activities directed against others. Anxiety and guilt feelings as well as hostility may lead to violent behavior.

Just as important is the exploration of the absence of guilt feelings when they should be present to prevent violent behavior. This is where the influence of social forces, including education and the mass media, plays a decisive role.

Psychotherapy can be successful only if it deals not just with feelings alone, but also pays serious attention to the child's thoughts and ideas. False ideas instilled in children play just as important a part in causing violent behavior as unrestrained feelings. In *The Circle of Guilt*, a study of an adolescent boy involved in a gang murder, Wertham stresses that "many delinquents are not 'bad'; they are poisoned" (1956, p. 156). It is therefore imperative for the psychotherapist to find out how the child justifies his violent acts. Many children have been led to believe that they can only assert themselves and prove that they are worth something by violence. To them, a violent act is heroic; it is a good act. (See pp. 284–285 under Juvenile Delinquency.)

Close cooperation by the psychotherapist with parents and teachers is especially important for the successful treatment of violent behavior. They should convey the same ethical principles to the child and help him to clarify his confusions about what is right and what wrong. As an adolescent girl with a reading disorder and arrests for participation in stealing and destructive acts told me sadly when I asked her what bothered her most; "I am all mixed up about right and wrong!"

To help these children resolve their moral dilemma, adults caring for them should keep Freud's definition of a decent, moral person in mind. He wrote: "A person has a high moral sense when he does not even give in to a temptation he only senses inwardly" (1978, p. 273—author's translation).

Play-group therapy or treatment in a talking group is sometimes the most successful therapeutic approach. Many children reveal their violent behavior and the reasons for it only in the presence of other children. Treatment is therefore most successful in such a setting (Daniels, 1964) (See pp. 287, 334). (See Figures 7.1, 7.2.)

Special Problems of Psychotherapy of Organic Reading Disorders and Other Organic Symptoms

Psychotherapy cannot heal the underlying organic impairments, but it can influence their psychopathologic manifestations and help the child cope with his handicap or to utilize it in some constructive way and live with it. Too many children are deprived of this vital form of treatment because of the erroneous assumption that organic disorders by their very nature preclude psychotherapy. The psychotherapeutic methods used for the treatment of these children must be based on a detailed knowledge of their organic symptoms as well as the psychologic symptoms caused by the organic defects. This form of therapy is doomed to failure otherwise.

Anna Freud has found that even psychoanalysis, which is such a special form of psychotherapy, is applicable within certain definite limits to children

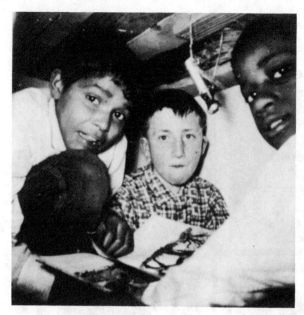

FIG. 7.1.   Three 11-year-old boys in play group therapy, reading and listening spontaneously in a "house" they built themselves; they picked the book out of the clinic
library. The boy who is reading is recovering from an organic reading disorder. The
boy in the middle had aphasia; the reading disorder of the boy on the right was
psychogenic. (Photo by Hilde Mosse.)

with organic disorders. In her book, *Normality and Pathology in Childhood*,
she writes that

> even in cases with organic defect (birth injury, minor brain damage) improve-
> ments are brought about in the severe impairments of personality formation.
> Where a comparatively normal ego exerts excessive pressure on a very impover-
> ished drive constellation, the child profits from the stimulation of fantasy and
> opening up of outlets for id derivatives which are by-products of the analytic
> situation. Where average drive activity is insufficiently controlled by an under-
> developed ego, the analyst's role and action as "auxiliary ego," another by-
> product of analysis, come to the patient's help (1965, p. 232).

This does not mean that psychotherapy can cure an organic reading and
writing disorder. As a matter of fact, it can help the child best if it is combined
with different forms of corrective education, casework treatment of the parents, and drug therapy, if indicated—or whatever other treatments the child
and his family need.

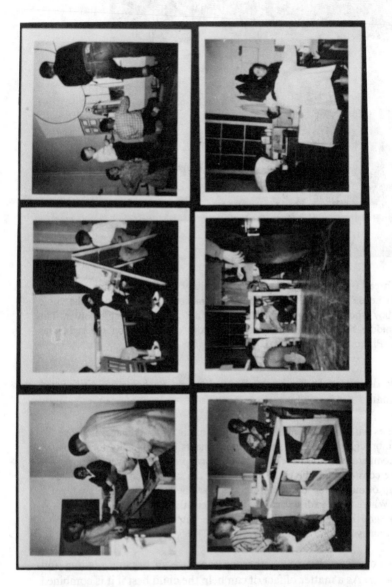

FIG. 7.2. Scenes from play group therapy. The three boys in Fig. 7.1 are here too. Most of the other children have various reading disorders associated with unspecific organic or/and severe behavioral symptoms. Boy with glasses playing with the sandbox has psychogenic mutism. (Photo by Hilde Mosse.)

Psychotherapy alone usually cannot cure a child with a psychogenic or a sociogenic reading disorder either. The technical basis of reading and writing English is just too difficult to grasp, so that many of these children also need reading treatment.

Psychotherapy as the Only Treatment for an Organic Reading Disorder

However, psychotherapy alone can be of considerable help to a child with an organic reading disorder, even though it may not cure the disorder completely. Its success with 8-year-old Orlando shows how this can be done.

ORLANDO, 8 YEARS OLD: HIS ORGANIC READING DISORDER WAS ALLEVIATED WITH PSYCHOTHERAPY ALONE.   Orlando was referred to me because he was distractible, excitable, had a short attention span, clowned, and provoked fights with his classmates. His teacher reported that he had "obviously no interest in learning to read, write, or remember, but he loves to look at books and to be read to." She thought he might be mentally retarded and eligible for placement in a CRMD class.

I found him to be suffering from a severe organic reading and writing disorder. He could not read any word and had barely managed to memorize how to write his first name. He could copy slowly and with great effort, but could write no other word either to dictation or spontaneously. He was a comic book addict, of course only to the pictures because he could not read. Fortunately he was also fascinated by what he called "library books" and wanted very much to learn to read. The psychologist found that he was not retarded, and my examination also showed no sign of this. His severe reading disorder together with his neurotic and behavioral symptoms prevented his intelligence from developing normally.

Orlando's behavior disorder and neurotic symptoms were caused not only by his inability to learn to read, but also by a traumatic family situation, and especially by his mother's negative attitude toward him. He had never seen his father, who abandoned his mother before he was born. He had two older brothers whom his mother had practically abandoned. They were being raised in Puerto Rico by their grandmother. Another brother, age 6, had a different father. His mother preferred this brother. From the age of 2 until 5, Orlando was boarded out by his mother together with his younger brother. She visited, but the boys lived apart from her. This separation from his mother came at an age when children are especially vulnerable to it. Orlando never felt comfortable with and accepted by his mother after that. She thought of him as "crazy" and felt that she could not do much about that.

By the time I examined him, he and his brother lived together with their mother again. There was a new stepfather (not the father of his younger brother) who was not particularly fond of him. The language spoken at home was Spanish. Orlando had a mild speech defect in both English and Spanish.

I found that he was immature for his age and tried hard to cover up a deep-seated free-floating anxiety that made him restless, fidgety, unhappy, and unable to concentrate on anything, either work or play. He had anxious dreams. He was friendly and in good contact and reached out for help. He had episodes of excitement that he could not control. At times he could not distinguish fantasy from reality.

I made the diagnosis of an organic reading and writing disorder, aggravated by a neurosis. I recommended corrective reading treatment, preferably on an individual basis, psychotherapy for him, and casework treatment for his mother.

The social worker kept in close touch with Orlando in school and with his teachers. She did her best to reach his mother, but she was not really interested in any consistent contact. She came only on an emergency basis, when she could not stand the pressures and conflicts at home, or when Orlando was in trouble in school. It was impossible to find a corrective reading teacher or a special class for him, and individual psychotherapy also could not be arranged. This was the reason I accepted him for group psychotherapy. He was not getting any better and something had to be done for him.

Orlando attended one of my play-therapy groups. He came regularly and entirely on his own. His mother refused to bring him since she was working and felt she could not take any time off. He was an active member of the group from the very beginning and was very much involved emotionally. Separation anxiety was an outstanding symptom, which took almost an entire schoolyear to overcome. He became excited, anxious, and uncontrollable when it was time to go home. He did not want to leave the clinic, hid under furniture and in the hallways, and ran back into the building many times before I could persuade him to go home.

Play-group therapy improved his behavior as well as his reading to such degree that his sixth-grade teacher (who had known him throughout elementary school) wanted to know how we had taught him to read. His reading was then almost at the fifth-grade level. At first she would not believe that no member of the clinic staff had ever taught him to read, but this is exactly what had happened.

The reason that Orlando learned to read without corrective reading treatment was that psychotherapy brought about emotional changes that allowed him to concentrate and to figure out the reading process on his own and with his teacher's help. Psychotherapy had freed him from his anxiety, had given him a feeling of stability and self-confidence, and had taught him how to get along with other children without his former overwhelming feelings of jealousy and inferiority. He felt no need to clown any more to get attention, and he no longer confused reality with fantasy.

Psychotherapy was discontinued when he entered junior high school. He visited the clinic on his own initiative from time to time after that. When I saw him last, he was 19 years old. He came to the clinic to translate from Spanish into English for a family we knew. He told me that he had dropped out of high school and worked at several jobs before he realized that he would never make enough money without some special training. Therefore he joined the Job Corps voluntarily and was being trained as an x-ray technician. He liked it very much and seemed calm and content and free of any neurotic or behavioral symptoms.

The case of Orlando shows the efficacy of psychotherapy in organic reading disorders, but it also shows its limitations. Had Orlando also had corrective reading treatment, he would have caught up with his classmates long before the sixth grade, and he probably would not have dropped out of high school. For even though his reading improved, it remained cumbersome for him so that he had to take a course in reading in the Job Corps. (See Psychotherapy of Psychogenic Mutism, Vol. II, p. 407 under Speech Disorders; Psychotherapy of Hyperactivity, Vol. II, p. 666; Psychotherapy of Psychogenic Reading Disorders, p. 253; Psychotherapy of Sociogenic Reading Disorders, p. 287.)

The prognosis for the treatment of all reading disorders is excellent. Only a small number of children with the severe organic type cannot be completely cured.

References

Adey, W. R. Neural information processing: Windows without and the citadel within. In *The proceedings of an international symposium on biocybernetics of the central nervous system.* Boston: Little, Brown & Co., 1969, Chap. 1.

Admiral Says U.S. Navy Is Hindered by Illiteracy, *New York Times,* July 5, 1977.

American Psychiatric Association. *Diagnostic and statistical manual of mental disorders* (3rd ed.) (DSM-III). Washington, D.C., 1980.

Ames, L. B., & Ilg, F. L. *Mosaic patterns of American children.* New York: Hoeber Medical Division, Harper & Bros., 1962.

A nation of illiterates? *New York Times,* September 30, 1979.

Artley, A. S. Yearbook of N.E.A. 1955. school page, *New York Herald Tribune,* September 28, 1955.

Barclay, L. G. Diagnosis and treatment of reading disorders. In *Realizing the potential of the individual in the great society.* Proceedings of the Bureau of Child Guidance All-Day Institute on Mental Health and Education, Board of Education of the City of New York, January 28, 1966.

Barclay, R. L. Dyslexia: A footnote (Letters to the Editor). *American Journal of Psychiatry,* 1967, *124,* 408.

Barger, W. C. An experimental approach to aphasic and nonreading children. *American Journal of Orthopsychiatry,* 1953, *XXIII*(1), 158–169.

Barger, W. C. Late reading in children. *Cerebral Palsy Bulletin,* 1959, *7,* 20–26.

Barger, W. C. *The mirror technique for difficult readers.* Ft. Lauderdale: Barclay, 1960.

Barger, W. C. Neuropsychiatry and pediatrics: Diagnostic entities. *Abstracts, VI World Congress of Psychiatry, Honolulu, Hawaii,* 1977, *1124,* 205.

Barness, L. A. Malnutrition in children beyond infancy. In W. E. Nelson (Ed.), *Textbook of Pediatrics* (11th ed.). Philadelphia: W. B. Saunders Co., 1979, p. 215.

Barr, D. *Who pushed Humpty Dumpty? Dilemmas in American education today.* New York: Atheneum, 1971.

Beeson, P. B. The development of clinical knowledge. *Journal of the American Medical Association,* 1977, *237,* 20.

Bender, L. Problems of conceptualization and communication in children with developmental alexia. In S. G. Sapir & A. C. Nitzburg (Eds.), *Children with learning problems.* New York: Brunner-Mazel, 1973, chap. 33. (Also in P. H. Hoch & J. Zubin, *Psychopathology of communication.* New York: Grune & Stratton, 1958, chap. II.)

Benson, F. D., & Geschwind, N. Developmental Gerstmann syndrome. *Neurology,* 1970, *20,* 293–298.

Benson, F. D., & N. Geschwind. The alexias. In P. J. Vinken & G. W. Bruyn (Eds.), *Handbook of clinical neurology,* vol. 4. New York: American Elsevier Publishing Co., 1969.

Best, C. H., & Taylor, N. B. *The physiological basis of medical practice* (3rd ed.). Baltimore: The Williams & Wilkins Co., 1943.

Birch, H. G., & Belmont, L. Lateral dominance, lateral awareness and reading disability. *Child Development,* 1965, *36,* 57–71.

Blair, G. M. *Diagnostic and remedial reading.* New York: The Macmillan Co., 1956.

Bloch, A. M. Combat neurosis in inner city schools. *American Journal of Psychiatry,* 1978, *135* (10), 1189–1192.

Brain, Sir Russell, *Speech Disorders,* Washington, D.C.: Butterworth Inc., 1961.

Brobeck, J. R. Higher neural functions, neural control systems. In J. R. Brobeck (Ed.), *Best & Taylor's physiological basis of medical practice* (9th ed.). Baltimore: The Williams & Wilkins Co., 1973, chap. 8, section 9.

Brückner, A., & Meisner, W. *Grundrisse der Augenheilkunde für Studierende und praktische Ärzte.* Leipzig: George Thieme, 1920.

Bucy, P. C. Electroencephalography's proper role (Editorial). *Journal of the American Medical Association,* 1956, *160,* 14.

Buder, L. Decline continues in reading ability of pupils in city. *New York Times,* November 19, 1972.

Bureau of Elementary Curriculum development, New York State Education Department. *The elementary school curriculum, an overview.* 1954.

Capeci, J. Wins 500 G for "retarded" tag. *New York Post,* November 7, 1978.

Carnine, D., & Silbert, J. *Direct instruction reading.* Columbus, Ohio: Charles E. Merrill Publ. Co., 1979.

Chagall, D. The child probers. *TV Guide,* 1977, October 8–14, pp. 8–12.

Chall, J. S. *Learning to read: The great debate.* New York: McGraw-Hill Book Co., 1967.

Chall, J. S. *Reading 1967–1977: A decade of change and promise.* Bloomington, Ind.: The Phi Delta Kappa Educational Foundation, 1977.

Charles, C. M. *Teacher's Petit Piaget.* Belmont, Calif.: Fearon Publishers, Inc., 1974.

Cheating on the I.Q. test. *New York Times,* November 6, 1978.

Chess, S., Korn, S. J., & Fernandez, P. B. *Psychiatric disorders of children with congenital rubella.* New York: Brunner-Mazel, 1971.

Clark, D. The nervous system. In W. E. Nelson (Ed.), *Textbook of pediatrics* (9th ed.). Philadelphia: W. B. Saunders Co., 1969.

Conrad, K. Beitrag zum Problem der parietalen Alexie. In *Ein Querschnitt durch die Arbeit der Tübinger Nervenklinik.* Berlin: Springer Verlag, 1949.

Crandall, B. Decline in reading of the classics in public schools causes concern. *New York Times,* May 29, 1977.

Critchley, M. *The parietal lobes.* London: Edward Arnold Publishers, Ltd., 1953.

Critchley, M. Isolation of specific dyslexic. In A. H. Keeney & V. T. Keeney (Eds.), *Dyslexia, diagnosis and treatment of reading disorders.* St. Louis: C. V. Mosby Co., 1968, chap. 3(1).

Critchley, M. Topics worthy of research. In A. H. Keeney & V. T. Keeney (Eds.), *Dyslexia, diagnosis and treatment of reading disorders.* St. Louis: C. V. Mosby Co., 1968, chap. 14 (2).

Critchley, M. *Developmental dyslexia.* London: William Heinemann Medical Books, Ltd., 1964.

Critchley, M. *The dyslexic child.* London: William Heinemann Medical Books, Ltd., 1970.

Cronkite, W. Cronkite faults papers and TV, citing coverage. *New York Times,* April 26, 1979.

Cureton action reading. Boston: Allyn and Bacon, 1977.

Daniels, C. R. Play group therapy with children. *Acta Psychotherapeutica,* 1964, *12,* 45–52.

Delacato, C. H. *The treatment and prevention of reading problems.* New York: Charles C Thomas, 1959.

Diak, H. *Reading and the psychology of perception.* New York: Philosophical Library, 1960.

Diak, H., & Daniels, J. C. The nature of reading skill. In C. C. Walcutt (Ed.), *Tomorrow's illiterates.* Washington, D.C.: Council for Basic Education. Boston: Little, Brown and Co., 1961.

The Doman-Delacato treatment of neurologically handicapped children. (Statement approved by: American Academy for Cerebral Palsy, American Academy of Neurology, American

Academy of Pediatrics, American Academy for Physical Medicine and Rehabilitation, American Congress of Rehabilitation Medicine, American Academy of Orthopedics, Canadian Association for Children with Learning Disabilities, Canadian Association for Retarded Children, Canadian Rehabilitation Council, National Association for Retarded Children.) *Developmental Medicine and Child Neurology,* 1968, *10,* 243–246.

Doman, R. J., Spitz, E. B., Zuckman, E., Delacato, C. H., & Doman, G. Children with servere brain injuries. *Journal of the American Medical Association,* 1960, *174* (3), 257–262.

Dörken, H. The Mosaic test: A second review. *Journal of Projective Techniques,* 1956, *20*(2), 164–171.

Eames, T. H. Physical factors in reading. In G. Natchez (Ed.), *Children with reading problems.* New York: Basic Books, 1968, chap. 11, pp. 37–143.

Editorial. *Journal of the American Medical Association,* 1968, *206,* 3.

Engels, F. *Dialectics of nature.* Moscow: Foreign Languages Publ. House, 1954.

Falvo, C. E., & Flanigan, J. M. Child Health Assurance Program, Study in duplication and fragmentation. *New York State Journal of Medicine,* April 1979, 721–724.

Feuchtwanger, E. In Kraus, Brugsch (Eds.), *Die Arteriosklerose des Gehirns und Rückenmarks,* Chap. in *Spezielle Bathologie und Therapie innerer Krankheiten.* Berlin, Wien: Urban u. Schwarzenberg, 1929.

Fish, B. Involvement of the central nervous system in infants with schizophrenia. *Archives Neurol.,* 1960, 115–121.

Fiske, E. B. Study cites student writing deficiencies. *New York Times,* February 23, 1977.

Fiske, E. B. City pupils remain behind in reading—Official asserts the tests suggest difficulty in early grades. *New York Times,* March 8, 1979.

Flesch, R. *Why Johnny can't read and what you can do about it.* New York: Harper & Bros., 1955.

Flesch, R. Why Johnny still can't read. *Family Circle,* November 1, 1979.

Flexner, A. *Medical education in the United States and Canada.* New York: Carnegie Foundation for the Advancement of Teaching, 1910.

Footnote, The New Yorker, March 18, 1967.

Freud, A. *Normality and pathology in childhood.* New York: International Universities Press, 1965.

Freud, S. The interpretation of dreams. In A. A. Brill (Ed.), *The basic writings of Sigmund Freud.* New York: Random House (The Modern Library), 1938.

Freud, S. [Character and anal erotism] In *Collected papers* (vol. II). London: Hogarth Press, 1942, pp. 45–50. (a) (Originally published, 1908.)

Freud, S. [On the transformation of instincts with special reference to anal erotism] pp. 164–171. In *Collected papers* (vol. II). London: Hogarth Press, 1942, (b) (Originally published, 1916.)

Freud, S. [Dostojewski and patricide] *International Journal of Psycho-Analysis,* 1945, *XXVI,* 1–8.

Freud, S. Dostoevsky and patricide. In *Character and culture.* New York: Collier Books, 1978, pp. 273–293.

Freud, S. [Formulations regarding the two principles in mental functioning] In *Collected papers* (vol. IV). London: Hogarth Press, 1946, chap. 1, pp. 13–21. (a) (Originally published, 1911.)

Freud, S. [A note on the unconscious in psycho-analysis] In *Collected papers* (vol. IV). London: Hogarth Press and Institute of Psycho-Analysis, 1946, pp. 22–29 (b). (Originally published, 1912.)

Freud, S. Der Wahn und die Träume in W. Jensens "Gradiva." In *Gesammelte Werke* (vol. VII). London: Imago Publ. Co., 1947, pp. 31–125. (Originally published, 1907.)

Freud, S. Die Traumdeutung. In *Gesammelte Werke* (vol. II/III). London: Imago Publ. Co., 1948. (Originally published, 1900.)

Freud, S. Das Ich und das Es. In *Gesammelte Werke* (vol. XIII). London: Imago Publ. Co., 1955, pp. 246–289. (Originally published, 1923.)

Freud, S. [On aphasia] In S. G. Sapir & A. C. Nitzburg (Eds.), *Children with learning problems.* New York: Brunner-Mazel, 1973, p. 461. (Originally published, 1891.)

Frostig, M. Teaching reading to children with perceptual disturbances. In R. M. Flower, H. F. Gofman, & L. I. Lawson (Eds.), *Reading disorders, a multidisciplinary symposium.* Philadelphia: F. A. Davis Co., 1965.

Gattegno, C. *Words in color, background and principles.* Chicago: Encyclopedia Britannica Press, 1962.

Gattegno, C. *Teaching reading with words in color.* New York: Xerox Corp., 1968.

Gellner, L. Correspondence on the backward child. *British Medical Journal,* 1953, *5.*

Gellner, L. Some contemplations regarding the border country between "mental deficiency" and "child schizophrenia." *II International Congress for Psychiatry,* Congress report (3). Zurich, Switzerland: Orell Fussli Arts Graphiques, 1957, pp. 481–487.

Gellner, L. *A neurophysiological concept of mental retardation and its educational implications.* Chicago: The Dr. Julian D. Levinson Research Foundation for Mentally Retarded Children, 1959.

Gerstmann, J. The syndrome finger agnosia, right-left confusion, agraphia and acalculia. *Archives of Neurology,* 1971, *24,* 476.

Gerstmann, J. The symptoms produced by lesions of the transitional area between inferior parietal and middle occipital gyri. In D. A. Rottenberg & F. H. Hochberg (Eds.), *Neurological classics in modern translation.* New York: Hafner Press, 1977, pp. 150–154.

Gindin, A. R. Spelling performance of medical students. *Bulletin of the New York Academy of Medicine,* 1974, *50*(10), 1120–1121.

Goldberg, H. K. Vision, perception, and related facts in dyslexia. In A. H. Keeney & V. T. Keeney (Eds.), *Dyslexia, diagnosis and treatment of reading disorders.* St. Louis: C. V. Mosby Co., 1968, chap. 10, pp. 90–109.

Gondor, E. I. *Art and play therapy.* Garden City, N.Y.: Doubleday & Co., Inc., 1954.

Goodenough, F. L. Measurement of intelligence by drawings. In *Measurement and adjustment series.* Yonkers, N.Y.: World Book Co., 1926.

Goodman, K. S. Do you have to be smart to read? Do you have to read to be smart? *Reading Teacher,* 1975, *28,* 625–632. (a)

Goodman, K. S. *The Reading Informer,* 1975, quoted in vol. 3, 2, p. 4. (b)

Grewel, F. The acalculias. In P. J. Vinken & G. W. Bruyn (Eds.), *Handbook of clinical neurology: Disorders of speech, perception, and symbolic behavior* (vol. 4). New York: American Elsevier Publ. Co., 1969, chap. 9, pp. 181–194.

Grinker, R. R., & Bucy, P. C. *Neurology.* Springfield, Ill.: Charles C Thomas, 1949.

Groff, P. The new anti-phonics. *The Elementary School Journal,* 1977, pp. 323–332 (Chicago: Univ. of Chicago Press).

Grunebaum, M. G., Hurwitz, I., Prentice, N. M., & Sperry, B. M. Fathers of sons with primary neurotic learning inhibitions. *American Journal of Orthopsychiatry,* 1962, *XXX-II*(3), 462–472.

Gurren, L., & Hughes, A. Intensive phonics vs. gradual phonics in beginning reading: A review. *The Journal of Educational Research,* 1965, *58*(8), 339–346.

Hallgren, B. Specific dyslexie, a clinical and genetic study. *Acta psychiatrica et neurologica,* Suppl. 65, Kopenhagen, Denmark, 1950, pp. 1–287.

Hanauer, J. What TV is doing to your child—the abuses. *New York Journal-American,* October 13, 1965, p. 20 (quoting R. Narkewicz, & S. N. Graven, The tired child syndrome).

Harris, A. J. *How to increase reading ability.* New York: Longmans, Green & Co., 1956.

Hawley, R. A. Television and adolescents: A teacher's view. *American Film,* October 1978, 53–56.

Hecaen, H. Cerebral localization of mental functions and their disorders. In P. J. Vinken and G. W. Bruyn (Eds.), *Handbook of Clinical neurology: Disorders of higher nervous activity* (vol. 3). New York: John Wiley & Sons, Inc., 1969, chap. 2.

Hecaen, H., & de Ajuriaguerra, J. *Left-handedness: Manual superiority and cerebral dominance.* New York: Grune & Stratton, 1964.

Hermann, K. *Reading disability.* Copenhagen: Munksgaard, 1959.

Himwich, W. A., & Himwich, H. E. Neurochemistry. In A. M. Freedman & H. I. Kaplan (Eds.), *Comprehensive textbook of psychiatry.* Baltimore: The Williams & Wilkins Co., 1967, section 2.2, pp. 49–66.

Hopkins, J. M. *Teaching a child to read.* Mimeographed letter to the parents of P. S. 7, Bronx, N. Y., February 6, 1962.

Horn, M. *The world encyclopedia of comics* (vol. 2). New York: Chelsea House Publishers, 1976.

House, E. L., Pansky, B., & Siegel, A. *A systematic approach to neuroscience.* New York: McGraw-Hill Book Co., 1979.

Hymowitz, C. Remedial bosses. Employers take over where schools failed to teach the basics. Courses in English and math offered to help workers master their equipment. *Wall Street Journal,* January 22, 1981.

Jackson, J. Discipline in our schools (Interview). *New York Amsterdam News,* April 16, 1977.

Jarvis, V. Clinical observations on the visual problem in reading disability. In *The psychoanalytic study of the child* (vol. X-III). New York: International Universities Press, 1958, pp. 451–470.

Jelliffe, S. E. The MNEME, the engram and the unconscious, Richard Semon: His life and work. *The Journal of Nervous and Mental Disease,* 1923, *57*(4), 329–341.

Jellinek, A. Acoustic education in children. In E. Froeschels (Ed.), *Twentieth-century speech and voice correction.* New York: Philosophical Library, 1948, chap. VIII, pp. 103–109.

Kawi, A. A., & Pasamanick, B. Association of factors of pregnancy with reading disorders in childhood. *Journal of the American Medical Association,* 1958, *166,* 1420–1423.

Kawi, A., & Pasamanick, B. Prenatal and paranatal factors in the development of childhood, in: Reading disorders, *Monographs of the Society for Research in Child Development,* 1959, *24*(4, Serial No. 73), 1–80.

Kimmis, H. Los Angeles lawsuit court upholds curb on crime comics. *Christian Science Monitor,* March 24, 1959.

Klasen, E. Das Syndrom der Legasthenie [*The reading disorder syndrome*] Bern, Switzerland: Hans Huber, 1970.

Kleiman, D. Educators turning away from out-of-class help. *New York Times,* June 13, 1979.

Kline, M. *Why Johnny can't add: The failure of the new math.* New York: St. Martin's Press, 1973.

Koch, C. *The Tree test: The tree-drawing test as an aid in psychodiagnosis.* New York: Grune & Stratton, Inc., 1953. (Originally published, 1952.)

Kolansky, H., & Moore, W. T. Clinical effects of marijuana on the young. *International Journal of Psychiatry,* 1972, *64*(10/2), 55–67.

Kraepelin, E. *Psychiatrische Klinik* (vol. I, 4th ed.). Leipzig: Johann Ambrosius Barth, 1921.

Kurzweil, R. *Print to speech.* Cambridge, Mass.: Kurzweil Computer Products, Inc., 33 Cambridge Parkway, 1980.

Lane, R. See ed board appeal in mistaken retarded case. *New York Daily News,* November 7, 1978.

LaVietes, R. Psychiatry and the school. In A. M. Freedman & H. I. Kaplan (Eds.), *The child: His psychological and cultural development* (vol. 2). New York: Atheneum, 1972, chap. 21.

Leischner, A. The agraphias. In P. J. Vinken & G. W. Bruyn (Eds.), *Handbook of clinical neurology: Disorders of Speech, perception and symbolic behavior* (vol. 4). New York: American Elsevier Publ. Co., 1969, chap. 8, pp. 141–180.

Lhermitte, F., & Gautier, J. C. Aphasia. In P. J. Vinken & G. W. Bruyn (Eds.), *Handbook of clinical neurology: Disorders of speech, perception and symbolic behavior* (vol. 4). New York: American Elsevier Publ. Co., 1969, chap. 5, pp. 84–104.

Liebman, M. *Neuroanatomy made easy and understandable.* Baltimore: University Park Press, 1979.

Lowe, H. R. The whole-word and word-guessing fallacy. In C. C. Walcutt (Ed.), *Tomorrow's illiterates.* Washington, D.C.: Council for Basic Education; Little, Brown and Co., 1961, chap. 4.

Luria, A. R., & Yudovich, F. Ia. *Speech and the development of mental processes in the child.* Harmondsworth, Middlesex, England: Penguin Books Ltd., 1971.

Machover, K. Personality projection. In *The drawing of the human figure.* Springfield, Ill.: Charles C Thomas, 1948.

Maeroff, G. L. State overhaul proposed for secondary education, Fleischmann panel says system leaves thousands of graduates unequipped to hold jobs or continue schooling. *New York Times,* October 3, 1972.

Maeroff, G. L. A solution to falling reading scores continues to elude big-city schools. *New York Times,* May 27, 1973.

Maeroff, G. L. *New York Times,* August 4,. 1973.

Malnutrition during pregnancy causes learning disabilities among the offspring. *Obstetrical and Gynecological News,* July 1, 1979.

Mautner, H. *Mental retardation, its care, treatment and physiological base.* New York: Pergamon Press, 1959.

McKay, J. R. Diseases of the newborn infant: Premature and full term. In W. E. Nelson (Ed.) *Textbook of Pediatrics* (11th ed.). Philadelphia: W. B. Saunders Co., 1979, pp. 423–424.

Medical News, *J.A.M.A.,* 1973, *223*(12), 1323–1324.

Medicine around the world, artificial vision. *M.D.,* April, 1974, p. 63.

Mitchell, J. E., Hong, K. M., & Corman, C. Childhood onset of alcohol abuse. *American Journal of Orthopsychiatry,* 1979, *49*(3), 511–513.

Montessori, M. *The Montessori Method.* New York: Schocken Books, 1964.

Moolenaar-Bijl, A. Cluttering. In E. Froeschels (Ed.), *Twentieth century speech and voice correction.* New York: Philosophical Library, 1948, pp. 211–224.

Moskowitz, R. San Francisco, Oakland "fail" in reading tests. *San Francisco Chronicle,* November 12, 1971.

Mosse, H. L. Aggression and violence in fantasy and fact. *American Journal of Psychotherapy,* 1948, *II*(3), 477–483.

Mosse, H. L. The Duess test. *American Journal of Psychotherapy,* 1954, *8*(2), 251–264.

Mosse, H. L. Die Bedeutung der Massenmedien für die Entstehung Kindlicher Neurosen [Mass media as causes for childhood neuroses]. *Monatsschrift Kinderheilkund,* 1955, *102* (2), pp. 85–91.

Mosse, H. L. Modern psychiatry and the law, proceedings of the Association for the Advancement of Psychotherapy. *American Journal of Psychotherapy,* July 1958. (a)

Mosse, H. L. The misuse of the diagnosis childhood schizophrenia. *American Journal of Psychiatry,* 1958, *114*(9), 791–794. (b)

Mosse, H. L. Creativity and mental health. *Curriculum and Materials* (Board of Education, City of New York) March/April 1959, *XIII*(4), 6. (a)

Mosse, H. L. Testimony for County of Los Angeles Crime Comic Book Ordinance. *Katzev vs. County of Los Angeles* (2nd District, Div. 2), Calif. District Court of Appeal. In *Advance California Appellate Reports* (cited ACA-168 ACA 1, 204), March 6, 1959. (b)

Mosse, H. L. Child reading (Letter to the Editor). *M.D.,* December 1962. (a)

Mosse, H. L. Reading disorders in the United States. *The Reading Teacher,* November 1962, pp. 1–5. (b)

Mosse, H. L. Review of *Narrative of a child analysis*, by Melanie Klein. *American Journal of Psychiatry*, 1962, *119*, 1. (c)

Mosse, H. L. The influence of mass media on the mental health of children. *Acta Paedopsychiatrica*, 1963, *30*(fascicule 3), 103–111. (a)

Mosse, H. L. [Childhood reading disorders as an international problem] Köln, W. Germany: *Ärztliche, Mitteilungen*, 1963, *60*(fascicule 8), 428–429. (b)

Mosse, H. L. Review of *The psychology and teaching of reading*, by Fred J. Schonell; *Reading and the psychology of perception*, by Hunter Diak. *American Journal of Psychotherapy*, 1963, *XVII*(1), 147–149. (c)

Mosse, H. L. *Observations of reading disorders in Europe*. Fourth Annual Reading Reform Foundation Conference Report. New York: Reading Reform Foundation, August 5, 1965.

Mosse, H. L. The influence of mass media on the sex problems of teenagers. *Journal of Sex Research*, 1966, *II*(1), 27–35. (a)

Mosse, H. L. Lineare Dyslexie. In K. Ingenkamp (Ed.), *Lese-und Rechtschreibschwäche bei Schulkindern*. Weinheim und Berlin, W. Germany: Julius Beltz, 1966, pp. 54–55. (b)

Mosse, H. L. Die pathogene Bedeutung der Ganzheitsmethoden. In C. F. Schmitt (Ed.), *Die Lése-Synthese*. Frankfurt, W. Germany: Verlag Moritz Diesterweg, 1966, chap. 10. (c)

Mosse, H. L. Zur Symptomatik und Ätiologie der Legasthenien. In K. Ingenkamp (Ed.), *Lese-und Rechtschreibschwäche bei Schulkindern*. Weinheim und Berlin, W. Germany: Julius Beltz, 1966, pp. 30–33. (d)

Mosse, H. L. Review of R. S. Eisler, A. Freud, H. Hartmann, & M. Kris (Eds.), *The psychoanalytic study of the child*. *American Journal of Psychotherapy*, 1967, *XXI*, 1.

Mosse, H. L. Individual and collective violence. *American Journal of Psychoanalysis in Groups*, 1969, *2*(3), 23–30.

Mosse, H. L. Massen Medien. In H. H. Meyer (Ed.) *Seelische Störungen*. Frankfurt, W. Germany: Umschau Verlag, 1970, pp. 201–210. (a)

Mosse, H. L. Viewpoints: What are the effects on children of overhearing sounds of lovemaking from the parents' bedroom? *Medical Aspects of Human Sexuality*, 1970, *IV*(9), 12. (b)

Mosse, H. L. The psychotherapeutic management of children with masked depressions. In S. Lesse (Ed.), *Masked depression*. New York: Jason Aronson, 1974, chap. 11.

Mosse, H. L. An international view of children's reading disorders. Based on a study of over 400 children age 4–19 in U.S.A. and Europe. *Abstracts, VI World Congress of Psychiatry, Honolulu, Hawaii*, 1977, *1046*, 192. (a)

Mosse, H. L. Terrorism and mass media. *New York State Journal of Medicine*, 1977, *77*(14), 2294–2296. (b)

Mosse, H. L. The media and terrorism. In M. H. Livingston (Ed.), *International Terrorism in the Contemporary World*. Westport, Conn.: Greenwood Press, 1978, pp. 282–286.

Mosse, H. L., & Daniels, C. R. Linear dyslexia, a new form of reading disorder. *American Journal of Psychotherapy*, 1959, *XIII*(4), 826–841.

National Education Association and American Medical Association. Dispensing medications in school. Guidelines passed by Joint Committee on Health Problems in Education of the NEA and AMA. *New York State Journal of Medicine*, September, 1974, p. 1806.

Newby, H. A. Clinical audiology. In L. E. Travis (Ed.), *Handbook of speech pathology and audiology*. New York: Appleton-Century-Crofts, 1971, chap. 13.

Noback, C. R., & Demarest, R. J. *The nervous system: Introduction and review* (2nd ed.). New York: McGraw-Hill Book Co., 1977.

Open Court Basic Reader for Grade 1:1. La Salle, Ill.: Open Court Publ. Co., 1963.

Open Court Program Evaluation, Second Conference, Fourth, Fifth, and Sixth Grade Evaluations, P.S. 108, Manhattan. Mimeographed minutes, February 22, 1971.

Orton, S. J. *Reading, writing and speech problems in children*. New York: W. W. Norton, 1937.

An overview of the elementary school curriculum. Bureau of Elementary Curriculum Development, The New York State Education Department, 1954.

Pavlov, I. P. *Pawlowsche Mittwochkolloquien, Protokolle und Stenogramme physiologischer Kolloquien* (vol. III). Berlin, Germany: Akademie- Verlag, 1956.

Pearson, G. H. (Ed.). *A handbook of child psychoanalysis.* New York: Basic Books, 1968.

Pearson, G. H. J. Inverted position in children's drawings, report of two cases. *Journal of Nervous Disease,* 1928, *68,* 449–455.

Pearson, G. H. J. A survey of learning difficulties in children. In *The psychoanalytic study of the child* (vol. VII). New York: International Universities Press, 1952, pp. 322–386.

Penfield, W. Engrams in the human brain, mechanisms of memory. *Proceedings of the Royal Society of Medicine,* 1968, *61,* 831–840.

Peterson, I. College textbooks being simplified to meet the needs of the poor reader. *New York Times,* November 7, 1974.

Piaget, J. *The child's conception of number.* New York: Humanities Press, 1952.

Pincus, J. H., & Glaser, G. H. The syndrome of "minimal brain damage" in childhood. *New England Journal of Medicine,* July 7, 1966, *275,* 27–35.

Preston, R. C. A foreign image of American reading instruction. *The Reading Teacher,* 1962. *16*(3) 158–162.

Rabinovitch, R. D. Reading and learning disabilities. In S. Arieti (Ed.), *American handbook of psychiatry.* New York: Basic Books, 1959, chap. 43.1.

Rabinovitch, R. D. Reading problems in children: Definitions and classifications. In A. H. Keeney & V. T. Keeney (Eds.), *Dyslexia. Diagnosis and treatment of reading disorders.* St. Louis: C. V. Mosby Co., 1968, chap. 1.

Rambert, M. L. *Children in conflict.* New York: International Universities Press, 1949.

Raymond, D. On being 17, bright—and unable to read. *New York Times,* April 25, 1976.

Rogovin, A. *Learning by doing: An illustrated handbook for parents and teachers of children who learn slowly.* Johnstown, Pa.: Mafex Associates, Inc., 1971.

Rosenbaum, D. E. Allen sets a 1970's goal: Every pupil able to read. *New York Times,* September 23, 1969. (a)

Rosenbaum, D. E. Mrs. Nixon honorary chairman of U.S. right-to-read project. *New York Times,* September 24, 1969. (b)

Rosenbaum, D. E. Federal project in reading gains. *New York Times,* August 18, 1970.

Rosenberg, P. E. Audiologic correlates. In A. H. Keeney & V. T. Keeney (Eds.), *Dyslexia. Diagnosis and treatment of reading disorders.* St. Louis: C. V. Mosby Co., 1968, Part 4, pp. 53–59.

Rosenthal, J. Functional illiteracy found high in U.S. in study at Harvard. *New York Times,* May 20, 1970.

Roswell, F., & Natchez, G. *Reading disability: Diagnosis and treatment.* New York: Basic Books, 1964.

Schilder, P. *The image and appearance of the human body.* New York: John Wiley & Sons, Inc., 1964. (Originally published, 1950.)

Schmidt-Kraepelin, T. *Über die juvenile Paralyse.* Berlin, Germany: Julius Springer, 1920.

Schmitt, C. F. Theorie des Leseprozesses auf der Grundlage des bedingten Reflexes. In C. F. Schmitt (Ed.), *Die Lese-Synthese.* Frankfurt, W. Germany: Verlag Moritz Diesterweg, 1966, chap. 6. (a)

Schmitt, C. F. Über Rückkopplung beim Lesen. In C. F. Schmitt (Ed.), *Die Lese-Synthese.* Frankfurt, W. Germany: Verlag Moritz Diesterweg, 1966. (b)

Schoenberg, B. S., Mellinger, J. F., & Schoenberg, D. G. *Arch. Neurol.,* 1977, *34,* 570–573.

Schuell, H., Jenkins, J. J., & Jiménez-Pabón, E. *Aphasia in adults, Diagnosis, prognosis, and treatment.* New York: Brunner-Mazel, 1975. (Originally published, 1964.)

Sellers, T. J. English, not dialect. *New York Times,* June 9, 1972.

Semon, R. W. [*Mnemic psychology*] London: George Allen & Unwin, 1923. (Originally published, 1920.)

Sequential levels of reading growth in the elementary schools. Division of Elementary Schools, Board of Education of the City of New York, February 1963.

Sharpe, W. *Brain surgeon.* New York: Viking Press, 1954.

Siegel, S. Subway crime, interview of muggers. *CBS-TV,* March 24, 1979.

Siepmann, C. A. Lectures on communication and education. *Image* (program guide of Public Television Channel 13, New York City), November 1969, *VII*(1), 21–23.

Silverman, J. S., Fite, M. W., & Mosher, M. M. Learning problems, clinical findings in reading disability children—special cases of intellectual inhibition. *American Journal of Orthopsychiatry,* 1959, *XXIX*(2), 298–336.

Simpson, E. *Reversals: A personal account of victory over dyslexia.* Boston: Houghton-Mifflin Co., 1979.

Smith, F. *Understanding reading—a psycholinguistic analysis of reading and learning to read.* New York: Holt, Rinehart & Winston, Inc., 1971.

Smith, N. B. Some answers to criticisms of American reading instruction. *The Reading Teacher,* 1962, *16*(3), 146–150.

Spalding, R. B., & Spalding, W. T. *The writing road to reading* (2nd rev. ed.). New York: William Morrow & Co., Inc., 1969. (First rev. ed. 1962.)

Sperry, B. M., Staver, N., & Mann, H. E. Destructive fantasies in certain learning difficulties. *American Journal of Orthopsychiatry,* 1952, *XXII*(2), 356–365.

Sperry, R. W., Gazzaniga, M. S., & Bogen, J. E. Interhemispheric relationships: The neocortical commissures; syndromes of hemisphere disconnection. In P. J. Vinken & G. W. Bruyn (Eds.), *Handbook of clinical neurology: Disorders of speech, perception and symbolic behavior* (vol. 4). New York: American Elsevier Publ. Co., 1969, chap. 14, pp. 273–290.

Stanford achievement test. New York: Harcourt, Brace & World, Inc., 1964.

Stern, C., & Stern, M. B. *Children discover arithmetic.* New York: Harper & Row, 1971.

Students decline in reading ability. New York Times, December 10, 1952.

Study finds children's TV more violent (quoting George Gerbner). *New York Times,* April 23, 1979.

Stutte, H. von. [Psychopathology of children following hemispherectomy] Jahrbuch Jugendpsychiatrie 4, Bern, Switzerland: Hans Huber 1965, pp. 85–97.

Substitutes for sight. *M.D.,* 1970, *14*(12), 49–51.

Taylor, E. A. The spans: Perception, apprehension and recognition as related to reading and speed reading. *American Journal of Ophthalmology,* 1957, *44*(4), Part I, 501–507.

Terman, L. M., & Merrill, M. A. *Measuring intelligence.* Boston: Houghton-Mifflin Co., 1937.

Terman, S., Walcutt, C. C. *Reading: Chaos and cure.* New York: McGraw-Hill Book Co., 1958.

Thompson, L. J. *Reading disability, developmental dyslexia.* Springfield, Ill.: Charles C Thomas, 1966.

Tinklenberg, J. R., Murphy, P. L., Murphy, P., Darley, C. F., Roth, W. T., & Kopell, B. S. Drug involvement in criminal assaults by adolescents. *Archives of General Psychiatry,* 1974, *30,* pp. 685–689.

Vereeken, P. Inhibition of ego functions and the psychoanalytic theory of acalculia. In *The psychoanalytic study of the child* (vol. XX). New York: International Universities Press, 1965, pp. 535–566.

Vick, N. A. *Grinker's neurology* (7th ed.). Springfield, Ill.: Charles C Thomas, 1976.

Walcutt, C. C. The reading problem in America. In C. C. Walcutt (Ed.), *Tomorrow's illiterates.* Washington, D.C., Council for Basic Education; Boston: Little, Brown and Co., 1961.

Walcutt, C. C. (edit.) Tomorrow's illiterates (editor's note). Washington, D.C.: Council for Basic Education; Little, Brown and Co., 1961.

Walcutt, C. C. Reading: A professional definition. *Elementary School Journal,* 1967, *67,* 7.

Walcutt, C. C. The major structure of an effective reading method. In C. C. Walcutt, J. Lamport, & G. McCracken (Eds.), *Teaching reading.* New York: Macmillan Publ. Co., 1974, chap. 7.

Weinschenk, C. [*The hereditary reading and writing disorder with its social-psychiatric implications*] Bern, Switzerland: Hans Huber, 1965.

Weinschenk, C. *Rechenstörungen: Ihre Diagnostik und Therapie.* Stuttgart, W. Germany: Verlag Hans Huber, 1970.

Wertham, F. A psychosomatic study of myself. *Journal of Clinical Psychopathology,* 1945, *7*(2), 371–382.

Wertham, F. Thrombophlebitis with multiple pulmonary emboli, psychiatric self-observation. *American Journal of Medical Sciences,* 1946, 211.

Wertham, F. The psychopathology of comic books. *American Journal of Psychotherapy,* 1948, *11*(3), 472–490.

Wertham, F. A psychosomatic study of myself. In M. Pinner & B. F. Miller (Eds.), *When doctors are patients.* New York: W. W. Norton, 1952, chap. 11.

Wertham, F. Psychotherapy in disorders of the gastrointestinal tract. *The Review of Gastroenterology,* August 1953, *20,* 8. (a)

Wertham, F. Review of *Adolf Meyer, The Collected Papers. Journal of the History of Medicine and Allied Sciences,* 1953, *VIII,* 2. (b)

Wertham, F. The curse of the comic books. *Religious Education,* November/December 1954.

Wertham, F. Reading for the innocent. *Wilson Library Bulletin,* April 1955.

Wertham, F. *The circle of guilt.* New York: Rinehart & Co., 1956.

Wertham, F. The Mosaic test technique and psychopathological deductions. In L. E. Abt & L. Bellak (Eds.), *Projective psychology.* New York: Grove Press, 1959, pp. 230–256. (Originally published, 1950.)

Wertham, F. The scientific study of mass media effects. *American Journal of Psychiatry,* 1962, *119* (4), 306–311.

Wertham, F. *Dark legend.* New York: Duell, Sloan & Pearce, 1966.

Wertham, F. Battered children and baffled adults. *Bulletin of the New York Academy of Medicine,* 1972, *48*(7), 887–898. (a)

Wertham, F. *Seduction of the innocent.* New York: Rinehart, 1954; Port Washington, N.Y.: Kennikat Press, 1972. (b)

Wertham, F. *A Sign for Cain.* New York: Warner Paperback Library, 1973. (Originally published, 1966).

Wertham, F. Medicine and mayhem. *M.D.,* June 1978, 11–13.

Wertham, F., & Wertham, F. *The brain as an organ.* New York: The Macmillan Co., 1934.

What does research say about reading? *Curriculum and Materials* (Board of Education, City of New York), 1954, *VIII*(3), 2.

Wheeler, T. C. *The great American writing block. Causes and cures of the new illiteracy.* New York: The Viking Press, 1979.

Wiener, N. *Cybernetics or control and communication in the animal and the machine.* Cambridge, Mass.: The M.I.T. Press, 1965.

Wing, L., & Wing, J. K. Multiple impairments in early childhood autism. *Journal of Autism and Childhood Schizophrenia,* 1971, *1*(3), 256–266.

Woodworth, R. S. *Experimental psychology.* New York: Henry Holt and Co., 1938.

Words and science. *M.D.,* February 1959, pp. 77–78.

Zucker, L. The clinical significance of the Mosaic and Rorschach methods. *American Journal of Psychotherapy,* 1950, *IV*(3), 473–487.

Index

Key to Children's Names in *Volume I*

The Complete Handbook
of Children's Reading
Disorders

VOLUME II

Contents

Acknowledgments

Grateful acknowledgment is made to the authors and publishers for permission to reprint excerpts from the following material:

Arieti, S. (Ed.), *American handbook of psychiatry*, vols. 1 and 2. New York: Basic Books, Inc., 1959:
  Gerard, R. W. Neurophysiology, brain and behavior.
  Goldstein, K. Functional disturbances in brain damage.
  Mulder, R. W. Automatisms (psychomotor seizures) in psychoses with brain tumors and other chronic neurologic disorders.
  Papez, J. W. The reticular system.
Chall, J. S. *Learning to read: The great debate.* New York: McGraw-Hill Book Co., 1967.
Chess, S., Thomas, A., & Birch, H. G. *Your child is a person.* New York: Viking Penguin Inc., 1965.
Critchley, M. *The parietal lobes.* London: Edward Arnold Ltd., 1953.
Critchley, M., & Henson, R. A. (Eds.), *Music and the brain.* London: William Heinemann Medical Books Ltd., 1977:
  Benton, A. L. The amusias.
  Critchley, M. Ecstatic and synaesthetic experiences during musical perception
  Critchley, M. Musicogenic epilepsy.
  Gooddy, W. The timing and time of musicians.
  Scott, D. Musicogenic epilepsy.
  Wertheim, N. Is there an anatomical localization for musical faculties?
Ehrlich, P. P., & Feldman, S. S. *The race bomb, skin color, prejudice, and intelligence.* New York: Times Books, 1977.
Feingold, B. F. *Introduction to clinical allergy.* Springfield, Ill.: Charles C Thomas, 1973.
Freud, A. *Normality and pathology in childhood.* New York: International Universities Press, 1965.
Jenkins, J. J., Schuell, H., & Jiménez-Pabón, E. Aphasia in adults. Hagerstown, Maryland: Medical Department Harper and Row, Inc., 1964.
Kilmer, W. L., McCulloch, W. C., & Blum, J. Embodiment of a plastic concept of the reticular formation. In: L. O. Proctor (Ed.), Biocyber-

375

netics of the central nervous system. Boston: Little, Brown and Company, 1969.

Proust, M. The past recaptured, translated by F. A. Blossom. New York: Random House, Inc., 1932.

Slater, E., & Roth, M. Clinical psychiatry. London: Bailliére Tindall, 1969.

Vinken, P. J., & Bruyn, G. W. (Eds.), Handbook of clinical neurology, vol. 3. Amsterdam: Elsevier/North-Holland Biomedical Press B.V., 1969:

Frederiks, J. A. M. Consciousness.

Frederiks, J. A. M. Disorders of attention in neurological syndromes.

Gooddy, W. Disorders of the time sense.

Hernández-Peón, R. Neurophysiologic aspects of attention.

McGhie, A. Psychological aspects of attention disorders.

Poeck, K. Pathophysiology of emotional disorders associated with brain damage.

Pribram, K. M., & Melges, F. T. Psychophysiological basis of emotions.

Vinken, P. J., & Bruyn, G. W. (Eds.), Handbook of clinical neurology, vol. 4. Amsterdam: Elsevier/North-Holland Biomedical Press B. V., 1969:

Ingram, T. T. S. The development of higher nervous activity in childhood and its disorders.

Lhermitte, F., & Gautier, J. C. Aphasia.

Wechsler, D. The measurement of adult intelligence. New York: Oxford University Press, 1944.

Part I

Specific Disorders and Syndromes Frequently Associated with Reading Disorders on an Organic Basis

The plight of the child with an organic reading disorder cannot be understood completely unless symptoms, syndromes, and disorders frequently associated with these reading disorders are also diagnosed and treated. These associated disorders, syndromes, and symptoms may be classified into two groups: specific and unspecific or general. The specific group consists of speech disorders, mental deficiency, convulsive disorders, cerebral palsy, musical ability disorder, and rhythmic ability disorder. The other group includes slowing down of all reactions, impairment of automatic mechanisms, inability to tolerate disorder, inability to shift, perseveration, attention disorders, hyperactivity, hypoactivity, fatiguability, irritability, mood disorder, and free-floating anxiety. The specific disorders will be circumscribed in Part I.

Chapter 1

Speech Disorders

All types and degrees of speech disorders in children should be taken seriously and diagnosed as early as possible, because not only do they make learning to read more difficult for the child, they also tend to affect his entire emotional and intellectual development. Even a mild speech defect should not be ignored on the assumption that it will disappear on its own. Only a diagnostic examination that includes hearing tests and an evaluation by a speech therapist can determine whether or not speech therapy is indicated.

Early speech therapy can sometimes prevent a reading disorder, and speech therapy alone can correct a reading disorder in certain cases. This important preventative and corrective role of speech therapy should be more widely recognized. A speech therapist should always participate in the planning for prevention and treatment of reading disorders in children, especially when the disorder has an organic basis. Many school systems such as that of New York City recognize the importance of speech therapy and employ speech teachers. But school officials usually are not familiar with the importance of this service for improving reading. I routinely refer children who have even the mildest speech defect (whether I examine them in schools, mental hygiene clinics, or in private practice) to a speech therapist for diagnosis, and, if indicated, for treatment. I have even asked speech teachers in schools to take a child with a reading disorder on for treatment where there was no clear speech defect. The training in auditory discrimination and in clear articulation in which these teachers specialize is exactly what such a child needs. It especially helps children with organic reading disorders and those whose defective reading is caused by whole-word teaching methods. (See section on Spelling, Vol. I, p. 115.)

Frequency

How frequently the combination of reading disorders with speech disorders occurs is difficult to determine. Statistics obviously depend on the diagnosis of both conditions. Most studies either do not evaluate their material statistically in this respect, or do not differentiate between reading disorders on an organic and on a non-organic basis. Reading and speech disorders are not recorded together in statistics partly because different professional workers deal with each disorder, they do not communicate with each other, and they write about them separately. Another important fact is that speech disorders are frequently not diagnosed at all or are omitted from the final recording of the diagnosis that is used in clinics and hospitals for statistical purposes; thus they are under-reported.

My own study shows that of the 222 children with an organic reading disorder, 96 (76 boys, 20 girls) also had a speech disorder. This amounts to 42.8%. Only a little over 8%, that is, 18 (16 boys, 2 girls) of the 223 children with a psychogenic or a sociogenic reading disorder also had a speech disorder. This indicates that the cerebral speech and reading apparatuses are frequently impaired together, because they are so close anatomically and overlap.

The relationship between speech and reading disorders seems to be especially close in the small hereditary group among the organic reading disorders. Both disorders occur in such families through several generations, but not necessarily together in the same family member (Schiffman, 1966, p. 245).

International statistics invariably show that boys have reading disorders more frequently than girls. They also show that speech disorders are more frequent among these boys. Hallgren in his well-known study found that 41% of the boys and only 32% of the girls with severe organic reading disorders also had speech disorders (1950); Klasen found 5% more boys than girls (Klasen, 1970, pp. 51–52). My own statistics agree with these findings.

Delayed Onset of Speech

It is important to distinguish delayed speech development from a speech disorder. The onset of speech is not always delayed in children with speech disorders. Stuttering, for instance, usually starts between the ages of 3 and 5 and, as Froeschels states, "never at the start of speech" (1948, p. 194). On the other hand, delayed speech development may be entirely within normal limits. It does not necessarily interfere with learning to read, and when it is found in the history of a child with a reading disorder, cannot be used in the absence of other data as evidence for the organic basis of the reading disorder.

We have no statistics to show how many children who read well had a delayed speech onset. We know, however, that delayed speech onset is very frequent among children with organic reading disorders; it varies between 30% and 39% (Klasen, 1970, p. 52). The "developmental lag" theory of the causation of reading disorders is partly based on such statistics. (See section on the "developmental lag" theory, Vol. I, p. 54.)

Classification

A speech disorder on an organic basis is called aphasia. Translated from its Greek origin, it means absence of speech; the term stems from adult neurology.

The word "aphasia" should not be taken literally. The majority of these patients—adults or children—are not mute. They can utter speech sounds or complete words and sentences. However, their speech is difficult to understand or completely unintelligible. Their grammar is defective and they may use words that do not express what they wanted to say. The symptomatology of aphasia is very complicated and difficult to disentangle and understand. That is why there is such confusion internationally about its classification, especially as it refers to children.

Aphasias in adults and in older children who already spoke before becoming aphasic, differ from those occurring in a child who is learning to speak. Here we must assume that the cerebral speech apparatus was so damaged before, during, or after birth that the child cannot learn to speak. Critchley and others therefore object to the diagnosis "aphasia" in children altogether. He suggests that "congenital disorder in the acquisition of speech" be substituted (p. 169, 1968b). Other neurologists and psychiatrists use the terms "Specific Developmental Disorder of Speech," "Linguistic Retardation," or they put the prefixes "developmental," "congenital," or "idiopathic" before the term "aphasia." Some neurologists prefer the term "Aphasoid," meaning aphasic-like. In the French literature we find the diagnosis "aphasie d'evolution," "aphasie d'integration," or "Trouble du Development du Language."

The term sensory or motor "audimutitas" (Audimutité in French and Hörstummheit in German) is also frequently used. It means mutism of a child who can hear. This is quite similar to the confusion reigning in the classification of organic reading disorders.

Progress in diagnosis, treatment, and prevention of aphasia in children rests, even more than in organic reading disorders, on the accessibility of all data internationally and on an exchange of findings and easy communication among all professionals (neuropathologists and -physiologists, neurologists, pediatricians, psychiatrists, psychologists, speech therapists, educators, nurses, etc.) who come in contact with the aphasic child. This should not be complicated by a confusion of terms. It is therefore better to stick to the traditional diagnosis of aphasia, while explaining what age and level of speech development is meant and what the symptoms are.

Aphasia and Mental Deficiency

Aphasia is due to malfunctioning of the cerebral speech apparatus. It has a profound effect on the child's emotional and intellectual development, which depends to such a large extent on speaking and on understanding what others say. Since aphasia stunts the child's entire mental growth, it is sometimes indistinguishable from mental deficiency. It affects so many fundamental functions that it blends into a dementia (i.e., a diffuse general intellectual defect). Many aphasic children function for all practical purposes on the level of mental deficiency, especially when their aphasia either is not diagnosed and treated at all or incorrectly, or does not respond to treatment and cannot be corrected. However, aphasias, like organic reading disorders, can also be found in children who are mental defectives. Most mental defectives are not aphasic; their cerebral speech apparatus functions within the limits of their intellectual capacity. (See Mental Deficiency, p. 409.)

Because we can best learn from the severest symptoms how to recognize mild or rudimentary forms, I will describe severe cases of aphasia associated with organic reading disorders. These children present great diagnostic, therapeutic, and educational puzzles. They fortunately belong to a small group among both these disorders.

Localization

The selection of training techniques for children with aphasia with or without mental deficiency, which utilize trainable parts of the appropriate cerebral apparatuses, depends on a detailed defect diagnosis. This requires some understanding of localization. Familiarity with the "aphasic zone" in the cortex, with its intricate interconnections, is however not sufficient for the diagnostic analysis of all such children. As Schuell, Jenkins, and Jiménez-Pabón point out in their standard book, *Aphasia in Adults,* "In spite of the functions assigned to different areas of the cortex, the importance of subcortical structures as integrating mechanisms should never be forgotten" (1975, p. 95). This applies especially to children because the subcortical white matter of the brain is particularly vulnerable in the fetus and the infant. (See section on the Relationship Between Cerebral Hearing, Speech, and Reading Apparatuses, Vol. I, p. 92.)

Correlation of Clinical Symptoms with Cerebral Localization in Childhood Aphasias

The neuropathologist and psychiatrist Lise Gellner has made the most significant attempt to connect these children's symptoms with subcortical lesions as she did with childhood agnosias and apraxias (see Vol. I, p. 95) (Gellner, 1953, 1957, 1959).

Based on her clinical observations, she differentiated two diagnostic groups, "word-sound deafness" and "word-meaning deafness." She found neuropathologic evidence of subcortical damage in or near brain-stem ganglia that receive and integrate impulses of crucial importance for speech. Ganglia are clusters of nerve cells arranged in a number of layers. Each ganglion has at least three functions: the accumulation and thereby strengthening of incoming impulses; the integration of impulses arriving from various sources; and the transmission of newly integrated impulses into various directions (Gellner, 1959, p. 3).

The ganglia implicated by Gellner in childhood aphasias are:

1. The inferior colliculi, which deal with audio-proprioceptive impulses. These arise in the inner ears; in the organs of hearing as well as the organs of balance; and in muscles, tendons, and joints.

2. The medial geniculate bodies, which deal with audio-autonomic impulses. These impulses also arise in the inner ears, in the organs of hearing as well as the organs of balance, and in the inner organs, which transmit them via the autonomic nervous system.

All these ganglia are connected with the cortex. Gellner also found cortical lesions in some of these children's brains. They were small areas of atrophic sclerosis and appeared to be like the ones found in people born blind or deaf with normal intelligence. She explained them as secondary changes resulting from the primary subcortical injury (Gellner, 1959, p. 16) (see Figure 1.1).

All these ganglia are small in size so that tiny injuries—for example, small hemorrhages that were too minute to cause the death of the fetus or newborn infant, or brief, nonlethal episodes of anoxia (lack of oxygen)—can damage them severely. They form a part of the vital relays or shunts in the brain, whose damage invariably causes clinical symptoms. They are especially vulnerable to birth injuries because they lie next to the great cerebral vein, which is (according to Gellner and other neuropathologists) "the very center of all birth injuries" (Clark & Anderson, 1961; Gellner, 1959, p. 15). Gellner explained this vulnerability further by stating that

> the most common cerebral birth trauma occurs in the dorsal region of the midbrain—where the corpora geniculata and the corpora quadrigemina lie in the closest proximity to each other and directly above the hypothalamus. The latter may have some bearing on endocrine and metabolic disturbances frequently found in these children (Gellner, 1959, p. xx; House, Pansky, & Siegel, 1979, pp. 24–25, Figs. 1–26–27 and pp. 472, 475, Fig. 24–8; Liebman, 1979, p. 51, Plate 14–1).

Many children I examined with severe organic symptoms, including students at a public school for aphasics, made a subcortical, "stonebound" pattern on the Mosaic test. In some, a subcortical pattern could be clearly distinguished from a cortical one. This indicated that both levels of the brain were affected. These test results provide some clinical indication at least, that subcortical pathology may underlie these groups of symptoms. (See section on Organic Mosaic Patterns, Vol. I, p. 28.)

Of course the children we examine survived their birth injuries or whatever caused their brain damage, and the correlation of their symptoms with the subcortical damage suggested by Gellner cannot be validated by autopsies; it must remain hypothetical. However, historically, much of what was once hypothetical in neuropathology has ultimately been proven correct. Gellner's clinical observations are not hypothetical at all. They are well-founded, and the terminology she suggests describes these children's basic impairment so well that it facilitates understanding and therapeutic planning.

Word-Sound Deafness

Children who have "word-sound deafness" can hear, but the integration of hearing with proprioceptive impulses (which arise in muscles, tendons, and

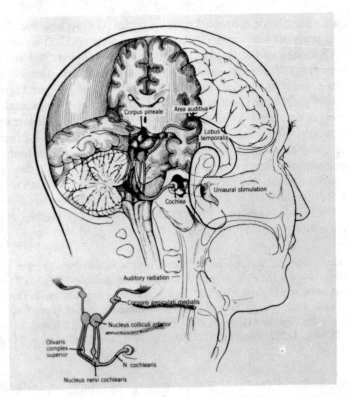

FIG. 1.1.   Schematic illustration of locations and connections of the medial geniculate bodies and the inferior colliculi whose defective functioning is implicated by Gellner in causing word/sound and word/meaning deafness.

joints), and with the speech areas in the cortex is defective. The damage is supposed to lie in the inferior colliculi, which mediate the auditory-somatic system. Complete destruction of such a ganglion is fortunately rare. Even complete interruption of fiber tracts is infrequent. We are primarily dealing with partial damage. Where no communication between the inferior colliculi and the cortex is possible at all, the child cannot learn to speak. He is mute. Children with partial damage may be capable of repeating articulated sounds, but they cannot use them in a meaningful way. They cannot learn to speak by listening. They cannot feel the sounds they produce themselves.

The speech defects of these children vary greatly in severity. All of them can understand what is said to them better when gestures are used. Their impairment involves the hearing of all sounds produced by muscular movement such as speech, as well as their own production of speech sounds. Most can distinguish pure tones made by singing or by playing a musical instrument. They may even be capable of learning to sing and to play a musical instrument. This is another example of the irrelevance of the question of cerebral dominance for children within these diagnostic groups. Some such children can learn to use their mouth muscles to chew and to whistle; others cannot. Most of them can learn to speak by kinesthetic and visual methods. They can observe the formation of different sounds in others or, by looking at films or pictures, can imitate what they have seen and check the positions of their own speech organs by looking in a mirror. They can get an appreciation of the vibrations of the larynx and the tongue and of the type of breathing required by touching as well as by visual observation.

All these children must be taught lip reading since they cannot learn to distinguish one word from the other in any other way. They need this visual bridge to connect one speech sound with the other. Some such children never learn to speak intelligibly, and many can only be taught soundless speech.

Characteristic for this and all other forms of aphasia is that the impairment is quite uneven. The child may understand one word and not another one that is equally difficult or easy, and even this performance varies from one day to the next and within one single day. These children can always understand short and familiar words better than new words, especially when they are long, but even this fluctuates. Fatigue and any other physical or emotional stress decreases their understanding and may even extinguish it completely. This may lead to severe emotional outbursts where the child seems completely out of control and becomes destructive to himself and others.

To prevent such panic reactions and to help these children, one must understand that they are much worse off than deaf children because they constantly hear sounds they cannot analyze, distinguish from each other, and understand. Frequently they cannot even localize sounds (i.e., know what direction the sound is coming from) and cannot distinguish different noises from speech. Even when the impairment is mild and consists only of an imprecision in speech sound analysis, it causes severe anxiety because the child can never be quite certain whether or not he interpreted the sounds he heard correctly— that is, whether the other person really said what he figured out had been said. The confusion and uncertainty, the feelings of insecurity, doubt, and anxiety aroused by this disorder are at their peak in emergency situations and whenever fast communication is required. These children cannot respond with speed to any incoming spoken message. Their frustration involves outgoing messages as well, because they cannot express themselves clearly and fast, especially when they need it most—namely when they are in danger or very anxious for other reasons, or in general emotional turmoil. Their psychologic management is therefore very difficult, and their emotional symptoms can be so severe that parents cannot cope with them at home and hospitalization or institutionalization has to be considered.

Impairment of Reading and Arithmetic

Some children in this group cannot learn to read, and reading is very difficult for all of them. The phonetic route is obviously closed to them. They constitute the only diagnostic group for whom the word-picture method of teaching reading is indicated, because the visual route is the only one open to them. Some of them can and even must be taught to read before it becomes possible to teach them to speak. They can be taught to write by copying and can eventually write spontaneously, but writing to dictation is either impossible for them to learn, or very difficult. These children sometimes do very well in written arithmetic, but cannot learn to recognize numbers when they are called out—that is, by ear.

Maternal Rubella as a Cause of Word-Sound Deafness

Maternal rubella (German measles) transmitted to the fetus seems to play a special role in causing this and probably also other forms of aphasia. Ames, Plotkin, Winchester, and Atkins, pediatricians and rehabilitation specialists at the Children's Hospital in Philadelphia, studied such children. They did not use the diagnosis "word-sound deafness," but the symptoms fit into this classification.

In their paper, "Central Auditory Imperception, a Significant Factor in Congenital Rubella Deafness," they describe 30 children (13 boys, 17 girls) who suffered from what they called "pure central auditory imperception with no associated peripheral hearing loss or blindness." All these children had failed to learn to speak. All had a significant rubella antibody titer, which means that they had rubella in utero. They also had rubella retinopathy but no blindness. They showed little ability to localize sound. Their responses to pure tone presented both by air and bone were normal, but not their response to speech, sudden noise, and various other sounds. All had a normal pure-tone audiometric evaluation and a normal performance on a psychologic evaluation done with the same modifications used for children with peripheral hearing loss. The authors make a plea for the early identification of this condition by physicians who should "identify the child when the mother seeks his help in finding the cause of his failure to speak." Because this paper appeared in the *Journal of the American Medical Association,* one has reason to hope that this plea will be heard (1970, pp. 419–421).

Crucial Role of Physicians

The physician's position is indeed a crucial one not only in the diagnosis of all forms of children's speech disorders, but also in seeing to it that these children get the appropriate treatment. The authors of this paper did not stop at recognizing that these children needed special education urgently and long before school age. They also took action by starting small classes for them in their hospital and setting up a cooperative educational program together with the Philadelphia school system. This was in 1970. The date alone shows how neglected children with aphasia still are. Not only are they too frequently misdiagnosed for too long a time, but when the diagnosis is finally made, special classes and other therapeutic facilities to take care of them frequently do not exist. This means that their impairment remains uncorrected, and that the psychopathologic process invariably set in motion gets worse; thus their eventual fate is institutionalization, either in a mental hospital or in a state school for mental defectives.

Word-Meaning Deafness

Children with word-meaning deafness can hear, but the defect lies in the integration of hearing with the inner organs, which is transmitted by the autonomic nervous system, and with the cortical speech areas. The damage supposedly lies in the medial geniculate bodies, which mediate the auditory-autonomic system. This type of aphasia resembles cortical receptive aphasia in adults, but has its own unique features. It is also called *acoustic agnosia* (which means inability to understand speech sounds) or *sensory audimutitas.*

It is sometimes impossible to make the differential diagnosis between word-sound and word-meaning deafness when a child is completely mute or manages to learn only a few words, which he pronounces poorly. Such a child's response to training alone can determine whether he has an aphasia because he cannot analyze speech sounds and therefore cannot repeat them, or whether he does not speak because he cannot understand the words even though he hears them perfectly clearly. In many cases, especially in the most severe forms, receptive and expressive features occur together anyhow, just as in the adult forms of aphasia. Anatomically, the colliculi and the geniculate bodies lie fairly close to each other, so that the same injury (hemorrhage, anoxia, etc.) may damage several of them or all of them simultaneously. These ganglia are not vital for the support of life, so that a fetus or a newborn infant may survive their damage.

The medial geniculate bodies constitute part of the cerebral speech and reading apparatus. The tracts connecting them with the cortex end in Heschl's transverse gyrus, where the sensory speech center is located, and which lies at the periphery of the reading region. When this connection is completely interrupted, the child appears deaf, but his startle reflex remains intact and indicates that he can hear. Most children in this group, however, have only partial blocks, which involve interruptions of tracts leading from the ear to the medial geniculate body (afferent and efferent), and from there to and from the inner organs. The tracts leading to the inner organs belong to the autonomic nervous system (House et al., 1979, p. 472, Fig. 24–8; Liebman, 1979, p. 51, Plate 14–1) (Illustration, Figure 1.1).

The outstanding symptoms of these children are impaired speech and difficulty in understanding and remembering words. They have trouble finding words or naming objects. They can repeat words and sentences correctly and often enjoy talking, but what they say is irrelevant, does not fit the situation, and does not express what they want to say. Their speech is often like that of a parrot; they repeat what they just heard, including questions asked of them. This parrotlike speech can also be called "echolalia," a designation used to describe a symptom of adult and childhood schizophrenia.

This symptom, together with others—for instance, the tenuous contact with reality that these children find so difficult to understand, may lead to the misdiagnosis of schizophrenia. This can only be avoided by a most thorough examination and evaluation of *all* the symptoms shown by such a child. He may, for instance, be able to answer simple questions with some short, usually concrete words he has learned, but be unable to talk in complete sentences, and therefore be incapable of telling a story coherently. He may, however, show by his actions and behavior that he does understand a story or activity he can see and where he does not have to rely on hearing to figure out what is meant. All such children have trouble following long speeches and understanding less common and long words. A child with mild word-meaning deafness, for instance, may manage to convey the main events of a story using only short nouns and some verbs, but not complete sentences.

Unless one keeps in mind that this telegram style of telling a story may be due to aphasia, it may not seem pathologic, but only caused by the child's excitement aroused by telling an exciting story. Children who are immature or whose intelligence is limited, or for whom English is a second language, often talk in this style. Because overlooking an aphasia has such serious consequences for the child's entire life, one should always keep it in mind when making a differential diagnosis, even though it applies only to a small number of children.

Word-meaning–deaf children enjoy kinesthetic and muscular movements immensely. This is probably a compensation for their inability to enjoy inner sensations because impulses cannot flow freely to and from their inner organs due to their interruption by damaged medial geniculate bodies. These children delight in intricate finger movements right in front of their eyes even as infants, and they love to dance to music later on. Unfortunately they also enjoy rocking and head banging, sometimes to such a degree that they injure themselves. They may rock for hours on end while kneeling, so that they get blisters on their knees and toes, and may bang their head so vigorously that fractures, wounds, or hemorrhages result. High doses of tranquilizing medication may be needed to stop these habits. Deaf infants also enjoy these movements, probably because they cause pleasurable sensations in the labyrinth (the organ of balance) in the inner ear.

Serious rocking and head banging can be observed in patients in state schools for mental defectives as well as in mental hospitals. These rhythmic movements seem to be pleasures of last resort for children with the most severe brain defects, such as blindness combined with deafness, degenerative diseases, atrophies, defects after encephalitis. In deaf and in word-meaning–deaf children these are, as a rule, minor and only transitory habits, provided the diagnosis of deafness or aphasia is made early and a plan for appropriate education worked out and carried out. (See section on Rocking, under Hyperactivity, p. 598.)

Corrective educational management of these children long before they reach school age is crucial; otherwise they develop secondary symptoms that can be so severe that they can no longer be changed.

Impact of Parents' Attitude on Children Causing Either the Clinical Picture of Mental Deficiency or of Early Infantile Autism

Gellner made long-range studies of word-meaning–deaf children and their parents and found (1) that two different clinical pictures emerge by the time these children reach school age, and (2) that these pictures are caused by the contrasting reactions of their parents to their handicap. She observed that word-meaning–deaf children who grew up with concrete-minded, emotionally accepting parents who did not judge them by their intellectual achievements and did not push verbal communication, but used their own imagination to communicate with them in other ways—by gestures, tone of voice, visual expression—rarely had tantrums, seemed fairly happy and easy-going, and were not too difficult to manage. They enjoyed talking to themselves and tried to find ways of communicating with other children and with adults. Their inability to learn by listening and to use words in a meaningful way led to the diagnosis of mental deficiency. The underlying word-meaning deafness was not always diagnosed.

Word-meaning–deaf children who grew up with parents who insisted on early and differentiated verbal expression, however, developed differently. They eventually stopped talking altogether because they just could not find a way to please their parents by talking. They also withdrew emotionally. Their inability to communicate led to intolerable feelings of frustration and despair and to severe, uncontrollable tantrums. Some of these children had a panic reaction whenever the position of objects around them was disturbed. They seemed to need minute constancy in their environment to achieve a feeling of inner stability. Furniture; toys; objects on tabletops, in drawers, in the kitchen; eating utensils—all had to be in exactly the same spot every day. They were also dependent on the sameness of their daily routine (Gellner, 1957, pp. 481–487; 1959, pp. 35–36).

These children present the clinical picture of Kanner's early infantile autism, a childhood psychosis of uncertain origin. They are indeed "psychotic" in the sense of suffering from a major mental disorder. Their basic organic handicap is so obscured by a secondary reaction that it is most difficult to diagnose, so that they are usually diagnosed as having early infantile autism or childhood schizophrenia. (See section on Inability to Tolerate Disorder, p. 478.)

Relation to Early Infantile Autism

Gellner's astute observations are important additions to the growing body of evidence that early infantile autism is not a clear-cut entity, that it is a combination of symptoms of differing, predominantly organic origins. Gellner has shown that it can develop when an aphasic child is inappropriately managed by intellectual, highly verbal, and emotionally remote parents.

When Kanner first described this syndrome he felt that it was caused by exactly this type of parent, that its origin probably was psychogenic. This theory was widely accepted and did great harm. I have observed its long- and short-range effects in many families. Psychoanalysis or other forms of psychotherapy were routinely recommended for such a child as well as for his parents. The children did not improve and the parents never got over their feelings of guilt. Many marriages could not survive the chronic turmoil and the unending, guilt-ridden strain. (Cox, Rutter, Newman, Bartak, 1975).

His personal experience with this approach led Jacques M. May, a famous physician, to write a critical book, *A Physician Looks at Psychiatry* (1958). Dr. May had twin sons suffering from early infantile autism. He described his experience with psychiatrists, psychologists, and social workers. All agreed

> that the fundamental cause of the disorder was an unconscious rejection of the children. This belief was not even challenged. Any scrap of information that could be turned into evidence of parental guilt or rejection was used indiscriminately in support of the theory (pp. 46–47).

No wonder that, as he stressed, "The blow to my wife was a ferocious one" (p. 47). I saw both boys years later in a private institute for autistic children founded by Dr. May. They suffered unquestionably from the severest word-meaning deafness form of aphasia. They did not speak, hardly responded to any commands, and were still most difficult to control even with the latest tranquilizers.

Another group of word-meaning–deaf children also demonstrate behavior resembling early infantile autism. They learn to speak very early and have an excellent rote memory. They can pronounce and remember the most difficult words that children normally do not use. They learn to recite passages from Shakespeare and other poets long before they are of school age, and their parents understandably think that their child is a genius. It soon becomes clear, however, that the child does not really understand what he says. He does not answer even simple questions and only repeats what is said to him. These children belong to the group called "idiots savants" (see sections on Hypermnesia, Hyperlexia, and Hypercalculia, Vol. I, pp. 69, 396, 226).

An ever-increasing number of studies show that the causes of early infantile autism are usually organic. An analysis of the original 11 cases on which Kanner based his first description of this syndrome already points in this direction. His follow-up study after 28 years indicates that 2 of the 11 unquestionably had an organic disorder (cases 10 and 11); they developed convulsions. Five other children had signs of Gellner-type aphasias, especially case 6, Virginia S. Two children (cases 1 and 2) probably had schizophrenia, and two could not be followed up. These also showed symptoms that might have been organic (cases 4 and 8). Seven of nine children who were followed up therefore probably had an organic disorder (Kanner, 1971). (See also Deykin and Macmahon, 1979.)

An exceptionally thorough study was done by Doris Weber (1970). She examined, treated, and followed up 66 children. Twenty-seven of them (41%) had clear-cut signs of organic causation. Some had anoxemia before or during birth. Three children had phenylketonuria, which is an inborn error of metabolism; a pair of twins had fetal rubella encephalitis because their mother had German measles during her pregnancy; one child had whooping cough encephalitis at the age of 3 months. At least one of these patients demonstrated the type of fingerplay characteristic for word-meaning–deaf children. I had the opportunity to examine some of these children myself when I was on my Fulbright Lectureship at the University of Marburg, Germany, and agree with Weber's conclusion that early infantile autism is a "polyetiologic" syndrome (i.e., a syndrome with diverse causes). She based this conclusion on sound clinical evidence.

Fetal rubella encephalitis seems to play a special role among the causes of this syndrome. It has provided clear-cut evidence that a specific organic disease can cause the symptoms of early infantile autism.

The child psychiatrist Stella Chess, in her study of 243 children with congenital rubella (German measles) found a high prevalence of early infantile autism among them. She reports the results of this study, which she carried out together with two psychologists, in *Psychiatric Disorders of Children with Congenital Rubella* (Chess, Korn, & Fernandez, 1971).

All these children had, of course, a diseased brain; it had been invaded by the rubella virus before they were born. Their autism therefore undoubtedly had an organic cause. When discussing the etiology of childhood autism in general, Chess feels that there is an "inescapable implication" in her data, namely that her findings "would appear to support the argument in favor of an organic etiology as against other lines of inquiry" (p. 122). (See also section on Maternal Rubella as a Cause of Word-Sound Deafness, p. 388.)

Relation to Schizophrenia

A fuller understanding of organic conditions, especially those that affect the cerebral speech and reading apparatuses, is indispensable for advancing our knowledge of both early infantile autism and childhood schizophrenia. We know that schizophrenia, whether it occurs in children or in adults, is not caused by organic cerebral defects. It is a chronic and usually progressive mental illness characterized by periods of remission that vary in length and in degree of social recovery. Its typical age of onset is adolescence and young adulthood. It is rare in childhood, but does occur. Its cause is unknown.

In my paper, "The Misuse of the Diagnosis Childhood Schizophrenia" (1958), I pointed out that "the present trend to diagnose children with severe emotional and mental symptoms as schizophrenic is scientifically wrong and has had serious practical consequences." I found that "even mild forms of agnosia, apraxia, aphasia, impairment of auditory perception and dyslexia may cause severe learning and behavior disturbances and lead to the erroneous diagnosis of childhood schizophrenia." This has been amply confirmed internationally since then.

So many children diagnosed as suffering from childhood schizophrenia have organic signs, that Goldfarb and others differentiate between an "organic" and a "non-organic" type (1961, pp. 55, 280). Of course, schizophrenia may occur in association with an organic condition, for instance with mental deficiency or an organic reading disorder, but this does not mean that both conditions are identical. (See case of Chester under Hyperactivity, p. 631.)

Attempts have been made to diagnose schizophrenia in infancy, but the symptoms described are so similar to those outlined by Gellner in her four diagnostic groups, that these infants undoubtedly suffer from organic conditions that we will eventually be able to diagnose and localize with more precision than we can at present, so that we can differentiate them from schizophrenia (Fish, 1960).

All children classified as suffering from early infantile autism or schizophrenia who show unquestionable evidence of the organic causation of their symptoms, should be removed from these diagnostic categories. This is of great practical clinical importance because it inevitably affects the therapeutic and educational management of these children, and with it, their entire life.

Therapeutic Management

Word-meaning–deaf children are so severely handicapped that they need supervision and care all of their lives. They seldom can be taught to read because they need a visual approach that has not yet been developed.

STEFAN, 11 YEARS OLD: WORD-SOUND AND WORD-MEANING DEAFNESS.
Stefan is an example of how severely handicapped these children are and how little help they receive. Stefan was 11 years old when I examined him for the first time. He was brought to me by his mother because he had to be formally exempted from school, which he had never been able to attend.

Stefan was delivered by forceps. He was not blue at birth and showed no other obvious signs of injury. He walked late (at 13 months) and his gait was insecure, but he did not bump into things. He never talked. He cried when he was unhappy or frightened, but had no tantrums. A doctor told the parents when Stefan was 4 years old that he would talk "when he makes up his mind." The parents took him to a hospital for speech disorders from the ages of 5 to 9, but he did not learn to talk. A psychologic examination at that time showed that he "gave evidence of abilities up to average with considerable scatter" and that he "often does not respond to sounds, even though there is evidence that he has sufficient hearing." The diagnosis, however, was not aphasia, but "autism"; and the parents were advised to have him committed to a mental hospital. They did not follow this recommendation, but kept him at home, and his mother trained him as best she could. His father worked. He had a 14-year-old healthy brother. His mother eventually took him to a chiropractor as she despaired of medical advice. He found what chiropractors usually find—namely, "rotary scoliosis of entire spine and upper cervical and dorsal misalignment"—and he worked on the boy's spine. He gave the mother good advice in one respect, at least: he suggested she teach Stefan to blow out matches and candles. In this way he learned to make some sounds. His mother taught him to dress himself, to eat with a fork, to brush his teeth. She told me that he was a good-natured boy and that he liked music. During my examination he sat quietly and played with his fingers in front of his eyes. He smiled from time to time, but did not respond to any question or command. He seemed to respond only to his mother's gestures.

I made the diagnosis of aphasia of both the word-sound and word-meaning–deaf type, with mental deficiency. Only if we should succeed in developing methods of corrective education for these children, can we ever hope to determine whether their general intelligence can develop beyond defective levels.

I re-examined Stefan 2 years later when he was 13 years old. There had, of course, been no change. The familial and social implications of this handicap are profound. The mother, who obviously loved this child, cried and told me that she did not mind taking care of him, but that the neighbors did not help her, but reproached her for not teaching him how to talk, and that the children in the neighborhood teased him and attacked him. She and her husband realized that they could have him committed to a state school for mentally defective children as soon as they felt they could not take care of him any longer, but both were afraid to take this final step. They loved him and would have felt guilty if they had sent him away. Very many parents of defective or psychotic children have the same unsolvable conflict. Because management becomes increasingly more difficult as these children enter adolescence and adulthood, and as their parents get older, institutionalization eventually becomes inevitable. The care in such institutions unfortunately is sometimes so inadequate and inhumane that good parents take their child home again, even though his care is almost beyond their strength. Good medical care should include decent and humane inpatient care of incurably mentally ill or mentally defective children and adults.

Hyperlexia

A small group of children have a peculiar reading symptom that we do not yet understand. Their disorder certainly belongs to the aphasias. Their cerebral speech and reading apparatuses are disordered in such a way that they can read but cannot speak spontaneously. They only speak when they read. Some such children read very early, before the age of 3, and no one remembers ever having taught reading to them. They often read words, including foreign words, that they could not possibly have heard their parents or other people use in their conversations. They pronounce these words, which are sometimes long and complicated, correctly. It remains a mystery what organic and psychologic mechanism enables them to do this.

An important study involving probably the largest number of hyperlexic children ever recorded was done by the neurologists Mehegan and Dreifuss (1972). They studied 12 children (11 boys, 1 girl) ages 5 to 9; two of these children read before the age of 3; 10 by the age of 5. Only three of these children had any spontaneous speech, but only one of these could use words meaningfully. Two children also had hypercalculia. The authors described the reading habits of these children in the following way:

> Upon entering the examination room, they would instantly seize reading matter if it were present. This choice was indiscriminate, ranging from telephone directories to drug brochures. Failing this, posters upon the wall attracted attention. All material was read in a compulsive, ritualistic fashion, and attempts to divert them to another task met with great resistance. Even several hours after their activity had been successfully interrupted, they would, if given the opportunity, return to the approximate point of interruption and continue. The material was rendered aloud in an identifiable, repetitious rhythm with alternating crescendo-decrescendo qualities, reminiscent of a primitive Gregorian melody. Inflection was appropriate and punctuation marks were generally respected (p. 1106).

The authors observed further that

> most could handle material from *The New Yorker* and *Newsweek* with 60 to 70 percent accuracy. In the event of encountering an unmanageable word, phonetic

breakdown by the examiner insured accurate recall as long as several weeks later. Only one child was considered to have normal articulation. Speech was generally interfered with by one of several dysarthric defects, primarily lingual or labial in origin. Of considerable interest was the habitual to-and-fro rocking movement that accompanied each rendition. Once again, efforts by the examiner to abolish this met with great resentment, and successful suppression of motion frequently resulted in the patients' abandoning the reading exercise (p. 1106).

All children had definite abnormal neurologic signs. The authors emphasize this by stating: "In no instance were the results of the neurologic examination completely normal." Only one child had a severe cerebral defect. A pneumoencephalogram showed agenesis of the corpus callosum. However, this does not explain the hyperlexia. Mehegan and Dreifuss end their excellent description with the remark that "this condition would appear to be a relatively unique disturbance of language development" (p. 1111). However, they could not correlate their organic findings with these children's hyperlexia.

This fortunately is such a rare condition that I have seen only two such children: one in a clinic, the other on the children's ward of a mental hospital.

JERAD, 7 YEARS OLD HYPERLEXIA. I examined Jerad on the ward of a state hospital where I taught childhood psychoses to 4th-year medical students. Jerad usually sat in a corner by himself and was delighted when someone paid attention to him. He liked to draw, and read proudly from practically any book or newspaper presented to him, but he did not talk otherwise. He did not answer questions but responded to simple commands, was friendly, and tried to convey by gestures what he wanted, or just went and got it. It was impossible to find out whether he understood anything he read. He did not respond to written commands. He could write his name and some words, (e.g., "BATMAN AND ROBIN") in large print, with somewhat uncertain strokes, but in the right direction. He did not reverse any letters.

His drawings indicated that his intelligence was above the level of mental deficiency and probably average. On one subtest of the Wechsler Intelligence Scale for Children (WISC) namely Block Design, he even earned an I.Q. of 128; on Coding—which requires writing, visual discrimination and visual memory—he was defective.

Jerad had devoted parents who had sought help since he was 18 months of age and had taken him to many specialists. He learned to feed himself at the age of 2, to control his urine at the age of 3, to dress himself at the age of 4. He soiled himself until the age of 6. He had such severe tantrums at home that he had to be hospitalized. It is possible that he had the type of verbally demanding parents Gellner describes, and that this played a role in causing his disturbed behavior.

On the ward he was observed whispering to himself. He eventually learned to name objects and to use some words. He always spoke clearly. The correct diagnosis most likely was word-meaning deafness with hyperlexia. Only prolonged observation and maximal training can determine the diagnosis and the prognosis in such severely handicapped children.

Jerad had been referred to this hospital for observation because the diagnosis could not be established on an outpatient basis. The tentative diagnosis was "pseudoretardation" which means that the child appears to be mentally defective, but is not. He had not been diagnosed as suffering from childhood schizophrenia, but there always were a number of children on this ward (as there are on all mental hospital wards for children and adolescents) with this diagnosis who actually had aphasia.

ELAINE, 6 YEARS OLD: A MISERABLE ODYSSEY OF APHASIA MISDIAGNOSED AS SCHIZOPHRENIA.   I saw Elaine for the first time on the children's ward of a mental hospital when she was 6 years old. The ward psychologist asked me to examine her because the tests she administered gave evidence of expressive and receptive aphasia and not of schizophrenia. She also found that Elaine was of average and possible superior intelligence. I examined her and presented her before a group of medical students. She was a friendly girl, in good contact, who tried to please the adults around her and was eager to communicate with them. She spoke Spanish at home and struggled valiantly to find words that said what she wanted them to say. Her words were not clearly pronounced in either language and did not always mean what she obviously wanted to say. She understood what objects were and what their use was, but could not always find the correct word for them. She had no schizophrenic symptoms at all. She was not withdrawn or suspicious, had no bizarre fantasies or ideas, and could distinguish fantasy from reality quite well. There was no evidence of hallucinations.

The nurses, attendants, and psychiatrists who observed her behavior found that her comprehension was much better than her speech, and that she understood words she could not repeat or use in her own conversations. She even made it clear by gestures and sounds when a word was mispronounced by others. For instance, she could not pronounce her own name clearly, but indicated quite unmistakenly when it was mispronounced by others.

Elaine had been sent to the hospital because of her severe behavior and learning disability in school. She was first referred to the school psychologist for placement in a class for mentally retarded children. She was then in the first grade and the teacher complained that she had crying and laughing spells, jumped up and down, and did not work. She imitated other children's behavior but not their speech. She could not count and recognized a few words in reading, but mostly "seems to be unaware of what is going on." The teacher also noticed Elaine's "poor pronunciation" and "irrelevant talking" and reported that she knew only a few words and did not begin to talk in sentences until almost the end of the first grade. The school psychologist stated in her report that "her speech is poor, she has her own pronunciation, she seems to be making up words, she has neologisms" (this latter term indicates a schizophrenic symptom of inventing bizarre words). She found that Elaine was not mentally retarded, but that "her emotional problems appear to impede the use of her at least average intellectual potential at this time." She did not diagnose or even suspect aphasia.

Elaine lived under very stressful family and economic conditions. She was the oldest of four sisters. She was very fond of her father, who deserted the family when she was 5 years old. He had been working, but became ill and felt that he could no longer take care of his family. The mother complained that Elaine hit and scratched her younger sisters, that she clung to her and could not sleep at night. She had nightmares and rocked in her bed.

Elaine was born after a long and difficult labor that lasted 12 hours. She walked at 18 months, said a few unintelligible words at age 3. When she was 5 she pronounced some Spanish words so that one could understand them. A remark in the social history shows that the mother understood Elaine's key problem better than many of the experts who saw this child before and after hospitalization. It states that the mother "is of the opinion that Elaine can understand but that she cannot pronounce words and becomes anxious when she cannot say a word. The same thing happens when she tries to say a word in Spanish. She said that Elaine's problem is 'in talking.' " Aphasia had not occurred even as a differential diagnosis to any of the physicians, psychiatrists, psychologists, social workers, guidance counselors, and teachers who had been in contact with her since the age of 4. The reason for this is a defect in the training of all these professionals. Aphasia is considered too specialized and too difficult for all but a small group of neurologists, neurosurgeons, and child psychiatrists. This proved to be disastrous for Elaine, as it is for so many other aphasic children.

The hospital psychiatrists agreed with my diagnosis, sent her home with the official diagnosis "Developmental Aphasia," and recommended placement in an appropriate class. She was then young enough to be immediately admitted to the special public school for aphasic children, and her prognosis would have been favorable. I assumed that this had been done, but 4 years later a social worker consulted me about a girl with the same name who was so severely disturbed in a class for mentally retarded children that the school asked to have her suspended. This was the same Elaine, now 10½ years old, and her behavior had become more disorganized. At home, she took care of household chores and even helped her mother with the care of her siblings, including a baby brother; but on the street and in school she provoked other children and showed a precocious interest in adolescent boys. She dressed like an adolescent. She still could not communicate verbally, was very anxious in new situations, and could not defend herself after provoking other children. This social worker was new to the case and did not know the history. I searched through Elaine's clinic chart, which had grown to about 70 typewritten pages. It included numerous psychiatric and psychologic reports and letters to various officials. I wanted to find out what went wrong and when the wrong turn had been taken. The long and detailed letter from the hospital was hard to find, but it was in the record. It had either not been read by all the experts who examined Elaine later on or had been ignored. All I found was a laconic remark in the social worker's notes stating that "The diagnosis of expressive aphasia was not accepted here and Elaine was placed on home instruction." I read the long and conscientious reports sent by the various home teachers, which continued to carry the diagnosis of "aphasia." Their observations provided even more evidence for this very diagnosis. They reported that

> her chief problem is speaking. She has great need to communicate and will use every resource at her disposal, gestures, pointing, she is quick to mimic. She does read, but whether she comprehends the story I cannot tell. She appears to understand illustrations.

Elaine saw a number of psychiatrists who gave her the following diagnoses: "Organic Brain Syndrome" (age 7); "Retarded emotional, neurological and even mental development whose etiology is not possible to determine at this time" (age 8); "Perceptual-motor defect (language barrier) probably organic in origin. Superimposed adjustment reaction of childhood" (age 9). By the age of 9, her I.Q. had deteriorated to the defective level (62). This invariably occurs when an aphasic child is not treated appropriately. The psychologist who examined her at that time did not diagnose the aphasia either, but was misled by her Spanish-language background into thinking that this fact explained her speech disorder. A clinic that specialized in the diagnosis and treatment of mentally defective children recommended that she be placed in a class for brain-injured children because she was not mentally defective. They, too, did not diagnose the aphasia. There was no place for her in such a class. The teachers of these classes are in any case not trained to teach aphasic children, who need special teaching techniques.

It was not the home teachers' fault that Elaine had not learned either arithmetic or reading beyond the first-grade level. They felt that she did not respond to them and should be tried in a classroom. Her mother also wanted her to learn to get along with other children and not to stay with her all day. For these reasons she had been admitted to a class for mentally defective children, a so-called CRMD (Children with Retarded Mental Development) class.

At the age of 10, Elaine landed in the same type of class to which she had been referred when she was 6. It had been inappropriate for her then, and it certainly was inappropriate for her 4 years later when the psychopathologic process set in motion by the untreated underlying aphasia had become so severe that she could no longer be expected to function in any classroom situation. The prognosis for a normalization of her behavior was now very poor, and she might have to bě readmitted to a mental hospital.

Treatment Techniques

Special Class Placement

I have observed excellent results achieved by specially trained teachers with the help of a psychologist and a psychiatrist specializing in organic disorders. They taught in a school for aphasic children organized by the New York City Public School System with the help of the school psychiatrist William Calvin Barger, a specialist in the treatment of children suffering from organic reading disorders. He invented the Barger Mirror-reading Board, which also helps some of these children. (See section on this board, Vol. I, p. 104.)

Special classes for "language-impaired" children were organized in numerous schools later on, using the original school as a model. These teachers came from the local school for the deaf. Licensed speech teachers were also assigned to these classes. The training of both groups of teachers provided an excellent background for working with aphasic children. Two very helpful practical books came out of this teaching experience. Hortense Barry, who was the "key" teacher in the original experimental classes, wrote *The Young Aphasic Child* (1961) and John Marsh, one of the teachers, wrote *Your Aphasic Child,* for parents (1961).

I referred a number of children to these classes, observed them in the classroom, and followed their progress. Not all aphasic children can respond even to such small specialized classes. A trial period is sometimes needed to determine the child's capacity to respond. This does not depend on the severity of the aphasia alone. The level of the child's general intelligence is just as important. Trial teaching in such a class is sometimes the only practical way to determine this.

Speech Treatment on an Individual Basis

The speech therapist is an indispensable member of the staff of child psychiatric community or hospital clinics for staff training, diagnoses, and treatment.

My experience at the Lafargue Clinic has taught me how important it is to have such a therapist as an integral member of the staff.

When Wertham started this clinic, he asked Augusta Jellinek (a PhD in speech therapy) to join the staff. She had done important work on the education of hard-of-hearing children, on acoustic education of children, on Amusia (central disorder of the musical function), and on "Phenomena Resembling Aphasia, Agnosia and Apraxia in Mentally Defective Children and Adolescents." In keeping with Wertham's concept that a mental hygiene clinic can carry out its task of diagnosis, treatment, and prevention of mental disorders only if all staff members work closely together and understand each other's clinical specialty, Dr. Jellinek gave seminars to which all staff members were invited. As the clinic was a voluntary organization where no staff member received any remuneration, these seminars were also free of charge.

The first seminar was held in 1946, the year of the founding of the clinic. I have talked to many former staff members since then and met them in hospitals, schools, and clinics while they were doing their work in education or in the mental health field. All remembered the staff conferences and seminars they participated in in great detail. As far as speech disorders are concerned, all retained an awareness of their diagnostic and therapeutic importance far beyond that of most of their colleagues. One can only wish that all mental hygiene clinics (which are now called Community Mental Health Centers) would follow the example of the Lafargue Clinic in this respect as well as in so many others.

MARIE, 10 YEARS OLD: APHASIA NOT RESPONDING TO PSYCHOANALYSIS, TREATED SUCCESSFULLY.   One of the most dramatic successes of Dr. Jellinek's speech therapy at the Lafargue Clinic was with Marie, the daughter of a well-known French writer from one of the Caribbean islands. She had been brought to the United States by relatives who hoped that her condition could be diagnosed and possibly cured. They came to the Lafargue Clinic after they had exhausted all their funds and their visa was about to expire.

Marie did not speak until she was 7 years old. At the age of 10, she could utter only a few words in French that were almost unintelligible. She had been variously diagnosed as a mental defective or suffering from a severe neurosis. A psychoanalyst told her parents that Marie's recovery depended on the cure of her mother's neurosis. Psychoanalysis for mother and child was urgently recommended. After a year of psychoanalysis with no improvement and with their funds running out, the family consulted this free clinic. The clinic asked for an extension of the child's visa, and Dr. Jellinek treated her. Within 3 months, Marie spoke 60 words in French, soon learned an equal number of words in English, and eventually was able to speak both languages and to resume normal schooling. Dr. Jellinek's therapy included reading as soon as the child had acquired a minimal speech vocabulary.

Cluttering

A type of speech disorder of special relevance to reading disorders is cluttering. The clutterer's speech is so rapid under pressure of excitement that his enunciation is indistinct; words are run together and syllables are slighted or dropped out. It is sometimes called "agitolalia" (English & English, 1961).

Cluttering is unfortunately not well enough known among psychiatrists, psychologists, and teachers, to the detriment of the children suffering from this speech disorder. Parents and teachers usually think the child just talks too fast, or that his speech has remained immature and will mature with time. This attitude leads to procrastination, which may have serious consequences for the child's reading and for his speech, because stuttering may be superimposed on cluttering. The clutterer's speech is extremely fast, indistinct, badly differentiated, and characterized by many repetitions. One word runs into the other and each word by itself is indistinct. The clutterer's intonation is monotonous, either too soft or too loud so that he is often hoarse. Clutterers are saliva-spitters and get in trouble because of it, although they do not do this on purpose.

It is characteristic for cluttering that these children are not at all aware of their speech disorder. As repetitions are a normal part of speech development in early childhood, the clutterer's repetitions are easily mistaken for infantilisms. The clutterer, however, does not simply repeat syllables and words, but slurs them. The recognition of these children's speech as abnormal is especially difficult because cluttering always starts when the child begins to speak. There is never an interval of normal speech as there is in stuttering. Children who speak a language other than English at home present an especially difficult diagnostic problem. Their cluttering may easily be mistaken for speaking English with a foreign accent. I have examined many such children and puzzled over the diagnostic significance of their poor pronunciation of English. Where I had the slightest doubt, I asked a speech therapist for help in establishing the diagnosis.

Differentiation of Cluttering From Speech Defects Due to Hearing Loss

Cluttering is a more severe speech defect than speech that is merely slurred and indistinct. The latter speech defect points to a hearing loss. I have made the tentative diagnosis of hearing loss many times by listening carefully to a child's (or an adult's) speech. In most cases the patients knew about their partial deafness but had not told me about it.

In other cases, no one before me had suspected defective hearing. For this reason, when I teach child psychiatry to residents and others, I point out how important this type of technical acoustic listening to the patient's speech is in addition to the customary listening to the content of what he says. (See section on Examination, Vol. I, p. 20.)

There is agreement among speech therapists and other professionals in this field that cluttering, in contrast to stuttering, always has an organic basis. This is so important because many reading and speech specialists are guided by superficial explanations—for instance, that the child's speech disorder is due only to uncontrolled excitement. These children have word-finding difficulties, they do not hear speech sounds clearly (not even their own), and they have a poor auditory memory. This comes close to word-sound deafness.

Repetition of Nonsense Syllables as a Test for Cluttering

One test that demonstrates the above difficulties and on which clutterers always do badly, is the repetition of nonsense syllables. They do not hear the syllables clearly and cannot remember what they just heard. They do better with syllables and words they know, but they can only repeat them clearly when told to speak slowly.

In order to evaluate the repetition of nonsense syllables, one must know what can be expected at different ages. This test has been correlated with stages of development. A 4-year-old child can repeat four nonsense syllables, a 7-year-old five, a 10-year-old six, and a 14-year-old (like an adult) seven (Moolenaar-Bijl, 1948, p. 212).

Localization

It must be emphasized that clutterers are not hard of hearing. Their organic impairment does not lie in the organs of hearing, but is centrally located in the cortical "aphasic zone," in subcortical areas, or in pathways connecting all parts of the cerebral speech apparatus. In other words, clutterers are "borderline cases of receptive aphasia," as Jellinek states (1951, p. 19). Their disorder may not be exclusively receptive, however, because they tend to think faster than they can speak; this means that they cannot find and/or pronounce words fast enough to keep pace with their thinking. This is why they cannot repeat stories well. They tend to leave out entire sentences or part of the plot or garble the chronologic sequence of the events (Moolenaar-Bijl, 1948, p. 214).

A Reading Disorder Characteristic for Cluttering

The clutterer's reading disorder reflects his speech defect. He reads too fast, with poor and monotonous intonation, neglects punctuation marks, omits or inserts words or syllables. He has no trouble learning the correct direction of letter shapes and of the letter sequence within words. He has no directional difficulties, but has trouble combining letter forms with sounds, and spelling is especially hard for him (Moolenaar-Bijl, 1948, pp. 215–216).

Relationship Between Cluttering and Stuttering

There is a marked contrast between cluttering and stuttering. They are at opposite poles psychologically. The clutterer is relaxed, unaware of his defect, not anxious about it, and never has associated movements. A clutterer can become a stutterer, however, if, according to Jellinek, "he begins to worry about his symptoms and tries to suppress them" (1951, p. 19). This is why it is so important to diagnose cluttering correctly and early, and to start the appropriate treatment right away. Only in this way can later stuttering and other neurotic symptoms be prevented. The clutterer differs also in other respects from the stutterer. He speaks more clearly when he talks to strangers, because he then slows down his speech automatically and pays more attention to his pronunciation, whereas stuttering is always worse in the presence of strangers. That is why cluttering may be overlooked by psychiatrists and others who only examine the child once. The clutterer may pay attention to his speech, slow it down, and speak fairly clearly during one such examination.

The juxtaposition of symptoms of cluttering and stuttering given in Table 1.1 shows the most important differential diagnostic areas (Moolenaar-Bijl, 1948, p. 220).

It is interesting to note that stuttering does not occur in mentally defective children. Apparently a certain level of intelligence is needed for the development of this symptom. However, cluttering does occur in these children.

Prognosis

Since the prognosis for cluttering is excellent, it is especially important to diagnose it correctly. It can be cured, and often responds to relatively brief speech therapy. It is best for clutterers if the same therapist treats their speech and their reading, because there is such a strong connection between them. Writing should also be part of the therapy. It slows the clutterer's thinking and teaches him to combine vision, hearing, the kinesthetic-motor movements of his hand and speech (he should articulate the word while he writes it). For reading, a slit the size of a syllable or a word should be cut out of an unlined piece of paper or a 3 X 5 card, which should be moved over the text while the child reads. Through such a window he can see only one syllable or one word at a time, both his reading and his speech are slowed down, and he is forced to focus his attention on one small detail instead of diffusing it (Moolenaar-Bijl, 1948, p. 222). This remedial technique is also very good for children with other forms of reading disorders (See Window Card, under Linear Dyslexia, Vol. I, p. 131.)

Psychogenic Speech Disorders

The speech disorder of a very large number of children is either a symptom of a neurosis or of benign developmental delays; for example, the child does not want to part with baby talk. Other forms of speech disorders due to physical causes (e.g., cleft palate), even though they may be of great importance for the child's emotional development, do not affect his reading.

TABLE 1.1. Comparison of Symptoms of Stuttering and Cluttering

	Stuttering	Cluttering
Awareness of defect	Present	Absent
Calling attention to speech	Aggravates defect	Improves defect
Free and uninhibited conversation	Improves	Worsens
Speaking to strangers	Worsens	Improves
Brief answers are . . .	Difficult	Easy
Asking child to repeat words or sentences	No improvement	Improvement
Reading disorder	Usually absent	Always present
Chief therapeutic technique	Distraction of attention from speech	Focusing attention on speech

Vocal Cord Nodules

These nodules apparently have a psychologic basis. Children with such nodules have a history of shouting too much or of talking incessantly in a very tense way. They are often middle children with a number of siblings who feel that their only chance of being heard is to shout. Frank B. Wilson, Ph.D, Director of the Division of Speech Pathology at Jewish Hospital of St. Louis, presented an interesting report at a meeting of the American Academy of Pediatrics. Of 33,000 youngsters he surveyed during a 5-year screening project in St. Louis County, 525 had vocal nodules. This study found that schoolchildren who had vocal cord nodules tended to be three times more talkative than their peers who didn't have nodules. Their teachers reported that these students were among the most difficult to manage. The study also indicated that boys generally suffer laryngeal disorders twice as often as girls (Wilson, 1971, p. 2085).

In my study of 445 children with reading disorders, only one child, a 9-year-old boy, had vocal nodules. His reading disorder had an organic basis. He also had difficulties learning to write. However, there was no correlation between these disorders and his vocal cord nodules. The cause of his difficulties with reading and writing was a mild word-sound deafness.

Children with such nodules usually need psychotherapy in addition to speech treatment. Surgical removal of the nodules alone is not enough, inasmuch as the nodules tend to recur unless the poor vocal habit is corrected.

Psychogenic Mutism

This speech disorder occurs very frequently. It is usually classified under the Neuroses and not under speech disorders. It is also called *Elective Mutism.* These patients do not talk at all (i.e., they are mute) under certain conditions.

Freud called this disorder "Aphonia." His famous patient, Dora, was mute when her lover was away. Freud described this case in "Fragment of an Analysis of a Case of Hysteria" (1943). He also described other hysterical patients he observed at Charcot's clinic who wrote instead of talking (1943, p. 50).

Psychogenic mutism in children may have several causes. It may be the symptom of a depression. It was the most common symptom among children who witnessed extreme cruelty during World War II, such as the shooting to death of their entire family. This severe depressive mutism is complete; the children do not speak at all for months or longer. Such a severe form is rare.

The most frequent kind of mutism is elective. It occurs only in certain places or under specific circumstances. The majority of these children are mute only in school, and they usually make up for these hours of silence by talking incessantly at home. Many of them whisper to other children and/or give them written messages to convey to their teachers. They are usually of at least average intelligence and work silently in the classroom.

There are variations of this school-related mutism. Some of these children talk to other children, but *never* to adults other than their parents. A smaller group talks only to selected adults outside their home and not to other children. These adults are usually their teacher, some relatives they like, and eventually their therapist.

These children's mutism is due to a mixture of anger, anxiety, and negativism. It is sometimes combined with a school phobia. The majority of these children have a rigid emotional attitude, which is also expressed in marked physical tenseness. Many of them are chronically constipated. They do not like to share, and have difficulty establishing close contact with people outside their family. This disorder seems to affect boys and girls equally. It sometimes seems to be an especially severe form of shyness.

TREATMENT. The treatment of choice is either individual or group psychotherapy. In the playgroups I organized, there were invariably one or two children suffering from psychogenic mutism. This seems to be the most efficient treatment method. The other children in the group usually sense the needs of mute children and try their best to open an avenue of communication. They often try to humor the mute child into talking. Eventually, they ask him to open his mouth so that they can see whether or not he possesses a tongue. The mute child complies quite willingly at this point. Later on they ask him to move his tongue and lips and to make some sounds. This is often the first time such a child smiles at the other children. All this may not lead to speech right away, but it opens up closer communication. The mute child starts to use gestures, whispering or writing little notes.

Psychogenic mutism can also be deliberate. It may be an act of defiance or affectation. However, this does not usually last long, because all basically healthy children love to talk.

Mental Deficiency

I am using the term Mental Deficiency throughout this book, even though it has been changed to Mental Retardation in the *Diagnostic and Statistical Manuals* of the American Psychiatric Association, (DSM-II) 1968 and (DSM-III) 1980. The term "retardation," like the term "developmental," is too easily misunderstood. The diagnosis mental deficiency indicates an inborn limitation of intellectual capacity and functioning. It means that the upper limits within which development is possible are abnormally low. It does not mean a retardation that is capable of acceleration beyond these abnormal limits. Because these upper limits are so difficult and sometimes impossible to establish, many clinicians prefer the more hopeful-sounding diagnosis "mental retardation."

Mental deficiency is measured in terms of an intelligence quotient, which is derived from psychologic tests. The I.Q. level below which a child is declared legally mentally defective or mentally retarded is not primarily based on clinical judgment, but on legal conventions. The cut-off point is 70 in some school systems and states, and 75 in others. In scientific clinical terms, however, mental deficiency is not only quantitatively but qualitatively different from normal intelligence. It is not a question of a little more or a little less intellectual ability; it does not mean stupidity, for instance. At some point, which may well coincide with an I.Q. of 70 or 75, a child's general intellectual functioning becomes so limited that his entire intellectual and with it his emotional capacity differs qualitatively from the norm.

This diagnostic category, whether it is called mental deficiency or mental retardation, has become unsatisfactory. We now know that it covers different syndromes with varied symptoms and etiology, for instance, chromosome anomalies, inborn errors of metabolism, enzyme deficiencies, and so on.

Localization

There is a core group of mentally defective children and adults whose intellectual functioning is uniformly below normal. All aspects of their intelligence are depressed to the same extent. These patients do not have focal symptoms, such as a reading or speech disorder; their speaking and reading is affected by their mental deficiency, but it operates efficiently within their intellectual limits. In strict neuropathologic terms, these patients have a dementia. This term indicates a diffuse intellectual defect.

No specific macroscopic or microscopic pathology has been found in this core group. Many studies have compared the size and weight of the brains of these children and adults with those of people with normal intelligence. No difference in size or weight has been found. It can be assumed that the limited intellectual functioning of mentally defective children is not due to gross anatomical or microscopically visible defects, but rather involves much finer, not yet measurable, defects, probably of a biochemical or physiologic nature. The speed of impulses and messages transmitted from one part of the brain to another is most likely a major factor. These children are uniformly slow in all their actions and reactions and in their general development. This is one of the basic symptoms of mental deficiency. (See p. 462 under Slowing Down of All Reactions.)

So many different faculties are involved in the process of intelligence that its underlying cerebral basis must also be very widespread. The psychologist David Wechsler defines intelligence as

> the aggregate or global capacity of the individual to act purposefully, to think rationally and to deal effectively with his environment. It is global because it characterizes the individual's behavior as a whole; it is an aggregate because it is composed of elements or abilities which, though not entirely independent, are qualitatively differentiable (1944, p. 3).

All forms of learning are part of the process of intelligence. Being able to choose appropriate actions and ideas is one of its most important aspects. Memory and attention play a fundamental role. A mentally defective child who has learned to pay concentrated attention to what he is doing functions on a higher level than another child with the same type of limited intelligence who is distractible and cannot concentrate. The use a child can make of all his senses is also important. Mentally defective children have difficulty forming mental images. Their intellectual and fantasy world consists only of their *immediate* sensory impressions. They cannot think much beyond their immediate life situation. They think in simple, concrete terms.

It can therefore be assumed that the entire brain is in some way involved in causing the symptoms of this core group of mental defectives. The cortical projection fields of all senses as well as the connections between them function on a low level. All areas concerned with memory and those parts of the reticular formation dealing with attention must be in some way involved. It was formerly assumed that intelligence was primarily located in the frontal lobes. However, frontal lobe lesions do not necessarily cause dementia. Intellectual functioning also involves emotions. Subcortical areas, for instance the limbic system, may therefore possibly also be affected in children suffering from mental deficiency.

Role of the Cerebral Apparatuses

The examination of children in special classes for mentally defective children and in state schools shows that very many of them have symptoms pointing to localized cerebral defects. A very large number has a speech disorder; others suffer from apraxia, agnosia, and various forms of reading disorders. A large number also has specific neurologic defects such as spasticity of some muscle groups, which falls under the diagnosis of cerebral palsy, or various paralyses. Some of these children suffer from all these handicaps. The defects of others are not so widespread. The severity of these defects varies in mental defective children just as it varies in children with normal intelligence. As Wertham observed, "Reading disability is an analyzable part of mental deficiency and not a finding which contradicts this diagnosis" (personal communication). These patients were formerly classified under "Mental Deficiency with Focal Symptoms." This precise diagnosis is unfortunately not used any more.

In addition to the malfunctioning of all the systems in the brain underlying intelligence, these children have specific localized impairments in their various cerebral apparatuses. It is therefore of the utmost importance to examine these children very carefully so that all their defects can be determined in great detail and corrective measures taken.

Reading Ability

Children belonging to the core group with diffuse mental deficiency can usually learn the mechanics of reading and writing to the point where they can read and understand simple stories, work instructions, and signs. This is crucial in making them employable and able to take care of themselves when they become adults. This does not apply to children with a very low I.Q. and to those with a defective reading and/or speech apparatus.

Diagnosis

It is sometimes difficult to determine with certainty that a child's intelligence falls into the defective range. All these children are very difficult to test because they are so slow and because so many of them have many other specific organic and psychologic symptoms that interfere with their test performance. Only experienced psychologists can sort out those responses on intelligence tests indicating that the child's intelligence is within normal limits, and then differentiate them from those that are depressed by the child's specific organic handicaps.

For instance, a child who is only slow in his reactions has normal intelligence when his performance on the intelligence tests is within normal limits except for a uniformly slow reaction and performance time. Frequently one can only find out what the total intellectual capacity of such a child is by giving him the very best corrective training and by observing his responses to it.

Role of I.Q.

It is important to realize that an intelligence quotient is not an absolute number. It can never be as accurate as test results are in chemistry or physics. The units that were compared when the tests were standardized are not so clearly defined as a chemical formula or a unit in physics. Human psychology and psychopathology cannot by its very nature be as precise. There are far too many individual and social variables. An intelligence quotient is only a statistical number, sometimes arrived at on the basis of questionable statistics.

Two intelligence tests are customarily used to determine the I.Q. of a child, the revised form L-M of the Stanford-Binet and the revised Wechsler Intelligence Scale for Children, (WISC). Both are administered individually.

THE STANFORD-BINET FORM L-M.   The I.Q. is determined on this test by the mental age of the child multiplied by 100 and divided by his chronologic age.

The Mental Age Concept.   The use of the mental age stems from Binet, whose basic assumption was that a person is thought of as normal if he can do the things persons of his age normally do, retarded if his test performance corresponds to the performance of persons younger than himself, and accelerated if his performance level exceeds that of persons his own age (Terman and Merrill 1972, p. 5). This is reflected in the scoring of the Stanford-Binet where, for example, every test passed between age 3 and 10 contributes 2 months to the mental age score of the child.

The very concept of mental age must be questioned, because it is much too rigidly defined. Not all 6-year-olds or 10-year-olds perform the same task in exactly the same way and on the same level of competence and intelligence. Their life experiences, even within the same country, economic and social class also vary. We now know that clinically mental deficiency is more complicated than that. It is not a fixation on a certain developmental level. A mentally defective man of 30 is a man physically, and in some respects psychologically. He is not the replica of a 6- or 12-year-old child, as the use of the mental age in tests would indicate. Wechsler therefore discarded this concept. However, the Stanford-Binet Form L-M is still an excellent intelligence test, in spite of this flaw. It is in some ways superior to the WISC. It is more thorough and detailed and often gives a more accurate picture of the child's functioning and capacities.

THE WISC.   The I.Q. of children examined with this test is based on the average performance of a large number of children of the same age on the verbal and performance tasks used in this test. The results of the child's performance on these subtests are then converted into an I.Q. score (Wechsler, 1944, p. 7; 1974, p. 4).

THE EQUIVALENCE OF TEST ITEMS.   Both the Stanford-Binet Form L-M and the revised WISC give numerical equivalence to test items that are quite different. The child earns the same score irrespective of whether the test passed calls for a repetition of a series of digits, the copying of a square, the definition of a word, or the correct reply to a commonsense question. Wechsler stresses that "to all intents and purposes, the simple addition of these groups necessarily assumes an arithmetical equivalence of the test items so combined" (Wechsler, 1944, p. 7). He also states that what he calls the "functional equivalence of the test items" is "absolutely necessary for the validation of the arithmetic employed in arriving at a final measure of intelligence" (1944, p. 6).

The equivalence of some test items can be questioned. An item may indeed be indispensable for intelligence tests, but it must be used and evaluated with caution. For instance, words play a crucial role in arriving at test results. Children who speak a dialect or a foreign language at home therefore test lower than children with the same level of intelligence who are familiar with the words used on these tests and the way the psychologist pronounces them.

To prove this point, A. Dove, a social worker in Watts, California, devised the "Chitling Test of Intelligence" as a half-serious idea to show that most whites would perform poorly on a test patterned after other standard intelligence tests but slanted toward a nonwhite, lower-class experience. The test has 29 items such as:

3. A "Gas Head" is a person who has a _____
   a) fast-moving car
   b) stable of "lace"
   c) "process"
   d) habit of stealing cars
   e) long jail record for arson

5. If you throw the dice and "7" is showing on the top, what is facing down?
   a) seven
   b) "snake eyes"
   c) "boxcars"
   d) "little Joes"
   e) eleven

8. "Down Home" (the South today for the average "soul brother" who is picking cotton in season from sunup until sundown), what is the average earning (take-home) for one full day?
   a) $0.75
   b) $1.00
   c) $3.50
   d) $5.00
   e) $12.00

12. Hattie Mae Johnson is on the County. She has four children and her husband is now in jail for nonsupport, as he was unemployed and was not able to give her any money. Her welfare check is now $236 per month. Last night she went out with the highest player in town. If she got pregnant, then 9 months from now, how much more will her welfare check be?
    a) $80.00
    b) $2.00
    c) $35.00
    d) $150.00
    e) $100.00

15. The opposite of square is _____
    a) round
    b) up
    c) down
    d) hip
    e) lame

The correct answers are:

3. c, 5. a, 8. d, 12. c, 15. d.

According to Dove, a score below 20 suggests a low ghetto I.Q. Dove says, "As white middle class educators put it, 'You are 'culturally deprived' '" (Ehrlich and Feldman, 1977, pp. 85–87).

Wechsler uses the following classification of intelligence levels, which has been generally accepted (1974, p. 26, Table 8).

130 and above	Very superior
120–129	Superior
110–119	High average (bright)
90–109	Average
80–89	Low average (dull)
70–79	Borderline
69 and below	Mentally deficient

This classification is too rigid and unclinical. The importance of the differences in I.Q. scores that are within normal limits has been exaggerated out of all proportion. This has harmed very many children for the rest of their lives. I have treated adolescent and adult patients who never got over their feelings of inferiority, incompetence, and hopelessness because they had been told that their I.Q. was only 115, that they were therefore not "college material," and that their vocational choices were limited. Others maintained an unjustified feeling of superiority. However, it is often helpful to know when a child's intelligence is very superior or close to the mental defective range. Education can be planned within those parameters, provided the enormous power of a child's interest in a subject and in a career, his talents, and his ability to persevere are taken into account.

I am opposed to revealing I.Q. scores to children or their parents. Such figures are prone to misinterpretations and they haunt both child and parents for the rest of their lives. The significance of the entire psychologic examination should be carefully explained to the child and his parents. If his I.Q. is within normal limits, he should be told so, and it should be stressed that there are no limits to what he can accomplish in life as far as his intelligence is concerned, that it depends entirely upon his interests and opportunities.

The accuracy of an intelligence quotient is never absolute. It cannot by its very nature determine the intellectual capacities of entire populations. It ought to be considered valuable and accurate only within the framework of clinical science. Mental deficiency is a clinical and not a psychometric diagnosis. Great harm has been done by using the I.Q. for generalizations about people or races in the social sciences.

The influence of Sir Cyril Burt, a famous British psychologist, is one example of many for the misuse of unscientific group I.Q. tests for the propagation of the crudest forms of prejudice. He based his thesis that I.Q. levels are inherited and therefore fixed and unalterable on I.Q. statistics that he interpreted as proving that working class people, women as a group, the Jews, and the Irish, were less intelligent than the English middle and upper classes. His theories were widely accepted as absolute truths for decades. They had a profound influence on education in many countries. The British education law of 1944 was partly based on his theories. It set up three educational tracks that differ qualitatively. The American psychologist Jensen and the physicist Shockley used Burt's I.Q. studies as one more proof for their thesis of the inherent inferiority of the intelligence of black children.

It has now been proven beyond doubt by the professors of psychology Leon Kamin of Princeton and D. D. Dorfman of the University of Iowa and others, that Burt did not err in the interpretation of his statistics, but that he deliberately "beyond a reasonable doubt" fabricated them for political reasons, to propagate the thesis of the superiority of the white upper classes ("Cheating on the I.Q. Test," 1978; "Intelligenz," 1978, p. 265; Kamin, 1974).

Clinically, intelligence tests are indispensable in spite of their limitations. They are needed for the determination of mental deficiency and for finding out whether or not a child's or an adult's intelligence is within normal limits. Lower or higher levels of intelligence within these normal limits are also helpful indicators, but only if they are not taken as absolutes.

Experienced clinical psychologists do not determine an I.Q. mechanically. They weigh the child's responses on all subtests of intelligence tests carefully, and evaluate them together with his performance on other tests, before they make the diagnosis of mental retardation or mental deficiency. If only *one* test shows evidence of normal intellectual functioning, the child does not belong in the mentally defective group. A good example of this is 10-year-old Marie, who was referred to the Lafargue Clinic as hopelessly defective. Her Rorschach test showed normal intelligence with a possibility of organic weakness. I described her cure by Dr. Jellinek in the section on Aphasia. Had she been treated like a mentally defective child, she would probably have had the same fate as Elaine, who got very much worse and probably spent most of her life in mental hospitals. I described her plight also in the section on Aphasia (pp. 382–385).

Mosaic Test

The Mosaic tests of these children provide a visual picture of the simple level on which they function. It has been standardized for mental deficiency by a number of psychologists. Ames and Ilg point this out in their book, *Mosaic Patterns of American Children* (1962), where they state:

> Probably the most clear-cut usefulness of the Mosaic, in designating intelligence, that has thus far been demonstrated is its effectiveness in distinguishing defective from normal subjects (1962, p. 27).

Children belonging to the core group of mental defectives without any focal symptoms make many small designs on the mosaic board. The organization of all their designs is good, but very simple. Each design is made up of pieces of only one shape; for example, a "ball" is made of equilateral triangles, "tiles" are made of squares, a kite consists of two oblong triangles, a fan of equilateral triangles, and so on. The color scheme is usually enumerative, one piece of each color being used for each design. Small designs scattered over the entire tray also indicate that the impairment lies in the cortex. Mentally defective children do not make subcortical patterns unless these areas are also affected, as they frequently are in children who also have aphasia (Figure 2.1).

The Goodenough I.Q.

Scoring a Goodenough Figure-Drawing Test for an I.Q. can also be helpful, but primarily as a screening device. The Goodenough is usually lower than a Wechsler or Stanford-Binet in children with organic defects. It is also low in children with mental deficiency. However, it should not be used as the only test to determine a below-normal I.Q. A child with apraxia may score in the defective range on this test, while his I.Q. may be within the normal range on the WISC or the Stanford-Binet. (See section on this test under Writing Disorders, Vol. I, p. 219.)

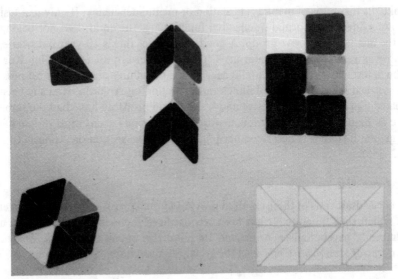

FIG. 2.1.   This Mosaic is typical for *mental deficiency.* Only one shape is used in each design. Enumerative color scheme. A number of small separate designs. (Color plate of Figure 2.1 follows p. 432.)

Group Tests

Such tests are totally inadequate for the diagnosis of mental deficiency. Their use in school systems has done great harm. Far too many children all over the country have been put in classes for retarded children just on the basis of group tests. These tests discriminate especially against children who speak one of the American dialects or a foreign language.

Treatment

Special Class Placement

There are different degrees of mental deficiency. Some school systems such as that of New York City recognize this. They put these children into different classes and on different educational tracks, one for "educable" and the other for "trainable" retardates. The educable group can learn reading, writing, and arithmetic and some other subjects; the trainable group can be expected to learn only to take care by themselves of their basic needs, such as washing and dressing themselves, toileting, feeding themselves, and orienting themselves in their environment by reading simple signs.

I was involved in the sifting out of children with normal intelligence and removing them from CRMD classes in New York City. Areas such as Harlem with large black populations had an exceedingly large number of these classes. The reasons were prejudicial as well as financial. The school system apparently got financial compensation for children in CRMD classes from the state and indirectly from the federal government. The larger the classes, the greater the compensation.

At the Lafargue Clinic and later at the Bureau of Child Guidance, very many of these children were tested individually, and the intelligence of many of them was found to be within normal range. Some even had a superior I.Q. All of these chidren were removed from CRMD classes. The psychologists at the Bureau of Child Guidance in charge of these operations, Dr. Dorothy B. Lee and Mrs. Alroy Rivers, also succeeded in establishing classes for intellectually gifted children, so-called IGC classes, in the districts of Harlem that were under our care. Their I.Q. had to be above 130.

That the misplacement of children with normal intelligence in these classes has not changed is demonstrated by the award of $500,000 to such a student in 1978. It was the first educational malpractice award in New York State. The student was 27 years old by then. At the age of 6 he scored 74 on an I.Q. test, one point below the cutoff, and was placed in a CRMD class. He remained in these classes till the age of 18 when he was abruptly dismissed because he earned an I.Q. of 94 on retesting.

He should not have been placed in such a class in the first place because he had earned an I.Q. of 90 when tested in a hospital before the first school test. If the school and the hospital psychologist had communicated with each other, the boy might have been saved from this debilitating miseducation.

As reported by the *New York Daily News* and the *New York Post,* this boy also had a severe speech disorder that remained untreated. Apparently he shared the fate of so many children with such a disorder, as described in the section on Aphasia (Capeci, 1978; Lane, 1978).

There are many thousands of children referred to school psychologists all over the country for placement in classes for mental defective children. The psychologic staff is never large enough to give individual tests to all these children. Screening devices are therefore essential. These are, of necessity, group tests. Only experienced clinical psychologists are really qualified to devise and evaluate such tests and to select those children who need to be tested individually.

Entirely too many children are referred for placement in these classes. Most of them are not mentally defective at all, but have severe reading and/or behavior problems. Teachers and school administrators frequently know that these children are not mentally defective, but try to use these classes to remove troublesome children from other classrooms. They are not entirely to blame for these maneuvers, because they are not given enough help to deal with these troublesome children in other more constructive ways.

Institutionalization

Some mentally defective children, especially those with a low I.Q. and others with many focal impairments, are very difficult to raise at home. The presence of such a child in a family with other children may be so destructive to the entire family that it is best to remove such a child. The present trend of the treatment of mentally retarded children is to have them stay at home and train them on an outpatient basis. Unfortunately, parents are now frequently not told that there is an alternative to home care, that they have a right to have their defective child admitted to a state school. This decision is extremely difficult to arrive at, especially as many of these institutions are poorly administered. The care these children receive is often neglectful and inhumane. This places an intolerable burden on the parents of these children, who feel guilty about institutionalization in any case. However, the solution is not to close these state schools, but to organize them in such a way that mentally defective children and adults receive humane and constructive care throughout their lives. (See case of Stefan under Word-Sound Deafness, p. 395.)

Prognosis

Many educable mentally retarded children can be made self-supporting, provided they get excellent education and training.

The number of mentally defective children will hopefully become smaller. We have already almost eliminated cretinism by treating such thyroid defects early, and we will eventually have the same success with many inborn errors of metabolism. Most cases of mongolism can now be prevented by amniocentesis and abortion. The prevention of fetal nutritional deficiencies, infections, and birth injuries should also decrease the incidence of mental deficiency. Better diagnostic and therapeutic understanding of aphasia, agnosia, apraxia, and organic reading, writing, and arithmetic disorders should make it possible for many such children to function close to normal as adults.

Chapter 3

Convulsive Disorders

421

A convulsion affects the entire brain. It is a diffuse symptom which may be induced by a localized lesion. A child with a convulsive disorder has a reading disorder only when the brain injury, disease, or other defect underlying his convulsions also damaged his cerebral reading apparatus. It is a question of the localization of the cerebral impairments.

Among the 222 children with an organic reading disorder I studied, 16 (14 boys, 2 girls) had a convulsive disorder. Only one of these boys had epilepsy; another had petit mal. One of the children in this group was Richard, the 10-year-old boy whom I describe in the section on Linear Dyslexia (Vol. I). He had a severe organic reading disorder with Linear Dyslexia and symptoms of cerebral palsy following a subdural hematoma due to a birth injury. His convulsions did not start until he was 13 years old (Vol. I, p. 129). It is important to realize that children with such a severe head injury may not have convulsions until many years later. They should, therefore, be re-examined at regular intervals for years.

The EEG is an important test for these children. It shows the presence or absence of a convulsive disorder even when the child has no convulsions. A child or an adult may have a convulsive disorder such as epilepsy and currently have no convulsions. The neurologist and specialist in convulsive disorders, Frederic A. Gibbs, stressed that for every adult epileptic he examined who had convulsions, he saw 10 who never had convulsions or only a few in their childhood and whose EEGs were typically abnormal (Alvarez, 1972, p. 9).

Walter C. Alvarez made the same observations in his *Nerves in Collision* where he described the plight of over 300 convulsive and nonconvulsive epileptics of all ages, whom he diagnosed and treated in his medical practice. He wrote:

> It is very important to note—as the experts have established—that for every one person with abnormal electroencephalograms and a history of convulsions, there are ten epileptics with abnormal electroencephalograms but *no* history of convulsions who are almost never diagnosed as epileptic (1972, p. 58).

Anticonvulsive medication is indicated for these patients. This does not affect children's reading disorders, which still have to be treated with special remedial techniques. (See section on EEG in Examination, Vol. I, p. 36. See also case of 11-year-old Morris, with Convulsions after a Head Injury in section on Attention Disorders, under Concentration, p. 67.)

Only one child among the 177 children in my study with a psychogenic reading disorder had a history of convulsions. This was a 10-year-old boy who apparently had had one febrile convulsion before the age of 4. No causal connection between this convulsion and his reading and behavior disorder could be established. (See discussion of Febrile Convulsions in section on

422

Hyperactivity, p. 308.) Among the 46 children with a sociogenic reading disorder there was no history of convulsions.

It is important to realize that epilepsy or any other convulsive disorder can cause hyperactivity. The problems of such children are described in detail in the section on hyperactivity (See also case of 8-year-old Ramon, p. 621.)

Epilepsy

This is a diffuse brain disorder without any demonstrable microscopic or macroscopic anomalies. Its cause is unknown, but there is an important hereditary component. It starts in childhood or adolescence up to the age of 20. According to Slater and Roth, about 40% have their first fit between the ages of 1 and 10 years, and a further 30% between the ages of 10 and 20 years (1969, p. 450). It lasts during the entire life of the patient unless it is treated. It is a good example of the fact that a brain disease or impairment may cause a number of severe symptoms, but not have damaged the cerebral reading apparatus, so that the child's reading ability remains intact.

In addition to convulsions, epileptics have a number of the unspecific organically caused psychologic symptoms circumscribed in special sections. These are: the slowing down of most reactions, the inability to tolerate disorder, the inability to shift, the morbid irritability, and the sudden unmotivated mood swings. These children may read slowly, but their reading may not be impaired otherwise. They can, of course, also develop a reading disorder on a psychogenic basis.

My statistics tend to show that children with an organic reading disorder only rarely have epilepsy. It affected only one boy among the 222 children in my study. However, this does not mean that reading disorders are that infrequent among epileptic children. The low incidence in my statistics may be due to the fact that I did not work in special clinics for children with convulsive disorders. These children are traditionally examined and treated in these special clinics, which are run either by pediatricians or neurologists. They are rarely cared for in child psychiatric clinics. In private practice, they are also usually treated by pediatricians or neurologists. This has disadvantages for the total care of these children, because the communication between these specialists and child psychiatrists, psychologists, and educators is unfortunately too often poor. The reading, writing, and arithmetic disorders and the general psychopathology of these children are consequently often not diagnosed and treated with sufficient care.

An exception was a special unit of the Bureau of Child Guidance charged with the supervision of the education of all children with convulsive disorders in the school system of New York City. This unit consisted of a child psychiatrist, a social worker, and several psychologists. Its work helped these children, their parents, and their teachers. It was in close contact with their clinics or private physicians. It was unfortunately dissolved for administrative rather than clinical reasons.

Many school systems such as New York City's have the sensible policy of teaching epileptic children whenever possible in regular classrooms. According to statistics cited by Alvarez, 80% of epileptic children can attend school, and about one-half of these can function in regular classes throughout their schooling (1972, p. 82).

Unfortunately these youngsters sometimes have abnormal episodes and may not take their medication regularly, so that they are difficult to teach. It is often difficult and time-consuming for guidance counselors and others assigned to this task to make certain that these children take their medication regularly and at the proper time, and that they remain under the care of a clinic or private physician and do not miss their appointments. Parents are often negligent in this respect, especially when overburdened with financial and other worries.

I know the extent of these usually chronic difficulties through my own experience. Receiving a complete case history listing all physicians, clinics, agencies the child attended, all tests, diagnoses, and medications and how long the child actually took them, often requires endless telephone calls, written requests, and generally a form of detective work. This is also true for other children with complicated physical and psychologic symptoms.

It has been the fate of many adult and child epileptics not to get the very long-range care they need, especially those who cannot afford private care. Some agencies and clinics do not accept them, and their parents are sometimes confused about what clinic to attend regularly. Because of their irritability and tendency to mood swings, often combined with very pedantic behavior, they are difficult patients as well as pupils, even after their convulsions have been controlled. They are in great need not only of physical and neurologic, but also of psychologic care.

Because of their inconsistent and fragmentary treatment, there is very little information about the frequency of reading, writing, and arithmetic disorders among epileptics. Alvarez made a statistical study based on records of 274 adults (129 men, 145 women) who were "largely episodic, nonconvulsive" epileptics. Only 1% had difficulties learning to read (1972, pp. 36, 38). The frequency of reading disorders among convulsing epileptic children still needs to be studied.

Reading Epilepsy

Reading may induce a special type of convulsion, which is sometimes called "sensory precipitation" or "reflex epilepsy." It is a very rare disorder.

Forster and Daly (1973) described this form of epilepsy in identical twins. They were sisters who had jaw-jerk vocalization and frequently lost their place in the text when reading. These seizures occurred with binocular as well as monocular reading, whether they read horizontally or vertically, and whenever they read unfamiliar material. Reading memorized material did not evoke the seizures. This indicates that the attention process may be involved in this form of epilepsy. Reading new material requires the most concentrated intellectual attention. (See section on Concentration Disorder, p. 68.)

The twins also had seizures while writing, even when blindfolded. There was a jerking or freezing of the writing hand. Reading musical scores without words also induced seizures. One of the twins had learned to read Braille in order to avoid seizures, but she had reading epilepsy even while reading Braille. The location of the seizures apparently depended on the muscles used for the activity. These girls had hand seizures while writing or playing music, and jaw-jerks while reading texts, Braille, or musical scores. No other neurologic defects were found, and the twins seemed healthy otherwise. They had three unaffected siblings.

Epileptic seizures can indeed be triggered by music. This is called "musicogenic epilepsy." Macdonald Critchley, in his comprehensive book *Music and the Brain* (1977b), states: "Musicogenic epilepsy is without doubt a clinical entity but a rare one" (p. 349). The combination of this form of epilepsy with reading epilepsy is apparently so extremely rare that Critchley does not mention it in this book.

Localization and Causation

The cerebral localization and the cause of this form of convulsions is not known. Forster and Daly suggest that it may be due to a "very discrete cerebral lesion," and that it may be of genetic origin.

This paper was presented at a meeting of the American Neurological Association. The neurologist Reginald Bickford said in the discussion that he had studied such cases for about 20 years and that the twins were a good example of a "primary reading epilepsy syndrome," which appears to have a genetic cause. He also said that the EEG discharge of some of his patients was limited to the parietal region and that it was more widespread in others.

He described two types of techniques being used to investigate this type of disorder: evoked potentials related to saccadic movements of the eyes during reading, and spectral analysis of the entire reading process. However, these investigations so far have failed to lead to a better understanding of this form of epilepsy.

Television Epilepsy

Television may induce convulsions. The frequency of this form of epilepsy is not known. It was at first assumed that either the flicker that occurs when the TV picture slips, or other malfunctioning of the set, induced these seizures. We now know, however, that properly functioning sets, black and white as well as color, may cause them.

Slater and Roth describe the type of reflex epilepsy to which TV-induced convulsions belong.

> Flashing lights prove to be an effective provoking agent of epileptic seizures in certain susceptible individuals who may suffer attacks of epilepsy at the cinema or whilst watching television. It is this group too who may develop epileptic phenomena whilst driving along a tree-lined avenue in the setting sun. Flicker produced by stroboscopic lamps is used as a method of provoking epileptiform discharges in the electroencephalogram (1969, p. 451).

The British clinical neurophysiologists Stefansson, Darby, Wilkins, Binnie, and colleagues examined 32 patients aged 6 to 31 who had reflex epilepsy induced by various light patterns, television among them. They used stroboscopic lamps and other methods. Sixteen of these patients had a history of major or minor seizures associated with TV viewing. Six of them had seizures only when sitting close to the screen; the others also when sitting at a distance. They tested their EEG while resting, when eyes were open or closed, and during TV viewing at different distances. They came to the conclusion that "properly functioning domestic television sets may induce seizures in epileptic patients" (1977). They stressed that the modern urban environment contains so many patterns of light "that the possible effect of these stimuli may be unrecognized by the patient or relatives." They observed that many seemingly spontaneous seizures are actually induced by light patterns, including those produced by television (1977, p. 88). This means that television epilepsy may be more frequent than has been recognized so far.

Chapter 4

Cerebral Palsy

Freud pointed out as long ago as 1897 that this is not a disease entity. He reported his findings in six different papers summarized in *Die Infantile Cerebrallähmung,"* (*Infantile Cerebral Palsy*) where he evaluated the literature on these disorders as well 35 of his own patients. He concluded that the cerebral localization of these disorders is not uniform. He stressed that all forms of cerebral palsy are due to damage to the brain either during the fetal period, during birth, or immediately after, and that the localization of the damaged areas of the brain varies (Freud, 1897; Spehlmann, 1953, pp. 41–45).

Freud's conclusions are still valid. Some neurologists, orthopedists, and pediatricians therefore no longer like to use the term cerebral palsy. They classify these children according to their symptoms, just as Freud did. However, Nelson's and other pediatric textbooks continue to use it and it has remained a popular term. It was formerly called Little's Disease.

The pediatrician John B. Bartram defines cerebral palsy as

> a group of non-progressive disorders resulting from malfunction of the motor centers and pathways of the brain, characterized by paralysis, weakness, incoordination, or other aberrations of motor function which have their origin prenatally, during birth, or before the central nervous system has reached relative maturity (1969, p. 1311).

He also stresses that it is a "nonfatal, noncurable condition that is frequently benefited by therapy and by training and education" (p. 1312).

Organic Basis

The underlying cerebral lesions or defects vary and with them the child's symptoms depending on the nature and extent of the injuries or other damage. Cortical areas in the frontal as well as in the parietal lobes, which control motor movements and integrate motor patterns, are usually affected; and so is the cerebellum, whose malfunctioning causes unsteady gait, difficulty with voluntary movements generally, an inability to perform rapidly alternating movements, delays in initiating and stopping movements, and an inability to coordinate muscular activities. It is assumed that these symptoms are due in part to impaired integration of the functions of the cerebellum with the functions of the vestibular apparatuses (the organs of balance) in the middle ear and with pertinent subcortical and cortical areas.

Children with this disorder frequently also have involuntary muscle contractions due to defects in the basal ganglia. These are choreiform (i.e., fine, irregular, arrhythmic, and jerky) or athetotic (i.e., slow, tonic, and wormlike). These involuntary movements are called hyperkinesias. They are sometimes difficult to detect, but they can be diagnosed with certainty through electromyography. (See section on Hyperactivity, p. 585.)

The high incidence of convulsions (25%) and mental deficiency (about 50%)

among children with this disorder shows that the underlying cerebral pathology is often diffuse (Bartram, 1969, p. 1312).

Role of Cerebral Apparatuses

These various apparatuses are unfortunately often involved, which makes it especially difficult for these children to function. Their speech apparatus is most frequently impaired. Their defective speech is sometimes only due to malfunctioning of their speech muscles, but frequently the cerebral speech apparatus is also involved, so that these children may have different forms of aphasia such as word-meaning or word-sound deafness.

The frequent visual difficulties may not only be due to eye muscle dysfunction, but also to involvement of cerebral areas leading to agnosia. The same is true for defects in hearing, which are very frequent.

Reading, writing, and arithmetic often present special problems for these children. Difficulties learning to write are especially prevalent because of the abnormal motor movements of their fingers, hands, and arms. Teaching them to type is sometimes the best solution. However, agraphias and apraxias due to malfunctioning of areas in the parietal lobes are also frequent.

Children with cerebral palsy may have any form of an organic reading disorder due to malfunctioning of their cerebral reading apparatus. The areas underlying arithmetic sometimes also malfunction. It is interesting in this connection that Gerstmann syndrome (acalculia, finger agnosia, disorientation of right and left on one's own body and on others, and agraphia) is apparently more frequent among this group of children than any other. (See Gerstmann syndrome, Vol. I, p. 175.)

These children invariably have a number of the general and unspecific symptoms found in all other patients with any kind of brain disease or other damage, including hyperactivity.

Classification

Four forms of cerebral palsy can be distinguished: (1) a hypertonic form, where spasticity is the outstanding symptom, the legs being more frequently involved than the arms; (2) an ataxic form where ataxia is the outstanding symptom; (3) a dyskinetic form that is characterized by poor coordination and by difficulty with chewing, swallowing, and speaking because of muscle weaknesses and abnormal accompanying movements; and (4) mixed forms, which are by far the most frequent (Matthes, 1973, p. 317).

Diagnosis

Diagnosis of cerebral palsy is based on the neurologic examination. It is very important to analyze all the child's many handicaps, motoric and otherwise, with the utmost care. This cannot usually be done in one session because of these children's extreme fatiguability, irritability, perseveration, and anxiety.

A psychiatric examination is usually also indicated because these children's many disabling physical handicaps invariably lead to psychopathology of varying severity. Close collaboration among the child's pediatrician, neurologist, and psychiatrist is of the utmost importance for the diagnosis and long-range treatment of cerebral palsied children.

Psychologic Tests

Testing is very difficult to carry out in these children, but is extremely important at the same time. The difficulties found by psychologists are summarized by Ingram:

> In patients with moderate or severe motor deficits as a result of cerebral palsy, it may be still more difficult to distinguish between failures on tests which are due to perceptual difficulties, failures which are the result of mental retardation and failures which are attributable to motor handicaps (1969, p. 363).

Psychologists working with these children develop an expertise in unraveling all these factors.

FIGURE DRAWINGS AND MOSAIC TESTS.   The handicaps of cerebral palsied children are usually revealed in their drawings, provided their arms are not too spastic or ataxic to draw. For instance, they draw one limb much shorter than the other, or just draw a line for the diseased limb. The Mosaic test shows the cortical and/or subcortical basis for these children's symptoms.

Incidence

Bartram points out that the group of diseases subsumed under cerebral palsy is one of the leading causes of crippling in children (1969, p. 1312). It is estimated that the prevalence rate is 100 to 600 cases per 100,000 population. Most of these patients are under 21 years of age. Bartram stresses that "the care and support of these children, who usually have multiple handicaps, present an important economic and social as well as a medical problem" (p. 1312). The medical, social, economic, and educational significance of cerebral palsy is even greater, because an unknown number of children have mild forms with handicapping symptoms that are frequently not diagnosed.

A good example for this is 8-year-old Eddie, whose reading and other disorders are described in the section on A Reading Disorder Specific for Hyperactive Children with Choreiform Movements, p. 586. Eddie had minimal choreiform movements as well as athetosis. Prechtl classifies all children with these symptoms under cerebral palsy. He was first to describe a Choreiform Syndrome in children, which is usually associated with hyperactivity

(1962). This was true for Eddie, who was born with an especially severe form of jaundice called Kernicterus. This is known to cause involuntary movements, because it damages the basal ganglia (Pearson, 1969, pp. 1060–1061).

Causes

The causes of cerebral palsy are exactly the same as those assumed to underlie reading disorders on an organic basis. Evidence for anoxia, or at least hypoxia (periods of low oxygen supply) is found frequently in the birth history of these children. Kernicterus and prematurity are known causes of cerebral palsy. Subdural hemorrhages due to a birth injury are especially prone to cause these disorders. The neurosurgeon William Sharpe (1954), who was especially interested in cerebral palsy, thought that these disorders could be prevented by a spinal puncture test done soon after birth, when a hemorrhage was suspected. This was supposed to indicate not only bleeding, but also an elevated pressure, which should be relieved by draining spinal fluid. However, it is unfortunately still not possible to prevent the consequences of all subdural hemorrhages. An example for such a failure is 10-year-old Richard, whose plight is described in the section on Linear Dyslexia, Vol. I, p. 129. He was born with such a hemorrhage and a subdural hematoma was removed soon after birth. However, he had only minimal symptoms of cerebral palsy throughout his life. He had nystagmus, mild ptosis of one eyelid, right abducens weakness, mild right facial paralysis, and mild spasticity of his right arm and hand. He also developed convulsions at the age of 13. His organic reading disorder and his attention disorder evidently had the same organic basis.

Treatment

These children need treatment by a number of specialists, including orthopedists; pediatricians; medical specialists in physical rehabilitation; physical therapists; occupational and speech therapists; specialists in perceptual training; educational therapists for the treatment of these children's reading, writing, and arithmetic disorders; neurosurgeons to correct the small number of children who can be helped through this specialty; psychologists; and child psychiatrists.

It is of the utmost importance to have *one* clinic and *one* specialist in charge of coordinating the child's entire treatments throughout childhood and adolescence and later on in life. Saturen and Tobias stress this point especially:

> There is danger of "fragmenting" the child into a complex of unrelated disabilities as he is parceled out among clinics or taken from office to office. One physician, be it the family doctor or pediatrician, should provide continuity of care to meet the child's changing needs, calling on the various disciplines for consultation. He should know and use the community's resources for rehabilitation and special education (1961, p. 591).

These children are usually worse off as far as fragmented treatment is concerned than even children suffering from epilepsy or other convulsive disorders ("World of Medicine," 1979). (See section on Convulsive Disorders, p. 423.)

Close cooperation between the various specialized clinics dealing with these children and child psychiatric clinics is important both for the children and the staff. I was in charge of such a clinic, called the Combined Evaluation Clinic. It was run jointly by the Child Psychiatric and the Pediatric Clinic specializing in physical rehabilitation.

Psychologists, pediatricians, and speech and educational therapists who work with children suffering from cerebral palsy, are especially helpful in figuring out the diagnosis and treatment plan of children referred to their own or the child psychiatric clinic with severe and multiple symptoms that are difficult to disentangle and to diagnose. (See section on Specialized Mental Hygiene Clinics under Treatments, Vol. I, p. 291.)

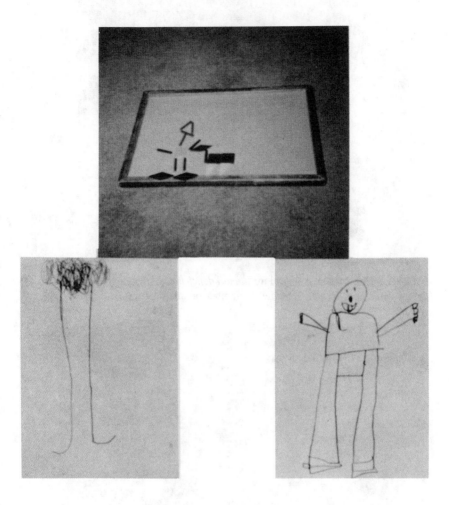

FIG. 13.1. Perry, age 7½. Psychogenic reading disorder, severe hyperactivity with anxiety. *Mosaic test title:* "A boy pulling his wagon." The boy moves fast. This is typical for hyperactivity; so is the overstepping of all limits—the boy's shoes are on top of the margin of the Mosaic tray. *Drawings:* They are expansive and grandiose. This is typical for hyperactivity. The lack of a neck on the man shows a lack of any restraining influence exerted by thinking over acting.

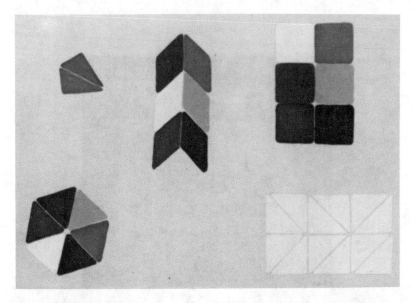

FIG. 2.1. This Mosaic is typical for *mental deficiency.* Only one shape is used in each design. Enumerative color scheme. A number of small separate designs.

FIG. 13.2. Ned, age 8, psychogenic reading disorder and reactive hyperactivity. *Mosaic test title:* "That's a robot. He is going through the hills." It is typical for Mosaics of hyperactive children that the design moves and that red pieces are in prominent positions. The robot walks on red legs, and his left side consists of three red pieces with a white piece in the middle.

FIG. 13.3. A moving bus made by Adrian, age 10, on his Mosaic test. (Color plate of Figure 13.3 follows p. 432.)

FIG. 13.5 Different stages of Chester's schizophrenia and hyperactivity as reflected in his drawings and in his Mosaic test. *Age 8:* Typical drawings indicating hyperactivity. They are also bizarre, which is typical for schizophrenia. The Mosaic design is also expansive and grandiose. It reaches the upper margin of the tray. Title: "A building. It talks to the space ship. It got transmitters to talk back and forth. That's the planet earth [line of oblong pieces], so it can take off! It is about two thousand billion feet long, two thousand billion people come into it, too!"

FIG. 13.7. *Chester, age 9.* Hyperactivity has lessened. The schizophrenic process is worse. His reading disorder has remained static. He is too preoccupied with his bizarre fantasies. His drawings are now static and constricted. His body image has become so poor that he dares draw only simplified stick figures. The Mosaic test is also severely constricted. It indicates a severe process. Red center pieces invariably indicate a tendency to serious violent outbursts. Chester had to be hospitalized.

FIG. 13.9 *Chester, age 15.:* His hyperactivity has subsided completely. It is a self-limited symptom, confined to immature organisms only. He has made an excellent social recovery from schizophrenia after years in a residential treatment center. However, the Mosaic design is still constricted and indicates that a schizophrenic process is continuing beneath the surface, and that his remission may not be long-lasting.

Chapter 5

Musical Ability Disorder

The neurologic term for this disorder is Amusia. Literally translated from Greek, it means complete lack of musical ability. However, these patients are not completely amusical; only certain parts of their musical ability are malfunctioning.

Amusia is a very rare disorder. It has been diagnosed almost exclusively in adults who were musicians or had some musical training, and its causes have been verified by autopsies. Cerebral lesions due to injuries, vascular accidents, or tumors were found. It is unquestionably an organic disorder and not due to psychopathology. Neuroses that interfere with the function of musicians have different symptoms.

Amusias are important in relation to children's organic reading disorders because both disorders may occur together. The musical disorder is usually overlooked because children are just not tested for defects in their musical function. A correct diagnosis would facilitate the child's treatment and recovery, because reading, spelling, and writing have musical elements. Recovery is delayed if these elements are not treated or used when they function well. They are rhythmic and tonal flexibility while reading, and an ability to distinguish minute differences in speech sounds, which is also crucial for spelling and writing. The reading of a child with a good musical ability can be improved with the use of auditory memory aids such as rhyming, melodies, chants, and all sorts of word/sound associations. (See section on Auditory Memory Aids, Vol. I, p. 74.)

A child with a reading disorder and good musical ability and training who can read notes, can transfer the sign/sound combination he has learned for note reading, to letter and word reading. The same holds true for learning sequences, which is so difficult for many children with an organic reading disorder. If their musical ability is intact they can often learn musical sequences such as singing or whistling scales or melodies easier and earlier than the alphabet and the letter sequences in words. Sequencing in the realm of music helps them with the sequencing needed for reading and arithmetic.

It must be stressed that Amusia does not mean complete absence of musical ability, which is extremely rare. It also has nothing to do with the so-called monotone syndrome, namely an inability to carry a tune. Augusta Jellinek and other authorities in this field point out that even such an inability is often amenable to instruction. In her classic study of Amusia she stresses that "there is no genuine constitutional defect or lack of musical ability, but only a lack in the motor skill to transpose correctly into singing what has been heard" (1956, p. 124). She also states that complete lack of musical interest and activity is extremely rare, and that an individual's actual musical capacities depend to a great extent on his or her education, training, and cultural background.

Children in the United States are surrounded by music. They hear it on radios, records, television, and are without exception interested in it and fascinated by it. It is a great pity that this interest is not used more constructively in schools as a basis for teaching more about music, including reading notes, distinguishing different styles, sight-singing, the basic elements of harmony, and the historical development of music.

The development of musical faculties is important not only for an increased esthetic enjoyment of life; it may also help learning some subjects. A child may for instance struggle valiantly with learning to speak a foreign language, but without success. An impaired musical ability, for example the inability to carry a tune, may contribute to this difficulty. Training whatever musical ability he has may help with the pronunciation of foreign languages.

Music is not a general human activity like speech, though it comes close to it. It is a faculty that must be trained in order to develop. If systematically taught, it also trains other faculties that are important for the child's intellectual as well as his emotional attention, his ability to listen, his motor skills when he sings or plays an instrument. He also learns to coordinate all his senses. It helps with the harmonious development of the child's mental, emotional, and physical faculties. However, only comparatively few children possess a musical talent that makes it possible for them to rise above amateur enjoyment and performance. The level of musical talents varies; ideally, all children should have the chance to develop theirs to the fullest.

The Organic Basis of Musical Ability

The faculty of hearing and understanding pure tones is central to all musical functions. This requires the intactness of Heschl's transverse gyrus and of other parts of the temporal lobes. It must be stressed that the faculty of hearing and understanding pure tones has a different cerebral location from that of hearing speech sounds and noises.

The temporal lobe areas underlying hearing, speech, and musical tones are connected with the organs of hearing in the inner ears and with almost all other parts of the brain. The neurologist N. Wertheim, who is an authority on the neuropathology and neurophysiology of musical functions, stresses that the organic basis for musical ability is very widespread and to a great extent still unknown. He writes:

> It is obvious that any attempt to find a representation in the brain for musical faculty encounters considerable difficulties and our present knowledge is far from sufficient to enable us to give definite answers to the many problems in this field (1977, p. 294).

He also stresses that

> considering the modern findings concerning the bilateral hemispheric representation of different cerebral functions, we must rather admit that the lesional sub-

stratum of musical dysfunction is much wider than is generally assumed, affecting concomitantly several functional systems of the brain (1969, p. 204).

(See also Dominance for Musical Ability, Vol. I, p. 61.)

Role of Emotions

The musical faculty is intimately connected with emotions. The limbic system, which is assumed to be at least in part the organic basis for emotions, is therefore undoubtedly involved in all aspects of music.

Role of Vision

There is also a close relation between vision and music, not only for reading notes and performing, but because music itself evokes colors and patterns in many people.

These visual sensations are perfectly normal. They are called synaesthesias. This is how Critchley describes them:

> The same melodic phrase may possess secondary sensations which change according to the key selected by the instrumentalist. That major and minor keys should differ in this context is not surprising. Some have spoken of minor keys being associated with grey or black photisms, major ones being green, blue, pink or red. To some subjects major chords are "brighter" than minor. But to those gifted with a more elaborate faculty of synaesthesia, highly specific differences may result according to the particular key chosen, whether it be major or minor.

It is interesting to note that blindness promotes these sensations (1977a, pp. 222–223).

Synaesthesias are intersensory sensations. They are especially vivid in children and in adults who are particularly gifted in this respect. Not only color vision when hearing music but also color hearing has been observed. Stimuli can apparently travel from one sense organ to another under circumstances and via pathways that are still unknown (Critchley, 1977a, pp. 219–230).

Some children and adults actually hear word for word during silent reading without moving their lips, tongue, or—so far as they can tell—their vocal cords. This is a special form of synaesthesia.

Unfortunately, children are not usually tested for these synaesthesias. Their extent, the role they play in children's fantasies and musical development, is therefore not known. We also do not know whether and under what circumstances they continue into adulthood. Some students of these phenomena believe they tend to be suppressed later on in life similar to eidetic phenomena (Critchley, 1977a, p. 230).

Children with organic reading disorders and other organic impairments usually do not possess these intersensory faculties. This is one reason for their difficulties with shifting. (See section on Intersensory Shifts, p. 483.)

The Cerebral Basis of Amusia

The cerebral reading, speech, and musical apparatuses can function independently. A malfunctioning of one is not necessarily accompanied by a malfunctioning of the others. Because the hearing and understanding of pure tones is localized in both hemispheres and apparently not confined to only one, diseases and injuries to either hemisphere may leave the musical ability of the patient completely intact.

I treated a 58-year-old orchestra conductor who had a stroke affecting the left side of his brain that led to aphasia. He was right-handed and had a right upper-arm paralysis. His aphasia was mostly expressive. He had spoken six languages before his stroke; afterwards, he could speak only one language, not his native language. He retained partial understanding of the other five languages, but could not speak them. His reading and writing were impaired in all languages. His musical ability was not affected at all. He learned to conduct with his left hand, even though he had been right-handed. He remembered musical scores by heart, and could read notes fluently. Within about a year after his stroke he was again able to conduct orchestras in different countries.

The relative independence of musical ability from speech, reading, and writing as observed in this patient, though rare, is not unique. Clinical studies have also shown that musical ability can sometimes function independently of intelligence. Some mentally defective children have a remarkably good musical ability.

Relation to Aphasia

The musical ability of children suffering from different forms of aphasia may or may not be impaired. Some aphasic children and adults can respond to music by singing or humming tunes and by dancing. This indicates that their musical ability has remained partially intact and that it can, to a certain extent, function independently from speech. Benton stresses the importance of these clinical observations. He writes that despite the close qualitative and quantitative association between disorders of music and speech,

> there is incontrovertible evidence that the two spheres of activity are mediated by distinctive neurobehavioural systems. The long-standing observation that patients with severe expressive language disorder are able to sing is in itself sufficient proof of this. The same dissociation may be observed in patients with receptive language disorder (1977, p. 390).

The intactness of the interaction of the pure-tone areas in the temporal lobes with the medial geniculate bodies and with the inferior colliculi is apparently just as important for an unimpaired musical function as it is for speech.

The medial geniculate bodies mediate the auditory-autonomic system. When their function is impaired, the word-meaning–deafness form of childhood aphasia is thought to result. The understanding of music is apparently also impaired, although it is very difficult and sometimes impossible to test these children's musical functions. Their singing may be especially affected because of its close connection with the autonomic nervous system. The vocal cords are smooth muscles that are innervated by nerves belonging to this system, and not by motor nerves as are the striated muscles of mouth and tongue.

The inferior colliculi integrate hearing with impulses arising in muscles, tendons, and joints. When they do not function properly, the word-sound–deafness form of childhood aphasia is assumed to result. This may affect not only speech sounds but also pure tones. (See section on The Autonomic Nervous System, p. 91; and sections on Word-Sound and Word-Meaning Deafness, pp. 385–386.) (Figure 1.1)

Role of Memory

Memory is an integral part of musical ability, and of fundamental importance. The musical memory of my conductor patient, for instance, remained completely intact, while he could not remember the language he had grown up with and other languages he had learned. Some children have an excellent memory for music, but find it very difficult to remember the forms of letters, how to spell and blend, and other aspects of memory connected with reading, writing, and arithmetic. Their musical memory can help these children also with other subjects. Musical engram complexes apparently can strengthen other engrams. Rhyming and singing, for instance, are excellent memory aids for other than musical facts. (See section on Memory Aids, Vol. I, p. 74.)

Classification

Two forms of Amusia can be distinguished. *Receptive* amusia consists of disorders of musical perception, recognition, memory, evaluation, and enjoyment. The symptoms of *expressive* amusia are difficulties in singing, whistling, playing instruments, and in producing rhythmic patterns. The difficulties in playing instruments belong to the apraxias. This symptom is also called instrumental apraxia. Most patients have symptoms of both forms.

Diagnosis

The diagnosis that the child has any musical difficulty requires first and foremost taking a detailed history of his musical experiences, training, interests, and enjoyment. This may reveal deficits no one, not even the child himself, may have noticed. A child who has no training in music does not notice that he has a musical disorder. He may never become aware of it, unless he needs musical ability for his work later on in life, or he wants badly to enjoy music and to perform for other reasons. His parents are also not likely to worry about his musical ability, unless he is a child prodigy and they are concerned about his future.

A child may also reveal spontaneously or in response to questions that he feels badly about not being able to sing or to perform in other ways like his friends or like performers he admires. I have examined and treated many adolescents who wanted to quit school and do nothing else but play the guitar and sing to become as famous, wealthy, and admired as the popular singer on whom they had a crush. These were invariably completely unrealistic expectations, but no lack of musical ability, proven by tests, could dissuade them. These are psychologic and social, not organic problems. They have nothing to do with Amusia.

The musical ability of all children with an organic reading disorder and/or other organic impairments should be tested, especially when such a child has aphasia. Music teachers usually test their students so that they can teach them more successfully, as well as to identify those children who are unsuited for their classes. These tests are adequate for healthy children with no organic impairments. Testing for Amusia requires special tests.

Psychiatric examinations or routine psychologic tests, including tests for aphasia, do not reveal Amusia. When a musical ability disorder is suspected, arrangements should be made for special testing.

Tests

It is essential that the child's hearing be tested before administering these special tests. A thorough and repeated audiologic examination is essential for every child with an organic reading disorder anyway. It should also be determined whether such a child can differentiate speech sounds, noises, and pure tones.

These tests should be administered by psychologists or speech therapists who have had musical training and experience, or by music teachers or musicians interested in this field. It is of advantage for a correct diagnosis for the psychologist or speech therapist to test the child together with a musician. Testing requires playing the piano and singing.

Before testing is started, the child or other patient should be classified according to his musical development. The neurologists Wertheim and Botez propose such a classification. They accordingly adapt their tests, the Wertheim-Botez system of examination of musical function disturbances (Wertheim 1969, pp. 200–203). They distinguish four developmental levels:

1. Musical persons without theoretical or instrumental musical training.

2. Professional musicians who lack musical training or knowledge of musical notation ("empirical" musicians, usually employed in dance bands, etc.).

3. Amateur musicians with theoretical and instrumental knowledge and highly trained professional musicians.

4. Persons lacking elementary musicality (who were never able to reproduce a simple song, to sing, or to whistle more or less correctly) (Wertheim, 1969, p. 200).

They stress that their testing system is not suitable for the fourth category "as the persons composing this category have in fact no investigable musical function" (Wertheim, 1969, p. 200). This applies also to children.

Augusta Jellinek also devised a testing system, which allows the analysis of primitive as well as of the very highest musical abilities. I have selected those test items from both systems that are most suited for children and adolescents.

No scoring should be attempted of any results of musical ability testing. Only individual findings are valid in individual cases. Jellinek emphasizes this point: "No mean measure of 'normal' musicality has been found. There is not, as in speech, a normal average of performance" (1956, p. 130).

Only those test items should be selected that are appropriate for the child's level of musical development. Testing should in any case be spread over several days, since it is too strenuous for one single session.

TESTS FOR GENERAL MUSICAL CONCEPTS

1. Recognition and definition of musical forms such as rock and roll, jazz, and jingles used for radio and television commercials, as well as symphonies, operas, sonatas, and so on.

2. Evaluation of musical samples and criticisms of the performance. The arbitrary use of wrong tempi, wrong expressive moods, and so on, should be added.

3. Attributing of musical samples to a composer and to a definite period and style.

4. Description of the affective tone of musical pieces, whether it is pleasant or unpleasant and to what type of music it belongs, for example, church music, dance, marching, and so on.

TESTS FOR MUSICAL PERCEPTION AND MEMORY

1. Identifying melodies sung or played.

2. Imitation in singing or playing of known or unknown melodies. The number of tones remembered within each melody should be recorded. Tonal and atonal tunes should be presented. A second repetition of the same melody that was imitated should be attempted.

3. Imitation of single tones produced by voice or an instrument.

4. Comparison of the patient's evaluation of an isolated tune with that of the same tune when accompanied on an instrument.

5. Observation of capacity to evaluate arbitrarily made mistakes, when a well-known piece is played.

6. Identifying instrumental sounds (original instruments if possible; use records or tapes of various instruments).

7. Identifying tones presented by voice or on an instrument as being high or low.

8. Identifying musical intervals.

9. Identifying major and minor chords (simultaneously played or in arpeggio).

10. Testing perception of tonality (does patient notice arbitrary changes of key in a tune or not?).

11. Identifying a tune when played in a key different from the first exposition.

This part of the test also helps evaluate other aspects of memory. It should be compared with other memory tests. (See section on Memory, Vol. I, pp. 64–70.)

TESTS FOR MUSICAL PRODUCTION AND EXPRESSION

Singing.

1. Spontaneous singing (tunes of the patient's choosing, tunes asked from but not sung for him; vocalisms; intervals).

2. Imitation by singing of known and unknown melodies and vocalisms, which are either sung, whistled, or played for the patient on an instrument.

3. Singing of well-known tunes after hearing only the lyrics without music (relating of text to melody).

4. Singing of identical musical phrases with and without words in various articulatory positions (on the vowels ah, oh, etc. or on syllables la la, mi mi, etc.).

5. Singing with accompaniment of the piano or another instrument; singing simultaneously with recorded music.

6. Testing of capacity to imitate staccato and legato singing.

7. Testing of capacity to transpose a tune sung to the patient in a higher or lower tonality.

Whistling. Use the same tests as under Singing above, with the exception of those concerned with articulation.

Mastery of an Instrument.

1. Touching of a piano key named to the patient (or blowing on a wind instrument, playing on a string, etc.); production of a wanted tone on an instrument he is familiar with.

2. Naming of piano keys, strings, and so on, and explanation by the patient how the single tones are produced on the instrument.

3. Spontaneous playing of melodies of patient's own choosing and of melodies requested by the examiner (on an instrument with which the patient is familiar).

4. Imitation on an instrument of melodies that had been sung, whistled, or played for the patient.

5. Playing with an accompaniment.

6. Playing with both hands; in octaves; polyphonic music (different in both hands). (This is not to be tested in cases afflicted with paralysis or paresis of one hand.)

TESTS FOR PERCEPTION AND PRODUCTION OF RHYTHMS, BEATS, AND TEMPI
(TEMPORAL ORGANIZATION)

1. Evaluation of the tempo of a musical sample played or sung for the patient (slow, fast, etc.).

2. Evaluation of time and rhythm (starting from simple dance music).

3. Testing the perception of changes in tempo (ritardando, accelerando) and rhythm.

4. Testing of patient's capacity to change his tempo on request, while performing music.

5. Imitation of rhythms (which are presented as noises, tapped, etc.) and second repetition of this imitation.

6. Imitation of rhythms presented on a constant musical pitch, and second repetition of this imitation.

7. Imitation of rhythms contained in melodies, and second repetition of this imitation.

8. Conducting or beating time with music that is either played or sung to the patient (demonstration of rhythmic accents).

9. Identifying the time signature (3/4, 4/4, 2/4, etc.) of conducting movements that are shown to the patient.

10. Reading of rhythm from printed music.

11. Reading, imitation of, and understanding of rhythmically organized speech (verses).

12. Imitation of rhythms in tactile presentation (tapped on patient's skin) and repetition of this imitation. The patient should also be asked to tap the rhythms on the examiner's hand, on a hard surface, and to tap simultaneously with both hands. These are important neurologic tests for a rhythmic disorder. This disorder is circumscribed in a special section (see p. 448.)

TESTS FOR READING OF MUSIC AND UNDERSTANDING OF MUSICAL TERMS
(TEST FOR A MUSICAL READING DISORDER AND MUSICAL APHASIA)

1. Capacity to sing or play from printed music.

2. Identifying the pitch and duration of single notes.

3. Interpretation of keys, signs, measures, and the like.

4. Orientation on a printed sheet of music; putting together staffs belonging to one instrument; identifying the instrument for which a line is printed from the whole context of the page (reading of a musical score).

5. Patient's interpretation of the letters and words appearing in printed music, as to their musical significance (f., pp., crescendo, etc.).

6. Explanation of musical terms, which though belonging to a foreign language are internationally used as musical terms (andante, allegretto, pianissimo, etc.).

TESTS FOR MUSICAL WRITING

1. Copying of a score.

2. Transcription on music paper of a known melody.

3. Writing notations to dictation.

4. Writing a melody spontaneously.

The principles in the testing of musical reading and writing are the same as for word reading and writing.

All these tests should be recorded on tape, so that they can be replayed and re-evaluated for a more refined analysis.

Even after such careful testing it is often very difficult and sometimes impossible to determine whether the musical defects of a child or an adolescent are due either to a lack of inborn ability or a lack of musical training, or are caused by pathologic changes in the brain. The differential diagnosis rests on the severity of the defects, on the presence of other definitely organic symptoms, and on indications of organicity in other tests. When the conclusion has been reached that specific musical training might help the child overcome other organic handicaps (e.g., a reading disorder), it should be undertaken regardless, without waiting for a complete clarification of the diagnosis.

Relation to Reading

The loss of the ability to read musical notations is apparently always associated with an inability to read texts. However, a dyslexia for texts is not invariably associated with a notation reading disorder. This has been observed in adults who were fluent in both kinds of reading before the onset of their brain disease, hemorrhage, tumor, or other disorder. The impairments differ in children, where these disorders constitute mostly defects in learning and not loss of functions already learned. Children may have difficulty learning both types of reading, or they may be capable of learning one and not the other, all on an organic basis. For instance, a child with a reading disorder on an organic basis may be capable of learning to read music and to play from a score. This may help him learn to read texts. He may also have both disorders.

The frequency of these various combinations is not known, because testing these children's musical abilities is the rare exception. The school psychologist Saunders is one of the few clinicians and educators specializing in reading disorders who mention the possibility of an association of reading disorders with a musical notation reading disorder. In a chapter entitled "Dyslexia: Its Phenomenology," in *Reading Disability,* edited by John Money, he writes: "There may or may not be failures in other symbol-association tasks, such as in learning musical notation" (1962, p. 39). In *Learning Disabilities: An Overview,* Lloyd J. Thompson refers to the possible association of a reading disorder with a musical ability disorder. However, he does not actually mention a musical ability disorder. Rather, he writes: " 'Tone deafness', with its varying degrees, suggests other disabilities in music, such as a poor sense of time or a shallow inner resonance for melody or harmony" (1973, p. 397). Kurth and Heinrichs made the largest study to date of the musical faculties of children with reading disorders. They studied 30 such children ages 9 to 11, and compared them with a group of 30 children who could read. They found differences that were statistically significant. The children with a reading disorder had an impaired memory for tunes. Their ability to distinguish tonal qualities and differences in loudness was also impaired. They had a musical ability disorder, which was not found in the control group (1976). More such studies are needed to clarify the relationship between organic reading disorders and different forms of Amusia.

Musicogenic Epilepsy

This disorder is so rare that it has been called "something of a neurological curiosity" (Scott, 1977, p. 363). Convulsions precipitated by reading musical notations belong to reading epilepsy. The convulsions of the twins described in the section on reading epilepsy occurred after both kinds of reading, of notes or words (p. 000). The hearing of very special melodies or tones elicits convulsions in the musical form. Its onset is usually at the age of 20 or older, but it does occur in children (Kruse, 1973, p. 407). It is apparently usually not associated with reading epilepsy or other forms of organic reading disorders.

Treatment

Music and dance therapy for organically handicapped, psychotic, or neurotic children has developed into a nonmedical specialty. It has been very difficult to develop techniques that direct these treatments at specific symptoms, and to correlate the treatment process with the clinical progress of the child. This is not only due to the unfortunately inadequate collaboration between clinicians and music therapists, but to the complicated structure of music itself and the even more complicated human reactions to it.

In an important paper on *Music as Adjunct to Psychotherapy,* Emil A.

Gutheil, MD, formulated this problem. In writing about research in this field he wrote:

> Its main problem lies in the fact that music represents a compound of variables, that the listener, the prospective recipient of musical stimulation, is also a complex phenomenon, and that the effects to be achieved by music are multidimensional.

He chose the lullaby as an example and wrote:

> It is known that the lullaby has a soporific effect; yet it is difficult to isolate its "active ingredients" scientifically. What is it in a lullaby that is soporific? Is it the tune? its calm melody? or the fact that the tune is produced by a protective figure, like that of a mother? or is it its rhythmic or melodic design which so often imitates the rocking motion of the cradle? (1954, p. 95).

Psychoanalysts tend to answer these questions strictly within the framework of their theories. Anna Freud writes: "It is not unknown that early contact with the mother through her singing has consequences for later attitudes to music and may promote special musical aptitudes" (1965, p. 87). These are speculations not yet based on long-range clinical observations. The answer to Gutheil's questions probably is that all the characteristics he mentions contribute to the soporific effect of the lullaby. Musical effects cannot be fractionated in this way.

What makes this type of research especially difficult is that musical experiences cannot be entirely and satisfactorily expressed in words. These are sensual and emotional experiences of great depth, certainly involving the unconscious. Composers use words when they feel a need for them. Their main method of communication, however, is musical (i.e., nonverbal). This very fact gives music the power to stir emotions and to assist in healing emotional disorders.

Historically, music was medicine. Chanting and dancing were part of magic rituals that were supposed to combat the evil influence of demons, which were thought to have caused the disease.

General Effects of Music Treatment

Depending on the type of music played, it can stir excitement in child or adult patients or decrease anxiety and create a calm, pleasant atmosphere conducive to the release of tensions and to healing distressed and depressed emotions. One of the healing factors in music is that it can create a feeling of harmony. Gutheil stressed this factor especially:

> Music shares with biology not only rhythm but also *harmony.* In biology, the latter is called equilibrium. It entails a balanced relation between parts. In

biology, there is a trend toward maintaining such an equilibrium, called "homeostasis," while in music, we find a similar trend toward maintaining harmony. As in biology, where all humoral, glandular, metabolic and emotional processes are ultimately striving toward the perpetuation or restoration of the original relations, so also in music, all intermediary "movements" of chords and intervals ultimately strive toward a harmonious solution and standstill of movement (tonica). Without such a solution, the listener has a subjective feeling of dissatisfaction and frustration (1954, p. 100).

This indicates what type of music should be played for and by patients. Rock and roll has no place in music therapy of hospitalized physically or emotionally ill children, or in their outpatient treatment. It appeals to the crudest emotions only and makes already overexcited children or adolescents even more excited. Especially children with organic impairments, who are too excitable anyhow, should be shielded from such emotional overstimulation with no harmonious solutions.

Music is also a socializing force. Singing and playing music and even listening together with others creates a feeling of common interests, of harmonious group relationships, of belonging. This is of special importance for organically impaired as well as neurotic children who tend to feel isolated, lonely, and different. Musical participation sometimes opens these children's lines of communication with others. It may help them overcome their fear of talking, or occasionally even a schizophrenic withdrawal.

Specific Curative Effects

Children or adults with specific musical defects need special training to overcome these defects. The choice of musical form and method of practice depends on the symptoms. There are excellent methods of teaching music to very young children, beginning with the age of 3. Some of these methods can be modified to help a child overcome his musical disorder. For instance, a modified Dalcroze method can be applied to such a child. It is especially useful because of its emphasis on teaching the experience of music through all the senses, based on body movements. It develops an excellent feeling for rhythms and tempi and teaches the value of notes in a way a young child can easily understand. Notes are called "galloping," "running," or "walking." The children carry a large drawing of such a note and are taught to listen carefully to the tempi played on the piano to find out when the time comes to gallop, run, or walk, depending on the note they are studying (Flaste, 1976).

The effects of such specific music treatment on children with a musical disorder still need to be studied. This requires the closest collaboration among all adults caring for the child: pediatricians, neurologists, child psychiatrists, psychologists, speech and music therapists, teachers, parents. It is the same kind of collaboration that is so essential for the correction and possible cure of all the symptoms of these children.

Chapter 6

Rhythmic Ability Disorder

Rhythm is an integral part of music, but it can also exist independently. It was historically the first stage in the development of music. It represents the "drum" stage. Gutheil stressed this point:

At the beginning, there was probably only rhythm. It is biologic in origin, and many physiologic processes show a rhythmic pattern. Our sense of rhythm is biologically anchored; it may be lost under pathologic conditions (1954, p. 99).

A rhythmic ability disorder may exist without a musical ability disorder. Some children who are very musical find it difficult to imitate rhythmic sounds and rhythmic body movements. Others with practically no musical talent can pass tests for rhythmic ability easily (Jellinek, 1933, p. 287). In her study on Amusia, Augusta Jellinek stresses these relationships especially: "Rhythmical reactions can be very well developed in persons with poor musical gifts, while it is difficult for many musically talented subjects to abstract the rhythmic pattern of a tune" (1956, pp. 130–131).

Rhythmic ability disorders are especially common among children with cerebral palsy because of the involvement of the cerebellum, which plays a role in rhythmic activities (Wertham, 1929).

The Organic Basis of Rhythmic Ability

Rhythmic activity is a basic somatic as well as cerebral function. It is so widespread and of such fundamental importance for health, that it cannot possibly be based on a cerebral apparatus. It is such a fundamental function of the central nervous system that the entire system has been regarded as a clock. The neurologist William Gooddy discusses this cerebral function in relation to disorders of the time sense. He states that the nervous system "provides both the anatomical structure and the physiological activity essential for clock mechanisms." He gives the following reasons for this:

1. because of its fundamentally rhythmic type of activity (associated with the all-or-none phenomenon of nervous transmission); 2. because the nervous system mediates sensory and motor activity, and thus is completely integrated with the reception and creation of rhythmic phenomena (e.g., light and sound waves; habitual movements such as walking or breathing [the sleep-wake cycle]; 3. because the nervous system is the final mediator of the person's awareness of all the clock systems derived from rhythmic activity, not primarily nervous (1969, p. 235).

The EEG shows that the brain actually is in constant rhythmic activity. Gooddy stresses the importance of this test as additional evidence for the clocklike rhythmic activities of the brain. He writes:

448

> By this instrument (for amplifying the normal electrical activity of the brain) we find the brain in constant rhythmic activity. The EEG patterns alter with observable changes in the state of health and alertness of the subject under test. When "the clocks are stopped" or otherwise affected by, for example, injury, a fit, sleep, death, alcohol or other drugs or even by lack of sleep after long journeys, the brain rhythms will alter into patterns completely different from that subject's normal or habitual patterns (1977, p. 138).

The majority of these rhythmic activities are involuntary. We do not notice them when they function normally and cannot alter most of them deliberately. They take place below the threshold of awareness. Rhythmic ability is voluntary. It has a sensory and a motor component. It consists of the perception, recognition, evaluation, and enjoyment of rhythm, as well as the ability to express it (i.e., to produce rhythmic patterns). Its expression is a voluntary, deliberate motor activity, such as tapping, singing, drumming, playing a musical instrument, and so on. It can also be expressed without rhythmic motor movements (as when a composer writes music) or entirely visually (in paintings or on film).

Constructivist painters such as Eggeling, Mondrian, Albers, and others were interested in the relation of music to visual experiences, and especially in the portrayal of rhythms in paintings. The painter Walkowitz expressed this interest in the following way:

> Pure abstract art is wholly independent of picturization in any form or of any object. It has a universal language, and dwells in the realm of music with an equivalent emotion. Its melody is attuned to the receptive eye as music is to the ear (1947).

The futurists, who were preoccupied with the analysis of movement, were also especially interested in the visual representation of rhythms.

The cerebral basis for rhythmic ability can therefore be assumed to consist of a widespread system that includes sensory projection fields as well as cortical and subcortical areas that mediate motor activities. The cerebellum is apparently also part of this system. Children and adults with cerebellar diseases such as tumors, encephalitis, and the like, have a rhythmic ability disorder. Wertham stressed the association of rhythmic ability disorders with cerebellar diseases. This localization was verified surgically in the patients he studied. In a paper on "A New Sign of Cerebellar Disease," where he described a new apparatus for recording rhythmic movements, he wrote: "The inability to perform rhythmic movements continuously by tapping (arrhythmokinesis) seems to be associated with disorders of the cerebellar system" (1929, p. 493).

Diagnosis

A rhythmic ability disorder cannot usually be observed during the psychiatric or routine psychologic examination. Teachers and parents may report that the child speaks and reads in a peculiar way, that he does not pause normally, and that his emphasis is also unusual, so that it is not always easy to understand him. Where a rhythmic ability disorder is suspected, special tests should be administered. The specialists familiar with these tests may be psychologists, reading therapists, or speech therapists. Some reading therapists administer tests for the child's rhythmic ability as a routine part of their examination. This should certainly be done for every child with a reading disorder. These disorders cannot be corrected successfully if a rhythmic disability is overlooked.

There are two forms of rhythmic ability disorders: a receptive form where the perception, recognition, memory, evaluation, and enjoyment of rhythm is defective; and an expressive form where the child has difficulties producing rhythmic patterns. These disorders may be part of a receptive or expressive amusia, but they may also exist independently. Children or adults usually have symptoms of both forms.

Tests

Rhythmic ability may be disturbed in two ways. The patient may be capable of repeating a rhythmic pattern correctly, but at too slow or too rapid a pace. Or his speed may be correct, but he may be incapable of repeating the rhythmic pattern correctly.

Rhythm has a speed factor and a regularity factor. One or both may be defective. Memory also plays a role. It should be recorded how many times a rhythm has to be repeated before the patient can perform it correctly or after which the patient still performs it incorrectly.

Test results should not be scored, but should instead be evaluated on an individual basis, just as in tests for musical ability. The specific tests for a rhythmic ability disorder are outlined in the section on Tests for Perception and Production of Rhythms, Beats, and Tempi (Temporal Organization), under the Tests for a Musical Ability Disorder, p. 439.

When evaluating these tests, it is important to realize that other organic symptoms may interfere with the child's rhythmic ability. Foremost among them is a difficulty in sequencing. A rhythmic pattern is a sequence. A child may not remember and perform rhythmic patterns accurately because he has trouble with all forms of sequencing. His rhythmic ability disorder may be part of his defective sequencing. The children I examined who had a rhythmic ability disorder, invariably had trouble also with learning other sequences.

The slowing down of most reactions often also interferes with a child's ability to perform rhythmic patterns. He may tap or clap rhythms correctly, but at too slow a pace. Children with defective automatic mechanisms may also have trouble performing rhythms correctly, because these have an automatic component.

Relation to Reading

Lack of rhythmic ability interferes with reading and speaking. It even affects silent reading, because this, too, requires a rhythmic sense. These children do not sense the rhythmic patterns that are an integral part of reading. They do not alter their speed appropriately or pause when the text requires it. They usually have trouble realizing when one thought or one sentence ends, and another begins. They may rush through the text at too great a speed to find a comma or a period, where they feel they can catch their breath. This interferes with their reading comprehension.

Nine-year-old Morris had this difficulty. His symptoms are described in Concentration Disorders (p. 557). He had numerous organic symptoms after a head injury. Another child was 8-year-old Renato.

RENATO, 8 YEARS OLD: A SEVERE RHYTHMIC ABILITY DISORDER. This disorder was not his worst symptom, but it interfered seriously with the correction of his reading disorder.

Renato's rhythmic disability was not part of a musical ability disorder. He loved to rhyme and sing, and learned reading, writing, and arithmetic partly through rhyming.

He had a number of other severe organic symptoms that impeded his ability to learn to read. He needed a visual and a tactile approach because he had great difficulty with auditory perception. He could not distinguish speech sounds and was a clutterer (i.e., he had mild receptive aphasia). (See Cluttering, pp. 402–405.)

His reading therapist treated him twice a week. He was very attached to her and made a great effort to learn. However, he had a severe attention disorder and an increased fatiguability. In the beginning he could pay attention for only 5 minutes at a time. It was the reading therapist who noticed his rhythmic ability disorder. His reading improved finally, when she beat a rhythm for him. It had been unintelligible before this. Eventually he learned to tap the rhythm by himself during reading.

The therapist also used other corrective methods for the numerous organic impairments that impeded his reading. He had a severe directional difficulty. He could remember the shape and direction of letters only after he had formed them many times out of clay and put them on a line, which she had drawn for him on a piece of paper. Blending was also difficult for him, and he had a severe sequencing problem. He could not recite the months of the year and did not even remember the number sequence in his address. When he was asked to name the letter he was looking at, he closed his eyes and imagined the entire alphabet in order to find that one letter. (See Sequence Writing, Vol. I, p. 152.)

In spite of the numerous organic symptoms, Renato's intelligence was within the average range; some subtests were even superior. The psychologists noticed that he needed visual clues. The cause of Renato's reading disorder and his other organic symptoms could not be established with certainty. It was probably due to a difficult delivery during which mid-forceps were used.

Such a rhythmic ability disorder that affects a child's reading, is much more frequent than has been reported, because it is often overlooked or considered only a minor symptom.

Part II

Unspecific and General Symptoms Frequently Associated with Organic Reading, Writing, and Arithmetic Disorders

This psychopathology consists of symptoms that are unspecific; this means that they are found in almost all children and adults suffering from any kind of organic brain disorder, irrespective of its cause or extent. They are unspecific also because they are not specific for any particular brain disease, injury, or defect. These symptoms are "general" because they pervade the child's entire behavior. They interfere in a general way with his emotional and intellectual development.

In "Pathologic Basis of Organic Reading Disorders" I have defined what "organic" means. I want to stress again that "organic" does not necessarily mean that a lesion shows up neuropathologically either macroscopically or under the microscope. "Organic" also means nonpsychological—that is, that the disorder is not caused by traumatic experiences in the patient's life that damaged him psychologically (Vol. I, p. 42).

The relationship of these general and unspecific psychologic symptoms with their organic cerebral basis is as follows.

In all patients suffering from brain diseases or defects we find primarily two kinds of symptoms: those that are physical and others that are psychologic in nature. Both can occur on the same organic basis. The psychologic symptoms would not exist except for the organic disorder. They are not due to the patient's reaction to the consequences of the impairments caused by his brain disorder, but are manifestations of the brain disorder itself. A brain disease or defect can manifest itself clinically in different ways. Psychologic symptoms constitute one form this manifestation takes. Tremor; paralysis; localizable perceptual disorders such as deafness, visual defects, and so on are physical symptoms. Anxiety, inability to concentrate, and morbid irritability are examples of some of the psychologic symptoms found in organic disorders.

Any damage to the brain (traumatic, neoplastic, inflammatory, circulatory, biochemical, etc.) can cause psychologic symptoms, regardless at what age it occurs, prenatal, during birth, or at any time later on in life. This damage may be localized or diffuse. Even a small, localized brain disorder can cause general and unspecific psychologic symptoms in adults as well as children. Of course these symptoms have different consequences in children because they interfere with the child's development, but they are basically the same. As a matter of historic fact, our knowledge of them stems from clinical and neuropathologic studies of adults.

These general and unspecific psychologic symptoms are, as a rule, either entirely omitted in studies of reading disorders, or are presented in such a fragmented way that their nature and impact cannot possibly be properly evaluated. In order to study them one has to look them up one by one in various textbooks (of neurology, psychiatry, psychology, both of adults and children, and of pediatrics). They are also classified under different diagnoses, namely "Chronic Brain Syndromes," "Nonpsychotic Organic Brain Syndrome," "Minimal Brain Damage or Dysfunction," "Primary" and "Secondary" Symptoms of "Organic Pathology" (Bradley, 1955, p. 89); "Behavioral Manifestations of Cerebral Damage in Childhood" (Eisenberg, 1964, p. 61) and "The Organic Psychosyndrome," a term used primarily by European neurologists, psychiatrists, and pediatricians. The reason for this diagnostic and semantic confusion is that the basic fact that these symptoms are psychologic manifestations of brain disorders is either not understood or not explained with sufficient clarity.

When we examine a child with a reading disorder we must therefore differentiate between physical (defects of speech, vision, hearing, neurologic signs, etc.) and psychologic symptoms, and also distinguish between the nature of a symptom and its cause. A symptom may be psychologic in nature and have an organic cerebral cause. These differentiations are important not only for the diagnosis of diseases of the central nervous system but also for many other diseases that affect the brain only indirectly. Hypoglycemia (abnormally low blood sugar), for instance, causes such unspecific psychologic symptoms, which have an entirely biochemical cause. They are well described from the pediatrician's point of view in *Nelson's Textbook of Pediatrics,* where it is stated that

> psychic disturbances such as irritability, negativism, drowsiness and alterations in behavior are common in older children. In the ranks of emotionally disturbed

children there are certainly some unhappy, ill-behaved or maladjusted children requiring sugar as well as guidance (DiGeorge & Auerbach, 1969, p. 1169).

Exactly the same unspecific and general psychologic symptoms (except, of course, for the drowsiness) are found in children with organic reading, writing, and arithmetic disorders and other kinds of brain disorders. This shows how misleading it is to subsume such symptoms under the term "Minimal Brain Damage," as is at present customary. One can understand these symptoms only if one realizes that they are psychologic in nature and can have either psychologic or different physical (including organic cerebral) causes.

The diagnostic term "Minimal Brain Damage" or "Minimal Cerebral Dysfunction" was coined primarily to cover these general and unspecific psychologic symptoms. The clinical basis for this diagnosis is so unclear that there is no agreement on its definition. A variety of symptoms are subsumed under this term, some of them physical (i.e., organic cerebral), but most of them psychologic in nature. I have found no clear differentiation between them. A pamphlet distributed to enlighten parents states quite correctly: "MBD (Minimal Brain Damage) is difficult to pin down" ("Helping Your Hyperkinetic Child," 1971). But these symptoms can and should be pinned down, and this is what I intend to do. Children have all sorts of brain disorders, diffuse or localized, general or specific, with a great variety of symptoms. These disorders and symptoms should be differentiated from each other and *named,* and not hidden within such a vague category. An international study group held at Oxford, England, in 1962, came to a majority conclusion that the term "minimal brain damage" should be abandoned. This has unfortunately not been universally accepted. I agree with Slater and Roth, who state in their textbook *Clinical Psychiatry,* that the term "minimal cerebral dysfunction" "does not lend itself for the categorization of any clinically significant group of cases" (1969, p. 688). Actually, this diagnosis has done great harm. It is so ill-defined that it seems uncanny and frightening to parents and teachers, and has created unnecessary anxiety in them. All they need hear is the word "damage," and no matter how optimistically the child's condition is explained to them, the doubt about their child's normality remains with them forever, and the child is stigmatized for life. The diagnosis "minimal brain damage" has also been much abused to conceal superficial and imprecise examinations and a lack of understanding of the true nature of the child's difficulties. I find this term entirely useless. I agree with Dr. Dominick P. Purpura, Director of the Rose Kennedy Center for Research in Mental Retardation, who said during an interview on a television program that he liked to think of Minimal Brain Dysfunction as Maximal Brain Ignorance (1973; see also B. Schmitt, 1975, González, 1980).

A striking example for this general and unspecific psychopathology on an organic basis is the syphilitic encephalitis (inflammation of the brain) called

General Paresis. This is a well-studied brain disease that has a depressed, an elated, and a demented form. Depression and elation are, of course, psychologic symptoms. Anomalies of the pupils and dysarthric speech are two of the physical symptoms characteristic for this disease. I am using this example from adult psychiatry because it leaves no room whatsoever for any doubt. General Paresis is a brain disease whose symptoms, course, cause, and cure are known completely.

The proof for an organic causation of these general and unspecific psychologic symptoms rests on:

1. The presence of neurologic signs (e.g., fixed pupils in General Paresis).
2. Other physical symptoms that have an organic cerebral cause (e.g., dysarthric speech in General Paresis).
3. Specific organic mental symptoms such as the defects in reading, writing, and arithmetic I have described in detail.
4. Tests (e.g., a low blood-sugar level in hypoglycemia, a positive blood and spinal fluid Wassermann test in General Paresis, or the various organic responses on psychologic tests in organic reading, writing, and arithmetic disorders.

The very presence of one or several of these symptoms does not indicate that the child's reading disorder is necessarily organic or that he has a reading disorder at all. As I have pointed out before, an organic reading disorder is caused by the defective functioning of the child's cerebral reading apparatus. A brain disease, injury, or other impairment may cause general and unspecific psychologic symptoms. It may, however, not have damaged the reading apparatus so that the child's reading ability remains intact. Epilepsy is a good example of this (see pp. 423, 424).

That these psychologic symptoms are manifestations of brain disease or other cerebral impairments does not mean that one can take their organic causation for granted. As a matter of fact, only 4 of the 12 symptoms are found exclusively in adults and children with brain pathology. These are:

1. The slowing down of all reactions.
2. The impairment of automatic mechanisms.
3. The inability to shift freely.
4. The perseveration.

All the other symptoms may also have a psychologic cause. The attention disorder, the hyperactivity, the morbid irritability, and the free-floating anxiety may, in addition, be symptoms of schizophrenia.

Early Infantile Autism must be especially mentioned in this connection. In the section on Speech Disorders I point out that this is not a disease entity, but a syndrome with very massive symptoms and different causes. I agree with Slater and Ross, who state that our knowledge has advanced to the point "where it seems fairly safe to classify the condition among organic disorders"

(1969, p. 680). That some of the cardinal symptoms of this syndrome belong to this unspecific and general psychopathology supports this point of view. These are: the inability to shift freely, the perseveration, the attention disorder —which in these cases is quite specific—and especially the inability to tolerate disorder—which is considered one of its most characteristic symptoms. (See Speech Disorders, pp. 381, 391; also Inability to Tolerate Disorder, p. 475 and Vol. I, p. 66.)

There is one more possible cause for some of these symptoms, namely somatic diseases (i.e., physical diseases not originating in the central nervous system, e.g., hypoglycemi a). The attention disorder, the hyperactivity, the hypoactivity, fatiguability, irritability, and free-floating anxiety may have such a cause.

The differential diagnosis of these causes will be discussed in the sections dealing with each individual symptom.

Each symptom in this general and unspecific psychopathology cannot be understood sufficiently in isolation. It can only be properly evaluated as one of a number of psychologic manifestations of the organic reading disorder and of whatever other organic disorders are associated with it. That is why it is so important to present this psychopathology in its entirety. The confusions and disagreements in this entire field are largely due to the separate and isolated presentations of reading disorders and the various psychopathologic symptoms of children with these disorders. Children suffering from the various manifestations of this psychopathology can be helped only if the adults caring for them understand that there is not only an intimate interaction between these symptoms and between them and the reading disorder, but frequently also a causal relationship. The impairment of these children's automatic mechanisms, for instance, is largely responsible for their slowness generally and for specific difficulties they have with reading; their attention disorder also has a crucial effect on reading and is influenced by and worsens some of the other symptoms. The circumscription of each symptom will deal with these interactions.

The general and unspecific psychologic symptoms characteristic for cerebral pathology are the following:

1. The slowing down of all reactions. The child's reactions themselves are slow, and they are initiated slowly because his response to all stimuli is retarded.
2. Impairment of automatic mechanisms.
3. Inability to tolerate disorder.
4. Inability to shift freely from one activity to another.
5. Perseveration.
6. Attention disorder.
7. Hyperactivity.
8. Hypoactivity.

9. Fatiguability.
10. Irritability.
11. Mood disorder.
12. Free-floating anxiety.

A child with an organic reading, writing, and arithmetic disorder does not necessarily have all these symptoms, but he invariably has some of them. The symptoms he has may be so mild that they are easily overlooked. However, it is important for the child's education and treatment to diagnose each one of them.

The Slowing Down of All Reactions

The slowing down of all reactions is a fundamental symptom and a terrible handicap for the child or adult patient. It is a retardation of the speed of response to all outside stimuli, and the responses themselves are slow. This symptom is only rarely discussed in detail. It is apparently taken for granted that these children's reactions are slow and that this is simply due to an impairment of their general intellectual efficiency. But this symptom is not that simple diagnostically, therapeutically, or educationally, especially for the patients. It affects the child's entire mental, physical, and emotional life. All his intellectual and most emotional responses are slow, including his thinking and comprehension, while his intellectual capacity is, as a rule, not impaired.

Reaction Time

The reaction time of these patients, adults as well as children, has been investigated with different clinical and experimental methods. Various response apparatuses have been constructed, where the patient has to press different buttons in response to visual and other stimuli. Not only do patients with organic cerebral impairments react significantly more slowly than the controls who have no cerebral defects, but it takes them increasingly longer to respond the greater the number of stimuli they must distinguish and the number of responses from which they must choose (Lee & Allen, 1972). This is of profound importance for the management and education of these children.

There is always a delay before such a child can respond to any stimulus. This delay is uniform and has nothing to do with the content of the stimulus, for instance a question. There is a pause before the child can answer even the most unimportant, routine, or trivial question. These children cannot even nod or shake their head right away, and they can only answer *one* question, carry out *one* command, or remember *one* errand at a time. Too many stimuli confuse them and slow their response even more. These children should be taught in quiet rooms with only a minimum of auditory and visual stimuli. Classroom walls with a variety of announcements and diverse learning materials confuse them. Such visual overstimulation alone makes it more difficult for them to learn. They should also be given a chance to work at their own pace. Everything goes much too fast for them in a regular classroom.

Reaction to Television

Television bombards children with this symptom with too many stimuli and may therefore be harmful to them. It should be cut down to a minimum of selected programs. The popular film technique of cutting one picture off abruptly and switching to another one is especially difficult for them to follow.

These children cannot react with speed in any situation. They are at their worst when there is a crisis or an emergency. They can therefore not be left alone and need adult help, supervision, and protection for a much longer period than other children.

It is wrong to urge such a child even in a subtle way to perform faster; this makes him anxious and insecure and inhibits his reactions even more. Parents, teachers, and all other adults coming in contact with such a child must understand that he has no choice but to work and to respond slowly, step by deliberate step.

Relation to Hypoactivity

It must be stressed that this symptom is not the opposite of hyperactivity. These children are not necessarily hypoactive or hypokinetic as described by De Hirsch, Klasen, and others. This so-called hypoactivity is actually more like lethargic or apathetic behavior. Such children are sleepy and difficult to arouse and to interest in anything. They are not spontaneous, almost never enthusiastic about anything, and have a passive attitude to life. Their general muscle tone is frequently flabby. Their emotions and impulses are depressed, but their reactions to stimuli are not necessarily abnormally slow. This lethargic behavior differs from the symptom I am describing. Children whose reactions are uniformly slow may have a normal or an abnormal impulsivity or emotionality. Some are hyperactive, others are lethargic, most of them are basically even-tempered. Some run around wildly in the classroom and are difficult to control; most sit in their seats quietly, trying hard to do what the teacher tells them to, and to present no behavior problem. Their slowness is in any case not caused by abnormal emotions or impulses (see Hypoactivity, p. 669).

Diagnosis

The diagnosis of this symptom can be made by the careful observation of the child's responses during the psychiatric examination, by classroom and playroom observations, by an evaluation of the teachers and the parents' reports, and by tests.

Word-Association Test

The psychologic test best suited for the diagnosis of this general slowness is the word-association test. This is an important projective technique that has unfortunately been neglected. Its value for children suspected of organic slowness lies in its ability to show that the child's responses are uniformly slow, independent from emotions. It is also helpful for the detection of areas of special psychologic sensitivity and for finding clues to neurotic complexes.

In this association test the child is asked to respond to a so-called stimulus word. The time it takes him to say anything that comes to his mind is measured and his response recorded. His reaction time is influenced by conscious as well as unconscious factors. As a general rule, the more painful and deeply repressed the emotions and thoughts aroused by the stimulus word are, the slower is the reaction. Children whose long reaction time is caused primarily by organic impairments and not by emotions, react slowly also to neutral stimulus words. Of course there is no completely "neutral" word. Each word carries an emotional connotation, but the examiner should select words which are least disturbing for the child being tested. The entire average reaction time is considerably longer in children with this general and unspecific psychologic symptom than in others. Timed responses on other tests (e.g., on subtests of intelligence tests) are also uniformly slow and help to establish the diagnosis.

Child's Relation to this Symptom

The child himself is often painfully aware of this symptom and can describe it better than anyone else. He realizes that he cannot do or say anything right away and that unless he pauses for a moment, he cannot get anything said or done. These children think of themselves as "stupid." They should be told that they are not "stupid," just slow in acting and reacting. They should also be told to take all the time they need to finish whatever they are doing. Parents, siblings, teachers, and friends must learn to be patient with them.

Parents' Role

Parents, as a rule, think the child's slowness is deliberate dawdling, that he is angry and disobedient, or that he daydreams too much and is in poor contact with reality. These children get punished quite unjustly. This slows them down even more and causes them to become angry, depressed, and negativistic.

Teacher's Role

The slowness of all the child's reactions is usually the first symptom noticed by the teacher. She also observes fairly early that the child stops responding altogether when she suggests that he work faster or when even the mildest and gentlest pressure is exerted on him. Then she begins to wonder whether he is just slow in his development, whether he is stupid, or whether he is mentally defective and belongs in a special class for such children.

Relation to Mental Deficiency

Slowness of all reactions is, of course, one of the basic symptoms of mental deficiency (see p. 410). It is therefore of crucial importance to find out whether or not the child's intellectual capacity is within normal limits. Sometimes it is very difficult to determine this with certainty, and the child may have to be observed over a prolonged period of time to find out what are the true limits of his intelligence. All these children are very difficult to test because they have so many other organic and psychologic symptoms that interfere with their test performance. Only experienced psychologists can sort out those responses on intelligence tests that indicate that the child's intelligence is within normal limits, and differentiate them from those that are depressed by the child's specific organic handicaps. For instance, a child with only this slowness as a symptom has normal intelligence if his performance on intelligence tests is within normal limits, except for a uniformly slow reaction and performance time. Such pure cases, of course, do not exist in practice. Projective techniques such as the Rorschach or figure drawings can be reliable indicators of normal intelligence in these children. The Mosaic test is of great help here, too (see Vol. I, p. 25). It is not influenced by the speed of the child's performance, and mental defectives make very typical mosaic designs (Figure 2.1). It can therefore confirm or rule out mental deficiency. In any case, it requires great skill and a lot of clinical experience with testing to pinpoint those areas where the child functions normally.

Careful observation of the child during the psychiatric examination, in the classroom, and at home can also pinpoint those actions and thoughts of the child that are within normal intellectual limits for his age. These are the same difficulties one invariably encounters when the differential diagnosis between mental deficiency and an organic cerebral disorder in a child with basically normal intelligence has to be made. (See sections on Mental Deficiency and on Special Classes for Mentally Defective Children, pp. 418, 409.)

ALEX, 7 YEARS OLD: HE HAD SUPERIOR INTELLIGENCE BUT HIS SLOWNESS GOT HIM INTO TROUBLE. The troubles of 7-year-old Alex show how this symptom affects a child with superior intelligence and how difficult it is even for medically trained parents to understand the child's plight.

Alex's father was a physician, his mother a nurse. His slowness was not their only complaint, but it was a major worry. His mother told me that he was slow in everything. When I asked for specific examples she said: "He eats very slow, he ties shoelaces slowly, he dresses himself slowly and seems to be always dreaming about something."

Alex had a number of other general and unspecific psychologic symptoms that fall into the core group I am discussing. These were a difficulty in concentration; morbid irritability practically every afternoon when he came home from school, often ending in temper tantrums; a mild difficulty in shifting freely: and a tendency to perseverate, which the parents interpreted as stubbornness.

His specific organic symptoms were as follows. There was a difficulty in sequencing: he could not recite the days of the week or the months of the year. He also had trouble with constructional activities. He could not read or draw the clockface (i.e., he could not tell time), and he could not remember the rules of games. This, combined with poor gross motor coordination (he could not skip, do jumping jacks, hit or catch a ball), made it impossible for him to play games with the other children. He was completely isolated on the playground in school and was so afraid of the gym teacher that he complained of stomachaches to his mother whenever he had gym in school. He told me very sadly: "I can't play," and also said that he did not like sports at all. He explained his dislike for gym in the following way: "We have a tough gym teacher. Whenever you don't throw the ball, you get yelled at." Thus he explained his inability to perform with a fear of the teacher. Another organic symptom was his inability to distinguish right and left on other people.

Alex was not referred to me because he had a reading disorder. He was in the second grade and was reading above his grade level. An educational therapist had tested him and found that his oral reading level was grade 3.9, his silent reading and his spelling were on third-grade level. He did, however, have a writing disorder. His letters were poorly drawn, and he had directional difficulties. He frequently wrote a word or even an entire sentence from right to left. His arithmetic was on grade level. His mother told me that she had begun to wonder whether he might have a learning disorder when the teacher told her that he daydreamed or "tuned out" in class, and because he hated to do homework. He refused to do it alone, and she felt she had to sit with him every afternoon and help him. This created intolerable conflicts between them.

What worried the parents more than anything else was that he was such an unhappy child. His mother told me sadly: "I am unhappy because Alex is so unhappy. He has such a poor image of himself." Both parents described him as basically a sweet, affectionate, and friendly child who seemed to be always anxious and tense.

Alex was tested by a psychologist who reported that he earned an I.Q. of 131 on the WISC with a verbal score of 134 and a performance score of 121. His responses were very superior on similarities and on information, and his vocabulary was very good. On block design he reached a 14, and on coding a 12-year level. As I have pointed out before, children with an organic reading disorder sometimes do especially poorly on these two subtests. However, she found the following indications of organicity: a poor body image; poor auditory memory for sequencing; a poor motor memory; poor body concepts on figure drawings; and perseveration, confused order, and poor planning on the Bender Gestalt test. (See Perseveration, p. 486.)

The parents had also consulted a neurologist, who found a mild cortical sensory loss in the right hand. The boy's reflexes were generally brisker on the right side, and he had a bilateral Babinski sign. The neurologist concluded that Alex had minor focal neurologic abnormalities.

When I examined him he was a very sad, tense, and anxious boy who felt inferior and inadequate to practically any task. He thought that nobody liked him because he was so inadequate. He said he had only one friend in his class, but that no one wanted to play with him, not even his two brothers. He had an 8-year-old and a 5-year-old brother and a 1-year-old sister. His mother had told me that all his siblings seemed much brighter and faster than he.

Alex had two main areas of conflicts: his dislike of and unhappiness in school; and his relationship with his older brother who was his exact opposite. His parents looked on this older brother as the perfect child. His mother described him as "very outgoing, very bright, overly confident, very good in sports," and Alex felt he could not possibly live up to him. He spoke freely and coherently and was not overly slow in his responses. His slowness became apparent only when he had to perform a task. He read well, but slowly. He made no mistakes and sounded out every word carefully. He understood what he read. He had been taught entirely phonetically and not with a sight-word method. This saved him from developing a reading disorder—combined, of course, with his superior intelligence. His writing was very slow and deliberate. He could form letters correctly only when his movements were slow and the letters very large. He confused some letters, and had difficulty spelling in writing. His oral spelling was on a somewhat higher level. (See Spelling, Vol. I, p. 115.) His drawings showed anxiety, insecurity, and a poor body image. The arms of the figures came directly out of the head, almost like the drawings of 3-year-old children, and were the only shaded part of the body. This showed an enormous amount of anxiety concentrated on his arms, which he felt he could not use properly—for instance, for writing, for playing, for defending himself, for fighting. Arms stand for mastery of the environment. Many children with reading and writing disorders express their concerns by the way they draw arms. (See section on Drawings, Vol. I, p. 214.)

Alex's Mosaic test showed his superior intelligence combined with constructional difficulties on an organic basis. He worked very slowly, had no plan, and put pieces on top of each other. He finally made an imaginative construction which was so poorly put together that it collapsed right away.

He wrote with his right hand, but could use both hands equally well (or poorly). Hand dominance had not been established. He also had no dominant eye. (See Hand Dominance, Vol. I, p. 179.)

Diagnosis. My diagnosis was that Alex had a number of organic defects whose effects he had largely overcome so far as reading was concerned, but which still affected his writing and spelling. That he read well in spite of his organic defects was due to excellent teachers using the most appropriate methods (primarily phonics) and to his superior intelligence. It was a remarkable achievement in any case.

This favorable result was in marked contrast to very many other children with the same superior intelligence and similar organic defects who would have developed a reading disorder. What made the difference was excellent teaching in school and careful education at home, with a stress on a large and varied vocabulary and clear and correct pronunciation. A child from an impoverished, deprived home where a dialect is spoken, attending a school with poorly trained teachers using haphazard and inappropriate teaching methods, would invariably have developed a serious reading and writing disorder in spite of the same superior intelligence. Alex's parents' emphasis on studying and on learning to read and write also helped, even though the pressure they exerted on him provoked a psychopathologic reaction.

Psychopathologic Reaction to Slowness and Other Unspecific Symptoms.
Alex had developed reactive symptoms to his organic defects. His slowness had a negativistic overlay. He was tense, anxious, and often depressed. He daydreamed too much and tuned out in school, because he felt he could not cope with reality. He suppressed strong feelings of anger because he was afraid of punishment and condemnation. He was a sensitive boy who was easily hurt and took everything very hard.

I discussed my findings with both parents and made the following *recommendations:*

1.   Alex did not need individual educational treatment for his writing and spelling disorder and his slow reading. I felt that he would overcome these disorders completely with continued good classroom teaching, provided his teachers and his parents understood his handicaps and managed them properly.

Alex himself had a great desire to overcome the handicaps and tried very hard. No further pressure should be exerted on him at home or in school. His teachers and his parents should understand that he could not help his slowness and that he needed a pause before he could respond. He should be encouraged to work slowly, at his own pace, and he should have no homework, at least for one school year. The hours he spent in school put him under all the stress he could be expected to endure. Homework had, in addition, undermined his relationship with his mother to a dangerous degree. Intrafamilial tensions should at all costs be alleviated and avoided.

2.   He should have *individual psychotherapy* as soon as possible, so that he could learn to understand himself better, including his need for slowness and his other organic handicaps. This form of treatment would also cure his reactive symptoms, and possibly prevent the development of more serious neurotic symptoms. It was my impression that he would respond within a comparatively brief period of time.

3.   He should have his own room, so that he would not be constantly under the influence of his domineering older brother.

4. He should not be forced to participate in any sport unless and until he himself asked for this.

I also told Alex's parents that it was my impression that his organic handicaps and his reaction to them would disappear completely if these recommendations were carried out.

Importance of the Diagnosis of this Symptom

The case of Alex shows how important it is to diagnose this one fundamental organically caused psychologic symptom. The slowness of all their reactions affects the ability of all these children to learn reading, writing, and arithmetic even when their cerebral reading apparatus is not directly damaged. This symptom makes it difficult for them to respond fast enough to each single letter when they are trying to sound out a word, so that they have trouble blending letters into words. Once they have mastered word reading, they tend to read each word slowly and to pause too long before reading the next word.

It is difficult for them to read fluently orally or silently, so that they have trouble understanding the entire text. This lack of comprehension makes them even more suspect of being mental defectives. Of course their slowness also interferes with the learning of other subjects, and is a major handicap during all tests.

These children cannot complete any test within the required period of time. The tensions and anxieties inherent in any test situation make it extremely difficult for them to respond, so that their answers are invariably below their capacity. Their group I.Q. tests are therefore always low. These children are unjustly rated as far below average in intelligence and consequently in learning ability unless it is recognized that it was their slowness and not a lack of knowledge and intelligence that depressed their test performance.

Children's Reactions to this Symptom

Some children are not particularly distressed by it. They are basically easygoing and proceed at their own pace without being self-conscious about their slowness. Most children find it difficult ever to feel sure of themselves. They tend to feel insecure, incompetent, and inferior to other children. They therefore have a great need to cling to adults and to make sure that they are loved and protected by them. They often are attention-getters and need this attention to stabilize their emotions, so that they can perform the tasks before them. Many of these children are chronically depressed. They cry quietly in school and often stop participating in the classroom altogether. They give up and become passive. Their attitude is one of quiet and desperate resignation, occasionally interrupted by angry tantrums. Their slowness makes most of them angry at themselves.

These reactions are not specific for this symptom alone. They are typical psychologic responses to many other symptoms in this core group and to the reading, writing, and arithmetic disorder itself. I want to stress again that such psychopathologic reactions can be prevented or at least minimized only by diagnosing each symptom and defect carefully and early, and by teaching and managing the child accordingly.

Relation to Impairment of Automatic Mechanisms

One reason these children are so slow is that their automatic mechanisms are impaired. They have to do deliberately, step by step, what others can do automatically, without having to pay any attention. These two symptoms are interrelated in a vicious circle. The slowness makes more difficult the formation of automatic mechanisms, including conditioned reflexes, and the lack of automatic mechanisms slows the child down. This is the next symptom to be circumscribed.

Chapter 8

Impairment of Automatic Mechanisms

An activity (e.g., tying shoelaces or reading) has become automatic when we can perform it without having to figure out how to do it and without having to pay attention to every detailed step needed to carry it out. The cerebral areas that are in charge of each such activity do the required work for us with their afferent and efferent connections and their patterns of associations. They are able to direct these activities on their own, below the threshold of consciousness.

Some of these mechanisms also start automatically; others may be initiated by deliberate, willful acts. The neurophysiologist R. W. Gerard describes automatic mechanisms in the following way:

> The vast bulk of responses to stimuli are executed automatically, reflexly, and without conscious attention. This is true of complex learned behaviors, as in skilled motor sequences, as well as of the more general unlearned responses. When scratching eliminates an itch, the entire episode can occur without consciousness; routine repetitive automatic behavior has eliminated the disturbance. But if the routine response fails to achieve this end, innovative or creative behavior is called for, and awareness enters the picture (1959, p. 1633).

We can understand the extent of the handicap caused by an impairment of automatic mechanisms only by realizing that by far the greater part of our ordinary daily activities consist of automatic mechanisms. We are conscious of only a tiny fraction of these activities or completely unaware of them. These mechanisms are involved in dressing, eating, washing, climbing stairs, winding watches, locking and unlocking, closing and opening doors, turning lights on and off, tying ties and shoelaces, packing a suitcase, catching a ball, playing all sorts of indoor and outdoor games, and (on a higher level) in speaking, reading, writing, calculating, and in all other learning processes as well.

These automatic mechanisms are great time and energy savers. Therefore when they do not function properly, children fatigue much sooner than do healthy children. This is one of several reasons for their fatiguability, and another example for the interconnection of the unspecific psychologic symptoms in this core group. (See Fatiguability, p. 312.)

Thinking and paying attention are closely linked. Automatic mechanisms free our attention from routine and more trivial tasks and make thinking on a higher level possible during that time. For example, we may be preoccupied with solving a problem (i.e., thinking about it) while approaching our home. We may take the keys out of our pocket, stop in front of the house, walk to its entrance, unlock the door, walk upstairs, unlock the door to the apartment, and enter it without having been aware of any of these acts. They had become automatic and we did not have to pay any attention to them. We could rely on our central nervous system to do them for us.

470

We could have paid attention to these activities if we had wanted to, and we would have had to if something had gone wrong, if there had been some obstacle interfering with the routine. This shows that these mechanisms are linked to attention in a very special way. They can be brought into the focus of attention automatically or at will. Whenever such a mechanism cannot be completed automatically, attention is focused on it instantly without any conscious effort—that is, automatically. A mechanism has become completely automatic only when it also turns attention away from itself and returns it automatically. These transitions are smooth unless the entire act is interrupted willfully.

Healthy adults and children have the choice of letting automatic mechanisms proceed or of interrupting them at will. They can focus their attention on them whenever they need or want to. Children with a defect in these mechanisms have no choice. They have to pay deliberate attention to all details. When they let their attention slip, they cannot proceed with the activity. They might have to restart from the beginning and again figure out each step. Neither the focusing nor the diversion of attention nor the act itself is automatic with them. Of course not all such mechanisms are affected in each child. The higher level acts, such as reading, writing, and speech, are apt to be more seriously affected than lower level mechanisms such as scratching.

Conditioned reflexes form the basis for many of these automatic mechanisms. In the section on conditioned reflexes I have explained how they are formed, what role they play in reading, and how they cause reading disorders when their formation is defective. To function properly, elements of reading such as linear eye movements and the return sweep must become automatic mechanisms. Conditioned reflexes make this possible. However, not all automatic mechanisms can be explained by conditioned-reflex formation. They occur on so many different psychologic levels that we must assume that different levels of the central nervous system and different cerebral systems are involved. Their close link to awareness and attention means that cerebral areas responsible for these functions probably also play a role. It is assumed that a special cerebral system, called the "reticular-activating system" or a "nonspecific projection system for awareness" plays a role in initiating and maintaining states of arousal, awareness, and attention. This system deals with basic mental states. It is not known whether it is defective in patients whose automatic mechanisms are impaired. What we do know is that these children have a more complicated attention disorder than just the routinely diagnosed "short attention span." They have an organic attention disorder that manifests itself in a number of ways. One way is that focus and release of attention does not become automatic or not as automatic as it ought to be. (See Automatic Attention, p. 513; and The Reticular Formation, p. 502.)

Automatic mechanisms must be differentiated from symptoms that the neurologists call "automatisms." These are forced involuntary movements or automatic activities while the patient is in a state of impaired consciousness, for example during a convulsive seizure (Mulder, 1959, p. 1149).

Relation to Apraxia

Impaired automatic mechanisms differ from apraxias. These children can perform all motor patterns they need, but they cannot learn to do them automatically. They must guide each motor activity deliberately and usually visually. Some can also perform them without watching each step visually, but can control these movements through mental images.

"Automatic" should not be confused with "unconscious." Automatic mechanisms are brain mechanisms easily made conscious through the faculty of attention. Unconscious mechanisms are repressed and can be brought to consciousness only with special methods, for instance the psychoanalytical method of free associations, dream interpretations, and so forth. (See Conditioned Reflexes, Vol. I, pp. 78–89; and Free-Floating Attention, p. 545.)

Relation to Speech Disorders

In the sections on conditioned reflexes and on speech disorders, I have described the role played by conditioned and unconditioned reflexes in speech formation. A possible defect in the formation of automatic mechanisms should therefore be kept in mind when a child's speech defect is examined. A child with such a defect speaks slowly and deliberately because he must pay attention to his articulation; it has not become automatic. It is especially difficult for him to pronounce words clearly when he is excited and wants to say something fast. These children are therefore often difficult to understand. This speech defect can easily be confused with cluttering.

The word-finding ability of these children may also be impaired when the associations among objects, actions, feelings, and words have not become automatic. This symptom can easily be misdiagnosed as a form of aphasia. Of course a child can have both, an aphasia and a defect in the formation of automatic mechanisms. Speech therapy cannot be successful if this symptom is overlooked, as it so often is. (See Conditioned Reflexes and Speech Disorders, Vol. I, pp. 78–89, and p. 379.)

Automatic mechanisms are established through repetition. These children can repeat an activity over and over again and it does not become automatic. This symptom therefore interferes seriously with their learning ability on all levels, because repetition is basic to learning. Rote learning and reciting are especially affected. Reciting the alphabet, the months of the year, the days of the week, or arithmetic tables is very difficult for these children. In the section on writing I have mentioned writing automatisms and the importance of "familiar sequences" ("geläufige Reihen"). These are distinct series memorized at a very early age, which persist into later life and are not forgotten even after severe damage to the brain. Some children's ability to form automatic mechanisms is so impaired that not even these relatively simple sequences (e.g., days of the week, months of the year, counting and arithmetic up to ten, multiplication tables, address, telephone number, names and age sequence of siblings, etc.) become automatic. This is a great complication in such a child's life.

Role of Parents and Teachers

When trying to find out whether or not the child knows these sequences one must, of course, make sure that he is old enough to have learned them and that they have been taught properly. This throws light on how important it is for the teacher (and the child's parents) to find out by which route the child learns best: the visual or the auditory. Many children of the visual type cannot learn anything they only hear, but must see it in pictures or in writing. They cannot, for instance, remember even these simple sequences when teachers or parents just say them and have the child repeat them. An auditory-type child, however, can learn them with ease in this way. (See Visual and Auditory Types of Memory, Vol. I, p. 69.)

Testing Familiar Sequences

When testing the child's knowledge of these familiar sequences we should not only have him recite them forwards, but also backwards. Only in this way can we be sure that he does not just repeat them by rote but that he also understands the meaning of the sequence and that he has a firmly established mental image of it.

Helping the Child to Cope with this Symptom

An impairment of his automatic mechanisms is a handicap for the child long before he enters school, and it should be diagnosed at that time so that special remedial measures can be started as early as possible. The consequences are grave when this diagnosis is missed. Parents, teachers, and especially the child himself, must learn to understand the nature of this symptom. They should also be made aware of the attention difficulty. They must understand that the child's attention is not focused automatically on certain activities, and that he must learn to focus it deliberately. This includes the simplest acts such as opening a door. The child must eventually learn to pay attention on his own, without relying on his parents' or teachers' commands. Some children can accomplish this only when they tell themselves orally what to do and how to perform each step of the activity. This requires great effort, patience, and persistence by the child. The attention span of some of these children is fortunately not necessarily short; only its initiation may be difficult.

Some automatic mechanisms remain throughout life without continuous practice, for instance those underlying swimming or bicycle riding; others are lost when not used. Even a healthy child who has not tied his shoelaces or his ties for awhile, or has not read anything during the long summer vacation, may have to figure out the required techniques again as if he had never learned them. A child with impaired automatic mechanisms who has acquired these mechanisms laboriously after a long period of practice, loses them after a much shorter period of disuse than a healthy child. (See also Conditioned Reflexes, Vol. I, pp. 78–89.)

Relation to Inability to Tolerate Disorder and to Slowness

Children who are slow and whose automatic mechanisms do not work properly function best in well-structured surroundings. They cannot tolerate disorder. Their dependence on orderliness slows them down, so that these three symptoms (slowness, impairment of automatic mechanisms, and the inability to stand disorder) are connected in a cause-and-effect and in a vicious circle relationship. They tend to aggravate each other. The slower the child, the more impaired are his automatic mechanisms and the greater is his need for orderliness, which, in turn, slows him down. This third unspecific psychologic symptom, the inability to tolerate disorder, will be circumscribed next.

Chapter 9

Inability to Tolerate Disorder

Children with any form of brain pathology cannot stand disorder around them. They need the certainty and predictability that an orderly daily routine provides. Disorder interferes with the efficiency of their performance. It disturbs them deeply, creates enormous anxiety, and may throw them into a panic. Thus they find it very difficult and sometimes impossible to function. Order gives them a structure in which they can live. Children with this symptom therefore function best in structured situations and do best on structured tests. Free choice unnerves them. They can have feelings of security and peace of mind only when they know in advance exactly what will be the daily sequence of their activities, and when they are certain that the chores they have to perform are familiar to them. Planning, which is so enjoyable for most healthy children, is very difficult for them to do. They should therefore not be expected to plan their work in school, but should be told quietly what to do next. The teacher also ought to explain to such children in great detail exactly what is expected of them and what they themselves have to expect. In the absence of such guidance, these children either become disruptive or very passive and incapable of doing anything. This is yet another example of the importance of teaching teachers all the symptoms that can be associated with reading disorders. Not only teachers of special education, but all elementary school teachers should be familiar with these symptoms so that they can at least recognize them and refer the child for examinations.

Relation to Obsessiveness

Their slowness, the impairment of their automatic mechanisms, and their need for orderliness forces these children to become obsessive. They must worry about the tiniest details in their daily activities. They can manage only when they perform their daily chores always in exactly the same way. Each step is important for them and they must check it to make sure it is the right one, performed at the right time, and in the correct manner.

They must, for instance, put their clothes on in exactly the same way every day. They cannot fall asleep except after following the same routine every night. They must make sure that the clothes they will need in the morning are put in the same place and arranged in the same sequence. They must pack their briefcase, unpack it in school, and arrange the materials on their desk in exactly the same way. They become anxious, bewildered, and confused when there is interference with these routines. Strauss and Lethinen call this symptom "meticulosity" in their book, *Psychopathology and Education of the Brain-Injured Child* (1947, p. 25). Charles Bradley, who was especially interested in the role organic factors play in the psychopathology of children, observed these children's "preoccupation with details—a sort of pathologic interest in keeping things in a precise orderliness" (1955, p. 91).

476

Differentiation from Obsessive-Compulsive Neurosis

Obsessive symptoms of this type can occur on an organic or on a psychologic basis. The differentiation between the two can be very difficult, especially when they are mild. What complicates this differential diagnosis even further is that a child with organic impairments can, of course, also have an obsessive-compulsive neurosis that developed independently from the organic disorder. This organic obsessiveness is therefore unfortunately sometimes misunderstood as the symptom of an obsessive-compulsive neurosis. In these children it is not caused by a neurotic process, however, but by their injured or otherwise diseased brain. It is actually the child's way of managing and in this way overcoming his handicaps. It is an attempt at self-healing.

We can be sure that the child's obsessiveness has an organic basis when it is only one of a group of organic symptoms, and when clinical examinations and tests show that these obsessions are the child's way of coping with his general slowness, the impairment of his automatic mechanisms, and his need for orderliness. The child's obsessiveness disappears as soon as the underlying symptoms have been alleviated or cured with special education, practice at home, or whatever form of treatment the child needs. (See Vol. I, pp. 289–343 Treatments.)

Any change represents disorder to these children. It unnerves them and they resist it. They experience severe emotional reactions when they have to move to a new apartment, another school, another city. They become very anxious and unable to function, show signs of depression (insomnia, loss of appetite, mutism, hypochondriasis), or become a severe management problem because of tantrums and destructiveness. The behavioral changes of these children differ, but adults taking care of them must in any case expect a severe reaction before, during, and after moving or any other important change in the child's and the family's life.

These children's intolerance for change includes the introduction of different people into their environment. No two people do things in exactly the same way. Pavlov observed that his dogs behaved differently with different attendants, even though these attendants had been carefully trained to use exactly the same procedures with each dog. The dogs clearly reacted to minute differences in the way they were being approached, in the tone of voice, the gestures, the way of walking, and the like, of their handlers. Children who cannot tolerate disorder can be thrown into despair and become panicky when someone to whom they are not accustomed, for instance a visiting relative or a baby-sitter, takes care of them, or when their teacher is sick and a substitute takes over.

It is also for this reason that the adjustment to the birth of a sibling is more difficult for them than for other children. Their struggle is not only with the conflicts common to all children when a new baby comes into the family. To them this event presents a major and profound disorder because it disrupts theirs and their family's routine; in addition to this, they have to get used to a new human being.

Relation to Early Infantile Autism

There is a severe form of the inability to tolerate disorder that is fortunately very rare. Children with this form react with a panic to the slightest change in the arrangement of even tiny objects in their surroundings: this can include their own room, other rooms in their home, their classroom, and any place they visit more than once (e.g., doctors' offices, etc.). They behave in this respect exactly as do children diagnosed as suffering from Early Infantile Autism. As a matter of fact, this symptom is considered one of the two main symptoms of this childhood psychosis. Kanner and Eisenberg emphasize this point in their classic paper, "Notes on the Follow-Up Studies of Autistic Children" (1955), which was decisive in the establishment of this syndrome. They state that Early Infantile Autism has "two principal diagnostic criteria" from which the other clinical manifestations stem: "extreme self-isolation and the obsessive insistence on sameness." They also stress these children's "insistence on adherence to routine" (pp. 227, 237). Even though they do not call this symptom an "inability to tolerate disorder," the behavior they describe is the same. Stella Chess et al. refer to autistic children's "frantic attempts to maintain the sameness of environmental details" (1971, pp. 30, 31). In a later study Eisenberg writes that among the three most characteristic symptoms of these children is an "anxiously obsessive desire for the maintenance of sameness" (1967, p. 1435). These and other child psychiatrists undoubtedly have the same symptom in mind, which I call an inability to tolerate disorder.

In the chapter on Speech Disorders I have discussed the differential diagnosis of Early Infantile Autism and pointed out that an increasing number of studies have established that most children with this diagnosis suffer from some form of central nervous system pathology, for instance the consequences of rubella encephalitis contracted in utero. I consider these children's extreme inability to tolerate disorder a psychologic symptom with an organic cerebral cause; this may not be true for all of these cases, but is probable in the vast majority. It is one more piece of evidence for the organic basis of this syndrome. (See Speech Disorders, pp. 391–394, 456–457.)

Relation to Reading Disorder

Reading is affected in a special way by the inability to tolerate disorder. To a healthy adult, reading presents order. It does not provoke anxiety unless he has an aphasia and/or an alexia. Reading has been a routine part of his daily life since childhood; its structure and Gestalt are familiar to him; he can read automatically, without breaking up its Gestalt. To any child, reading means disorder, until he reads fluently. He can recognize an object (e.g., an apple) once he has become familiar with its Gestalt, color, consistency, taste, and so on. It then represents order to him. The word "A P P L E," however, is a broken-up, disordered jumble for him. The very appearance of a written or printed page seems a disorganized mystery to him, it does not have a cohesive Gestalt. Children who cannot tolerate disorder therefore approach reading with especially severe anxiety and great bewilderment. They must be taught very slowly and patiently as to the structure of this seemingly disorganized jumble, so that it eventually takes on a familiar and orderly form.

Management

Children who cannot tolerate disorder are obviously very difficult to live with. Great patience and loving understanding is needed to help such a child. He feels emotionally and intellectually paralyzed and regresses when he is hurried along too fast, or when he is punished, ridiculed, humiliated, and otherwise treated with disdain and contempt because of his orderliness and obsessiveness.

These children have the need to finish one activity completely and to make sure that it has really been finished, before they can start another one. This makes their behavior rather rigid and makes it difficult for them to shift freely from one activity to another. This difficulty with shifting is another symptom common to this core group.

Inability to Shift Freely

Kurt Goldstein considers a patient's failure to "shift reflectively from one aspect of a situation to another" (p. 774) one of the basic symptoms of brain pathology that indicate an impairment of what he calls the "abstract attitude" (p. 773). (He postulates that normal individuals have two kinds of attitudes toward the world: the concrete one and the abstract one.) Without going into the details of his theory of brain function, his description of this symptom helps us understand how these patients function and suffer.

He states that such a patient is

> unable to shift from reciting one series (for instance, numbers) to another (days of the week), because active shifting is impossible for him. He can follow or even take part in a conversation about a familiar topic or a given situation, but if he has to shift to another topic—even one equally familiar—he is at a complete loss. He may be able to read a word and, at another time, spell it, but when asked first to read and immediately afterwards to spell, he is unable to do so (1959, pp. 774–775).

This is exactly what children with this symptom cannot do. It also explains, at least in part, why children with all sorts of organic pathology function so unevenly. Teachers frequently complain that the child can, for example, spell or multiply perfectly well on one day and not on another, and that his performance often fluctuates even within one day. This may, of course, be due to uneven attention on a psychologic or an organic basis. The child's shifting ability, however, should be examined in all such cases because it is so easily and so very frequently overlooked. It is such a fundamental impairment that the child's performance in all areas cannot be improved unless the teacher understands the nature of this symptom.

Children with this symptom find it difficult to shift from one activity to another regardless whether they like what they are doing. It is, of course, more difficult for them to stop and to start something else when their present activity is exciting and interesting. Purely psychologic factors influence this organically caused psychologic symptom too.

This shifting difficulty is not confined to motor activities. It includes thinking, fantasies, and, to a certain extent, emotions. The emotionality of these children is often also rigid and cannot be shifted with ease. When they get angry, they cannot get over their anger for hours or days at a time; when they get excited, an abnormally long period of time is required to calm them down. They get stuck in their emotions.

The child's inability to shift freely can be observed when he is supposed to switch from undressing to taking a bath, from playing to washing up for dinner, from storytelling to gym, from arithmetic to social studies, from reading to writing or spelling, and so on. Of course healthy children also often resist changing from one activity to another when they like what they are doing or dislike what they are supposed to start. The children I am describing, however, cannot shift freely and smoothly even when they want to. As a matter of fact, the more they want to shift, the less they are able to. They want very much to act like other children but cannot. In their desire to be as fluid and as fast as the other children in their class, they become very tense, angry, and anxious. This increases their rigidity, so that they find it more difficult to make any move intellectually or physically. Their entire body becomes tense, their hands start to tremble, they can't do anything, and they often begin to cry.

A child with a shifting difficulty has to overcome two hurdles: stop his current activity and start the new one. Once the child has stopped and succeeded in freeing his attention from what he was doing, he may find it difficult to focus that attention on a new task. Thus his shifting problem is aggravated by his attention disorder. Such a child dreads anything new anyhow, because he fears he cannot perform it or otherwise cope with it. It threatens the feelings of security, satisfaction, and competency he had laboriously achieved by finishing the previous task. These children cannot stand surprises. They need a pause before they can start with another activity. There is a certain danger in such a pause because of their distractability, however, because their attention is attracted by anything and everything around them, and a pause provides an opportunity for their attention to wander. Many children are aware of this complication and find out by themselves how to prevent it. They sit quietly with their eyes closed for a few moments before they proceed. This makes shifting much easier for them. Unless teachers, parents, and classmates realize that the child needs this pause, they may think that he is just stalling, dawdling, or daydreaming. (See Distractability, p. 572–581.)

These children are so obsessive, so fixed on a daily routine, and find shifting so difficult, that they do not dare be spontaneous. They are fearful of making mistakes, of doing things awkwardly, and of being ridiculed. All children are afraid of being laughed at; this is an especially hurtful type of humiliation. This fear is multiplied in children who have shifting difficulties and other organic handicaps because they have so often experienced all kinds of humiliations. Many of them are aware of their handicaps and see their own actions as ridiculously awkward and inept. They are therefore tense and anxious even in the kindest and most understanding of surroundings. All this makes it hard for them to get along with other children. Many of them cannot even play free and imaginative games with others, and this makes them feel isolated, lonely, and unhappy.

Relation to Reading

Reading, writing, and arithmetic are invariably affected by this symptom because each of these skills requires a great deal of shifting. The child must shift from one letter to another, from one word to the next, from sentence to sentence, paragraph to paragraph, number to number, from addition to subtraction, and on and on. Ability to blend letter sounds into words may be severely affected because it requires an especially fluid form of shifting, and, in addition, a shift from one sense to another—namely, from vision to speech sounds.

Intersensory Shifts

Intersensory shifts (e.g., from vision to hearing, speaking to listening, taste to touch, etc.) present special problems for many of these children. Birch and his collaborators studied intersensory transfer and integration in healthy and in organically impaired children. They found that infants cannot integrate information received by different senses, and that this faculty develops gradually, is almost completed by the age of 5, and improves steadily until about the age of 11. Organically impaired children may develop this faculty incompletely or only at a later date. They may then find it difficult to determine whether an object they are examining with their hands, with eyes closed, is identical with or different from the one they just looked at (McGhie, 1969, p. 142, Birch and Lefford, 1964, p. 48).

Diagnosis

The child's inability to shift freely can be diagnosed like most of the other unspecific symptoms: by observation of the child during the psychiatric examination, at home, and in the classroom; and by tests. This symptom shows up in intelligence as well as projective tests. David Wechsler referred especially to the "loss of shift" as one of the most important symptoms of organic brain disease in his book, *The Measurement of Adult Intelligence,* which dealt with the construction and use of the Wechsler-Bellevue intelligence test (1944, p. 153). The shifting difficulty becomes apparent not only when the child has to switch from one subtest to the next, but also from one Rorschach card to the other and from one test to another. It slows the child's entire test performance and makes the evaluation of his true intellectual capacity difficult.

Mosaic Test

The Mosaic test performance of these children is also influenced by their difficulty with shifting. They may make a "stone-bound" design where there is a fixation on the form, and often also on the color of the individual piece after it is put on the tray. The child puts down one piece and then carefully selects only pieces of the same shape and color. He cannot shift to other forms and colors, even though this fixation makes it impossible for him to achieve a design he had in mind. This indicates, on another diagnostic level, that the child's organic disorder is localized in subcortical areas. Some such children can make a design, usually a simple one, but would like to make something else. They talk about this, but can only repeat the first design. This means that they perseverate. (See Organic Mosaic Test Patterns, Vol. I, p. 30.)

Rorschach Test

These children may react to some Rorschach cards in a similar way, namely by just repeating what they saw on the previous one. They may, for instance, have seen a "bat" on one card, and say "this is a bat" when they see the next card, which actually looks entirely different.

Management of Children with this Symptom

There is sometimes a marked contrast between these children's inability to tolerate disorder, their rigidity, their obsessiveness, their inability to shift freely, and the lability of their emotions. It is important to understand that such children can be both rigid and emotionally labile, and that both these seemingly contrasting aspects of their behavior are based on their cerebral pathology.

Their rigid and often unyielding behavior makes these children appear willfully stubborn, negativistic, absent-minded, not willing to listen carefully to what the teacher says, and disobedient. They are easily misunderstood and treated unjustly unless the nature of their symptoms is recognized. Their despair leads some of them to hit out wildly, to run around the classroom destroying what is in their way. Some may just run out of the classroom to cry by themselves in the hall or toilet.

This explosive reaction does not, of course, occur only with this symptom. All kinds of frustrations, organic or psychogenic, can cause it. Children with shifting difficulties are most prone to react in this explosive way during transitions from one subject or activity to another. These explosive reactions are a part of other unspecific symptoms, namely free-floating anxiety or morbid irritability with a tendency to sudden rages or panics. Such emotional outbursts should be prevented at all cost; they are too destructive for the child himself and for everyone around him. It takes much too long for the child and for his classmates to re-establish their equilibrium afterwards. Prevention requires, above all, an understanding of the symptom.

All symptoms in this group leave a mark on the child's character, less so the earlier he can be helped to overcome them. Inability to shift freely forces the child to become stubborn, rigid, and inflexible in his general attitude. When such a child says, "I won't!" we cannot be sure that he does not really mean "I can't!". He probably says "I won't!" because he thinks he can't do what is asked of him. This is, of course, true in very many situations and not characteristic for children with this symptom alone. It is, however, especially important for the management of these children that teachers and parents understand that the child may mean he cannot when he says he will not.

Such a child needs a lot of reassurance. He should be told quietly that the adult knows he is capable of performing the task in question. It should also be explained to him that he really means "I can't." Reassurance, however, only works when it has a realistic and honest basis. Teacher or parent must be certain that the child can do it, in case of a new task, or that he has been able to do it in the past. It helps the child in any case when the adult promises to sit next to him and to help him. Another child can sometimes perform this helpful and reassuring function just as well or better than an adult.

The child's inability to shift freely is so intimately connected with the other core symptoms I have described that it also improves when they do. My previous suggestion that the teacher explain all the details of the daily schedule to the child in advance and give him plenty of time to go through with them, helps alleviate this symptom as well. Shifting is made easier for the child when he knows in advance exactly when to shift and to what activity. In this way shifting becomes an integral part of his daily routine. Parents should proceed in the same way, with the understanding that the child cannot tolerate sudden changes or surprises.

Relation to Perseveration

Children who can't shift freely find it very difficult to free themselves from what they are doing or thinking, and to stop. They have the urge to continue doing or thinking the same thing over and over again, that is to perseverate. This is how these two core symptoms, the inability to shift freely and the perseveration, are interconnected.

Chapter 11

Perseveration

Perseveration is automatic repetition that adult or child patients find difficult to stop. Attempts have been made to explain this symptom neurologically. The neurologists Lhermitte and Gautier suggest that perseveration "would appear to result from an absence of the normal inhibition which normally follows the activation of neural circuits." They call it a "general disorder which is found in all varieties of sensorimotor disorganizations: apraxias, agnosias, aphasias" (1969, p. 91). Schuell, Jenkins, and Jiménez-Pabón, in *Aphasia in Adults, Diagnosis, Prognosis, and Treatment,* state that perseverative responses are "probably due to abnormal duration of a past pattern of excitation" (1975, p. 123). It is a common symptom in other organic disorders as well, and is found in almost all children whose reading disorder has an organic basis.

Perseveration must be distinguished from repetitions healthy children normally make when they begin to learn reading, writing, and arithmetic. The differential diagnosis must also rule out the tendency to repetitions of especially anxious, tense, insecure children. These children are not sure that their work is correct and therefore repeat words, numbers, sentences, and so on. For them this is a way to practice to improve their performance.

What often complicates the differential diagnosis between harmless repetitions on a psychologic basis and organically caused perseveration is the fact that perseveration, too, is influenced by psychologic forces such as anxieties and feelings of insecurity. A child may, for instance, perseverate only when he is upset. Kurt Goldstein's observations on brain-damaged adults are pertinent here also. He states that

> perseveration occurs particularly when the patient is forced to fulfill tasks with which he is unable to cope. For instance, a patient who has difficulty with arithmetic may be able to answer promptly as long as he has to solve problems which are within his capacity. The moment he is given a problem which he is unable to fulfill, he may either be thrown into a catastrophic state and not react at all, or he may repeat the last correct result or part of it, that is, he perseverates. If he is then given an example, however, which he is able to solve, he may again answer correctly, and all perseveration will disappear" (1959, p. 792).

This is as true for children as it is for adults. It is one of many examples showing that the causation of a symptom is not necessarily psychologic just because it occurs only under stress and disappears when anxiety has been relieved.

Differentiation from Schizophrenia

Perseveration must also be differentiated from the stereotype behavior found in schizophrenia. This is sometimes difficult because, as Eugen Bleuler pointed out in his classic treatise, *Dementia Praecox or The Group of Schizophrenias,* these patients occasionally "demonstrate a perseveration similar to that seen in organic brain disease" (1950, p. 457). This symptom is called "verbigeration," when the patient repeats the same word or phrase monotonously for hours, days, or even longer. Epileptics sometimes also verbigerate, so that this symptom is not typical for either schizophrenia or organic brain disease. That a child's repetitions are schizophrenic stereotypes and not perseverations on an organic basis can be seen by their bizarreness (the child may, for instance, repeat peculiar gestures, odd sounds, or words he made up) or by the bizarre, fantastic, or magic explanations he gives for them. In case of doubt, the presence of other symptoms of schizophrenia—that is, withdrawal into a peculiar fantasy life, poor contact with reality and with other people, morbid suspiciousness, auditory hallucinations, and so on, as well as tests—clinch the differential diagnosis.

Relation to Reading

Perserveration is a general symptom that may affect all aspects of the child's motor and intellectual activities. It especially hampers reading, writing, and arithmetic. Thus it is very important for teachers to recognize that the child's mistakes are not due to lack of comprehension or carelessness, nor are they done on purpose to annoy. The child may seem to be stubborn, angry, and defiant when he is actually suffering from perseveration and an inability to shift freely. Such a child has an urge to continue writing the same word over and over again and to perseverate during other tasks, while playing, in games, and the like. This is not willful behavior. The child can stop perseverating only when his feelings of anxiety and insecurity are relieved, when he no longer feels either rushed or threatened with failure. Feelings of anger and defiance eventually enter into the child's behavior and aggravate his perseverations, but they are secondary to the perseverations and to his difficulty with shifting.

While perseveration may affect all the child's activities, depending on the circumstances, four main types can be distinguished. The child may have several or all of them, depending on the severity of the symptom and on the amount of pressure he has to endure.

Perseveration of an Act

This type of perseveration is also called Perseveration *of an attitude,* or *of a determining tendency.* It can be observed during the various daily activities of the child, such as dressing, bathing, eating, playing, gym, all sorts of sports, singing, or playing an instrument. The child's reading, writing, recounting of events, and storytelling may be affected by it. Such a child sometimes gets stuck in the middle of a narrative and repeats the last sentence or everything he has just said over and over again, at such length that he often forgets what he was about to tell.

Interruptions are especially hard for these children to tolerate. They cannot simply stop, continue where they left off, or start something different. They must start their story over again from its beginning or at least repeat part of what they just said. They perseverate in the same way when reading or writing.

This type of perseveration, however, does not consist only of repetitions. The child's activity remains the same in *principle* even though he has been told to do something quite different. After storytelling time, for instance, the teacher may ask the children to spell orally. The perseverating child will persist in telling a story or in spelling the required word, but in the framework of a story, as though he had not heard the teacher's request. He seems not to be listening. His "lack of cooperation," however, is not an act of willful or careless disobedience, but the result of this type of perseveration, which is beyond his control. He can respond to the teacher's request and rejoin the other children with their work only after his perseverations have subsided. This takes time. These perseverations leave the child in a confused and anxious state from which he can recover only by a quiet, peaceful pause, during which he is permitted to sit at his desk without doing anything, closing his eyes for awhile if he so desires. As I have stressed before, a number of these core symptoms, including perseverations, can be prevented by allowing these children such a pause after each task has been completed, and before they start on a new one.

Impact on Arithmetic

The mechanisms involved in the perseveration of an act, an attitude, or a determining tendency can best be seen in the way arithmetic is affected by them. Children with this symptom persist in doing what the previous arithmetic or mathematical example required. Where the first example called for multiplication, for example, they continue to multiply all following examples regardless of what operation each actually calls for. Their arithmetic work may therefore look like this: $2 \times 2 = 4$; $2 + 4 = 8$; $3 - 3 = 9$; $10 \div 2 = 20$, and so on. (See also Arithmetic Disorders, Vol. I, p. 226.)

Perseveration of a Word or a Number

Children who perseverate in this way tend to rewrite or reread words and numbers. These perseverations occur primarily at the end of sentences, pages, or paragraphs, wherever the child sees a "stop" sign and feels that he has to start something new. They affect the child's reading whether or not he is familiar with the text, but are less frequent and bothersome when he has read it before.

Periods present special obstacles for these children, both when reading or writing. Such a child sometimes rewrites the last word of each sentence several times before he can get himself to put the period down and to start with the new sentence. This perseveration is, of course, connected with the difficulty in shifting. Both symptoms, the shifting trouble and the perseveration, are aggravated by these children's basic doubt about their ability to do any work correctly. They have trouble finishing any assignment, whether it is easy or difficult. That is why such a frequent referral complaint of their teachers is: "He (or she) rarely completes an assignment."

DOUG, 10 YEARS OLD: HE PERSEVERATED WHEN WRITING.   A good example for this type of perseveration is the book report written by Doug when he was 10 years old and in the fifth grade. I have already described the plight of this boy in spelling (Vol. I, p. 97). He was referred to me when he was 9 years old and suffered from a severe, hereditary, organic reading and writing disorder with Linear Dyslexia.

Doug wrote this book report with great effort, being very careful to do it just right. His handwriting showed the care he took in forming his letters. Sometimes he started a letter, then gave up and started writing it over again. He did not erase. Apparently he had been told not to. He wrote letters and words, crossed them out, rewrote them, and repeated this many times, until he finally let the word stand. For instance, he wrote the word "promoted" eight times and crossed it out six times. He obviously did not cross it out because he had misspelled it; this had happened only once, when he spelled it "pronoted." It seems that the act of crossing out had also become perseverative. These two perseverative acts (the repetition of letters or words and the repetitive crossing-out) were especially striking in one simple sentence, which was supposed to read: "I'm so glad it came in time." What he wrote was this: "In- I In I'm so glad a glad glad glad it came came in ¢ ¢ ¢ ¢ time." The unevenness of his crossing-out lines showed how unsure he felt.

In another part of his book report Doug not only crossed out the same word four times because he had misspelled it, but also put a frame (two horizontal and two vertical lines) around these mistakes. This made them even more conspicuous. What he had in mind, however, was to parenthesize them so that his teacher would understand that they were not to be considered a part of his report (Figures 11.1 and 11.2).

Doug's public school teacher was especially interested in children with reading disorders and tried to help them. It was she who sent me the book report with the following note: "This is part of a book report. D. did a tremendously involved job of 3 pages worth of writing. I did recognize his great effort by giving him an 'A.' However, you can see his tendency to *perseverate* (underlined by her) —which shows up in all his writings." This note showed her understanding and concern. Doug remained in regular classes and was

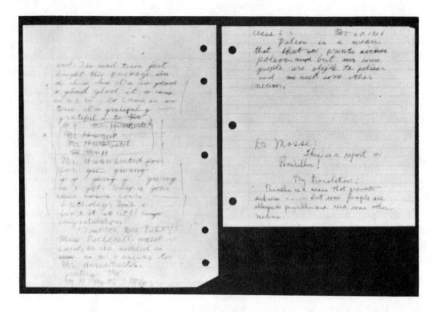

FIG. 11.1.

FIGS. 11.1 AND 11.2. Writing examples from Doug, age 10, in 5th grade. Perseverations are outstanding in one example. He perseverates letters, words, and lines over his writing. He suffers from the hereditary type of an organic reading disorder. He recovered completely, got a master's degree. Drawings show his concern about his eyes with disconnected eyeglasses. The boy has different eyes, one with a large pupil. Doug had severe linear dyslexia and was aware of this difficulty. He had accommodation and fusion difficulties and received eye training with special exercises in addition to reading treatment and psychotherapy. Drawings also show his poor body image and reflect his feelings of incompetency in the thin, ineffectual arms with only four fingers on the left hand. He was right-handed but very awkward with tools due to mild apraxia.

promoted in spite of his handicaps. By the age of 14 his troubles were forgotten and he was able to study like all his classmates. He had overcome his reading and writing disorder through psychotherapy with me and also educational treatment. He did well in college and eventually earned a PhD.

Children with this type of perseveration also have trouble with their arithmetic. They have a tendency to repeat numbers mechanically without using them for their calculations. Their examples may therefore look like this: 5 X 4 = 24; 60 + 19 = 69; 7 X 7 = 47; 39 + 27 = 59. (See Arithmetic Disorders, Vol. I, pp. 220–242; Gerstmann Syndrome, Vol. I, p. 175.)

FIG. 11.2.

Perseveration of a Rote

A child who perseverates in this way continues to recite a poem, the days of the week, or the months of the year, and the like, after the teacher has changed the subject. During the psychiatric examination the child may, for instance, answer "January, February," and so on, when asked where he lives, if he had been asked to recite the months of the year beforehand. The same is true for arithmetic. He may have been reciting the tables or counting and continues to recite or to count when other kinds of calculations are called for. When asked to add after having counted to 16, the child may, for instance, do this addition in the following way: $16 + 6 = 17$.

The different ways in which arithmetic is affected by perseverations show how very important it is to analyze each child's mistakes with the greatest of care. Teachers and parents should never assume that they know why the child got wrong results on his arithmetic examples. They should take the time to ask the child to explain the reasoning behind his calculations step by step, from beginning to end.

Perseveration of an Answer

Children who perseverate in this way give the same answer for awhile no matter what the questions are. This affects all subjects in school, again including arithmetic where the child clings to the result of a former sum.

The diagnosis that the child perseverates requires close observation of his behavior during the psychiatric examination, in school, and at home. Psychologic tests play a special role in relation to this symptom. They may be severely affected by it so that they are difficult to administer, and they may be the only means of finding out that the child perseverates.

Impact on Psychologic Tests

Projective as well as intelligence testing becomes quite difficult when a child perseverates, because he tends to stick to the same type of response through numerous test items. The test situation itself creates so much anxiety that it provokes perseverations. However, there are exceptions. This symptom may be so mild that it is easily overlooked. The test most sensitive to perseverations is the Bender Visual Motor Gestalt test, which often shows perseverations where no other test does. It even reveals, according to Bender, three different types of perseveration, namely perseveration of motor impulses, of rhythmic movements, or of forms.

EUGENE, 6 YEARS OLD: HE PERSEVERATED ON A DRAWING TEST. The case of 6-year-old Eugene shows the value of tests for the diagnosis of perseveration and is an example for the minor but important role often played by perseverations in children with more massive symptoms.

Eugene was a boy of high-average intelligence who had the following general and unspecific psychologic symptoms (other than perseveration) on an organic basis: a severe attention disorder with a short attention span and distractibility, inability to shift freely, a tendency to sudden mood swings, free-floating anxiety, and hyperactivity.

His specific organic symptoms were those outlined in the following paragraphs.

1. A writing disorder, in part due to constructional apraxia. He could not trace or copy and wrote letters into each other. He also reversed letters and numbers and confused the two.

2. A reading disorder. He could not blend letters into words, confused the direction of letters, transposed letters in words, and could not spell at all. Many 6-year-old children have these difficulties, but Eugene's were much more severe and intractible.

3. A severe arithmetic disorder. He did not even know the value of coins. He had no number concept at all, could not understand the position value of numbers, and got numbers and letters mixed up.

4. His body image was impaired. This was reflected in his drawings. He confused his right and his left hand because no dominance had been established. He wrote with his left hand but could perform some skills with his right hand, such as eating or ball throwing. He could not distinguish right and left

on others. However, he had no finger agnosia. (See Gerstmann Syndrome, Vol. I, p. 175.)

Neither Eugene's parents nor his teachers had observed perseverations, but the psychologist found that he perseverated on subtests of the WISC and on the Bender Gestalt test.

During my examination he perseverated only on the drawing tests, not on the Mosaic test nor while reading or writing; and not when he talked.

Drawing Test.   In the drawing tests, which are a routine part of my examination, I asked Eugene to draw a tree first, before the figure drawings. Each drawing is done in pencil on a separate sheet of paper. Eugene's first drawing showed a poorly formed tree, completely open at its base with a squirrel hole in its trunk and a squirrel hovering alongside it without touching any part of the tree (see figure 11.3). When he had finished it, I gave him another sheet of paper and asked him to draw a person. This is when he perseverated because he again drew a tree. I said nothing since I did not want to interrupt him and wanted to observe what he would do on his own.

He finished the tree first, and then, almost as an afterthought, drew a very small stick figure of a boy (see Figure 11.3). When I gave him a third piece of paper and asked him to draw a woman he no longer perseverated. That he perseverated was only a minor revelation of his drawing tests, just as it was a very minor handicap in his daily life. His drawings showed much more important organic and psychologic impairments.

As I have pointed out in the section on Drawings (Vol. I, p. 214), a purely descriptive analysis of the form of the drawings should be made first, before the more exciting psychodynamic interpretations; otherwise important diagnostic signs such as perseverations are overlooked. The very poor forms of Eugene's drawings reflected his constructional apraxia and his poor body image. Stick figures are simplifications, evasions of having to draw a two-dimensional body. They show that the child avoids drawing the body because he feels uncertain of the image of his own body, because he prefers to deny the existence of his body for neurotic or psychotic reasons, or because he is physically very ill. Eugene's drawings also revealed severe psychopathology.

Psychopathologic Interpretations.   The completely open tree bases indicated a feeling of rootlessness, of insecurity, of lack of protection. Many children draw squirrel holes, and they have various meanings. Often a happy squirrel looks out of the hole. Eugene's squirrel was certainly not happy, but was totally isolated and exposed. It is very unusual for a child to draw a squirrel without any support whatsoever, suspended in air like a bird.

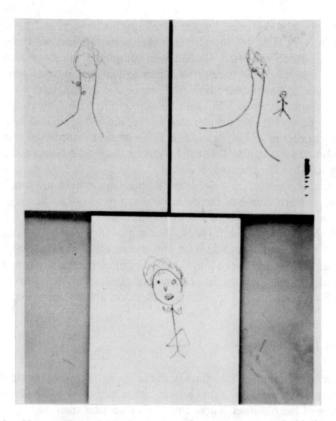

FIG. 11.3.   He perseverated drawing a tree. After drawing a tree in his first drawing, he drew another tree when asked to draw a person next. After that he added a boy. The drawing of a woman reflects his fear of his overwhelming and cruel mother. The structure of the drawings indicates an organic disorder. The rootless trees with an open bottom; the tiny boy, standing in the air; and the squirrel, in the air, outside his treehole show how lonely, helpless, abandoned, and exposed to all dangers this boy felt.

Children identify with animals, and this was probably how Eugene felt: isolated, exposed, without support. This interpretation is supported by the figure of the boy who is very small, without mouth or feet, standing in the air. The drawing of the woman is enormous in contrast to the boy. She has a very large head, a big mouth showing many sharp teeth, and arms with muscles. Her body is visible through her dress; this is attributable partially to the poor body image, but also indicates sexual curiosity. This figure can be interpreted as a reflection of Eugene's fear of his mother, whom he saw as an overwhelmingly angry and threatening person with great physical strength.

These drawings expressed Eugene's feelings, his history, and his traumatic experiences very well. He literally trembled when his mother threatened to punish him, which was often. He had been completely uprooted when he was 2 years of age, when his mother took him to her own mother who lived in another state, and abandoned him. She reappeared 3 years later when he was 5 years old and uprooted him again by taking him with her, away from his beloved grandmother. No wonder that he wet his bed again and had a severe behavior disorder in school, in addition to his organic disorders. Perseveration was the least of his troubles, but it had to be diagnosed because therapeutic planning had to take it into account.

Children who perseverate need more time than others to complete their work and to learn. Some of the other core symptoms—the slowing down of all reactions, the impairment of automatic mechanisms, the inability to tolerate disorder, the inability to shift freely, the fatiguability—also slow down these children's work so that a child with any one or all of these symptoms must concentrate harder and over a longer period of time to learn the same material. This is unfortunately what most of them find extremely difficult to do because their abilities to focus and to maintain attention are also impaired.

Relation to Attention

The perseveration itself interferes with the smooth flow of attention because the starting of new tasks, thoughts, or other activities is hindered by the persistence of the old ones. These children's attention span may appear to be unimpaired because they spend so much time perseverating, but this is deceptive. The length of time they can pay attention varies in different situations and with differing circumstances, just as it does in other children. These variations, however, are extreme in children with an attention disorder on an organic basis. Kurt Goldstein described this aspect of organic attention disorders: "Attention may seem to be sometimes grossly disturbed, and yet the same patient, under other conditions, may appear attentive or even abnormally so" (1959, p. 771).

Relation to Attention Disorders

Perseveration therefore is not incompatible with an attention disorder, as, for instance, Bartram suggests. He states such children have, among other symptoms, "a short attention span for the age (or the converse—perseveration)" (1969 (1), p. 111). A child may have both symptoms (perseveration *and* an attention disorder); many children with an organic reading disorder do. I want to stress again that all organically caused psychologic symptoms can occur together in the same child and that they do not exclude each other. For instance, a hyperactive child may be very slow when he attempts a concrete task.

Attention Disorders

Attention is an extremely important, much neglected aspect of almost all reading disorders and accomplishments. It is a misleading oversimplification to refer to attention disorders as just a "short attention span." This is what most textbooks and other publications dealing with this subject do, whether they are written by educators, psychologists, child and adult psychiatrists, or pediatricians. Focusing and maintaining attention are not simple acts that can be understood just by measuring the time they take. They are complicated neurophysiologic and psychologic processes that operate on different cerebral and psychologic levels. Their impairment causes a number of symptoms, of which a short attention span is only one. Concentration difficulties and distractibility are other signs of the impairment of the child's ability to pay attention. A concentration difficulty is an inability to concentrate one's *attention*, and distractibility means distractibility of *attention*. These symptoms should therefore not be discussed separately as they usually are, because they are part of a defective attention process. What children with attention difficulties suffer from, therefore, is a complex and multifaceted attention disorder.

Structure of the Attention Process

The ability to focus and to maintain attention belongs to the highest mental activities. Attention is a mental quality that can be attached to almost all physical and psychologic activities. It is attracted by stimuli coming from the world around us or from within (i.e., by physical or psychologic impulses). Physical pain, for instance, directs our attention to the painful area, and psychologic pain (caused by conflicts, trauma, guilt feelings, etc.) directs it toward the psychologically distressing areas. We pay attention to something almost every waking moment and also in our sleep, when we dream.

Attention is such a basic human faculty that it has aroused the interest not only of neurologists, psychiatrists, psychologists, neurophysiologists, and educators, but also of philosophers such as Descartes, Leibniz, Schopenhauer, and Herbart. Some of the pioneer studies of attention were made by the psychologist Wilhelm Wundt. William James, who was a student of Wundt, defined attention from the psychologists' point of view in his classic work *Principles of Psychology*. His definition was that

> attention is the taking possession by the mind, in clear and vivid form, of one out of what seem several simultaneously possible objects or trains of thought. Focalization, concentration of consciousness are of its essence. It implies withdrawal from some things in order to deal effectively with others, and is a condition which has a real opposite in the confused, dazed scatterbrained state which is called distraction ([1890] 1950, Vol. 1, pp. 403, 404).

This definition contains some of the most important elements of the attention process: its selectivity, the effort connected with it ("taking possession by the mind"), the clearness that is part of it, the concentration it requires, and the distractibility that occurs when it is not operative. Attention is indeed, as James stated, closely connected with consciousness; but it also occurs during states of altered consciousness—namely in dreams, during hypnosis, and in epileptic and other fugue states. The attention process is an indispensable part of memory formation and of thinking and is therefore fundamental for learning. Where it does not function properly, the child's entire intellectual and emotional development is seriously impaired. To understand its normal and abnormal functioning, it is necessary to analyze its structure and to describe each component separately with its pathology.

Organic Basis of the Attention Process

The attention process cannot function unless its basis in the central nervous system is intact. It has so many components and is so all-pervading that its organic basis must be widespread. It can therefore not be as relatively circumscribed as the cerebral reading, writing, and speech apparatuses. The very concept of a system or an apparatus does not fit this process. All senses with their cortical projection fields and many other areas and levels of the brain, as well as sensory and motor pathways, participate at one time or another in the attention process. The nature and location of the object of attention determines which specific parts are involved. The cerebral mechanisms underlying the attention process are not yet completely understood.

When attention is focused on a stimulus, something must obviously happen to its perception by the sense organ and to the transmission of this perception. We must assume that both the perception and the transmission along afferent pathways are altered in some way, not only speeded up but changed so that perception becomes apperception. How this comes about chemically, electrically, or in some other way, is not known. It is assumed, however, that a special cerebral system, called the "reticular activating system," the "nonspecific projection system for awareness," or "the reticular formation" lies at the core of the attention process and is active whenever attention is paid to anything. McGhie stressed this in a chapter entitled "Psychological Aspects of Attention Disorders," where he wrote: "there seems little doubt that this (the reticular formation) is a vital part of the nervous system for the maintenance of attention" (1969, p. 150).

The Reticular Formation

The reticular formation is very widespread anatomically. Papez describes its localization in the following way:

The reticular formation is a primitive diffuse system of interlacing nerve cells and fibers which form the central core of each half of the brain stem. It occupies the central parts of the medulla, pons and midbrain tegmentum. It is continued upward into the intralaminar and reticular nuclei of the thalamus and the ventral thalamus. At all levels there are side-to-side connections, so the functions are bilateral even at the cortical level (1959, p. 1607).

It is assumed that this formation plays a role in initiating and maintaining states of arousal, alertness, and awareness, and that it is essential for the maintenance of consciousness as well as attention. Apparently it does not itself transport specific sensory information, but renders transportation possible by an adequate waking reaction to the peripheral stimulus. Frederiks points this out especially clearly in the chapter "Consciousness" in the *Handbook of Clinical Neurology* (1969a, Vol. 3, p. 53). Arousal, alertness, and consciousness are prerequisites for attention, except when it occurs during states of altered consciousness (i.e., in dreams, during hypnosis, or in epileptic and other fugue states).

Because of the close relationship between alertness and attention, the neurophysiologist Hernández-Peón defines attention as "a state of specific alertness" (1969, p. 156). He uses animal behavior to show what he means by this.

The presentation of a novel or unexpected stimulus to a dog or cat produces an alerting reaction designated "orienting reflex" by Pavlov. By pricking up its ears, sniffing, and visual searching, the animal adopts an exploratory attitude towards the immediate environment, and therefore, it becomes receptive to a great deal of stimuli through most sensory channels. There are rapid oscillations of sensory transmission in this state. It is only later on, when the animal recognizes the meaning of the most significant stimulus, that alertness becomes specifically and steadily oriented, i.e. that attention ensues. Therefore, whereas the "orienting reaction" is a state of unspecific alertness, attention corresponds to a state of specific alertness (1969, Vol. 3, pp. 155, 156).

Great caution must be observed when transferring results of animal experiments to the behavior of human beings. The concept of "specific alertness," however, is useful for understanding the organic basis of attention also in human beings. It can be assumed that the role of the reticular formation differs in these two states—that is, during unspecific and specific alertness. Some restraint is apparently exerted on the alerting mechanism itself when specific alertness occurs. It is important to note in this connection that, so far as is known, only certain parts of the reticular formation are involved in attention. McGhie points this out when he writes: "It now seems likely that the brain-stem component performs an alerting operation, while the thalamic sections mediate the focussing and shifting of attention" (1969, p. 139).

In the same chapter McGhie also describes how the reticular formation is thought to function during attention in relation to the cortex, the senses, and sensory pathways. He writes that neurophysiologic research has demonstrated

> that the reticular system is capable of blocking stimulation along sensory pathways near the receptors. However, the regulatory role of the cortex in input processing is also becoming increasingly more apparent. It is now established that pathways from the cortex to the reticular system allow the cortex to exert both a facilitating and inhibiting influence on the reticular system. Other work supports the suggestion that information reaches the cortex prior to its arrival in the reticular system so that the cortex may analyse input and then inhibit its passage through the reticular system, thus blocking attention (1969, p. 139; see also Hernández-Peón, 1969, Fig. 10, p. 176; Liebman, 1979, Plate 17-1, p. 61).

It must be stressed that these are primarily assumptions and that we still know very little about the complicated interaction among cortical areas, sense organs, sensory and motor pathways, and parts of the reticular formation that undoubtedly takes place during every act of attention.

Information Theory

Experimental psychologists are trying to understand the organic basis of attention with the help of information theory. Broadbent and others have developed filter models of the attention process that attempt to show how the brain selects stimuli to attend to, then filters, analyzes, and stores them. Stimuli can be defined as pieces of information; these models are based on this concept. They serve as working hypotheses for experiments. It is hoped that they will be able to approximate ever more closely the actual performance of the brain, and that they can eventually be correlated with clinical symptoms.

Other cybernetic studies have also investigated the functions of the reticular formation, including its role during attention. In *Biocybernetics of the Central Nervous System,* Kilmer, McCulloch, and Blum made the following observations:

> The reticular formation receives relatively unprocessed information from all of the sensory and effector systems as well as from all of the autonomic and vegetative systems. It puts out control signals that direct and tune and set the filters on all inputs. This is the structure that decides what way to look and, having looked, what to heed. It controls the thalamic relays at the information anteroom to the cerebral cortex and even the cortex itself (1969, p. 213).

They wrote this in the chapter entitled "Embodiment of a Plastic Concept of the Reticular Formation," where they also emphasized that

> only the RF has a wealth of direct or monosynaptic connections to and from all

other central nervous structures. Only the RF is able to arouse, put to sleep, and turn off (override in a crisis) the rest of the forebrain. And only the RF has the position and connectivity to possibly make computations wide enough (of sufficient scope) and shallow enough (in logical depth) to enable it to arrive at good gross modal decisions within a fraction of a second (1969, p. 215).

It cannot usually be determined exactly what parts of the brain are diseased or malfunctioning in a child with an attention disorder on an organic basis. It can be assumed, however, that sections of the reticular formation are active and interacting with the cerebral reading apparatus when a child or an adult reads attentively. The reticular formation is probably also involved in the recall of memory images that takes place during reading. (See section on Memory, Vol. I, p. 66–68.)

Whatever its organic basis, attention is an inborn faculty of the brain whose application to specific tasks and to special circumstances is acquired. The neurologist Rabbitt used the computer to illustrate the relationship between an inborn faculty of the brain, such as attention, and the actual performance of an individual. He wrote that "to behave as though the translation from neurology to performance were unmodified by life experience of an organism would repeat the error of confusing a computer's programme with its hardware" (quoted by McGhie, 1969, p. 147). In this analogy the cerebral basis of the attention process can be looked on as the computer, life experience as the programme.

Classification of Attention Disorders

Attention disorders in childhood are at last about to be officially acknowledged as classifiable clinical entities in the *Diagnostic and Statistical Manual of Mental Diseases,* published by the American Psychiatric Association in 1980 (D.S.M.-III). The previous manual (D.S.M.-II) did not mention them. They are now classified under "Disorders Arising in Childhood" and called "Attention Deficit Disorder." Three subheadings are added: "with hyperactivity," "without hyperactivity," and "residual type." This classification is still not satisfactory. No provision is made for the differentiation of an organic from a psychologic causation, and the disorder most consistently associated with an attention disorder is not even mentioned. An attention disorder invariably affects a child's ability to learn. Other subheadings—"with a reading disorder," "with an arithmetic disorder"—should therefore be added. This association is very much more frequent than the one between an attention disorder and hyperactivity. Almost all the 445 children with a reading and writing disorder I studied had some kind of attention disorder, but only 29 of them also suffered from hyperactivity.

The association between an attention disorder and hyperactivity is, however, very close indeed when examined from the point of view of hyperactivity. A hyperactive child invariably has an attention disorder. He usually cannot pause long enough to pay attention, especially intellectual attention, which is indispensable for learning. So close is this association that it is frequently very difficult to determine whether a child is hyperactive because he is so distractible and "stimulus-bound," or whether he cannot concentrate because he is so hyperactive—that is, cannot control his drive towards continuous motor activity. A child can, of course, also suffer from both symptoms. (See Distractibility, pp. 575, 581.)

Measuring Attention

Tachistoscopy

Some of the oldest experiments in psychology were devised to measure how many dots, beans, or other uniform objects could be grasped within one span of attention. At that time psychology was still closely linked with philosophy, and these experiments were inspired by the philosophic question whether the mind could apprehend more than one object at a time. The psychologist Robert S. Woodworth described these experiments and their philosophic background in detail in his book, *Experimental Psychology*. He and other experimental psychologists defined span as "one glance" or "one momentary act" (1938, p. 686). They did not use the customary educational and clinical definition of attention span as the length of time a person can concentrate on a task. Tachistoscopes were used for these experiments because they made it possible to see objects at one brief glance, before the eyes had time to change their fixation point (Woodworth, 1938, pp. 687, 688, 689).

Tachistoscope, translated from the Greek, means an apparatus that makes the quickest seeing possible. "Tachistos" is the superlative of "quick." Tachistoscopes have a shutter whose speed can be regulated so that words, pictures, and other materials can be exposed for measured periods of time. These exposures range from one second or more to fractions of a second. The child looks through a stationary window and fixes his eyes on a marked fixation point.

Tachistoscopes were originally constructed by the experimenters themselves. Teachers can still make hand tachistoscopes on their own, as Roswell and Natchez point out in *Reading Disability: Diagnosis and Treatment* (1964, p. 84). More sophisticated machines have been developed, some hand-operated, others power-driven. Some make it possible to project the test material on a screen and to use films so that eye movements can be recorded while the child reads. (See Treatments, Vol. I, pp. 138–139.)

The Perceptoscope is such a specialized tachistoscope. It can project an entire text by moving it line by line from left to right across the visual field. The child sees one or more words at a time moving from left to right. The beginning of the next line can be set somewhat lower so that he also learns the return sweep. (See Linear Dyslexia, Vol. I, p. 127.)

These machines can test a child's reading speed for a diagnostic evaluation. They can also be used for treatment of reading disorders or to increase the reading speed of children whose reading is just too slow and not otherwise defective.

Tachistoscopy showed that between 6 and 11 distinct objects can be seen at one glance. A person does not always see the same number. How many objects he sees depends on his attitude, his alertness, the duration of afterimages, the amount of information he has to record, and the arrangement of the objects (Woodworth, 1938, pp. 692, 693).

A much greater number of objects is seen when they are not scattered about at random, but are assembled in groups or arranged in another systematic way. For instance, three times as many letters can be seen when they are grouped together as words, and twice as many words are noticed when sentences are shown (James, [1890] 1950, pp. 405, 407, his Vol. 1).

Relation to Teaching

These findings have a bearing on teaching techniques. The best use is made of the child's attention when items are presented in an organized way and the rules or principles underlying this organization are explained to the child. Disconnected bits of information should never be taught in any subject. Children should be instructed to look for interconnections, principles of organization, and systems. This applies to classroom teaching as well as to television and other visual aids.

Numbers or letters should not be shown scattered helter-skelter over the blackboard or over the television screen. This is especially important for learning arithmetic and mathematics. Numbers ought to be shown from the first day on in their relationship to each other, so that their numerical value and later on their position value can be remembered by the child with unquestioned clearness. (See Arithmetic Disorders, Vol. I, p. 227.)

I have examined many intelligent children who were totally confused by disconnected, bit-by-bit teaching. No wonder that they looked at the items they were supposed to learn over and over again in a desperate attempt to memorize them, and that their teachers complained that they were slow.

Measuring Reading Speed

While measuring the speed of a child's reading, tachistoscopes also measure his attention process. Eye-movement photographs during reading show that the eyes move with alternating pauses and quick movements called saccadic movements. The pauses are called fixations, and it is assumed that reading takes place during these fixations. The amount the reader can see during each fixation is called the recognition span. (See Linear Dyslexia, Vol. I, p. 127.) It can be assumed that each fixation corresponds to the smallest unit of the attention process, to the "span of attention" of experimental psychologists.

Slow readers have about six, more rapid readers about four fixations per second. The length of their span therefore varies from .16 to .26 per second. However, this does not really give an accurate measure of the speed of the child's reading or the movement of his attention because the recognition span varies so. For instance, one child reads three or four words during each fixation, another child only one syllable. The number of words read per second therefore measures reading speed and movement of attention more accurately. Reading speed of course varies with the subject matter, the ease or difficulty of the style, the child's interest in the text, how alert or fatigued he is, and many other factors.

There is no normal or average speed of reading or of attention. A rate of 250 to 300 words per minute is considered adequate for general reading. Rapid readers cover 10 to 13 words per second and 500 to 600 words per minute. Rates as fast as 1,000 words per minute have been reported. These exceptional rates refer to silent reading only. To reach maximum speed, it must be done entirely without lip, tongue, or vocal cord movements. (See Silent Reading, Vol. I, p. 112.)

These rates can be assumed to measure also the maximum speed at which a child's or adult's intellectual attention moves because, as Woodworth pointed out long ago, "one of the most rapid processes that occur in human beings is silent reading" (1938, p. 696).

Rapid reading, in itself, does not rule out a reading and/or an attention disorder. As Roswell and Natchez stress,

> Rate scores must always be evaluated in connection with comprehension. For instance, students who score in the 90th percentile in rate and the 20th percentile in comprehension are bound to run into trouble in high school and college, obviously not because of rate, but because they get so little from their reading (1964, p. 170).

Comprehension requires that the basic reading technique has become automatic, including an automatic withdrawal of attention from it so that the child is free to concentrate on content rather than on the deciphering of individual words. It also requires that the child's intellectual attention is intact and that he does not lose the thread of the text in spite of the rapid sequence of his responses to the print. What psychologists call a "set" must remain steady through the shifting from one word, paragraph, or page to the next.

Attention "Set"

A "set" is a fixed, stable, attentive attitude focused exclusively on the content of a text or a film, a television story, a lecture, as it unfolds. It is accompanied by a certain amount of intellectual, emotional, and physical tension. This attentive attitude links the small pieces of a text together, guarantees its cohesion, and makes sustained attention possible. Anyone who has written a paper, an essay, or a book knows what a "set" is, even though he or she may never have heard of it. The writer knows that it is imperative that the "set" be kept going and firmly fixed on the sequence of what is being written. He or she must try to ward off all distractions because it may take hours or days to find the thread again once the attention "set" is lost. That is why writers are so difficult to live with, including students who have to write something for school or college. Knowing of the necessity of keeping an attention "set" together makes it somewhat easier for parents and others to live through these periods.

How much of a text a child can read and understand at one sitting indicates the length of time he can sustain intellectual attention. A tachistoscope is not indispensable for measuring this. It is simpler and much cheaper to use a stopwatch, especially when testing the speed of a child's oral reading.

Scanning

Scanning is a special form of rapid reading. It requires a firm but also flexible attention "set." The scanner concentrates on headlines, captions, and key words only, but does not read the text. He or she makes a fast and superficial assessment of main ideas only with the purpose of locating what, if anything, should be read in detail, and of finding out roughly what new information the text may offer.

Scanning is a valuable skill that should be taught and practiced so that it can become really useful. It is indispensable for high school and college students, and for all those whose work requires a lot of reading. It is, however, neither a reliable indicator of a child's reading ability nor of the intactness of his attention process. I have examined many children who only scanned and could not read any text fluently. They had developed such skill in guessing the content or in inventing it outright, that their parents and their teachers assumed that they could read.

Scanning is easier and much faster than reading for all children, whether or not they have a reading disorder. It is tempting to scan rather than to read any text. Scanning inhibits learning to read fluently when it is permitted too early, namely before the child can read silently with ease and understanding. It is usually introduced much too early and without the necessary safeguards. A child who cannot read fluently should be permitted to scan only when he has a reading disorder and is in treatment, so that his reading therapist can supervise his scanning and make sure that it does not become his only way of reading. Scanning may actually be very important for such a child because it helps him to recognize at least the main theme of a text.

Comic books condition children to scan because they induce them to picture-gazing and to surveying one or two pages before they settle down to read a caption, provided they read the text at all. A study of how children read comic books by C. R. Daniels and myself showed that they scan the pictures first and read captions primarily where pictures do not tell the story. Frequently they do not read every word in the caption either. Comic books are powerful conditioners because children look at them long before they start school and during their school and college years as well. Statistics show that more comic books than textbooks are read, perhaps not by all, but by most children during these years. (See Linear Dyslexia, Vol. I, p. 132; and Mass Media, Vol. I, p. 275.) Comic books inhibit reading in a number of ways. Conditioning to scanning is only one of their damaging effects.

Permitting children to scan from elementary school on, together with other poor curriculum practices—for instance, the complete absence of dictation, the neglect of composition writing, whole-word teaching of reading, the use of comic books for reading practice—has contributed greatly to the superficiality of the general knowledge of vast numbers of children, and to their indifference to accuracy. High school and college teachers are complaining bitterly about these shortcomings and often find that it is too late to correct them. They may outlast the child's school years and become ingrained traits (Wheeler, 1979).

Diagnostic Tachistoscopy

Tachistoscopes are helpful but not indispensable for reading therapy. A child's reading disorder can be cured without them. The technique of tachistoscopy, however, is of great value for neurologic diagnosis and for research. It can test the nature of the patient's visual perception, his visual fields, his binocular vision, his attention, and his memory. For instance, a number of test cards can be shown to him in quick succession to find out how many he can remember and for how long. This also tests his ability to sustain a "set" of attention, his retention, and his fatiguability. Tests for attention usually also test memory (see Memory, Vol. I, p. 76), and vice versa.

Tachistoscopy can help with the differential diagnosis of visual agnosia. Patients are instructed to describe, identify, and make a sketch of the picture or other material they saw. Their defects can be observed and recorded with this method.

For the test of binocular vision, test pictures can be projected so that they overlie the fixation point of one eye or both. The role of each retina, what Helmholtz and others called "retinal rivalry," can then be investigated. By projecting the test material a little to one side of the fixation point, one homonymous (i.e., entirely on one side) visual field can be investigated and compared with the other. This is important for the diagnosis of brain tumors and other focal brain lesions, of unilateral cerebral damage, and of brain diseases.

Tachistoscopy is also of great value for the study of the different functions of both hemispheres. The right visual field involves the nasal side of the right retina and the temporal side of the left retina. The fiber tracts of both these retina sides reach the visual center in the left hemisphere. A study of the right visual field therefore tests the performance of a part of the left hemisphere. A study of the left visual field tests the right hemisphere. (See Hemispheric Dominance, Vol. I, p. 58.)

Macdonald Critchley describes the use of the tachistoscope as a test in clinical neurology in his standard book, *The Parietal Lobes.* He writes that "the technique of tachistoscopy has still not received the attention it deserves at the hands of clinical neurologists" (1953, p. 322). This is true also in regard to child neurology, psychiatry, and psychology.

Effect of Attention on Reaction Time and Speed of Performance

That attention shortens reaction time can be shown with the word-association test (see Slowness, p. 461). Wundt, who was one of the originators of experimental psychology, found that the reaction time could be shortened when a warning signal preceded the stimulus to which the subject was supposed to react. He wrote that "the perception of an impression is facilitated when the impression is preceded by a warning which announces beforehand that it is about to occur" (quoted in James [1890] 1950, Vol. 1, p. 428). He attributed this to the preparatory tension of attention, which gets mind and body ready to react at an instant. However the strain of this tension can be so great that it leads to premature or erroneous reactions. Wundt described this in the following way: "When the strain of attention has reached its climax, the movement we stand ready to execute escapes from the control of our will, and we register a wrong signal" (quoted in James [1890] 1950, Vol. 1, pp. 428, 429).

Tension Preparatory to Attention

This can be readily observed when the ready signal is given to start an event in competitive sports. It also plays a role during tests in school, especially when the results are crucial for the child's promotion or for his career. The preparatory tension can be so painful and intolerable that it results in wrong answers. Very many children complain that their mind "goes blank" at the moment they start a test and that it does not recover at all or takes too long to become clear again. These children cannot release their preparatory tension; they cannot overcome it, relax, and free their attention in order to concentrate on the test. Feelings of insecurity and anxiety, sometimes to the degree of terror, underlie this inability. Unconscious factors play a large role in arousing these feelings.

As a rule, attention shortens reaction time and increases the speed of all physical and intellectual performances. This applies also to children with organic reading and writing disorders and other organic defects. However defective their performances may be, they can carry them out faster when they pay attention to them. (See Slowness, p. 459; and Mental Deficiency, p. 409.)

Evaluation of Attention on Intelligence Tests

The Stanford-Binet Intelligence Scale Form L-M apparently is the only intelligence test requiring a formal evaluation of attention. The Wechsler-Bellevue Intelligence Test, which is used much more frequently, does not mention attention at all in its original or the revised form (1974). On the Binet, attention must be rated on a sliding scale that extends from "absorbed by task" to "easily distracted." Such specific evaluation helps understand the child's test performance and his general behavior. Psychologists usually include an evaluation of the child's attentiveness in their reports, regardless of what tests they have administered. However, far too often their only reference to attention is that the child has "a short attention span." (See Mental Deficiency, p. 409.)

Psychiatric Examination

Careful observation during the entire psychiatric examination will reveal the level of functioning of most components of the attention process. It will demonstrate the ease or difficulty of arousing the child's attention; how long he can sustain it and during what activities; what interests arouse it; what distracts him; and whether or not he is preoccupied. It also reveals the nature and quality of his intellectual attention; that is, whether it is more powerful than his sensory attention or whether he responds mainly to sensory stimuli. For a more formal testing of his concentration ability, he should be asked to perform the following intellectual tasks in his mind, not on paper: recite the days of the week and the months of the year in reverse order, providing, of course, he can say them in the right order; count from 1 to 20 forwards and then backwards; do simple arithmetic problems requiring carrying over, for instance $112 - 25$, $6 + 7$, and so on, or subtract serial 7 from 100. The answers given and the time taken should be recorded. These problems have been chosen because the answers cannot be given merely by automatic rote memory; they require a "set" of attention. Of course these tests also test the child's memory and his fatiguability. (See Memory, Vol. I, p. 76; also, Fatigue, p. 312, and Fatiguability, p. 671.)

The child's physical behavior during attention should also be observed. It reveals how tense he becomes when he pays attention; whether he grimaces, fidgets, or makes other gestures that show that he is in distress; or remains at ease and relaxed.

When evaluating a child's attention process, one should keep in mind that it may be adequate or better during the psychiatric examination and impaired in other situations, especially in school. The reverse can also occur: a child may be very anxious and therefore inattentive and distractible while he is with the psychiatrist, and his attention may be quite adequate when he is at home or in school.

Automatic Attention

The automatic release of attention is an integral part of every automatic mechanism. Conditioned reflexes have not been securely established and habits not permanently formed until the acts in question can be performed without the help of attention. As soon as the basic technique of reading, for instance, has become automatic, the child does not have to withdraw his attention from it deliberately. He reads without noticing how he does it. His attention is automatically freed so that he can concentrate on the text and on the images, feelings, and thoughts it arouses. (See Vol. I: Conditioned Reflexes, p. 78; Word Reading, p. 82; and Linear Dyslexia, p. 126.)

The focusing of attention can also become an automatic act. For instance, whenever something goes wrong with the conditioned response of the habitual act, attention is automatically focused on it.

The automatization of parts of the attention process is of great importance in our daily lives since it enables us to do several things at the same time. Experimental psychologists have studied this faculty while trying to determine how many acts a person can perform simultaneously. They found that the number depended on how habitual the various acts were. Actually we are always engaged in several activities simultaneously. We may, for instance, walk, carry a briefcase in one hand, gesticulate with the other hand, talk, see, and hear. Our attention is probably only focused on talking; all other acts are habitual and need no attention. It has been automatically diverted from them. It will return automatically when something goes wrong, for instance when we drop the briefcase or stumble.

It is unlikely that two completely different and original acts or thoughts can be dealt with simultaneously within one single unit of attention. What may appear to be a simultaneous performance—for example dictating a letter while writing something else—is actually accomplished by a very rapid oscillation of attention from one act to the other. (See Impairment of Automatic Mechanisms, p. 469; Distractibility, p. 572; and Conditioned Reflexes, Vol. I, p. 78.)

Passive, immediate attention is also automatic. It is an alerting mechanism that may be life-saving. It is inborn and not acquired as is the attention aspect of automatic mechanisms.

Acquiring automatic attention is difficult for children who have trouble establishing any automatic mechanism. Management at home and teaching should take this into consideration. Such a child needs to be aware of this handicap because he must learn to focus and to withdraw attention deliberately until it has become automatic. (See Impairment of Automatic Mechanisms, p. 469.)

Perceptual Changes During Attention

The attention process renders every object attended to more clear and distinct. This is one of its most important qualities. William James pointed this out: "there is no question whatever that attention augments the clearness of all that we perceive or conceive by its aid" ([1890] 1950, Vol. 1, p. 426). The details of a landscape, for instance, become more clear and distinct when attention is focused on them. Even a distant object, only dimly seen without attention, may become clearer when it is deliberately attended to, of course only within the limits of the visual acuity of the viewer and the brightness of the object.

Attention cannot make clearer an object that lies beyond the eye's capacity to see clearly. The greater clarity produced by attention is, however, also of help to an incapacitated sense organ. A person who is hard of hearing, for example, hears a sound more clearly when paying attention to it; a child with poor eyesight sees the text he is reading more clearly when he is concentrating on it; and so on.

Clearness

This quality of greater clearness produced by attention has interested philosophers such as Schopenhauer, psychologists such as Wundt, and physiologists since Helmholtz.

Apperception

Wundt defined the perceptual changes brought about by attention as "apperception" because attention makes it possible to perceive something in addition to something else. Apperception has been used as a synonym for attention. In his paper, "General Principles of Psychosomatic Relations of the Eye," Otto Lowenstein describes what apperception means from the psychiatric point of view. He writes:

> Normal vision includes not only physical process, but also a psychological attitude. In order to see it is not enough that the eye and its afferent and efferent pathways are unimpaired; it is necessary that the individual adopts an active attitude towards the target. By means of this active attitude, perception becomes apperception, i.e. the object is not only recognized but is included in the totality of preceding experiences (1945, p. 433).

What he calls "active attitude" includes the attention process. When a child reads without this active attitude, that is purely mechanically, without paying attention, his perception does not become apperception and he neither understands nor remembers the text.

The neurophysiologic mechanism underlying apperception is still far from clear. It is an integral part of the entire attention process, which is still only partly understood. (See Organic Basis of the Attention Process, p. 502.)

The neurophysiologist Hernández-Peón explains the neurophysiologic basis of clearness in the following way:

> Because clearness of perception depends on the degree of attention, it is obvious that sensory impulses triggered by the attended stimulus must be facilitated somewhere along their trajectory from the receptors up to the integrating circuits underlying conscious experience (1969, p. 156).

He also states that "in the awake brain the activation of specific sensory neurons is strictly related to the process of attention" (p. 157). He summarizes his theory of this aspect of the attention process in this way:

> During attention induced in experimental animals, transmission of sensory signals triggered by the attended stimulus is facilitated both at the specific and unspecific or polysensory afferent pathways from the receptors up to the cerebral cortex. The net result is the arrival of more accurate information not only to the analyzer mechanisms of the specific cortical receiving areas, but to widespread areas of the brain including the integrating neural circuits involved in memory and other aspects of behavior (1969, Vol. 3, p. 157).

Whatever the underlying mechanism, the greater clearness produced by attention indeed provides more accurate information, and with it facilitates the formation of memory and of judgment. It also has a profound influence on thinking generally and indirectly on various aspects of behavior. (See Memory, Vol. I, p. 66; Intellectual Attention, p. 540; and Concentration, p. 554.)

William James' definition of clearness clarifies its psychologic role. He states that

> clearness, so far as attention produces it, means distinction from other things and internal analysis or subdivision. These are essentially products of intellectual discrimination, involving comparison, memory and perception of various relations. The attention per se does not distinguish and analyze and relate. The most we can say is that it is a condition of our doing so ([1890] 1950, Vol. 1, pp. 426, 427).

It is an indispensable condition.

Without the greater clearness provided by attention, we may see or hear many things, but we do not *notice* them. They remain part of a diffuse impression. Sensory stimuli, if not made clearer and more distinct by attention, tend to fuse with each other into a confused and confusing general impression. Each separate sensation, if not attended to, makes others even less distinct. This is true for all senses. No wonder that a child with a severe organic attention disorder is in a constant state of confusion and turmoil. He feels insecure and anxious and has no clear concept of the reality about him and how to master it. In reading, he cannot distinguish one letter from another or one word from the next.

Implications for Education

The awakening of a child's attention to things he never noticed before is one of the basic tasks of education. We are apt to notice only those stimuli whose significance and importance is known to us beforehand. This is one basic reason children who have not been taught reading, writing, arithmetic, and other subjects clearly and understandably have such limited outlook and ways of thinking. They do not know what to notice. William James expresses this principle very well and clearly:

> Men have no eyes but for those aspects of things which they have already been taught to discern. Any one of us can notice a phenomenon after it has once been pointed out, which not one in ten thousand could ever have discovered for himself. . . . In Kindergarten instruction one of the exercises is to make the children see how many features they can point out in such an object as a flower or a stuffed bird. They readily name the features they know already, such as leaves, tail, bill, feet. But they may look for hours without distinguishing nostrils, claws, scales, etc., until their attention is called to these details; thereafter, however, they see them every time ([1890] 1950, Vol. 1, pp. 443, 444).

One reason for the damaging effect of the whole-word method of teaching reading is that it ignores this principle. How is a child supposed to notice the letters "o" or "r" in the word "horse," for instance— or any of the other letters —when neither their form nor their sound has been pointed out to him? That so many thousands of children leave school with an extremely limited vocabulary is also partially due to the neglect of this fundamental aspect of teaching. These children have not been taught properly, from nursery school on, to notice details of objects and ideas and to name them correctly. To have been taught to notice something is, of course, the basis for recognizing it later on. Recognition of objects, thoughts, feelings is dependent on memory and on the greater clearness produced by attention. Paying attention is the most important step for memorizing something, both in reading and in listening. Children should be told that the best way to remember a lecture, a discussion, a concert, a play, is by listening *attentively*.

It is possible to train oneself to notice objects at the periphery of one's vision and hearing, without the help of the greater clearness provided by undivided attention. One can learn to notice such marginal objects without moving one's eyes or head and while concentrating one's attention on objects in the center of the visual field. Teachers acquire this habit of necessity. They cultivate a special form of emotional, visual, and auditory readiness to react to subtle clues, so that they can notice what goes on in the remotest corners of their classroom even when their backs are turned. The attention process also produces another perceptual change in that it intensifies all sensations. This greater intensity is very difficult to distinguish from the greater clearness, because attention also changes the relative intensity of two objects. The one attended to seems louder, brighter, sharper, stronger, and the like. The tune played by one instrument in an orchestra, for instance, seems not only clearer but also louder when we give it our full attention deliberately.

These perceptual changes also affect imagination. Concentration on imagined objects can give them almost the brilliancy and intensity of real objects, especially in children and in artistically gifted adults. Experimental psychology has shown that such vivid mental images can leave afterimages just like real objects. Children who can produce such vivid images find it often difficult to distinguish reality from fantasy. They are not sure whether imagined stories or other fantasies are real. Such experiences are entirely within normal limits and should not be confused with pathologic hallucinations.

The greater clearness and intensity produced by attention sometimes does not help children with an attention disorder and other impairments on an organic basis to distinguish objects properly. They see objects perfectly clearly, but they find it difficult to distinguish them from other visual stimuli that surround these objects. The same is true for hearing and the other senses. Even the most intense concentration does not always help such children distinguish what Kurt Goldstein calls the "figure" from the "ground." He defines these terms in the following way:

> We call the excitation in the stimulated area the f i g u r e and the excitation in the rest of the organism the g r o u n d. All performances of the organism, as well as all experiences, are so organized. Figure and ground are intimately interconnected; to every figure belongs a definite ground (1959, p. 777).

He also stresses that "all damage to the nervous system, especially brain damage, disturbs the figure-ground organization in general or in a part which belongs to a definite performance field" (1959, p. 777). This disturbance is more of a handicap for children than for adults because it affects so many aspects of learning. It can best be diagnosed through tests.

One can, for instance, show the child a drawing of the outline of a familiar object such as a cup with the background structured with wavy lines. A child with this disturbance will find it much more difficult than a healthy child to identify the cup. Strauss and Kephart describe such tests in their book, *Psychopathology and Education of the Brain-Injured Child.* They summarize the consequences of this disturbance in the following way: "He cannot hold the form if the background is also patterned and his difficulties increase as the patterning of the background becomes stronger ... his difficulties in form recognition are increased when the contrast between figure and the background is decreased" (1955, pp. 60–61). It is possible that this disturbance is at least in part due to the malfunctioning of these children's attention process, which does not produce the greater clearness and intensity necessary for normal functioning.

The greater clearness and intensity of sensory impressions provided by attention also has psychologic implications. These two qualities make the objects of attention more exciting and interesting, so that the effort connected with attending seems more pleasurable and less cumbersome. This touches emotional components of the attention process that are an integral part of its functioning.

Selectivity of the Attention Process

Being able to select one stimulus or a group of stimuli for attention and to pay no attention to all others is vital for survival. It protects us from being overwhelmed and confused by a massive onslaught of physical and psychologic stimuli and makes it possible to respond immediately to stimuli that indicate an emergency. The selection of which stimulus to attend to depends on many physical, psychologic, and social factors.

The physiologist Helmholtz formulated a general law stating that we leave all impressions unnoticed that are valueless to us as signs by which to discriminate things. This is an inborn physiologic selection. We are not aware of the fact that we screen out many stimuli in compliance with this law. We are, however, aware of the fact that objects are easier to discriminate, distinguish, and recognize when we focus attention on them.

The greater clearness produced by attention is dependent on its selectivity. Once a stimulus has been selected for attention, it becomes more clearly outlined and can be both more accurately perceived and more easily distinguished from its surroundings.

Relation to Reading

This selectivity has a bearing on reading. A child must learn to ignore everything on the page that interferes with the discrimination of letters from their background and from each other. He must be taught that pictures (especially when arranged all over the page as in comic books), that lines surrounding a text as in comic book balloons, and that anything else he sees on the page have no value for reading. He should be told to make a deliberate effort not to attend to any of these items while he is reading. (See Letter and Word Reading, Vol. I, pp. 31, 82.)

The selection of stimuli for attention is either voluntary or involuntary, for example when a sudden unexpected sound, sight, or other sensation arouses attention. Physiologic and psychologic studies by Luria and others have shown that inattention—that is, the screening out of unnecessary or irrelevant stimuli —is accomplished by inhibition, that it is an active and not a passive process. It is done consciously and deliberately or occurs automatically without the person's awareness. It is a form of self-restraint that serves to conserve energy that would otherwise be squandered on too many stimuli. However, the inhibition of irrelevant stimuli also requires energy and therefore contributes to the feeling of effort connected with attention and to the fatigue it produces. (See Physical Changes During Attention, p. 521; and Distractibility, p. 572.)

There is a very thin line between variations in selectivity that remain within normal limits, and pathologic selections. What people select for attention is normally sensitive to anxiety, mood changes, feelings of guilt, and other emotions. Unconscious forces play a large role in this. Varying interests and points of view also determine selections.

A woman raising children, a worker, a teacher, a physicist, a businessman, and so forth, are apt to pay attention to different aspects of the same conversation, lecture, or event, and consequently to remember, repeat, and evaluate them differently. This creates great problems in communication. Some people hear only what they want to hear, deliberately or due to unconscious needs. So far as children are concerned, adults can never be entirely certain that a young child heard, absorbed, and understood accurately what he was told or overheard, especially when the content was highly emotionally charged. To avoid misunderstandings, it is best to ask the child to repeat, in his own words, what was said. This method can, of course, be effective only in an atmosphere of complete trust. Damaging and lasting misunderstandings between children and adults often occur because it was assumed that the child paid attention to every word said, while anxiety, anger, shame, depression, preoccupation with his own problems, and so on, made the child's attention highly selective. (See Concentration, p. 554; Distractibility, p. 572; and Emotional Components of the Attention Process, p. 546.)

To prevent misunderstandings and other problems in communication, children should be taught to listen and to observe carefully, and to report what they saw, heard, or read *accurately.* They must learn to restrain their emotions and personal preferences while listening to their teachers and to others as well as while reading a text. Methods of teaching reading that permit substitution of words instead of insisting on accurate reading are damaging in this respect, too, as they are in so many others (Groff, 1977). (See Spelling, Vol. I, p. 115; and Vol. I, p. 268 under Sociogenic Reading Disorders.)

What children select to attend to differs with their age, the level of their intelligence, their individuality, and their talents. An attempt should be made to determine each child's mode of selection and to help him diversify it. It is especially important to recognize, appreciate, and encourage the highly original selections of gifted children. On the highest level of scientific, artistic, and literary creativity, the act of selection itself is, according to Wertham, the act of creation.

In his masterpiece, *A La Recherche Du Temps Perdue (The Past Recaptured)*, Marcel Proust describes these kinds of selections. He writes:

> Impelled by the instinct that was in him, long before he thought he might some day be a writer, he systematically ignored so many things which caught the attention of others that he was accused of being absentminded and himself thought that he could neither listen nor observe. But all the while he was instructing his eyes and ears to retain forever what seemed to others to be childish trifles—the tone in which a sentence had been spoken, the facial expression and movement of the shoulders of someone about whom perhaps he knows nothing else—all this many years ago and only because he had heard that tone of voice before or felt that he might hear it again, that it was something enduring, something which might recur; it is the feeling for the general which in the future writer automatically selects what is general and can therefore enter into a work of art. For he has listened to the others only when, however mad or foolish they were, by repeating parrot-like what people of like character say, they had thereby become the spokesmen for a psychological law. He retains in his memory only what is of a general character (1974, p. 33).

See also Thomas Mann's masterful short story, "Tonio Kröger," which deals with artistic creativity.

Selective Inattention

Pathologic selection of what to attend to is called "selective inattention." In "Clinical Manifestations of Psychiatric Disorders," Louis Linn defines this symptom as

> an aspect of attentiveness in which the subject blocks out those data of consciousness that generate anxiety, guilt and other unpleasant feelings. It is synonymous with the psychological defense mechanism known as denial (1967, p. 557).

A striking example for this kind of inattention is the story of a young man who maintained an erroneous notion about the anatomy of the sex act through-out childhood and early adolescence, even though his mother and father had repeatedly explained it to him openly and accurately. His father was a gynecologist and obstetrician deeply involved in promoting anatomically accurate and psychologically constructive sex education. It therefore came as a great shock to him when his own son, at the age of 20, reproached him bitterly for never having explained the sex act accurately, so that he got the impression that what the man does is urinate. He had obviously selected from what his parents told him only what he could tolerate emotionally and what fitted into his own childish sex theories. Such distortions of sex information given entirely in good faith are not at all unique and not necessarily neurotic. The topic itself arouses so much anxiety and touches on such conflicting, intimate, and often repressed emotions, that it is apt to cause selective inattention. Misunderstandings and distortions are therefore the pitfalls of all sex education.

Neurotic selections are often difficult to distinguish from the normal. What schizophrenic adults and children select to attend to, however, is usually so bizarre and inappropriate that it differs greatly from the norm. Children and adults whose brain does not function properly find it very difficult to select relevant stimuli and to focus their attention only on them. They have trouble inhibiting other stimuli and preventing their attention from wandering from one object to another. They are "stimulus-bound" and distractible. (See Distractibility, p. 572; Concentration, p. 554; and Inability to Shift Freely, p. 480.)

Physical Changes During Attention

Attention is accompanied by a feeling that is difficult to describe. The psychologist Wundt called it a "peculiar feeling." He wrote that "we always find in ourselves the peculiar feeling of attention" (quoted in James [1890] 1950, Vol. 1, p. 440). Kretschmer calls it "consciousness of activity." In his *Textbook of Medical Psychology* he defines attention as "this preferment of certain psychic material which is accompanied by the consciousness of activity" (1934, p. 108). This feeling has also been called a strain, a sense of tension, or a feeling of effort. We speak of straining our attention as if it were a physical activity such as straining a muscle. This feeling comes indeed very close to being a physical sensation. We even localize it in different parts of the body. We feel it, for instance, inside and around our ears when we listen attentively to music, and usually localize it inside our head or on our forehead during intellectual attention. Its intensity varies with the degree of concentration. When we transfer our attention or mode of attending from one sense to another, we have a sensation of altered physical direction.

The entire attention process, including the feeling that accompanies it, is so closely linked to the senses, to physical sensations such as pain, motor activities, etc. and to emotions, that it invariably provokes subtle physical changes. Kretschmer describes the relationship of attention to these physical changes in the following way:

> The quite trivial shifts of feeling which accompany attention, tension or relief of expectancy, the touching on affectively toned "complexes" (by certain spoken words, for example) betray themselves by slight innervational changes which can be experimentally recorded, although they may pass unnoticed by an onlooker or even by the subject himself (1934, p. 54).

These are changes in pulse rate, blood pressure, in the secretion of endocrine glands, in the tension of muscles, in the electrical conductivity of the body as measured by the psychogalvanic reflex, in the pupils, and so forth. They are truly "psycho-somatic" manifestations. This is what biofeedback instruments measure.

Changes in the Autonomic Nervous System

These physical changes can occur only with the participation of a specialized part of the peripheral and central nervous system, namely the autonomic nervous system, which is also called "vegetative" cr "involuntary." This system is spread throughout the entire body. It reaches and influences all organs, senses, and somatic systems (i.e., the circulatory, respiratory, digestive, urinary, musculoskeletal, and reproductive systems). Its central regulation is located in the region of the hypothalamus where areas regulating arousal and sleep, muscle tonus, metabolism, reproductive functions, automatic functions, emotions, and the like are situated. These areas have connections with the cortex, which can exert an influence on them and, indirectly, on the autonomic nervous system—which, in turn, sends messages and stimuli to cortical areas via the same indirect anatomical route.

The autonomic nervous system performs functions that are vital for the maintenance of health and of life. For instance, it helps to maintain the uninterrupted function throughout life (without cessation even during sleep) of the heart muscle, the intestinal muscles, and other rhythmically innervated muscles; it regulates metabolism, body temperature, pulse rate, blood pressure, secretion of endocrine, sweat and other glands, and plays an important role in the function of all senses.

We might notice an accelerated heartbeat, increased perspiration, or other effects of overstimulation or imbalance of this system; but this is unusual. Normally we do not notice its activities. They go on without our conscious awareness and independent from our will. We cannot influence them deliberately: we cannot, for instance, widen or narrow our pupils at will. Their reaction to light and accommodation, which is so important for seeing and reading, is a function of the autonomic nervous system and is entirely beyond our control. (See Organic Basis of the Attention Process, p. 502; Hyperactivity, p. 582; and Drug Therapy, Vol. I, p. 330 and p. 657.)

The autonomic nervous system consists of two antagonistic systems: the sympathetic system, also called thoracolumbar because of its anatomical location; and the parasympathetic or craniosacral system. The sympathetic system is also called adrenergic because noradrenaline (also called norepinephrine) transmits the impulses at its nerve endings. The parasympathetic system is called cholinergic because acetylcholine is the transmitter substance at its nerve endings (Brobeck, 1973, pp. 59–60; Liebman, 1979, pp. 38–42, Plates 12-1, 12-2).

It is an oversimplification to call the interaction of the two systems only antagonistic; it is much more complicated than that. Taken as a whole, the activities of the sympathetic nervous system, according to Wertham, prepare the body for action (e.g., for flight or fight, for sexual activity, or for any other active behavior), while the parasympathetic nervous system prepares the body for less emotionally colored, more passive pursuits such as sleep or digestion (1953a). The sympathetic nervous system has also been called the mobilizing system, while the parasympathetic nervous system is thought to be involved in energy-conserving processes (Pribram & Melges, 1969, p. 320).

A good example of these differing functions is the antagonistic action of the two systems on the pupils. The effect of parasympathetic stimulation is contraction, which is appropriate for sleep, while sympathetic stimulation causes dilatation, which is indispensable for attention. It also provides a larger visual area for seeing the outside world, so that appropriate action can be taken when necessary.

Another important example is the action of the two systems on the digestive tract. Sympathetic stimulation inhibits peristalsis and glandular secretions and contracts the vessels of the esophagus, the stomach, and the small and large intestines; it therefore inhibits digestion. Parasympathetic stimulation dilates the vessels of the entire digestive tract, increases peristalsis and glandular secretions, and enhances digestion. It makes possible healthy digestion while eating or sleeping. The decreased appetite of children and adults on sympathomimetic drugs (i.e., drugs that stimulate the sympathetic nervous system) such as Benzedrine, Dexedrine, or Ritalin, as well as their trouble falling asleep when they take them too close to bedtime, stems from sympathetic stimulation. (See Hyperactivity, p. 657; and Drug Therapy, Vol. I, p. 330, 331.)

RELATION TO ATTENTION DISORDERS. The autonomic nervous system of children suffering from an organic reading, writing, and arithmetic disorder, an attention disorder, and other symptoms on an organic basis, is usually not examined at all or not with sufficient care, so that its malfunctioning is not diagnosed. Changes in its tonus, imbalance between the two systems, over- or understimulations are therefore frequently overlooked and symptoms neglected or misinterpreted as psychogenic. This affects the attention process especially.

Attention is so intimately linked with the sympathetic nervous system that an attention disorder on an organic basis invariably indicates that this system does not function properly. Malfunctioning of the sympathetic nervous system, on the other hand, usually causes an attention disorder. Establishing the current status of the child's autonomic nervous system should therefore be part of the diagnostic examination whenever organic impairments are suspected. It also helps to understand the child's general behavior, because this is affected by the tonus and reactivity of the system. The tonus of each system is normally subject to change, and the balance between the systems may also vary physiologically. The differential diagnosis between physiologic and pathologic variations is therefore frequently difficult. A detailed examination is thus even more important.

REACTIVITY OF THE AUTONOMIC NERVOUS SYSTEM.   The basic reactivity of a child's (or adult's) autonomic nervous system may be within normal limits, yet may deviate sufficiently to make a noticeable difference in his physical and emotional reactivity and excitability. Some children and adults are vagotonic (parasympathotonic) throughout their lives; others are sympathotonic; most have a well-balanced autonomic nervous system. The parasympathetic system of vagotonic children has a stronger tonus and is more easily stimulated than their sympathetic system. Their heartbeat tends to remain slow, their blood pressure low, their digestion uninhibited, and so on, in response to stressful situations. This is in contrast to the reactions of sympathotonic children, whose faces turn pale sooner, whose hearts beat faster, whose blood pressure rises higher and is generally more labile, and whose digestion is inhibited sooner when they are anxious, excited, and under stress, than occurs in children who are vagotonic or have a well-balanced autonomic nervous system.

SYMPATHOMIMETIC DRUGS.   Most studies of children with attention, reading, and other disorders on an organic basis, whether classified as MBD (Minimal Brain Dysfunction or Damage) or not, do not even mention the autonomic nervous system as part of the syndrome. Yet the drugs invariably recommended for treatment are sympathomimetic; that is, they stimulate primarily the sympathetic nervous system. An examination of these children's autonomic nervous system before, during, and after treatment with these drugs should therefore be mandatory; this is however grossly neglected in practice and in a large proportion of the scientific literature. Some studies deal only with the autonomic nervous system as a whole and do not distinguish between sympathetic and parasympathetic functions in the analysis of their data.

An example for this type of study is the paper by Zahn, Abate, Little, and Wender on "Minimal Brain Dysfunction, Stimulant Drugs, and Autonomic Nervous System Activity" (1975). The authors make no distinction between the two systems and refer only to "autonomic" base levels, responsivity, arousal measures, and so on. To call dextroamphetamine (Dexedrine) and methylphenidate (Ritalin) just "stimulant drugs" is also inaccurate. They stimulate the sympathetic nervous system primarily and influence the parasympathetic nervous system only indirectly, as a response to sympathetic stimulation. In this as in other such studies the autonomic nervous system as a whole is not really investigated— only some selected reactions. The balance between the two systems and their respective tonuses was completely ignored. No wonder that the results of these studies are vague, usually contradictory, confused, and confusing.

The basic error made by these investigators is that they treat as uniform and therefore comparable entities conditions that are not entities at all but that consist of entirely different parts. "Minimal Brain Dysfunction" is not a clinical entity and the autonomic nervous system is not a physiologic entity.

Progress in this complicated field requires studies in detail of all the various functions involved, and of their interactions. It also requires taking the "Law of Initial Value" (Wilder) into consideration. This law is of such fundamental importance in psychophysiology because it makes certain reactions to psychologic, physiologic, or pharmacologic stimuli understandable and predictable.

Law of Initial Value

This law was first observed by the neurologist and psychiatrist Joseph Wilder as long ago as 1930. Its validity and usefulness have since been confirmed by numerous investigators all over the world. They use a variety of stimuli and physiologic as well as psychologic functions. The law states, according to Wilder, that

> the higher the initial (pre-stimulus) level of an organismic function the smaller the response to function raising, the larger the response to function depressing stimuli. Beyond a certain medium range of initial values (levels) we encounter reversals of the usual type of response, increasing in frequency with the extremeness of initial values (1965, p. 577).

In his paper on "Modern Psychophysiology and the Law of Initial Value," he states that the law deals, among other aspects,

> with the antagonism between excitation and excitability: the higher the excitation, the smaller the remaining excitability or, in terms of energy: the higher the

kinetic the smaller the potential energy (1957, p. 3348–3352; 1958, p. 200; 1967, Chap. 1; see also Janisse, 1977, p. 10).

Applied to children with an overexcited sympathetic nervous system with a very high tonus, as is typical for so many children with an organic reading and attention disorder who are also hyperactive, this means that any psychologic, physiologic, or pharmacologic stimulus (i.e., Dexedrine, Ritalin, etc.) that makes them more excited may either have no effect at all or, paradoxically, may calm them down. It explains why sympathomimetic drugs, which act as stimulants for an unexcited, well-balanced sympathetic nervous system, act as sedatives for hyperactive children. This is also the reason sedatives (e.g., barbiturates) sometimes cause excitement in some children and adults.

The "Law of Initial Value" is especially important for investigations dealing with the autonomic nervous system, because its tonus varies so much physiologically. Studies of this system that ignore this law are therefore totally unreliable and misleading. The reaction of the parasympathetic or the sympathetic nervous system to any drug or other stimulus depends entirely on the tonal level that existed *before* the drug or other stimulus was administered. Wilder stresses that the following basic principles of the interaction of the two parts of the autonomic nervous system have been established, based on the "Law of Initial Value." He writes:

> Every disturbance (stimulation) in the sympathetic system causes, by successive induction, a stimulation in the opposite (parasympathetic) system. The initial level determines the extent of response in each system; it also determines whether the oscillation will level off quietly in damped waves, or whether the tolerance limit of a system will be reached and the leveling-off take place in form of a crisis, a paradoxic reaction, an "attack" (1958, p. 201).

IMPLICATIONS FOR DRUG THERAPY.   Because the Law of Initial Value is too often ignored in clinical, animal, and experimental studies of the effect of sympathomimetic drugs, we still do not know whether they stabilize the autonomic nervous system of children with an organic attention disorder, hyperactivity, and so forth, as is often claimed, or whether they destabilize it even further. The widespread practice of prescribing these drugs after the most cursory physical examinations, often without any neurologic or psychiatric examinations—and with equally superficial re-examinations—has harmed very many children. It has also retarded progress in constructive clinical management and in pharmacology. (See Hyperactivity, p. 582; and Drug Therapy, Vol. I, pp. 330–331 and Vol. II, p. 657.)

THE ATTENTION REFLEX.   So closely is attention connected with the sympathetic nervous system that it elicits a sympathetic reflex called the attention reflex. It consists of the dilatation of the pupils whenever attention is paid, often accompanied by very fine contractions at their margins. These fine contractions are called pupillary restlessness (Pupillenunruhe in German), or hippus. They are not visible to the naked eye; they can be seen only through a magnifying glass (Best & Taylor, 1943, p. 1708). These and other pupillary reactions can be recorded and studied with special instruments that magnify, photograph, and/or film them. These instruments are so sensitive that they record the size and speed of even the finest pupillary contractions. The recording of pupillary movements is called pupillography. Pupillographic studies have shown that attention is not the only psychologic stimulus eliciting pupillary dilatation. Pain, fright, strong sensory stimulations, and generally strong and sudden emotions have the same result. This reflex is therefore often called the psychologic pupillary reflex. It is, however, indistinguishable from the attention reflex because all these sensations and emotions evoke attention immediately, and with it, the attention reflex. This is a normal reflex in any case and does not indicate any pathology.

Pupillography. Psychiatrists, neurologists, psychologists, and neurophysiologists have studied the behavior of the attention reflex during various somatic, organic cerebral, and mental diseases. Both Kraepelin and Bleuler refer to pupillographic studies in their textbooks and state that this reflex is very often completely absent or at least markedly diminished in schizophrenia. This is probably due to the poor emotional reactivity of schizophrenics, as well as to their lack of contact with other people and with their environment generally. Kraepelin thought that this indicated a poor prognosis (Bleuler, 1930, p. 105; 1950, pp. 172, 314; Kraepelin, 1921, p. 135).

The earliest extensive pupillographic studies were done by the neurologist and psychiatrist Otto Lowenstein. The pupillographic equipment he used is illustrated in a paper he wrote together with the neurologist E. D. Friedman, entitled "Pupillographic Studies. Present State of Pupillography; Its Method and Diagnostic Significance" (1942, pp. 969–993). It was built in the neurologic department of New York University College of Medicine (p. 972).

Lowenstein showed pupillographically what profound influence attention and other emotional stimuli have on the function of the eye. The attention reflex—that is, the sympathetic stimulation by attention—is so powerful that it causes an exhausted pupil to react again. He called this the "psychosensory restitution phenomenon." In a symposium on "Psychosomatic Problems in Ophthalmology" (1945), he describes this phenomenon. He states that

when finally the pupillary reflex is exhausted by means of a great number of light stimuli regularly repeated at the same interval—this exhaustion can be suddenly overcome when a psychological or sensory stimulus is interposed between two light stimuli. Such a psychological stimulus really defatigues the exhausted pupil. This phenomenon, which I called the psychosensory restitution phenomenon, is based on a real brain reflex. Its center is located in the posterior part of the hypothalamus. Its effect is based partly on the liberation of adrenaline in the periphery, partly on central disinhibition of the parasympathetic (p. 435).

Lowenstein also emphasizes that this phenomenon has far-reaching implications for the scientific understanding of the relationship between psychologic and physical processes generally. In the same symposium he states that this phenomenon

> shows that psychological processes have a direct—and not only an indirect—biological importance. The mechanism as represented by the psychosensory restitution phenomenon is to be kept in mind when you will be told about psychologically initiated phenomena occurring in an area far removed from consciousness, such as for instance, the influence of emotions on the intraocular pressure, or possibly the development of exophthalmus (1945, pp. 435–436; see also Janisse, 1977, p. 4).

That psychologic processes can have a direct physical impact as shown by the psychosensory restitution phenomenon, supports the original idea of Richard Semon (1923) that any stimulus, physical or psychologic, changes the part of the brain it reaches chemically, electrically, or in some so far unknown way. He called this change an "engram." Other neurophysiologic studies also tend to confirm Semon's engram theory. (See section on the engram under Memory, Vol. I, pp. 64–67, 80.)

The psychosensory restitution phenomenon also shows at least one neurophysiologic mechanism through which any emotional turmoil (e.g., over a reading disorder) may affect a child's eyesight. It also demonstrates the enormous effect a psychologic stimulus, such as arousal of interest in a text (i.e., motivation) has in counteracting visual fatigue. This is, of course, possible only within the limits of the physiologic capacity of the eyes. (See Emotional Components of the Attention Process, p. 546; and Fatigue, p. 312.)

Pupillography is not just an instrument for research; it also has clinical and pharmacologic applications. It can, for instance, assist in localizing lesions in the brain and can help diagnose brain diseases, sometimes while they are still in a preclinical stage—that is, before clinical symptoms appear. Otto Lowenstein, together with E. D. Friedman, an outstanding clinical neurologist, also showed that it is possible to distinguish organic from psychogenic causation with pupillography in some cases, for instance in children with postencephalitic symptoms. This is, of course, the fundamental problem in the differential diagnosis of all reading disorders (1942, pp. 984, 985).

It is also possible to assess the general functioning of the autonomic nervous system with pupillography and to study the effects of various drugs on this system. The tonus of the sympathetic nervous system can, for instance, be assessed in this way, as Lowenstein points out. In a paper on "Pupillographic Studies, Periodic Sympathetic Spasm and Relaxation and Role of Sympathetic Nervous System in Pupillary Innervation," he writes that "a certain functional sympathetic tonus is necessary in order that a maximal sympathetic reaction, for example, a maximal psychodilatation reflex, may be guaranteed" (1944, p. 93). Pupillography is therefore a method that can establish the initial value— that is, the level of the sympathetic tonus—before sympathomimetic drugs are administered. It can also register tonal changes while the drug is active and after the drug has been discontinued, and in this way help establish the drug's usefulness in compliance with the Law of Initial Value (Janisse, 1977, pp. 130, 131, 153; Rubin, 1962).

Psychiatrists have given up pupillographic examinations of their patients because they seemed unproductive. However, the mechanisms underlying changes of the pupils in response to psychologic factors and the meaning of these changes during schizophrenia and other mental diseases are still largely obscure. Pupillography of children is difficult to perform, but it can be managed. Children with organic reading and writing disorders and other organic impairments could benefit from such examinations, because they provide a sensitive test of their attention process and of the functioning of their autonomic nervous system. An absent attention reflex and/or psychosensory restitution phenomenon would indicate a defective attention process and help determine whether it has an organic or a psychologic basis.

It must be stressed that both pupils must react to light and to accommodation: these reflexes are essential for the normal functioning of the eyes. They have nothing to do with the attention reflex, which, compared to them, is a minor and subtle phenomenon. Its absence is also a minor event, while the absence of a reaction to light and/or accommodation is always a major and very serious symptom. For instance, one of the cardinal symptoms of general paresis (dementia paralytica) is the absence of the reaction of both pupils to light, while they continue to react to accommodation.

Each child with an organic reading disorder and/or other organic impairments should in any case have a thorough eye examination by an ophthalmologist, including fundi and visual fields when indicated. This is also the specialist most likely to notice when a child's pupils do not react to psychologic stimuli such as attention. (See Chapter 1, Examination, Vol. I, pp. 34–35.)

Pupillographic studies have continued with far too little correlation with clinical symptoms and diseases and with reactions to pharmacotherapy. Janisse has made the most detailed and comprehensive study of pupillometry from its beginning. This study includes research in relation to children and to mental diseases (1977).

Eye Movement Changes.

Changes in Direction.   Attention causes the eyes to move in the direction of the visual object that is of interest. These movements are often so swift and automatic that they resemble a reflex. The ophthalmologist Kestenbaum describes the mechanism underlying such eye movements in a paper on "Psychosomatic Factors in Eye Movements." He writes:

> For instance, an object situated at the right excites the attention of the person. This object is imagined on the left part of the retina of each eye, the stimulus carried backwards to the cortical center of vision in the left occipital area. From here, a motor impulse is elicited which runs downward to the eye muscles in such a manner that the eyes are turned to the right, exactly in the direction of the seen object. The entire process is similar to a simple reflex; there is a centripetal pathway, a transmission, and a centrifugal pathway. But this "reflex" occurs only if the object has attracted the *attention* of the subject. Many objects are seen peripherally but the eyes do not turn towards them. Thus we see that a purely psychological factor, the *attention,* plays a deciding role in the course of an apparently somatic reflex (1945, p. 453).

Thus, the very close link of attention to physical activities is evident also with regard to eye movements. Voluntary as well as automatic eye movements play a crucial role in reading. Neither functions properly unless the child focuses his attention on the text. Lack of attention therefore interferes with a primarily physical phenomenon— eye movements—and in this way undermines the entire reading process.

Changes in Fixation of the Eyes.   Attention is the main factor in the complex mechanism of the eye's fixation on an object. Looking in the direction of an object and fixing one's eye on it are two different matters. Kestenbaum describes the mechanism of fixation in the same paper in the following way:

> In "fixation" the tonus of all external eye muscles is increased, in order to hold the eyes more exactly in the proper direction. One can "fix" one's eyes to a higher or lesser degree; that is to say, the tonus of the eye muscles can be increased to a higher or lesser degree. The amount by which the tonus of the muscles is increased depends directly on the strength of attention the subject is paying to the object (1945, p. 454).

ATTENTION TEST.   The relationship between eye movements, eye fixations, and the attention process is so close and constant that it can serve as a basis for an attention test. The test material consists of a rotating drum with vertical stripes or a series of pictures. The child looks at the drum while it moves and is told to fix his eyes on a stripe or on a picture and to follow it as long as he possibly can. His eye movements, which are recorded, alternate between a movement following a stripe or a picture, and a returning movement by which they try to follow another stripe or picture.

The more attention is given to a single stripe or picture, the farther the eyes will follow it, and the greater will be the amplitude of the to-and-fro movement. The extent of this amplitude is directly dependent on the factor of attention, quantitatively and qualitatively. This fact offers us, according to Kestenbaum, "the strange opportunity of measuring the purely psychological phenomenon of attention by the size of eye movements, measurable in degrees or millimeters" (1945, p. 455).

A rapid to-and-fro movement of the eyes leads to a short amplitude, which indicates that the child cannot maintain his attention and suffers from an attention disorder. Such a child invariably has a reading disorder based on his attention defect alone, even if he has no other impairments, because he cannot fix his eyes on any part of a text long enough to read it or, if he can read the words, long enough to understand it. (See Linear Dyslexia, Vol. I, p. 127.)

Changes in the Electroencephalogram

Attention abolishes the alpha rhythm, one of three normal, spontaneous rhythms (alpha, beta, delta) recorded by the EEG. The alpha rhythm consists of rhythmic oscillations occurring at a frequency of 8 to 10 per second. It occurs normally in an inattentive state, that is, in drowsiness or light sleep, during a narcosis, or when the eyes are closed. As soon as the eyes are opened or when attention is aroused by any stimulus at all or focused on any mental effort, for example an arithmetic problem, the amplitude of alpha oscillations decreases markedly and the waves become more rapid and irregular. Normal alpha waves recur as soon as the eyes are closed and attention ceases (Grinker, 1949, p. 63).

Attention also alters evoked potentials. This is electrical activity registered by the EEG that is not spontaneous but rather is provided by stimulating sense organs or various parts of the brain. Evoked potentials have been studied primarily by neurophysiologists who found, according to Hernández-Peón, that "focusing of attention on a given stimulus produces changes in the amplitude, scalp distribution, and multiplicity of waves of the corresponding evoked response" (1969, p. 158).

An enormous amount of data has been accumulated since then using this same method, but progress has been minimal in clinical terms. In a comprehensive chapter on "Evoked Potentials and Learning Disabilities," Evans warns that "until there have been successful replications [of published research], most will be open to criticism that significant findings resulted from the fact that many measurements were taken and some statistically significant ones, therefore, would have been expected because of chance alone (1977, p. 87). Not even the limits of normal responses have been outlined, especially in regard to children, and correlation with clinical symptoms and diseases has been sparse and unreliable. Mirsky has apparently done the most extensive research using EEG, evoked potentials, and other experimental methods in relation to attention. In "Attention: A Neuropsychological Perspective," he makes an attempt to correlate attention disorders with clinical entities (1978, p. 56). However, the results remain tentative and are not applicable to practical clinical work.

What hampers progress in this type of research is a deplorable lack of clear-cut clinical entities that can be compared accurately with each other. Mirsky uses such unscientific classifications as "Hyperkinetic children," "Mother with schizophrenia 'high risk,'" "Hyperkinetic behavior," "Psychosurgery patients" (1978, p. 56). Apparently all these researchers use the vague and inaccurate term "learning disability" instead of a precise diagnosis of the child's reading, writing, and arithmetic disorder. Their correlations are therefore no correlations at all, and are clinically and educationally useless.

Neither attention disorders nor reading disorders cause abnormal EEG patterns or, so far as is known, pathologic evoked potentials. They can therefore not be diagnosed with these methods. (See EEG, Vol. I, p. 36.)

Changes in the Muscular System

The attention process and the muscular system have an especially close relationship. Physiologically, attention requires motor inhibition and control. The neurophysiologist Hernández-Peón points this out. He writes: "During unspecific alertness facilitation rapidly oscillates among sensory and motor pathways. In contrast, during specific alertness, facilitation is steadily restricted to selected parts of the afferent pathways activated by the object of attention, and *immobility is the usual motor adjustment*" [emphasis added] (1969, p. 156). These findings are based on the observation of animals. They can, however, be transferred to the attention process in human beings.

These observations are especially relevant for the understanding of those hyperactive children who seem to be in a constant state of "unspecific alertness." Their behavior indeed oscillates between brief periods of sensory attention, and motor movements. This is characteristic for the organic type of hyperactivity. Learning to exert motor control is absolutely necessary for these children, otherwise they cannot overcome either their hyperactivity or their attention disorder. That is why daily physical exercises should be an essential part of their treatment and why gymnastics, whether or not they have been especially designed for this purpose, help all inattentive children to concentrate better. (See Distractibility, p. 572; and Hyperactivity, pp. 582, 666.)

The motor apparatus participates in the process of attention in other ways as well. The entire apparatus is of necessity tense during passive immediate sensory attention, especially when danger is expected, and during the preparatory tension of attention when mind and body are ready to act at an instant. Muscular tension is also increased when attempts are being made to ward off distractions and to continue to attend.

The entire body is sometimes also tense during ordinary attention, especially when the task is difficult and/or unpleasant, and during intellectual or physical fatigue. The "peculiar" feeling of strain accompanying attention tends to express itself in muscle strain that is normally so slight that it remains unnoticed. Its existence can, however, be demonstrated with special recording devices. Facial muscles reflect the degree of strain felt and the attitude towards the object of attention. One can observe the changes in the child's or adult's face when he is paying attention or at least making an effort to attend. Grimacing, shutting one's eyes, or frowning are common during attention. These facial expressions often become so habitual that they accompany any kind of attention, pleasant or unpleasant, and play a large role in the development of characteristic and permanent facial lines and features.

Stress and Tension Syndrome

It is important for parents and teachers to know and for the children themselves to understand that there is a feeling of effort connected with paying attention and that the tension and strain they often feel in various parts of their body is not necessarily abnormal. However, when this feeling of effort becomes exceptionally strong and leads to prolonged and unrelieved muscle strain, it may result in headaches, a stiff neck, or pain in other parts of the body, especially shoulders and back. These symptoms are part of the "stress and tension syndrome," which in adults plays a role in the causation of heart disease, high blood pressure, various gastrointestinal symptoms, and other so-called hypokinetic diseases (diseases caused by lack of exercise). The prevention as well as the cure of these unpleasant consequences of physical changes during attention lie in arousing the child's emotional and intellectual interest in his work, in making it exciting for him, and in relieving his anxieties, which usually stem from his conviction that he cannot accomplish the required task. Emotional excitement about the task and pleasurable anticipation of success can eliminate the unpleasant and exaggerated character of the "peculiar" feeling of attention and with it the painful muscle tension. Regular physical exercises also contribute to prevention and cure (Kraus, 1972).

Fatigue

Children who have to strain their attention because it is difficult for them to concentrate for organic or psychologic reasons are, of course, more prone to develop muscle strain with its diverse symptoms than healthy children. They also fatigue much sooner because both the feeling of effort and the muscular tension are very tiring. Fatigue sets a vicious circle in motion. It increases the feeling of strain and the tenseness of muscles, which, in turn, increases the fatigue. Such a child should not be pushed to do work that is beyond his capacity, and the time devoted to any task should remain below his fatigue threshold. He should be taught to stop before he gets tired, not afterwards. (See Fatiguability, p. 671.)

CURATIVE PHYSICAL EXERCISES. Systematic physical exercises in the form of special gymnastics or calisthenics are indispensable for treatment as well as prevention of the muscle strain and the fatigue caused by an attention disorder, and for alleviating the disorder itself. These exercises should be coordinated with other forms of treatment as an integral part of each treatment plan.

Any form of gymnastics or calisthenics, practiced daily or at a minimum every other day, has a considerably curative and preventive effect. To be most helpful to all children, these exercises should be started as soon as the child enters school, preferably as early as nursery school when children are 2 or 3 years old. Some organic symptoms can be diagnosed at that age. The great advantage of these exercises is, however, that they help all children, and that they can prevent numerous mild organic impairments from developing into major symptoms even when these impairments have not been diagnosed.

These exercises should, of course, be gauged to the child's age and physical development. They improve every child's motor control, body image, ability to pay sensory and intellectual attention, skill in performing practical physical tasks, and self-confidence; in addition, they have a beneficial effect on his general physical and emotional development. They also provide other benefits: they can prevent obesity; calm a child who is overexcited, overstimulated, restless, and/or hyperactive; and make some children less inhibited.

These exercises must be structured and cohesive, and must involve all muscle groups systematically. Their preventive and curative effect depends on the application of these principles. The current gym practices of letting the children play games or permitting them just to run about wildly to let off steam are not at all helpful in this respect. They may tire the children out physically and make them easier to manage in the classroom. However, this usually makes them less, not more, attentive. Free games tend to strengthen these children's habit of paying only immediate sensory attention. They make them more, not less, excited and excitable and do not guarantee a harmonious motor development of the entire body either.

Competitive sports have no curative effect either. They make a child who is anxious and feels incompetent for any reason (organic or psychologic) more anxious, angry, and tense. Neither is it sufficient merely to let all children in a classroom stand up from time to time, stretch and breathe deeply, and then sit down again. Many teachers use these exercises quite informally and casually because they have found that this relaxes the children, wakes them up, and makes them more attentive.

Curative exercises, to be really effective, should be special daily lessons, done preferably in gym suits, with enough free space for each child and with mats on the floor so that the children can lie down on the floor and rest between each group of exercises. Such a rest and relaxation period is an integral part of all these exercises; it should last for at least 2 consecutive minutes.

Pediatricians, physiotherapists, and physical educators have devised special exercises to increase the concentration span of children and adolescents. They are called concentration exercises ("Konzentrationsgymnastic" in German). These exercises help not only children and adolescents with an attention disorder on an organic basis, but also those who are inattentive for various psychologic reasons; in addition, they help all children who are tense, anxious, easily excited, overly inhibited, unstable, or hyperactive. They cannot possibly harm any child and should be used routinely in special classes for emotionally disturbed, organically impaired, and mentally retarded children. They can also benefit children in regular classes. Elementary school teachers as well as gym instructors should be familiar with them.

Concentration Exercises. Concentration exercises combine body movements with relaxation, breathing, and rest periods. All movements are connected with a logical thought or idea so that the child has to keep a "set" of attention in mind while he is exercising. This strengthens his concentration span. In the beginning the teacher or therapist has to direct each exercise orally, until the child has learned to direct himself. This requires careful and exact listening and the ability to keep the correct sequence of the movements in mind. This helps the child learn sequencing, which is so difficult for organically impaired children. It also improves his ability to shift smoothly from one movement to another.

Various forms of concentration exercises have been devised. Prominent among them are imitation exercises ("Nachahmeübungen" in German), which were first developed in Switzerland. They call for carefully designed imitations of familiar daily activities such as washing, brushing teeth, putting on various garments (stockings, pants, coat, tying shoelaces, etc.), running to school, getting on a bus or in a car, sitting on an imaginary chair, jumping an imaginary rope, imitating movements made when bicycling, playing tennis, and so on.

These exercises require simultaneous concentration on body movements and on the mental image of these movements, so that the child exercises his kinesthetic-motor as well as his intellectual attention. All children love to dramatize, and these imitations are a form of dramatization. Children can and should perform them long before they enter school, from the age of 2 on. These and other similar exercises stimulate children's imagination in addition to improving their general physical strength, their motor coordination and control, their body image, their self-confidence, and the enjoyment of their own body, which is such a bothersome stranger to organically impaired and also to many neurotic children. These and other forms of gymnastics also have a calming effect on children's emotions and improve their general behavior (Pototzky, 1926; Prudden, 1972, 1979).

It is a pity that gymnastics for all children and curative exercises for organically impaired and emotionally disturbed children have been sorely neglected in schools and treatment centers (residential and ambulatory) all over the United States. This has undermined the healthy physical development of all children. It has also interfered with their optimal emotional growth. Hans Kraus, an orthopedic surgeon specializing in rehabilitation medicine, and the physical therapist Sonya Weber demonstrated this. They administered a test developed by them, namely the "Kraus-Weber Test for Minimum Strength and Flexibility of Key Posture Muscles," to thousands of healthy children aged 6 to 16 in the schools of the United States. They found that over half of them failed one or more test items, which meant that their motor development was below what it could and should be. Other testers have come to the same conclusions, among them the physical fitness expert Bonnie Prudden. In her report to President Eisenhower she stated that

> Failure to pass (the Kraus-Weber Test) indicates both weakness and tension, and children laboring under these disadvantages are plagued with fatigue, short attention spans, poor retention, and a high degree of absenteeism (Prudden, 1972, pp. 40, 41).

The damage has been much greater in regard to organically impaired children because general or special gymnastics are a therapeutic necessity for them. Not even the otherwise excellent book by Ernest Siegel on *Helping the Brain-Injured Child* (1962) mentions physical exercises. (See section on Distractibility, p. 572ff.) Strauss, Lethinen, and Kephart do not mention them in the two volumes of their *Psychopatholgy and Education of the Brain-Injured Child* either (1947, 1955).

Some teachers of special classes for brain-injured, mentally retarded, or behaviorally disturbed children are rediscovering the value of daily physical exercises on their own. They are finding that the general behavior of all their students improves and that there is a more relaxed and attentive attitude in their classroom. Physical exercises, however, are too valuable a method of education, prevention, and treatment to be left to chance and random use. Elementary school teachers, teachers of special education and of physical education, as well as physiotherapists, pychologists, pediatricians, neurologists, and child psychiatrists should be familiar with them, recommend them, and apply them as part of the child's corrective education and treatment.

Other physical changes are also part of the attention process. They are connected only with the senses and have an organic cerebral, not a somatic basis. (See Perceptual Changes During Attention, p. 514.)

Passive or Involuntary Attention

This form of attention is focused passively, without a deliberate effort. The inner or outer stimuli that get such a passive response are either very intense, massive, or sudden; or they have all three qualities. They may interrupt active attention because of their striking qualities. The very nature of a stimulus may also be so compelling that it attracts passive attention in spite of conscious efforts to ignore it. Sexual and other pleasurable stimuli, pain, and danger signals, for instance a fire alarm, an oncoming car, etc., have such compelling quality.

In the beginning an infant's attention is primarily passive. It takes time, effort, experience, and some teaching to overcome this passive, reflexlike reaction to unselected inner and outer stimuli. Some children take longer than others to learn to direct their attention actively and to keep it in focus. Such a delay may be entirely within normal limits.

The transition from passive and involuntary to active and deliberate attention is difficult for all children suffering from any kind of organic cerebral impairment. As Wertham points out in "Projective Psychology" when discussing organic patterns on the Mosaic test, "In the normal brain there is a plastic utilization of inner and outer stimuli. The patient with impaired brain function becomes excessively dependent on outer stimuli at the expense of his inner goal" (1959, p. 249). These children suffer from a "bondage to the stimulus" ("Reizgebundenheit"), as Kurt Goldstein called it. Their attention is excessively attracted to outer stimuli and to physical and emotional impulses extraneous to the goal they want to achieve. Any task they want to or have to attend to is therefore constantly interrupted against their will and intent.

Active or Voluntary Attention

Attention can be directed actively, deliberately, and purposely toward any stimulus, activity, thought, emotion. This requires that irrelevant stimuli are deliberately kept out of the field of attention. An infinite number of outer and inner stimuli are constantly with us and vie for our attention. They overwhelm and confuse adults as well as children unless a deliberate effort is made to select only one or a group of related stimuli, focus attention on it, keep it there, and ignore all others.

An infant cannot pay active attention. It develops this faculty gradually and to a large extent on its own, through experience, ever-widening interests, and with the help of parents and teachers. The higher the level of active attention, the less likely it is to develop spontaneously. It must be taught and practiced. Deliberate teaching has an important role to play in helping the child overcome his tendency towards passive attention, which keeps him at the mercy of every passing stimulus or impulse.

William James expressed an educational principle that still applies. He wrote that "this reflex and passive character of the attention which makes the child seem to belong less to himself than to every object which happens to catch his notice, is the first thing the teacher must overcome" ([1890] 1950, Vol. 1, p. 417). I know from classroom observations and through talks with teachers that the nature of attention and practical methods of teaching children to pay attention are sorely neglected topics in teacher education. Lack of skillful teaching should therefore be considered as a possible cause of a child's attention disorder.

Children whose attention disorder has an organic basis have more difficulty with active attention than with any other element of the attention process. These children, as a rule, want to pay attention actively but cannot, or can do it only by exerting strenuous and very fatiguing effort. However, once such a child has been successful in ignoring all stimuli except those needed to accomplish the task before him, he will often stick to it with greater tenacity than healthy children and have trouble shifting to something else.

What Kurt Goldstein observed in brain-damaged adults also applies to children. He wrote that such a patient "may even appear abnormally attentive, because under such circumstances he might often be totally untouched by other stimuli from the environment to which normal persons would unfailingly react" (1959, p. 789). Which task such a child can attend to is not determined primarily by the ease with which he can accomplish it. The process of attention, whether healthy or malfunctioning, is driven by emotions that determine which stimuli, impulses, tasks, and so forth, the child or adult chooses to attend to.

Any child selects that task which seems most exciting, interesting, worthwhile to him. This is what a child with an organic attention disorder also does. That is why such a child can sometimes pay attention to a difficult and complicated task better than to an easier one. Whatever he is asked to do must, however, be within the limits of his capacity; otherwise his self-confidence and with it his ability to pay active attention to anything at all is shattered.

Immediate Attention

Attention is immediate when the topic or stimulus is interesting in itself, without relation to anything else. It is spontaneous and not planned. It is usually passive and involuntary, but can also be voluntary, namely when a deliberate selection of topics of immediate, instant, current interest is made.

It is easy to pay immediate attention. That is why this mode of attending is characteristic for young children who still live day by day and whose world is limited to their immediate surroundings. As soon as the child's horizon and perspectives widen and he can plan, he ceases to be tied to objects and experiences of immediate interest only, and can pay attention with a distant goal in mind. He is then ready to pay derived attention.

Derived Attention

Attention is derived when the stimulus or topic owes its interest primarily to its association with something else that is interesting and important. The target of derived attention is not the immediate object, but the goal it leads to. This mode of attending is active and voluntary when a deliberate effort is required to attend to something solely for the sake of some remote interest it will serve.

Derived attention can also be passive and involuntary when a stimulus arouses attention, not because of its own intrinsic interest, but because it is connected with something else, for instance an interesting experience, a thought, a feeling. We may, for example, be driving along a road paying attention only to driving the car until we notice a house that reminds us of some painful or otherwise important experience. Both types of derived attention are, of course, part of everyday life.

Voluntary derived attention requires the ability to plan and to postpone pleasure and gratification if necessary, as well as an understanding of the importance of the goal to be reached. This highlights the importance of explaining to children, in words and concepts they can understand, why they should pay attention to something even though it may seem boring and an unnecessary bother to them.

Relation to Reading

Learning to read and write requires derived attention. Unless the child really wants to be able to read and write he will have trouble concentrating on the cumbersome basic technique. Paying attention to the shapes and sounds of letters is bothersome and not particularly exciting, especially for children who find this difficult to learn. To make reading and writing important and exciting is often difficult in an era where children communicate through the telephone and the tape recorder and see no need to read or write. It requires a lot of effort and imagination from parents and teachers to convince these children that reading and writing are still valid and valuable means of communication.

Some teachers can make any task seem an exciting challenge, and many children pay attention only to please their parents and teachers. This purely emotional motivation works, especially when the distant goal is still beyond the child's comprehension, for instance the reason for learning another language, for studying some mathematical concepts, and so on. It is, however, not the ideal kind of motivation because it does not give a sufficiently solid basis for the increasingly more intense efforts needed for derived attention in the higher grades and later on in life. An intellectual as well as an emotional relationship to distant goals must be instilled in each child.

Paying derived attention is difficult for some, but not all, children with organic impairments. Some of these children practice very hard and long to reach the goal of reading and writing, which is indeed very distant for them. Some neurotic children, especially those who have been infantilized by their parents and cannot plan or postpone gratification, also find it hard to do.

Sensory Attention

This mode of attending deals with sense impressions coming from outside the body or from within. It plays a role in the child's relationship to his own body. A child who cannot or does not want to pay attention to the kinesthetic-motor sensations and movements of his body and to other bodily sensations has an impaired body image. Such impaired sensory attention may be the symptom of an organic cerebral disorder or may indicate a schizophrenic process. A fear of paying attention to some sense impressions is sometimes found in anxiety or hysterical neuroses.

To pay sensory attention is easier than intellectual attention. However, these two modes of attending cannot be schematically separated from each other. Listening to music, looking at a painting, watching movies or television require sensory attention, but it also involves the intellect. However, the distinction between sensory and intellectual attention is useful for an assessment of a child's entire attention process.

Intellectual Attention

The objects of intellectual attention are thoughts, ideas, images, fantasies, imagined objects, and so on. It is the highest form of attention. It does not develop spontaneously to its fullest, but must be taught formally and practiced. Poor teaching and general schooling makes it very difficult for a child to overcome his childish dependence on immediate sensory attention. A child's entire intellectual development is stunted when his ability to pay intellectual attention is inhibited by poor schooling, by organic impairments, or by neurotic inhibitions.

There is an intimate relationship between thinking and intellectual attention. Being able to pay intense and prolonged intellectual attention is a prerequisite for thinking. The English language reflects this close relationship. One of Webster's definitions of attention is "thought," and one of its definitions of "to concentrate" is "to collect or focus one's thought." The words "thought" and "attention" are sometimes used interchangeably, for instance in such popular expressions as "give it a moment's thought," which also means "pay attention to it," and "deep in thought," which also means "in a state of concentrated attention."

Intellectual attention is involved in thinking at all levels, from solving simple practical problems to the highest, most complicated, and abstract questions. There is a close relationship between the power of applying intellectual attention and level of intelligence. Philosophers and psychologists have debated the interaction between these faculties. Some went so far as to state that "genius is nothing but a continued attention." William James disagrees with giving attention such exaggerated importance. He writes that

> it is their genius making them attentive, not their attention making geniuses of them. And, when we come down to the root of the matter, we see that they differ from ordinary men less in the character of their attention than in the nature of the objects upon which it is successively bestowed ([1890] 1950, Vol. 1, p. 423).

A superior faculty of attention is indeed an integral part of a superior intellectual capacity. Attention alone cannot solve problems, but no problem can be solved without intellectual attention. Attention makes problem solving possible, provided the selection of what to attend to is appropriate. Attention is selective; it deals with specific topics. A child with a high level of intelligence has an infinitely greater number of topics, ideas, and so forth to choose from to which to pay intellectual attention, than another child whose intelligence is more limited. Of course a child's life experiences and level of education also play a role in the variety of these choices.

Whatever the level of a child's intelligence, it cannot develop to its fullest unless he learns to pay intense sensory and intellectual attention to his inner world and to the world around him. This holds true for a genius just as for a mentally defective child. No child can reach the limits of his innate intellectual and emotional capacity without developing all facets of his attention faculty. For instance, a mentally defective child who cannot learn to pay sustained attention or who has not been taught how to do it remains much more handicapped than he needs to be.

Because attention affects thinking and general intelligence so deeply, its malfunctioning depresses the intelligence quotient a child earns on intelligence testing. It is difficult to determine a child's true intellectual capacity when his attention wanders. Psychologists take this into consideration when they report their findings. (See Mental Deficiency, p. 409.)

Being able to pay sensory and intellectual attention also plays a role in a child's relationship to other people. Paying attention to others is obviously essential for establishing a relationship with them. Some children are so preoccupied with themselves that they pay no attention to others. A pathologic form of preoccupation is found in some neuroses and in schizophrenia.

Some children with an attention disorder on an organic basis cannot concentrate their sensory and/or intellectual attention long enough to find out how others think and feel. This isolates them from children and adults, makes them feel anxious, insecure, and rejected, and often is at the root of their disturbed behavior.

Sensory and intellectual attention assist each other, but they can also be in conflict and compete with each other. The younger the child, the more he prefers sensory attention, which is therefore apt to distract him from intellectual work. This is why there is a risk in providing constant background music on educational television shows. This music is supposed to arouse and maintain the child's attention and to give him a pleasant feeling of excitement and expectation. Music does serve this purpose well, unless it is too loud and exciting and arouses the child's sensory attention to such a degree that it prevents him from paying intellectual attention; if this happens he does not learn what the show is supposed to teach him.

A good example for this are some sections of "Sesame Street" where the music overshadows the letters, words, numbers, and so forth the child is supposed to learn. Such a show charms the children's senses but not necessarily their intellect. Children must learn to pay intellectual attention without the gimmick of sensory stimulation. Applying their intellect should be made exciting for them in and of itself.

Simultaneous Stimulation of Sensory and Intellectual Attention

Children with organic reading, writing, and arithmetic disorders and/or other organic impairments cannot learn when sensory and intellectual attention are stimulated at the same time. They get confused and distracted and cannot concentrate on either. Because it is so difficult for them to form automatic mechanisms, they cannot get used to habitual background noises such as street traffic, birds singing, an elevator moving, and the like, and cannot shut them out of their field of attention. That is the reason background music on educational television shows may distract them from learning anything, rather than arouse their attention.

Children and adults with a healthy central nervous system, on the other hand, often find it easier to concentrate intellectually while listening to music. Music relieves tensions and produces pleasant moods. This works best when the music is carefully selected to produce such a mood, and when it is familiar so that it requires only passive sensory attention. As soon as it sounds novel and too exciting, it attracts active attention and disrupts intellectual work.

Parents often wonder how their children can study seriously while their hi-fi is going full blast. The secret is habituation. These children are so used to hearing this type of music that they feel something is missing when they don't hear it, and this silence distracts them. However, many of them actually do their work only casually and superficially, because the music envelops their senses to such a degree that they cannot pay full intellectual attention.

Warding Off Distractions

Special habits help some adults and children to ward off sensory distraction. These are repetitive and by themselves senseless movements, for instance pacing the room, playing with keys, chewing gum, and so forth. These rhythmic physical activities provide pleasant sensations, but not so pleasant that they draw off intellectual attention. They also relieve tension. There may be a neurophysiologic as well as a psychologic reason for these habits. Hernández-Peón observes that

> Conceivably, sensory inhibition occurring before the onset of and during voluntary movements may serve to prevent interference of motor pathways by constantly arriving sensory signals. This mechanism might also account for the common observation that in order to maintain intellectual attention, sensory distraction can be counteracted by various meaningless movements such as pacing the room, playing with keys, vibrating foot, etc. (1969, p. 165).

Noisy Classrooms

Intellectual attention develops best when learning is made exciting for the child and an effort is made to keep distracting sensory stimuli away from him while he is studying. Noisy classrooms may seem attractive to some parents and educators because of the obvious emotional excitement of the children, but they do not stimulate intellectual attention. Typical is the reaction of a 10-year-old boy who had spent four grades in such classrooms before his parents put him in another school where children had to sit still, pay attention to the teacher, and do their work quietly. No talking or running around were permitted. His parents were anxious and worried how he would react to this new, "strict" school atmosphere. There was no need to worry. The boy came home in a state of happy excitement and said that for the first time in his life he had been able to concentrate in school because it was so quiet, no one ran around, no one yelled, and no one fought!

Visualization to Train Intellectual Attention

There are some special exercises that help young children in Kindergarten and the lower grades develop their intellectual attention. As I pointed out in teaching reading and writing, visualization helps children remember the shapes of letters, and is essential for oral spelling and for mental arithmetic.

Children should be encouraged to visualize (with their eyes open or closed) first concrete objects (e.g., a toy), then larger areas (e.g., their room at home), then moving objects and entire stories, and at last, abstract forms such as letters and words. They should be taught to try to see all the details before their mind's eye. Children love to do this anyway; all they need is encouragement and practice. This will expand their intellectual attention in depth and breadth.

Intellectual attention can become so intense that it leads to absentmindedness. This is a benign attention disorder that affects children and adults when they are preoccupied with solving intellectual problems or emotional conflicts. It is a self-limiting condition. When the problem has been solved or the work completed, the preoccupation stops.

Relation to Behavior

The systematic development of a child's intellectual attention has a profound effect on his behavior. A child who has not learned to think first and act later cannot rise above primitive, impulse-driven behavior. Such a child acts immediately, without the delay provided by thinking, and therefore without regard to the effects of his actions on others or on himself. These children are apt to relieve their inner tension, which accumulated for any reason whatsoever, by hitting other children without provocation, by wildly running around school or home, by throwing things, and the like.

Freud stresses the fundamental importance of thought for delaying motor (i.e., physical) action when he discusses the role played by the reality principle in healthy mental functioning. In his paper, "Formulations Regarding the Two Principles in Mental Functioning," (1911) he writes:

> Motor discharge, which under the supremacy of the pleasure-principle had served only to relieve the mental apparatus from an accumulation of stimuli, . . . was given a new function, namely the purposeful change of reality. It was converted into planned action. This necessitated a delay of the motor discharge (i.e. action) which was made possible by the process of thinking, which grew out of imagining. Thinking was endowed with qualities which made it possible for the mental apparatus to tolerate the heightened tension which accumulated during the delay (1946a, p. 16; 1948, p. 233) (author's translation).

Freud sees the development of the reality principle and of thinking in historical perspective, as part of the history of mankind, which is being repeated to a certain extent in the growth process of each individual child. The mental life of the infant and young child is, according to Freud, largely governed by the pleasure principle. The reality principle develops later and forms the basis for the entire ego structure. He stresses the role education must play to make this development possible. He describes the task of education in this connection as "inspiring children to overcome the pleasure principle and to replace it with the reality principle" (1946, p. 19); 1948, p. 236. (author's translation)

Educators should heed this principle. Far too many children go through all their years of schooling without any change in pleasure-principle–dominated behavior. They do not learn to pay intellectual attention and to think. The overwhelming majority of them have no organic impairment that makes it difficult for them to learn to pay intellectual attention. Their disordered behavior is due to overwhelmingly negative family and societal influences, inadequate teaching prominent among them.

The importance of helping a child develop intellectual attention for the prevention of violent and destructive behavior alone can hardly be overestimated. Violence cannot be stopped or prevented without stressing this aspect of education. (See Juvenile Delinquency, Vol. I, p. 284, 282.)

Relation to Reading

There are, of course, many opportunities during every schoolday and throughout all grades to stimulate a child's intellectual attention, and numerous ways to do this. There is no better way, however, to accomplish this than to teach children how to read early, efficiently, and with such skill that they love to read from the very beginning. No activity equals reading in stimulating intellectual attention and thinking with all its implications and applications. A child who cannot read cannot possibly develop his innate intelligence to its fullest. That is why a reading disorder has such far-reaching consequences for the child's life and why it is so important to correct it early and well.

Free-Floating Attention

This is an extreme form of passive, sensory and, to a lesser degree, intellectual attention. Attention never rests while we are awake. It drifts from one sense impression, thought, or fantasy to another when it is not being focused. The physiologist Helmholtz made the following observations about the unsteadiness of attention:

> The natural tendency of attention when left to itself is to wander to ever new things; and so soon as the interest of its object is over, so soon as nothing new is to be noticed there, it passes, in spite of our will, to something else (quoted in James [1890] 1950, Vol. 1, p. 422).

Since the discoveries of Freud we know that there is another dimension to free-floating attention. It does not only respond passively to sense impressions, but is also driven by unconscious forces. That is why it became an integral part of the psychoanalytic method of free association, which Freud devised to uncover the content of the unconscious. (See also section on Memory, Vol. I, p. 71.)

Free-floating attention is not identical with distractibility. In contrast to the more alert, tense, and active behavior of a distractible child, it requires a relaxed, passive, and primarily introspective attitude. It also differs from preoccupation, which is an extreme form of voluntary, derived intellectual attention.

It is quite pleasant to let one's attention wander without purpose. Such a relaxed state facilitates daydreaming and may lead into a twilight state between waking and sleep. Considerable effort is sometimes needed to snap out of it. Children, just like adults, love to let their attention float, especially when they are supposed to focus it on some difficult or distasteful task, or when the reality around them is too painful and confusing.

It is an especially tempting mode of attending for those children who suffer from organic impairments or neurotic conflicts. All children must, of course, learn to limit the time devoted to this pleasant state. William James thought that learning to do this had fundamental importance for education. He wrote that

> the faculty of voluntarily bringing back a wandering attention, over and over again, is the very root of judgment, character and will. No one is compos suis if he have it not. An education which should improve this faculty would be the education par excellence. But it is easier to define this ideal than to give practical directions for bringing it about ([1890] 1950, Vol. 1, p. 424).

Teachers, parents, and the children themselves know how difficult it is to reach this ideal. They struggle with it daily.

Emotional Components of the Attention Process

Emotions accompany this process. Sensory as well as intellectual attention arouse emotions and are also driven by them. We bestow our attention on people, objects, thoughts, and all sorts of other stimuli largely because they interest us. Interest in this context means a feeling of intense concern or curiosity. It is emotional as well as intellectual. The psychoanalyst Gutheil describes the relationship between emotions, interest, and attention briefly and very accurately. He writes: "It is the affect that creates interests, and interests form the basis of attention" (1945, p. 479).

Interest and Motivation

Psychoanalytic studies have shown that interest has conscious as well as unconscious sources. The attention process functions best when both the conscious and the unconscious motives, that is the driving forces behind the interest, are in harmony. Motive means the driving force, the reasoning behind a thought or an action.

Motives are either hidden in the unconscious, or overt, that is known to the child or adult. Educators prefer to talk about "motivating" the child rather than about arousing his interest. What a child or adult pays attention to and how long he can concentrate on it depends largely on his motivation. A child's derived intellectual attention, which is essential for learning, functions best when his motivation is emotional as well as intellectual. Attention for only emotional or only intellectual motives does not function as well and requires greater effort to maintain.

To motivate a child means to make learning exciting for him by arousing his intellectual and his emotional curiosity and interest so that he himself wants to pay attention and to learn. Children should be given something that is worth remembering, not the trivia that fill most primers and far too many of the first-, second-, and third-grade readers. To have a 6-year-old read over and over again such sentences as: "Mother said: 'Look, Look. See this,' " or " 'Oh, oh,' said Sally," or " 'Yes, yes,' said Jane," or " 'Oh Jane,' said Sally," or " 'Look Mother,' said Jane," and so on, ad infinitum, wastes a child's attention and time and tends to destroy rather than enhance his motivation for learning to read. Such poor style and trivial content are typical for all primers based on the whole-word or sight/word teaching method, because they use only a limited number of words, which children are supposed to learn to read through endless repetitions (Chall, 1967, pp. 220–223).

Motivation should be built on what Maria Montessori called the child's "instinctive love of knowledge." In the book in which she describes her experiences with teaching the children attending the "Casa dei Bambini," a special school for poor and neglected children, she writes: "We have had most beautiful proof of an instinctive love of knowledge in the child, who has often been misjudged" (1964, p. 371). Children's thirst for knowledge is quite unlimited unless it is smothered. They want to know about and to understand everything that goes on around them, and their searching questions should be answered immediately. Their interests are aroused by innumerable aspects of their daily lives, many of them connected with reading. No interest should be left to die, but should be encouraged as it arises.

Interest in Reading

A child's interest in reading is usually aroused first by street signs and numbers, house and apartment numbers, nameplates, addresses and names on letters, titles of books, headlines and captions of pictures in newspapers, and so on. These items are part of the child's daily life and of his everyday use of language. They should be read to him whenever he asks what they mean or say, irrespective of his age. This is the best way by far to teach and to learn reading. All that is required of the child's parents and other adults caring for him is an ability to read and a little patience, because the same items must be read over and over again. Children as young as age 3 can learn the basic elements of reading and writing in this way, namely letters and the act of blending them into words. They will never forget what they learned in this way, and how exciting and pleasant it was. They will find reading and writing challenging and interesting from then on, unless poor teaching spoils it for them.

Positive emotions such as pleasure in working on a task and trying to master it, hopeful expectations, a generally cheerful mood, delight in success, and so forth, support the attention process; negative feelings such as anxiety, anger, hatred, feelings of inadequacy and doubt, depression, feelings of hopelessness following failure, and so forth, undermine it. Success is the best stimulant for attention. This is one reason why it is so important to help each child achieve success and to alleviate his fear of failure and other anxieties he may have. (See Vol. I, pp. 253–254, 331 Treatments.)

Importance of Classroom Atmosphere

The emotional basis for the attention process receives its most solid support from a peaceful, secure, noncompetitive and noncombative atmosphere in the classroom. Children concentrate best when they feel secure and happy among the other children in their class, like the other children, and feel liked by them. What the great educator Makarenko called the "pedagogic collective" provides the soundest emotional support for the ability of all children to pay attention. The formation of such collective spirit presupposes a decent social orientation and a certain degree of self-discipline.

Self-Discipline and Work

The processes of attention and of self-discipline are closely connected. A child who is interested in his work and concentrates his attention on it exerts self-discipline at the same time. Maria Montessori pointed out how important it is to teach discipline indirectly in this way, through paying attention to work. She wrote that

> the first dawning of real discipline comes through work. At a given moment it happens that a child becomes keenly interested in a piece of work, showing it by the expression on his face, by his intense attention, by his perseverance in the same exercise. That child has set foot on the road leading to discipline (1964, p. 350).

This holds true for every child who learns to read early and with pleasure and to concentrate long enough to read an entire book.

Role of Sexual Arousal

An emotion that invariably undermines the attention process is sexual arousal. Sexual feelings are overwhelming feelings that make it impossible to pay attention to anything else. That is why it is best for a child's emotional and intellectual development when sexual activity and sexual interests remain dormant until the beginning of puberty.

Freud called the period from the completion of the Oedipus complex at about the age of 3 or 4 to puberty the "latency" period because he assumed that the sexual drive remained repressed and inactive during that time. Actually, sexual feelings are not so dormant during that period as he thought them to be. It is, however, important that they remain in the background during childhood. This is unfortunately not true for the majority of children growing up in the United States and in many other countries as well. Even where parents try to protect their children from too early sexual arousal, they cannot prevent the intrusion of erotic and frankly sexual material into their children's lives through the mass media, television, comic books, films, magazines, many with frankly pornographic text and pictures (Mosse, 1966a).

It is not a question of suppressing a normal, healthy instinct, but of too early sexual overstimulation of children who cannot be expected to understand fully and master actual or fictional sex experiences. These can only cause confusion and anguish in the child and make it more difficult for him or her to concentrate on what is their main task during that period of their lives, namely to learn reading, writing, and arithmetic and other subject matter basic for their entire life.

Today's children have less time for accomplishing this anyhow, because childhood has become shorter in all industrialized countries. For reasons that are still obscure, girls start to menstruate at the age of 9, 10, or 11, instead of between 12 and 18; and boys' puberty often starts as early as age 11.

Sexual feelings have the greatest urgency during adolescence and are apt to interfere most with the attention process during that time. Adolescent patients and adults looking back on their adolescence told me that these feelings interfered with their ability to pay attention in the classroom more than any other preoccupation, to the degree where they sometimes had to find an excuse to leave the room in order to masturbate somewhere in private.

However, overt or hidden sexual curiosity is actually one of the most powerful of all motivating forces for reading and other intellectual interests, often seemingly unrelated to sex. Freud assumed that all interests stem ultimately from sexual curiosity that has been sublimated, that is transformed into other, morally more acceptable interests.

Damaging Roles of Humiliation and Fear

Some parents and teachers have the mistaken belief that fear of humiliation and dread of punishment (corporal or other) are the best motivators. They are sometimes not even aware of the fact that humiliation is part of their daily routine, that they are trying to improve their student's learning and behavior through ridiculing and belittling. This technique crushes the child, destroys his self-confidence, and may leave a permanent scar. Motivation is enhanced by encouraging the child to develop his own initiative, by giving him responsibilities, and by strengthening his self-concept—not by weakening it through constant humiliations.

Fear is indeed a powerful motivating force, but an entirely negative and destructive one. An atmosphere of fear in the classroom or at home paralyzes the emotions and thinking of most children to such a degree that they cannot concentrate sufficiently to do their best. Children with a reading disorder and/or other impairments on an organic basis cannot pay attention at all under such circumstances. Harsh and especially unjust punishment produces not only fear but also anger, an emotion that invariably disrupts the attention process. One of the fundamental tasks of education is to instill in children a sense of justice. This cannot be done entirely without punishment. When it is just, brief, and followed by forgiveness, however, it need not create an atmosphere of fear and anger. It can cleanse the atmosphere and promote attention rather than destroy it.

Strong motivation can alleviate even an organically caused attention disorder. It is sometimes extremely difficult, however, to arouse an interest in reading in a child with a reading disorder who has experienced nothing but failure for many years. It is sometimes even impossible for such a child to overcome his aversion against reading until life itself compels him to read.

CLEMENS, 12 YEARS OLD: LACK OF MOTIVATION IN A CHILD WHO COULD NOT READ AT ALL. Numerous colleagues and I tried quite unsuccessfully to explain to Clemens why he should learn to read and write.

Clemens had a severe organic reading and writing disorder and could neither read nor write. This disorder had not been diagnosed until he was 9 years old. By then he had developed such a severe behavior disorder that he was committed to a state hospital with the completely erroneous diagnosis of childhood schizophrenia. (See Aphasia, p. 379, 382, 385 and Mosse, 1958a.)

With the help of the Lafargue Clinic he was discharged 3 years later with the diagnosis of "Primary Behavior Disorders, neurotic traits." The hospital had wanted to transfer him to a state school for mentally defective children. The intervention by the staff of the Lafargue Clinic prevented this move, which would have ruined this boy's life forever.

His intelligence was average or slightly higher. He tested lower on some subtests of intelligence tests only because of his severe reading disorder. (See Mental Deficiency, p. 409.) The clinic assumed legal responsibility for his care after his discharge from the state hospital, which in 3 years had not succeeded in teaching him even the basic techniques of reading and writing. He received individual psychotherapy and remedial reading treatment at the clinic, and a social worker treated his family. He did not respond at all to the diligent efforts of several educational therapists, and they asked me to help break his resistance against reading and writing. He felt so angry and discouraged that he could not concentrate on it.

Clemens loved to come to the clinic and to talk, but when it came to reading he was mute. Because he loved his family and his friends and liked to talk to them, I thought I could motivate him to concentrate on writing by suggesting how nice it would be if he could at last write to them when he was away at camp during the summer. He gave me a puzzled and amused look and said: "But when I want to talk to them I call them by phone!" He was right, of course. He had no need for writing in his daily life except in school. Reading and writing are needed for higher intellectual activities and for more remote practical purposes, such as filling out application forms for work, and the like. All this was of no immediate interest for him.

Clemens managed to get through junior high and high school with but a minimal knowledge of reading and writing. His interest in really overcoming his disorder was aroused only many years later, by life itself. He became fascinated with the theater, worked as a stage manager, and finally realized that he could not get by forever with his excellent auditory memory and the telephone.

Token Economy

The great difficulty with motivating children with reading, writing, and arithmetic disorders and others who do not pay attention in school for neurotic or other reasons has led to a search for successful methods, the so-called "token economy" among them. Its use has become popular in schools all over the country. In classes and institutions using a token economy, good behavior and learning are rewarded with tokens that can be exchanged for money, for goods such as candy or toys, or for various privileges.

Token economy is a variant of punishment/reward methods of teaching. It grew out of the theories of behaviorism and operant conditioning, and is supposed to be a form of conditioning through reinforcing desirable and extinguishing undesirable behavior. It was originally used only in mental hospitals. Children frequently see it as a form of bribery and react accordingly. They are apt to threaten not to do any work at home or in school unless they are paid for it. Such an entirely materialistic and selfish attitude may remain with them and dominate their relationships to other people and to work for the rest of their lives.

The motivation encouraged by token economy is entirely selfish, materialistic, devoid of any decent social orientation, and dependent only on immediate gratification. There is too much of a trend in this direction anyhow. The experience reported to me by a school psychologist is unfortunately no exception. She told me how shocked she was when a child she was supposed to test refused to leave the classroom with her unless she paid him. What shocked her even more was that all the children in the class backed him up and yelled, "Pay him! Pay him!" They meant it seriously; it was not supposed to be a joke. One can't blame these youngsters; they were only reflecting the attitudes of the adult society around them. Children should be motivated to study and to do other work not only for immediate material and selfish rewards. They ought to learn to postpone immediate gratification for distant goals with uncertain rewards. As the great educator Makarenko wrote in his book, *Road to Life*, a classic in the world literature on education, "That person whose behavior is ruled by the most immediate gratification—today's dinner, (today, be it understood!) —is the weakest of men" (1951, Vol. 3, p. 284).

To avoid the danger of instilling undesirable attitudes permanently, token economy should be used as a last resort only, when all other methods of motivation have failed, and only for a limited time, as a transition, until the child's own interest in reading and other subjects has been awakened sufficiently.

Teaching Attention

Attention, like discipline, is best taught indirectly, by arousing interests in work and thinking. However, it also needs to be taught deliberately to make sure that the child's attention span increases as he gets older, and that he can also concentrate on something in which he is not necessarily terribly interested. How often have I heard high school and college students complain that they never learned "how to study"! What they meant was that they were never taught how to concentrate their attention for as long as necessary to learn something in which they were not interested. They had not learned to shut out more interesting and exciting inner and/or outer stimuli. This is, of course, infinitely more difficult for children suffering from an attention disorder, on either an organic or a psychogenic basis.

Motivation and Education

An understanding of the nature and vicissitudes of motivation and of other aspects of the emotional basis of the attention process is indispensable for successful teaching of any subject. It is unfortunate for children and their teachers that courses in education do not deal with these subjects in sufficient depth. An important educational principle is therefore not sufficiently adhered to. William James stresses its importance, and it is as valid today as it was when he formulated it. He writes:

> The only general pedagogic maxim bearing on attention is that the more interest the child has in advance in the subject, the better he will attend. Induct him therefore in such a way as to knit each new thing on to some acquisition already there; and if possible awaken curiosity, so that the new thing shall seem to come as an answer, or part of an answer, to a question preexisting in his mind ([1890] 1950, Vol. 1, p. 424).

I know of a junior high school teacher who was told that she had to teach Hamlet before the end of the term. There were only a few weeks left. About half of her eighth-grade students had such severe reading disorders that they could barely read simple fourth-grade books. They could not possibly read *Hamlet* or even understand most of the words. She could certainly not be expected to "knit" (as James recommended) *Hamlet* in some way onto any of the children's previous knowledge or experience. She struggled valiantly to arouse and maintain their attention. It is likely, however, that this antipedagogical curriculum requirement spoiled *Hamlet* for these children forever. This is not an isolated incident.

A brilliant high school sophomore once asked me to help her write a report on Voltaire. She had been given this assignment without any preparation; it was totally unrelated to anything she had ever read. She had not been taught the pertinent French or general European intellectual history or literature and therefore could not fully understand the text. No wonder she was unhappy with this assignment and could not get herself to concentrate on it. She forced herself to work on it only because she did not want to spoil her excellent grade-point average, and forgot all about it as soon as she handed her paper to her teacher. Such disconnected and poorly understood studies are usually not remembered. Failure to adhere to the pedagogic maxim so masterfully expressed by James is one of the numerous preventable reasons why so many junior and senior high school students cut classes, truant, or drop out of school altogether in disgust.

Fulfilling the requirements of the pedagogic principle bearing on attention is difficult and requires great skill. The teacher must have a wide range of knowledge, skill in presenting it, and a thorough understanding of the students' prior knowledge and of their psychology and way of thinking. To a certain degree it is an art as well as a skill. Students do not daydream, let their attention wander aimlessly, or fall asleep in a class taught by a teacher who has mastered this principle.

Lack of Continuity of Curricula Interfering with Attention

Not only are subjects all too frequently not taught in accordance with this principle by individual teachers; there is also too often no continuity of the curriculum from one grade to the next and from one school level to another. Children who move to a different school district or to another city are even worse off. There is usually no curriculum coordination among different school systems.

In his thorough critique of school programs in the United States in *What Ivan Knows That Johnny Doesn't,* Arthur Trace, Jr. deals with this discontinuity. He comes to the conclusion that "American students are deprived of a solid knowledge of literature, foreign languages, history and geography," and gives four main reasons for this deprivation. One of the reasons is that "the continuity of the basic subjects from grade to grade is commonly not only lacking, but often times the study of the subject itself is interrupted for semesters or years at a time" (1961, pp. 176, 177).

These practices make it unnecessarily difficult for teachers to arouse and maintain their students' attention, and for students to concentrate. This, like any other discontinuity, makes paying attention and remembering especially difficult for all children who have an attention disorder, a reading disorder, and any other symptom on an organic basis.

Organic Basis of Motivation

Neurophysiologic studies show that motivation is also an integral part of the organic basis for the attention process. Hernández-Peón stresses this when he writes:

> Attention can only be focused upon significant stimuli be they either physic or psychic, and therefore attention is intimately associated with motivation and learning. It should not be surprising to find functional interactions between the neural mechanisms underlying each of these processes (1969, p. 156).

Concentration

Concentration is the highest form of active attention. The ability to concentrate is, of course, essential for daily living, for learning, and for any kind of work, especially when it is original and creative. Children develop this ability gradually with increasing emotional and intellectual maturity and widening interests. The more complicated the task, the more complex the intellectual activity it requires, the older the child will have to be before he can concentrate on it.

It is not possible to determine an exact developmental timetable that indicates at what age and for how long a child should be able to concentrate on a certain task. Too many factors in the child's life, most of them entirely beyond his control, further the development of concentration or inhibit it. For example, concentration requires a certain degree of emotional stability. A child whose emotions are in turmoil, who is overexcited and constantly over-stimulated in any way cannot possibly learn to concentrate on anything. Emotional stability in the home therefore furthers an early development of a child's power of concentration. Emotional turmoil, chaos, and constant tensions, on the other hand, may make it impossible for the child to concentrate on anything.

The level of a child's intelligence also plays a role. The more intelligent a child, the wider the range of his interests is likely to be, so that he will want to concentrate earlier and longer on a greater variety of activities than other children.

The physical illnesses a child has are also important. A child with a fever or in constant pain cannot concentrate. Many physical diseases in close succession impair any child's power of concentration. However, children who are bedridden for any length of time or are otherwise immobilized (for instance by a cast) sometimes learn of necessity to concentrate earlier and more intensely than other children their age. Books and reading may become very important for them.

Implications for Teaching

The number of practical and intellectual activities on which children of the same age can concentrate and the length of time they can do it therefore varies. It is one of the most important tasks of teachers to see to it that all children in the same class reach the level of concentration they need to study and to remember the curriculum of their grade. The emotional climate set by the teacher plays a fundamental role here, among other factors.

Only where the emotional basis of attention (both at conscious and unconscious levels) has been involved, steadied, and calmed, can concentration take place. This is the reason healthy as well as disturbed children can sit still and concentrate on their work with *one* teacher or *one* psychologist, psychiatrist, or parent, and not with another. Some adults have a natural and/or carefully cultivated ability to calm children's emotions and to create the atmosphere in which concentration can take place. The most confused and anxious child feels safe, protected, at ease, and at peace in the presence of such an adult. Feelings of insecurity, inferiority, doubt, anxiety, envy, resentment, hatred—that is, all negative feelings, and especially anger—shatter such a peaceful emotional climate and destroy the concentration process. Competition is apt to arouse such negative feelings and should therefore be avoided, especially for children with organic disorders.

Concentration Disorder

Concentration difficulties or "weaknesses" ("Konzentrationsschwäche" in the German literature) are very common. This highest form of active, voluntary attention is the most vulnerable element of the entire attention process. What parents, teachers, guidance counselors, and others sometimes call a short attention span or distractibility may, on close examination, actually be a concentration disorder.

Concentration difficulties are usually entirely within normal limits. Everyone's power of concentration is at times impaired. All sorts of tensions, anxieties, conflicts, excitements, sad or happy events, worries, and so forth make concentration normally difficult or impossible. It continues to be a struggle throughout life to concentrate on matters that seem uninteresting, unnecessary, too difficult, and/or generally unpleasant. Children as well as adults know from their own experience how painful it is not to be able to concentrate, and can sympathize with anyone who suffers from a genuine concentration disorder.

The difference between the usual concentration difficulties and a pathologic concentration disorder is quantitative and not qualitative, except when a child has a global concentration disorder and cannot reach this level of active attention at all. This is fortunately very rare. A child's concentration difficulties should be considered pathologic only when they are severe, involve a wide range of practical and intellectual activities, and/or interfere with learning.

RELATION TO READING. A concentration disorder may involve only *one* activity. As a rule, this activity is something the child finds difficult and/or dislikes. That is why the concentration disorder of children with organic reading and writing disorders often involves only reading and writing. A widespread concentration disorder, on the other hand, can make it impossible for a child to learn to read and write, even though his cerebral reading apparatus is intact. I have examined children who could not read just because they could not concentrate long enough to learn it.

A concentration disorder may therefore be the cause of a reading disorder, but it may also be its consequence. Children who have trouble reading on an organic or on a psychogenic basis almost invariably develop concentration difficulties. Reading is so cumbersome for them and takes so much time that they fatigue sooner than proficient readers. This decreases the time they can concentrate. Their comprehension is also affected because they usually have to concentrate so hard on the techniques of reading that they cannot pay much attention to the content.

Such children become susceptible to any pleasurable or potentially pleasurable outer or inner stimulus and gladly let their mind wander away from reading. They start to daydream and to find an endless number of activities to do and to think about that are more exciting than reading. Strauss and Lethinen give a typical example of this behavior. They write that

> teachers often remark that a child knows many words but cannot read them in continuity as a sentence or story, that he is interrupted after a few words by a strong urge to talk about his own affairs, to look at the picture, to leaf through the book, or to attend to other activity in the classroom (1947, p. 180).

Such a concentration disorder often does not remain confined to reading, but spreads to other activities, especially those involving intellectual attention. The fact that a child who cannot learn to read often has no confidence in his ability to think also plays a causative role. A reading and writing disorder may in this way cause a more general concentration disorder, especially in beginning readers in the lower grades.

DIAGNOSIS. Concentration is not a diffuse, but a selective and specific process. Therefore, in order to determine whether a child's difficulties are normal or pathologic, each task on which he cannot concentrate should be carefully recorded together with the setting in which this failure occurred, and the length of time concentration lasted. It is also helpful to make a list of all activities the child can concentrate on and for how long. This makes it possible to survey the child's entire concentration faculty and to plan corrective measures for teaching, management at home, and psychotherapy. Children's concentration disorders persist much longer than they need to because such detailed evaluation is usually not made.

The examination of a child's concentration disorder should also list all those other components of the attention process that are most difficult for him to do.

For example, a 9-year-old boy with a severe organic reading, writing, and arithmetic disorder following a birth injury could not concentrate on intellectual work and also found it most difficult to sit still long enough for practical activities. When taken to a concert of classical music, however, which he had never heard before, he sat quietly through the entire performance in fascinated concentration. Music touches emotions and requires auditory attention. This boy's immediate voluntary sensory attention and concentration was therefore intact so far as music was concerned. His immediate and derived intellectual attention and concentration were impaired. A corrective educational and management plan can be built on the basis of such diagnostic analysis.

Sometimes a concentration disorder involves only parts of an activity or just a particular setting. A child may, for instance, be incapable of concentrating on reading in school, but concentrate adequately on it at home in his own room. Another child may have trouble concentrating on reading in any setting, but be capable of listening to a story read to him for hours with such intensity that he can retell it word for word.

I have observed children with organic reading and writing disorders who could not concentrate for more than a few minutes on reading or writing except when it came to rhyming. This fascinated them so that they made up the rhyming word and wrote it down with great care and intense concentration. Educational therapists assess their students' concentration preferences and base their corrective techniques on them in an imaginative way. (See Educational Treatment, Vol. I, p. 229.)

Impact of Somatic Factors

Toxic, metabolic, endocrine, nutritional, and other somatic (in contrast to organic brain) disorders may damage a healthy brain indirectly by breaking through the hematoencephalic (blood–brain) barrier. A concentration disorder may be caused in this indirect way. (See this barrier, Vol. I, p. 55; and Physical Diseases and Memory Disorders, Vol. I, p. 72.)

FOOD ADDITIVES.   Food additives present an entirely new set of nutritional factors beyond the control of any individual or family. They may cause an entirely new form of malnutrition that has to be considered when a child with a concentration disorder is examined. Their role in relation to memory disorders and hyperactivity is circumscribed in these sections.

It has been estimated that some 3,000 different substances are added to prepared foods, and that the food industry uses more than a billion pounds of these chemicals a year. This amounts to 5 pounds per person. These staggering numbers apply only to substances added to food directly during processing. They do not include hormones and other substances (e.g., antibiotics) fed to animals, which enter the food chain and become additives in this indirect way (Rappaport and Calia, 1974).

Exact figures are not known because they are apparently impossible to obtain. They are not publicized by the food industry, and there is as yet no law requiring labels on all packaged foods stating exactly what additives they contain ("Food Facts and Fancies," 1973, pp. 59–61; O'Connor, 1973). These chemicals are added to food to color, flavor, preserve, thicken, emulsify, acidify, and sweeten it, among other things ("Food Additives: Health Question Awaiting an Answer," 1973).

Ingestion of additives has increased steadily with increased consumption of processed packaged foodstuffs such as snacks, sodas, "convenience" foods, items on the menus of franchised food services, and the like. Fresh produce from farms and dairies, which used to be the main items in the diets especially of children, has largely been replaced by these prepackaged foods. The decisive change came in 1970, when Americans for the first time in history spent more for manufactured and prepared foods than for fresh produce ("Food Additives: Health Question Awaiting an Answer," 1973, p. 73).

Millions of children are therefore growing up on a diet unbalanced in favor of additive-saturated processed foodstuffs, sometimes from the day they are born. Too many parents do not know that such a diet can harm their child; others cannot or do not want to take the time it takes to prepare fresh food. It is therefore not unusual to see a 6- or 7-year-old child come to school in the morning with a bottle of coke or soda in one hand and potato chips in the other. That is his or her breakfast, and he eats it while walking to school, in the school bus, or in his parents' car while being driven to an expensive private school. I have observed this many times, and any teacher can give innumerable examples of such malnourishing breakfasts. Food-additive malnutrition is not limited to children of any one socioeconomic group.

The children's parents are not entirely to blame for this form of malnutrition. Children want these foods because massive television advertising has made them seem more attractive and exciting to eat than other foods. Mothers often have a difficult struggle to overcome their children's mass-media–conditioned appetites. They themselves are, of course, also influenced by these commercials, which tend to allay their doubts and fears (Sheraton, 1979).

Effect on Central Nervous System. That food additives may affect the child's central nervous system and cause organic symptoms such as a concentration disorder, as well as a variety of somatic symptoms, has been shown by physicians in their clinical work and by medical and biochemical researchers. Monosodium glutamate (MSG), for instance, a favorite food additive, may cause the so-called Chinese Restaurant syndrome, which is essentially neurologic. It consists of burning sensations in the neck and forearms, chest tightness, and headaches. MSG is added because it intensifies the taste of protein-containing foods. It does this supposedly because of its ability to excite nerve cells, that is those nerve endings that are responsible for the sense of taste. However, a substance that excites only one small group of sensory nerve endings without affecting other nerve cells as well, is not known. The effect of MSG cannot possibly be limited only to the nerve endings on tongue and palate, and animal research has shown that it also reaches other parts of the central nervous system. Studies of its effects on infant animals revealed that MSG can cause brain damage, dwarfing, obesity, learning deficits, retinal defects, and necrosis of neurons ("Food Additives: Health Question Awaiting an Answer," 1973, p. 78).

Monosodium Glutamate Damage. That a diet containing MSG can harm the brains of human babies was shown by Dr. Marguerite Stemmermann, an internist at the Owen Clinic Institute for Nervous and Mental Disorders in Huntington, West Virginia. She examined and treated a 1-year-old girl with multiple daily convulsions of the petit mal type. This girl had begun sharing the family's food at the dinner table when she was 6 months old. Convulsions resembling shuddering fits appeared shortly after that and increased in frequency. At 1 year of age she was having more than 100 such fits a day. Repeated EEGs revealed no cortical brain disorder. When MSG was eliminated from her diet her fits stopped within 3 days. She had been given heavy anticonvulsant medication, which was gradually withdrawn after the fits stopped. Then, after 1 year without symptoms, she was experimentally given half a frankfurter. In 3 hours, a shuddering fit occurred. A week later, a bit of spaghetti sauce brought on a similar reaction ("Food Additives: Health Question Awaiting an Answer," 1973, p. 73).

Clinical and experimental evidence showing the damaging potential of MSG, especially on the growing brains of infants and children, became so strong and irrefutable that baby food manufacturers finally decided to remove it voluntarily from their products. It had not been added for the infant's benefit anyhow, since it is valueless in this respect. It was used to please the mother's palate so that she would feed the product to her child and continue buying it. The Food and Drug Administration has not yet officially forbidden its use.

No one knows how many children's brains were and still are damaged by MSG and other food additives, how many convulsive seizures, attention disorders, hyperactive behaviors, reading disorders, and other organic symptoms were caused by them. The necessary clinical and biochemical studies have simply not been done. One reason for this lack of data is that pediatricians, neurologists, psychiatrists, and other physicians are not yet sufficiently aware of the enormous number and variety of food additives, of their chemical composition, or of their harmful potential. They may therefore make no attempt to find out what their patient's daily additive intake is and what his history is in this respect. As a consequence, not enough patients are put on an elimination diet. This is the only way to determine whether or not the symptoms are caused by the substances removed from the diet.

Another reason additives may be falsely considered harmless is that these organic symptoms are sometimes so mild that they are not noticed by parents and teachers, and no physician is consulted. The incorrect assumption can then be made that the brain of this particular child was not damaged. Clinical studies such as the case reported by Dr. Stemmermann that correlate food additives with clinical symptoms are therefore of inestimable value ("Food Additives: Health Question Awaiting an Answer," 1973, pp. 73–80).

The pediatrician and allergist Ben F. Feingold and his co-workers at the Kaiser Permanente Medical Center have made such studies. He presented their findings first at the Annual Convention of the American Medical Association in 1973, and then in his book, *Why Your Child Is Hyperactive* (1975). He based his conclusions on a study of over 100 children and adolescents suffering from hyperactivity, an attention disorder, and reading, writing, and arithmetic disorders. His study dealt primarily with hyperactivity; concentration difficulties were involved only in conjunction with this other, major symptom. Both these symptoms disappeared simultaneously when these children were put on an additive-free diet ("Food Additives Are Linked to Child Behavior Problems," 1973; "Food Facts and Fancies," 1973, pp. 59–61; O'Connor, 1973; González, 1980) (see also Hyperactivity, p. 627).

From the public health point of view, all potentially harmful substances should be removed from children's diets regardless of the number of children they may damage, unless these chemicals are of vital importance—for example, for preventing infection of the food. The vast majority of additives do not meet these requirements. Many of them are entirely unnecessary additions anyhow. As Dr. Jacobson, a former research associate at the Salk Institute points out,

> When a food has to have nitrite added for flavor, along with other taste enhancers and coloring, and requires BHA (butylated hydroxyanisole) and BHT (butylated hydroxytoluene) to keep it from becoming rancid, it is just not fit to eat. Steering away from these substances has a positive nutritional advantage in addition to avoiding possible harmful effects ("Food Additives: Health Question Awaiting an Answer," 1973, p. 80).

The evidence is so convincing that food additives can cause a concentration disorder in children and other organic symptoms, that a detailed diet diary covering at least 2 full weeks should be routinely requested when a child with these symptoms is examined. An elimination diet should be prescribed when the diagnosis of food-additive malnutrition has been made, or even when it is only suspected. (See Hyperactivity, pp. 627–630.)

HUNGER

"We don't go to sleep hungry, we just *be* hungry."
—10-year-old boy

So far as chronic hunger as a cause for a concentration disorder is concerned, a chronically hungry child is always the victim of parental and/or social neglect. His parents or guardians are either too poor to buy enough food; or they are physically or mentally sick and incapable of taking proper care of him; or they are cruel, "battering" parents who starve him deliberately.

BATTERED CHILDREN. Most of the so-called battered children I have examined were malnourished because they were also neglected and not fed properly, or because they were starved deliberately as punishment for nonexistent or minor transgressions, or with the intent of starving to death. This finding is not sufficiently stressed in the literature on these children. Children whose parents are drug addicts as a rule also suffer from chronic starvation and are malnourished.

Free school lunches are an absolute necessity for all these children. They are the only decent meal many of them get all day, providing that the composition of the lunch is really nourishing. This is unfortunately less and less the case. In a newsletter put out by a community school board in October 1974, for instance, a 9-year-old girl is shown eating what is clearly a prepackaged lunch. The caption of the picture states that the school also serves "frozen TV dinners," which are notorious for their saturation with unhealthy food additives. Schools usually employ dietitians, who ought to know better or, when they do, ought to be listened to more carefully. The children's parents usually do not know and cannot be expected to know what additives school meals contain, and that these chemicals can harm their child.

School lunches, however, do not still the hunger of those children who come to school hungry because they have not had breakfast and have not eaten anything substantial since lunch the day before. This makes it extremely difficult for them to concentrate on their work. Some schools and parent associations are therefore offering free breakfast. This practice should be mandatory for all who need it, so that no child has to endure hunger with all its physical and emotional consequences—headaches, stomachaches, fatigue, dizziness, irritability, inability to concentrate, and so on—while sitting in the classroom.

It is important that adults in charge of children can recognize when they are malnourished. Teachers whose schools are in the poorer districts can usually tell when a child is inattentive due to malnutrition because his appearance is typical. The pediatrician Barness describes it in "Malnutrition in Children Beyond Infancy." He writes that such a child's "muscular development is inadequate, and the poor tone of the flabby muscles results in a posture of fatigue, with rounded shoulders, flat chest, and protuberant abdomen. Such children often look tired; the face is pale, the complexion "muddy," and the eyes lack luster." He also stresses that these children cannot concentrate and "do poorly in schoolwork" (1979, p. 215).

FATIGUE. Fatigue is another one of the somatic conditions that cause concentration difficulties in adults as well as children. Malnutrition is only one of its many causes. Anything that interferes with sleep causes fatigue. Occasional sleep difficulties are an unavoidable part of every child's life. Fatigue should therefore not be considered abnormal unless it is a chronic condition and interferes with the child's learning, and with his general physical, emotional, and intellectual development.

A chronically fatigued child should first of all have a physical examination, because a number of physical diseases (anemia, tuberculosis, etc.) lead to fatigue. When he is found to be physically healthy, a search for the psychologic cause or causes of his lack of sleep should be made. Anxiety and/or depression are the most frequent psychologic causes for a child's insomnia. They may be transitory reactions to stressful situations (e.g., impending tests, failure in school, fear of punishment, pending divorce of parents, sickness of a parent, and very many others) or symptoms of a neurosis. There are, however, also powerful social causes for fatigue that do not stem only from the unique life and family situation of the individual child but affect great masses of children.

Television Fatigue. One can observe children in almost every classroom who are chronically fatigued and cannot concentrate because their parents lose the nightly battle around the television set and let their child watch the shows he wants to see until all hours of the night. A large number of these children cannot fall asleep afterwards even though they are dead-tired, because the violent and shocking actions they have seen have overexcited and over-stimulated them and/or made them so fearful that they are afraid to shut the light off and go to sleep. Nightmares and long, frightening dreams provoked by the shows they watched are likely to interrupt what little sleep they get. The effects of this excessive and late television viewing due to parental mismanagement may remain with the child throughout the next day. Not only is it very difficult for such a child to concentrate on his schoolwork because of fatigue, but he is likely to be still so preoccupied with the shows he saw that he cannot concentrate on anything else. Every teacher from elementary through high school can cite many examples of this.

A substantial number of children, poor and affluent alike, manage to watch television through most of the night without their parents' knowledge. They make-believe they are sleeping or wait until their parents are asleep, then watch on their own set or on the family's set in the living room.

Tired-Child Syndrome. Excessive television viewing can get so out of hand that it may result in what the pediatricians Narkewicz and Graven called a "tired-child syndrome." They studied a group of children between the ages of 5 and 9 who were brought to them by their worried parents because of "nervousness," chronic fatigue, abdominal pains, and sleep and appetite disturbances. When they found that not one of these children had any positive physical findings, they probed further and discovered that all of them were such excessive television viewers that they could be called television addicts. They also observed that these children's viewing time increased with their increasing fatigue and sleeplessness so that they were caught in a vicious cycle. The anxiety produced by the television shows interfered with their sleep so that they were much too tired the next morning to do their schoolwork, to play, or to eat properly. They could not cope with anything except television and watched it for an ever-increasing number of hours. This interfered more with their sleep, and so on. All these children recovered completely when this cycle was broken by not letting them watch any television for at least 1 entire week. The symptoms invariably returned when television watching was again permitted without any restraint (1965, p. 20).

Fatigue Due to Noises. Another important social factor causing fatigue in far too many children because they cannot get enough sleep is noise pollution in their own home or in their neighborhood. No one can sleep soundly when television sets, recordplayers, and radios are blaring, when people are fighting, when sirens pierce the air, and so on.

Hunger, fatigue, and noise pollution cause a reactive concentration disorder that affects children who are basically organically and emotionally healthy. This is the most frequent type of concentration disorder, and it is caused by all sorts of stressful life situations. It is a constant symptom of reactive disorders, including reactive depressions.

NEUROTIC CONCENTRATION DISORDERS.   Most neuroses also cause a concentration disorder, which then interferes with the child's learning. Reading, writing, and arithmetic disorders on a psychogenic basis are primarily due to such a neurotic or to a reactive concentration disorder. An inability to learn a specific subject is only rarely a neurotic symptom. Children can suffer from a school phobia, but a reading, writing or arithmetic phobia is extremely rare. (See chapter on Psychogenic Reading Disorders, Vol. I, p. 248–249.)

SCHIZOPHRENIC CONCENTRATION DISORDERS.   Schizophrenia and manic-depressive psychosis both undermine the attention process. The very core of the schizophrenic process, namely the withdrawal from contact with others, the retreat into a bizarre fantasy life, the coming apart of the ego structure, makes it extremely difficult for the child (or the adult) to concentrate actively and voluntarily for any length of time.

MANIC AND DEPRESSIVE CONCENTRATION DISORDERS.   An inability to concentrate is one of the most distressing symptoms of any depression, whether reactive, neurotic, or psychotic. A manic patient cannot, of course, concentrate on anything. He is much too excited, elated, hyperactive, and distractible.

An inability to concentrate is often the very first symptom patients with any one of these diseases, including organic cerebral defects or diseases, complain about, and the first impairment noticed by their parents, teachers, and others who live with them. The patient's description of this symptom is unspecific and does not reveal the underlying cause. The differential diagnosis rests on symptoms that are specific for these diseases, and on tests.

RELATION TO MEMORY DISORDERS.　There is a very close relationship between these two disorders. A concentration disorder invariably affects memory. The formation of a stable engram requires concentrated attention. Damage to concentration therefore causes a memory defect.

Among the many causes of both disorders are anoxia and a number of chemical substances such as alcohol, LSD, heroin, cocaine, barbiturates, marijuana, bromides, and most other drugs prone to be abused or to cause addiction. (See Memory Disorders, p. 66.)

CHEMICAL CAUSES

Bromides.　Bromide intoxication may come about quite innocently. The patient may not know that the tablet, powder, or elixir he became used to taking for minor discomforts such as a feeling of fullness after meals or minor aches and pains, contains bromide, or that this drug is dangerous. Chronic bromide intake causes a severe psychosis that ends in death unless it is diagnosed and speedily treated.

That bromides have become an abused drug was shown by McDanal, Owens and Boldman, among others. They reported their findings in the *American Journal of Psychiatry,* warning that some drugs containing bromides, for example Alva Tranquil, Lanabrom Elixir, and Miles Nervine, can be bought without prescription and that only one of the popular bromides, namely Neurosine, must be prescribed. They stressed what has also been pointed out by other physicians for a long time, namely that there is no longer any responsible medical use for bromides, and that they should be removed from the market (1974, pp. 913–915; Brenner, 1978).

LSD.　LSD and other hallucinogenic drugs also cause a toxic but usually nonlethal psychosis. The entire attention process disintegrates while the user is in this psychotic state. A concentration disorder and other symptoms, for example recurrent hallucinations, frequently persist long after the psychosis has subsided and the drug has been excreted.

I have examined adolescents and young adults who complained months and in some cases years after their last LSD "trip" that they had trouble concentrating. Some of them had also taken other drugs and smoked marijuana habitually. They could not steady their attention long enough to concentrate adequately. They made strenuous efforts to stabilize especially their intellectual attention, but could not prevent it from vacillating. The highest level of the attention process—namely their voluntary, derived intellectual concentration—was invariably most severely affected, while the lower, more primitive elements, especially their immediate voluntary sensory attention, had remained intact.

The innumerable studies of drug users do not stress this symptom sufficiently, if they mention it at all. These patients are unfortunately not examined carefully and thoroughly enough clinically, especially during follow-up reexaminations. A concentration disorder therefore frequently remains unnoticed, especially when the patient himself does not complain about it. Drug users are often not aware of the impairment of their ability to concentrate. They are under the illusion that drugs have freed their mind so that it can wander without restraint and interruption from one thought and feeling to another and do not realize that they cannot concentrate adequately any more. Yet, a concentration disorder of varying severity sometimes is a permanent consequence of their drug experiences. (See Memory Disorders, Vol. I, p. 70–74.)

A concentration disorder is one of the compelling reasons why so many drug users fail in school and college and eventually drop out. The destruction of the emotional basis for the attention process by LSD, marijuana, barbiturates, heroin, cocaine, and the like, also plays a major role in this. Apathy, lack of interest and initiative, and total preoccupation with one's own feelings are outstanding consequences of drug use.

It must be stressed that marijuana alone, smoked habitually for months or longer, causes all these symptoms, without any other drug intake. The psychiatrist Kornhaber stresses this point. In a discussion of a paper by Kolansky and Moore on "Clinical Effects of Marijuana on the Young" (1972), he summarizes the symptoms caused by marijuana alone and their effect on school performance. He states that:

> the major symptoms—regression to early modes of conceptualization (from logical mathematical modes to magical and omnipotent thinking), decrease in concentration span and frustration tolerance, poor impulse control, psychomotor retardation, disorientation in time, judgment breakdown, signs of depressive illness (sleep disturbance) —are first apparent in the school environment (1972, p. 80; Kolansky & Moore, 1975).

Drug-using students with these symptoms invariably state that they don't care about anything anymore. As a 19-year-old boy told me: "LSD is a great change in value judgment. Things that used to be important are no more important. *Nothing* is important anymore." He had dropped out of college; was confused, vague, depressed; could not concentrate; and had recurrent hallucinations. He was also a habitual marijuana smoker and had tried other drugs. This multiple drug use is typical for the vast majority of these youngsters. The combined effect of these drugs is not just additive but cumulative.

They worsen each other's effects and cause more severe chemical injuries to the brain.

There were a number of writers or would-be writers among my patients. Their style was usually the "stream-of-consciousness" type without any structure or consistent storyline. I found that often there was primarily a clinical and not an artistic reason for this. The brain of these writers had been so damaged by the various drugs they had taken or were still taking that they could not concentrate long enough to develop a storyline and to stick to it. They were under the illusion that they had freely chosen this style because it seemed the most "free," advanced, and progressive. In reality their choice was dictated by the symptoms of their damaged brain. Anyone who has read diaries and other writings of many drug users has noticed how similar they are.

What characterizes them is their vagueness; their free association of confused, vague, and abstract ideas; their absence of a logical sequence and logical reasoning; and often a pretentious use of erudite-sounding abstract words, usually poorly understood by the author. The 19-year-old boy I mentioned before who found that nothing was important anymore wrote such a diary. When describing LSD "trips" he wrote, in part:

> After the trip an individual may well be absolutely unable to function due to new juxtapositions of verbalizations that have changed his verbalized concept of the world in such a way as to make his verbalized view of the world diverge further from the abstraction. Of course, the reverse may be true also, in that an individual's verbalized concept of the world may approach the abstraction more closely.

He also talked in this confused, vague, and abstract way during my psychiatric examination. He was trying hard to understand what had happened to him but could not organize his thoughts sufficiently to describe simply and concretely how he felt. He recovered from the effects of drugs within 1 year with psychotherapy and complete abstinence from all of them, including marijuana. Seven months after my first examination he wrote me a well-organized letter in clear style in which he stated: "I have no desire to mess with drugs anymore. I no longer smoke either cigarettes or marijuana." As is essential in the psychotherapy of all drug users, I had tried to instill in him the will to stop taking them.

HEAD INJURIES. A concentration disorder on an organic basis can also be caused by a head injury. This is usually only a transitory impairment, but it can persist for years where the trauma was severe. This is unfortunately what happened to Morris, whose plight I discuss in the section on Specialized Mental Hygiene Clinics, Vol. I, p. 291. I examined him when he was 11 years old and re-examined him at the ages of 13 and 15. His concentration disorder did not improve. He had the following history and clinical findings. (See Memory, Vol. I, p. 72.)

MORRIS, 9 YEARS OLD: A NUMBER OF LASTING ORGANIC SYMPTOMS AFTER AHEAD INJURY, INCLUDING CONCENTRATION DISORDER.   At the age of 9, Morris tripped on a carpet and fell over a banister. He landed on his head and arm one floor below on marble and passed out. He was rushed to the hospital where he remained unconscious for several hours. When he regained consciousness he was drowsy and confused and could not speak properly. He spoke jibberish that no one could understand. This type of aphasia lasted for 2 weeks. His speech remained slow for awhile, but returned to normal.

He had episodes of great agitation and violence before he could speak again. He also wet his bed and his gait was ataxic (i.e., unsteady) because he could not coordinate his movements. He also had a left hemiparesis (a spastic paralysis of his left arm) and seizures involving only this arm.

His head was tilted to the right and he had a facial weakness on the left side of his face. The x-rays of his skull were negative and there were no signs of increased intracranial pressure, but his EEG showed an abnormal pattern on the right side of his brain.

Morris was discharged from the hospital after 1 month when all his gross neurologic symptoms had subsided. He was referred for outpatient care to the Pediatric Division of the Department of Physical Rehabilitation, where he received perceptual training because tests had shown mild to moderate perceptual impairments. His hospital diagnosis was: "Cerebral Contusion"; the prognosis was considered "guarded."

Morris was referred for psychiatric examination at the age of 11 because his behavior in school had deteriorated after the accident. He was restless and inattentive, did not listen to the teacher, disturbed the class by his embarrassed laughing when he was called on and could not answer, and fought with the other children. His marks in all subjects had gotten worse. Before the accident he had been interested in reading and ahead of his class. Since then it took him much longer to do the same work and he was not really interested in learning anymore. He was now 1 year behind his classmates in reading, and his arithmetic was also far behind. His performance was too slow to pass any tests in school. His current memory had become quite poor. He had a tutor who reported that he forgot what she taught him from one lesson to the next, even though he tried hard to concentrate.

The psychiatric and the psychologic examinations at the ages of 11, 13, and 15 and the speech and educational evaluations showed the following symptoms:

Physical Symptoms.   His physical balance was impaired. He had trouble roller-skating. He had been well coordinated before the accident.

Perceptual Defects. His spatial orientation and his visual-motor coordination were poor. On some Frostig tests for perception he functioned on the 7-year level. For several months after the accident he could not control his pencil well. This had improved with practice.

Psychologic Symptoms on an Organic Basis. 1. An attention disorder primarily involving his ability to concentrate, which was severely impaired. It affected all intellectual activities including reading and arithmetic. He was quite distractible.

2. A slowing down of reactions and activities involving mostly learning, that is, intellectual work. It took him much longer to do any schoolwork in class and at home.

3. *Memory Defect.* He had trouble recalling events of the immediate past. His retention was especially impaired for current details. His ability to retain learned intellectual material was most severely affected.

4. *Free-Floating Anxiety.* This caused his great restlessness and his readiness to strike out at other children. He was always afraid they would laugh at him and call him "stupid," which they often did. Medication decreased this somewhat but not enough for him to function adequately. His parents' and his younger brother's attitude towards him made him more anxious. He was extremely attached to his mother who did not really understand him. She spanked him, called him "stupid face" and sometimes told him she suspected that he had jumped over the banister on purpose just to irritate her. His father, who was a hard-working engineer, could not accept the fact that he had a handicapped son and punished him severely for his bad report cards. Casework treatment of the mother modified her attitude but could not change the father's.

Specific Organic Symptoms. 1. *Reading Disorder.* Morris's reading disorder was only partly due to his difficulty with concentrating. The technical aspects of reading had been affected by his head injury. He was ahead of his grade before, but was 1 year behind in his overall reading ability after the accident. He had trouble blending. His comprehension was also below grade and his oral reading rhythm was impaired. He read very rapidly with no pause and no punctuation. (See section on Rhythm Disorders, p. 447.)

2. *Arithmetic Disorder.* Morris perseverated frequently, and could no longer do mental arithmetic. He had to write the examples down in order to solve them. He understood more complicated problems only when he was alone with a tutor, not in the classroom with other children around him. His anxiety, distractibility, and slowness interfered with his performance in the classroom. He did poorest on tests because they took him too long.

Psychologic Tests. When Morris was 9, 11, and 12 years old, tests showed evidence of brain damage. They also revealed severe psychopathology, especially depression. There was free-floating anxiety, body preoccupation, and a tendency to retreat into his own fantasy world. His verbal intelligence quotient on the WISC was 99, performance 85; full-scale I.Q. was 91. The psychologists felt that his intellectual endowment was average.

Rorschach. One response on a Rorschach card was especially revealing and showed that he had not gotten over the emotional shock of the accident a year and a half after it happened. He described what he saw in the following way:

> There is blood here, a boy who had an accident. It's a hole in the head, the head was cracked, it is bleeding. You know there is no blood in the brain. Only when the skull is fractured is there blood. It is falling, it is falling.

He said this reminded him of a recurrent nightmare he had had since the accident. He always dreamt that he was falling off some high place. He had apparently overheard the doctors say that he had no bleeding in his brain after the accident and concluded from this that there was no blood in the brain. He was clearly still preoccupied with and worried and confused about the effects of the accident on his head.

Mosaic Test. The Mosaic tests I gave him also showed organic patterns (cortical as well as subcortical) and severe anxiety.

Psychiatric Examination. My psychiatric examination showed a severe depression with occasional suicidal thoughts in addition to the organic symptoms. Morris spoke freely and was in good contact. His depression was not only a reaction to the trauma and its consequences, but was also due to conflicting family relationships of long standing. He was jealous of his younger brother whom his father preferred. This preference had gotten much worse since the head injury because his father refused to accept the fact that Morris had organic handicaps that were beyond his control. He continued to blame and to punish him, and Morris had found no sure way to please him. He had always been very close to his mother, but now she tended to blame him for the accident. Both parents disagreed on how to manage him and frequently did not talk to each other for days.

Diagnosis. My diagnosis was that Morris suffered from a neurotic depressive reaction to his accident in addition to its organic sequellae.

Treatment Plan. I recommended tranquilizing medication, individual psychotherapy, casework treatment of his parents, and individual educational treatment.

Follow-Up. The two follow-up examinations when he was 13 and 15 years old showed only minimal improvements, even though an attempt had been made to carry out the treatment plan. His depression had subsided but his neurotic fantasies, fears, and confusions remained. He did so poorly in school and his behavior remained so disruptive that he was sent to a special private school for brain-injured children. His organic symptoms, including the concentration disorder, persisted and could not be expected to improve substantially anymore, 4 years after the accident.

Relation of Organic to Neurotic and Familial Factors

Whether a child with Morris' organic symptoms can improve depends not only on the severity of these symptoms. Emotional problems outside the organic sphere are important and sometimes decisive factors in facilitating or inhibiting the child's recovery.

Morris' family situation made it extremely difficult for him to overcome his handicaps. Added to this was evidence of neurotic symptoms even before the head injury. The constructive efforts of the staff of the clinic could only show limited results without the parent's, especially the father's, cooperation, which was never completely obtained. The father did not want the boy to attend the clinic because to him and to other people who might hear of this, it meant that his son was "crazy."

The mother felt uncomfortable attending her sessions with the social worker. Many appointments were therefore not kept and it was very difficult to maintain the prolonged contact with the family that the boy needed. This does not mean, however, that mental hygiene clinics should not make the most strenuous efforts to help such a child even without parental cooperation. I have witnessed many good results that were achieved—not without the parent's consent, because it is not only illegal but also bad clinical practice to work without it—but in spite of their uncooperative attitude.

OTHER CAUSES OF ORGANIC CONCENTRATION DISORDERS. Head injuries and chemical damage to the brain are, of course, not the only possible causes of organic concentration disorders in children. Tumors, vascular accidents, or infections can also cause this symptom. I want to mention particularly syphilitic infections of the brain, including juvenile paresis. Syphilis has again assumed epidemic proportions after having been almost completely wiped out. Many patients are not treated sufficiently, and it is therefore entirely possible that juvenile paresis will again affect children between the ages of 10 and 15.

An organic impulse disorder may underlie an inability to concentrate. Such children have the need to move constantly, are distractible, and cannot sit still. This organic form of hyperactivity does not let the child slow down long enough to concentrate. The psychogenic type of hyperactivity is also invariably associated with a concentration disorder. (See Hyperactivity, p. 645.)

Incidence of Concentration Disorders Among Children with Reading Disorders

Klasen in her excellent study of reading disorders found that a concentration disorder was the second most frequent psychopathologic symptom among the 500 children she studied. The most frequent symptom was anxiety. Her statistics are more extensive and thorough than most others. She found a concentration disorder in 39% of these children. There was also a statistically significant difference between elementary-school–age children and older youngsters. A concentration disorder was more frequent among the younger children. The older ones had apparently overcome their concentration disorder or learned to concentrate in spite of their reading disorder. Other studies, all involving fewer than 70 children, found concentration disorders in from 28.8% to 50% of their patients (1970, pp. 132, 133). These percentages would be even higher if all components of the attention process had been examined and included.

One of the most frequent complaints about the children with reading disorders referred to me for examination was that they were inattentive in school. I found that those with an organic reading disorder invariably had trouble with one or more components of the attention process. The majority of children whose reading disorder had a psychogenic basis also had attention disorders.

Distractibility

Defined with the composition of the entire attention process in mind, distractibility is immediate, involuntary, sensory attention. Children or adults with this symptom cannot delay their response to outer or inner sense impressions. They find it most difficult to pay voluntary, derived, and intellectual attention. It is hard for them to wait and to plan and to keep a distant goal in mind.

Immediate, sensory, involuntary attention is a primitive way of attending characteristic for infants and very young children. Occasional episodes of distractibility in older children may therefore indicate no more than a transitory regression to an earlier stage of development that is usually entirely within normal limits.

It takes some children longer than others to overcome their infantile distractibility. Some remain easily distractible throughout their lives. As William James remarks about the "reflex and passive character" of children's attention, "It never is overcome in some people, whose work, to the end of life, gets done in the interstices of their mind-wandering" ([1890] 1950, Vol. 1, p. 417).

Stella Chess points out that some children are more distractible from birth on than others. She describes the behavior of distractible children in *Your Child Is a Person,* where she records the following observations:

> The distractible infant, crying when hungry or hurt, could be diverted with a rattle or by being picked up or talked to. The nondistractible one continued to bellow until he tasted milk. No amount of juggling, cooing, or stroking would alter his direction of behavior (Chess, Thomas, & Birch, 1965, p. 31).

She followed these babies up for 10 years and found that their basic behavior patterns, which she calls "temperaments," did not change. She states that

> The toddler who put on one shoe, then saw a block that needed replacing on his barn; put on another shoe, then looked out the window; went to his mother to get his shoes tied, but saw the cat and stopped to pat him on the way ... got his lessons learned, too, but in brief, frequent sessions (Chess et al., 1965, p. 156).

Pathologic distractibility is either organic or psychogenic. The psychogenic form differs from the norm only in extent and severity. Organic distractibility has specific features that are not just an exaggeration of immature behavior.

A child or adult whose distractibility has an organic basis is stimulus-bound and cannot help but respond to unselected stimuli in his immediate surroundings or within his own body. Any visual, auditory, tactile, or any other kind of stimulus evokes an immediate response. These children find it difficult to focus their sensory or their intellectual attention on anything, learning or play, for any length of time because even the most trivial occurrence around them attracts their attention. They cannot stabilize and direct their attention voluntarily sufficiently to bring it in line with the goal they want to or are supposed to reach.

Their distractibility is not due to suspiciousness or anxiety. They are stimulus-bound whether or not they are anxious, angry, sad, or happy. Of course anxiety, tensions, excitement—any emotional turmoil—worsen this symptom, too, just like all others. The distractibility, however, usually only lessens, and does not disappear completely when the anxious or overexcited mood subsides.

The ability to pay voluntary, derived, intellectual attention is impaired in the organic as well as the psychogenic form of distractibility. The selectivity is also impaired in both forms, but for different reasons. The psychologically distractible child selects what he attends to and what he screens out on the basis of conscious or unconscious (neurotic) preferences. Children who suffer from the organic form cannot distinguish important from unimportant stimuli. They cannot decide which stimulus to select to pay attention to, and which to screen out. From the point of view of brain function, this is an inability to inhibit inappropriate responses.

The clinical and experimental psychologist A. R. Luria developed choice-response tests that showed this. He found that children with organic cerebral defects either failed to respond to any signals, or they over-responded to appropriate as well as inappropriate signals. Normal children of a younger age sometimes also had difficulty inhibiting inappropriate responses. Normal children of the same age as the patients, however, coped easily with the test tasks. (Quoted in McGhie 1969, p. 142). Neurophysiologists seem to agree with Luria. Hernández-Peón, for instance, states that: "Elimination of irrelevant responses is undoubtedly accomplished by active inhibition" (1969, p. 167).

This organic inability to select appropriate stimuli creates a psychologic dilemma for the child. It puts him in a state of emotional and intellectual confusion and leads him to doubt his senses. These children are usually aware of their inability to decide what to notice and what to ignore. This undermines their feelings of self-confidence and self-worth in a special way. They tend to generalize their difficulty in making decisions about the trivial details of their daily lives and to feel that their judgment about more important matters is also unreliable. Some distractible children are easygoing and not especially unhappy. Others are conflicted, unhappy, and torn by doubts.

Distractibility on an organic basis is especially severe and difficult to overcome when it is combined with an impairment of automatic mechanisms. This is unfortunately a rather frequent combination. The distractibility itself interferes with the formation of these mechanisms. A distraction interrupts what the child is doing, and thus prevents the repetitions needed for automatization. Pavlov observed in his experiments that the dogs lost their conditioned response temporarily after having responded to a distracting stimulus with what he called their investigatory reflex (Woodworth, 1938, p. 707). Distractions are so frequent in these children that they are bound to interrupt conditioned reflex formation, and to make the conditioning less stable once it has been acquired. This alone makes it harder for them to learn reading and writing, which require so many conditioned responses. (See section on Conditioned Reflexes, Vol. I, p. 471.)

Automatic focusing and releasing of attention is inherent in all automatic mechanisms. The automatic mechanism of habituation makes it possible to ignore the stimuli we have gotten used to and do not need for the task at hand. Habituation is a mechanism that is basic for mental and physical health; its malfunctioning is a major handicap. Hernández-Peón emphasizes this from the neurophysiologic point of view. He states that habituation is a "fundamental and pervasive process in the animal kingdom necessary for adaptive behavior and independent of nervous complexity." He also stresses that it is an acquired, not an inborn process. Only the *capacity* for developing habituation is inborn. "Habituation consists in learning not to respond to a stimulus which by meaningless repetition loses significance for the organism" (1969, p. 167).

Children with organic distractibility have great difficulty learning this. They must be helped to acquire habituation; otherwise they remain distractible. (See Impairment of Automatic Mechanisms, p. 469.)

Relation to Hyperactivity

Some distractible children are restless and move about constantly in pursuit of various stimuli. Their distractibility makes them hyperactive. This hyperactive behavior, however, is not due to an impulse disorder or to overwhelming anxiety. It is an unrestrained response to unselected stimuli. Far too many of these children are simply diagnosed as hyperactive and the cause of their hyperactivity is not investigated. This differential diagnosis cannot be made just by observing the child in the classroom and elsewhere. It requires careful psychiatric and psychologic examinations.

Hyperactivity is such an overwhelmingly disturbing symptom that the accompanying or underlying distractibility is easily overlooked. Children who are hyperactive because of organic drivenness or neurotic anxiety have, of course, also an attention disorder, but they are not necessarily stimulus-bound. It is harmful for the child to diagnose only the hyperactivity and to miss the distractibility. Each of these two symptoms requires a different educational and therapeutic approach. Drugs may calm the child and make him less hyperactive, but they do not necessarily touch the distractibility.

Relation to Reading

Not all distractible children are restless and hyperactive. The distractibility is less obvious and more difficult to detect in many of them. Many children with organic reading, writing, and arithmetic disorders are most distractible when confronted with these tasks. They sit quietly at their desks and seem to be completely absorbed in their work. However, the work they produce is quite deficient. They never finish an assignment and their answers are never complete.

They start to answer a question, stop and give it up, start with another one, give up again, and so on. Their writing looks sloppy and lacks continuity. There are the usual erasures, words crossed out, and perseverations. (See case of Doug in section on Perseveration, p. 490.) (Figure 11.1) Teachers are apt to think that such a child is careless, unconcerned, defiant, and a daydreamer unless they take enough time to observe his work habits minutely and sympathetically. Such close observation will show that the child is constantly diverted from doing his work by numerous tiny details that other children do not notice at all. Flaws in the texture of the paper, page numbers, marks or specs on his pencil or fingers, dust on the desk, slightly uncomfortable clothes, the pictures in his book, and so on, attract his attention to such lengths that he has no time to concentrate on his work. Such a child's attention never rests. As Strauss and Lethinen point out, such a child is at the mercy of "any features of the material which are, for the normal person, additional or irrelevant" (1947, p. 129).

A global, all-pervading distractibility is fortunately rare. Most children's distractibility varies in different situations. What Kurt Goldstein observes in brain-injured adults is also seen in children. He writes:

> The patient's attention is usually weak in special examinations, particularly so at the beginning, when he has not as yet become aware of the approach to the whole situation, something he can get only through concrete activity. When he has done so, has entered the situation concretely, his attention is usually satisfactory, and he may even appear abnormally attentive, because under such circumstances he might often be totally untouched by other stimuli from the environment to which normal persons would unfailingly react. In other situations he will seem to be very distracted, as, for instance in those which demand a change of approach. He seems distracted because he is incapable of making a choice. Consequently, it is not correct to speak of a change in attention in such patients in terms of plus or minus. The state of the patient's attention is but part of his total behavior and is to be understood only in connection with it (1959, p. 789).

Parents, teachers, and all other adults caring for the child should therefore record in what situations and during which activities he is distractible, and under what circumstances his distractibility lessens or stops. Such a child should never be judged by group tests in school, and should be given a lot of time during individual testing.

Psychologic Tests

Psychologists examine such children several times on different days and make certain that each child can respond to the tests under, for him, the best circumstances. Psychologic tests should determine the upper limits a child can reach, not only his failures. This applies not only to tests but also to psychiatric examinations and educational evaluations. Too many school-guidance records and psychiatric charts show only what the child cannot do, not what he is good at and loves to do. Yet, knowledge of the upper limits such a child can reach in anything, the tasks he performs well, and those he thinks he does well and likes to do, is essential for educational and therapeutic planning.

Treatment Techniques

For instance, a child who is least distractible while copying should be encouraged to copy letters, words, and sentences— of course only on lined paper. (See Teaching of Writing, Vol. I, p. 184.) The length of time he copies should be gradually increased, and with it, his attention span. Increasing the length of time such a child can pay sustained attention to anything strengthens his attention span also for other tasks. Of course the quality of his writing should be improved at the same time, and he should be taught to say the sounds of the letters, words, and sentences while he is copying them. By building on what he can do best, he will eventually learn to read and write and overcome his distractibility. Any other best performance of such a child can be built upon with similar techniques.

Distractibility is not incompatible with a shifting difficulty. Any event, for instance someone entering the classroom, which also distracts healthy children, is a much more serious interruption for these children. Once their attention is diverted, they cannot easily return to what they were doing. They tend to stick to each distraction longer than others do.

Treatment of organic distractibility can succeed only if it is based on a diagnosis of all the detailed features of this symptom. The therapeutic principles are the same as for other psychologic symptoms with an organic basis. Everyone caring for the child should be very patient with him and give him plenty of time to prepare for each activity and to carry it out. All activities should be planned for him and together with him in advance, step by step. Surprises and interruptions should be avoided. To help the child fight his distractibility, any potentially distracting stimulus should be removed from his classroom and his room at home. This pertains to visual as well as auditory stimuli. The room where the child does his homework and the classroom should be quiet. Radio, recordplayer, television should be turned off while he is studying or involved in other activities, for instance playing games, building with blocks, and so forth.

One of the basic principles of corrective education and of psychotherapy is explaining the mechanism of his symptoms to the child and encouraging him to invent his own methods of getting around them, of overcoming them entirely if possible, or of living with them when they cannot be changed. Children are not given enough credit for their ability to understand what is wrong with them and to come up with their own solutions. They should be given a chance to think things through on their own. Such an approach stimulates their derived intellectual attention, strengthens their self-confidence, and tends to calm their often chaotic emotions.

In his book, *Helping the Brain-Injured Child,* published by the Association for Brain Injured Children, the teacher, Ernest Siegel, gives excellent practical advice for the management of distractibility and other organic symptoms. He states:

It is necessary to have the child's *full* attention and to give him our *full* attention. Many people can do several things at the same time, but the brain-injured child, being so distractible, is often unable to divide his attention. To understand what is being said, he must focus his attention completely on the speaker. If he is watching television, we turn the set off before talking to him. If he is drawing, he must put the pencil down before he is ready to listen to us. If he is playing ball, he must stop before he can pay attention to us. We must look directly at the child and speak slowly and briefly (1962, p. 72).

This is indeed sound advice! Siegel gives many other concrete suggestions for the training and education of these children.

His description of how to help distractible children acquire healthy eating habits is especially pertinent. He writes:

Vases, flowers, patterned table cloths, and such embellishments have no place at his table—at least during the training period. Even some of the essentials must be eliminated: he should not receive the four pieces of silverware at once; he should not be served more than one course at a time. Servings should be kept small, and not too many different foods placed in the plate. Salt, pepper, water and various condiments placed at the table would distract him (1962, p. 54).

This is a good example of how simplified the training and education of these children need be and what careful attention to details it requires.

Like many other educators, Siegel unfortunately recommends word/picture teaching of reading before phonics are introduced. However, this helps only the comparatively small group of children whose auditory-discrimination defect is so severe and/or whose ability to combine the sight of letters with their sounds is so impaired, that they cannot learn to blend. He also recommends that writing be taught only after the child has made substantial progress in sight reading. This late teaching of writing, however, is appropriate only for children with severe defects in visual-motor coordination and intersensory integration. The writing road to reading is the best for these children, too, just as it is for healthy children. (See Movement Blindness, Vol. I, p. 167.)

THERAPEUTIC EFFECT OF MOTOR ACTIVITIES.   Children are less distractible during all kinds of motor activities, for example during physical exercises, while using tools, building with blocks, playing with toys, and the like. Motor activity also counteracts organic distractibility. Writing is a motor act: it forces the child's attention on what his fingers and his arm produce on paper. It keeps the senses of vision and of touch busy and therefore less subject to distractions. Use of the sense of hearing should be added by letting the child say the word or the letter sound while he is writing it. This adds another motor activity, namely speech. These children should not be permitted to copy, trace, or write silently in the beginning.

Writing as a Treatment Technique.   Writing is an excellent remedial technique. Not only does it help the child ward off distracting impulses and stimuli; it also makes it easier for him to learn the left-to-right direction and conditions his eye movements to staying on a straight line. Siegel points out that most children with organic defects do better when script is taught from the beginning. Script is superior to print because it forces a left-to-right direction, presents each word as one kinesthetic-motor unit from the start, makes spacing easier, and prevents reversals. Lower case "b" and "d," for instance, cannot possibly be confused in script (1962, p. 103). (See Teaching of Writing, Vol. I, p. 184.)

Reading aloud also counteracts distractibility, partly because it, too, is a motor activity. It makes it easier for the child to concentrate, since the mind has a tendency to wander during silent reading. Normally, as soon as we notice that our minds are far removed from what we are reading, we restore attention by reading aloud, by whispering, or by articulating the word we are reading. This also helps distractible children. They should not read silently until they have overcome their distractibility during oral reading, and they should be encouraged to whisper or to articulate while reading by themselves.

It is sometimes impossible for an organically distractible child to learn to read silently without moving his lips or whispering. This, of course, slows down his reading forever, as it does the reading speed of innumerable other children and adults who also fail to learn it. This is not necessarily a disadvantage, however. Accuracy may be more important than speed later on in life: oral reading, whispering, or just articulating guarantee it. Silent reading is not as accurate. Mistakes are easily overlooked when printers' proof, for example, is read only silently. (See Oral and Silent Reading, Vol. I, pp. 182, 112.)

Motor acts such as writing and reading out loud also have other advantages for distractible children. They help them remember what they are reading or writing, because they strengthen sensory impressions generally. William James describes his own experience in this respect in the following way:

> I can keep my wandering mind a great deal more closely upon a conversation or a lecture if I actively re-echo to myself the words than if I simply hear them; and I find a number of my students who report benefit from voluntarily adopting a similar course ([1890] 1950, Vol. 1, p. 447).

This motor aid is especially useful for distractible children because they tend to rush from one impression to the next, so that each one is vague and poorly outlined. (See Memory, Vol. I, p. 74; and Perceptual Changes During Attention, p. 514.)

To prevent distractions during reading and writing, some precautionary measures should be taken. The desk should be cleared of all items except for the pencil, the paper, and the book. Pictures invariably distract. A distractible child should therefore read only books without pictures, or pictures should be covered while he reads. Comic books are especially harmful for such children. They should be kept out of their sight as much as possible, and should most certainly not be used for remediation as is at present customary. (See Linear Dyslexia, Vol. I, p. 127; and Mass Media, Vol. I, p. 275.)

Some children are so distracted by all the words on the page that they cannot read one paragraph or even one single line in continuity. They need a cover card to cover the lines of type above and below the line they are reading. A window card is the best device for them (Frostig, 1965, p. 122). (See descriptions of window card, Vol. I, p. 316.)

It is sometimes best not to give such a child a book at all but to type short paragraphs on separate sheets of paper so that only one sheet at a time is in front of him when he reads.

The distractibility of children and adolescents is sometimes so severe that they cannot function in a group situation and need individual instruction until they improve. Others can function in a classroom, provided an adult can sit next to them when they read or write or do other work requiring intense concentration. This helps them to calm down and to focus their attention only on the task at hand. It protects them from having to react to all sorts of tempting stimuli. Another child who feels sure of himself, concentrates well, and feels friendly towards the distractible child can often be as helpful as an adult in this situation.

Distractibility on a Psychologic Basis

This form of distractibility can be just as disturbing as the organic one. It is usually due to anxiety stirred up by realistic or neurotic fears and tends to be transitory. When the anxiety, the depression, or the inner turmoil and overexcitement subsides, the distractibility disappears.

Persistent forms of psychogenic distractibility may result from poor management at home where the child was so infantilized that he could not overcome his immature immediate reaction to sensory stimuli. Such a child follows every pleasurable or potentially pleasurable stimulus; he remains at the mercy of the pleasure principle. (See Intellectual Attention, p. 540.)

Children whose home is chaotic and whose family relationships are constantly shifting also may react with persistent distractibility. Such a child may have difficulty structuring his feelings and his thinking inside or outside his home. These children are often torn by doubts and by feelings of insecurity. They overreact to all sorts of stimuli because they are not sure what is and what is not important.

Whether such a child becomes distractible or reacts in the opposite way, by becoming apathetic and withdrawing into fantasies and daydreams, depends on many factors. The constitutional type of the child may play a role in this because it may express itself in a tendency to resolve tensions and conflicts with increased motor activity. Such a child is more likely to react with distractibility than a quiet, passive youngster who tends to work out his problems by withdrawing into his own fantasies and daydreams. The latter child may become absent-minded and preoccupied, while the other child becomes distractible.

Distractibility on a Schizophrenic Basis

There is a special form of potentially malignant distractibility that is rare, but it can occur as early as age 5. It is due to suspiciousness. A child who is mistrustful and suspicious must respond immediately to whatever he sees, hears, or suspects so that he knows what is going on and can protect himself. Such a child has a heightened sensitivity to unselected stimuli because he suspects that they are in some way directed against him. These children feel that they must be on the alert constantly so that they can ward off attackers. This abnormal suspiciousness may be the first sign of a beginning schizophrenic process. It may be the forerunner of delusions or already indicate delusional thinking. It can, however, also be the reaction of a child whose life is actually constantly in danger, for instance from cruel parents, street gangs, and so on.

The treatment of psychogenic and schizophrenic distractibility must, of course, deal with the underlying pathology. Educational and managerial measures that help organically distractible children are often also helpful for these children.

Relation to Hyperactivity

The close association between hyperactivity and attention disorders has led the neurologist Frederiks to classify hyperactivity in children under attention disorders. In "Disorders of Attention in Neurological Syndromes (sensory extinction symptoms: the hyperkinetic syndrome)," he wrote that the hyperkinetic syndrome probably is a "global attention disorder" caused by "some sort of disorder of the function of the reticular formation" (1969, p. 197).

Whatever its organic basis may be, hyperactivity is a distinct symptom. It differs from distractibility and other symptoms caused by a diseased or malfunctioning attention process, even though the underlying cerebral pathology may be the same, and sections of the reticular formation may be affected in both conditions. Hyperactivity is primarily a motor-drive disorder. It should be classified and diagnosed separately. It belongs to the core group of organically caused psychologic symptoms and will be circumscribed in the following chapter.

Hyperactivity, Also Called Hyperkinesis

"Hyper," translated from Greek, means "over," that is, above the norm. Hyperactivity therefore means overactivity. "Kinesis" means motion; thus, Hyperkinesis means above normal motion. This latter term describes this symptom much more accurately. These children are not abnormally active in the sense of being busy doing something all the time. They are, as a matter of fact, incapable of performing structured activities for any length of time because of their overwhelming motor drive. They are constantly in motion and find it very difficult to slow down and to stop their urge to walk, run, climb, jump, touch, to keep their muscles moving in any way possible.

This symptom has also been called: "motoric," "pathologic," "developmental" or "chronic sustained" overactivity; "psychomotor" or "impulsive" restlessness; "organic drivenness"; "hyperkinetic impulse disorder"; and "abnormer Bewegungsdrang" or "dranghafte Unruhe" (abnormal movement drive, driven restlessness) in German studies. It was classified under "Behavior Disorders of Childhood and Adolescence" and called "Hyperkinetic reaction of childhood (or adolescence)" in the *Diagnostic and Statistical Manual of Mental Disorders* published by the American Psychiatric Association in 1968 (D.S.M.-II). In D.S.M.-III(1980) hyperactivity is classified only under "attention deficit disorder with hyperactivity."

The diagnosis Hyperkinesia has also been used; this is a misnomer. Hyperkinesias are abnormal involuntary muscle movements such as myoclonic jerks or twitchings of individual muscle fasciculi found in diseases of the basal ganglia (Drew, 1968, p. 919; Grinker, 1949, p. 295). They are physical and not psychologic symptoms. Hyperkinesis is a psychologic symptom that involves the motor drive as a whole, not single muscles or muscle groups (Charlton, 1972, p. 2059).

Choreiform Movements

A small group of hyperactive children, however, has mild choreiform movements in some muscles, in addition to the involvement of their motor drive as a whole. These movements are involuntary. The child cannot stop or initiate them at will. They are invisible when the muscles are relaxed, but their presence can be demonstrated with electromyography. They probably occur much more frequently than most studies indicate because they are so easily overlooked.

These movements are fine, irregular, arrhythmic, and jerky. They involve muscles of the tongue, face (including eyes), neck, trunk, arms, and legs. These children do not have a history of rheumatic fever and do not suffer from Chorea Minor, which is a delayed manifestation of rheumatic fever; their choreiform movements must therefore have another causation. We can assume that whatever caused their hyperactivity also underlies their choreiform movements. So far as localization is concerned, these movements indicate that the

585

child's basal ganglia are involved, specifically the putamen or the caudate nucleus (Prechtl, 1962, p. 126).

A Reading Disorder Specific for Hyperactive Children with Choreiform Movements

The neurologists Prechtl and Stemmer studied hyperactive children with such chorealike twitchings. They felt that these children presented a "uniform neurologic syndrome," which they called "The Choreiform Syndrome in Children." They diagnosed these children's choreiform movements not only clinically during their neurologic examination, but also with the help of electromyography and EEGs. They found that almost all of these children's eye muscles were affected. This made reading difficult for them, caused a reading disorder, or seriously aggravated any other reading disorder. In their paper on this syndrome, which was based on the careful study of 50 children, they wrote:

> In 92% of the children the eye muscles were also affected, resulting in disturbances of conjugate movement and difficulty in fixation and reading. In some cases we could correlate errors in word recognition with the occurrence of involuntary eye movements (Prechtl & Stemmer, 1962, p. 122).

This shows again how very important it is to examine the eye movements of children with a reading disorder with the greatest of care. (See sections on Word Reading, Vol. I, p. 82; on Linear Dyslexia, Vol. I, p. 127; and on Hyperactivity and Reading Disorders, p. 602.)

EDDY, 8 YEARS OLD: CHOREIFORM MOVEMENTS.   One of the 29 hyperactive children in my study, 8-year-old Eddy, had choreiform movements, and also grimaced. He had a severe organic reading, writing, and arithmetic disorder. His eye muscles did not seem to be involved. However, electromyograms and electrooculograms were not made; EEGs were not studied with this possibility in mind. The neurologist found that Eddy also had "minimal athetosis." Athetotic muscle movements are also involuntary. They are slow, tonic, and wormlike.

Eddy was born with jaundice. He had severe erythroblastosis fetalis, a hemolytic disease of the newborn due to Rh factor incompatibility. This disease affects the brain especially seriously because it leads to kernicterus—that is, yellow staining of brain cells with bilirubin. Eddy's kernicterus was so severe that he had to have an exchange transfusion—that is, a complete replacement of his blood—to save his life. Kernicterus is known to cause athetosis in children (Carter & Gould, 1968, p. 883; Clark, 1969, p. 1266). It seems likely that Eddy's other organic symptoms—his choreiform movements; his hyperactivity; his speech defect; his reading, writing, and arithmetic disorder—also resulted from his kernicterus. It is interesting in this connection that 8% of the children studied by Prechtl and Stemmer also had had kernicterus. However, not all these children had athetosis. According to Prechtl and Stemmer, athetosis occurs only in severe cases where the pallidum is damaged in addition to the putamen and/or caudate nucleus. Because of the specific muscle symptoms of these children, Prechtl and Stemmer classified the "Choreiform Syndrome in Children" under cerebral palsy. (See Cerebral Palsy, p. 427.)

Diagnosis

More confusion surrounds the symptom hyperactivity than any other in the core group of organically caused psychologic symptoms. Actually, it is much easier to diagnose than some of the others because it is so noticeable. Its uniqueness is frequently obscured by linking it with a variety of other, mostly minor, symptoms and subsuming it under the ill-defined diagnostic category of MBD. The relationship between hyperactivity and MBD is usually not clarified either; In fact, both are sometimes used interchangeably. For instance, a pamphlet for parents with the title, "Helping Your Hyperkinetic Child," states that they are "parents of an MBD child" (1971). (See discussion of Minimal Brain Damage, under Unspecific and General Symptoms Associated with Organic Reading, Writing, and Arithmetic Disorders, p. 454.)

The diagnoses "Hyperkinetic Syndrome" or "Hyperactive Child Snydrome" have actually replaced Minimal Brain Damage or Dysfunction in numerous studies, even though this is not stated specifically. The symptoms that make up this syndrome differ in different studies. "Overactivity," "impulsivity," "excitability," and, so far as attention is concerned, "distractibility," "poor concentration," or "short attention span" are the symptoms most frequently mentioned.

An example for the unclinical and unscientific approach that has crept into this entire field are the symptom lists widely used as a basis for diagnosing this "syndrome" and for evaluating treatment, primarily drug therapy. These lists were compiled for easy feeding into a computer to facilitate statistical evaluations, not with a well-defined clinical syndrome in mind. They are very broad and do not contain pathologic symptoms alone. The most widely used list has 28 so-called symptoms; some have as many as 55! The presence of a certain number of these "symptoms" (six or more on one list) is supposed to clinch the diagnosis of Hyperkinetic or Hyperactive Child Syndrome.

The items on these lists include normal variations of children's behavior such as "easily upset," "hard to get to bed," "fears," "teases," "always into things," "wakes early," "talks too much," "restless in MD's waiting room," and so on. What child is not at times "defiant," "heedless of danger," "impatient," "disobedient," all categorized as symptoms on these lists! Behavior is also listed that has nothing whatever to do with hyperactivity: for example, "lies often," "takes money, etc.," "wets bed," and so forth. A hyperactive child may also wet his bed, lie, or steal, but not because he is hyperactive. This type of behavior is not characteristic for hyperactivity.

These lists are especially harmful and misleading when they are used as questionnaires to be scored by teachers or parents or used as a basis for structured interviews. Information obtained in this way can only be superficial and quite unreliable. This method is the opposite of a clinical examination, which guides mother and child carefully towards spontaneous expression of thoughts and feelings, in addition to observing the child's behavior in different situations. (See chapter on Examination, Vol. I, p. 20.) Diagnoses, treatment plans, drug evaluations, and all sorts of theories are far too often based on scores obtained by this method alone, instead of on thorough and repeated psychiatric and psychologic examinations of children (Cantwell, 1972; Stewart, Pitts, Craig, & Dieruf, 1966; Stewart, Thach, & Freidin, 1970).

These symptom lists usually do not mention reading, writing, or arithmetic disorders, even though their association with hyperactivity is much more frequent and significant than that of many other items on these lists. So vague and confused is the writing on this topic that the false impression is sometimes conveyed that all children with learning disorders (fashionably abbreviated "LD") are hyperactive, or that a child cannot have a serious reading disorder unless he is also hyperactive. No wonder parents and teachers are not only understandably distressed but also confused. This misunderstanding may especially hurt the quiet, obedient, well-behaved children with a reading, writing, or arithmetic disorder; their parents and teachers may assume that they cannot possibly have difficulties with reading, so that their reading disorder is overlooked. This is the same group of children whose learning and other troubles tend to remain unnoticed anyhow because they do not irritate the adults around them.

The diagnosis of hyperactivity is actually not difficult to determine, especially its organic form. No symptom list is needed. It is a severe and major symptom, not a mild and minor one. It should not be stretched to include all sorts of other behavior difficulties. Only those children are hyperactive or hyperkinetic who, for whatever reason, cannot control their motor drive, *even when they want to.* Children who run around the classroom, into the halls, and up and down the stairs deliberately to annoy their teacher, or just for the fun of it, do not suffer from hyperactivity. They can stop this misbehavior at any time, if and when they want to, in response to firm and decisive management of their teachers and parents.

Hyperactivity can be episodic (i.e., occur only at certain times during the day) or constant, during every waking hour, as it is in severe cases. Its diagnosis requires, first and foremost, familiarity with the behavior of emotionally healthy children with an intense motor drive.

Healthy Children with an Intense Motor Drive

The need for muscular activity is an inborn drive that is present in all children, girls as well as boys. It appears very early in infancy, long before the child has learned to walk, and varies greatly in intensity. The normal variability of this drive and the fact that it is part of the child's constitution is often not taken into consideration when the differential diagnosis between a very active child whose motor drive is still within normal limits, and hyperactivity is made. This accounts, at least in part, for a damaging overuse of the diagnosis of hyperactivity. It is, however, often quite difficult to differentiate between a child with an intense motor drive who is difficult to manage and educate, and genuine hyperactivity.

In *Temperament and Behavior Disorders in Children* (1968) and *Your Child Is a Person* (1965), books written together with Thomas and Birch, Stella Chess describes children with an intense motor drive and the educational problems they present. She calls them children with a "high activity level" (Thomas, Chess, & Birch, 1968, p. 116). She bases her descriptions largely on her observations during a 10-year research study of 231 children whose psychologic development she followed from infancy on. In *Your Child Is a Person,* she writes that

> some babies were from early infancy onward much more active than others. Even in the period toward the end of feeding, when most babies are quiet and sleepy, they moved their arms, lifted their heads, kicked, or—if they were on their backs —moved their whole bodies till the covers were off. This went on right to the moment their eyes shut. Even when asleep they frequently moved spot to spot in the crib. Their mothers could never turn away for a moment if these infants were on the bathinet, for fear they would squirm off. Diapering was a problem because they twisted and turned so much (1965, p. 28).

She also observed that the intense motor drive of these infants often persisted into their school years. She writes: "The highly active toddler who wriggled in his high chair long before his meal was over and always preferred running to walking sometimes became the restless first-grader who was constantly finding excuses to leave his seat" (1965, p. 157). Any pediatrician can confirm these observations. I have seen many such infants in my previous pediatric practice; they most certainly did not suffer from hyperactivity.

This type of child is not headed for a reading, writing, and/or arithmetic disorder either. He is quite capable of paying intellectual attention, provided his motor needs are recognized and managed constructively. Chess points this out, too:

> Teachers size up the children and give the more active ones some extra room in which to breathe. Even when the group is large, the skillful teacher will give the active child more work at the board, more errands to do, more chance to use his

muscles. She will also try to avoid blanket demands on the class as a whole for absolute silence and immobility.

Her conclusions are that:

the highly active child should not be protected from the normal demands of a typical school day. If he is allowed so much leeway that he turns school into an extended play period, he will not learn to accept school work as necessary and desirable. Without gradual, systematic training in the work of learning, his entire educational progress may be jeopardized (1965, pp. 162, 163).

This is quite true, but often difficult to carry out.

One cannot blame a teacher for referring to such a child as "hyperactive" and for requesting that he be put on medicine to calm him down, when that teacher has to cope with an overcrowded classroom with numerous disturbed and undisciplined children. Many teachers are desperately looking for help that is usually not forthcoming, and are confused about the meaning of "hyperactivity." What they have been taught, heard, and read about this condition is apt to be very confusing indeed. So much has been written and discussed in the mass media about "hyperactive" children and the supposedly striking results of drug therapy, that teachers and parents are apt to suspect this symptom as the cause for all sorts of misbehavior. The majority of these children are not hyperactive at all, but healthy children with an intense motor drive; or children who are restless, fidgety, inattentive, preoccupied, disobedient, or aggressive for all sorts of reasons, organic or psychologic, but not because of an uncontrollable motor drive. Hyperactivity has unfortunately become a fashionable diagnosis covering all sorts of children who cannot sit still and do not conform. As a consequence, far too many children are receiving drug therapy. (Egerton, 1978)

Manifestations

As a rule, there is a great contrast between a child suffering from hyperactivity and any other child, including normally highly active children. Such a child is not just restless, fidgety, and impatient. He is not a "fidgety Philipp" ("Zappel-Philipp" in German), one of the bad children immortalized in the classic children's book, *Der Struwwelpeter*, which was published in 1847. This fictitious character has recently been honored in some American and German articles on hyperactivity as the first hyperactive child ever described. However, Dr. Heinrich Hoffman, the physician who wrote and illustrated this book, most certainly did not have a pathologic symptom in mind. He wrote poems about typical troubles of children, or of parents with their children, such as not wanting their hair or fingernails cut, not watching where they were going, playing with fire, not eating properly, being cruel, making fun of dark-skinned children, sucking their thumb, and so on. These were cautionary poems warning children in a humorous way of the dire consequences of bad behavior. The story of Fidgety Philipp warns of the terrible consequences of not sitting still at the dinner table and not obeying one's father. Philipp rocks back and forth on his chair until he falls backwards and pulls the tablecloth down over himself. Plates break, the food spills over, and everyone goes hungry. Some hyperactive children also rock at the dinnertable, but this is not their most disturbing or most characteristic behavior (Cantwell, 1972; Feighner, 1974; Schmidt, 1973).

The symptomatology of hyperactivity in children was quite dramatically described during the 19th century, not in fiction, but by such famous neuropsychiatrists as Maudsley, Wernicke, and Emminghaus, who wrote the first textbook of child psychiatry (*Die psychischen Störungen des Kindes*), published in 1887. These early descriptions dealt only with the severest forms of organic hyperactivity in children with epilepsy and/or mental deficiency. Hyperactive mental defectives were called "agile" or, in German, "erethische" idiots.

In 1870 Maudsley described the behavior of a hyperactive 8-year-old epileptic girl. He wrote that this physically strong and healthy girl moved constantly, like an engine that never stops. She touched everything within her sight. She did not hold anything in her hands for any length of time, but dropped it and looked for something else right away. Her hyperactivity did not improve. Her care required the undivided attention of one adult and all the energy he or she could muster (Kramer & Pollnow, 1932, p. 2). We can nowadays calm down many such severely hyperactive epileptic children with anticonvulsive medication and various tranquilizing drugs, but unfortunately, still not all of them.

The girl described by Maudsley suffered from the most severe form of hyperactivity. The motor drive of these children is completely disinhibited, uncontrolled, and chaotic. Whatever enters the child's vision becomes the target of the drive, independent of his interests or any goal he might like to pursue. Any change in the child's immediate environment determines the direction of the drive.

Not all these children are also stimulus-bound. It is the motor drive searching for a target, not so much the target (i.e., the stimulus) attracting the child. When such a child sits down or lies down he continues to move. He fidgets, wriggles, is restless, and is usually unhappy. This type of restlessness has been called "ill-humored" restlessness ("unlustvolle Unruhe" in German). These children may seem to be running around and moving about happily, but this is deceptive. Many hyperactive children feel that their constant drivenness is unpleasant. This makes them grumpy and irritable and sometimes angry at themselves for not being able to stop their motor drive. Tantrums and other destructive outbursts are at times due to the child's helpless anger and self-hatred. (See Chapter 16, Morbid Irritability, p. 675.)

Some hyperactive children, however, enjoy their motor drive. They run about, jump, dance, climb, and so forth, happily. They are not conflicted about their drive. The hyperactivity of one group of these children resembles the behavior of manic adults. However, manic attacks are exceedingly rare in childhood, if they exist at all. I have never seen a manic child. None of the 29 children in my study had this manic type hyperactivity. It is very unlikely that the cause of such anxiety-free, exuberant hyperactivity is ever a manic-depressive psychosis in a preadolescent child.

Age of Onset

INFANCY AND EARLY CHILDHOOD.   The child's abnormal motor drive sometimes becomes apparent as soon as he can walk. However, the onset may be even earlier, in infancy. This invariably indicates a severe form that may be difficult to control. Three boys in my study were so hyperactive as infants that they had to be tied down in their crib.

SCHOOL AGE.   Hyperactivity invariably becomes a major problem as soon as the child joins a group of children, in a day-care center, in nursery school, in Kindergarten, or in first grade. That is why parents and other adults frequently date the onset of the child's hyperactivity from the beginning of some kind of schooling. This is often incorrect. The parents may not have noticed that their child's motor drive was abnormal, but may have thought that he just needed a lot of physical activity and would eventually calm down. This was the date of onset given by the parents of 14 of the 29 children in my study. The family life of some of them was so chaotic, however, that their parents would have noticed only an extreme case of hyperactivity. All their children were more or less out of control. It was not possible, however, to prove an earlier onset in spite of careful evaluation of the history, including home visits. It therefore seemed likely that the beginning of school was the actual time of onset. (See Reaction to a Chaotic Home, p. 648.)

Age at Time of Disease

When a child's hyperactivity is caused by physical or mental diseases (e.g., encephalitis, epilepsy, schizophrenia, etc.), its onset depends on how old he was when he had this disease. (See appropriate sections.)

The onset of hyperactivity is in any case confined entirely to childhood; it does not begin in adolescence or adulthood. States of agitation, excitement, motor disinhibition that occur later on in life are essentially different.

Role of Anxiety

Hyperactivity can be caused by anxiety, it can itself cause anxiety, and it can exist entirely without anxiety.

HYPERACTIVITY WITHOUT ANXIETY. Many hyperactive children are not only not anxious, but have a pathologic lack of anxiety in situations where they ought to be anxious. These children take terrible risks when racing across streets; when climbing on closets, stoves, windowsills, trees, walls, and roofs; when jumping over obstacles, and so on. They are always in danger of hurting themselves and need constant supervision. This is difficult to do because they are so fast that it is hard to keep up with them. Accidents can therefore not always be prevented.

One of the 29 children in my study, an 8-year-old hyperactive boy, came to his psychiatric examination with his right leg in a cast. He had raced across the street much too fast, and had fallen and broken his ankle. Another boy who was 9 years old when I examined him had a history of having frequently broken windows at home and elsewhere since the age of 2, when his hyperactivity started. This was not done in anger, or deliberately for other reasons. It occurred quite by accident, as a consequence of climbing or jumping on windowsills much too fast and carelessly. He hurt his hands and arms each time.

Such accidents would be even more frequent if hyperactive children did not usually have such excellent motor coordination. As Maudsley observed, these children, as a rule, are robust with strong and well-coordinated musculature. Parents and teachers frequently describe the child, boy or girl, as "very muscular," and the children themselves like to show off the strength and agility of their muscles. They usually learn to ride a bike very early and with great ease.

HYPERACTIVITY WITH ANXIETY

Hyperactivity Causing Anxiety. Hyperactivity generates anxiety in many children. Their inability to stop their motor drive frightens them, and the conflicts aroused by their uncontrolled behavior make them angry, insecure, and anxious. Anxiety worsens this symptom, as it does all others, making it more difficult for the child to calm down and to restrain his movements. This creates a vicious circle that must be broken, otherwise the hyperactivity gets steadily worse.

It is best to deal with the anxiety first through calm, reassuring, and consistent management at home and in school, combined with psychotherapy. Anxiety-reducing medication may also help, but is often not needed. Decreasing the child's drivenness with medication may also break the vicious circle. The conflicts and anxieties caused by long-standing hyperactivity, however, frequently persist after the hyperactivity has subsided, and must still be dealt with. Alleviating anxiety helps all symptoms anyhow, organic or psychogenic. It is therefore a basic requirement for the treatment of all symptoms in this core group, and for helping these children overcome their reading, writing, and arithmetic disorder as well.

Hyperactivity Caused by Anxiety. Antianxiety measures are crucial also for the treatment of those hyperactive children whose hyperactivity is caused by anxiety. A very large group of children are hyperactive mainly on a psychogenic (neurotic or reactive) basis. Their anxiety is usually overwhelming and all-pervading. It is a so-called "free-floating" anxiety—that is, it is not focused on a specific object or special situation. (See chapter on Free-Floating Anxiety, p. 687.)

An especially severe form of this anxiety can occur on an organic basis and is found in schizophrenic children as well. This is a disabling form of anxiety that disorganizes these children's feeling of wholeness and integrity. It undermines their ego structure or does not let it develop, drives them into chaotic moving about and into touching things, and makes them generally restless, fidgety, and unhappy. They often get completely disorganized in a classroom situation where they are together with other children because they are afraid of them, and their anxiety is increased to an unbearable degree. These children's motor movements are usually tense and not as well-coordinated and free-wheeling as those of the other hyperactive children, and they are not as likely to take the same risks running, jumping, or climbing. Many of these children have specific fears (of the dark, of dogs, etc.) in addition to their free-floating anxiety. It is not their motor drive that is disinhibited in these children; their anxiety drives them. Adults, too, walk back and forth when they are anxious. Motor activity is pleasurable in that it expresses anxiety and relieves it at the same time. That is one reason sports and other physical exercises have such a calming effect on these children. (See Curative Physical Exercises, p. 535.)

Whether or not anxiety underlies a child's hyperactivity can usually be detected during the psychiatric examination by what the child himself says and by observing his behavior. Many children complain that they are "nervous." "Nervous" usually means anxious. A 6-year-old boy who told me that he was "nervous," explained that this meant "like a panic." When the child manages to cover up his anxiety, psychologic tests will invariably reveal it. These children make frame designs on the Mosaic test or have their design hug the margin of the tray as much as possible. The Rorschach and other projective tests will also show the level and extent of their anxiety.

It is often not possible to determine whether a hyperactive child's anxiety is the cause of his hyperactivity, a reaction to it, or stems from other factors within himself or in his environment. Moreover, it may not be necessary to make these distinctions. Any reduction in anxiety will invariably decrease a child's hyperactivity except in the severest nonanxious cases, just as any form of excitement, caused by happy or by distressing circumstances, invariably increases it.

It is unfortunate for hyperactive children that so many papers dealing with this subject, whether or not the results of drug therapy are also evaluated, do not mention anxiety. The results of any study of the effect of drugs on hyperactive children must be questioned when the children's anxiety (or lack of it) is not also investigated. This is especially important in relation to sympathomimetic drugs (e.g., the amphetamines, Ritalin, Cylert, etc.).

Anxiety is closely bound to the sympathetic nervous system. Any increase in the tonus of the system— chemically by drugs or psychologically by threatening experiences, and so on—increases anxiety, at least up to a certain level. That is why "Drug Information on Ritalin" warns that "marked anxiety" is one of the contraindications for this drug (1975). Anxious children can become completely disorganized by these drugs. Unfortunately, children with other symptoms sometimes have the same reaction. This happened to a very anxious 6-year-old boy I examined. He had been put on Dexedrine in another clinic and had gone completely wild, according to his mother. He described the feeling he had in the following way: "I felt wild, like an untamed animal, like a lion." This wild behavior lasted for 24 hours. It was impossible to get him to sleep during that time.

Reaction to Physical Restraint

Severely hyperactive children resist any physical restraint on their movements. They cry, scream, bite, and make frantic efforts to get free. They try to wiggle out from under a restraining hand or arm, and slide out of chairs and under desks when forced to sit down. Children whose hyperactivity is primarily based on anxiety, however, often welcome being made to sit down and to remain seated, since it decreases their anxiety.

Attraction to Moving Objects

Hyperactive children are fascinated by moving objects. They like to watch anything that moves: cars, trees moved by the wind, airplanes or birds flying, and so on. This is when they can sit still, at least for a while. There is a certain danger in their preoccupation with moving and flying. Hyperactive children have tried to fly out of windows, or from less dangerous heights, for example radiators. These were not necessarily mentally defective children. Emotionally healthy children also like to watch flying and have been known to experiment with flying to see whether they can fly like Superman. I have examined many children who were not hyperactive and got hurt during such attempts.

Hyperactive children, however, are apt to be more reckless in their attempts to fly, and their preoccupation is much more intense and longer lasting. Fascination with flying and attempts to fly were observed as characteristic features of hyperactivity in children long before comic books and television stimulated children's imagination in this direction. For example one of the 45 hyperactive children, a 7-year-old girl, described by Kramer and Pollnow in their classic paper, "A Hyperkinetic Disease of Childhood" ("Über eine hyperkinetische Erkrankung im Kindesalter"), died falling out of a window. She wanted to fly like a bird. This paper was published in 1932; it was a milestone in the clinical investigation of hyperactivity in children. Some forms of hyperactivity in childhood have since been called the Kramer-Pollnow Syndrome.

Hyperactive children like also to move things about. That is one reason they like to push chairs around, to open and close doors, to turn keys in locks, and to turn light switches off and on, watching it get light and dark with the utmost delight. Healthy children enjoy these activities too, but get over them at a younger age; they don't consider these activities as important either. The behavior of a 7-year-old hyperactive boy was typical in this respect. His mother told me that he was a "light-switch-player," and that he also liked to swing the closet doors in his room back and forth. His parents could tell what he was doing while they were sitting in their living room because they heard the rhythmic squeaks of the door hinges. The rhythmicity of these movements is typical for hyperactive children. When they push, swing, hammer, knock, they do it with a certain repetitive rhythm.

These children also love to open water faucets and to flush toilets to watch the water rushing down. Their favorite toys are cars, trains, any toy that moves. When they build with blocks, they tend to build very high towers, only to topple them over right away to watch the pieces fall.

Hyperactive children unfortunately like to throw things. They do this often in anger, just like other children. Their enjoyment, however, also stems from the fact that throwing releases motor impulses. They throw pillows and blankets out of their bed and all sorts of objects (e.g., soap, milk, eggs, etc.) out of windows. In the classroom they like to climb on chairs, tables, radiators, and windowsills, and to throw self-made paper balls and other objects about.

It is characteristic for hyperactive children to sit still inside anything that moves: cars, trains, merry-go-rounds, pushcarts, toy wagons, and the like. This is not always true of planes because there is very little feeling of movement. Their motor drive seems to be satisfied so long as their body is in movement, actively when they themselves move or passively when they are being driven.

Kramer and Pollnow's patients were also light-switch players, liked to swing doors open and shut rhythmically and to turn faucets off and on, and sat still in toy carts or other moving vehicles.

Speech

Many hyperactive children talk incessantly. Speaking is, of course, a motor activity, and their nonstop talking is another expression of their motor drive. Some of these children make all sorts of noises with their lips, tongue, and vocal cords while moving about. This is especially disturbing for their teacher and for the other children in their class.

Fascination with Keys

This fascination with keys seems to be characteristic for hyperactive children. Kramer and Pollnow were the first to point this out. Keys are, of course, exciting also for other children since they convey great power over adults. One can lock them in or out, even against their will, and hiding or holding them makes adults furious and helpless and gets them into a chase with the child.

Hyperactive children are incredibly adept at stealing keys right out of adults' pockets without being noticed. They enjoy the noise keys make, the way they wiggle on the keyring, and the fact that they can turn them back and forth in keyholes. There is a certain danger in this fascination especially where car keys are concerned. One 5-year-old hyperactive boy I was treating stole his parent's car keys, rushed to the car, and started the engine before they could stop him. He also released the hand brake. What saved his life was that he was too short and too scared to step on the gas when the car started rolling. The car fortunately stopped on its own. He was one of the 29 children in my study.

Fascination with Windows

Windows have a special attraction for hyperactive children. Kramer and Pollnow pointed this out, too. These children climb or jump on windowsills wherever they find them and are in constant danger of falling out. They are so fast that it is usually not possible to stop them before it is too late. These children are not suicidal; they do not want to fall out. They like to look out of closed or open windows to watch the cars and everything else that moves down below. They also like to throw things out and watch them fall, and to rock or in other ways balance themselves.

A 7-year-old hyperactive boy I examined ran up and down the stairs in school and in and out of classrooms searching for an open window. When he found one, he pulled himself up on the windowsill, bent over until half of his body was outside, and then proceeded to rock up and down like a see-saw.

It did not occur to him that he might fall out and die. So dangerous and difficult to control is this attraction that windows have to be locked when these children are around. This is what the mothers of two of the 29 children in my study had to do. Both were severely hyperactive boys. One 5-year-old, Ramon, had a convulsive disorder of unknown origin; the other, 10-year-old Adrian, suffered from hyperactivity following encephalitis.

Once, when Adrian was 11 years old, his parents forgot to lock the window and he fell out. They lived on the 14th floor. Fortunately he was able to hold on to the ledge and the police could rescue him. Locking their windows was a great hardship for both families, especially during the summer. Both were very poor and had no air conditioning.

Five-year-old Ramon's fascination with windows was so strong that he talked about them incessantly while working on his Mosaic test. He was so hyperactive that he could not stop himself from moving the pieces about on the tray. As soon as he achieved a form, he moved the pieces apart again. Any open space between pieces he called "a window." (Detailed case histories of both boys appear on pp. 616 and 621.)

Rocking

Rocking is a rhythmic motor movement that also satisfies a hyperactive child's motor drive. It is sometimes used as a substitute for running around freely when the child is forced by adults or by his own fatigue to sit or to lie down. However, it also has a calming effect because it is an autoerotic activity, and children enjoy the slight dizziness it often causes. Many healthy children rock themselves to sleep, especially during periods of anxiety and conflicts. Children who are deaf or hard of hearing are especially prone to rock for prolonged periods of time. It is thought that the stimulation through rocking of their inner ear, particularly of the vestibular apparatus that controls balance, gives them special pleasure. It is interesting in this connection that two of the four hyperactive children in my study who rocked were hard of hearing in one ear.

Hyperactivity does not necessarily cause rocking. Only 4 of the 29 children in my study rocked, and hyperactivity was not the only cause of their rocking. It is therefore important to investigate all possible causes of a hyperactive child's rocking so that treatment can be successful. Rocking can then sometimes be stopped before the hyperactivity subsides. It might also persist when the child is not hyperactive anymore, unless its causes are dealt with.

Tantrums

Not all hyperactive children have tantrums. The hyperactivity of 8 (all boys aged 5 to 10) of the 29 children in my study was complicated by tantrums. Tantrums are a severe complication indeed, because they make the already difficult management of a hyperactive child even more complicated. Tantrums are dramatized emotions that also provide a release of motor impulses. They express a child's feelings of helpless anxiety or of furious anger and frustration because he feels that nobody listens to him or pays attention to him. Tantrums are an extreme form of communicating usually chaotic emotions. Some children and adolescents, however, throw tantrums quite deliberately to upset the persons around them and to win their power struggle over them.

The complicated mechanisms underlying tantrums render it highly unlikely that they are ever caused by hyperactivity alone. Anxiety plays an important part in all tantrums. Children with the nonanxious form of hyperactivity therefore do not seem to have tantrums. All eight children with tantrums in my study had a high degree of anxiety, and none of the very severely nonanxious hyperactive children ever threw a tantrum.

Tantrums occur in places where the child experiences the kind of frustrations he finds most unbearable. The location of a tantrum therefore gives a clue to its cause. Four of the eight hyperactive children in my study who had tantrums had them only at home; three only in the classroom; one both at home and in school.

The classroom tantrums of the three children were triggered by frustrations related to their severe reading and writing disorder. All three were boys, aged 7, 8, and 10. The 10-year-old read only a few words; the 7-year-old could not even recognize letters and had great difficulty copying and writing to dictation. The 8-year-old could not read or write at all. He was in the third grade and had managed only to memorize one first-grade reader. When given another book to read he just repeated what he had memorized and did not realize that his words and the text did not match. (See Position Reading, Vol. I, p. 112.)

All three boys also had a severe arithmetic disorder including difficulties with writing and reading numbers. All three were painfully aware of their difficulties with learning, felt hopeless and defeated, and were angry at themselves. The 8-year-old had been on Dexedrine and the 7-year-old on Ritalin for almost 1 year before I examined them. These drugs had decreased their hyperactivity only minimally. They had not helped their reading, writing, and arithmetic disorder or diminished their tantrums, and should not have been expected to. Tantrums do not disappear until their cause, in these cases the reading and arithmetic disorder, has been eliminated.

Tantrums frequently respond to an improvement in parental and/or educational management. Psychotherapy is indicated where these measures do not work. Playgroup therapy is often better than individual psychotherapy for these children, provided they are not too hyperactive. Tantrums need an audience. That is why a child may not have any tantrums when he is alone with his therapist, but continue to have them in the classroom or at home in front of a number of people. Group therapy tends to provoke tantrums: thus the therapist has a better chance to understand them and to help the child get over them.

As with rocking, tantrums do not automatically disappear when the child's hyperactivity has subsided. Children whose tantrums occur only in the classroom need correction of their reading and arithmetic disorder. When tantrums also take place in the home or are confined to the home, treatment of the underlying family conflicts is indicated.

Sleep

Hyperactivity does not necessarily cause sleep difficulties. No single sleep disturbance by itself is characteristic for hyperactivity since it can also be found in many other children. The sleep disturbance of each hyperactive child should therefore be carefully examined to determine what role, if any, his hyperactivity has in causing it.

Only those forms of hyperactivity that have certain chemical or endocrine causes are invariably accompanied by severe sleep difficulties. Foremost among them are infants born addicted to morphine, heroin, or methadone. Hyperthyroidism sometimes also causes hyperactivity together with insomnia, and abuse of cocaine, marijuana, or amphetamines by children, adolescents, or adults can have the same consequences.

One group of severely hyperactive children needs a lot of sleep and sleeps well. This was first reported by Kramer and Pollnow. The deep, peaceful, and uninterrupted sleep of these children is quite a contrast to their hyperactivity during the day. Of the 29 hyperactive children in my study, nine (seven boys aged 6 to 10, and two girls, aged 5 and 6) belonged to this group. This had nothing to do with their anxiety level. Three of the nine belonged to the very anxious group; all others were nonanxious. Two of these children, boys aged 6 and 9, were so exhausted when they came home from school that they slept soundly for 2 or 3 hours. They woke up around 5 or 6 P.M., stayed awake for another 2 or 3 hours, and fell asleep as soon as they were in bed. They did not wake up early either, as do many hyperactive children. These children needed so much sleep not only because their relentless hyperactivity tired them out; they also suffered from increased fatiguability. Their schoolwork and other structured activities were difficult and tiring for them. Their fatiguability was just one more of the psychologic symptoms caused by their organic impairments. (See Chapter 15, Fatiguability, p. 671.)

The excessive need for sleep of some hyperactive children may also have other organic causes. We know through pathologic studies that the motor drive area and the sleep area in the midbrain are both affected in some brain diseases, for instance in certain types of encephalitis. Both areas are located in close proximity to each other. During the epidemic of epidemic encephalitis (Economo's disease) in 1918, for instance, many patients, especially children, became hyperactive and had severe sleep disorders as well. Autopsies showed that subcortical sleep and motor drive areas were involved. It can therefore be assumed that other, noninfectious, brain disorders may sometimes also affect both these areas.

The seven other children with healthy sleep patterns went to bed early and fell asleep right away. None of the nine children in this entire group was on drug therapy when I first examined them. Their sound sleep was not due to drugs. Treatment of these children's hyperactivity had to be planned so that their sleep habits would not be adversely affected. Sympathomimetic drugs such as Ritalin, amphetamine, and so forth, have to be given with special caution to these children because they often interfere with sleep, especially when they are given too late in the afternoon. Stimulation of the sympathetic nervous system prevents sleep, which is based on parasympathetic activities. (See Role of the Autonomic Nervous System, p. 522.)

Restless sleeping was frequent among the children I studied. One 7-year-old boy even jumped in his sleep. This is, of course, also found in other children. However, the cause of this sleep pattern in hyperactive children is probably their unrestrained motor drive, which is not quiescent even during sleep.

SLEEPWALKING. Sleepwalking is usually caused by unconscious forces that have nothing to do with hyperactivity. Hyperactivity was, however, the determining factor so far as 9-year-old Rafer, one of the 29 children I studied, was concerned. He walked very fast in his sleep and threw objects about, just as he did during the day. He was a severely hyperactive mentally defective boy who could not read or write and had to be watched constantly. His sleepwalking most likely was but the continuation of his hyperactivity during the day. It was mainly due to his unrestrained motor drive.

Hyperactive children have nightmares and frightening dreams that wake them up just like many other children, caused by reactive or neurotic factors that may or may not have anything to do with their hyperactivity. Of the 29 children I studied, 13 suffered from frightening dreams and/or nightmares that woke them up almost every night.

Only three children in my study, boys aged 5, 7, and 8, found it difficult to fall asleep. The 7-year-old boy was afraid to fall asleep because of fear of ghosts and of dying. These were neurotic fears that had nothing to do with his hyperactivity.

Whatever sleep difficulty a hyperactive child may have, lack of sufficient sleep invariably increases his hyperactivity. A child who wakes up tired and is sleepy in school cannot concentrate on learning and is more hyperactive than he would be after a good night's sleep. As a matter of fact, insufficient sleep alone can make a child hyperactive. It is therefore imperative for the successful treatment of hyperactivity to remove any obstacles interfering with the child's sleep.

SLEEP DEPRIVATION CAUSED BY TELEVISION VIEWING. The most important cause of sleep deprivation of hyperactive children, as it is for far too many other children, is too prolonged, too late, and too unrestrained television viewing. Two 9-year-old severely hyperactive boys in my study watched television every night till 1 A.M. and sometimes all night long, with or without their parents' knowledge. Both were emotionally and physically severely neglected and suffered from free-floating anxiety. They could not read or write at all. One cannot hope to alleviate such children's hyperactivity and to make it possible for them to learn to read unless and until television has been completely eliminated from their lives, or at least severely and consistently restricted to about 1 hour in the afternoon.

The effect of television on hyperactive children is almost entirely destructive anyhow. Television shows, with their fast action and their violent or otherwise emotionally exciting and disturbing content, overstimulate these children who are already much too excitable and emotionally unstable. That many of them can sit still only in front of the television screen does not mean that viewing decreases their hyperactivity. It stops it for awhile, but almost invariably increases it afterwards. Most shows stimulate these children's imagination almost entirely in a destructive direction. Their difficulties with falling asleep and many of the disturbing dreams that wake them up, can often be traced directly to television viewing.

Evening and nighttime television viewing plays such an enormous role in sleep disturbances of hyperactive children that the importance of hyperactivity as a cause of these disturbances cannot be scientifically studied unless television viewing has been considered, or better yet, eliminated as a factor. I have not found one single study where this was done. Symptom lists used for the diagnosis of hyperactivity contain items such as "wakes early" and "difficult to get to bed," but not a word is usually said about television in the accompanying text.

The treatment of hyperactivity requires first and foremost that the child gets a long period of uninterrupted sleep every night. It is therefore often necessary to prescribe a sedative for bedtime and to persuade the parents to eliminate television entirely until the child has improved, or at the very least not to permit viewing after dinner. These measures are sometimes more effective than sympathomimetics or tranquilizers given during the day.

Reading Disorders

Hyperactivity occurs with or without a reading disorder. Many hyperactive children can read and write. Their hyperactivity may have started after they learned to read, or it may have been so episodic that they could learn during the calm intervals when they could pay attention.

Whether a hyperactive child can learn to read and write depends not only on his ability to pay attention. It is primarily determined by the condition of his cerebral reading apparatus. When it is defective, he will invariably have a reading disorder. When it functions well, he will not, provided his hyperactivity stops long enough so that he can pay attention and learn. The level of the child's intelligence is important in this respect. The higher it is, the better his chance to learn to read even during brief attentive periods.

A SPECIFIC READING DISORDER ASSOCIATED WITH HYPERACTIVITY. Some hyperactive children, however, may have reading difficulties even when their cerebral reading apparatus is intact. These difficulties may arise when hyperactivity affects the child's eye muscles and consequently his eye movements. Cohen, Bala, and Morris worked on a research project that tried to answer the question "Do Hyperactive Children Have Manifestations of Hyperactivity in Their Eye Movements?" They reported their preliminary findings in the *Bulletin of the New York Academy of Medicine* of November 1975.

They found that these children were generally unable to hold their eyes steady in either direct, forward, or lateral gaze, appeared to have more saccadic interruptions of pursuit movements than normal children, tended to continue to use head movements at a late age when solving problems, and had more saccadic movements in darkness. Apparently they did not examine these children's eye movements during reading and did not distinguish hyperactive children with choreiform movements from those without. Their preliminary findings alone, however, indicate that these children might have difficulty learning linear reading and the return sweep. This may make them prone to develop Linear Dyslexia. (See Linear Dyslexia, Vol. I, p. 127.)

The eye-movement problems observed by Cohen, et al. might make it difficult for these children to move their eyes steadily from left to right on the line, to fixate them when needed, and to time their quick forward saccadic movements properly. There is as yet no clinical evidence for this, however. Only 1 of the 29 hyperactive children in my study, for instance, had Linear Dyslexia. The reading disorder of many of them was so severe, however, that they had no chance to develop it. They could read only isolated words and had never read full sentences or paragraphs. They had not yet practiced linear reading and the return sweep. (See section on Linear Reading, p. 126.)

So far only Prechtl and Stemmer have demonstrated that some hyperactive children can have reading difficulties specific for hyperactivity, if they also have choreiform muscle movements. They recorded these children's eye movements during reading with a electrooculogram and found that these patients had a disturbance of conjugate eye movements and trouble with fixation. This made reading difficult for them. The choreiform twitchings of their eye muscles seemed to be the cause of these difficulties. It made their eye movements irregular at times.

Prechtl and Stemmer could correlate periods of such irregular eye movements with errors of word recognition in some of these children. These movements were entirely involuntary. The children were not aware of them and could not control them (Prechtl, 1962 (1), p. 191).

Abnormal eye movements of hyperactive children cannot be detected just by observing the child. Special recording devices are needed to find them. The eye movements of all hyperactive children who have a reading disorder should be examined with such instruments. Only when this is done on a large scale will it be possible to determine how widespread eye-movement disorders are among these children and how their reading is affected by them.

Violent Behavior

Hyperactive children are more likely than others to act or react violently, because violent acts involve motor movements. Wertham points this out in *A Sign for Cain.* He discusses the neuropathology of violent acts in the chapter "Why Men Kill," where he writes:

> Violence is always based on physical movements. These tendencies to movement, which we call motor drives, can be greatly increased in rare instances through specific damage to the brain. In the early 1920's, for example, there was an outbreak of epidemic encephalitis. Children were observed who had a tremendous tendency to overactivity and who in some cases committed violent acts. Their destructive aggressiveness was beyond the control of their willpower. They suffered from a specific brain infection. In occasional instances, milder forms of this disease are a factor in otherwise unexplainable outbursts of juvenile violence (1966, p. 24).

This applies to all children with severe hyperactivity on an organic basis. These children tend to be violent and destructive primarily for two reasons, as outlined here.

1. *Unintended Destructiveness.* Violent acts committed by hyperactive children may be just unintended by-products of their unrestrained motor drive. These are accidents and not deliberate acts. These children tend to bump into people and objects while running around wildly. Objects fall and break, there are spills, people get hurt, and the child may injure himself. These children also like to touch, poke, push, pinch, and slap other children while running past them—not necessarily out of hostility, but playfully, as a motor release that seems harmless to them. It often surprises them when the other children get angry and hit back. Their classmates sometimes get used to this behavior, do not take it seriously, and tolerate it good-naturedly. However, they can hardly be expected to put up with it throughout an entire schoolday. The danger of the provocation of serious fights is always present. Whether deliberate or not, this type of motor release creates hostility and undermines the hyperactive child's relationship with other children, with his teachers, and with other adults caring for him.

2. *Immediate Motor Response to Conflicts.* Because of their uninhibited motor drive, hyperactive children are likely to hit out at once when they get angry, and to solve conflicts with immediate and unthinking physical action. Their hitting is often wild and disorganized. They have trouble learning intellectual attention anyhow, and it is especially difficult for them to overcome reacting only according to the most primitive pleasure principle. (See Intellectual Attention, esp. p. 540.)

It must be stressed, however, that, as Wertham states, the committing of a violent act is truly beyond the control of a hyperactive child only in very severe and rare cases. It is the exception rather than the rule. Rarely does a child's hyperactivity alone explain a violent act. In the vast majority of such children, other forces are operative and usually crucial in causing a violent act.

Hyperactive children are subject to the same violence-fostering factors within themselves, in their family, and in society generally as are other children. They do not commit violent acts unless something other than their hyperactivity happens in their life that encourages them to be violent. They may have witnessed violent behavior among their parents, in school, or on the street and imitate it. They may have been encouraged to react violently, to settle verbal insults or misunderstandings by hitting out. They may also not have been discouraged sufficiently from being violent. They are, of course, exposed to an overwhelming stimulation of their imagination with violence and crime through television and other mass media just like other children. They are, however, much more susceptible to these stimuli because of their increased excitability and their tendency to act out right away what they saw on TV, in comic books, or in real life. (See Mass Media, Vol. I, p. 275.)

No violent act is in any case ever committed for just one single reason. Behind it is always a constellation of psychologic (conscious as well as unconscious) and social factors interacting with one another. In children or adults whose brain is malfunctioning, organic factors may also play a role. Purely statistical correlations among a number of hyperactive children and the number of violent acts they committed explain nothing. That is another reason why the presently so popular symptom lists are so misleading. They contain items indicating criminal and violent behavior, such as "lies often," "takes money, etc.," "neighborhood terror," "reckless, daredevil," "sets fires," and so on. Such a list gives equal weight to delinquent acts that differ widely psychopathologically and legally, and conveys the impression that all of them have the same cause, namely the child's hyperactivity. This is mechanical, superficial, and entirely unclinical reasoning. It cannot be taken for granted that because a child is hyperactive, his hyperactivity explains why he stole, lied, or set a fire. (See discussion of symptom lists at the beginning of this section; and also Fire Setting, p. 609.)

Hyperactivity is such a distressing symptom that the error is all too often made of seeing it as the only cause for all the child's troubles. I have examined many hyperactive children who had been on stimulants or tranquilizers for years. This had calmed them down and made them somewhat easier to manage, but their reading disorder persisted and their violent behavior continued. The impairments underlying their reading disorder and the conflicts underlying their violent actions had never been treated.

Murderous Acts Against Siblings

KIRK, 6 YEARS OLD: A HYPERACTIVE BOY WHO COMMITTED VIOLENT ACTS AGAINST HIS BROTHER AND HIMSELF.   An especially sad example for the omissions discussed above is 6-year-old Kirk, who was referred to me privately by a pediatric neurologist. His plight shows how very important it is to investigate the violent behavior of a hyperactive child (and, of course, also of any other child) with the greatest of care so that its various causes become clear. One needs the details of a complete case history referring to all the different dimensions in order to understand, treat, and prevent such a child's violent behavior. Computerized additions of selected symptoms cannot accomplish this. Unfortunately, this method is used almost universally in studies of hyperactive children.

When I examined Kirk, he was 6 years old and had been on Dexedrine or Ritalin continuously for 2 years, since the age of 4. These drugs had been prescribed by his pediatrician. They had decreased his hyperactivity, but he had lost his appetite, and mealtimes had turned into battles. His weight gain and his growth had stopped. His severe temper tantrums persisted; his jealousy of his older brother, now 8, had gotten worse; his violent behavior at home had reached the crisis point. His parents told me that he had made numerous suicide attempts since the age of 4, by trying to jump out of a window. He actually jumped out once, but was not seriously hurt. He had threatened to commit suicide many more times. His most serious recent act of violence made them feel particularly furious at him and helpless at the same time. He had gone to bed, then gotten up secretly, climbed onto a kitchen chair, grabbed two knives, run into his brother's room, and cut him. Then he ran up to his grandmother and held a knife to her neck. His father restrained him, however, and serious injuries were prevented.

Kirk's parents found it very difficult to say anything positive about him. He got along best with his 13-year-old sister and his housekeeper, who had also been his baby nurse. He was in the first grade in school and loved it.

His report cards had always been good, even in Kindergarten. He was not violent or disruptive in school, but restless and somewhat overactive without his medication. However, he had great difficulty with reading and writing.

Kirk was born prematurely, during the 7th month of pregnancy and had to be kept in an incubator for 2 months. His speech was late, at age 2, and at first indistinct. His hyperactivity started early: he had to be tied down even in his crib, and harnessed later on in his high chair. As soon as he could walk, he ran out of the garden into the neighborhood and got into many accidents. He was fascinated with keys and locks. His parents locked windows and closet doors wherever possible, and especially their car. He managed to release the car brake once and the car crashed into a wall.

His parents were more angry at him than worried about him. He had been an unwanted child anyhow. His hyperactivity had made their feelings toward him more ambivalent and negative. He was mainly raised by the housekeeper. His father was quite openly fed up with him. He told me: "I have given up putting soap in his mouth and beating him." The boy himself and his mother told me that the father had thrown him bodily out of the house many times, even in winter, and had threatened to send him away forever. There was great tension between the parents. They did not get along. The mother felt quite helpless and reacted with bouts of alcoholism.

When I examined Kirk, he was in good contact. He spoke freely and truthfully about his troubles, which he summarized by saying: "It's about being bad." He felt quite guilty and unhappy, and was extremely anxious, restless, and somewhat distractible. He tried very hard to please. He talked freely about his desire to die. He told me that he was sure that his mother and father did not like him and that they preferred his brother and sister, which was unfortunately true. He was not hyperactive during my examination.

I found the following organic symptoms: an attention disorder that was at least in part due to psychologic factors; free-floating anxiety, also, in part, due to non-organic troubles; a difficulty with shifting that made it hard, for example, for him to play games with other children; a body image problem, expressed in very poorly formed figure drawings; a reading and writing disorder unquestionably on an organic basis. It was fortunately mild and Kirk did his best to overcome it. His hyperactivity was also organic in origin, but seriously aggravated by profound psychologic difficulties.

This boy's organic impairments, including his hyperactivity, were completely overshadowed by his severe psychologic pathology, which needed attention first and foremost. No drug could possibly be expected to alleviate them.

Kirk was suicidal. He was in a constant rage against himself and against his parents, felt unloved, and consequently, insecure and anxious. Frequently he saw no other way out of the intolerable tensions within himself and in his family than through committing some violent physical act, directed against himself or against members of his family. He was in urgent need of individual psychotherapy. This should have been recommended 2 years previously, when he was 4 years old, together with, or even without, drug therapy. Individual psychotherapy of this boy could not, however, be expected to succeed without the sincere and profound involvement of both parents. It was also imperative to stop all sympathomimetic drugs, and to give him anxiety-reducing drugs if and when needed. (See Treatments, Vol. I, pp. 657, 663.)

Relation to Window Fascination

The symptoms caused by a child's hyperactivity sometimes determine not so much the cause for a violent act, but how it is carried out. This applies especially to children who are fascinated with windows. Kramer and Pollnow were first in observing this. One of the 45 children in their study, a 3-year-old boy, tried to throw his baby sister out of a window. Kirk threatened or attempted suicide only in connection with a window. Another one of the children I studied, 5-year-old Ramon, actually threw his 4-year-old brother out of a window. This brother luckily did not die. He held on to the window bars and was pulled back into the room by his mother. Ramon was one of the two boys in my study who had the severest form of window fascination. His mother usually kept all windows locked. It was not clear whether Ramon really wanted to kill his kid brother, whether he even understood what death meant, or whether he just wanted to watch him fall. Both motives may have been operative even though his mother reported that there was very little overt hostility between the two boys, that they usually played well together. (See complete case history under Convulsive Disorders, p. 621.)

Another one of the 29 children, 4-year-old Stan, was suspected of having killed his 2-year-old brother by pushing him out of a fifth-floor window. The police officers who questioned him were satisfied that this was an accident. However, his mother was not so sure. He had lifted his brother onto the radiator right underneath the windowsill many times before and he did not fall out. Whether or not it was an accident, Stan was so upset by this event that his hyperactivity got much worse. When I examined him 3 years later, when he was 7 years old, he still talked about it a lot, even in school. He still felt so guilty that he had tears in his eyes while talking about it. His reaction was so severe and long-lasting that it became especially difficult to treat his hyperactivity, his organic speech disorder, and his severe organic reading and writing disorder.

One cannot conclude from these case histories that hyperactive children are more prone than others to hate their younger siblings and to try to kill them. It also does not mean that only hyperactive children find windows interesting and use them for murderous acts. There are no statistics to indicate how many children of such tender age have attempted to or have actually killed another child, by throwing them out of windows or otherwise. Reports indicate, however, that their numbers may tragically be on the increase.

For instance, Lester Adelson, a county coroner, reported the murder of five infants less than 1 year old, by six children under the age of 8. Two of them were 2, another two were 5, and one each were 7 and 8 years old (Adelson, 1972).

Violent and other criminal acts committed by hyperactive children are, as a rule, carried out with great speed, suddenly and unpredictably. They are not planned. A child usually has no time to plan while he is hyperactive. Planned violent and other criminal acts such as planned burglaries or thefts are therefore usually not committed by hyperactive children. These children are, as Kramer and Pollnow already pointed out, fast and efficient pocketbook searchers—mainly for keys, but, of course, also for other desirable objects (e.g., money). (See Fascination with Keys, p. 597.)

Fire Setting

All children find fire fascinating and play with matches at some time during their childhood, with or without their parents' knowledge. No one knows how many fires are started accidentally in this way. Fire is especially attractive for hyperactive children because they love to watch anything that moves. The constantly moving and expanding flames also reflect these children's inner turmoil, and their almost constant state of excitement. It is therefore possible that they tend to set fires more frequently than other children. My statistics point in this direction. Twelve of the 29 hyperactive children in my study, all boys, were fire setters. They were not just innocently playing with matches. They usually set their fires alone at home, on the street, or in school—wherever and whenever they thought they could get away with it without being observed.

A few, but by no means all, of these fires were set in anger, to hurt someone in school or at home. For instance, an 8-year-old boy set fire to the papers on his mother's desk. He told me: "I wanted to see her mail burn." This boy was an only child and very jealous of his mother. He resented any outside contact she had, by mail, by phone, or in person. The most serious fire was set by 13-year-old Adrian, who suffered from the nonanxious form of postencephalitic hyperactivity. He was one of the two boys in my study who had the most severe form of window fascination. He set fire to the office of the school psychologist because he was angry at him and at the school in general. It was a large and very dangerous fire in which the building had to be evacuated. This was the last and most serious of a number of disruptive and destructive acts and led to his suspension from the special class and school he was attending. He had to be sent to a day school in a mental hospital.

Twelve children out of 29 is a large group, about 40%. Of the 416 non-hyperactive children with reading and writing disorders in my study, only 41 (10%) set fires. It therefore seems that fire setting is the only violent act committed more frequently by hyperactive children than by others.

DIAGNOSIS AND TESTS.   It is very important to examine each hyperactive child for fire setting since my material shows that so many of them commit this violent act. This requires special care. The child's parents may not know about it; often they just forget to mention it, so they should be asked specifically about it. The child himself will usually not reveal it unless it is one of the reasons for his referral to the psychiatrist or psychologist. Even then he may deny it because he feels guilty and is ashamed. Sometimes dreams show a child's fascination with fire even while they show his fear of it. Psychologic tests sometimes give the only indication that fire plays too prominent a role in the child's fantasies. Fire may be the child's response on Rorschach cards. His T.A.T. (Thematic Apperception Test) stories and/or his drawings may also deal with fire. A predominantly red Mosaic test, or red pieces in prominent positions—for example a red tip on an arrow or red in the center of a design—sometimes point to fire setting. Such Mosaics show inner turmoil, excitability, and explosiveness with a tendency to violent outbursts. They are typical for many hyperactive children. Many children and adolescents I have examined were not known to be fire setters until such a Mosaic aroused suspicion. Such a child should then be asked whether he likes to watch fires. A fire setter will most likely confirm this and eventually admit that he has set fires.

Special Methods of Examination

The key to the diagnosis of hyperactivity is the observation of the child. No other technique is needed. When the child is not hyperactive during the psychiatric, pediatric, psychologic, or educational examination, he should be observed in the setting where the hyperactivity occurs: at home or in school. Some children are hyperactive only in the presence of other children, not when they are alone with one adult.

Far too many children are diagnosed as hyperactive and put on drug treatment on the basis of parents' and teachers' complaints alone, without direct observation by the physician prescribing the drug or other collaborating clinicians. Such observation is time-consuming but indispensable. Hyperactivity has become a popular complaint; it is frequently merely a cry for help by teachers and parents who cannot manage a difficult child. It sometimes also indicates poor management at home and/or poor teaching. The description of the child's actual behavior by parents and teachers may be imprecise and misleading for many reasons. It should not be exclusively relied upon for such a serious diagnosis.

It is easier to arrange the observation of such a child in a group setting in a mental hygiene clinic than in private practice, provided there are playgroups. Observation of a child in such a group is an excellent technique to confirm or to rule out hyperactivity in doubtful cases. Playgroup therapy is also often indicated for the treatment of such a child. (See Treatments, Vol. I, p. 334; and Vol. II, p. 666.)

While the diagnosis of hyperactivity may not be problematical, further examinations often are. The difficulty may start with getting the child into the examining room. Contrary to what I suggest in the examination chapter (Vol. I), one cannot leave it to the child to decide whether he wants to hold on to one's hand. There usually is no time for this. The child may be running around in the waiting room, forcing one to catch him and to grab his hand. (See Examination, Vol. I, p. 18.)

My examination of many hyperactive children in schools has shown that this presents special problems. These children often hide under tables in the classroom or run around wildly. They must be caught and led by hand through halls and up and down stairs to the examining room. One can never let the child run about freely. The danger is that he will run away, create a disturbance by running in and out of classrooms, and eventually run out of the building.

Once the child is in the examining room, the door must be closed. An open door is an invitation to running out. Windows should be closed before he comes in; they should be opened only in such a way that he cannot possibly reach them.

Hyperactive children can sit down and pay attention better when they lean against something steady and solid, for instance the side of a desk. Some can stand still easier when they lean against a wall. It helps to suggest this to the child if he has not discovered it on his own. He should, of course, not be reprimanded for squirming about on his chair and for moving his legs constantly. He cannot be expected to talk freely when he has to use all his energy just to sit still; just sitting is already a great strain for him. One hyperactive child put into words exactly how all these children feel when he said: "When I sit still I get tired. When I move around, I feel good!" Such a child should therefore be permitted to get up and walk around from time to time during the examination.

It helps to give these children moving toys to play with while they talk, since this satisfies at least part of their motor drive. Small cars are ideal for this purpose. The child can play with them on top of the desk or get on the floor and race them and still talk, because this play does not consume too much of his attention. Some children in my study remained seated for a while and began to talk freely while drawing. The arm and hand movements involved in this activity evidently helped them.

Hyperactive children tend to talk much too fast and to answer too quickly. Their answers are therefore often irrelevant. They say anything that comes to their mind just to get this unpleasant situation over with as fast as possible so that they can get out and run around again.

Tests

ELECTROENCEPHALOGRAM. No EEG tracing is specific for hyperactivity.

Even children with the severest organic form of hyperactivity may have a normal EEG. An abnormal EEG, on the other hand, does not necessarily indicate that the child's hyperactivity has an organic basis. The relationship between the EEG and hyperactivity is the same as that with all other psychologic symptoms in this organic core group, and with reading, writing, and arithmetic disorders on an organic basis as well. (See EEG, Vol. I, p. 36.)

MOSAIC TEST.   The Mosaic test is not specific for hyperactivity either. Hyperactive children have a special liking for this test because it is nonverbal and involves moving pieces of different colors around with their hands. It is so attractive for them that one can get them to sit down sometimes by starting the examination with it. Ramon, one of the most severely hyperactive children in my study, sat down only while working on his Mosaic. He was one of the two boys with the severest form of window fascination. At the age of 5, he just moved the pieces about constantly and called the open spaces "windows." (See Fascination with Windows, p. 597.)

Children generally prefer the color red to most other colors; hyperactive children have a special liking for this color. They may use many red pieces or put them in central or other crucial positions in their design. Red expresses their state of constant overexcitement, their inner turmoil, their emotional overstimulation. It also indicates explosiveness and a tendency to violent outbursts, including fire setting.

Sometimes these children's Mosaic goes beyond the margins of the tray. This indicates expansiveness, a feeling of grandiosity, and generally a lack of consideration for boundaries. Seven-year-old Perry made such a Mosaic. The title of it was, "A Boy Pulling His Wagon." The form of this design was excellent. It showed that his intelligence was above average. He put the boy's shoes, indicated by two black diamonds, on top of the lower margin. Red was a conspicuous part of his Mosaic. The boy's arms and legs and the top of the wagon were red. (See Figure 13.1.) Perry was a severely hyperactive boy whose behavior indeed knew no boundaries. He was also a fire setter.

Another boy in my study, 8-year-old Ned, made what he called "A robot going through the hills." He was through with it in 5 minutes, got up, ran around, and refused to explain the details of his Mosaic. He would not point out where the robot was supposed to be; he just indicated that the entire design moved. He started with a large, red triangle that hugged the left margin. This made his mosaic what Wertham calls "margin-bound," indicating anxiety. Almost a third of his Mosaic pieces were red. He put them in important places, at the left margin where his design and its movement started, and jutting out underneath his entire Mosaic. It looked as if his robot was moving on top of them or as if they were his legs. (See Figure 13.2.) Ned's Mosaic was not so well organized as Perry's, indicating a somewhat lower level of intelligence.

FIG. 13.1.   Perry, age 7½. Psychogenic reading disorder, severe hyperactivity with anxiety. *Mosaic test title:* "A boy pulling his wagon." The boy moves fast. This is typical for hyperactivity; so is the overstepping of all limits—the boy's shoes are on top of the margin of the Mosaic tray. *Drawings:* They are expansive and grandiose. This is typical for hyperactivity. The lack of a neck on the man shows a lack of any restraining influence exerted by thinking over acting. (Color plate of Figure 13.1 follows p. 432.)

His hyperactivity was just as severe, however, and he was also a fire setter. (See Ned's case history on p. 648.)

It must be stressed that one cannot make the diagnosis of hyperactivity on the basis of such a Mosaic alone. Children who are not hyperactive may make the same kind of Mosaic. This indicates that they, too, are overexcited and in

FIG. 13.2.   Ned, age 8, psychogenic reading disorder and reactive hyperactivity. *Mosaic test title:* "That's a robot. He is going through the hills." It is typical for Mosaics of hyperactive children that the design moves and that red pieces are in prominent positions. The robot walks on red legs, and his left side consists of three red pieces with a white piece in the middle. (Color plate of Figure 13.2 follows p. 432.)

emotional turmoil and have a tendency to explosive outbursts of violence, including fire setting.

The Mosaic test is very reliable in showing whether the child is suffering from the anxious or the nonanxious type of hyperactivity. Anxiety comes out clearly in the design, rather than being hidden as in other projective tests. In the chapter, "The Mosaic Test," in *Projective Psychology,* Wertham describes how this test reveals anxiety. He writes:

> Anxiety may be expressed by clinging to the margin or by designs that take the form of a picture frame. This may be coupled with an avoidance of the open area of the central space, or there may be a small design in the middle which the frame encloses. It is interesting that the same kind of complete or incomplete frame occurs in the Navajo sand paintings in which the central picture is "tied in," as the Indians express it, "to keep out the evil" (1959, p. 241).

Anxious hyperactive children make "margin-bound" Mosaics.

The Mosaic test also helps establish the cause of the child's hyperactivity, whether it is organic or psychogenic or based on schizophrenia. (See Examination, Vol. I, pp. 25–29; and other sections dealing with the Mosaic test.)

KOCH TREE TEST AND FIGURE DRAWINGS. It is not possible to infer from these children's drawings that they are hyperactive. Their trees and figures may show more movement than those of other children, but this is not conclusive. A number of hyperactive children in my study drew very large, expansive trees and figures that covered the entire page. This reflects their expansiveness and feelings of grandiosity and power. Seven-year-old Perry, for instance, whose Mosaic went beyond the limits of the tray, drew a huge tree and enormous human figures. He called the figures "Mr. and Mrs. Frankenstein" in a facetious way, attempting a joke. Their enormous legs can be interpreted as expressing his hyperactivity, that is his constant running about. The lack of a neck is typical for a lack of intellectual control. The small, thin arms showed how inadequate he felt when it came to (1) manual skills, including writing; and (2) reaching out to other people. (See section on Drawings, Vol. I, p. 214; and see Figure 13.1, p. 613.)

Other projective tests such as the Rorschach and the TAT are also not specific for hyperactivity. The child's behavior during these tests is more diagnostic for this symptom than is the test content.

Organic Causes

A child may be hyperactive for different reasons. His hyperactivity may have organic causes (e.g., encephalitis). When such a child dies, one finds lesions in his brain. He may also be hyperactive on a somatic basis, through some infectious, toxic, or metabolic disorder that affects the brain indirectly. (See Concentration Disorders, pp. 556–558.) The same symptom can also occur in schizophrenia or entirely on a psychologic basis.

Localization

Hyperactivity is fortunately not a lethal symptom; autopsies are therefore very rare. Most hyperactive children who died and whose brain was examined had encephalitis. Hyperactivity was, of course, not their only organic symptom and the lesions found at autopsy were widespread. Structures near the ventricles, the medulla, the midbrain, and the diencephalon were usually affected. The substantia nigra and the hypothalamus were the site of the most severe involvement. It has therefore not been possible to establish exactly what lesions are responsible for the hyperactivity exclusively. It is probable, however, that they lie in the neighborhood of the substantia nigra and the basal ganglia because damage to these structures causes other involuntary motor symptoms, for instance choreiform and athetotic movements. (See Choreiform Movements, p. 585.)

The neurologist Frederiks assumes that a disorder of the reticular formation underlies the organic form of hyperactivity. He writes:

> Obviously an anatomically verifiable lesion as well as a disturbance of the function without a clear anatomical basis can produce a disturbance of the function of the reticular formation in such a way that perception and behavior become structureless (1969 (b), p. 197).

These assumptions have so far neither been confirmed nor refuted by autopsy findings or in other studies.

Encephalitis

An enormous number of children all over the world contracted encephalitis following the worldwide epidemic of influenza in 1918. Hyperactivity was one of the most distressing and persistent postencephalitic symptoms. This symptom may follow any type of encephalitis, whether caused by a virus (e.g., after influenza, measles, chicken pox, mumps, vaccinia, etc.) or a bacterium (e.g., after whooping cough, etc.).

ADRIAN, 10 YEARS OLD: A HYPERACTIVE CHILD WHO HAD ENCEPHALITIS.
The hyperactivity of 1 of the 29 children in my study was due to encephalitis, the cause of which was never established with certainty. The pediatricians and neurologists treating him assumed that it was a virus. This child was Adrian, whom I examined first when he was 10 years old. (See sections on Fascination with Windows, p. 597; and on Fire Setting, p. 609.) He had no reading disorder and was not hyperactive before his attack of encephalitis at the age of 9. He was critically ill, could not talk or swallow, and had to be tube-fed. He developed a paralysis of his left arm and leg and had trouble walking and putting on his clothes, when he was able to get out of bed. He also had a left facial paresis. The EEG showed bilateral hemisphere disease. The diagnosis made by the neurologist based on the EEG and on clinical examinations was: "Diffuse encephalitic process." Adrian was agitated and unmanageable on the pediatric ward and in school later on.

When I examined him he had just been suspended from school because he ran in and out of the classroom and whistled constantly. He was in constant movement and had urinated on the classroom floor because he could not stop moving long enough to use the toilet. He sometimes yelled, "I can't breathe," and asked the teacher to open the window. He had a severe form of window fascination and the teacher was afraid he might jump out. The thought of jumping out was definitely on his mind because he mumbled from time to time, "I'll be in pieces."

He also asked all day long for something to eat. His appetite had become insatiable only since his illness and he had gained a lot of weight. This symptom indicated that the encephalitis involved subcortical structures that regulate endocrine functions. During my examination he was restless and fidgety, but did not run around. He talked freely and told me that he heard voices that frightened him, especially a man's voice saying: "Adrian, you are going to cut my head," or "Adrian, kill yourself on the 10th floor," to which he himself replied: "I'll be in pieces." He said that he had tried hard to talk to the voices to make them go away. He described how he argued with them and emphasized that he had never done what they told him to do. He had no visual hallucinations and did not see the men or women who seemed to talk to him.

Mosaic Test. Adrian talked constantly during the Mosaic test. He said to himself: "Don't listen to your voice, I might kill myself. I am making a house. Pretty, pretty, not so pretty. These are different colors. A car, a little car. I am going to make the wheels." His final title was, "This Is a Bus." The entire test took only 1 minute. He spoke incessantly and very rapidly, like many other hyperactive children. It was very difficult for him to make a design resembling a truck. This inability to achieve an adequate form indicated a cortical disorder. His Mosaic was also stone-bound: he used only oblong pieces, which is characteristic for a subcortical involvement. He put three red pieces next to each other so that they stood out more than those with other colors. This could be interpreted as a reflection of his excitability. (See Figure 13.3.)

Drawings. Adrian's figure drawings and the tree showed his anxiety, his poor body image, and his preoccupation with movement. The tree swayed, and the man he drew and called "my father" waved his arms. He indicated this by a line drawn around the entire upper part of the body. The woman walked in some kind of enclosure and waved her arms. Pronounced shading on the tree and the woman indicated anxiety. The drawings also showed that he was struggling against his hyperactivity. The long necks indicated an attempt at intellectual control of movements and emotions. The circle he drew around his figures seemed to restrain them, to put limits on their movements. (See Figure 13.4.)

Adrian also had other psychologic symptoms caused by his encephalitis. These were his facetious, jocular mood; his irritability; his perseveration; his severe memory defects, which involved memory for recent events as well as retention; his free-floating anxiety; and his attention disorder. It was so difficult for him to concentrate and his memory was so poor that he had not been able to learn anything in school during the year since his illness. This also made the evaluation of his intelligence very difficult. He was not tested before his illness, but had functioned adequately in regular classes in school. One could assume that his intelligence had been average, since there were no reports to

FIG. 13.3.   A moving bus made by Adrian, age 10, on his Mosaic test. (Color plate of Figure 13.3 follows p. 432.)

dispute this assumption. His I.Q. after the encephalitis was 72 on the WISC with a verbal quotient of 66 and a performance of 83. The psychologist reported, however, that these numbers were meaningless as it had been impossible to evaluate his true intellectual potential because of his lack of attention.

Reading, Writing, and Arithmetic Disorder.   Adrian had been in the fourth grade prior to his illness. One year later his reading barely reached the third-grade level. His writing and his arithmetic were also defective. He could not do even simple calculations mentally anymore, but had to write them down. (See Arithmetic Disorders, Vol. I, pp. 227–229.)

I made the diagnosis of a psychosis following encephalitis and recommended drug treatment, home instruction until he could function in a special class in school, and casework treatment of the family. Adrian had two older sisters and one younger. His mother had had surgery several times and had still not recovered completely. His father had abandoned the family and visited only rarely. These severe family stresses aggravated Adrian's condition and delayed his recovery.

I put him on tranquilizers, first on Thorazine, later on Phenergan. The voices disappeared and he became calmer and more manageable. Dexedrine had been tried before and made him worse. He was maintained on Mellaril later on, sometimes combined with Ritalin. He never hallucinated again, but his hyperactivity improved only sporadically. He barely functioned in a special class with only three other children.

I had an office in the school where the special class was located, and Adrian visited me regularly. I also observed him in the classroom. His teachers, his social worker, the school psychologist, and I worked together closely to help

FIG. 13.4.   Adrian, age 10, organic reading disorder with postencephalitic hyperactivity. All pictures move. The tree waves in the wind, the "father" waves his arms wildly, the girl jumps up and down. The lines surrounding the figures indicate an attempt at limiting movements.

him. When he wanted to tell me something in private, he came racing down the stairs and through the long halls. He stopped barely long enough to say hello, then ran around the office while we talked. He loved the small cars I had in a desk drawer. Playing with them made it easier for him to slow down and eventually to sit down. We made a game out of this and I timed how long he could sit. He tried valiantly to improve on this time period, but it never exceeded 3 minutes.

His improvement was so minimal that he had to be suspended even from this special class when he was 13 years old, after he set a dangerous fire in the psychologist's office. (See section on Fire Setting, pp. 609–610.) This was 4 years after the encephalitis. He was then sent to a day school in a mental hospital.

When he was re-examined at the age of 15, he was no longer hyperactive; he was only somewhat restless when he sat down. His other organic symptoms had also disappeared. He seemed at last to have recovered from all the sequelae of his encephalitis. His mother said that this recovery had come about very gradually, without the help of drugs. She had not given him any during the past 2 years because she was afraid he might become an addict like so many youngsters she knew. Not all cases of postencephalitic hyperactivity have such a favorable outcome.

Meningitis

In most cases of meningitis there are also lesions in the brain substance. The cortex is usually most affected, but subcortical areas, the basal ganglia, the diencephalon, and so forth, may also be involved (Wertham, 1934, p. 423). This explains why hyperactivity may occur following meningitis.

LANA, 8 YEARS OLD: POSTMENINGITIS HYPERACTIVITY.   One of the children in my study, a girl named Lana, was 8 years old when I examined her. She had had meningitis at the age of 2 and had been hyperactive and a severe management problem at home. Since then, and in school later on, she also had exhibited other organically caused psychologic symptoms, namely free-floating anxiety with sudden states of panic, an attention disorder, irritability, persever-ation, and a severe reading, writing, and arithmetic disorder.

She could not function in a regular or even in a special class, and had to be on home instruction until her hyperactivity subsided at the age of 13 when she began to menstruate. Hyperactivity is mainly a childhood symptom, confined to an immature organism. It tends to subside spontaneously with the onset of puberty, even in severe organic cases.

Lana's anxiety also diminished and her attention disorder became less severe. Her reading and arithmetic disorder improved, but did not rise above the fourth-grade level. She did not recover completely from all the sequelae of her meningitis.

Convulsive Disorders

Epilepsy or any other convulsive disorder may cause hyperactivity. (See Convulsive Disorders, p. 620.)

Hyperactivity may start immediately after the first convulsion, or much later, months or even years. It is therefore sometimes difficult to determine whether or not the child's convulsions, which he may have had years ago, and his hyperactivity have the same organic basis. An EEG typical for a convulsive disorder is the most important diagnostic test in these cases. It proves that a convulsive disorder underlies the child's hyperactivity. It is important to real-ize that a child or an adult may have epilepsy and currently have no convul-sions. This is especially important for the diagnosis and treatment of those hyperactive children who had only one or just a few convulsions in their infancy or early childhood. These are usually febrile convulsions (i.e., they occur only during a fever). These convulsions used to be considered inconsequential. We now know, however, that about 30% of children who have febrile convulsions will have spontaneous seizures later on. The number of these convulsions is important in this respect: the risk after only one of them is 6%; after 4, 60% (Millichap, 1968).

Each hyperactive child with such a history should therefore have an EEG and be carefully examined also for other signs of a convulsive disorder, especially seizure equivalents. When the diagnosis of a convulsive disorder has been established, the child should be treated with anticonvulsive drugs in addition to educational and other forms of treatment he may need.

Hyperactivity is a serious complication of a convulsive disorder. Not only is the management of such a child at home and in school much more difficult; it also complicates drug therapy. For instance, Dilantin, one of the most effective of all anticonvulsive drugs, sometimes causes a form of hyperactivity. The child may become slap-happy and difficult to control. Sympathomimetic drugs, on the other hand, may lower the child's convulsive threshold and cause convulsions. Dexedrine and Benzedrine are not supposed to have this effect; Ritalin does, however. The product information printed by the drug company warns specifically that Ritalin may lower the convulsive threshold in patients with or without prior seizures. Tranquilizers must also be given to these children with great caution. Mellaril and the phenothiazines, for example, may cause convulsions (Kalinowsky & Hoch, 1961, p. 32, Itil & Soldatos, 1980).

Four of the 29 hyperactive children in my study had convulsions, three of them only the febrile type. A girl who was 5 when I examined her had had one febrile convulsion at the age of 1; an 8-year-old boy had one at the age of 3; and an 11-year-old boy had two at the age of 4 during scarlet fever. A causal connection between their febrile convulsions, their hyperactivity, and their other organic symptoms could not be established. These children had no convulsions later on, and no other evidence for a convulsive disorder.

There seemed to be such a connection, however, between the convulsive disorder of the fourth child, Ramon, and his hyperactivity: they apparently had the same organic basis, though obscure.

RAMON, 5 YEARS OLD: HYPERACTIVITY DUE TO A CONVULSIVE DISORDER.

Ramon was one of the two boys in my study with the severest window fascination, and the child who threw his 4-year-old brother out of a window. (See Fascination with Windows, p. 597; Violent Behavior, p. 604; and Mosaic Test, p. 612.) He also had tantrums, was fascinated by keys, and set fires. All his organic symptoms were severe: convulsions, attention disorder, free-floating anxiety, perseveration, directional confusion (he could not distinguish right from left on himself or on other persons), speech disorder, and reading, writing, and arithmetic disorder.

He had had three convulsions by the age of 8 when I examined him for the last time. All were typical grand-mal seizures. The first, at the age of 2, lasted 1 hour; the second, at 3 years of age, lasted about 4 hours; the third, at the age of 7, lasted about 30 minutes. He was brought to a hospital each time because the convulsion could not be stopped at home. His EEG was "very dysrhythmic" and slow for his age, according to the neurologist. It was not typical for a convulsive disorder but did not rule it out either. Ramon probably suffered from epilepsy, even though the age of onset was somewhat earlier than is usual. His twin sister also had convulsions and an older sister had died during a convulsion. The incidence of epilepsy in families of epileptics is high, as high as 60% according to some studies (Alvarez, 1972, p. 40).

Repeated psychologic examinations showed that Ramon's intellectual capacity was within the average range in spite of his multiple organic impairments. I examined him at the age of 5 and again when he was 8 years old because he failed to respond to outpatient treatment. The very skillful child psychiatric fellow who worked with me told me that Ramon was the only child she had ever examined whom she could not control. No one else could either. Various drugs had not calmed him down sufficiently. He was unmanageable in a number of special classes and his mother could not manage him at home. The only feasible therapeutic plan was to send him to a psychiatric hospital.

Children suffering from a convulsive disorder with hyperactivity are severely handicapped and require special care. Kramer and Pollnow wrote about this long ago. Nineteen of the 45 children they studied had convulsions (1932). Yet textbooks of pediatrics, pediatric neurology, psychiatry, child psychiatry, or neurology either do not mention the association of a convulsive disorder with hyperactivity at all or refer to it only casually. Careful studies of a large number of such children are needed, so that we can help them better than is now possible.

Mental Deficiency

Some mentally defective children are hyperactive. This is a serious complication that makes their management and education even more difficult. These children are hyperactive when the cerebral defects underlying their low intellectual capacity also involve the areas in the diencephalon regulating their motor drive.

RAFER, 9 YEARS OLD: HYPERACTIVITY AND MENTAL DEFICIENCY.   Only 1 of the 29 hyperactive children in my study was a mental defective. This was 9-year-old Rafer, who was severely hyperactive during the day and also at night when sleepwalking. (See Sleep, pp. 600–602.)

He was referred by his school because he had learned very little since Kindergarten, could not pay attention, and was extremely restless. He had been held over in the second grade, but his reading had remained at pre-primer level. His hyperactivity had started at the age of 2. He was fascinated with windows and had broken quite a few of them. He was also a fire setter: he had started a fire in his apartment by looking for a shoe with a lighted match under his mother's bed. It was fortunately quickly put out by neighbors and the fire department. Just a few days later another apartment in the same house caught fire, and he was under suspicion for having set it. I found that he was preoccupied with fire; this was understandable because his family had been burnt out of a building 2 years before. However, he was not afraid of fire, but excited and fascinated by it. (See Fire Setting, p. 609-610.)

Rafer's I.Q. on the WISC was 65 with a verbal quotient of 67 and a performance of 69. The level of his intelligence was definitely within the defective range. His organic symptoms, however, were more severe than in many other children with the same abnormally low intellectual capacity. His reading, writing, and arithmetic disorders were unusually severe; so was his attention disorder, his fatiguability, and his anxiety. This severity may have been due, at least in part, to the terrible social conditions under which he and his family had been living.

He hardly knew his father, who visited only sporadically and never gave any financial help. He lived with his mother and older brother in great poverty. After having been burnt out of one building, they moved into an abandoned house without heat or hot water and remained in it for about 1 year. When Rafer was about 8, they moved into a tenement house with no light in two of their four rooms. He was too thin when I examined him and obviously poorly nourished. He had been treated for anemia the year before, probably caused by malnutrition. Chronic malnutrition itself can cause hyperactivity, fatiguability, anxiety, and an attention disorder. (See Concentration, p. 554.) Even though his mental deficiency and his specific organic symptoms were not caused by these damaging social conditions, they were seriously aggravated by them.

I recommended placement for Rafer in a class for mentally retarded children, a pediatric examination, treatment of his malnutrition, dental care (he had many cavities), drug treatment for his hyperactivity, and social work treatment for the entire family. I felt that he also needed individual educational treatment for his reading, writing, and arithmetic disorder. These disorders were too severe to respond to classroom teaching alone.

Toxic Causes

Only those toxic substances cause hyperactivity that damage the cerebral basis for the motor drive in some way. Some drugs, for instance cortisone, may cause hyperactivity in some children, while not causing this symptom in adults. Others may also cause this symptom in adults.

Exogenic Psychoses

Hyperactivity is a symptom of some toxic psychoses, with or without hallucinations and disorientation. Hallucinogenic substances such as marijuana, cocaine, psilocybin, mescaline, LSD, glue, or gasoline frequently cause episodes of severe hyperactivity (Slater & Roth, 1969, pp. 421, 429).

I have examined glue sniffers 11 years old and younger who were admitted to the pediatric ward because they danced around wildly and could not stop. Overuse of sympathomimetic drugs may also cause hyperactivity. Even small doses sometimes cause this symptom in adults and in some children. An example for this reaction is the 6-year-old boy who felt and acted like a "wild lion" after he took Dexedrine. (See Hyperactivity with Anxiety, p. 593–595.)

Accidental Poisoning

The incidence of accidental poisoning of infants and young children has increased phenomenally and with it, toxic damage to the central nervous system, leading in some cases to hyperactivity. According to the pediatrician Einhorn, this has become a leading health problem, accounting for more than 3,000 deaths annually in the United States, and the number of nonfetal poisonings is estimated to exceed one million a year. Einhorn writes about this topic in *Pediatrics* (1968), where he stresses that many children who survive the ingestion of poison are left with permanent disabilities. He emphasizes that

> some of these deficits may be subtle and are often overlooked. Intellectual impairment, for example, may result from chronic lead intoxication. It may, however, be secondary to poisoning by any product that affects primarily the central nervous system.

He goes on to warn that "this type of handicap may only become apparent when the child enters school" (1968, p. 527). These handicaps do not necessarily include hyperactivity, which Einhorn does not mention at all in this context. They do, however, include reading, writing, and arithmetic disorders, which become apparent only when the child enters school. The organic impairments on which they are based often are not noticed before that time.

Lead Poisoning

Lead poisoning is being studied as a possible cause of hyperactivity. Some investigators suspect that chronically elevated lead levels in blood, urine and teeth that are too low to cause symptoms typical for lead encephalopathy, may lead to hyperactivity and other psychologic symptoms subsumed under the term "Minimal Brain Dysfunction" (Needleman et al. 1979; Lin-Fu 1979). There is no sufficient clinical proof as yet for this hypothesis. We do not know, for instance, how low these lead levels can be and still cause any adverse effects. This was pointed out by Anita Curran, MD, Director of Lead Poison Control of the Department of Health of New York City, at a meeting of the Public

Health Committee of the Medical Society of Queens County (April 1976). Furthermore, hyperactivity is the opposite of the symptoms produced by lead encephalopathy. *Hypo*activity characterizes a child suffering from this poisoning, which has an insidious onset with anorexia, apathy, anemia, hyperirritability, incoordination, subtle loss of learned skills, and sporadic vomiting. Unless the diagnosis is made during this stage and the child treated promptly, a severe encephalopathy sets in with ataxia, forceful vomiting, periods of lethargy or stupor, and, eventually, coma and convulsions. All too frequently the end result is death (Chisholm, 1968, p. 544).

Lead poisoning is a preventable disease. It can and should be eradicated. Children contract it by eating substances containing lead (e.g., paint) or by inhaling it (e.g., through car exhausts, when storage batteries are burnt, etc.). Children can also be poisoned in this way by ingesting fruit covered with insecticide, fruit and beverages improperly prepared or stored in lead-glazed ceramic containers, or water from lead pipes; or through exposure to lead nipple shields, face powders containing lead, lead soldiers and other toys. Some crayons, watercolors, chalk, and modeling clay contain lead and are dangerous when the child chews or swallows them.

Poor children 3 years old or younger are especially vulnerable, since they are apt to live in dilapidated housing painted long ago with lead paint. This paint flakes off unless it is removed or painted over. Several tiny flakes may contain 100 mg of lead or more. These flakes spread lead poisoning among all children who eat them by chewing plaster or by nibbling on cribs and other furniture, on windowsills, and so on. Infants and very young children habitually put objects into their mouth and lick or chew them. This habit is called pica when it persists longer than usual. Pica may also be due to hunger or other forms of malnutrition (Chisholm, 1968, pp. 543, 544). Lead poisoning itself may increase the child's need to chew because it causes loss of appetite and with it, malnutrition.

One of the 29 hyperactive children in my study, 6-year-old Mona, had a history of lead poisoning. An analysis of her organic symptoms shows how difficult it is to prove or to disprove that lead caused her hyperactivity or any of her other symptoms.

MONA, 6 YEARS OLD: HYPERACTIVITY AND LEAD POISONING. Mona was referred at the age of 6 at the end of the school year by her Kindergarten teachers. They wanted to know whether she should enter first grade or repeat Kindergarten. They complained about her hyperactivity, her distractibility, her awkwardness with pencil and paper, and her unintelligible speech. Her mother and her baby-sitter were worried because they found her difficult to control and, at times, too fearful.

Mona was an only child whose mother worked. She did not know her father because he had abandoned her mother while she was pregnant. She had been born in the breech position after a difficult labor. Such deliveries sometimes injure the brain of the fetus. She was born with mild clubfeet and had to wear orthopedic shoes for awhile. Her speech started late, at the age of 2, and was indistinct; it had improved during the school year with the help of her teachers, however.

Mona was treated for lead poisoning at the age of 5, 1 month before she entered Kindergarten. Her neurologic examination at the age of 6, 10 months after her treatment, was entirely negative. Psychologic testing indicated that her intelligence was probably within average range. However, a valid I.Q. could not be obtained because of her hyperactivity, her attention disorder, her anxiety, and her perseveration. The speech therapist found a speech disorder on an organic basis.

Psychiatric Examination.   Mona was restless and distractible during my examination. Her hyperactivity subsided as soon as her anxiety decreased with improved contact and feelings of trust and security. Her speech also became understandable, she was friendly, and she talked freely. She could barely hold a pencil and wrote straight upwards, vertically. She had trouble copying letters and could not draw a tree or figures. She could not read and her number concepts were also poor. She managed to count to six. Her Mosaic test showed marked anxiety: she made a frame design that was also stone-bound, indicating an organic, subcortical disorder. She felt badly about her inability to perform and got angry at herself. Her relationship with her mother was fraught with conflicts: Mona felt rejected by her and was often afraid her mother would leave her.

Diagnosis.   Mona suffered from a reading, writing, and arithmetic disorder on an organic basis. Her writing disorder was especially severe, and was due to constructional apraxia. Her other organic symptoms were: hyperactivity, free-floating anxiety (partly on a psychogenic basis), perseveration, a speech disorder, and an attention disorder.

Recommendations.   I recommended transfer to a therapeutic Kindergarten, speech therapy for Mona, and social work treatment for her mother to alleviate the conflicts between her and the child.

Analysis of Causation.   It was not possible to determine which of Mona's organic symptoms, if any, were caused by lead poisoning. The speech disorder definitely antedated the poisoning, as did her anxiety and her attention disorder. One could not be so sure about her other symptoms, however. Her perseveration, her constructional apraxia, and her difficulty with number concepts were first noticed in Kindergarten. Lead poisoning may have caused or at least aggravated them. She had had no pediatric, neurologic, psychologic, or psychiatric examination before the poisoning, so that it was impossible to find out whether these symptoms pre-existed. Only her hyperactivity seemed definitely to have started afterwards, after she entered Kindergarten. Was this only a coincidence, or was there a causal relationship? Not even this could be answered with certainty.

Many children are hyperactive only in group situations, in the presence of other children, especially when they suffer from the anxious form. Mona's hyperactivity clearly belonged to this form. The onset of hyperactivity when a child enters Kindergarten is therefore not at all unusual. In Mona's case, this time of onset certainly could not be used as evidence for its causation by lead poisoning. It is quite possible, but cannot be proven beyond doubt, that lead poisoning caused none of Mona's symptoms, that it left no pathologic trace in her brain. Long-term follow-up examinations including lead levels of blood and teeth and EEGs of many such children are essential to clarify the relationship between lead poisoning and hyperactivity. Even these studies may remain inconclusive unless it is possible to determine what organic symptoms, if any, the child had before the lead poisoning.

Food Additives

(See Food Additives, under Attention Disorders, p. 558.)

That food additives can cause hyperactivity in some children was shown by the pediatrician and allergist, Ben F. Feingold. In his textbook, *Introduction to Clinical Allergy* (1973), he wrote that he had noticed that disturbing psychologic symptoms sometimes disappeared together with allergic manifestations in patients for whom he prescribed a diet free from food additives. The allergic children who responded in this way had the following psychologic symptoms: "hyperactivity, lack of concentration, distractibility, impulsivity and learning difficulties" (p. 193). They had been referred to him because they had pruritus or urticaria, and not for their disturbed behavior. He found that their skin allergies were due to the ingestion of synthetic flavorings and colorings from various types of soft drinks, artificially colored and flavored breakfast and other foods, chewable vitamins, and so forth. The elimination diet he prescribed had the following results:

> Not only were the pruritus and urticaria controlled, but in addition the parents observed a striking and at times dramatic change in the child's behavioral pattern. The parents reported that the child became docile, was better adjusted to its home environment and showed a definite improvement in achievement at school.

Proof that the ingestion of synthetic flavors and colors had really caused these behavioral symptoms came when "several of the children under observation experienced a return of symptoms with a reversal of the behavioral pattern following the inadvertent ingestion of the additives" (p. 193). Feingold stresses that "the emotional and behavioral disturbances observed in this group of patients were coincidental findings, noted upon developing the history, while the psychological improvement followed treatment directed to the chief complaint" (p. 193). Such incidental observations, based on meticulous clinical work, have often led to new discoveries in the history of medicine and psychiatry.

The observation that hyperactivity can be treated with a food-additive–free diet in some allergic children, led Feingold to study the effect of this diet on hyperactive children with no allergic manifestations on their skin or elsewhere. He points out that sensitivity to chemical food additives cannot be diagnosed through skin tests because it is not really an allergic reaction. He explains it in this way:

> Since the food chemicals are low molecular weight compounds, their involvement in an immunologic reaction would mean they are serving as haptens (incomplete antigens). Since haptens cannot be demonstrated by skin testing, this procedure is not helpful in the diagnosis (1973, p. 157).

He emphasizes that the diagnosis must therefore be based on "(1) an awareness that colors and flavors are a common cause of adverse reactions, and (2) a high degree of suspicion which follows the exclusion of all other possible factors" (1973, p. 157). A careful history and a diet diary for a period of 7 to 10 days are, of course, also indispensable (González, 1980; Brody, 1980).

Feingold studied over 100 hyperactive children with or without skin manifestations. He reports his findings in *Why Your Child Is Hyperactive* (1975), where he stresses that "whether the patient is an adult or a hyperkinetic child, there is no natural body defense against the synthetic additives" (p. 14). A child who reacts with hyperactivity or other symptoms to these substances can therefore not be desensitized. The only cure is their complete elimination from his diet.

The typical diet of these children does not differ from that of millions of other children in the United States. Their breakfast consists of cereal loaded with nonessential flavors and colors added to entice the child; a beverage, either chocolate or other drinks, most of which are rich with many artificial flavors and colors; pancakes made from a mix, frozen waffles dyed with tartrazine (FD&C Yellow #5), or frozen French toast. The conscientious mothers of these children almost invariably give them vitamins, usually chewable, which are also loaded with additives. School lunch also provides a large supply of these substances, consisting of hot dogs, luncheon meats, ice cream, and various beverages.

ROLE OF SCHOOL LUNCHES. The policy of school systems in New York City and elsewhere to discontinue cooking fresh food for breakfasts and luncheons in favor of prepared frozen foods and mass meal packs is important in this respect. It is potentially damaging for millions of children. It has not only decreased the nutritional value of these meals and made them unappetizing, as the *New York Times* reported (Sheraton, 1979). It has also added vast amounts of chemical food additives.

Fortunately not all children who ingest such quantities of food additives become hyperactive or get other organic or somatic symptoms, not even all children in the same family. Why some children are sensitive to these substances and others are not, is not yet known. There is no test to distinguish those who are sensitive from those who can tolerate these substances. What we do know is that psychologic factors are not involved. However, we should protect all children equally from whatever may harm any one of them. This means eliminating nutritionally useless and potentially damaging food additives.

Feingold suggests that the increase in the number of hyperactive children (which indeed seems real and not only due to an increase in and overuse of the diagnosis) may be due to the increase in food-additive ingestion by children since 1970. It is, however, not known how many hyperactive children can be cured or improved by an additive-free diet. Feingold's own statistics show that

the best estimate, based on careful records, is that 50% have a likelihood of full response, while 75% can be removed from drug management, even if full response to other symptoms is not achieved. . . . That result alone would appear to make trial a worthy venture (1975, p. 71).

A diet diary should indeed be requested from every mother whose child is hyperactive. Such a diary might show a relationship between food intake and episodes of hyperactivity. Where such a relationship is even suspected, treatment with an elimination diet should be tried (González, 1980).

Feingold describes this diet, which he calls the "K-P (Kaiser-Permanente)" diet, in great detail with practical cooking instructions in *Why Your Child Is Hyperactive*. Many parents now put their child on this diet on their own—before seeing a physician—whom they consult only when their child fails to respond. I have examined a number of these children. Their mothers told me that they found the diet easy to prepare and not too time-consuming.

Two groups of food are eliminated by the "K-P" diet. Group 1 consists of foods containing natural salicylates. These are two vegetables (tomato and cucumber) and most fruits (almonds, apples, apricots, all berries, cherries, currants, grapes and raisins or products made from grapes such as wine and jellies, nectarines, oranges, peaches, plums, and prunes). Grapefruit, lemon, and lime are permitted. Unfortunately this eliminates most fruits that children like to eat and that are good for them in so many other respects. However, Feingold suggests that these foods should be restored to the child's diet slowly, one at a time, if he shows a favorable reaction to the total "K-P" diet.

Group 2 eliminates all food containing artificial colors and flavors. Food preservatives are not forbidden except for BHT (butylated hydroxytoluene), because an occasional child may show an adverse response. Such a diet requires careful reading of food labels and conferring with the marketer to find out which items are free from these substances.

Feingold's book includes a list of permitted foods. Cereals and bakery goods free from these chemicals are permitted. Most bakery goods, however, are not additive-free, and must therefore be prepared at home. Commercial breads, except for egg-containing and whole-wheat bread, are allowed. Flours, meats, fresh fish, poultry (except when stuffed) are allowed; so are home-made sweets (e.g., ice cream, chocolate syrup, gelatins made from pure gelatin, tapioca and other puddings, custards, candies without almonds). Milk, Seven-Up, grapefruit and pineapple juice, pear and Guava nectar, sweet butter, cooking oils and fats, honey, and all natural (white) cheeses are on the permitted list. This leaves out most highly advertised foods that have become children's favorites, such as soft drinks or frankfurters. However, children can be persuaded to accept this diet, especially when they themselves have experienced the connection between eating certain foods and distressing feelings.

Schizophrenia

Hyperactivity may be part of schizophrenia. This is rare, but has to be considered as a possible cause. What Bleuler called a "hyperkinetic form" of catatonic schizophrenia occurs in adults. These patients move constantly, but their movements are peculiar and bizarre and not due to a motor-drive disorder. Their behavior is more like a state of wild excitement (Bleuler, 1930, p. 308; Slater & Roth, 1969, p. 318). The movements of children whose hyperactivity is caused by schizophrenia are not necessarily bizarre or peculiar. The hyperactivity itself may not reveal the underlying schizophrenic process. Other aspects of the child's behavior show that he is suffering from this disease.

Schizophrenic symptoms sometimes become apparent only after the hyperactivity has subsided either as a result of drug treatment or spontaneously. Schizophrenic hyperactivity is often episodic, alternating with calm and withdrawn behavior. Its onset may be sudden and unpredictable, similar to the onset of catatonic excitement in adults. It is always severe and belongs to the anxious form of hyperactivity.

Reading Disorders
of Hyperactive Schizophrenic Children

Hyperactivity, regardless of its cause, makes learning to read difficult. When a child also has schizophrenia, his ability to learn reading may be even more seriously impaired. The schizophrenic process itself does not destroy a patient's ability to read, provided he learned it before the disease started. When it starts in preschool age, however, it often makes it difficult even for a nonhyperactive child to learn reading and writing because it causes such a severe concentration disorder and distractibility. (See Concentration, p. 554; and Distractibility on a Schizophrenic Basis, p. 581.)

The level of the child's intelligence also plays a role here. The higher such a child's intelligence, the more likely he is to learn to read and write in spite of his attention disorder and, in exceptional cases, even in spite of his hyperactivity.

The reading disorder of a schizophrenic child (whether he is hyperactive or not) may also have an organic basis. His cerebral reading apparatus may be defective for reasons that have nothing to do with schizophrenia. Some child psychiatrists, for example Bender, Fish, and Goldfarb, assume that the schizophrenic process damages the immature brain of an infant or young child in a way that does not differ qualitatively from any other organic damage, that it affects all parts of the brain including reading and speech apparatuses. However, most schizophrenic children learn to read perfectly well once they have overcome their attention disorder. Their cerebral reading apparatus has not been damaged. It can therefore be assumed that some schizophrenic children suffer from two different disorders, schizophrenia and a reading disorder on an organic basis that differs from schizophrenia (Goldfarb, 1961).

For the treatment of a hyperactive schizophrenic child it is important to determine whether or not his cerebral reading apparatus has been damaged. This can and should be done irrespective of what the cause may be. The cerebral reading apparatus is malfunctioning when such a child's reading disorder persists after the attention disorder has been alleviated. When an attentive schizophrenic child still has trouble learning to read, his cerebral reading apparatus must be defective.

The attention disorder of such a child usually responds to drug treatment, combined with careful management at home and in school. Individual psychotherapy in addition to these other measures is often also helpful. The persistent reading disorder can, of course, be corrected only with special teaching methods. (See Relation to Speech Disorders and Impact of Parents' Attitude on Children, under Word-Meaning Deafness, p. 389 Vol. I, pp. 131, 316 .)

CHESTER, 8 YEARS OLD: HYPERACTIVITY DUE TO SCHIZOPHRENIA. Only 1 of the 29 hyperactive children in my study, 8-year-old Chester, had schizophrenia. His plight provides an excellent example for the complicated relationship between hyperactivity, schizophrenia, and a reading and writing disorder. I am presenting his history in such great detail because it illustrates typical problems in the diagnosis, treatment, and prognosis of such a disturbed child.

I examined Chester when he was 8, 9, and 15 years of age. He was born prematurely, after 7 months' gestation. His birth weight was only 5 lbs, 4 oz, and he was kept in an incubator for several weeks. His physical health and development were good from then on. He started to speak early: words at the age of 9 months; sentences soon after his first birthday. He was toilet trained easily, before the age of 2, and had no relapses. He had to wear eyeglasses because his vision was poor in one eye and he had strabismus. Repeated neurologic examinations were negative, as were EEGs and an x-ray of his skull.

Family Situation. Chester was an only child raised by his mother with some help (or rather interference) from his maternal grandmother. His mother had wanted a child even though she was already 38 years old and had a malfunctioning heart valve. The father lost interest in his wife soon after she got pregnant and left her after Chester was born. He did not contribute to his support and saw him only rarely. This left the mother to fend for herself. She could not work because of her heart condition, became very depressed, and made two suicide attempts—one before Chester was born, another one soon thereafter. She went to a number of psychiatrists in various clinics, but unfortunately did not receive the guidance and psychotherapy she so desperately needed. They treated her only with drugs. She tried to rise above her stressful and depressing life situation by joining Jehovah's Witnesses. Her religious beliefs played a large role also in Chester's thinking: she took him to all meetings.

Mother and child were extremely close, but their relationship was not quite so pathologic as in the symbiotic type of childhood schizophrenia described by Mahler. Chester separated from her easily and liked to do things on his own. However, when I first examined him at the age of 8, they still slept in the same bed.

Chester's teachers observed that his mother sometimes talked to him as if he were her husband, not her son. That is how he acquired his adult and sophisticated vocabulary. The relationship between the two was quite ambivalent. Affection suddenly changed into angry and often violent outbursts. Chester would hit his mother with such force that she became afraid of him even though he was only a child. She was also often furious at him and hit him. She confessed to the social worker that she sometimes had murderous impulses against him, but she never hit him severely. He was definitely not an abused child. He was very jealous of her to the point where he set fire to her mail. (See section on Fire Setting, p. 609.)

When I first examined the mother, she was tense, irritable, anxious, and angry. She felt overwhelmed by her son's hyperactivity and his generally destructive and uncontrollable behavior. Although a very intelligent woman who tried to do her best, she could not control her son or herself. She was so irritable and angry that she reacted with violent outbursts against neighbors and strangers following minor incidents that had nothing to do with Chester. She had been diagnosed differently by different psychiatrists, the most recent diagnosis being anxiety neurosis. Other diagnoses were neurotic depression and schizophrenia. She was in good contact when I examined her and I found no evidence of delusions or hallucinations.

Hyperactivity and Other Symptoms. Chester was hyperactive almost from the time he could walk, when he was 15 months old. His hyperactivity remained episodic and manageable until he came in contact with a group of other children, at the local Head Start program, at the age of 4. He ran around, screamed, and had temper tantrums. He made no contact whatsoever with other children, but had an imaginary playmate and lived largely in his own fantasy world. Chester's anxiety in group situations and his inability to play with other children were caused even at that early age by morbid suspiciousness. This is a serious schizophrenic symptom in children and often a forerunner of delusions. (See Distractibility on a Schizophrenic Basis, p. 581.)

Chester was also very argumentative. His verbal ability had been superior from the beginning. All his teachers stressed his "exceptional verbal skills," referring to his advanced vocabulary and his superior, adultlike choice of words. However, he was incapable of learning anything systematically because he could not sit still and pay attention long enough. His behavior was impossible to control in Kindergarten also, so that he had to be suspended and referred for psychologic and psychiatric examinations.

First Psychologic Examination. The psychologist who tested him at the age of 5½ had to cope with the following behavior:

> Upon seeing the test material he became panic stricken. He ran around the room, crawled on the floor, banged on the blackboard with an eraser, screamed and seemed highly agitated. He spoke to me, but did not seem to hear my responses. He tried to run out of the room.

She succeeded in calming him down eventually, and came to the following conclusions:

> Because of his overwhelming anxiety it was not possible to obtain a valid quantitative score. However, it is my impression that his intelligence falls within the high average or superior range. His verbal ability is highly developed. He can generalize and categorize accurately. He uses language with an attempt at precision and with richness of expression. He has a well-developed ability to understand abstract ideas. However, he often responds inappropriately. Occasionally he makes nonsensical or bizarre statements. He makes up words and makes puns on words.

First Psychiatric Examination. The psychiatrist who also examined him at 5½ years noticed his morbid suspiciousness especially. He also reported that Chester used neologisms (words he invented), that he rhymed often and liked to talk in "rhythmic word series," and that he was "plagued by inner voices which he admits distract him." He made the diagnosis of childhood schizophrenia and recommended home instruction because the boy could not possibly function in a group situation.

Schooling. Chester was on home instruction from the age of 6 to 7 years. From 7 to 8 he attended a special private school for children who function on a retarded level but are actually not retarded, and who have some brain damage. This was at least the official policy of that school. In practice, however, it also admitted psychotic children. Chester's teachers were therefore experienced in managing very disturbed children, but he was too difficult even for them. They reported that he was hyperactive, that he fantasized about "a little friend," a "mechanical brain" and other "assorted devices," that he talked a lot about outer and inner space, and that he generally tended to substitute fantasy for reality. They complained that he expressed his ideas "dogmatically," and that he "went to fantastic lengths to prove even the most absurd point." Furthermore, he had no qualms about attacking anyone, adults or children. He kicked, scratched, or bit them. His teachers felt that they had no choice but to dismiss him. They referred him for re-examination and this is when I examined him.

Second Psychologic Examination. The psychologist who tested Chester at the age of 8 also found testing very difficult to accomplish because of his "enormous anxiety level" and his severe attention disorder. She could not obtain an intelligence score but thought that it was probably above average. She found that his comprehension was above age level, but that his digit span was poor, and he had a problem in digital ordering and some right-left confusion. This indicated to her that he had a "mild perceptual problem which is often associated with prematurity." Projective tests revealed his wild and bizarre fantasies and pointed to schizophrenia.

Speech Examination. The speech therapist who examined him, also when he was 8 years old, found no speech defect. However, she was the only clinician who could obtain a formal intelligence score. She gave him the Peabody Picture Vocabulary Test, where pictures have to be matched with the appropriate words. Chester earned an I.Q. score of 121. This confirmed what everyone suspected, namely that his intelligence was indeed superior.

Educational Evaluation. The educational evaluation was also done when

Chester was 8 years old. The educational therapist found that he could name most, but not all, letters and that he knew no sounds at all. He could read only two words on sight. He could write only his first name, but reversed letters. He also reversed numbers and the position of numbers. He told her somewhat facetiously, "I am a first-grade drop out!" His writing was very clumsy. The therapist had the impression that there was an organic basis for his reading, writing, and arithmetic disorder, that it was not caused merely by a lack of attention. The psychologists' findings of mild perceptual defects also pointed in this direction.

Second, Third, and Fourth Psychiatric Examinations. There were two psychiatric examinations after the first one; mine was the fourth. The second psychiatrist made the diagnosis of "Minimal Brain Damage"; the third felt that he suffered from (1) "Chronic Brain Syndrome" and (2) a "Reactive Disorder."

One of the pediatricians who had referred Chester for a psychiatric examination also thought that he had a "reactive behavior disorder." All these physicians apparently were impressed with his mother's abnormal behavior and thought that the boy was reacting to it, rather than being sick himself. This is a problem frequently encountered in child psychiatry. It is often very difficult to unravel the complicated mother/child relationship and to determine whether one or both is mentally sick. I, too, considered the possibility that the boy could be imitating some of his mother's behavior, that he might have picked up some of his fantasies from her. However careful observation of mother and child over about 1 year left no doubt that the boy was schizophrenic and not his mother.

That this boy was diagnosed so differently also shows how difficult it is to diagnose the disorder of such a young child with so many very severe symptoms. (See Word-Meaning Deafness, p. 389.)

Chester was not in good contact and quite negativistic during my examination at the age of 8. He walked around most of the time and could not sit still. He gave factual answers to simple, concrete questions about his address, his school, where he lived, and so forth; however, when a question aroused his anger or caused anxiety, he told long, disconnected stories that were part fantasy and part reality. They were impossible to follow. When I asked him about his father, for instance, he said, "That's a personal question, that's going a little too far!" He then started running around excitedly and talking very rapidly about disconnected episodes involving his father, a dog, himself, and others. This form of "looseness of associations" is a thought disorder typical for schizophrenia that is also found in adults.

Chester was fortunately not fascinated with windows. He was, however, interested in flying. Like so many other hyperactive children, he talked freely about "flying like a bird." He had told the psychologist, "My wings come out at night and then I do fly." He got angry when she did not believe him.

He told me that he had many frightening dreams. He was quite preoccupied with one about Senator Robert Kennedy (who had been murdered 2 years before). He said: "I saw Kennedy's casket, on top was a stone. There was a face on top of it. It said: "Kennedy is dead.' " He had the feeling that he was in some way responsible for this death. This may have been a hallucinatory experience rather than a dream, but it was impossible to clarify.

He interspersed neologisms in his narratives. My interruptions to ask what certain words meant met with evasiveness. He answered: "I forgot," or "Sometimes I don't understand what I say," or "Something I say comes out of nowhere." He remained silent when I suggested he might be repeating voices he heard. Often he moved his head as if he were responding to a voice. To a direct question about voices he responded: "I had a good voice. I had a spirit. It was Jehovah's spirit. It happens overnight, then the word comes out in the morning. Sometimes I say a word I am not thinking about, and my mother understands it, sometimes it happens to my mother." At this point I thought that we were dealing with "Folie à deux," that both he and his mother might be hallucinating. What the boy was referring to, however, might also have been the "speaking in tongues" practiced by some religious sects, and not a pathologic symptom. "Speaking in tongues," or glossolalia, consists of unintelligible sounds uttered in a state of religious trance or ecstasy. These utterances are supposed to come directly from a holy spirit that has entered the worshiper. It was generally impossible to determine how much of what he told me reflected his mother's religious beliefs, and what were his own, possibly delusional, ideas. He also said that he had seen "Satan, the Devil" at night, and some spirits of people who had died in the house where he lived.

Mosaic Test. Chester talked incessantly while working on his designs. He could not make up his mind about them and destroyed five before he settled on one. It took him 15 minutes to complete the test. When he finally decided to make a spaceship he said: "It's about to blast off. This opportunity is for the moon. A little grounding test. How the moon is gravitating. This is what the picture is about, so I must know everything about the moon. If they took this spaceship to the moon, they must have gl———" (unintelligible neologism). He refused to explain what he meant. The final title of the Mosaic was: "The Apollo 15 spaceship and a building. It talks to the ship. It got transmitters to talk back and forth. It's about 2,000 billion feet long, 2,000 billion people are in it." (This was after the moon landing.)

Chester's Mosaic test reflected his preoccupation with outer space and his grandiosity. There was no indication of organicity. The design rested on a baseline that extended from the right to the left margin. This showed anxiety. Chester called this line "the earth." Black and red pieces were in prominent places, indicating a tendency to emotional outbursts (e.g., tantrums) and to depression. The Mosaic was not typical for schizophrenia, but his drawings were. (See Figure 13.5.)

Drawings. Chester's drawings were grandiose and bizarre and showed a peculiar body image. (See Figure 13.6.)

Diagnosis. I felt that Chester was probably suffering from childhood schizophrenia, but that the extent of his mother's influence on his thinking and behavior had to be determined, as we might be dealing with a folie à deux situation. The danger also existed that the mother may make another suicide attempt and take the child with her. What Wertham called an "extended suicide" had to be considered and prevented.

Recommendations. The clinic staff and I thought that the safest plan was to send Chester to a psychiatric hospital or to a child psychiatric ward in a general hospital for observation. It was, however, impossible to obtain the mother's consent for this, even though she had an excellent relationship with the social worker and other staff members and trusted us. There was therefore no choice but to continue treating mother and child on an outpatient basis. Home instruction was the only possible plan so far as schooling was concerned.

Course. This treatment plan was pursued diligently by all staff members, but it did not work. Chester became more and more withdrawn and fantasy-preoccupied. His hyperactivity diminished, but the home teacher still could not work with him and asked that home instruction be discontinued. Chester merely ran around or just sat and fantasized; he did no work at all. He also told bizarre stories. At home he was so destructive and out of control that his mother finally asked to have him placed. She herself improved remarkably. Her emotions were stabilized: she had no depressions and behaved more adequately.

Second Educational Evaluation at the Age of 9. The educational therapist found that Chester still could not spell, even though he had a perfect score on auditory discrimination. This meant that he could not blend letter sounds into words, a typical finding in organic reading and writing disorders. He still reversed letters and numbers. He was also much more suspicious: when the therapist asked him to write his name, he said, "I can't sign anything. It might be dangerous. I have to look for the fine print. I have to show it to my mother." She thought he might just be kidding her, but he meant it seriously. He also sang throughout her evaluation, and frequently whispered, "I think I am crazy."

FIG. 13.5.

FIGS. 13.5 AND 13.6.   Different stages of Chester's schizophrenia and hyperactivity as reflected in his drawings and in his Mosaic test. *Age 8:* Typical drawings indicating hyperactivity. They are also bizarre, which is typical for schizophrenia. He drew a "vulcan man and a vulcan woman, a vulcan illogical. If he smiles long, he can die from it. He has human blood and he has vulcan blood." The Mosaic design is also expansive and grandiose. It reaches the upper margin of the tray. Title: "A building. It talks to the space ship. It got transmitters to talk back and forth. That's the planet earth [line of oblong pieces], so it can take off! It is about two thousand billion feet long, two thousand billion people come into it, too!" (Color plate of Figure 13.5 follows p. 432.)

Third Psychologic Examination.   The third psychologic examination, also done at the age of 9, showed that Chester was worse. Projective tests revealed that he felt disorganized, was very angry, and thought of himself as being a monster.

It was still impossible to obtain an I.Q. score except on the Peabody Picture Vocabulary Test. This test showed a drop of his I.Q. from 121 at the age of 8 to 111. Such a drop on any intelligence test is always a serious sign since it indicates a deterioration of the child's condition.

Drug Treatment.   By the age of 9, Chester had been on drug therapy (Dexedrine and tranquilizers) for almost 2 years, with unsatisfactory results. When I asked him how these drugs made him feel, he answered: "They help me stay still." His hyperactivity had indeed lessened, but he had become worse in every other respect. These drugs had not arrested the schizophrenic process.

FIG. 13.6.

Fifth Psychiatric Examination. Chester was much more anxious, suspicious and withdrawn when I re-examined him at the age of 9. He clowned and seemed to respond to voices coming from "spirits." It was almost impossible to establish contact with him. He was not spontaneous. Only the Mosaic test and the drawings seemed to arouse his interest. He worked very fast this time and made his Mosaic design in half a minute. However, he broke it up immediately, then made exactly the same design. While he worked, he repeated over and over: "Western insurance, insurance policy sign." This was supposed to be the title for his Mosaic. He did not elaborate. This was the kind of repetitive stereotypical behavior found in schizophrenia.

Chester's Mosaic test showed deterioration when compared with the previous one. He made a small compact design, using only six pieces: three of them red, three blue. He put the red pieces in the middle and surrounded them with blue triangles. This small design showed how constricted his mental life had become. It had none of the diversity and liveliness of the Mosaic he had made 1 year before, and it showed no anxiety. These were serious signs, and so was his choice of colors, which reflected his overwhelming inner turmoil and explosiveness. The blue outer pieces seemed inadequate to contain the red inner core. I have seen such Mosaics in patients of all ages who committed violent acts. (See Figure 13.7.)

Drawings. His drawings had also become more constricted and bizarre. He drew stick figures on his own, and made a drawing of a person with a full body only when I requested it. Stick figures are a simplification and an evasion. Chester could not face drawing a body because his own felt too peculiar, as

FIG. 13.7.

FIGS. 13.7 AND 13.8. *Chester, age 9.* Hyperactivity has lessened. The schizophrenic process is worse. His reading disorder has remained static. He is too preoccupied with his bizarre fantasies. His drawings are now static and constricted. His body image has become so poor that he dares draw only simplified stick figures. The lower right-hand picture in Fig. 13.8 was drawn when I suggested he put a body on the picture of the woman. The Mosaic test is also severely constricted. It indicates a severe process. Red center pieces invariably indicate a tendency to serious violent outbursts. Chester had to be hospitalized. (Color plate of Figure 13.7 follows p. 432.)

if its parts were not hanging together properly. (See Figure 13.8; see also section on Drawings, Vol. I, p. 214.)

Final Diagnosis and Treatment Plan. The diagnosis childhood schizophrenia had been established beyond doubt. It was also clear what had to be done: Chester had to be hospitalized.

Follow-up. Chester was admitted to the child psychiatric ward of a prestigious private hospital soon after I examined him. He was treated with high doses of phenothiazines, mainly Thorazine. He told me years later that this had been an unpleasant experience. He said: "Thorazine made me groggy. When I get groggy and sleepy I get off balance. These medicines kept me off balance, uncomfortable, and I like to be comfortable!" He also said that the drug dosage was invariably increased whenever a child misbehaved. Apparently this was the only method used to discipline the children. He put it this way: "The nurses were lazy. When a kid looked sassy, *up* with the medicine! When a child misbehaved, *up* with the medicine!" He and his mother also mentioned a very unpleasant side effect of his drug treatment. It caused priapism, a painful and persistent erection. This is unfortunately typical for the management of children on many psychiatric wards. They are filled with drugs to the point of toxicity. Educational and psychotherapeutic methods that in the long run are more constructive and less damaging are neglected, and the children are not properly examined for their physical and psychologic reactions to drugs.

At the age of 10 Chester was sent to a residential treatment center in the country. This was a cottage-type private institution for inpatient treatment of severely disturbed boys. He stayed there for almost 4 years, and loved it.

FIG. 13.8

He told me, "It was more like a resort." His mother said, "It was good for both of us." The psychiatrists at the center took him off all drugs and treated him entirely with psychotherapeutic and educational methods. His hyperactivity lessened, and stopped completely when he was about 12 years old. His violent behavior also ended. He was discharged to his mother's care when he was 14. He continued to visit the center and remained under its supervision for another year.

I re-examined him when he was 15 years old. His mother had called the clinic to say that she wanted to bring him "to show all of you what you did, how well it worked out. He is a normal teenage boy now, and he can learn!" With great pride she showed me his report card and his graduation certificate from a regular junior high school. He had done well in all subjects (77 in math, 80 in social studies, etc.) except reading. He still read only at the third-grade level. His teachers told her that he still had "Dyslexia," and that he still "does not see letters right." They meant that he still reversed letters while reading or writing. His behavior was now excellent in school and at home. He had made friends and was not isolated anymore.

Chester was somewhat guarded, cautious, and anxious during my examination. He was restless, but not hyperactive, and in good contact throughout. It was understandable that he was afraid of psychiatrists. He told me how much he disliked these psychiatric examinations. He said: "You make a lot of decisions when you talk to people. What you say can really get them in trouble. You are making decisions for the person that has not even made a decision yet!" He was afraid that I might detect that there still was something wrong with him, and that I would send him away again. I had the feeling that he himself still had doubts about his own sanity and that he tried hard not to show his doubts.

I found no evidence of delusions or hallucinations. He no longer used neologisms, but still interspersed words into his narratives that were out of context. For instance, when he was telling me how difficult it sometimes was to talk to his mother, he paused suddenly—said "protective"—paused again, then finished his sentence. He got angry and said, "It just slipped out!" when I asked him what he meant by "protective." It seemed that this was a residue of his schizophrenic thought disorder. A sudden inner pressure, originating in the unconscious, forced him to interject the extraneous word.

His fantasies now seemed reality oriented. Only his preoccupation with what he called "inner space," meaning the ocean, was still somewhat bizarre and unrealistic. He talked at length and with great excitement about submarines he wanted to build, repeating over and over that "power" was a great problem. I could not pin him down to specifics so I asked him to draw a blueprint. He drew only vague outlines, indicating that he would solve that problem by building it like an airplane. This was clearly only a grandiose and entirely unrealistic fantasy, since he had no knowledge at all of engineering or even of simple mechanics.

As he had done at the age of 9, he refused to write anything but his name. This he wrote twice, saying he had not done it correctly, when it was actually written clearly and with great care. Oral reading still aroused great anxiety: he read word by word very slowly, pausing after each word. He could not read securely on one line and execute the return sweep properly (i.e., he had Linear Dyslexia). His blending was still unsatisfactory. He left out parts of words: for instance, he read "to" instead of "took." He understood the content of small paragraphs immediately in spite of this, due no doubt to his superior intelligence.

When I asked Chester how he could get such good marks while reading so poorly, he told me that his teachers let him read silently because he reads better that way. He could not explain how it was possible to read and understand a word silently that he could not say orally. For instance, if he read "to" instead of "took" during silent reading without correcting himself, the meaning of the entire sentence would be changed. He said that his teachers always questioned him in great detail about what he had read to make sure he had read it correctly. I suspect that he skipped difficult words and guessed the content, as do so many other children with a reading disorder. (See Silent Reading, Vol. I, p. 112.)

Mosaic Test. Chester approached this test in exactly the same way as he had at the ages of 8 and 9. Not being able to make up his mind, he made one design after the other. He worked very slowly (it took him 20 minutes to complete the test), and broke up three designs. These three started at the right upper corner and hugged the margin, which showed his great anxiety. He turned the tray while making his final design, a sign of negativism, just like the turning of Rorschach cards.

Chester's final Mosaic had no title. He still did not seem satisfied. He took the blue and the yellow diamond off and said, "With these two off, it could look like a rocket." Then he put both pieces back.

Chester's Mosaic was just as compact as the last one. It had one more piece, seven instead of the previous six, but its structure was even less solid than 6 years before.

This Mosaic showed that his clinical improvement was not on solid ground, that the schizophrenic process was continuing beneath the surface. The Mosaic test is more sensitive to schizophrenia than any other projective technique. It is a reliable indicator of the quality of a remission. Wertham has shown this in the chapter on the Mosaic test in *Projective Psychology* (1959), as well as in other publications. (See Figure 13.9.)

Drawings. Chester's drawings reflected his clinical improvement. His superior intelligence and his creative talent finally surfaced. He drew a huge tree standing next to a stream that flowed over some rocks. The picture was well composed, and there was nothing bizarre about it. The enormous crown of the tree reflected his exuberant fantasy life. Its openness towards the top expressed the openness and vagueness of his fantasies and their drift away from reality, as well as his persistent grandiosity. The crown extended beyond the edge of the paper. Anxiety and feelings of insecurity were indicated by the fine, often interrupted lines he drew, by the exposed roots, and by the lack of a baseline. (See Figure 13.10.)

Chester had indeed fully recovered from his hyperactivity, and his schizophrenia was in remission. The hyperactivity subsided first, before the schizophrenia improved. This is just one more example of many showing that hyperactivity, whatever its cause, is a symptom of childhood only, that it subsides when childhood ends and adolescence begins. (See Course, Vol. II, p. 656.)

The prognosis of Chester's schizophrenia was much more problematical.

FIG. 13.9.   FIG. 13.10.

FIGS. 13.9 AND 13.10.   *Chester, age 15:* His hyperactivity has subsided completely. It is a self-limited symptom, confined to immature organisms only. He has made an excellent social recovery from schizophrenia after years in a residential treatment center. The beautiful tree next to a brook reflects his recovery. The crown shows his persistent exuberant and unrealistic fantasy life. However, the Mosaic design is still constricted and indicates that a schizophrenic process is continuing beneath the surface, and that his remission may not be long-lasting. (Color plate of Figure 13.9 follows p. 432.)

One could only hope that the remission would last for many years or that it might turn out to have been a full and permanent recovery. Only repeated follow-up examinations into and through adulthood could provide answers.

That his reading and writing disorder persisted so long, that it outlasted his hyperactivity and the remission of his schizophrenia, confirmed my impression that it had a separate organic origin and was not caused by schizophrenia.

I gave a paper on "The Misuse of the Diagnosis Childhood Schizophrenia" at the Second International Congress for Psychiatry, which was held in Zurich, Switzerland in 1957. It was published in the *American Journal of Psychiatry* (1958) and in German, in the *Jahrbuch für Jugendpsychiatrie und ihre Grenzgebiete* (Vol. 2, Hans Huber, Bern, 1960). It dealt with the erroneous diagnosis of childhood schizophrenia that was then widespread in the United States. I stressed that this hindered the progress of psychiatry as a clinical science, and that it presented a threat especially to those children who lived in a socially difficult milieu.

It has unfortunately come to the point where a paper on "The Misuse of the Diagnosis Hyperactivity" ought to be written. The same type of superficial clinical examinations combined with nosologic confusion underlie both misuses.

For instance, some hyperactive children who formerly would have been diagnosed as suffering from childhood schizophrenia (rightly or wrongly) are now apt to be diagnosed as simply hyperactive, or as having a "hyperkinetic reaction of childhood" or a "hyperactive child syndrome." The overuse of the diagnosis hyperactivity is not confined to children suffering from schizophrenia. This is actually the smallest group because the underlying schizophrenic process is often so difficult to detect. The greatest misuse occurs with regard to children whose symptoms have a psychologic basis, and to those who have an increased, but not a pathologic motor drive.

Psychologic Causes

Hyperactivity can occur entirely on a psychologic basis without any organic involvement. It may be part of a reactive disorder (e.g., a reactive depression) or of a neurosis. It falls invariably into the anxious category. These children express anxiety due to many different causes by being hyperactive. Their anxiety may be due to distressing life experiences; to neurotic distortions of these experiences; to a reading, writing, and arithmetic disorder; or to any number of other reality or unconscious factors. Like other dramatic and easily observable psychogenic symptoms, this one is, in part, a cry for help. This highlights the importance of diagnosing the psychogenic origin of this symptom correctly so that the child gets what he needs: treatment of the underlying psychopathology combined with elimination or at least modification of the damaging, anxiety-provoking familial and social factors. (See Hyperactivity Caused by Anxiety, p. 593.)

Psychogenic hyperactivity, too, occurs only in childhood. Adolescents and adults do not react to any form of anxiety with hyperactivity.

Differential Diagnosis

The diagnosis of psychogenic hyperactivity requires special care so that it does not become overused and abused. Children who suffer from all kinds of behavior disorders and neuroses are far too readily classified as hyperactive. This affects especially those children who are explosive, violent, and unpredictable, those who like to dramatize their fantasies and emotions, and all children who are generally difficult to control and to teach. Children with less dramatic symptoms—those who are just tense, restless, excitable, and inattentive—are also often wrongly called hyperactive. Close observation in different settings. will show that the motor behavior of all these children is actually tense and inhibited rather than out of control, and that they do not just run around wildly.

The erroneous diagnosis of hyperactivity would not be so harmful if a search for the underlying psychopathology were undertaken in any case. Unfortunately, however, most such children are treated only with drugs as a matter of routine as soon as the diagnosis of hyperactivity has been made; psychologic, familial, and social factors are ignored or neglected. It is, of course, simpler and cheaper just to give such a child drugs rather than to spend time unraveling and treating the underlying causes. But in the end it is much more costly for the child.

The plight of 6-year-old Kirk with his suicide and murder attempts shows the damaging effect of such one-sided and short-sighted approach. His hyperactivity had an organic basis, which at least justified the use of drugs. (See p. 606, 604 under Violent Behavior.) The harm is much greater when all symptoms are psychogenic and drugs are contraindicated, especially stimulants such as Dexedrine or Ritalin. (See Hyperactivity with Anxiety, p. 593; Exogenic Psychoses, p. 623; and Treatment, Vol. I, p. 330.)

Time Sense Neurosis

Children who suffer from what I call a *time sense neurosis* are especially prone to be misdiagnosed as hyperactive. This is an anxiety neurosis with an unconsciously distorted sense of time. It is very frequent also in adolescents and adults where, however, it does not cause the same motor symptoms. Real and fictitious time limits are intimately linked with a fear of death in the unconscious of these patients.

Children with this neurosis act as if they had to meet one deadline (in its literal sense) after the other all day long, as if death or some other terrible catastrophe awaited them if they overstepped this line. It is interesting in this connection that the word "deadline" was originally used for a line around a prison beyond which a prisoner could go only at the risk of death (i.e., of being shot by a guard). These children are therefore tense, feel driven, and are always in a rush. They tend to jump up and down in anxious anticipation of disaster while working at their desks. They run rather than walk from one assignment to the next.

They feel that they must finish whatever they are doing with the utmost speed, and claim much too soon that they are finished. Their work is therefore sloppy, superficial, and full of omissions. Their oral reading is hasty and inaccurate, and they only scan the text while reading silently, provided they could pay attention long enough to learn to read. Their handwriting is illegible because they write much too fast. Depending on the age of onset of their neurosis, they have trouble learning to read or, when it starts later, cannot read and write fluently, rapidly, and accurately. (See chapter on Psychogenic Reading Disorders, Vol. I, p. 249.)

To subsume the symptoms of these children under hyperactivity alone may retard or prevent the recognition of the underlying anxiety neurosis, and with it causative treatment. To alleviate the symptoms that could be misinterpreted as hyperactivity may not even require lengthy psychotherapy, provided the underlying neurotic time complex is recognized. These children do not know why they constantly feel so driven, rushed, and anxious. They are not aware of being afraid of deadlines. I have found that they usually respond with a feeling of immense relief as soon as they realize that what terrifies them are only imaginary deadlines, and their drivenness decreases or disappears. This can often be achieved in a few psychotherapy sessions because the deadline fear is usually not deeply repressed. This does not mean that the anxiety neurosis has been cured, but the child can function and learn much better in the meantime. (See Treatments, Vol. I, p. 331; and chapter on Psychogenic Reading Disorders, Vol. I, pp. 246–249.)

Reactive Disorders

1. *Reaction to a Chaotic Home* (Social Pressure Syndrome). A child's hyperactivity may be part of his reaction to a chaotic, disorganized, uncaring, socially and emotionally deprived family situation. At the Lafargue Clinic we used a special diagnostic category for symptoms caused by an extremely stressful, destructive, and generally hostile life situation: We called it a *Social Pressure Syndrome.* The hyperactivity of these children is part of such a syndrome. Like adults and adolescents with this syndrome, they, too, are helpless victims of a hostile environment. Such a situation may make a child depressed so that his hyperactivity may be part of a reactive depression. Preschool and early elementary-school-age children, however, may react to such a home with hyperactivity without being depressed. It is therefore useful to separate such a reaction from a reactive depression.

The hyperactivity of these children is due to immaturity and anxiety. They retain the motor and emotional behavior of 2-year-olds, especially when their motor drive is very strong. They continue to express their emotions immediately in dramatic muscular activity beyond the age when they should have learned to pay intellectual attention and to control motor expressions. (See Immediate, Derived, Sensory, and Intellectual Attention, pp. 538, 539, 540.)

Their general immaturity is due to emotional, intellectual, and often also physical neglect by their parents or by other adults charged with raising them. These adults are either too ignorant or do not care enough to train and to educate them so that they can mature. Many such children also want to remain babyish. The only happy and secure time free from anxieties they can remember was when they were a baby or a very young, helpless child. This was the only time in their lives when they had their usually overworked mother's undivided attention. There are, as a rule, several younger siblings who have occupied this place since then. Jealousy of these siblings and anger at their mother and their father, if he is in the home, as well as a feeling of having been abandoned as far as emotional support is concerned, also play a role in their hyperactivity and in causing other disruptive behavior at home and in school. The anxiety underlying these children's hyperactivity is due to a lack of rules or of any other structure in their homes. This creates emotional and intellectual chaos in the child. Ethical confusion is one of its most destructive aspects: these children literally do not know what is right and what is wrong for them or for others. They operate under their own, personal pleasure principle only. They do what they feel driven to do in order to survive.

These children's homes are without regular meals or bedtimes. They grab whatever they can find in the refrigerator at any time, day or night. They go to sleep when they feel like it, often with their clothes on. Many of them have no bed of their own.

It is quite common for them to continue wetting their bed and soiling their pants. Their clothes are often not kept clean and repaired, and they have not been taught to keep their body clean either. These homes are usually overcrowded, too hot in the summer and too cold in the winter, with not enough blankets to cover everyone. At least one television set is going all the time, day and night.

The punishment meted out to these children is usually erratic, sudden, unexpected, unpredictable, and often so severe that they actually are "battered" children. Alcoholism and/or drug addiction play a large role in causing such homes. However, one cannot put all the blame on the parents of these children; they, too, may suffer from the *Social Pressure Syndrome.* This does not excuse their mismanagement and cruelty, but it must be recognized for treatment planning.

The existence and actual conditions of such homes are not generally covered in studies of children's disorders. Yet they are a powerful cause of behavior and learning disorders, and are much more frequent than social studies and statistics indicate. I have visited such homes and studied their impact. Since concrete case studies of the milieu of such children are nearly always omitted in clinical research publications, a full and detailed description of such a home will be included here.

NED, 7 YEARS OLD: HYPERACTIVITY CAUSED BY A CHAOTIC HOME.   The hyperactive behavior of 7-year-old Ned was caused by just such a chaotic home. He was one of the six children in my study (all boys ages 7 to 10) whose hyperactivity had a psychologic basis.

Home.   Ned's teacher, the school nurse, and the social worker visited the home many times because the parents refused to come to school to talk about their children who were always in trouble. The conditions they found were always the same. The mother managed to keep the children and their tenement apartment clean, in spite of rats and overcrowding. However, what the workers called the "emotional tone" was invariably "chaotic." Ned and his three brothers, aged 1½, 9, and 11, ran around and did as they pleased. There was no set time for meals or for going to sleep. Fortunately, food was plentiful and the boys did not go hungry. However, all of them still drank out of baby bottles. This continuing babyish habit showed their desire to be taken care of and protected like babies, needs that had never been adequately fulfilled for any one of them.

Ned shared his bed with 9-year-old Manuel; 11-year-old Raymond slept on the couch together with his baby brother. None of the boys got enough sleep, because there was no set bedtime and the apartment was noisy. Two or all three of their television sets were often turned on to different channels at the same time, day and night. The children watched too many hours during the day and much too late into the night. They were sleepy in the morning, got up when they felt like it, and were always late for school. Frequently the parents did not bother to send them to school or did not make sure that they arrived there, even though the school was right across the street. The three school-age boys cut classes, often did not return to school after the lunch recess, and sometimes did not come to school at all for weeks at a time without being sick. Ned frequently ran out of the house and roamed the streets until late at night.

Father. The father was irritable and did not seem to like his children. He was hostile towards the school and said quite candidly that he did not care how they behaved and learned in school. He told the school staff that it was up to them to make his boys behave. Alcohol played a role in his irresponsible and destructive behavior: he was drunk on the few occasions when he visited the school. There were rumors among his neighbors that he was involved with drugs. All of them were afraid of him. He stayed home most of the day, unable to work because of some physical disability. The clinic staff could not find out what his diagnosis was in spite of many contacts with the Department of Welfare, which supported the family. This is but one example of the lack of exchange of important information between agencies dealing with child welfare. He stayed in or on top of the bed most of the day, being waited on by his wife, who spent most of her time taking care of him instead of her children.

Mother. No one in school had succeeded in establishing a relationship with her, so that she could be helped to manage her children better. Whenever she came to school she was so upset, anxious, angry, and confused that it was impossible to communicate with her.

She had been referred for a psychiatric examination many times, but had never gone to a psychiatric clinic. I made numerous attempts to reach her, but she came to my office in the school only once, when I examined 11-year-old Raymond. By then I had already examined Ned and started treating him, of course with her and her husband's written permission. As soon as she entered my office, she began to yell at Raymond and me. She would not sit down and talk quietly. She paced back and forth, repeating that her apartment would burn down with her husband in it, unless she went home right away. She was furious at Raymond for having put her in this position and called him "crazy"; he began to cry. I tried unsuccessfully to calm her down and to explain to her that her boys were not "crazy," but unhappy and confused and in need of help, as was she herself. She did not listen and ran out of the office without waiting for Raymond. It was, of course, impossible to diagnose her condition based only on this brief observation. It seemed to me that her dramatic behavior was, at least in part, deliberate, and that she was very anxious, angry, confused, and childish, but apparently not psychotic. Her intelligence seemed to be quite limited, so that I thought she might be mentally defective.

Just how incapable these parents were of controlling and protecting their children was shown by the following episode, which disturbed the school and the neighborhood deeply. A Kindergarten child had fallen from a roof to her death directly across from the school during lunch recess, in full view of parents, teachers, and children. All of them were still in a state of shock the next day when they saw Ned and his brothers run around on the ledge of the same roof. They yelled at them to get off, but the boys just laughed and continued their play. Their mother saw this and said nothing. She was standing on the street talking to neighbors. Her callous and stupid behavior shocked the school community. They yelled at her to make her boys get off and stay off that roof.

Punishment. Both father and mother lashed out at all the boys from time to time when they could no longer stand the chaos in their home. They beat them so severely that all three had scars. Ned came to school several times with his lips and nose bloody from these beatings. When I asked him how he was being punished, he told me: "My daddy hits me with a stick, my mamie with a belt." Then he showed me numerous scars on his arms and a long one on his right knee that had had to be closed with stitches. He told me he had thought he was going to die when he had to be taken to a hospital for these stitches. He also said that his brother, Raymond, once had to have eight stitches after his mother had hit him on the head with her shoe. I saw that scar on Raymond's scalp later on when I examined him.

Medical Neglect. Ned and his brothers were not taken to clinics for medical care when it was urgently needed. Ned had situs inversus, that is, his heart and major vessels were on the right instead of the left side of his body. He had been diagnosed as suffering from an "A 1" cardiac impairment. He was supposed to attend a cardiac clinic regularly, but his parents did not take him. They had not even taken him to a hospital when he had a severe foot infection.

Both he and Raymond needed eyeglasses and dental care, but this, too, was neglected. The school physician, the school nurse, the social worker, the psychologist, the teachers, and I tried in vain to get the parents to attend to the medical needs of their children.

School Behavior. Ned was in the second grade when I examined him. His hyperactivity had been noticed from the day he entered school, in Kindergarten. It had gotten so much worse that he had to be suspended many times. He also fought with other children, told lies, and had hit teachers. He had no window or key fascination, but he did set fires.

His teacher described his behavior to me in the following way:

I find it impossible to teach a lesson with him in the classroom. He runs around and out in the hall. He roams the halls and cannot be stopped by anyone. He cannot stay in his seat. He calls out constantly and makes animal sounds. He answers back and is rude. He clowns. When approached on a one-to-one basis he can be sincere, but at times he may find the whole situation funny. He has trouble reading and writing.

Even the gym teacher found him "wild" and could not control him.

Psychologic Examination. The psychologic examination showed that his intelligence was within the normal range. There were no indications of any organic involvement. His contact with reality was found to be adequate and there was no evidence on any test of schizophrenia. The psychologist found Ned to be "a boy with great anxieties for which he is poorly defended. He manages not to get overwhelmed by avoiding contact with people, and by using few fragile, counterphobic mechanisms." He made the following recommendations:

Some intensive therapeutic intervention with his family should help tip the balance so that Ned can at least tolerate and be tolerated in a normal school situation. If that is impossible (and judging from the parents' unwillingness to seek mental help it would seem almost impossible), he will most probably need to be put in a more therapeutic milieu than either his class or his home.

He had a residential treatment center in mind.

Psychiatric Examination. During my examination Ned was hyperactive and very distractible. He walked or ran around the office and sat down only when his arms and hands could be active, when playing with small cars, drawing, or during the Mosaic test. Through all this he was in good contact, talking incessantly, freely, and apparently truthfully.

He was a very sturdy, muscular boy with a great need for physical activity.

He looked like a little prizefighter. Soon after he walked into my office, he flexed his arm muscles to show me how big and strong they were and said: "Me, Hercules!" He admired the Superman-type heroes in comic books and on television and wanted very much to be like them. Some of his destructive actions were direct imitations of the behavior he had observed in these mass media.

Children with this type of physical makeup are more prone to react with hyperactivity than others. That is why Ned was the only one among the three school-age brothers who was hyperactive. His two older brothers were also always in some trouble in school, but they did not react with hyperactivity to their chaotic home. Instead they were depressed and anxious. Their anxiety found expression in tension, restlessness, fear of adults and other children, and daydreaming. They were rather thin and tall and not as muscular as Ned. While Ned expressed every emotion, fantasy, and thought immediately in some form of motor activity, they were introspective. All three boys had a severe attention disorder that caused their reading disorder.

Role of Physical Constitution.   The relationship between physical constitution and mental illness has been worked out quite thoroughly in adults. Children's pathologic and normal behavior is just as much influenced by their physical makeup. A study of this relationship in children has, however, unfortunately been sorely neglected. Stella Chess' concept of "temperament" is not identical with physical constitution.

Ned gave a realistic description of his home, including spiritualistic meetings that frightened him. He talked about frightening dreams and about his fear of ghosts. He was especially anxious at night, in the dark, because of all the disquieting noises in the apartment and outside in the hall. These seemed to be real experiences and not hallucinations; nor was there any evidence of delusions.

Reading, Writing, and Arithmetic.   Ned was a complete nonreader. He could not even write all letters. His arithmetic was a little better: He could add beyond 10, but had trouble subtracting; he loved to make money carrying packages and had managed to learn how many pennies were in a nickel, a dime, and a dollar. He did not know the value of a quarter, however; this is more difficult to comprehend.

Drawings.   The figures he drew were in movement: the boy was swimming, the girl jumping rope. This is typical for hyperactive children. That he had a body image problem was indicated by the poor form of all his drawings. (See Drawings, Vol. I, p. 214.)

Mosaic Test.   Ned's Mosaic also gave the illusion of motion. The emphasis on movement in the Mosaic test, as in the drawings, is a characteristic finding in cases of hyperactivity. When he made "A robot going through the hills," he put it together in a great hurry (only 5 minutes), got up, ran around, and refused to point out to me what the details of his Mosaic were supposed to represent. He just motioned that the entire robot moved.

His design was margin-bound: it hugged the left margin of the tray, an indication of anxiety. Red played a prominent role in his Mosaic, as it does with many other hyperactive children. Almost one-third of all the pieces were red, and all of them were in important positions. A large red triangle anchored the design to the left margin where the movement started, and six red diamonds jutted out underneath the entire Mosaic. They were either the legs of the robot or some mechanism that made it move. These red pieces expressed Ned's inner turmoil, his almost constant state of overexcitement, his emotional overstimulation. The form of his Mosaic showed that his intelligence was average. (See also a discussion of this Mosaic in the section on the Mosaic test under Hyperactivity, Tests, p. 611–615, and also Figure 13.2.)

Diagnosis. I made the diagnosis of hyperactivity on a reactive basis with a severe reading and writing disorder due to a severe attention deficit.

Ned and his brothers were subject to such emotional neglect and to such severe beatings by their parents that they might fall into the category of "battered children."

Recommendations. I made the following recommendations:

1. The protective services of the Department of Welfare should be alerted to the danger of child abuse in this family. This agency had the duty and the power to investigate whether charges of child neglect or abuse could or should be brought against these parents.

2. Pediatric re-examination, return to the cardiac clinic, an eye examination, and dental care. The school physician, the school nurse, the social worker, and I would work together to get the parents to take Ned to these clinics.

3. Placement in a class for emotionally disturbed children.

4. Reading treatment on an individual basis. Ned might never learn to read adequately without this additional help.

5. Psychotherapy on an individual basis.

6. Ned might benefit from drug treatment. A sedative at night seemed indicated because it was so difficult for him to fall asleep. This could be effective only if parental management could be changed so that all television sets within vision and hearing of the children were turned off before, during, and after their bedtime, which should be early and rigidly enforced. No drug could possibly be prescribed unless and until the parents cooperated fully with the

clinic staff. Otherwise they could not be trusted to give Ned any drug at the proper time.

7. If the parents continued to ignore and to sabotage the school's and the clinic's efforts, legal steps should be taken to force them to cooperate. Under existing conditions such administrative-legal measures are, of course, extremely difficult to carry out.

Course. I started to treat Ned psychotherapeutically, and he was eventually placed in a special class. No other recommendation was carried out. My effort failed and had to be abandoned. Ned did not even show up for his weekly sessions in my office in his school regularly, because he was so frequently absent without any excuse and could not be found in or around the school building. The social worker and the psychologist had the same experience with his two brothers whom they treated. It was impossible to involve the parents. The clinic staff was powerless and helpless in this situation.

During my many conferences with the principal and his assistants, I urged them to take administrative measures to help these children, such as calling a hearing in the office of the Assistant Superintendent. Parents can be forced to attend such a hearing and can be pressured into complying with the school's recommendations. These are extreme measures, however, and should be taken only where the physical and/or mental life of children is at stake, as it was in the case of Ned and his brothers. No such actions were taken. The Department of Welfare did not act either. No wonder that Ned's hyperactivity and his other disturbing symptoms did not improve during the following years, as long as I could keep in touch with his situation, namely until he was 12 years old.

It is unfortunately far from rare that those in authority who have the power and the duty to protect children and to save them from physical, emotional, and mental destruction take no action at all. No new legislation can change that. It is always easier to do nothing; it saves time, energy, and aggravation. Such administrative inaction and indifference is the enemy of children with a chaotic home almost as much as the brutality and callousness of their own parents. Here is an area of causal factors for juvenile delinquency and violence. (See section on Juvenile Delinquency in Sociogenic Reading Disorders, Vol. I, p. 284–285.)

Reactive Depression

Depression in children before adolescence does not always cause the classic and obvious symptoms. Many children who are truly depressed (not just temporarily sad) show a diverse symptomatology that includes hyperactivity. I have shown the problems connected with such "masked" childhood depressions in "The Psychotherapeutic Management of Children With Masked Depressions" (1974). This applies to reactive as well as neurotic depressions. An underlying depression should therefore be kept in mind during the examination of a hyperactive child.

Remschmidt and Dauner suggest a separate classification for these children. They classify them as suffering from an "Agitated-Depressive Syndrome" (1971, p. 19).

JOE, 8 YEARS OLD: HYPERACTIVITY DUE TO A REACTIVE DEPRESSION BECAUSE OF TUBERCULOSIS.   A reactive depression caused the hyperactivity of only one child in my study out of the six with psychogenic hyperactivity. This was 8-year-old Joey. I examined him on a pediatric ward for children with tuberculosis, where he had been for almost 1 year.

Tuberculosis is usually treated with drugs on an outpatient basis, but Joey had no home to which to go. Both parents and three siblings also suffered from tuberculosis; they had all gone home. His illness was more severe and there was no place for him in the overcrowded home. He had become so hyperactive and difficult to manage that the nurses, the physicians, and the teachers running the hospital school requested a consultation. Drugs had not calmed him down.

I found that Joey was sullen, restless, and hyperactive. However, it was possible to calm him down, and he was in good contact and eager to talk. No one had taken the time to let him talk about his worries. He was very much afraid of death. One of his sisters had recently died in a fire, and he thought the mysterious illness in his "chest," which gave him no pain or other discomfort, might kill him. His reading had remained on the primer level because he had missed so much school and could not concentrate in the hospital school. This also depressed him.

I have found that masked depressions, sometimes causing hyperactivity, lie behind most of the behavior disturbances so distressing to the nurses in their management of pediatric wards.

These childhood depressions are basically benign and can be cured, provided attention is paid to the child's plight. Psychotherapy can often be effective within just a few sessions. Sometimes the very act of talking about depressed feelings and thoughts may give enormous relief and help lift a depression. Depressed children are lonely children who have no one to whom they can talk seriously about their most intimate concerns. Giving names to mysterious emotions has a healing effect in all psychotherapy; this is certainly true for depressions. As soon as the depressive mood has been lifted, depressive symptoms such as hyperactivity disappear. This was true for Joey when he at last had a chance to talk freely about his feeling of being doomed physically and about his concern as to his intelligence. He felt very "dumb" because he could not read like the other children. His depression and that of so many other children with pulmonary tuberculosis and other physical diseases could have been prevented if only someone had listened to him.

Physically ill children must be given a chance to explain exactly what they think is wrong with their bodies. Physicians and other adults usually have no idea what the child's thoughts and fantasies are in this respect. Only if they listen carefully can they straighten out the many misunderstandings and fantastic ideas children usually have about their illnesses.

NEUROSES.   Hyperactivity can be part of a childhood neurosis. This does not occur in the rare obsessive-compulsive neuroses, but is fairly frequent in anxiety neurosis. Children with hypochondria or a hysterical neurosis usually are not hyperactive, nor are children with any one of the psychosomatic disorders (e.g., asthma).

Four of the six children in my study with psychogenic hyperactivity had an anxiety neurosis. The behavior of all of them was so disruptive that they had to be suspended from school numerous times. This is but one more proof of the clinical fact that neuroses can be just as severe and difficult to treat as psychoses. Two of these children had severe tantrums; all set fires and had nightmares.

JEFFREY, 6 YEARS OLD: SEVERE NEUROTIC HYPERACTIVITY.   Hyperactivity can be the expression of a child's terror of being abandoned by his parents, as was true for two of the children in my study with an anxiety neurosis. One of them had witnessed serious parental strife since birth; the other, Jeffrey, was actually boarded out from the age of 3 to 5 while his parents were separated. During that period he was in three different homes. One of his foster parents used to lock him up in a dark cellar where there were rats, or in a closet. His hyperactivity started after that, even though his parents reunited. Apparently he never fully overcame these traumatic experiences, which occurred so early in his life. His neurosis was so severe and so difficult to treat, and his general behavior was so violent, that he had to be sent to a psychiatric hospital. He had attempted suicide, set fires, and run after his mother with a knife. He was the only child in this group who had to be hospitalized. His hyperactivity subsided completely when he was 12 years old and did not recur. I followed him up until the age of 16: this boy's neurosis was so severe that it had not subsided completely even at that age. His reading had improved, but he still had Linear Dyslexia and his performance did not rise above the fifth-grade level in spite of his average intelligence.

Course

The course is invariably stormy while this symptom lasts. It disrupts the life of the child and of his family, even when it is comparatively mild. It was so severe in 13 (almost half) of the 29 children in my study, that they had to be suspended from school attendance, some of them numerous times. Six of these children (one girl, five boys) had to be put on home instruction because they could not function in any group, not even in special classes. Adrian and Chester were two of these children. (See pp. 616, 631.)

Hyperactivity can be so severe and so unresponsive to any form of treatment that the child has to be hospitalized. This happened to seven children in my study, all of them boys. They had to be sent to psychiatric hospitals or residential treatment centers. Ramon (p. 621), Chester (p. 631), and Jeffrey (p. 656) belonged to this group.

Outcome

The long-range prognosis for this symptom is favorable, even for the severest forms and whatever the cause. The pediatrician Sidney S. Gellis stressed this fact in an editorial in the *American Journal of Diseases of Children*, where he wrote: "Hyperactivity is self-limited. Follow-up studies indicate that whether treated or not the condition resolves to a great degree" (1975, p. 1324). My study confirms this. The severest forms of hyperactivity subsided in adolescence even when treatment had been discontinued. The postencephalitic hyperactivity of Adrian (p. 616), the schizophrenic form of Chester (p. 631), and the neurotic form of Jeffrey (p. 656) are examples of this outcome.

Hyperactivity is evidently a childhood symptom, confined to an immature organism and subsiding spontaneously with maturation. With treatment it usually subsides earlier. The reasons for spontaneous recoveries are not certain, but it can be assumed that cortical and subcortical impulses that restrain the motor drive become dominant when the organism matures. States of overexcitement and agitation occurring later on in life have a different structure. (See Organic Basis of the Attention Process, p. 502; and sections on Causes of Hyperactivity, pp. 615–623, 645–656, 647–654).

Treatment

Drugs

STIMULANTS. The action of so-called stimulants, such as amphetamine sulfate (Benzedrine), dextroamphetamine sulfate (Dexedrine), levoamphetamine succinate (Cydril), pemoline (Cylert), methylphenidate (Ritalin), and so on, is supposed to be specific for hyperactivity. A number of hyperactive children are indeed calmed by these drugs. The result is sometimes striking and may be apparent soon after the first ingestion of the drug. The reasons for this seemingly paradoxic reaction (i.e., inhibition of the motor drive through further stimulation) are still speculative. These are clinical observations that ought to be investigated by taking Wilder's "Law of Initial Value" into consideration. Most studies, including textbooks of pharmacology, unfortunately do not even mention this physiologic law. (See description of this law in section on Physical Changes During Attention, p. 525.)

What these drugs have in common is that they are sympathomimetic (i.e., they stimulate the sympathetic nervous system to varying degrees). This stimulation affects lower as well as higher levels of this system, including its central regulation and integration in the hypothalamus. It is also assumed that these drugs stimulate cortical areas and the reticular activating system. (See description of this system in section on Organic Basis of the Attention Process, p. 502; and under Organic Causes of Hyperactivity, p. 615.)

The stimulating effect of these drugs is quite apparent in adults, in children who are not hyperactive, and unfortunately also in many children who are hyperactive. These drugs are not really specific for hyperactivity; in fact, they may even increase the hyperactivity of hyperactive children and cause hyperactivity in children who are not hyperactive. They do not affect the motor drive in adults in the same way.

The "Law of Initial Value" can provide a more plausible explanation for these different reactions than any other physiologic mechanism. It is not known exactly how this Law works in relation to these complicated drug reactions. It can be assumed, however, based on this Law, that the reaction of the sympathetic nervous system depends on the level of its tonus or excitation before the drug was administered. The higher the excitation, the smaller the remaining excitability. Beyond a certain critical level of excitation, the system is not capable of reacting any more to any further stimulation and a reversal of its customary reaction takes place. Under these circumstances it remains on the same level of excitation for awhile and then relaxes completely (i.e., has a so-called paradoxic reaction).

Applied to the reaction of hyperactive children to sympathomimetic drugs, this means that their hyperactivity will subside only if their sympathetic nervous system was in a high state of excitation on all its levels before they took the drug. Some of these children will, however, remain just as hyperactive, because their sympathetic nervous system was incapable of responding to any additional stimulation, but had not yet reached the point of no return where a paradoxic reaction occurs. An increased dosage may then have the desired result.

Hyperactive children with a low initial level of sympathetic excitation will, of course, become more hyperactive. The critical tonal levels that determine these different reactions are not known. Tonal levels can be measured with pupillography and other techniques. It is a pity that the research needed for these determinations has not been done, and thus we cannot predict a hyperactive child's reaction to these drugs. The child's basic autonomic reactivity, whether he is vagotonic, sympathicotonic, or has a well-balanced autonomic nervous system, must also play a role here. (See Pupillography, p. 527; and Changes in the Autonomic Nervous System, under Physical Changes During Attention, p. 522–525.)

Until the autonomic nervous system of hyperactive children has been studied thoroughly before, during, and after treatment with stimulant drugs, no progress can be made in this complicated pharmacologic field, and children will continue to be harmed. I have seen psychotic reactions worse than the uncontrollable excitement and hyperactivity of the 6-year-old boy who felt "like a lion" and ran around wildly for 24 hours. (See Hyperactivity Caused by Anxiety, p. 593.)

In any evaluation of the reaction of hyperactive children to these drugs, it is also important to realize that a child's sympathetic nervous system, as well as the hypothalamic areas dealing with the motor drive, can become overstimulated by psychologic as well as organic stimuli. The fact that a child calms down in response to stimulating drugs can therefore not be used to differentiate organic from psychogenic hyperactivity, as has been suggested.

Undesirable Effects. By stimulating the sympathetic nervous system, these drugs invariably affect the entire autonomic nervous system and therefore also have other than antihyperactivity effects. This fact is not made sufficiently clear in the voluminous literature dealing with these drugs. Pharmaceutical firms advertise their respective drugs by stressing their "minimal" sympathomimetic effects. However, the actions of the sympathetic and of the parasympathetic nervous system are so finely and delicately balanced and so dependent on each other, that even minimal sympathetic stimulation affects the entire autonomic nervous system of the child.

These drugs disturb the balance between the two systems that is so vital for the child's development and general well-being. To call the ensuing symptoms "side" effects is a misnomer, since they are integral effects of sympathetic stimulation. It is, for instance, well known that these drugs interfere with sleep. The last dose must therefore be given no later than early in the afternoon, preferably right after lunch; otherwise the child will not be able to fall asleep. The reason for this is that the sympathetic nervous system keeps the body awake and ready for action, while parasympathetic activity makes sleep possible. This is clearly a sympathomimetic effect. The assumed stimulation of the reticular formation by these drugs also prevents sleep. (See Sleep, under Manifestations of Hyperactivity, p. 600.)

Another well-known effect of stimulant drugs is loss of appetite. For this reason they have been and unfortunately sometimes still are prescribed for adults who want to lose weight. In children such loss of appetite may have serious consequences. Safer, Allen, and Barr were first to point out that these drugs may retard the growth and weight gain of hyperactive children. The children they studied remained shorter and thinner than would normally have been expected. Their studies also showed that this growth deficit was not necessarily made up later on, after the drug had been discontinued (1972).

Children on these drugs often also complain of stomach aches, sometimes feel nauseated and vomit, and have other digestive disturbances. The imbalance of their autonomic nervous system apparently accounts for all these symptoms. The sympathetic nervous system inhibits the peristalsis and secretion of the esophagus, stomach, and small intestines, and constricts their vessels. It also decreases the motility and tonus of the colon and rectum. Its stimulation therefore causes loss of appetite and inhibits digestion.

Parasympathetic action, on the other hand, increases the motility and secretions of the esophagus, stomach, and intestines, and dilates their vessels; it makes normal digestion and bowel movements possible. Sympathetic stimulation by these drugs apparently prevents the parasympathetic system from becoming active at the right time and/or with sufficient strength to make normal digestion possible. This may take place without a stomachache or nausea, so that neither the child nor his parents notice that he does not eat and digest his food properly anymore. To minimize this effect these drugs should be given after meals, not before the child eats. This rule is not always observed because drug absorption is faster and more reliable when the stomach is empty, before meals (Carter & Gould, 1968, p. 881).

Children on these drugs frequently also show a number of other effects, for instance a characteristic facial pallor, a dry mouth, or focal sweating especially of the palms of their hands, which can be very embarrassing. Sympathetic stimulation constricts the capillaries of their face, produces thick saliva, and causes localized sweating. It may also cause headaches and dizziness by constricting cerebral arterioles; and palpitations and tachycardia by affecting pulse rate and blood pressure. Fortunately, not all children on these drugs have all these symptoms.

Since these effects are often only transitory and mild, they may not even be noticed unless the child is re-examined and followed up with great care. However, no matter how mild they are, they may still interfere in subtle ways with the child's development and have far-reaching consequences.

Addiction. It has been proven beyond any doubt that Dexedrine, Ritalin, and other stimulating drugs cause addiction in adolescents and adults. Whether this is called "abuse," "habituation," or "dependency," there is no doubt that these patients feel that they cannot function unless they take the drug they call "speed" or "uppers." No one knows what the youngest age for this form of addiction is, or whether any hyperactive elementary-school-age child on these drugs has ever become addicted. No such case has so far been reported, but long-range studies to determine this have not yet been done. We do know, however, that drug abuse has infiltrated elementary schools all over the United States. One can therefore not blame parents for being afraid to give their child such a drug, or for refusing this kind of treatment altogether.

Adrian's mother was such a parent. She was afraid he might become a drug addict like so very many children she knew. For 2 years she took the prescriptions given to her at the clinic, but either tore them up later on or had them filled at the hospital pharmacy and then threw the pills away. Adrian got over his postencephalitic hyperactivity anyhow, even though other symptoms continued. (See case of Adrian under Encephalitis, p. 616.)

This parental attitude has become widespread. It is also not at all unusual for parents to feel afraid or ashamed to talk about their fears and doubts openly with their child's physician, especially in busy and impersonal clinics. Their fears should therefore be anticipated and discussed freely and as a matter of course whenever a stimulant drug is prescribed.

The prevention of drug addiction in a wider sense also requires that these drugs not be given to children whose hyperactivity has a psychologic basis. These children must learn to master their behavior psychologically and not chemically. Television advertising has already conditioned them from preschool age on to feel the need for a pill whenever they experience tension, anger, anxiety, or frustration. Their psychologic defenses should not be weakened any further by stimulant drug treatment, which may prepare the ground from which drug addiction springs.

Contraindications. 1. Convulsive Disorders. All these drugs, except Dexedrine, lower the convulsive threshold. Thus they should not be given to children with convulsions or where a potential for convulsions is even suspected. (See Convulsive Disorders, p. 421.)

2. The anxious form of hyperactivity. Stimulant drugs worsen this form. (See Hyperactivity with Anxiety, p. 593.)

Prevention of Harm from Stimulant Drugs. The prescription of these drugs requires special caution because they affect such vital parts of the child's central nervous system in ways that are still largely unknown. They should be given only for severe forms of hyperactivity, and where no other potentially less harmful form of therapy is effective. Care must be taken that symptoms worse than hyperactivity are not produced. One should always keep in mind that this is a self-limited symptom that subsides spontaneously.

A child who has to take these drugs can be protected from harm only by thorough physical and psychiatric re-examinations at frequent intervals. The status of his autonomic nervous system should be included in these examinations. He should also be taken off the drug frequently to find out if his hyperactivity has subsided, so that he can function without them.

Such careful and conscientious care is unfortunately the exception rather than the rule, as has been shown by a number of investigations. A study by Gerald Solomons in Iowa, for instance, found that nearly half the cases sampled were followed up with *less* than two patient visits or *phone calls* in any 6-month period, and that the average length of medication was 3 years (1973)!

The use of stimulant drugs has increased enormously since then, even though the Bureau of Narcotics and Dangerous Drugs has prohibited the refilling of Ritalin prescriptions since that time. Ritalin is the most widely prescribed stimulant. Before this prohibition, telephone follow-ups or indefinite administration of this drug without any contact with a physician were very simple; thus one prescription could be refilled indefinitely. Some physicians, however, are unfortunately getting around this restriction by writing larger prescriptions, some for as many as 1,000 tablets at a time. This lasts for almost an entire year for a child taking two tablets a day, and 2 years for the one-a-day child. This means no re-examination at all and probably also no follow-up. (Schrag & Divoky, 1975, p. 250.)

This form of drug treatment has taken on mass proportions. No reliable statistics exist, and no one really knows how many children are on these drugs, how many of them have been helped, and how many harmed. Various prevalence estimates put the figure between 500,000 and 1 million children. These drugs are big business indeed. The pharmaceutical industry has not been helpful in producing precise figures of the number of children on these drugs; they try to keep a low profile to ward off criticism.

Misuse.   This mass prescription of stimulants to helpless children is especially ominous in that they are also prescribed for children with MBD (Minimal Brain Dysfunction) who are not hyperactive. I consider this a form of malpractice; these children suffer from reading, writing, and arithmetic disorders, which cannot possibly be cured pharmacologically. These drugs are not only ineffective in this respect; they may also cause hyperactivity and other symptoms in these children. (See Treatments, Vol. I, p. 330; and Hyperactivity, p. 657.)

Overuse.   My own experience shows that all these drugs are overused, and that too many hyperactive children are indeed kept on them for years without re-examinations, as in Kirk's case. (See sections on Diagnosis of Hyperactivity, p. 587; on Violent Behavior, p. 604; and on Psychologic Causes, p. 645.)

Successful Educational Treatment Without Drugs.   The experience of an elementary school principal who was also a clinical psychologist is a typical example for such drug overuse. He had been a member of the staff of the Lafargue Clinic and had worked closely also with other psychiatric clinics throughout his career as an educator. He knew the children in his school and their parents very well. They loved and respected him. Most of them were poor and had to struggle to survive economically and psychologically. They could not afford private care, so that he had to send disturbed children to the only city hospital psychiatric clinic available in his district.

Rarely, if ever, was such a child treated with psychotherapy or were his parents counseled by a social worker. Drugs were prescribed routinely, stimulants for all children diagnosed as hyperactive. This diagnosis was used so broadly that it involved almost all children he referred, whatever the teacher's complaints. He knew that these children did not learn and could not sit still because they were anxious, confused, frustrated, and often emotionally and physically neglected. Their problems were sociologic and psychopathologic, and drugs could not solve them. These children did not improve; in fact, some of them got even more restless, inattentive, and wild.

He pleaded with the psychiatrists and other members of the clinic's staff to initiate other forms of treatment, but to no avail. So he took matters into his own hands and tried an experiment. He knew that the motor drive of these children was chronically frustrated. They usually spent their off-school hours huddled in front of television sets, unable to move freely because of their overcrowded apartments. It was too cold to play outdoors in the winter, and too dangerous because of street violence in the summer.

He thought that more intense physical activity during their school day might calm them down sufficiently to function without drugs. So he arranged to have them taken off stimulants and added to their curriculum a daily free play period in the gymnasium. A gym teacher voluntarily gave up his lunch hour to watch them. These children's psychogenic hyperactivity was indeed gone after such a period. They sat still and paid attention. Although the play period did not cure their other symptoms, they were easier to teach and could be kept off all stimulant drugs during the remaining school year. I visited this school frequently and witnessed the result of this successful therapeutic educational intervention. (See Curative Physical Exercises, p. 534, under Attention Disorders.)

TRANQUILIZERS AND ANTIANXIETY DRUGS. These drugs may help children with the anxious form of hyperactivity, although they, too, have been overused and may do harm. Thorazine, Mellaril, Atarax, and other similar drugs may, for instance, cause convulsions. They should be prescribed cautiously and only where psychologic and educational measures have proven ineffective. It must always be kept in mind that almost any kind of drug may alleviate anxiety purely on a psychologic basis due to suggestion. The child's (or adult's) anxieties are often relieved just by knowing that something is being done to help him. Children are very suggestible, and the disturbing feeling most easily relieved by suggestion is anxiety. (See Hyperactivity Caused by Anxiety, p. 593; and The Organic Basis of Free-Floating Anxiety, p. 691.)

SEDATIVES. It is imperative that a hyperactive child get enough uninterrupted sleep, since lack of sleep alone can cause hyperactivity. If this cannot be achieved with sound bedtime management such as good timing, a calm and quiet period before bedtime without television, and so forth, sedatives should be prescribed. Barbiturates such as phenobarbital may help; they do not invariably cause excitement in these children (i.e., provoke a paradoxic reaction), as has been widely believed. We cannot yet predict how such a child will react to these drugs because they unfortunately have not been investigated clinically with the "Law of Initial Value" in mind either.

Antihistamines such as Benadryl, Phenergan, and others often work very well as sedatives. Tranquilizers and antianxiety drugs may also put the child to sleep. (See Sleep, p. 600.)

GENERAL PRINCIPLES OF DRUG ADMINISTRATION.   Drug treatment of hyperactivity requires special measures that should be adhered to routinely.

1.   The name, nature, and purpose of the drug should be explained to both parents in detail, and they should be given a chance to ask questions. An atmosphere of mutual trust must be established, otherwise drugs will not be administered properly. Parents have many fears about drugs, not only that their child may become addicted. They may, for instance, worry that the child's later sex life may be affected. The father of one of the 29 children in my study refused any form of drug treatment because of his fear that his son would become impotent. To run around wildly was, to him, an indication of his son's manly strength, which assured potency in adulthood. Parents may also have many other kinds of fears. The name of the drug should be clearly legible on the medicine bottle.

2.   The purpose of drug treatment should be explained to the child alone, not in the presence of his parents. The child, too, must be given a chance to express his fears, doubts, misconceptions. Many children are afraid the drug may make them "crazy," that it may influence their mind and control it, so that they will become helpless and incapable of controlling their own thoughts and actions. What they have seen in comic books, on television, and in movies also influences them greatly in this respect. These mass media show many stories where people's minds are being changed and controlled by drugs and all sorts of gadgets, where the brain of one person is transplanted into another, and so on. These children must be told that all the drug will do is calm them down, to make them less "nervous" (if the child has used this term to describe his disturbing feelings). They must be assured that the drug will not change their mind; that it will not make them think thoughts they do not want to think, hate people they don't actually hate, love people they do not really love, and so forth.

3.   The child must *never* have access to the drug; it should be given to him only by adults. He should never be put in charge of taking it by himself. Children have come to my office proudly pulling their pillbox out of their pants pocket. They have told me that they swap tablets with their friends, sometimes

take more just to see what might happen, take them whenever they feel like it or not at all. Some children also buy and sell them. It has been well documented that this happens in schools all over the country. This reflects totally irresponsible adult management.

Parents should give the child his drug before he goes to school. He should get his second dose when he comes home for lunch. If he needs a tablet at lunchtime and cannot come home, *one* professional person in the school should be given this task, preferably the school nurse. It has unfortunately become a widespread practice to have the classroom teacher dole out these drugs as a matter of routine. They are often given casually, like candy. Drugs should never become associated with candy in the child's mind. The danger of taking too many is too great, and their addiction potential is enhanced. Drug taking should remain something serious and special in the child's mind. He should be aware of the dangers involved in not taking them exactly as prescribed, and of their limited purpose ("Dispensing Medications in School," 1974, p. 180). Drugs must be kept in some securely locked container. It is too easy to steal them out of a teacher's desk.

These rules should be adhered to from Kindergarten through high school in the present social climate which furthers drug taking through advertising and by other means.

Nutrition

The nutritional status of each hyperactive child should be determined. A detailed diet diary over a span of at least 2 weeks should also be routinely requested to determine whether he might respond to the Feingold diet. (See Food Additives, under Hyperactivity, p. 558; and also Concentration, p. 554.)

Many hyperactive children are thin and wiry and do not take enough time to eat properly. Their appetite should be stimulated, and the amount and type of food they eat carefully monitored. Vitamin supplements are essential for these children, especially Vitamin B because it increases appetite and has a calming effect. The pediatrician and neurologist Mary Coleman reported at a seminar on Psychopharmacology With Children sponsored by The Department of Psychiatry of New York Medical College on March 10, 1977, that studies have indicated that vitamin B_6 may be just as effective for the treatment of hyperactivity as stimulant drugs.

Appetite monitoring and stimulation should be done with special care in all children on stimulant drugs, because many of them do not gain weight or grow properly.

One should also keep in mind that undernutrition and hunger may by themselves cause hyperactivity. (See Hunger, under Attention Disorders, Vol I, p. 73, p. 561.)

Physical Exercises

Systematic daily physical exercises are an essential form of treatment for hyperactive children. The experience of the principal who provided a daily gym period for these children shows how effective this approach can be. However, to let such a child simply run around freely and wildly may not be enough, because he must eventually learn to control and to master his motor drive. This requires systematic physical exercises such as gymnastics or calisthenics. The child needs to practice concentrating on deliberate, purposeful muscle movements. Games and competitive sports may also decrease his hyperactivity just by making him too tired to move. However, many of these children have difficulty shifting and perseverate, which makes it very difficult for them to participate in games. Those children whose automatic mechanisms are also impaired are even worse off. The anxieties and tensions inherent in competitive play and sports may, in addition, actually worsen their hyperactivity. (See Curative Physical Exercises, under Attention Disorders, p. 534; and case of Kirk, p. 606.)

Psychotherapy

The complex psychopathologic and social problems of hyperactive children very often require psychotherapy, individual or in a group. Indications depend on the severity of the psychopathology, on its duration, and on the importance of unconscious processes. The cause of the hyperactivity is less decisive in this respect, since psychotherapy does not only affect the psychogenic form, but may have a healing effect also on the other forms. Children suffering from any one of the organically caused psychologic symptoms in this core group and from a reading disorder on an organic basis are very often helped through psychotherapy. It must be stressed again in this connection that the decrease of a psychologic symptom with psychotherapy does not necessarily mean that its cause is psychologic. It may be organic. (See explanation of "organic" under Unspecific and General Symptoms Associated with Organic Reading, Writing, and Arithmetic Disorders, p. 543; and under Pathologic Basis of Organic Reading Disorders, Vol. I, p. 42.)

Parental Guidance

Counseling of parents is essential, no matter what treatments the child receives. Both parents should be involved, since they have to find out together how best to live with their hyperactive child and how to help him. Such a child needs a firm, calm, and noncontradictory routine. Conflicts within him and among his parents and siblings invariably increase his hyperactivity. All anxiety- and excitement-provoking factors should be eliminated from such a child's life as much as possible. This incidentally holds true for all children suffering from this core group of organically caused psychologic symptoms.

Television is one of these anxiety-provoking factors. Even its best programs tend to arouse excitement and anxiety in such children, including those who can sit still only in front of it. All these children are emotionally unstable; television viewing destabilizes them even further. Parents should therefore be advised to restrict their child's viewing or to eliminate it altogether, depending on his reactions. (See Sleep, p. 601.)

Special Class Placement

Many hyperactive children cannot function in a regular classroom and may have to be placed in special classes with few children and specially trained teachers. The selection of the appropriate class depends not only on the severity of the hyperactivity. Other symptoms are just as important, especially the presence or absence of a reading disorder. A hyperactive child with a severe reading disorder should be placed in a class run by teachers especially trained in the treatment of reading, writing, and arithmetic disorders; otherwise he will not learn to read. Far too many of these children are simply sent off to a class for emotionally disturbed children and no attention is paid to their reading disorder.

Some hyperactive children cannot function in any group. They have to be put on home instruction, provided their home is suited for such a plan; otherwise they have to be hospitalized or sent to a residential treatment center. (See Course of the Hyperactivity, p. 656.)

All these placements should be of limited duration. The child should be returned to a regular class as soon as his hyperactivity has subsided.

Individual Reading Treatment

Hyperactive children whose reading disorder is severe usually need individual reading lessons in addition to regular schooling or special classes. Their educational therapists must pay special attention to their eye movements, since the choreiform eye movements of many hyperactive children require special remedial techniques. (See Choreiform Eye Movements, p. 430; and Linear Dyslexia, Vol. I, p. 127.)

None of these treatment methods, individually or in combination, can be successful unless all adults involved with the child—their parents, teachers, pediatrician, social worker, psychologist, and child psychiatrist—work closely together and communicate with each other frequently. This is very difficult to arrange, but attempts in that direction should be made. (See chapter on Treatments, Vol. I, pp. 291, 298, 296.)

Chapter 14

Hypoactivity

Hypoactivity or hypokinesis is the opposite of hyperactivity. Hypokinetic children are apathetic, difficult to arouse and to interest in anything, rarely enthusiastic, and not spontaneous. In school they yawn alot and seem sleepy even when they slept well the night before. Their muscle tone is flabby, and it is difficult to mobilize them for any motor activity. They usually have a passive attitude toward life. Their hypoactivity is not necessarily due to a depression. It is a chronic and not an acute condition.

This symptom, too, may have an organic or a psychologic cause. It may occur with or without a reading disorder.

Hypoactivity is just as important as hyperactivity and may be more frequent. But because hypoactive children are only rarely referred to child psychiatrists and psychiatric clinics, this symptom is either not mentioned at all or appears to occur less frequently than it probably does.

Prechtl made a special study of the organic form. In *The Long Term Value of the Neurological Examination of the Newborn Infant,* he describes a "Hypokinetic Syndrome" (1960). The children he studied from birth on had perinatal hypoxia and other birth difficulties.

Children with the psychogenic form have given up trying. Years of failure, especially in reading, have so discouraged them that they feel they cannot master anything in life.

Hypoactivity is usually not mentioned in relation to reading disorders. Klasen apparently has the most extensive statistics on this symptom: she found it in 18.4% of the 500 children she studied, while 26.8% were hyperactive (1970). The speech and reading therapist Katrina De Hirsch also stresses the importance of this symptom in *Predicting Reading Failure.* Three of the eight children in her study were hypoactive. She writes that these three "had difficulty maintaining a sitting posture, and tended to slump. Their throwing was hypotonic; some of them could hardly hold a pencil" (De Hirsch, Jansky, & Langford, 1966, p. 47). (See The Slowing Down of All Reactions, p. 461.)

Diagnosis

Observation is the basis for the diagnosis of hypoactivity. This includes a report on the child's behavior and attitudes at home, when playing freely with other children, and in school. A physical examination is also essential to rule out physical diseases causing this symptom.

Treatment

1. The nutritional status of these children needs to be examined just like that of hyperactive children. They may be lethargic because they are underweight, and this should be corrected. Some children gain too much weight because the composition of their food is inadequate. They may actually be

malnourished. (See Hunger, p. 561, Vol. I, p. 73)

2. Hypoactive children need systematic, daily, noncompetitive physical exercises to improve their motor apparatus and to help them enjoy physical activities. This is a crucial form of treatment. They can rarely overcome their hypoactivity, or the attention disorder and the fatiguability invariably associated with it, without this form of therapy. (See Curative Physical Exercises, under Attention Disorders, p. 534.)

3. All hypoactive children with a reading disorder need reading treatment on an individual basis. Their hypoactivity prevents them from keeping pace with their classmates even in small special classes.

4. Psychotherapy, individual or in a group, may also be indicated. Many such children cannot overcome their hypoactivity or their reading disorder without it.

5. Parental guidance is as essential for children with this symptom as it is for all children suffering from a reading disorder and the other symptoms in this organic core group.

Hypoactivity is closely connected with fatiguability. As De Hirsch pointed out in her book on reading failure, "both hyper- and hypoactive youngsters showed a considerable tendency to fatigue. Toward the end of the testing session, they were altogether unable to function" (1966, p. 47).

The symptom of fatiguability will be circumscribed in the next chapter.

Fatiguability

This symptom is more severe and long-lasting than the occasional episodes of fatigue due to lack of sleep that are part of every child's life. These children are not just bored in school and yawn to show their boredom and distress for having to sit through their lessons. They usually try hard to fight their feelings of lassitude and sleepiness, and are ashamed of getting tired while their classmates are still full of enthusiasm and energy. Often they complain of headaches, but what they actually feel is not pain, but tenseness and fatigue. They feel they just cannot go on with their work and have to rest awhile.

Fatigue has a restorative function, indicating that the organism has reached the limits of its energy and must rest. Abnormal fatiguability means that the child needs more energy than normal to function properly.

Diagnosis

The correct diagnosis of this symptom is very important for the constructive management of the child. The behavior of such a child is usually at first mistaken for boredom, lack of interest in his work, and generally a negativistic and defiant attitude. Punishment usually follows such an evaluation. Such lack of understanding invariably increases the child's fatiguability; he begins to feel desperate about his inability to overcome this symptom, which actually overcomes him and which he dislikes. The ensuing depression may immobilize him to such an extent that he can no longer participate in any classroom activity. Careful observation of the child's behavior during the psychiatric and psychologic examinations, in school, and at home will show his abnormal fatiguability.

Psychologic tests are especially helpful because they require the type of sustained, structured and timed mental work that causes the child's abnormal fatigue. Tests such as counting backwards or doing arithmetic problems requiring carrying over and subtracting serial sevens from 100, and others designed to test memory and attention also test fatiguability. (See Psychiatric Examination under Attention Disorders, p. 512, Vol. I. p. 76–77.)

Fatiguability may have a somatic, a cerebral, or a psychologic origin. That is why children suffering from this symptom should first of all have a physical examination. Numerous physical illnesses can cause it, for example tuberculosis, other chronic infections, and anemias. (See Fatigue, under Attention Disorders, p. 562.)

Cerebral Fatiguability

Any malfunctioning of the brain through whatever cause leads to fatiguability during mental work. This cerebral fatiguability, however, also leads to physical fatigue, because the body is invariably involved in mental efforts through the attention process. (See Physical Changes During Attention, p. 521.)

672

All children suffering from a reading disorder on an organic basis have this symptom. Their fatiguability may be general and affect all their mental efforts, or specific and occur only when they read. It is specific for those children whose reading disorder is an isolated impairment, who do not have any of the other unspecific organically caused psychologic symptoms in this core group. For instance, children whose reading disorder is hereditary usually have this specific fatiguability.

The fatiguability of most children with an organic reading disorder, however, is more widespread. It is inherent in all the core group symptoms, including hyperactivity. A hyperactive child may seem indefatigable, but his fatiguability is invariably abnormal. The hyperactive child who said: "When I sit still I get tired. When I move around I feel good!" was aware of his special fatiguability. (See Special Methods of Examination, under Hyperactivity, p. 610.)

Fatiguability is especially severe and debilitating for children whose automatic mechanisms are impaired. They fatigue much sooner than children who do not have this symptom, because they need so much more time and energy for all their mental and physical activities. The same applies, to a somewhat lesser degree, to children who have difficulty shifting, and to those who perseverate. The large number of children with a reading disorder who have all these symptoms are very badly off indeed; they need a rest period after almost every effort. (See Impairment of Automatic Mechanisms, p. 469; Inability to Shift, p. 480; Perseveration, p. 486.)

Children who have an attention disorder are also especially handicapped, since fatiguability and an attention disorder interact in a vicious cycle. A child who has difficulty concentrating fatigues easily, and when he is tired, he has trouble concentrating. (See Fatigue, under Attention Disorders, p. 562.)

Psychogenic Fatiguability

Psychogenic fatiguability occurs very frequently. Almost every child (and adult) suffers from it at one time or another during life. This symptom may be reactive and transitory or neurotic and more chronic. It is an integral part of all forms of depression, including the "masked" type. A child may complain of being always tired, but close examination may show that he is depressed. The reason for his fatigue is insomnia, a cardinal symptom of depression, combined with depressive apathy and loss of interest in life.

Fatiguability on a neurotic basis is usually chronic and severe. These children are exhausted before the end of the schoolday, and sleepy, cranky, and irritable for the rest of the day. Sleep is for them a retreat from intolerable conflicts for which they find no solution, and from feelings they cannot face and do not dare express openly. Not to reveal their true feelings during an entire schoolday and/or at home requires all their energy. These are usually negative feelings, of anger, hatred, jealousy, often not deeply repressed into the unconscious, but readily accessible to the child. These children are often aware of their destructive emotions and suppress them deliberately.

Treatment

The most important aspect of successful treatment is a correct diagnosis. The child can be helped as soon as the diagnosis of abnormal fatiguability has been made. What he needs above all is the permission and encouragement to rest as soon as he feels tired. He should not be pushed or push himself beyond the *beginning* of fatigue. He should also be assured of uninterrupted sleep at night for as many hours as he needs to feel fresh when he wakes up. Activities that tire him unnecessarily should be avoided.

Such a child may need an afternoon nap throughout his elementary school years, either in school or after he comes home. Just resting his head on a desk during a rest period may not be enough. These children may need to lie down on a cot in school or in bed at home, with blinds drawn and no noise. I have sent such children to health-improvement classes if no other class was available. These classes are supposed to provide such rest periods after lunch, as well as mini-rest periods throughout the entire schoolday.

The parents of children with this symptom should also be advised to supervise their child's television viewing carefully so that he does not develop a "tired-child syndrome" on top of his fatiguability. (See section on Fatigue under Attention Disorders, p. 562–564.)

Cerebral fatiguability does not improve by itself, in isolation. Sufficient rest lessens it, but does not eliminate it entirely. Improvement depends on the lessening of all the other organic symptoms, including the child's reading disorder. Where the fatiguability is specific and involves only this disorder, it will disappear as soon as the child has learned to read.

Psychogenic fatiguability responds well to psychotherapy. Sometimes it subsides after a comparatively brief period of treatment, before the child's other neurotic symptoms have disappeared.

Fatigued children are irritable. Fatiguability and irritability are closely connected. Morbid irritability, another of the organically caused psychologic symptoms in this core group, will be circumscribed in the next chapter.

Chapter 16

Morbid Irritability with a Tendency to Sudden Rages

675

The study of this important symptom has been much neglected in adult and child psychiatry, in psychology, and in education. It is very frequent and very difficult to cope with. Every child with an organic reading disorder has periods of irritability or is chronically irritable.

The intensity of this symptom ranges from a minor emotional disturbance to a severe and sometimes dangerous symptom indicating serious underlying pathology. Its mild psychogenic form, which is part of nearly everyone's life, occurs during periods of physical and/or emotional stress that no child or adult can avoid. Anyone would become irritable if someone kept interrupting while he or she was talking to someone else. Noises that make it difficult to understand what is being said have the same effect; so do blinding lights that make it difficult to see, and all kinds of other stimuli that interfere with the orderly progression of thoughts and actions. A state of heightened emotional excitement is sometimes also accompanied by irritability. Fatigue, hunger, and pain are other ubiquitous causes. (See Fatigue p. 562; Hunger, p. 567; Fatigue Due to Noise, p. 542; and Noisy Classrooms, p. 543, under Intellectual Attention.)

The morbid form of irritability occurs during physical disease (e.g., hypoglycemia, hyperthyroidism, etc.); in epilepsy, general paresis, and all sorts of other cerebral impairments; in alcoholism, drug addiction, mania, depression, schizophrenia, and in some neuroses and reactive disorders. (See Hypoglycemia, p. 454, 456; General Paresis, p. 455–456; and Chemical Brain Damage, Vol. I, p. 73.)

This symptom consists of excessive sensitivity to minor and unspecific external stimuli. The minutest noise or other disturbance in their surroundings stirs up an irritating, unpleasant excitement in the child or adult. This excitement interrupts everything the child was doing, thinking, or feeling; it cannot be suppressed. It comes on very suddenly and provokes an immediate physical reaction that cannot be controlled either. It is involuntary, reflexlike, and primitive. The child startles, turns around, jumps up, trembles, cries out, swears; he may start to cry and to lash out wildly. It takes him a while to recover, to regain his equilibrium, and to return to what he was doing, only to react soon in the same way to an equally unimportant event or trivial stimulus.

These feelings and reactions are completely out of proportion to the magnitude and significance of the stimulus, and the child usually knows it. Irritable children are tense and are often in a constant state of heightened alertness. They feel vulnerable and quite helpless in relation to this symptom. Their hypersensitivity is beyond their control.

The child's or adult's perception is apparently altered during irritability, so that they notice more stimuli than when they are not irritable. There are also indications that they perceive stimuli as being more pronounced than they usually are. Light seems brighter, sounds louder, tactile stimuli sharper, movements of people more sudden and faster, and so on. This seems to be an exaggeration of the perceptual changes taking place during the normal attention process. (See Perceptual Changes During Attention, p. 514.)

Irritability affects the inner equilibrium, the sense of inner cohesion, of wholeness. It has an unsettling effect, and conveys a feeling of instability. These children feel that their inner balance is being threatened, or that they have already lost it. They worry whether they have gone insane, or are "going crazy."

The loss of inner balance may indeed be one of the causes of morbid irritability, for instance in schizophrenia, during mania so far as adults are concerned, in depression, in physical diseases, and so on. The coming apart of various mental functions—a loss of equilibrium—is a characteristic feature of schizophrenia; the manic patient has lost his emotional balance; depression is based on the decompensation of this balance; physical diseases tend to upset this balance. Irritability often indicates a worsening of the underlying disease. At the very beginning of such a disease its occurrence may have special diagnostic significance. It may, for instance, be a very early symptom of a brain tumor.

Irritability is an especially unpleasant symptom. These children feel very uncomfortable. Those who are aware of their hypersensitivity feel badly about not being able to control it, and are ashamed of being so "touchy."

This symptom is usually not chronic, but occurs in recurrent episodes. These episodes come on suddenly, without warning, and often without a precipitating event. It is sometimes impossible to figure out what caused them, or what made them suddenly disappear. One can predict them only if a child's irritability is usually associated with fatigue, hunger, pain, or fever; or when he is anxious or angry.

Most, but not all children with an organic reading disorder become irritable when their cerebral reading apparatus is too exhausted to function any longer. All the other organically caused symptoms and impairments may cause irritability in the same way, through fatigue and/or anxiety. However, many such children have episodes of irritability when they are not tired or anxious. Long-range studies of this symptom that could lead to an understanding of this as well as other aspects of its structure have unfortunately not been done. We can therefore prevent such episodes only when the underlying causes have been removed.

Role of Anxiety

A child who perseverates and is afraid that he cannot possibly finish his work, may become irritable. Time pressure is especially apt to cause irritability, the morbid as well as the less severe psychogenic form. Children with organic impairments have many such anxious moments during every schoolday, and may therefore also have repeated episodes of irritability. However, episodic as well as chronic irritability may occur entirely without anxiety. Anxiety is not necessarily involved in this symptom; in the organic form it is a consequence and not a cause.

Role of Anger

Morbid irritability is often misunderstood and consequently mismanaged and aggravated. Some textbooks erroneously call it primarily an "expression of anger" or a "special tendency to anger" (Bleuler, 1930, p. 81; 1950, p. 370; Linn, 1967, p. 570). Rather, it is a reflexlike, automatic symptom. The stimuli, the feelings they arouse, and the child's or adult's reactions are all unspecific. These patients experience irritability as forced upon them and as foreign to their nature or their usual behavior. Some of them wonder whether their hypersensitivity is not entirely physical.

Feelings of anger enter prominently into this symptom, but they are not primary except in some psychogenic forms. An angry child is not necessarily irritable, and an irritable child is not necessarily angry. Anger develops as a reaction to irritability and to the hostility it provokes in others.

Irritable children feel that there is something wrong with them, and wonder how they can steel themselves against interrupting stimuli. They desperately want to be left alone and undisturbed. Eventually they get angry at these interruptions and at themselves for not being able to ignore them. This leads to a feeling of smoldering anger or, in severe forms, of subdued rage that is ready to explode suddenly and unexpectedly in response to anything, and to be directed at anything or anybody in the child's immediate surroundings.

These children react very much like distractible children. They make desperate efforts to concentrate, and become enraged out of desperation. Small children react with temper tantrums. They may also hit out wildly, demolish furniture and anything else in the path of their fury, and attack anyone close by. Hostile reactions by other people also feed into their anger. Irritable children are difficult to live with. Their hypersensitivity makes other people angry, and it undermines the child's relationship with them. This may lead to a vicious cycle of mutual anger that is difficult to break and may continue after the child's irritability has subsided.

Anger also plays a role in episodes of irritability during all forms of depression: psychotic, neurotic, or reactive. Feelings of anger are often part of a depressive mood.

Anger, above all other emotions, shatters the concentration process. The irritable child who is angry finds it almost impossible to concentrate on anything, work or play. He should therefore be shielded from becoming angry at all costs. This requires that his classmates, teachers, and parents understand that his angry feelings are due to his anger at his own hypersensitivity, and that they are also a reaction to their annoyed and angry attitude towards him. They should also realize that minor overreactions are instantly converted into angry and potentially violent outbursts when such a child is punished because his irritability is mistaken for deliberate disruptiveness. The worst thing one can do is to talk to such a child in an angry tone of voice. This leads invariably to an escalation of mutual anger.

Irritability is contagious. Adults and children who watch an irritable child become themselves irritable. This is one of the factors that can lead to the battered child syndrome. The only way to avoid these complications is by understanding the involuntary and usually episodic nature of this symptom. It is best to ignore the child's touchiness, to leave him alone and as undisturbed and uninterrupted as possible, and not to pressure him to do any work. He might want to sit by himself somewhere for a while or to lie down in a quiet room, and these needs should be respected. Such careful and understanding management of an irritable child is also important from the point of view of violence prevention.

Role of Suspiciousness

Children suffering from morbid irritability may become overly suspicious. This is far more dangerous for their mental health than anger. They may misinterpret harmless disturbing stimuli as deliberately staged. Deliberate hostile acts by other children may then seem to confirm their suspicions. The crackling made by crumpling a piece of paper may, for instance, sound like a crackling fire or like cap-gun blasts to such a child, and he may feel that this is directed against him, playfully or with serious intent.

Teasing about his misinterpretations may make him more defensive and intensify his suspicious attitude. If his suspiciousness is not stopped at that point, he may eventually hold the outside situation entirely responsible for his inner tension and irritability, and blame others for his own angry outbursts. This morbid suspiciousness may still be accessible to psychotherapy. It may still be possible to help the child understand that his suspicions do not have a realistic basis. However, morbid suspiciousness may be a forerunner of delusions. Such a development is fortunately very rare in children under the age of 11. It must and can be prevented by dealing with unrealistic suspicions from the very beginning, and by helping such an irritable child to distinguish real from imaginary attacks. (See Distractibility on a Schizophrenic Basis, under Distractibility, p. 581.)

The Organic Basis for Irritability

Excessive dependency on external stimuli at the expense of inner goals is a sign that there is something wrong with the brain. A child or adult with an injured, diseased, fatigued, or otherwise malfunctioning brain suffers from this "bondage to the stimulus" ("Reizgebundenheit," as Kurt Goldstein called it). This pathologic way of reacting underlies the organic form of irritability. (See Passive or Involuntary Attention, p. 537; Distractibility, p. 572; and Selectivity of the Attention Process, p. 518.)

Irritability can also be understood as an attention disorder and classified under that heading. It can be looked at as a pathologic form of involuntary and immediate sensory attention, and as a special form of distractibility. The altered perception of stimuli during irritability also points to a disordered attention process. One can therefore assume that cerebral mechanisms underlying the attention process may in some way be malfunctioning during irritability and in this way help cause this special kind of "bondage to the stimulus."

It seems possible that the complicated interaction that takes place among cortical areas, sense organs, sensory and motor pathways, and parts of the reticular formation during every act of attention is somehow impaired. The restraining influences exerted on the thalamic section of the reticular formation by the cortex and by other parts of this mechanism might be malfunctioning. It is assumed that this section of the reticular formation mediates the focusing and shifting of attention. Its unrestrained activity might possibly have something to do with the hypersensitivity to unspecific stimuli so characteristic for irritability. (See Organic Basis of the Attention Process, p. 502; and Perceptual Changes During Attention, p. 514.)

The facts that episodes of irritability are typical for epilepsy and other convulsive disorders, and that they sometimes take the place of a seizure (i.e., are so-called convulsive equivalents), also point to diminished cortical restraints of subcortical impulses during these episodes.

Diagnosis

The diagnosis is made by observing the child's behavior during the psychiatric, pediatric, neurologic, and psychologic examinations; and by what the child himself reveals. However, observations of parents and teachers often provide the only evidence showing that he has this symptom.

It is characteristic for irritability that children as well as adults often do not realize that they are irritable. They may not be aware of it during an episode or in retrospect, after it has subsided. Often they also do not realize that an unpleasant, frequently violent incident was initially provoked by their irritability. It is therefore essential to ask very specific questions in order to diagnose this symptom or to rule it out, unless the child himself has said that he is irritable. Even then he should be asked to describe exactly what he means.

Some children say that they are "nervous" when they mean irritable. To describe their irritability they may use words such as "touchy," "jumpy," "jittery," or say that they fly off the handle for no good reason. Often they are genuinely puzzled by their hypersensitivity and try to find plausible reasons for their reactions. They should be asked to describe such an episode in great detail: to tell exactly what they heard, saw, felt, and thought. Such a child may, for instance, describe how he flew off the handle and almost hit his friend when all the friend had done was to crumple up pieces of paper. The loud crackling noise this made sounded like toy gun shots to him.

The adults taking care of such a child may also not realize that irritability was behind episodes of disturbed and disturbing behavior. They, too, should therefore be questioned in detail about their observations of the child's behavior.

Episodes of morbid irritability with a tendency to especially violent outbursts are characteristic for epilepsy and other convulsive disorders. It is therefore imperative to examine each child with this symptom for an underlying convulsive disorder. As many other epileptics, such a child may not have convulsive seizures. An EEG is needed to establish this diagnosis or to rule it out. (See Convulsive Disorders, p. 423; and Convulsive Disorders, under Hyperactivity, p. 620.)

Tests

There are no specific tests for irritability, although the child's behavior during tests may reveal this symptom. When the Mosaic and other tests show that the child is stimulus-bound, it can be assumed that he tends to be irritable. If this has not been revealed before, his history and the observations of his parents and teachers should be reevaluated.

Treatment

1. As with all the other organically caused psychologic symptoms, improvement requires that the child himself understand it. He must be given a chance to find his own way of coping with it.

2. Constructive management of the child at home and in school is the most important aspect of treatment. Whatever causes irritability under normal circumstances should be avoided: especially fatigue, hunger, time pressure, nagging, yelling, and other approaches that are irritating for any child. The child's irritability should be ignored as much as possible, and he should never be punished for it. During periods of irritability he should not be pressured to read or write or to do any other kind of work. He should be allowed to rest and to be alone if and when he wants to.

3. These children's environment should be made as nonirritating as possible. Noisy and chaotic homes and classrooms cause irritability and increase its morbid form to the point where the child cannot bear it any longer. Such surroundings provoke attacks of rage.

4. Systematic physical exercise and other physical activities may lessen

this symptom. However, some children are too irritable to carry out even simple and pleasurable physical exercises or games. Whether this form of treatment hurts or helps must be determined for each individual child.

5.   Sedatives or tranquilizing drugs may decrease these children's irritability. Their effect depends largely on the degree of anxiety involved in this symptom. They are less effective in the completely nonanxious forms. Stimulants should not be prescribed because they might worsen this symptom. They sometimes cause irritability in children who are not irritable, because the tonus of the sympathetic nervous system is increased during irritability.

Anticonvulsive drugs will eliminate this symptom completely when epilepsy or another convulsive disorder has been established as its cause.

6.   Psychotherapy may have a beneficial effect on this symptom, too. It can be effective by decreasing anxiety where this plays a role; by giving the child insight into the nature of his irritability and his reactions to it; by helping him to cope with anger and to overcome suspiciousness.

Irritability is sometimes associated with a sullen mood. A mood disorder is another one of the organically caused general and unspecific psychologic symptoms in this core group. It will be circumscribed in the next chapter.

Chapter 17

Mood Disorder

Mood disorders are a very frequent symptom among children with an organic reading disorder and other organic impairments. Their mood changes suddenly and unexpectedly, without a discernible reason or precipitating event. Nothing has changed in their life, yet they wake up in a low, sullen mood; or it overcomes them suddenly, attacklike, at any time during the day; and it lasts for hours or days until it lifts just as suddenly and unpredictably.

These children feel low and dispirited. They are cross, cranky, and displeased with themselves and with everybody and everything around them. Suddenly they are convinced that no one understands them, and nothing anyone does for them seems right. They become picky eaters or may lose their appetite altogether. They grumble and swear under their breath, and yell at or curse other people without provocation.

They realize on their own that they are in an "evil" mood and tell others to stay out of their reach. Sometimes they become restless and may have the urge to run away, to hide some place. They are preoccupied with themselves, avoid contact with others, and may become violent if approached in any way, even with the most loving intentions. They want strictly to be left alone. This is, as a rule, in great contrast to their ordinary behavior.

Ill Humor

The mood of these children is sullen, but they do not sulk. Children sulk when their feelings have been hurt, and they cannot or do not want to get over this hurt. Sulkiness has a specific and understandable reason, while sullenness is a general feeling not related to any event. These children are ill-humored, and suffer from a special kind of depression. When asked to describe how they feel, they say that they are in a bad or "evil" mood, not that they are depressed. Ill-humored adults describe their mood in the same way. Ill humor is an uncomfortable feeling that does not have the connotation of hopelessness, of apathy, of readiness to give up trying that is part of a depression. Ill-humored children are more ready to act than they would be if they suffered from another type of depression.

Ill humor is not necessarily accompanied by irritability. These children are not irritable during their periods of ill humor. However, ill humor is invariably accompanied by anger, in contrast to the organic form of irritability. These children are always ready to react with outbursts of anger. They also find it very difficult to concentrate on anything. They do their work poorly, if at all; and they fail tests. One should not force them to take tests in school when they are in such a sullen mood. Psychologic tests done during such periods also yield questionable results; they should thus be repeated later on, when the mood has subsided.

The child's sullen mood lifts as suddenly and unpredictably as it started, and he becomes his former self. His episode of ill humor disappears without leaving a trace.

Elated Mood

The swing to a low mood is far more frequent than a state of elation and exuberance. However, a child with an organic mood disorder may also have periods of unmotivated happy excitement that come on suddenly and unexpectedly, without a precipitating event, and cease just as suddenly. Elated and ill-humored periods occur quite independently; in rare instances, they may follow each other.

This symptom unfortunately recurs with great regularity. These children may have a period of ill humor once or twice a month, every few months, or every few days. The lengths of the free intervals may be identical or may vary, but this symptom apparently has a certain rhythm.

The mood disorder of children suffering from epilepsy or another convulsive disorder is especially severe and dangerous: it often leads to extremely violent behavior.

The Organic Basis of the Mood Disorder

The limbic part of the forebrain and parts of the thalamus and hypothalamus are assumed to play a role in stabilizing emotions. Papez described the limbic system and proposed the hypothesis that its malfunctioning may underlie emotional disorders (1959). How very limited the knowledge of the pathologic anatomy and physiology of emotions continues to be is summarized by the neurologist Poeck. He writes:

> The consideration of the anatomic relationships supports the hypothesis proposed by Papez (1937), of closed functional loops in the central nervous system, the intactness of which is necessary for balanced emotional feeling and behavior. The exact pathways of these functional loops are not yet known (1969, p. 363).

One might therefore assume that the limbic system or cortical impulses that restrain or otherwise regulate its function may be malfunctioning during periods of abnormal moods.

Diagnosis

The diagnosis is obvious when the child is examined while in an ill-humored mood. The history obtained from his parents and teachers will otherwise reveal this symptom. It must then be determined whether the child's moodiness is within normal limits, or whether it is neurotic or organic in origin. The severity, unpredictability, and periodicity of the mood disorder will determine the differential diagnosis. The cause is unquestionably organic when the child has a convulsive disorder. Other organic symptoms and tests clinch the diagnosis in other children.

Tests

Intelligence and projective tests may show the underlying organicity, and often also reveal the child's emotional lability. The Mosaic test is especially helpful also with this symptom: in addition to revealing or ruling out an organic disorder with such clarity, this test also shows the child's tendency to mood swings. These children prefer the colors red and blue and characteristically put them next to each other in prominent positions in their design.

Treatment

It is impossible to cheer up a child while he is in an ill-humored mood. He should be left to his own devices as much as possible, and frictions that lead to angry outbursts should be avoided. This is very difficult to do, since these moods are only rarely accessible to psychotherapeutic or special educational methods. Drug treatment may be more successful. Anticonvulsive drugs eliminate the mood disorder of epileptic children altogether, but they do not affect children with other organic impairments. Sedatives or tranquilizers may be effective and should be given on a trial basis. These children should be left alone but not *be* alone. They have to be watched, otherwise they may hurt themselves or others.

Free-Floating Anxiety with a Tendency to Panics

Free-floating anxiety, one of the most disabling of all the general and unspecific symptoms, is a diffuse and overwhelming form of anxiety that dominates the child's entire emotional and mental life. It is not focused on a specific object or special situation and is not caused by anxiety-provoking events. It is, however, aggravated by them. It invariably undermines the child's ego structure and does not let it develop normally. It also undermines his attention process, makes him distractible and restless, and may cause hyperactivity. Many of these children also have specific fears (of the dark, of animals, etc.). (See Hyperactivity with Anxiety, p. 593.)

This symptom also affects the child's physical well-being. He usually has some of the physical manifestations of anxiety, such as palpitations, pallor, sweating, trembling, dizziness, feeling faint and actually fainting, increased heart rate, urinary frequency, and diarrhea.

This malignant form of anxiety may indicate severe organic impairments or serious cerebral or somatic diseases, for example, leukemia, encephalitis, or other life-threatening illnesses. A child with this symptom should therefore first and foremost have a physical and neurologic examination. Children with an organic reading disorder suffer from this form of anxiety only when they also have several other organic impairments. It must be stressed that severe free-floating anxiety also occurs in childhood schizophrenia, and that a less severe form is found in anxiety neuroses.

Panics

These children have panic reactions when their anxiety is brought to the breaking point by situations that normally provoke anxiety, or by an accumulation of the many frustrations they have to face every day because of their organic impairments. Excessive fatigue due to the child's fatiguability may trigger a panic, as can minute frustrations no one else may have noticed. These panics are therefore difficult to predict or to prevent; they are also extremely difficult to manage once they have started.

Such a child feels that he cannot go on any longer, and a sudden emotional and motor discharge of his feelings of anguish and desperation follows. He screams and cries and is unconsolable; he may bite or hit himself, pound on his desk or on walls with his fists, run around the classroom sobbing, run out into the hall and out of the building to get home, and so on. Conscious or unconscious suicidal intent often underlies self-destructive acts during these panics. Like the rages associated with irritability, panics may also take the form of severe temper tantrums, where the child throws himself on the floor sobbing, trembling, yelling, shaking, kicking.

The conscious awareness of these children is sometimes diminished during a panic. Their perception of what goes on around them may be blurred, unclear, and confusing. This increases their anxiety and blurs their memory images of the episode. They therefore often cannot remember what happened to them and what they were doing. This sometimes makes it difficult to differentiate such a panic from a convulsion or an epileptic twilight state.

Close observation of several panics, the child's history, and tests will clarify the diagnosis.

It is often impossible to calm such a child just by talking to him quietly. Holding him sometimes helps; hitting only increases his frenzied desperation. It is sometimes best to take him to a quiet room where the adult can be alone with him, but this is also difficult to carry out. Prevention is therefore of utmost importance.

Such a panic takes its own time to subside. The child is often exhausted afterwards and may need to lie down and to sleep. He may also complain of a headache. This is exactly how epileptics feel after a seizure. Such postpanic behavior may also make the differential diagnosis difficult. Where the panic occurred in school, it might be best to send the child home. (See Convulsive Disorders, under Hyperactivity, p. 620.)

These panics are especially severe and frequent in children who cannot communicate clearly and fast enough, who suffer from a speech disorder. (See Speech Disorders, p. 379.)

Prevention of Panics

Free-floating anxiety is usually so severe and unresponsive to treatment with special education and other forms of psychotherapeutic management, that tranquilizing drugs have to be prescribed. These drugs may prevent panics. However, other forms of treatment are also needed to keep the anxiety level of these children low, prevent panics, and make learning possible.

Relation to Kurt Goldstein's "Catastrophic Reaction"

How these children can be helped can best be understood when these panics are compared with the specific anxiety reactions of adults with organic impairments that Kurt Goldstein called "catastrophic." He observed that these patients experience a sudden feeling of severe shock and anxiety and that their behavior becomes disorganized. In his book *The Organism,* he describes these reactions in the following way: "In these situations the individual feels himself unfree, buffeted and vacillating. He experiences a shock affecting not only his own person, but the surrounding world as well." He also stresses that:

after a catastrophic reaction, his reactivity is likely to be impeded for a longer or shorter interval. He becomes more or less unresponsive and fails even in those tasks which he could easily meet under other circumstances. The disturbing after-effect of catastrophic reactions is long enduring (1939, p. 37).

This is true also for children. They remain tremulous and frozen emotionally and intellectually for a while after a panic.

It is important that teachers and parents realize that such a child does not just have a trantrum, but that his behavior is due to his organic defects and that he cannot stop it once it has started. They should also know that the child needs a period of rest afterwards, when no demands whatever are made on him.

These panics are too often misinterpreted as an expression of the child's hostility, stubbornness, and negativism, and he is consequently reprimanded and punished. This worsens his anxiety, prolongs the panic and its aftereffect, and leads to more frequent outbursts. The training of teachers, even those with a degree in special education, is often defective in this as well as other respects. I have observed this far too many times during visits to special classes or special schools set up to teach children with reading disorders on an organic basis, as well as other organic impairments. Many such children are misdiagnosed as merely suffering from an ordinary behavior disorder, and are put in special classes dealing with these disorders. This invariably worsens their impairments and leads to more severe panics.

There are special educational treatment methods that can prevent panics. What Schuell, Jenkins, and Jiménez-Pabón described in their excellent book, *Aphasia in Adults,* applies also to children with free-floating anxiety, the majority of whom are not aphasic. These authors emphasize that all threatening situations have to be prevented, and that everyone caring for these patients must be alert to any sign of impending stress. They point out that

> there are innumerable ways to intervene to relieve tension. The clinician may change to easier materials or to a more familiar task. She may interrupt an activity with casual conversations, or suggest a break or stopping work for the day. It does not matter what she does, so long as she reduces the mounting tension, and gives the patient a chance to recover his equanimity. She should stay with him, however, until she is sure he is alright (1975, p. 318).

These preventive measures were so successful that these authors could state that "in fifteen years of working with aphasic patients, we have seen so few catastrophic reactions that it is difficult to think of good examples" (1975, p. 318). The same measures should be used with these children by teachers, educational therapists, speech therapists, psychologists, psychiatrists, nurses and attendants in hospitals where the severest cases sometimes have to be sent; and also by the child's parents.

So far as the schooling of these children is concerned, these therapeutic measures can be applied only in small, special classes or when the child is taught alone. Some children with this severe form of anxiety can learn only with individual instruction.

A panic is a sign of mismanagement of the child by the adults taking care of him. However, these extreme outbursts cannot always be prevented even with the most careful management. It is much more difficult to prevent them in a child whose emotional and intellectual development has been interrupted by free-floating anxiety and other organic impairments, than in an adult with a mature and firmly structured personality.

Panics and rages are the most distressing and destructive manifestations of organically based psychopathology. They are more difficult to tolerate and to control than any other type of behavior.

The Organic Basis of Free-Floating Anxiety

It does not seem that such a diffuse and all-pervading feeling can have just one circumscribed area in the brain as its basis. All the child's actions, thoughts, and other feelings are tinged by anxiety. Similar to the faculty of attention, anxiety can be attached to or withdrawn from any action, thought, or emotion. It can therefore be assumed that its organic basis is diffuse and facilitates mobility.

Anxiety is a response to danger signals, that is, impulses carrying the message that something is wrong or about to malfunction somewhere in the organism, or that it is being threatened from without. These impulses may come from sensory impressions, or from any location within the body, including the brain. They are apparently transmitted without letup during free-floating anxiety by a disorganizing somatic or cerebral process or by mental images where some form of disaster is only imagined.

Role of Autonomic Nervous System

The limbic system might be part of the organic basis of this symptom (Noback & Demarest, 1977, pp. 171–174). It is assumed to play a role in stabilizing emotions and might possibly be unstable during anxiety. These are only assumptions; what we know is that wherever the impulses carrying the alarming message originate and to whatever part of the brain they travel, exactly the same measurable physical process is set in motion that prepares the body for flight or fight via the autonomic nervous system. All levels of this system are apparently involved in this process, including regulatory areas in the hypothalamus. Its sympathetic part is especially active. Its tonus and all its functions are increased. (See the Autonomic Nervous System, under Physical Changes During Attention, p. 522; and Limbic System, under Organic Basis of the Mood Disorder, p. 685.)

Our knowledge of the organic basis of anxiety is still so limited that the pharmacologist and psychiatrist Robert Byck felt that he could state categorically, "the neurophysiological and biochemical basis of anxiety is unknown."

He made this statement in the 1975 edition of Goodman and Gilman's *Pharmacological Basis of Therapeutics* in the section on *"Drugs Used in the Treatment of Anxiety"* where he also wrote that: "The clinical popularity of these drugs apparently is the result of a mechanism of action that is as yet undefinable" (1975, p. 190). Some textbooks of physiology shy away from this complicated topic altogether. Anxiety cannot even be found in their indexes, yet it is one of the most frequent and important emotions normally, and part of all physical and mental diseases. Knowledge of its organic basis would be a major step in helping patients suffering from innumerable diseases.

Diagnosis

Observation of the child during the psychiatric or psychologic examination will reveal this symptom, especially when it is severe. However, the differential diagnosis between the organic, the schizophrenic, and the neurotic form may be difficult. The child's history and tests are helpful in this respect, combined with the presence or absence of other organic, neurotic, or schizophrenic symptoms.

Tests

The child's behavior during testing may be as revealing as the test results. Such a child may be too anxious for testing, or his obvious anxiety may render invalid the results of intelligence and achievement tests.

Projective tests are especially helpful in revealing the depth and breadth of the child's anxiety. These children invariably make a "frame" design on the Mosaic test, which indicates anxiety and also points to their need to surround themselves with some kind of protective wall. Such a child's anxiety may also be so severe that he cannot perform such an unstructured test. The Rorschach test is especially sensitive to anxiety and all its conscious and unconscious ramifications. It may also show its organic, schizophrenic, or neurotic origin.

Treatment

1. As with all other symptoms, the child suffering from this one should be helped to understand its mechanism so that he can develop his own ways of dealing with it and of avoiding panics. He can learn to stop when he begins to feel tense, to rest a while, and to change his activity. He can ask to be allowed to leave the room or to lie down. It is also possible to convey to him that his anxiety is not based on a real and present danger.

These goals can be achieved best with individual psychotherapy. It is, however, very important that all adults caring for the child—parents as well as teachers—also help the child alleviate this symptom.

2. Counseling of parents and teachers is essential and can sometimes be

effective even without individual psychotherapy. Parents should be made aware of all measures they can use to decrease the child's anxiety; so should his teachers.

3. Placement in a special class for organically handicapped children is also essential. Where the anxiety is very severe, the child may have to be put on home instruction, at least temporarily.

4. This severe form of anxiety can usually not be decreased without drug treatment. As Dr. Byck pointed out, we do not yet know the mechanism of action on the central nervous system of antianxiety drugs. Their action is even more obscure when it comes to children. These drugs should therefore be given cautiously, and the reaction of the child should be monitored frequently. Antihistamines sometimes decrease anxiety, but phenothiazines are most effective. As I stressed in the section on Drug Treatment of Hyperactivity, they should not be given to a child whose history or EEG indicates that he has a low threshold for convulsions.

5. Noncompetitive physical exercises usually have a calming effect on these children and should be part of their daily routine.

For descriptions of children with free-floating anxiety, see cases of Ramon, p. 621, Ned, p. 648, Lana, p. 620, and Kirk, p. 606.

Other forms of anxiety are described whenever they play a role, in relation to other symptoms and to the different reading disorders.

Chapter 19

Neurotic and Behavioral Psychopathology of Organic Reading, Writing, and Arithmetic Disorders

A child suffering from these disorders may also have behavioral and neurotic symptoms that are identical to those found in ordinary behavior disorders or neuroses.

These symptoms may be due to the child's reaction to the consequences of his reading disorder and of his other organic impairments. Neurotic symptoms develop from psychopathologic processes going on in the unconscious; an organic handicap may set such a process in motion. Behavioral symptoms are usually due to less complicated, more immediate reactions of the child to his handicap. A psychogenic reading disorder may cause the same kinds of neuroses or behavior disorders, so that the nature as well as the cause of these symptoms must always be carefully investigated.

Such a child's neurotic or behavioral symptoms may also stem from all sorts of traumatic life experiences that have nothing to do with his organic impairments. But these symptoms will invariably also be deeply affected by his organic reading disorder and by his other organic handicaps.

It is not always possible to disentangle the causation of each neurotic or behavioral symptom. Several causes are usually operative. For instance, a school phobia, which is a special form of anxiety neurosis, may be caused by a child's neurotic inability to face his organic reading disorder as well as by his infantile and ambivalent attachment to his mother. The diagnosis and especially the treatment plan must consider both causes.

Neurotic Symptoms

I have described the intimate interaction between neurotic and organic symptoms in a number of children, for instance in 7-year-old Emilio. He had a number of neurotic symptoms, namely nightmares, sleep talking, cross-dressing with a special interest in women's high-heel shoes, in addition to and independent from constructional apraxia and a severe organic reading, writing, and arithmetic disorder (Vol. I, p. 174). Other examples are 7-year-old Alfred's beginning psychopathologic reaction to his upside-down reading and writing (Vol. I, p. 107); 9-year-old Jose's hair-pulling (trichotillomania), skin picking, and anxious dreams, which were closely related to his untreated mirror-reading disorder (Vol. I, p. 105); and 9-year-old Morris' depression and suicidal thoughts, which were not caused exclusively by his head injury (p. 568). These interactions were also discussed in the sections on Rocking, Tantrums, and Sleep, under Hyperactivity (pp. 598, 600).

Behavior Symptoms

In the sections on Violent Behavior and on Fire Setting, I have described the interaction between behavioral and organic symptoms (pp. 604, 609). The analysis of 6-year-old Kirk's difficulties is the best example for this interaction.

His numerous organic symptoms—a reading disorder, free-floating anxiety, an attention disorder, a shifting difficulty, a distorted body image, and hyperactivity— could not possibly explain his suicidal attempts and his knife attack on his brother and grandmother. His behavioral symptoms were caused by parental strife, neglect, and cruelty. They overshadowed his organic impairments (p. 606).

References

Adelson, L. The battering child. *Journal of the American Medical Association,* 1972, *222,* 159–161.

Alvarez, W. C. *Nerves in collision.* New York: Pyramid House, 1972.

American Psychiatric Association. *Diagnostic and Statistical Manual of Mental Disorders* (D.S.M.-III), 1980; D.S.M.-II, 1968.

Ames, L. B., & Ilg. F. L. *Mosaic patterns of American children.* New York: Hoeber Medical Division, Harper & Bros., 1962.

Ames, M. D., Plotkin, S. A., Winchester, R. A., & Atkins, T. E. Central auditory imperception, a significant factor in congenital Rubella deafness. *Journal of the American Medical Association,* 1970, *213* (3), 419–421.

Barness, L. A. Malnutrition in children beyond infancy. In W. E. Nelson (Ed.), *Textbook of pediatrics* (11th ed.). Philadelphia: W. B. Saunders Co., 1979, 3 (27), p. 215.

Barry, H. *The young aphasic child, evaluation and training.* Washington, D.C.: The Volta Bureau Alexander Graham Bell Assoc. for the Deaf, Inc., 1961.

Bartram, J. B. Cerebral dysfunction ("brain damage"; learning disorders). In W. E. Nelson (Ed.), *Textbook of pediatrics* (9th ed.). Philadelphia: W. B. Saunders Co., 1969. (1)

Bartram, J. B. Cerebral palsy. In W. E. Nelson (Ed.), *Textbook of pediatrics* (9th ed.). Philadelphia: W. B. Saunders Co., 1969. (2)

Benton, A. L. The amusias. In M. Critchley & R. A. Henson (Eds.), *Music and the brain.* Springfield, Ill.: Charles C. Thomas, 1977, Chap. 22, pp. 378–397.

Best, C. H., & Taylor, N. B. *The physiological basis of medical practice* (3rd ed.). Baltimore: Williams & Wilkins Co., 1943.

Birch, H. G., & Lefford, A. Two strategies for studying perception in "brain-damaged" children. In H. G. Birch (Ed.), *Brain damage in children, the biological and social aspects.* Baltimore: Williams & Wilkins Co., 1964.

Bleuler, E. *Lehrbuch der Psychiatrie* (5th ed.). Berlin: Julius Springer, 1930.

Bleuler, E. Dementia praecox or the group of schizophrenias; *Monograph series on schizophrenia,* Vol. 1. New York: International Universities Press, 1950.

Bradley, C. Organic factors in the psychopathology of childhood. In P. H. Hoch & J. Zubin (Eds.), *Psychopathology of childhood.* New York: Grune & Stratton, 1955, pp. 82–104.

Brenner, I. Bromism: Alive in well. *American Journal of Psychiatry,* 1978, *135* (7), 857–858.

Brobeck, J. R. Higher neural functions, neural control systems. In J. R. Brobeck (Ed.), *Best & Taylor's physiological basis of medical practice* (9th ed.). Baltimore: Williams & Wilkins Co., 1973, Chap. 8, section 9.

Brody, J. E. New evidence links food dyes to behavior problems. *Science Times, The New York Times,* April 1, 1980.

Byck, R. Drugs and the treatment of psychiatric disorders. In L. S. Goodman & A. Gilman (Eds.), *The pharmacological basis of therapeutics.* New York: Macmillan, 1975, pp. 152–200.

Cantwell, D. P. Psychiatric illness in the families of hyperactive children. *Archives of General Psychiatry,* 1972, *27,* 414–422.

Capeci, J. Wins 500 G for "retarded" tag. *New York Post,* November 7, 1978.

697

Carter, S., & Gould, A. P. The static encephalopathies. In H. L. Barnett (Ed.), *Pediatrics* (15th ed.). New York: Appleton-Century-Crofts, 1968, pp. 879–905.

Chall, J. S. *Learning to read: The great debate.* New York: McGraw-Hill Book Co., 1967.

Charlton, M. H. Symposium: Minimal brain dysfunction and the hyperkinetic child. Clinical aspects. *New York State Journal of Medicine,* August 15, 1972, pp. 2058–2062.

Cheating on the I.Q. test. *New York Times,* November 6, 1978.

Chess, S., Korn, S. J., & Fernandez, P. B. *Psychiatric disorders of children with congenital Rubella.* New York: Brunner/Mazel, Inc., 1971.

Chess, S., Thomas, A., & Birch, H. G. *Your child is a person.* New York: The Viking Press, 1965.

Chisholm, J. J. Jr. Lead poisoning. In H. L. Barnett (Ed.), *Pediatrics* (15th ed.). New York: Appleton-Century-Crofts, 1968, pp. 540 –548.

Clark, D. The nervous system. In W. E. Nelson (Ed.), *Textbook of pediatrics* (9th ed.). Philadelphia: W. B. Saunders Co., 1969, Chap. 20.

Clark, D. B., & Anderson, G. W. Correlation of complications of labor with lesions in the brains of neonates. *Journal of Neuropathology and Experimental Neurology,* 1961, *20,* 275.

Cohen, B., Bala, S., & Morris, A. G. Do hyperactive children have manifestations of hyperactivity in their eye movements? *Bulletin of the New York Academy of Medicine,* 1975, *51* (10), 1152.

Cox, A., Rutter, M., Newman, S., Bartak, L. Comparative study of infantile autism and specific developmental language disorder: Parental characteristics. *Brit. J. Psychiatry,* 1975, *126,* 146 –159.

Critchley, M. *The parietal lobes.* London: Edward Arnold, Ltd., 1953.

Critchley, M. Topics worthy of research. In A. H. Keeney & V. T. Keeney (Eds.), *Dyslexia, diagnosis and treatment of reading disorders.* St. Louis: C. V. Mosby Co., 1968, Chap. 14, pp. 165–173. (b)

Critchley, M. Ecstatic and synaesthetic experiences during musical perception. In M. Critchley & R. A. Henson (Eds.), *Music and the brain.* Springfield, Ill.: Charles C. Thomas, 1977, Chap. 13, pp. 217–232. (a)

Critchley, M. Musicogenic epilepsy. In M. Critchley & R. A. Henson (Eds.), *Music and the brain.* Springfield, Ill.: Charles C. Thomas, 1977, Chap. 19, pp. 344 –353. (b)

Curran, A. Lead poisoning in New York City. *Bulletin of the Medical Society of the County of Queens, Inc.,* April 1976, pp. 80 –81.

De Hirsch, K., Jansky, J. J., & Langford, W. *Predicting reading failure.* New York: Harper & Row, 1966.

Deykin, E. Y., Macmahon, B. The incidence of seizures among children with autistic symptoms. *American Journal of Psychiatry,* 1979, *136* (10), 1310–1312.

DiGeorge, A. M., & Auerbach, V. H. Hypoglycemia. In W. E. Nelson (Ed.), *Textbook of pediatrics* (9th ed.). Philadelphia: W. B. Saunders Co., 1969, pp. 1163–1171.

Dispensing medications in school. Guidelines passed by Joint Committee on Health Problems in Education of the National Education Assoc. and the American Medical Assoc. *New York State Journal of Medicine,* September 1974, p. 1806.

Drew, A. L. Jr. The degenerative and demyelinating diseases of the nervous system. In H. L. Barnett (Ed.), *Pediatrics* (15th ed.). New York: Appleton-Century-Crofts, 1968, pp. 905–937.

Drug information on Ritalin. *Journal of the American Medical Association,* 1975, *30,* 10.

Egerton, J. M. Now schoolteachers are playing doctor. *Medical Economics,* April 1978, 119–124.

Ehrlich, P. R., & Feldman, S. S. *The race bomb, skin color, prejudice, and intelligence.* New York: Ballantine Books, 1977.

Einhorn, A. H. Poisonings in childhood—General. In H. L. Barnett (Ed.), *Pediatrics* (15th ed). New York: Appleton-Century-Crofts, 1968, pp. 527–537.

Eisenberg, L. Behavioral manifestations of cerebral damage in childhood. In H. G. Birch (Ed.), *Brain damage in children, the biological and social aspects.* Baltimore: Williams & Wilkins Co., 1964, pp. 61–76.

Eisenberg, L. Psychotic disorders I: Clinical features. In A. M. Freedman, H. I. Kaplan, & H. S. Kaplan (Eds.), *Comprehensive textbook of psychiatry.* Baltimore: Williams & Wilkins Co., 1967, Chap. 42, pp. 1433–1438.

English, H. B., & English, A. C. *A comprehensive dictionary of psychological and psychoanalytical terms.* New York: Longmans, Green & Co., 1961.

Evans, J. R. Evoked potentials and learning disabilities. In L. Tarnopol & M. Tarnopol (Eds.), *Brain function and reading disabilities.* Baltimore: University Park Press, 1977, Chap. 3, pp. 77–109.

Feighner, G. Multimodality treatment of the hyperkinetic child. *American Journal of Psychiatry,* 1974, *131,* 4.

Feingold, B. F. *Introduction to clinical allergy.* Springfield, Ill.: Charles C. Thomas, 1973.

Feingold, B. F. *Why your child is hyperactive.* New York: Random House, 1975.

Fish, Barbara, Involvement of the Central Nervous System in Infants in Schizophrenia, *Arch. Neurol.,* Vol. *2,* pp. 115–121, February 1960.

Flaste, R. For young minds, music without tears—or boredom. *New York Times,* August 13, 1976, p. A 12.

Food additives are linked to child behavior problems. *Medical Tribune,* July 25, 1973.

Food additives: Health question awaiting an answer. *Medical World News,* 1973, *14* (32), 73–80.

Food facts and fancies, *M.D.,* 1973, *17* (11), 59–61.

Forster, F. M., & Daly, R. F. Reading epilepsy in identical twins. In S. A. Trufant (Ed.), *Transactions of the American Neurological Association,* 1973, *98.* New York: Springer Publ. Co.

Frederiks, J. A. M. Consciousness. In P. J. Vinken & G. W. Bruyn (Eds.), *Handbook of clinical neurology. Vol. 3, Disorders of higher nervous activity.* New York: John Wiley & Sons, 1969, Chap. 4. (a)

Frederiks, J. A. M. Disorders of attention in neurological syndromes. In P. J. Vinken & G. W. Bruyn (Eds.), *Handbook of clinical neurology. Vol. 3, Disorders of higher nervous activity.* New York: John Wiley & Sons, 1969, Chap. 10. (b)

Freud, A. *Normality and pathology in childhood.* New York: International Universities Press, 1965.

Freud, S. *Die infantile cerebrale Kinderlähmung.* Wien: Holder, 1897.

Freud, S. Fragments of an analysis of a case of hysteria. In *Collected papers* (Vol. 3). London: Hogarth Press, 1943, pp. 13–146. (Originally published, 1905.)

Freud, S. Formulierungen über die zwei Prinzipien des psychischen Geschehens (Formulations regarding the two principles in mental functioning). In *Collected papers* (Vol. 4). London: Hogarth Press, 1946, Chap. 1, pp. 13–21. (a) (Originally published, 1911.)

Freud, S. Gesammelte Werke (Vol. 8). London: Imago, 1948.

Froeschels, E. Pathology and therapy of stuttering, XV. In E. Froeschels (Ed.), *Twentieth century speech and voice correction.* New York: Philosophical Library, 1948.

Frostig, M. Teaching reading to children with perceptual disturbances. In R. M. Flower, H. F. Gofman, & L. I. Lawson (Eds.), *Reading disorders, a multidisciplinary symposium.* Philadelphia: F. A. Davis Co., 1965.

Gellis, S. S. Editorial. *American Journal of Diseases of Children.* 1975, *129,* 1324.

Gellner, L. Correspondence on the backward child. *British Medical Journal,* April 1953, p. 5.

Gellner, L. Some contemplations regarding the border country between "mental deficiency" and "child schizophrenia." In *Congress Report III,* 2nd International Congress for Psychiatry, Zürich, Orell Füssli Arts Graphiques, 1957, pp. 481–487.

Gellner, L. *A neurophysiological concept of mental retardation and its educational implications.* Chicago: The Dr. Julian D. Levinson Research Foundation for Mentally Retarded Children, 1959.

Gerard, R. W. Neurophysiology, brain and behavior. In S. Arieti (Ed.), *American handbook of psychiatry* (Vol. 2). New York: Basic Books, 1959, Chap. 80, pp. 1620–1638.

Goldfarb, W. *Childhood schizophrenia.* Cambridge, Mass.: Harvard Univ. Press (published for the Commonwealth Fund), 1961.

Goldstein, K. *The organism.* New York: American Book Co., 1939.

Goldstein, K. Functional disturbances in brain damage. In S. Arieti (Ed.), *American handbook of psychiatry* (Vol. 1). New York: Basic Books, 1959, Chap. 39, pp. 770–794.

González, E. R. Learning disabilities: Lagging field in medicine. *Journal of the American Medical Association,* 1980, *243* (19), 1883–1892.

Gooddy, W. Disorders of the time sense. In P. J. Vinken & G. W. Bruyn (Eds.), *Handbook of clinical neurology. Vol. 3, Disorders of higher nervous activity.* New York: John Wiley & Sons, 1969, pp. 229–250.

Gooddy, W. The timing and time of musicians. In M. Critchley & R. A. Henson (Eds.), *Music and the brain.* Springfield, Ill.: Charles C. Thomas, 1977, Chap. 8, pp. 131–140.

Grinker, R. R., & Bucy, P. C. *Neurology.* Springfield, Ill.: Charles C. Thomas, 1949.

Groff, P. The new anti-phonics. *The Elementary School Journal,* March 1977, 323–332.

Gutheil, E. A. Psychosomatic problems of ophthalmology, a symposium. *Journal of Clinical Psychopathology,* 1945, *VI* (3, 4), p. 479.

Gutheil, E. A. Music as adjunct to psychotherapy. *American Journal of Psychotherapy,* 1954, *VIII* (1), 94–109.

Hallgren, B. Specific dyslexia, a clinical and genetic study. *Acta Psychiatrica et Neurologica,* 1950, *65* (Suppl.), 1–287.

Helping your hyperkinetic child. CIBA Pharmaceutical Co., 1971, 1974.

Hernández-Peón, R. Neurophysiologic aspects of attention. In P. J. Vinken & G. W. Bruyn (Eds.), *Handbook of clinical neurology. Vol. 3, Disorders of higher nervous activity.* New York: John Wiley & Sons, 1969, Chap. 9, pp. 155–186.

House, E. L., Pansky, B., & Siegel, A. *A systematic approach to neuroscience.* New York: McGraw-Hill Book Co., 1979.

Ingram, T. T. S. The development of higher nervous activity in childhood and its disorders. In P. J. Vinken & G. W. Bruyn (Eds.), *Handbook of clinical neurology. Vol. 4, Disorders of speech, perception, and symbolic behavior.* New York: American Elsevier Publ. Co., 1969, Chap. 18, pp. 340–376.

Intelligenz. *Der Spiegel,* 1978, *42,* 265–270.

Itil, T. M., & Soldatos, C. Epileptogenic side effects of psychotropic drugs. *Journal of the American Medical Association,* 1980, *244* (13), 1460–1463.

James, W. *The principles of psychology* (2 vols.). New York: Dover Publications, Inc., 1950. (Originally published, 1890.)

Janisse, M. P. *Pupillometry, the psychology of the pupillary response.* New York: Hemisphere Publ. Corp., 1977.

Jellinek, A. Beobachtungen bei Amusie und ihre musikpsychologischen Parallelen (Observation of amusia and its parallels in the psychology of music). Leipzig: Johann Ambrosius Barth, *Zeitschrift für Psychologie.,* 1933, *128,* 281–288.

Jellinek, A. Psychogenic disorders of speech. *Proceedings of the Rudolf Virchow Medical Society in The City of New York,* 1951, *10,* 15–20. Basel: S. Karger.

Jellinek, A. Amusia. *Folia Phoniatrica Separatum,* 1956, *8* (3), 124–149, Basel: S. Karger.

Kalinowsky, L. B., & Hoch, P. H. *Somatic treatments in psychiatry.* New York: Grune & Stratton, 1961.

Kamin, L. *The science and politics of IQ.* New York: Halstead Press, 1974.

Kanner, L. Follow-up study of eleven autistic children originally reported in 1943. *Journal of Autism and Childhood Schizophrenia,* 1971, *1* (2), 119–145.

Kanner, L., & Eisenberg, L. Notes on the follow-up studies of autistic children. In P. H. Hoch & J. Zubin (Eds.), *Psychopathology of childhood.* New York: Grune & Stratton, 1955, Chap. 13, pp. 227–239.

Kestenbaum, A. Psychosomatic factors in eye movements. *Journal of Clinical Psychopathology,* 1945, *VI* (3, 4), 453–458.

Kilmer, W. L., McCulloch, W. C., & Blum, J. Embodiment of a plastic concept of the reticular formation. In L. O. Proctor (Ed.), *Biocybernetics of the central nervous system.* Boston: Little, Brown & Co., 1969, Chap. 10, pp. 213–260.

Klasen, E. *Das Syndrom der Legasthenie (The reading disorder syndrome).* Bern: Hans Huber, 1970.

Kolansky, H., & Moore, W. T. Clinical effects of marijuana on the young. *International Journal of Psychiatry,* 1972, *64* (10/2), 55–67.

Kolansky, H., & Moore, W. T. Marihuana, can it hurt you? *Journal of the American Medical Association,* 1975, *232* (9), 923–924.

Kornhaber, A., Clinical corroboration of paper on marijuana by Kolansky, Moore. *International Journal of Psychiatry,* 1972, *10* (2), 80.

Kraepelin, E. *Psychiatrische klinik* (4th ed.), Vol. 1. Leipzig: Johann Ambrosius Barth, 1921.

Kramer, F., & Pollnow, H. Über eine hyperkinetische Erkrankung in Kindesalter. *Monatschrift für Psychiatrie und Neurologie,* 1932, *82* (1/2).

Kraus, H. *Backache, stress and tension. Their cause, prevention, and treatment.* New York: Pocket Books, 1972.

Kretschmer, E. *A Text-book of medical psychology.* London: Oxford Univ. Press, 1934.

Kruse, R. Epilepsien des Kindesalters. In A. Matthes & R. Kruse (Eds.), *Neuropädiatrie.* Stuttgart: Georg Thieme, 1973, Chap. 23, pp. 353–425.

Kurth, E., & Heinrichs, M. Zur Frage der musikalisch-rhythmischen Differenzierungsfähigkeit und Merkfähigkeit bei leserechtschreibschwachen Kindern (Contribution to the question of the ability of children with reading and writing disorders to differentiate and remember music and rhythms.). *Psychiatrie, Neurologie und Medizinische Psychologie,* 1976, *28,* 559–564.

Lane, R. See Ed Board appeal in mistaken retarded case. *New York Daily News,* November 7, 1978.

Lee, H., & Allen, M. W. Hemispheric differences in complex reaction time in patients with unilateral cerebral disease. *Transactions of the American Neurological Association,* 1972.

Lhermitte, F., & Gautier, J. C. Aphasia. In P. J. Vinken & G. W. Bruyn (Eds.), *Handbook of clinical neurology. Vol. 4, Disorders of speech, perception, and symbolic behavior.* New York: American Elsevier Publ. Co., 1969, Chap. 5, pp. 84–104.

Liebman, M. *Neuroanatomy made easy and understandable.* Baltimore: University Park Press, 1979.

Lin-Fu, J. S. Lead exposure among children—reassessment. *The New England Journal of Medicine,* 1979, *300* (13), 731–732.

Linn, L. Clinical manifestations of psychiatric disorders. In A. M. Freedman & H. I. Kaplan (Eds.), *Comprehensive textbook of psychiatry.* Baltimore: Williams & Wilkins Co., 1967, Chap. 13 (13), pp. 546–577.

Lowenstein, O. Psychosomatic problems in ophthalmology, a symposium. Introduction, general principles of psychosomatic relations of the eye. *Journal of Clinical Psychopathology,* 1945, *6* (3/4), 433–436.

Lowenstein, O. & Friedman, E. D. Pupillographic studies. *Archives of Ophthalmology*, 1942, *27*, 969–993.

Lowenstein, O., & Levine, A. S. Pupillographic studies V. Periodic sympathetic spasm and relaxation and role of sympathetic nervous system in pupillary innervation. *Archives of Ophthalmology*, 1944, *31*, 74–94.

Makarenko, A. S. *The road to life* (3 volumes). Moscow: Foreign Languages Publishing House, 1951.

Mann, T. *Tonio Kröger*. Frankfurt: Fischer publisher, 1976.

Marsh, J. *Your aphasic child. A practical guide*. New York: The Chorion Press, 1961.

Matthes, A. Infantile zerebral Paresen (Infantile cerebral pareses). In A. Matthes & R. Kruse (Eds.), *Neuropädiatrie*. Stuttgart: Georg Thieme, 1973, Chap. 21, pp. 316–338.

May, J. M. *A physician looks at psychiatry*. New York: The John Day Co., 1958.

McDanal, C. E., Owens, D., & Boldman, W. M. Bromide abuse: A continuing problem. *American Journal of Psychiatry*, 1974, *131* (8), 913–915.

McGhie, A. Psychological aspects of attention disorders. In P. J. Vinken & G. W. Bruyn (Eds.), *Handbook of clinical neurology. Vol. 3, Disorders of higher nervous activity*. New York: John Wiley & Sons, 1969, Chap. 8, pp. 137–154.

Mehegan, C. C., & Dreifuss, F. E. Hyperlexia, exceptional reading ability in brain-damaged children. *Neurology*, 1972, *22*, 1105–1111.

Millichap, J. G. *Febrile convulsions*. New York: Macmillan, 1968.

Mirsky, A. F. Attention: A neuropsychological perspective. In J. S. Chall & A. F. Mirsky (Eds.), *Education and the brain* (77th Yearbook of the National Society for the Study of Education). Chicago: The National Society for the Study of Education, 1978, Chap. 2, pp. 33–60.

Montessori, M. *The Montessori method*. New York: Schocken Books, 1964.

Moolenaar-Bijl, A. Cluttering. In E. Froeschels (Ed.), *Twentieth century speech and voice correction*. New York: Philosophical Library, 1948, pp. 211–224.

Mosse, H. L. The misuse of the diagnosis childhood schizophrenia. *American Journal of Psychiatry*, 1958, *114* (9), 791–794. (a)

Mosse, H. L. The influence of mass media on the sex problems of teenagers. *Journal of Sex Research*, 1966, *II* (1), 27–35. (a)

Mosse, H. L. The psychotherapeutic management of children with masked depressions. In S. Lesse (Ed.), *Masked depression*. New York: Jason Aronson, 1974, Chap. 11.

Mosse, H. L., & Daniels, C. R. Linear dyslexia, a new form of reading disorder. *American Journal of Psychotherapy*, 1959, *XIII*, 4, p. 826–841.

Mulder, R. W. Automatisms (psychomotor seizures) in psychoses with brain tumors and other chronic neurologic disorders. In S. Arieti (Ed.), *American handbook of psychiatry* (Vol. 2). New York: Basic Books, 1959, Chap. 55, pp. 1144–1162.

Narkewicz, R. M., & Graven, S. N. Tired child syndrome. In Hanauer, J., What TV is doing to your child—the abuses. *New York Journal-American*, October 13, 1965, p. 20.

Needleman, H. L., et al. Deficits in psychologic and classroom performance of children with elevated dentine lead levels. *The New England Journal of Medicine*, 1979, *300* (13), 689–731.

Noback, C. R., & Demarest, R. J. *The nervous system. Introduction and review* (2nd ed.). New York: McGraw-Hill Book Co., 1977.

O'Connor, J. J. TV: The agribusiness. *New York Times*, December 21, 1973.

Papez, J. W. The reticular system. In S. Arieti (Ed.), *American handbook of psychiatry* (Vol. 2). New York: Basic Books, 1959, Chap. 79, pp. 1607–1609.

Pearson, H. A. Diseases of the blood. In W. E. Nelson (Ed.), *Textbook of pediatrics* (9th ed.). Philadelphia: W. B. Saunders Co., 1969, Chap. 24, pp. 1060–1063.

Poeck, K. Pathophysiology of emotional disorders associated with brain damage. In P. J. Vinken & G. W. Bruyn (Eds.), *Handbook of clinical neurology. Vol. 3, Disorders of higher nervous activity.* New York: John Wiley & Sons, 1969, Chap. 20.

Pototzky, C. *Konzentrationsgymnastik.* Leipzig: Georg Thieme, 1926.

Prechtl, H. F. R. *The long term value of the neurological examination of the newborn infant.* (Little Clubs Clinics in Developmental Medicine.) London: Heinemann, 1960.

Prechtl, H. F. R. Reading difficulties as a neurological problem in childhood. In J. Money (Ed.), *Reading disability. Progress and research needs in dyslexia.* Baltimore: The Johns Hopkins Press, 1962, Chap. 13. (1)

Prechtl, H. F. R., & Stemmer, Ch. J. The choreiform syndrome in children. *Developmental Medicine and Child Neurology,* 1962, *4,* 119–127. (2)

Pribram, K. M., & Melges, F. T. Psychophysiological basis of emotions. In P. J. Vinken & G. W. Bruyn (Eds.), *Handbook of clinical neurology. Vol. 3, Disorders of higher nervous activity.* New York: John Wiley & Sons, 1969, Chap. 19, pp. 316–344.

Proust, M. The past recaptured (tr. F. A. Blossom). *M.D. Voices,* August 1974, *33.* (Originally published by Random House, New York, 1932.)

Prudden, S. *Suzy Prudden's family fitness book.* New York: Grosset & Dunlap, 1979.

Prudden, S., & Sussman, J. *Suzy Prudden's creative fitness for baby and child.* New York: William Morrow, 1972.

Purpura, D. P. (Rose Kennedy Center for Research in Mental Retardation) NBC research project on the maturing brain (interviewer, Frank Field). *NBC-TV,* July 23, 1973.

Rappaport, M. I. & Calia, F. M. The use of antibiotics in animal feeds (Editorial). *Journal of the American Medical Association,* 1974, *229* (9), 1212.

Remschmidt, H., & Dauner, I. Zur Ätiologie und differential Diagnose depressiver Zustandsbilder bei Kindern und Jugendlichen (The etiology and differential diagnosis of depressions in children and youths). *Jahrbuch für Jugendpsychiatrie,* 1971, *VIII,* 13–45. Bern, Stuttgart, Wien: Hans Huber.

Roswell, F., & Natchez, G. *Reading disability: Diagnosis and treatment.* New York: Basic Books, 1964.

Rubin, L. S. Autonomic dysfunction in psychoses, adults and autistic children. *Archives of General Psychiatry,* 1962, *7,* 27–40.

Safer, D., Allen, R., & Barr, E. Depression of growth in hyperactive children on stimulant drugs. *New England Journal of Medicine,* 1972, *287* (5), 217–220.

Saturen, P., & Tobias, J. S. Evaluation and management of motor disturbance in brain-damaged children. *Journal of the American Medical Association,* 1961, *175* (7), 588–591.

Saunders, R. E. Dyslexia: Its phenomenology. In J. Money (Ed.), *Reading disability: Progress and research needs in dyslexia.* Baltimore: The Johns Hopkins Press, 1962, Chap. 2, pp. 35–44.

Schiffman, G. Program administration within a school system. In J. Money (Ed.), *The disabled reader: Education of the dyslexic child.* Baltimore: The Johns Hopkins Press, 1966, Chap. 15.

Schmidt, M. H. Das hyperkinetische Syndrom im Kindesalter (The hyperkinetic syndrome in childhood). *Zeitschrift für Kinder- und Jugendpsychiatrie,* 1973, *3,* 250.

Schmitt, B. D. The minimal brain dysfunction myth. *American Journal of Diseases of Children,* 1975, *129,* 1313–1318.

Schrag, P., & Divoky, D. *The myth of the hyperactive child.* New York: Pantheon Books, 1975.

Schuell, H., Jenkins, J. J., & Jiménez-Pabón, E. *Aphasia in adults, diagnosis, prognosis, and treatment.* New York: Brunner/Mazel, Inc., 1975.

Scott, D. Musicogenic epilepsy. In M. Critchley & R. A. Henson (Eds.), *Music and the brain.* Springfield, Ill.: Charles C Thomas, 1977, Chap. 20, pp. 354–364.

Semon, R. W. *Die MNEME als erhaltendes Prinzip im Wechsel des organischen Geschehens (Mnemic psychology)*. London: G. Allen & Unwin, 1923. (Originally published, Engelman, Leipzig, 1920.)

Sharpe, W. *Brain surgeon*. New York: Viking Press, 1954.

Sheraton, M. "Junk food" plan widely criticized. *New York Times*, July 13, 1979.

Siegel, E. Helping the brain injured child. New York: Association for Brain Injured Children, 1962.

Slater, E., & Roth, M. *Clinical psychiatry* (3rd ed.). Baltimore: Williams & Wilkins Co., 1969.

Solomons, G. Drug therapy: Initiation and follow-up. *Annals of the New York Academy of Sciences*, 1973, *205*, 335–344.

Spehlmann, R. *Sigmund Freuds neurologische Schriften*. Berlin: Springer-Verlag, 1953.

Stefansson, S. B., Darby, C. E., Wilkins, A. J., Binnie, C. D., et al. Television epilepsy and pattern sensitivity. *British Medical Journal*, 1977, *21*, 88–90.

Stewart, M. A., Pitts, F. N. Jr., Craig, A., & Dieruf, W. The hyperactive child syndrome. *American Journal of Orthopsychiatry*, 1966, *36* (5), 861–867.

Stewart, M. A., Thach, B. T., & Freidin, M. R. Accidental poisoning and the hyperactive child syndrome. *Diseases of the Nervous System*, 1970, *31*, 403–407.

Strauss, A. A., & Kephart, N. C. *Psychopathology and education of the brain-injured child. Vol. 2, Progress in theory and clinic*. New York: Grune & Stratton, 1955.

Strauss, A. A., & Lethinen, L. E. *Psychopathology and education of the brain-injured child* (Vol. 1). New York: Grune & Stratton, 1947.

Terman, L. M., & Merrill, M. A. *Stanford-Binet Intelligence Scale: Manual for the third revision Form L-M*. Boston: Houghton-Mifflin Co., 1960, Norms Edition, 1972.

Thomas, A., Chess, S., & Birch, H. *Temperament and behavior disorders in children*. New York: New York University Press, 1968.

Thompson, L. J. Learning disabilities: An overview. *American Journal of Psychiatry*, 1973, *130* (4), 393–399.

Trace, A. S. Jr. *What Ivan knows that Johnny doesn't*. New York: Random House, 1961.

Walkowitz, *Abstract art from life to life* (catalog of exhibit). New York: Egan Gallery, Dec. 30–Jan. 20, 1947.

Weber, D. *Der frühkindliche Autismus unter dem Aspekt der Entwicklung (Early infantile autism from the developmental point of view)*. Bern, Stuttgart, Wien: Hans Huber, 1970.

Wechsler, D. *The measurement of adult intelligence*. Baltimore: Williams & Wilkins Co., 1944.

Wechsler, D. *Manual for the Wechsler Intelligence Scale for Children* (rev. ed.). New York: The Psychological Corp., 1974.

Wertham, F. A new sign of cerebellar disease. *Journal of Nervous and Mental Diseases*, 1929, *69* (5), 486–493.

Wertham, F. Psychotherapy in disorders of the gastrointestinal tract. *Review of Gastroenterology*, 1953, *20*, 8. (a)

Wertham, F. The Mosaic test technique and psychopathological deductions. In Abt, L. E., & Bellak, L. (Eds.), *Projective psychology*. New York: Grove Press, 1959. (Originally published, Alfred A. Knopf, New York, 1950.)

Wertham, F. *A sign for Cain*. New York: Macmillan, 1966. Warner Paperback Library, 1973.

Wertham, F., & Wertham, F. *The brain as an organ*. New York: Macmillan, 1934.

Wertheim, N. The amusias. In P. J. Vinken & G. W. Bruyn (Eds.), *Handbook of clinical neurology. Vol. 4, Disorders of speech, perception, and symbolic behavior*. New York: American Elsevier Publ. Co., 1969, Chap. 10, pp. 195–206.

Wertheim, N. Is there an anatomical localization for musical faculties? In M. Critchley & R. A. Henson (Eds.), *Music and the brain*. Springfield, Ill.: Charles C Thomas, 1977, Chap. 16.

Wheeler, T. C. *The great American writing block. Causes and cures of the new illiteracy.* New York: The Viking Press, 1979.

Wilder, J. Paradoxic reactions to treatment. *New York State Journal of Medicine,* October 15, 1957, pp. 3348–3352.

Wilder, J. Modern psychophysiology and the law of initial value. *American Journal of Psychotherapy,* 1958, *XII* (2), 199–221.

Wilder, J. Pitfalls in the methodology of the law of initial value. *American Journal of Psychotherapy,* 1965, *XIX* (4), 577–584.

Wilder, J. *Stimulus and response, the law of initial value.* Bristol, England: John Wright & Sons, Ltd., 1967.

Wilson, F. B. Emotional stress may cause voice anomalies in kids, medical news. *Journal of the American Medical Association,* 1971, *216* (13), 2085.

Woodworth, R. S. *Experimental psychology.* New York: Henry Holt & Co., 1938.

World of medicine, CP progress. *M.D.,* May 1979, pp. 47–50.

Zahn, T. P., Abate, F., Little, B. C., & Wender, P. H. Minimal brain dysfunction, stimulant drugs, and autonomic nervous system activity. *Archives of General Psychiatry,* March 1975, 32.

Index

706

Key to Children's Names in Volume 2